DATE DUE

DEC - 2 1998	

The Machete and the Cross

The Machete and the Cross

CAMPESINO REBELLION IN YUCATAN

DON E. DUMOND

UNIVERSITY OF NEBRASKA PRESS   LINCOLN AND LONDON

Publication of this book was assisted by a grant from the University of Oregon Foundation.

♾ The paper in this book meets the minimum requirements of American National Standard for Information Sciences—Permanence of Paper for Printed Library Materials, ANSI Z39.48-1984.

Library of Congress Cataloging-in-Publication Data

Dumond, Don E., 1929–

   The machete and the cross : campesino rebellion in Yucatan / Don E. Dumond.

    p. cm.

   Includes bibliographical references (p.) and index.

   ISBN 0-8032-1706-4 (alk. paper)

   1. Yucatán (Mexico : State)—History—Caste War, 1847–1855. 2. Mexico—History—19th century. 3. Yucatán Peninsula—History. 4. Indians of Mexico—Yucatán Peninsula—Government relations. 5. Mayas—Mexico—Government relations. I. Title.

F1376.D86   1997

972'.06—dc20   96-32949

                                                           CIP

For the girl I met in Uruapan

Contents

Illustrations

Plates

Figures

Maps

Tables

Preface

My interest in the campesino rebellion of Yucatan—the so-called Caste War—and the related cult that featured a Christian cross through which God spoke in Maya, was first piqued in the mid-1950s, when as a graduate student in Mexico I encountered *The Maya of East Central Quintana Roo*, by Alfonso Villa Rojas. I was delighted when Nelson Reed's *The Caste War of Yucatan* appeared a decade later.

By that time I was at the University of Oregon and teaching an interdisciplinary course in Mexican history and ethnology. While explaining the well-known "folk-urban continuum" of Robert Redfield, I became uncomfortable with Redfield's lack of attention to the rebellion and the effect it had in forming the attitudes of those remnant rebels of Tusik who were the subject of Villa's study in the 1930s. Not long afterward I attempted to treat this serious omission in a paper that focused on Redfield's conceptualization of Yucatecan society and social history (Dumond 1970).

But in preparing that paper during a sabbatical leave in Mexico, I was disappointed by the extremely secondary (or tertiary, even quaternary) nature of the sources available—in Spanish and well as English—and by the difficulty of getting behind even the nineteenth-century Yucatecan histories to find more primary sources. I decided then to begin a more detailed study.

Active archival research began in the winter of 1971–72, when my wife and I made our first trip to Belize City, where we spent exploratory time in the archives, and then moved to Mérida. There, with the generous assistance of the late Alfredo Barrera Vásquez, director of the Instituto Yucateco de Antropología e Historia, we were introduced to various library and archival sources, as well as to items in Barrera's own collection, and advised of the potential usefulness of the extensive communications reproduced (and preserved) in the official newspapers and gazettes of nineteenth-century Mérida and Campeche. This led us to the magnificent collections of the Biblioteca Carlos R. Menéndez. Trips to Mérida were repeated regularly, with the Menéndez resources supplemented by those of the Hemeroteca del Estado de Yucatán and by book and manuscript collections of the library of the Instituto Yucateco, later to form the Sección Yucateca of the Biblioteca Manuel Cepeda Peraza.

In 1977 a preliminary description of the rebel history was published in a version largely derived from a symposium held five years earlier (Dumond

1977). In 1976–77 a yearlong senior research fellowship of the National Endowment for the Humanities made possible further trips to Belize and Mérida and a first visit to the British Public Record Office in London. Although I had hoped to complete a book draft while so supported, the resources were so rich that the year was passed collecting data.

Unfortunately, administrative and other research commitments conflicted with a speedy completion. Although some work was done with colonial documents pertinent to the background of the rebellion (Dumond and Dumond 1982) and one paper was published regarding proliferation of the religious cult (Dumond 1985), I could not give sustained attention to the project until 1987–88, when another sabbatical year made possible the completion of a preliminary draft of the manuscript. Visits to London in 1988 and 1990, and another visit to the peninsula of Yucatan in the latter year, provided the last bits of data acquired first hand. These were supplemented by material from the rich holdings of microfilmed Mérida archives of the University of Texas at Arlington.

The extensive source materials I used are in both Spanish and English. The former consist of published secondary works such as the contemporary historical accounts of the nineteenth-century wars by Yucatecans; of military and other governmental dispatches published in the gazettes and official newspapers of Yucatan and Campeche; of commercial newspaper accounts; and of original archival documents. The materials in English are predominantly from two sets of holdings: the manuscript collection of the Archives of Belize that was designated "Archives of British Honduras" and systematized by a former governor of that colony, and the dispatches of British Honduras governors in the Colonial Office collection in the Public Record Office, London and Kew. The first of these sets pertains to the period from the beginning of the rebellion to the 1880s, although coverage is sketchy in the 1870s; documents of the second set were reviewed for the years 1870 to 1903.

The nature of sources relied on varies from part to part of the present work. For the relatively brief part 1, which deals with the colonial era, secondary sources are depended on for most of the historical events. More primary materials are used in considering relationships between social and legal categories of persons. Published materials in considerable variety, largely of the nineteenth century, provide most of the sources for part 2, which carries background material from the achievement of independence from Spain, through the beginning of the actual rebellion, to the maximum advance of the rebels toward the west in 1848. The early stages of hostilities draw also on official Yucatecan dispatches and on certain documents from the archives in Belize.

Part 3 carries the rebellion from the beginning of the retreat from the west in 1848 to certain events of 1853. Nineteenth-century histories from Yucatan are heavily supplemented by dispatches in the government gazettes. Archival material from the Public Record Office is added to that from Belize to provide the basis for relations between rebels and British.

Part 4 treats events from 1853 to the late 1860s. Because the nineteenth-century Yucatecan histories extend only to the period of Maximilian's empire, events of the last years of the 1860s are developed from primary sources, including extensive use of dispatches in Yucatecan gazettes and unpublished archival material in Mérida, Belize, and London. The main body of pacified but independent rebels of the south is treated at some length. No full and coherent history of this group has ever been written in any language, so the description of these events from archival sources breaks ground that has been scarcely touched in any published work.

Part 5 covers the last three decades of the nineteenth century. Sources used to bring this period to light include, again, Yucatecan dispatches published in gazettes of Mérida and Campeche, accounts in commercial Yucatecan newspapers—which by the end of the century were covering local news in a moderately efficient way—and especially the British Colonial Office documents from the Public Record Office. Again, no published history has ever dealt closely with the rebels of this period. This has tempted past commentators to project forward in time the religious and political organization of the *bravos* reported from the early 1860s, when the strength of those belligerent rebels was at its highest. As I show in these chapters, the result has been a serious lack of understanding of important later events.

In the work, spellings and related conventions have presented a continual problem, the normal variations between Spanish, English, and Maya orthography made much worse by the lack of systematization of spelling in nineteenth-century Yucatan. Generally, I have attempted to use what seemed to be the most common among available variants. I have corrected some spellings of the last century where the modern usage is clear: the given name *Venancio* for the more common nineteenth-century *Benancio*, for instance. On the other hand, I have retained some antiquated usages, such as *pacíficos del Sur*, which in present-day Spanish would carry no capital letter. With regard to map designations, very modern local usage tends to alter Mayan words to conform to Spanish expectations (as, by changing Chunpom to Chumpón); thus I have retained here a number of nineteenth-century spellings, especially when there is clear precedent in the anthropological or historical literature to do so. Where such precedents are not clear, however, I have stuck with most local usages, even when I suspect that they are etymologically erroneous (e.g., I use Chumbalché rather than Chunbalché). In general, I have used accent marks on Maya place-names, since they have been so widely adopted by Spanish-speaking Yucatecans, but I have not used them on Maya surnames. I have also refrained from using accents in cases in which a designator of a major geographic area is of common use in English but not when the designation is that of a city or town. Thus, Mexico and Yucatan carry no accents, but Mérida does.

Where I quote sections of Spanish-language works, the translations are my own unless otherwise indicated. When materials originally in Spanish or Maya are quoted from English sources, the translation is that of the source, unless noted. Although I encountered a few items in Maya, my own lack of facility with that language prohibited significant use of them. When the translation is not that of the source, I mention this—along with citations of all sources used—in the notes to each chapter.

Finally, I am pleased to acknowledge my debt to institutions and individuals. I have referred already to fellowship support from the National Endowment for the Humanities and to sabbatical leaves supported by the University of Oregon. I also thank the latter for such additional support as brief periods of released time and the clerical and administrative assistance without which I could have done nothing at all. I also gratefully acknowledge some last-minute financial support from the University of Oregon Foundation.

In the United States, Grant D. Jones coached me on my first approach to the archives in Belize. I thank him and Victoria Reiffler Bricker for information freely exchanged over the past two decades and more. Later, John Hudson, Robert Gambel, and Señorita Maritza Arrigunaga of the library of the University of Texas at Arlington helpfully provided access to microfilms and other materials in their collection. In Mérida I owe most to the late D. Alfredo Barrera Vásquez, whom I mentioned earlier, but a second debt as well to the late Doña Flora Menéndez de Moguel, former director of the Biblioteca Menéndez, and her son Nicolás Moguel Menéndez, who permitted access to the facilities at times that enabled my wife and me to make as much as possible of limited periods in Mérida. I owe appreciation also to the late Professor Antonio Canto López, to Professor Salvador Rodríguez Loza, to Lic. Rodolfo Ruz Menéndez, to Professor Roldán Peniche Barrera, and to Sr. Juan Francisco Peón Ancona; from time to time all of them provided significant pieces of information. Dr. Peter J. Schmidt of the Museo Regional de Yucatán, and Arq. Alfredo Barrera Rubio and Senorita Rocío Ximénez Díaz of the Centro Regional del Sureste of the Instituto Nacional de Antropología e Historia, united in facilitating access to graphic materials held by the Museum and under care of the Centro.

In Mexico DF I am grateful to Yolanda Mercader Martínez, former director, Biblioteca Nacional de Antropología e Historia; to Profa. Ann Staples de Pérez Priego of the Colegio de México; and to Maestra Lorena Careaga Viliesid, of the Instituto de Investigaciones Dr. José María Luis Mora. All have generously provided information of one sort or other. In Chetumal I acknowledge with gratitude the assistance of Antrop. Luz del Carmen Vallarta.

At a still later stage, Nelson Reed and Paul Sullivan informed me of crucial sources published after the manuscript was in penultimate draft. I thank both Professor Sullivan and an anonymous reader for comments on that draft. Additional acknowledgments are included in photograph and figure credits.

Last of all, and greatest rather than least, I thank my wife, Carol Steichen Dumond, who spent as many hours as I did in archives and libraries of varying degrees of discomfort. Indefatigable seeker of documents, sensitive critic, strenuous editor, meticulous translator, and eternal friend, she not only executed the maps that illustrate this work, but she performed at least 90% of the specialized map and textual research that made them possible. It is with more pleasure than I can possibly convey that I dedicate the final result to her.

The Machete and the Cross

Prospect

It is well known that in the years following 1810 Mexico, like other Spanish colonies of the Americas, was preoccupied with a war of independence through which the dominance of peninsular Spaniards was replaced by that of American-born Spaniards and mestizos. A century later, a military and social revolution disrupted the years following 1910 as campesinos sought to take their place among the rulers of the country. Both movements were bloody and traumatic.

Yucatan, although nominally a part of colonial New Spain and republican Mexico, danced to the beat of a different drum. Her accession to independence in 1821 was placid. The years following 1911 and the resignation of the longtime dictator of Mexico, Porfirio Díaz, were little more troubled.

But in the decades between Mexico's revolutions, Yucatan did have her rebellion, a violent campesino movement that came more than half a century before that of the country at large. As in central Mexico, the seeds of the inevitable Yucatecan upheaval had been sowed from the earliest years of the Spanish domination. But unlike events in Mexico, the rebels of Yucatan did not achieve ruling power even briefly, nor did they enlist members of a middle class who could unify them and who could have administered a government if the rebellion had succeeded.

The subject of this history is that rebellion in Yucatan. Commonly if inaccurately known as the *Guerra de Castas*, the "Caste War"—more adequately translated as "Race War"—it was a violent movement of campesinos who were predominantly, but by no means exclusively, Indians as so defined by Yucatecan law. The immediate result was a localized war that lasted for more than half a century, producing independent realms of varying degrees of rebelliousness around the margins of civilized Yucatan. The less direct result was the particular shape of Yucatecan history and economic development in the nineteenth century and after.

As in all such cases, the actual hostilities took place within and were conditioned by a geopolitical setting that included international as well as local factors: the relationship of Yucatan to Spain, of Yucatan to Mexico, of England to both Spain and Mexico, as well as local relationships between classes and differing economic postures. And because it is in the inception of the colony that the early seeds of the revolt are to be found, my examination here will begin with the colonization of Yucatan by the Spaniards. In a comparable way, a full account must also include some events after 1901, for the real end of active rebellion and rebel independence, like their effects, did not come as neatly as did the occupation of remnant rebel settlements and the establishment of the military government that marked nominal Mexican ascendancy.

Thus, part 1 deals briefly with the Spanish colony. The emphasis is on the attitudes of Spaniards toward Indians—that is, on the relations between those who before the law were full citizens or *vecinos* and those who were Indians, legal categories that distinguished the heritage of the conqueror from that of the conquered and carried gross differences in both status and taxation. But although the purely legal distinction between *vecino* and Indian remained clear and unambiguous, as time went on the less formal social line was not: by the end of the colonial period more than half of the rural *vecinos* could claim either a mother or a grandmother who came from a family legally Indian. A self-identified "Maya" might or might not be Indian before the law.

Part 2 carries the narrative from the achievement by the Latin American colonies of independence from Spain through the first year of the rebellion.

With independence came, on the one hand, the extension of basic citizenship rights to those classed legally as Indians and with it a rise in their overall expectations. On the other hand, campesinos were affected by a change in patterns of trade that encouraged the expansion of certain Yucatecan rural industries and the conversion of freely available farmland to more industrial use. But the early decades of independence also became a time of rivalry and altercation between Yucatan and Mexico and, on the peninsula of Yucatan itself, between the cities of Mérida and Campeche. These disputes led to a number of active military engagements in which men of the predominantly Indian lower classes from eastern Yucatan gained practical experience as military irregulars in a series of armed conflicts, in some of which they were a deciding factor.

A plot for an Indian rebellion was allegedly uncovered in the east, which then brought on locally repressive acts by the government followed by acts of rebellious banditry and murder by local eastern people in response. These culminated in a massive retaliatory repression all over Yucatan of those recognized legally as Indians, with withdrawal of rights and extensive persecution of their leaders. As a result, active fighting began in the east in mid-1847. In less than a year the conflagration swept over the eastern three-quarters of the peninsula of Yucatan, as the rebels drew to their cause possibly a fourth of the entire peninsula population. Frantic Yucatecan efforts to stem the rising tide elicited several lists of grievances from the rebels. To the extent that these complaints were articulated, they included high taxes and ill treatment of those defined as Indians; to a lesser extent they included the expropriation of lands that campesinos believed should be freely available to all subsistence farmers and the existence of debt peonage. Panic-stricken, the Yucatecan government offered to meet all demands presented, but the offer was refused by the rebels, who—now more interested in fighting than in concessions—battled on under several independent leaders until their advance stalled not far from Mérida, the capital of the peninsula.

In part 2 I also offer an explanation of why the rebellion occurred when and where it did, an explanation buttressed by evaluation of the early rebel demands—demands interpreted by Yucatan as sufficient conditions for peace but which when acceded to bought no peace from the rebels. I also attempt to show that the small but important component of *vecinos* who were in the rebellion from its inception, as well as the large number of those classed legally as Indians who refused to join the rebels, casts doubt on any characterization of the Caste War as a purely "Indian" rebellion, as that term has commonly been used in Yucatan.

In part 3 I carry the rebellion through its next stage, which began as Yucatecan forces rallied to throw the rebels back in late 1848 and continued into 1853. As the campesinos were driven eastward—back to the region where hostilities had begun—they lost through surrender about two-thirds of those who had joined their cause. Once in the east, the territory they held became relatively stable. During this phase of the war, the major demand of the rebels became political and physical separation from Yucatan, a claim they reiterated as the government army hounded them through the eastern forests. By now the importance to the rebels of munitions received from independent traders in British Honduras became unmistakable, although the Belize government decried the trade and attempted unsuccessfully to mediate between the rebels and Yucatan. Now, too, the rebels first asked to have their territory absorbed by the British colony and endured British refusal.

But the rejuvenated Yucatecan army was not able to occupy the eastern region permanently—a region that had never been fully integrated into the peninsula economy. With the rebels suffering severely from war and hunger, there appeared in late 1850 the miraculous cult of the crosses through which the Christian God spoke to his people in Maya, bringing about a resurgence of rebel spirit and the creation of a capital of their own at Santa Cruz—or Chan Santa Cruz—but no real improvement in their material condition.

But after months and years of Yucatecan pounding, roughly half the rebels declared for armistice with Yucatan and retired into the southern wastelands to live alone, independent and peaceful—except when they found it necessary to repel their former allies, now their foes, the active rebel *bravos* of the east. The conditions under which these new *pacíficos* made peace assured them of de facto separation from Yucatan, physically and politically.

The original rebels were now divided.

In part 4, I carry both active and pacified rebels through the 1860s. The *bravos*, revived by their religious cult, demonstrated the greatest strength, stability, belligerence, and tenacity witnessed in all but the first year of the war. Meanwhile, the Yucatecan government was forced to recognize its limitations in men and money, and its war effort flagged. Its attention was also drawn increasingly to the northwest of the peninsula and the growing market importance of fiber from the native agave, henequen, which flourished in the dry northwest corner of their territory, far removed from the war front. Some commentators have dated the end of a narrowly defined Caste War to this lessening of government effort in the mid-1850s.

But the war was far from over. The cult of the cross and its manipulators at Santa Cruz continued their climb to the apex of political power among the *bravos*. There were blood-curdling massacres of Yucatecan towns, punctuated by the wholesale kidnapping of prisoners, marked truculence by *bravos* toward the British Honduran government, and increased repression of their own people. This ordeal was lessened only when an internal revolt overthrew the cult manipulators.

A counterrebellion gave power to a threesome of leaders who enforced a measure of stability on the rebel government—although their displacement of the major cross cult from Santa Cruz to Tulum was to fuel the growth of a rival *bravo* center. Smoother relations with British Honduras were established, and the rebel dependence on that colony for munitions began to blossom into real friendship.

The establishment of Maximilian's empire in 1864 wrought significant but short-lived changes in government policy. Campaigns against the *bravos* were renewed, although to no avail, for the rebels at the height of their power inflicted serious defeats on the government forces. And government policy toward the *pacíficos* backfired: the result in the pacified south was unrest, a threatened rebellion, murder of a government official, and a declaration of *pacífico* independence from Yucatan. Part 4 ends at about the time of the redefection of half or more of the southern *pacíficos* to join again with the *bravos*.

Part 5 covers the last three decades of the nineteenth century. The Juárez government had broken diplomatic relations with London because the British had earlier recognized Maximilian. The ensuing period of diplomatic estrangement led to increasingly close and paternalistic relations between British Hondurans and the active rebels to their north, including newly sanctioned trading in armament. But *bravo* requests for incorporation by England continued to be refused.

At British urging, the active rebels became less and less aggressive, and raids on Yucatecan territory stopped almost altogether. This was matched by Yucatecan withdrawal from the rebel frontier, a physical move encouraged by a growing boom in the international fiber market that promised to mend the shattered economy through increased investment in henequen. Thus, social and natural factors coincided to produce extensive plantations in the northwest, while rebels quietly held on in the east.

For rebel society, these years were a time of stagnation and dissolution. Although external pressure remained insignificant, the population declined. In 1885 at Santa Cruz an internal revolt rocked a society already tottering, and at the end of the decade hostility and killing separated the two major rebel centers. As political divisions among the remnants grew more pronounced, emigration became chronic. While the rebel society dwindled, ties to the British grew closer.

With the complete entrenchment of Porfirio Díaz in the leadership of Mexico after the 1880s, his government placed major emphases on economic development and the elimination of pockets of rebellion in the country. A change for *bravos* and *pacíficos* alike came with the signing of the treaty between Mexico and Britain that established the boundaries of the British colony on terms favored by London and outlawed all powder trade with the rebels as demanded by Mexico. This was the beginning of the end of successful rebellion. Mexican military pressure was brought to bear on the active rebels, with Mexican forces allowed passage through the waters of British Honduras to establish a military presence in the southern portion of *bravo*-controlled territory.

Finally, in 1901, the Mexican army invaded the bush of eastern Yucatan, occupied the rebel pueblos, created the federal Territory of Quintana Roo, and began to force government on the eastern forests once nominally ruled by Yucatan but never really controlled by anyone except the rebels. Among *pacíficos* the loss of their independence came more slowly, if equally decisively, as a standard Mexican form of representative local government was gradually imposed upon them.

Following part 5, a final chapter provides some additional analysis.

Part 1. Sustaining the Colony, 1511–1821

1 / Beginnings

In 1511 a boatload of seventeen castaways, their ship splintered on a reef, washed up on the east coast of the peninsula of Yucatan, where they were captured by Maya Indians. This is the first recorded Spanish landing on the peninsula. Most of the perpetrators were killed immediately or died soon after.[1] But two of them survived and would make separate marks on the world.

Although Yucatan may have been touched briefly by a Spanish ship or two in the next few years, the first seriously purposeful visit was in 1517, when 110 Spaniards from the West Indies sailed under Francisco Hernández de Córdoba to continue a search for wealth that had been unrewarded in the metal-poor islands. Striking Yucatan on the northeast at Cape Catoche, they found unfriendly Indians and were forced to fight, and although they did not tarry they sighted baubles of low-grade gold stored in temples of stone masonry. Coasting to the western shore of the peninsula, at Campeche they landed again and to their surprise found cross-shaped symbols marked in color on the backs of idols—or, rather, glimpsed these crosses as they hastily embarked to avoid a second fight. At Río Champotón, they fought again even harder than before but were repulsed by the bellicose inhabitants with great losses. Captain Hernández and more than half his crew perished there or fled home to die of their wounds. This was the real "discovery" of Yucatan.

The reports of gold called loudly to stubborn Spaniards, however. In 1518 an expedition under Juan de Grijalva touched first at Cozumel Island on the east, then coasted the sandy shoals of the northern Yucatecan littoral toward the Gulf of Mexico. Landing near Champotón, Grijalva and his 240 followers found that the inhabitants of that area had mellowed not at all in the intervening year, but this time the Spaniards won the field. Continuing westward and north along the coasts of Tabasco and Veracruz, they traded for gold trinkets and heard of yet more to be had farther on, laying the groundwork for the third and crowning expedition.[2]

And so the following year Hernán Cortés set out from Cuba, evading an attempt by the governor of the island to revoke his commission as expedition

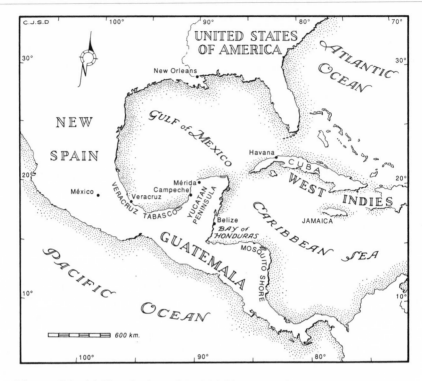

Map 1. Colonial New Spain and Its Neighbors. Based on general sources, with reference to Anonymous (1787) and López (1801).

leader, and rendezvoused his ships at Cozumel Island. Here he smashed idols and erected a cross. He also managed to send a letter to the Spanish castaways of 1511 and was joined by one of them, Gerónimo de Aguilar, now fluent in Maya, who was to claim fame as Cortés's first effective interpreter. While the second surviving castaway chose to follow his fate among the Maya of Yucatan, the 1519 expedition moved on to the conquest of Mexico, into history, and out of the present story.[3]

The Land

If these visitors could have seen Yucatan clearly and completely, they would have found not an island—as they took it to be—but a flat yet rugged limestone platform that ages before had been thrust above the oceans as the floor of the Atlantic jammed against the volcanic massif of the cordillera far to the south. Low of relief, the jumbled limestone emerges from the sea behind a marshy shoreline and shallow, treacherous bays, rising in slow, choppy waves toward the mountains. Overall, the elevation along the center of the peninsula increases only at the rate of about twenty centimeters per kilometer, or one foot every mile. To an observer in an airplane, the entire peninsula appears flat as a table.

In Yucatan proper, the single feature that has loomed larger to earthbound observers is a low ridge of hills: the *sierra*, as it is known locally, which rises for the most part no more than two hundred meters above sea level and spreads across the limestone plain as a spidery inverted V, the apex located sixty kilometers south of Mérida, one leg thrust southwest to Campeche, and the other southeast toward the geographic center of the peninsula. This scarp marks the north and east edges of what geographers know as the Yucatan Platform, upon which the land is even more knobby but continues to rise upward as it moves south.

As the land rises slowly from north to south, so does the annual rainfall, with less than five hundred millimeters (twenty inches) falling in the northwest but more than four times that amount in the south. Dumping moisture on the peninsula in summer and fall, the northeast trade winds bring less in winter and spring—seasons when none at all is likely in the northwest.

So it is that the dry, deciduous scrub of the northwestern third of the peninsula gives way to a taller rain forest on the east and south and finally to dense, high evergreen rain forest in a belt swinging south from the west coast around Champotón, east to the present boundary with Guatemala, then northeast to the Bay of Chetumal and the modern nation of Belize, the former British Honduras.

Several lakes and streams punctuate the wettest region of the south, where there is the most vegetation and the deepest soils, and the mouths of these waterways find the only bays of the peninsula deep enough to provide natural harbors. Northward, lakes are more scattered, localized in hollows where clays seal the porous limestone, and interspersed with savannas that become seasonal swamps. There are no watercourses here, however, because the porous limestone allows fast percolation, and streams are subterranean. Permanent water is often to be found only in the farthermost reaches of caves.[4] Yet on the northernmost rim of the peninsula—the driest and lowest region, with the least soil and most porous limestone— this hidden water is accessible even in the parching seasons. There, as along parts of the low eastern region where there are lakes and swamps, limestone caverns have collapsed to form the plentiful natural wells known as *cenotes*.

*Map 2. The Peninsula of Yucatan, Land Form and Vegetation. Based on Raiz (1964)
and Wagner (1964, fig. 1). Colonial period settlements here and in later maps
are from text sources, Anonymous (1848), and Heller (1847), with comparative
reference to Berendt (1878). The location of Tipu is from Jones (1989, map 2).*

Aside from settlements around Río Champotón on the west and Chetumal Bay on the east, at the time of the Spanish conquest most of the peninsula's native people seem to have lived north of the densest rain forest. But
unlike the central Mexican highlands, where an ethnically heterogeneous
population was dominated from the Basin of Mexico by the Aztec Triple

Alliance, the linguistically and culturally homogeneous Yucatec Maya were divided into a large number of separate and independent political units, differing substantially in size, strength, and organization—some ruled by hereditary nobles, some formed of more loose agglomerations of kin, but all without any overarching, tribute-collecting superpower.[5]

Had these first Spanish visitors been clairvoyant, they would have understood that the natives' fiercely maintained and decentralized independence would stall any hope of a rapid conquest when European invaders turned their full attention to Yucatan. According to some stories, it was in the support of Mayan independence that the remaining Spanish castaway of 1511, Gonzalo Guerrero—now a Mayan war captain, father of Mayan children, and with a tattooed body and pierced lip—stamped his impression on the world. These tales, however, may be legendary embellishment.[6]

Conquest

In 1526 Francisco de Montejo, a captain of Cortés who was filled with the usual speculative Spanish ambition, obtained royal appointment as *adelantado* (hereditary governor) of unconquered Yucatan. The following year he began his assault on the peninsula. But he found his ambition sorely tried, and two decades would elapse before he could claim success.

His first landing was on the swampy east coast, where climate and sickness more than bellicose Indians took their toll and came near to repulsing the invader, who for reasons of higher policy shifted his efforts to the west in order to work from a stable bridgehead at the Laguna de Términos, near the mouth of the Río Candelaria. The second campaign, at first more successful, moved along the west coast of Yucatan, where what was to be the city of Campeche was founded for the first time, and victory seemed destined to crown efforts in the north and east.

But as Indian resistance stiffened, a deathblow was dealt the campaign by news of the conquest of metal-rich Peru. The inevitable gold rush dissolved Montejo's army like magic. He abandoned Campeche and withdrew again to the Laguna de Términos.

Finally, in 1540 and 1541 a push up the west coast by a force commanded by both the son and the nephew of the aging Montejo and aided by Mexican Indian allies led to the reestablishment of Campeche as a Spanish strongpoint and ultimately to major capitulations by local Maya and the founding of Mérida. Advancing from there, all but the interior of the peninsula was subdued in short order, the southeast in a particularly cruel and bloodthirsty fashion by three members of the Pacheco family—a name that will appear again in later chapters.[7] But the tradition of local independence asserted itself in eastern Yucatan almost immediately through a widespread rebellion triggered by Mayan priests, one of whom was alleged by Montejo to have claimed to be the Son of God.[8] The revolt was put down, and a number of Indian leaders were burned, but the eastern Maya had earned a reputation for fierceness.

In 1547 Spanish occupation was finally permanent, based on four formally established settlements that between themselves governed the entire subdued territory of the peninsula: Mérida, the major capital, on the northwest, with the Spanish settlement rank of *city*; the regional capitals of Campeche on the southwest, Valladolid on the east, and Bacalar—or more properly Salamanca de Bacalar[9]—on the southeast, all with the rank of *villa*. These were to remain key centers throughout the colonial period and the nineteenth century. Although subjugating Maya as far southeast as the settlement of Tipu, the conquerers stopped short of those living around the central lakes in what is now the Petén district of Guatemala—speakers of the Yucatec language who professed to have moved south in response to internecine warfare and violence in pre-Hispanic times.

But although the Spaniards found temple buildings of stone everywhere —in centers surrounded by the thatch-roofed huts of common Maya people —the rugged limestone platform yielded no gold or other mineral wealth.[10] The new masters of the land, therefore, turned to secure riches in the only way possible, by allocating to themselves tribute from all adult Indians— tribute based on the regular agricultural labors of the native population.

And so the *encomienda*, as the allocation of tribute payers was called, came to be an institution that endured far past its life span elsewhere in New Spain, lasting in Yucatan through the eighteenth century, although with tribute payers periodically reallocated from one Spanish family to another. But with the passage of time many of the *encomiendas* would be taken over by the Crown; those that were not would be taxed for the royal benefit.

The Last Campaign and the First Canek

Not long after the conquest of Mexico, Cortés had made his disastrous overland journey to Honduras to punish his rebellious lieutenant Cristóbal de Olid. In doing so, he crossed the present Petén district of Guatemala at the location of Lake Petén, where in 1525—twenty years before the conquest of Yucatan to the north—he was entertained by Canek, the ruler of the local Maya.[11] Canek's people were by legend the offspring of immigrant ancestors from northerly Chichén Itzá, and were considered Itzá themselves. Whatever their origin, after the undisputed passage of Cortés they were left undisturbed and uncatechized by Spaniards for nearly a century, despite the attention being given to both conquest and conversion farther north and despite what must have been this undesirable pagan influence on the subjected Maya of the region south of Bacalar.

In the second decade of the seventeenth century a delegation of the Itzá appeared in Mérida wanting, they said, to treat of their submission. Presumably this was their attempt to seek fulfillment of native Maya prophecies that spoke of their eventual return to the north;[12] its certain result was that the Spanish began to proselytize in the south.

In 1618, two Franciscan friars, Bartolomé de Fuensalida and Juan de Orbita were dispatched by their order from Mérida through Bacalar and Tipu, immediately east of the central Petén lakes. Received with friendship by Canek (who was obviously not the same individual who hosted Cortés ninety-three years earlier), in the course of their visit they were shown idols to which they responded with impulsive disgust.[13] Although the priests were not ejected from the Petén capital immediately, they found it expedient to leave in a very few days.

Even so—perhaps because of the strength of native prophecy—they were allowed to return briefly the following year. But despite some indication that Canek himself was ready to negotiate a political as well as a religious peace, his countrymen were of a different mind, and the Franciscans were this time forcibly evicted. So much for prophecy.

This near miss, however, led in 1622 to an attempted military conquest. The armed advance in this case was preceded by a visit to Lake Petén by another fearless priest who—unauthorized—aimed to forestall the use of force against the Indians. For his pacific efforts he and his escort of friendly Maya from the Belize River were sacrificed to Canek's gods.

On news of this, the waiting military force poised for a thrust from their advance camp at Sacalum (or Sacluum), located somewhere north of Lake Petén.[14] Unfortunately for them, the soldiers had been at Sacalum long enough to more than wear out their welcome with nearby Maya. As the Spanish party celebrated a preliminary festival mass in their church they were massacred to a man, their bodies dismembered and in some cases their hearts torn out in the ancient Maya way.[15] Lake Petén remained unconquered.

At Spanish instigation, a large body of loyalist Maya from Oxcutzcab tracked down and captured a pagan priest and some followers who possessed incriminating items from the Sacalum church, as well as some of the late Spanish commander's own possessions. They were tried and hanged, and to underscore Spanish vengeance—as a foretaste of later reprisals when Maya would show themselves unappreciative of Spanish rule—their bodies were dragged through the streets, drawn, quartered, and decapitated, their heads displayed in Maya towns of the Sierra district as a warning to others.[16]

Not long after this, the formerly pacified Maya around Bacalar revolted, burned their villages, and fled south toward the Petén region.[17] It added to the easterners' reputation for fierceness.

Although this was the last shudder of the series of Indian rebellions that were the direct aftermath of conquest, ending it was not easy. When in 1641 Father Fuensalida made a final trip to lure them back to Bacalar, he and his party were warned off short of Tipu and spent anxious days during which most of their Maya escort melted away and Fuensalida and his fellow Franciscans were restrained, insulted, frightened, and finally sent packing. They learned that apostate native priests were celebrating a Mass of their own devising. It was not until 1656 that the dispersed Bacalar people were induced to receive a legitimate Christian priest.[18]

But by the 1680s the Yucatecan Spaniards had succeeded in congregating many of the scattered southeastern Maya into pueblos.[19] And in the next decade Tipu was brought again into Spanish orbit.

Finally, in 1697, a century and a half after the virtual completion of the conquest of Yucatan to the north, Guatemala and Yucatan, acting with poor coordination but to similar ends, mustered the strength that resulted in the nominal capitulation and conversion of the people of Lake Petén.[20] The recalcitrant Maya this time were vanquished, their island capital secured, while most of the people—in traditional Mayan fashion—scattered into the deep forests of the Petén.[21]

The Spanish success at Lake Petén marks the official end of the untidy conquest of Yucatan. Although it certainly did not mean the subjugation of all individual Maya, it meant the practical end of formal paganism on the peninsula. Thereafter all Spanish encounters with native Maya in Yucatan, no matter how far from Spanish settlements nor how well hidden in the rain forests of the east and south, would be encounters with baptized people, all bearers of Spanish given names, all at least nominal followers of Catholic Christianity.

Aspects of Aftermath

With the Maya inhabitants subjugated, the tasks remaining were instruction in Christianity (in which the *encomenderos* were expected to take the lead) and the establishment of governance. Each of these—conversion and governance—brought certain peculiar results that are of special importance to this history.

The result of conversion was the special significance that the Christian symbol of the cross achieved in the eyes of the converted Indians of Yucatan. This has been remarked by many writers, some of whom have traced this exceptional regard for the cross to practices of preconquest times—such as the use of cross-shaped marks like those noted by the Hernández party at Campeche or of more embellished crosses found in Mayan reliefs from much earlier periods.[22]

Other commentators have instead focused upon events of the period at or immediately after conquest. For example, both Grijalva and Cortés erected crosses on their first visits to Cozumel Island. Again, when in 1541 Montejo's forces received a most important public acknowledgment of fealty from the Maya Tutul Xiu and his teeming followers of Maní, they did not honor the occasion with a mass, but for some unclear reason celebrated it with the Good Friday ceremony of the Adoration of the Cross—even though it was January. The sight of all of the Spaniards prostrating themselves in unison to the cross was said to have had a profound effect on the onlooking Maya. Or yet again, as the pre-Columbian pilgrimage center of Izamal was converted to a Spanish religious seat and the major pyramid was dismantled to build a convent, the friars erected a thatched shrine on the remnant summit. A high wind struck the shrine and destroyed it, leaving—miraculously in the eyes of the Spaniards, at least—three standing crosses.[23] But most of these occurrences, however spectacular, could have impressed no more than a few of the Maya at any one time.

Potentially more convincing are situations that involved a greater number of Indians over a longer time. In the sixteenth century, for instance, it is said that the Franciscans traveled about through the whole of Yucatan unarmed save for "the cross and their staff."[24] But probably more to the point, it has been asserted that the first resident bishop of Yucatan ordered wooden crosses erected in the plazas and at the entrance to each pueblo, as well as at many points along the roads. The Indians were required to stop and prostrate themselves whenever they passed one, to teach them reverence.[25]

Whatever may have been the cause or causes, it is clear that the Christian cross was immediately embraced by the Maya,[26] although the context in which it was used in the early decades of their conversion was not always pleasing to the Spanish priests. For as conquered Indians made the difficult transition to Christianity, they were disturbingly inclined to relapse into idolatry. In one famous period in the 1560s several pueblos were accused of reverting under the leadership of members of the old Maya priesthood to the ritual sacrifice of children; in some innovative cases victims were crucified and their hearts cut out, the body-laden crosses then thrown into a cenote.[27] In any event, one of the symbols found most consistently in rural Yucatecan shrines and churches is a simple cross, a symbol that has also intruded into native family worship throughout the rural area, where the cross is often personified as a saint.[28]

The second of these results of the colonial experience worked more upon the dominant Spaniards than on the subjugated Indians, for it concerned the governance of the entire region. In 1561 Yucatan became a separate diocese, although its bishops remained suffragan to the archbishop of Mexico. In parallel fashion, its civil government, although subject to the viceroy of New Spain, did not experience direct viceregal rule; rather, Yucatan was a separate *gobierno*, a province with its own governor who held a direct appointment from the king. And in those frequent occasions when one royal appointment had lapsed and the next appointee had not yet appeared on the Yucatecan coast, the governing power was wielded by the vested town governments, the *ayuntamientos* of the four incorporated Spanish civil units, Mérida, Campeche, Valladolid, and Bacalar, each in its own area. Although in New Spain as a whole the early practice of government by local council had quickly yielded to appointive agents of the viceroy or, in the separate *gobiernos*, of the governor, in Yucatan the *ayuntamientos* jealously maintained their status as local governing bodies. The *cabildos* or councils of Mérida and the three original *villas* were thus the de facto local governing bodies in Yucatan through the entire period of the colony.[29]

All of this engendered a sense of independence in Yucatan that was not to be found in the provinces of central Mexico. Like the pervasive worship of the cross, it would have important repercussions in the nineteenth century, as New Spain flexed its muscles in freedom from colonial rule.

Yucatan in a Colonial World

Despite Yucatan's solid land connection with the mainland of America, not even a railroad joined the peninsula to the rest of Mexico until the mid-twentieth century, and the only practical communication with the outside world, including mainland New Spain, was by sea. Campeche was the single settlement of importance to function as a port city. Although that seaside *villa* had an obvious disability in its lack of a deepwater bay or estuary, it was nevertheless the most favorable port location on the populous west coast of the Yucatan peninsula, the shape of which gave the open roadway at that point at least partial shelter from the prevailing north and east winds. Its early maritime importance is attested by the sixteen separate raids it suffered from pirates in the two centuries following its founding.[30]

But the location of the major port so far south of Mérida, the capital, caused inconvenience to that city. Although ocean traffic between Havana and Veracruz passed closely by the northern Yucatecan coast, communication with that shipping from Mérida required a painful journey of 170 kilometers over excruciating roads to the seaport. In consequence, despite the danger of the open northern coast of Yucatan—exposed to the periodic winter "northers" of the Gulf of Mexico—the subsidiary port of Sisal was established north of Mérida before the sixteenth century was over. This at least permitted the capital to communicate more directly with both New Spain and Cuba, although Sisal did not begin to rival Campeche in commercial importance until the nineteenth century.

The results of these differing geographical situations were significantly divergent courses of development for the two major population centers— Mérida and Campeche—as Yucatan slowly emerged as an agricultural province. Colonial trade was forbidden with non-Spanish territories and severely restricted with all ports of the Spanish domains except Cádiz in Spain itself, with which communication was possible only by transshipment through designated colonial points of exit and only by means of the annual sailing of the official fleet from Veracruz. Campeche thus developed chiefly in communication with a handful of other centers of New Spain, in late colonial times shipping to them homely products such as rice, tallow, leather, salt, and cotton goods, as well as a certain amount of dyewood that was bound for Spain to be further transshipped to using countries. Mérida, on the other hand, exported only a few agricultural products through Sisal to Havana. While Campeche saw herself as a professional port, the focus of Mérida remained primarily toward the interior of the peninsula. This difference in the sense of exposure to the outside world, as well as a difference in immediate economic markets, would exacerbate friction between the two cities in the nineteenth century.

One of the most significant external relationships of Yucatan, however, was its link with the growing British presence to the southeast. Founded in 1544, the *villa* of Bacalar was located not far from a bay on the Caribbean that might have provided port facilities vastly superior to those of Campeche, save for the dangers of the lee shore on which it lay. But its major misfortune was to face not ports of New Spain with which Yucatan might legitimately conduct some colonial trade but the Caribbean islands that were home to either enemies or indifferent friends of Spain, with whom most trade was illegal. Not the least of those enemies was that floating population of freebooters attracted to the Caribbean by the very presence of Spanish shipping and colonies and the possibility of Spanish plunder.

At the time of conquest, this southern region had been heavily occupied, and although the violent aftermath of the eastern Indian rebellion of 1546 left portions of it only thinly populated, it was still important as a producer of cacao. Salamanca de Bacalar soon became the headquarters of a missionary endeavor that in the latter part of the sixteenth century planted a string of some twenty-two subsidiary mission establishments or *visitas* as far south as the Belize River.

The missionary impact, however, was still not permanent, for the Indian population—as I noted earlier—showed a marked tendency to rebel and drift still farther south toward the uncontrolled region that is now the Petén district of Guatemala.

There was also growing pressure from the Caribbean freebooters. As their raids on Bacalar reached a climax in the 1640s and 1650s, coinciding with troubles from local Indian rebellions, the Spaniards moved the *villa* of Salamanca inland to an intermediate location and then to the pueblo of Chunhuhub, where it remained for around sixty years.

This inaugurated some decades of general Spanish retreat. The withdrawal from Bacalar in the face of advancing freebooters who had added to their more famous enterprise of pillage the commercial cutting of dyewood, coincided with a Spanish withdrawal under the same circumstances from the Laguna de Términos in the southwest and from Cozumel Island in the northeast. In 1655 Britain captured Jamaica, underscoring her stake in the Caribbean. By 1670 enterprising woodcutters known to themselves as Baymen—predominantly English nationals, many of whom hailed from the British colonies of North America—had invested the entire east coast of the peninsula, from what is now southern Belize north to Cozumel Island and Cape Catoche, as well as the region around the Laguna de Términos.[31]

Late in the century, however, the Spanish contraction was reversed. As I mentioned earlier, Franciscan missions had moved south into the interior, and dispersed Indian populations were concentrated into pueblos, while Spanish forces finally subdued the independent Itzá on Lake Petén. In the 1680s and 1690s there were also Spanish attacks on camps of the Baymen around the Laguna de Términos, resulting in a number of the dyewood cutters being hauled off to Mexico. By 1717 the Baymen were successfully expelled from that region. Spanish Yucatecans took over their logging works and, in some cases, their black slaves.

In the east, most of the resident Baymen had apparently also been dislodged from regions north of old Bacalar. In 1727, when freebooters landed at Ascension Bay, fell on Chunhuhub, and attacked as far north as Tihosuco, the Yucatecan governor and military commander responded quickly and drove the attackers from the coast. That year the same active official reestablished Salamanca at its old site near Chetumal Bay; two years later he had the stone fortress of San Felipe constructed there, and from that time the *villa* began to function more as a post under Yucatecan military control than as an independent Spanish municipality. This advance discouraged the Baymen from occupying Yucatecan territory north of Bacalar, but it did not halt their incursions. There were raids on Chunhuhub as late as 1750.[32]

The region at the mouth of the Belize River south of Bacalar now became the major focus of Baymen activity. Spanish attempts to dislodge them there may have been made as early as 1718; Spanish thrusts increased between 1730 and 1750, but success was limited. The Treaty of Paris of 1763, ending the Seven Years' War in Europe, acknowledged English rights to cut logwood in the Belize River region, while forbidding the construction of fortifications. But it set no boundaries on the area of those rights, and by that time the woodcutters, now also interested in commercial cuts of mahogany, were working as far north as the Río Hondo.

In 1779, as Spain entered the North American War of Independence on the side of the colonies, a thrust at the English took the form of a Spanish fleet that landed at St. George's Cay, then the major Baymen settlement, located immediately off the mainland coast near what is now Belize City, and made prisoners of the entire establishment. The British settlement remained abandoned until the war's end, when the Treaty of Versailles of 1783 brought peace again and allowed the cutting of dyewood between the Belize and Hondo rivers. In a subsequent convention of the same year, Britain gave up her claims to the Mosquito Shore and recognized Spanish sovereignty over the entire coast of the Bay of Honduras, while Spain allowed the presence of English logging settlements on her soil between the Hondo and Sibun rivers but forbade the construction of fortifications and the establishment of plantations. When in the following decade war again broke out between England and Spain, a Spanish force attacked the Belize settlement but was repulsed. It did not, however, change the long-term agreement between Spain and England.

Thus was created the anomalous situation of the settlement of Belize,[33] where British citizens were allowed the right to cut timber and establish themselves, but ultimate sovereignty was reserved to Spain. Such was the condition under which the first appointed superintendent of the British settlement took office in 1786, and such was it to endure until the achievement of independence by the Spanish colonies in the nineteenth century. A partial explanation of Britain's tolerance for the position of the settlement must have lain in her growing conviction that the empire was founded on commerce, rather than territorial control, and that the only real value of colonies was their facilitation of trade.[34]

But with this foreign presence in the Caribbean came a broad problem for Spanish governors: traffic in contraband. With trade originally forbidden with any country but Spain or, in very restricted fashion, with other Spanish colonies, the temptation for Spanish colonists to deal for foreign goods by way of British ports in the Caribbean was irresistible. In 1713, furthermore, the Treaty of Utrecht had given Britain a monopoly on the transport of African slaves to Spanish America and provided for the necessary distribution stations, one of them at Campeche. These stations immediately became depots for contraband, and the term *free trade* could at the time be considered a synonym for smuggling. British participants in this trade included a number of North American colonists, some of whom were engaged in a complex series of exchanges beginning with salt fish from Newfoundland and ending with the purchase of logwood from English woodcutters trespassing on some portion of the peninsula of Yucatan. By these dodges, in the first half or so of the eighteenth century the British were said to have gained control of a full half of the commerce—legal and illegal—of the entire Spanish Indies.[35]

For Yucatan, the problem would not be solved with independence, for independence from Spain as a part of Mexico only brought higher tariffs—and increased smuggling. Here the position of Bacalar was particularly convenient, for this outpost against British incursions, separated from the rest of Yucatan by leagues of wilderness road, was a prime location for passing contraband. Goods entering the territory by that gateway were immediately spread to storehouses in the scattered eastern towns, among which Tihosuco was by the nineteenth century considered the major center for banking the necessary liquid capital. The illicit trade included, not only ordinary imports that could be obtained elsewhere by paying duty, but items that were banned outright, including raw cotton and many cotton goods, certain foodstuffs, and some firearms. So popular was the smuggling enterprise in Yucatan, especially in Bacalar, that according to one commentator the nineteenth-century monetary value of contraband in the peninsula rivaled that of legitimate trade.[36]

While Belize was not the only way station in this traffic, by the nineteenth century its surreptitious network of communication linking British Honduras and eastern Yucatan was of long standing. It would be drawn on heavily during the rebellion to come.

The difficult and ragged conquest of Yucatan cost the Spaniards decades of hard and bloody campaigning against a series of politically independent regions, and then brought them not metallic treasure but an impoverished agrarian realm supported by the tribute of Indian farmers. But this native population, notably more docile in the west than in the east, showed itself largely receptive to sincere, if sometimes imperfect, conversion to Christianity, especially to glorification of the symbol of the cross. Above the native Maya, the hierarchical society was dominated by its four Spanish municipalities, each of them exercising relatively independent jurisdiction over a share of the peninsula, each resistant to centralized control by the crown, each following divergent interests. Early differences were especially manifest between Mérida, the interior capital, and Campeche, the commercial port city.

During the first century of domination, sporadic rebellions by eastern Indians marred the peace. To Spanish discomfiture, the last violent outbreaks coincided with growing British pressure in the Caribbean, as freebooting woodcutters invaded much of the east coast of the peninsula as well as its southwest corner at the Laguna de Términos. Major Spanish military efforts of the late seventeenth century finally neutralized both intrusions and rebellions, and culminated in the conquest of the last independent and pagan Indian settlement at Lake Petén. After two centuries, Spanish control of the peninsula was finally complete, blemished only by the continuing British presence in the far southeast around the Belize River—a situation distasteful to Spanish officialdom but welcome enough to tax-evading Yucatecans and the smugglers who catered to them.

2 / Governing for God and King

The twin goals of the conquest were souls for heaven and riches for the living. Although in the eyes of many colonial participants there were not enough of either, both aims contributed to the foundations of the war that would tear the peninsula apart in the mid-nineteenth century.

Conquest by Contract

The Spanish empire in America had been created through a kind of free enterprise, as ambitious Spaniards, singly or in groups, financed their own campaigns of territorial gain under a royal patent that was obtained sometimes before, sometimes after, the fact of conquest. When Hernández de Córdoba and his company sailed, it was as a cooperatively floated venture for territory, for riches, or for slaves to be sold on the islands of the Spanish Indies, where native Indians were fast being exterminated by disease and domination. When Francisco Montejo set out on the conquest of Yucatan, it was at his own expense, armed beforehand with his royal appointment as *adelantado* and captain general (military commander) of the unconquered region but acting in effect as a privateer. When Hernán Cortés approached the American mainland it was at the head of an expedition financed by himself, by the other captains and some of the ordinary soldiers of the troop, and in particular by the governor of Cuba. Only after his spectacular conquest was Cortés appointed governor and captain general of New Spain and confirmed in his de facto overlordship—the result of a piece of chicanery that cut the governor of Cuba completely out of the enterprise, despite his investment. If the financial returns of the first two of these campaigns made no noticeable contribution to the royal coffers, at least the cost to the Spanish Crown of the military actions was negligible. But with the triumph of Cortés on mainland New Spain, the harvest of a treasure in objects of precious metal, and—in particular—the discovery of mines, brought the Crown an incredible return: precious metals were taxed directly by the king at the rate of 20 percent of the assayed value.

But the freebooting approach could work only if would-be conquerors saw clear hope of profit. So the hierarchical Spanish social system offered lesser and often more immediate rewards by way of grants of tribute from conquered towns or regions, paid in whatever goods were locally current. Thus, conquest brought into immediate being two great categories of residents: Spanish *vecinos*, citizens, who in fact or potential were those who collected the tribute, and *indios*, Indians, the conquered masses who inevitably paid it. After the successful third *entrada* into Yucatan, conqueror-governor Montejo assigned regions, towns, or parts of towns in *encomienda* to his supporters. And the *encomendero* after the manner of a feudal lord collected his tribute, governed his Indians, and—theoretically—saw them converted to Christianity.

The holder of an *encomienda* might be a harsh master, but his tributaries were at least in theory positioned well on the free side of slavery. By the time Yucatan was conquered, Indians had been declared the special wards of the Spanish monarch himself, and (in contrast to Africans) their enslavement could legitimately occur only under very special circumstances: specifically, slaves of conquered Indians could continue to be treated as slaves; Indians in rebellion could be reduced to slavery; and, as a subcategory of the last, Indians who refused to swear fealty to the Crown when formally and officially advised of the virtues of doing so (for they were by definition in rebellion if they refused) could be enslaved.[1] But even these exceptions were rare in practice. Traffic in Indian slaves was roundly and unanimously condemned by the clergy and by the bureaucratic Spanish officialdom who quickly came to administer Crown policies, and the great majority of Indians were at least nominally free.

The Church and *Congregación*

At the time of the conquest and for some time afterward, the basis of subsistence—and tribute—in the relatively heavily occupied northern rim of Yucatan lay with the slash-and-burn cultivation of agricultural crops, in particular of corn or maize (*Zia mays*).[2] Fields were cleared of brush, burned, planted with the aid of a digging stick, farmed two years or possibly three, then allowed to lie fallow until the *monte* or dry forest gained a sufficient height and density in the eye of the farmer to indicate the land could profitably be farmed again (about ten years in most cases).[3] Although recent research has demonstrated conclusively that cultivation regimes much more intensive than this were in use throughout much of the lowland area presumably inhabited by Maya-speaking peoples at the height of the pre-Hispanic civilization,[4] no such evidence exists for northern Yucatan, where the absence of watercourses or swamps, the paucity of moisture, and the porosity of the limestone ruled out the construction of drained fields, irrigation works, or even water-conserving terraces.

Appropriate to this basic, shifting agricultural practice, which required lands four to five times the extent of those in cultivation at any one time, was a relative dispersal of population. Even so, this was not a dispersal as complete as the slash-and-burn practice might be thought to render desirable, for the Maya still showed an obvious preference for living in small if scattered population clusters, each apparently based upon a set of patrilaterally related kin.[5]

The final result was that despite the existence in the 1530s of a number of Indian towns of fairly substantial size, the bulk of the native Yucatecan population was scattered among a multitude of hamlets, which would be referred to in Spanish as *ranchos*. And so in the 1550s, when the conquest was complete, the predominantly Franciscan clergy, seeking efficient conversion and religious control of the newly subject population, promoted the forcible relocation of hamlets into villages, and villages into towns, although preexisting territorial divisions were maintained and village landownership was not seriously disrupted.[6]

Although the policy was initially successful, the centrifugal effects of habit and agriculture worked against the continuation of these larger population clusters. There is evidence that within only a few decades individual Indian families were drifting away from the new centers to reestablish old hamlets, some of this movement apparently in response to disease epidemics, some to avoid Spanish labor requirements, most in order to be closer to active cornfields. By the end of the century it was necessary for the Franciscans to forcibly recongregate some areas.

But this conflict between nucleation for religious and administrative reasons and dispersal for subsistence and other reasons continued, causing sporadic efforts by church and government to collect outward-drifting Maya. It was never resolved,[7] however, and by the end of the colonial period the dispersal in ranchos may have equaled that existing at the time of conquest.[8]

The Naturalization of Christianity

Despite the difficulty of the military conquest of Yucatan, conversions to Christianity followed quickly and easily. Notions of God, the Trinity, and the Virgin Mary, as well as the symbol of the cross, were taken up immediately. Masses of people were baptized—including *principales* or nobles, with native priests among them—each person marked as a nominal convert by a Spanish baptismal name that was linked with the Maya lineage- or surname.[9]

But what the friars would see as true conversion demanded a radical reorientation in native ritual and civil life. Under the new regime blood sacrifice of animals as well as humans was forbidden, as was the wearing of masks and ceremonial costumes. Tattooing, body painting, the use of nose- and earplugs were outlawed. Caciques might be required to free their slaves in return for baptism. And so, despite the acceptance of baptism and Christian names by ostensibly willing converts, a real reorientation could be achieved only through the exercise of continued and close clerical surveillance. Given the magnitude of the task, this was impossible.

By the 1560s there were a dozen fairly substantial Franciscan establishments. With the added labors of the small number of secular clergy on the peninsula the Franciscans built small churches in many pueblos, and by the 1560s, there were nearly two hundred such native settlements. Most of them could not be served with regularity even as *visita* points on a large circuit.

With *congregación* there was also the establishment of schools for *principales*, the native nobility, in which were taught some prayers, the importance of the sacraments, and Spanish. It was to these newly and sketchily Europeanized intellectuals that the spiritual and educational care of most of the Mayan population was in turn entrusted.[10] This system resulted not in the reorientation of ritual life envisioned by the priests but rather in the incorporation of Christian teachings into a body of native belief and ritual from which only the elements most obviously repugnant to the Spaniards were eliminated.

It will not do to presume that the bulk of the conversions were not sincere on some level. Still, no matter how sincerely embraced, the new teachings were taken as an addition to, rather than a substitute for, more ancient practices. In time, the early native noble-instructors gave way to more regularized and specifically ritual practitioners in the persons of lay readers or *maestros cantores*, functionaries like those of today who in the absence of the priest perform subsacramental ceremonies in rural churches and who then may participate in pagan observances in the fields or even on the church steps. The end result of this system of delegated instruction is the syncretic body of ritual and religion that characterizes the present-day Maya of Yucatan and neighboring regions, in which saints are worshipped not only in church but also in fields, where they are joined by folk deities like the rain-powerful Chacs.[11]

Although in recent years this syncretism seems to have assumed forms at least tolerable to the regular Catholic priesthood, in earlier times the combinations of elements were often abhorrent. Reminiscent of that Mayan priest of eastern Yucatan who was said by Montejo to have claimed to be the Son of God (see chapter 1), in 1597 a native of Sotuta was condemned to death for inciting Indians to idolatry, on the complaint that he represented himself as another Moses, while secreting a boy in his house and passing the voice off as that of the Holy Spirit giving instruction. More organizationally inclined were a pair in 1610 who set themselves up as pope and bishop, ordained lesser priests, said mass in church vestments, gave communion, and confessed adults. Later in the same century, when Indians from Bacalar fled south and turned apostate, native priests were reported by Father Fuensalida to have treated their flocks to a mass in which tortillas and maize gruel replaced bread and wine.[12]

The Erosion of Local Power

The system of privateer captains who conquered in the name of the Spanish crown had definite financial advantages for the royal house. It also tended, however, to build a class of feudal lords that was anathema to a ruler such as the monarch known both as Charles I of Spain and Charles V of the Holy Roman Empire, who had a decided preference for absolutism. This begat a set of royal efforts designed to mitigate the strength of local rule in the new Spanish territories.

First there was the the Council of the Indies, formed to sit in Spain in charge of all the monarch's New World affairs. Then came the establishment of the New World *audiencias*, or superior courts, to which legal decisions of the governors were subordinate. The *audiencia* of Mexico, established less than a decade after the conquest, was thus the first local brake on the power of Cortés. And very quickly governing power was invested in a royally appointed viceroy, supreme over all New Spain.

Although the first of the *audiencias* was established only after Montejo received his original royal commission, it immediately assumed an intermediate position between him as *adelantado* of Yucatan and the Council of the Indies as agent of the king in Spain. By the end of 1550, only four years after the final conquest of the peninsula, the *audiencias* of Confines (with its seat in Central America) and of Mexico, which alternately held jurisdiction over Yucatan, had with royal approval removed Montejo as governor and stripped him of his *encomiendas*.

The same movement toward absolute rule by the crown led to significant changes in the nature of the *encomienda*, whereby *encomenderos* were separated physically and administratively from the pueblos that paid tribute into their pockets.[13] This did not, however, imply disapproval by the Crown of the position of Spanish colonists as overlords or of the tribute system per se, for revenues from vacated *encomiendas* were often pooled to provide incomes for Spaniards holding no *encomienda* directly. The system would survive in Yucatan through the eighteenth century.

Another aspect of the movement to impose royalist rule was the effort to lessen the power of the *cabildos* of incorporated Spanish towns through the appointment of regional officials responsible directly to the governor. In Yucatan, contrary to the situation in many parts of Mexico, this attempt met with little success, unlike the revisions to the local *encomienda* system that were just mentioned.

The Organization of Governance

Elected officers of the four Spanish-oriented *vecino* municipalities consisted of those termed *alcalde* (a justice, sometimes translated as mayor), *regidor* (councillor or alderman, usually representing a subdivision such as a ward), and *alguacil* (constable). These formed units of the self-governing Spanish segment of Yucatan, the *república de españoles*. Closely parallel to this organization was that of the *república de indios* or *república de indígenas*, which from the 1550s on served as the means of indirect rule of the Indian population of each pueblo.

As in the four *vecino* municipalities, elected officers of the Indian *república* in each pueblo consisted of a pair of *alcaldes*, three or four *regidores*, several *alguaciles*, and a few others; but there was also a professional scribe who was literate in Maya and sometimes in Spanish. Above these in each *república* was an Indian *gobernador* nominally appointed by the governor of Yucatan, although there is evidence that this *gobernador* was in fact commonly chosen by members of the *república*—usually from among the *principales,* those remnants of the preconquest nobility from which were selected the majority of all Indian officials.[14]

In addition to these officers, in the early years alongside the *gobernador* and probably above him appeared the local *cacique,* the traditional ruler whose position was inherited from preconquest times and still recognized by the conquerors, although the same *cacique* might also hold the office of *gobernador.* By the seventeenth century, however, the separate office of *cacique* seems to have disappeared, and thereafter the terms *gobernador* and *cacique* tend to be used interchangeably for the ranking officer of the Indian *república.*[15] Throughout the period, there was never any supravillage Indian organization, for above the *gobernador* the Indian pueblos were directly subject to representatives of the governor of Yucatan. Thus, the traditions of local autonomy that had been so difficult for the Spaniards to overcome in the conquest of Yucatan were perpetuated and even intensified by the particular mechanism of indirect rule that was integral to the colonial governing apparatus.[16]

With regard to the non-Indian population, the difficulties experienced by the governors of Yucatan in planting their own magistrates within the territorial jurisdictions of the four prideful and obstreperous Spanish municipalities were not overcome for more than a century. But with the seventeenth-century troubles from pirates and recalcitrant Indians, the governor began to appoint the local official called *capitán a guerra,* charged with organizing local militia (composed of *vecinos* rather than Indians), seeing to the manning of sentry posts, seeking out pirate bases, rounding up fugitive Indians, and so on. Because of its primarily military nature, the position conflicted less seriously with the civil-judicial functions of the *cabildos,* but nevertheless by the middle of the eighteenth century this infiltration of the hinterlands by the central government of Yucatan led to the presence of the quasi-political military *partido,* or district. These *partidos* thus did finally include centrally appointed magistrates with military and civil powers, in a governmental structure that existed alongside the *cabildos* of the original Spanish settlements.

Rather than superseding the broad areal jurisdiction of the *cabildos,* however, as occurred in many regions of Mexico, in Yucatan both municipality and *partido* continued to act in parallel and redundant fashion.[17] And parallel to both was the structure of the Indian *repúblicas*, which by reporting directly to the governor rather than to local officials were able to maintain autonomy.

Tribute, Tributaries, and Taxes

Initially, but with dwindling effect as the colonial period wore on and the numbers of Indians decreased, the basic support of the colonial structure was the civil tribute paid by Indian tributary and destined for the *encomendero* or, if the *encomienda* had reverted to the Crown, for the king. Not long after the conquest, tribute was set to include for each married male a certain amount of woven cotton cloth, an amount of maize, and two fowls (turkey and chicken), the cash equivalent of about twenty-four *reales* (with the Spanish *real* equal to one-eighth peso). Later this was modified to include lesser payments by more people—adult men and women, single or married. This was finally settled at a cash equivalent of fourteen *reales* per year for each male aged fourteen to sixty, and eleven *reales* for each female aged twelve to fifty-five, and so it continued until the late eighteenth century, when tribute for women was abolished.

To these must be added three recurrent lesser taxes, one for community expense, one to support nominally free legal service to Indians, and a third—religiously phrased but destined for civil coffers nonetheless—to purchase an indulgence permitting the consumption of meat on fast days. These have been estimated at thirty-eight *reales* per year for each married couple.

So much for the civil tribute, paid only by Indians and destined for support of both civil government and *encomendero*. There was also, however, a system of religious taxation that fell on both *vecino* and *indio*, although unequally.

Vecinos were traditionally charged a tithe. Actually collected by the civil government, a portion was allocated to the parish priest, but the bulk of it was forwarded to Mérida where most of it went to the bishop of Yucatan, while a percentage entered the channels of civil government. Again by tradition, the tithe was assessed against increases in livestock or other products of the land but not against cash wages if these were the sole income. A very poor *vecino* (and there were many as time went on) was in effect exempt. What was more consistently charged, however, was a set of fees for sacraments and other services—particularly baptisms, confirmations, marriages, and burials.

Having little property subject to taxable increase as tithes, both sexes among those legally classified as Indians were charged an annual head tax referred to piously as *limosna* or "alm" by the clergy, otherwise as *obvención mayor*. Payable in kind at various intervals and calculated at locally customary values for a variety of goods (cotton cloth, pigs, chickens, etc.), this tax went directly to the parish, and because customary parish values for goods were often significantly lower than the going market price in the urban centers, the obvention payments in kind might place the parish priest in position to engage in a profitable trade in commodities. These taxes were considered the equivalent of cash (in which some Indians came to pay them) in the amount of 12.5 *reales* for a male aged fourteen to sixty, 9 *reales* for a female aged twelve to fifty-five. Not only was the income so realized of crucial importance to the parish, but the labors of the Indians who served in menial capacities in the church establishment and in the quarters of the priests were remunerated by excusing them from payment of all or part of the obventions.

But here, also, there were additional taxes: particularly the weekly fees (an egg and a jar of oil) charged for instruction of each Indian child in Christian doctrine, and those scheduled fees termed *obvenciones menores* that paid for baptisms, confirmations, weddings, and burials. These, with the *obvenciones mayores*, have been estimated to total somewhat more than thirty-four *reales* per year for each Indian married couple.[18] Thus, the civil and religious taxes assessed against an Indian married couple for much of the colonial period totaled somewhat more than seventy-two *reales* per year, which in the calculation of one historian amounted to half or more of the Indian family's annual income.[19]

The obligations reportedly most odious to the Indian population, however, were not the civil head tax and obventions but rather a portion of the general set of labor obligations that might also be subsumed under the rubric of tribute. One of these was a labor draft.

One day's labor was required of one person of each family every week for local projects such as maintenance of the church building or for service to officials of the *república de indios*. At less specific intervals labor was demanded for major public works or for duty as a postal runner or as a litter bearer, if a priest needed to be carried from town to town. But it appears that these were accepted with equanimity. What was galling was the requirement of personal service to *vecinos*.

The *servicio personal* was a draft whereby each Indian pueblo was assessed a weekly quota of male and female workers (*semaneros*) who were assigned to individual *vecinos* by a permit that specified the number the *vecino* was permitted to employ. A wage was to be paid, but it was low, was often evaded in one way or another, and did not cover time spent traveling from pueblo to workplace. In addition, the term of work might be extended by the Spaniard against the inclination of the worker, and there were extra customary gratuities of labor and firewood that were expected to be paid by the Indian to the local official who was in charge of labor allocations.[20]

A second, hard-felt oppression was labor in the form of *repartimiento* common in Yucatan: Spaniards—often lieutenants of the governor—provided raw material such as cotton together with an advance of cash, in exchange for which Indian recipients were required in a specified time to return a finished product such as woven cloth.[21] With the customary price kept artificially low, with short supplies of the raw materials often foisted on the recipient, with long measure often required for the finished product, and with the Spanish party to the transaction able to enforce compliance through the threat of corporal punishment, it is no wonder that attempts to avoid *repartimiento* were blamed for a number of defections of Indians from pueblos in the vicinity of the Spanish towns.[22]

Such was the plight of the Indian taxpayer.

Indians in the Hierarchy

In the immediate aftermath of conquest, the Spaniards recognized the existence of a local aristocracy and made use of it to secure and maintain control over the mass of the Indian population. Loyalty of these *principales* was obtained by the granting of certain favors, such as a total or partial exemption from tribute. This had been the formula for the maintenance of peace and the extension of control throughout New Spain. One result of it was that the upper Indian classes were the first to become hispanicized and the first to be absorbed into the upper levels of colonial society, where in many regions they eventually disappeared from view as Indians.[23]

In colonial Yucatan as a part of this same approach, *caciques* were asked in the early days to lead their armed Indian followers into campaigns to subjugate those of their native fellows who resisted the domination of the Spaniards or who had fled from it to the forests of the interior. The most extreme and one of the best documented examples of this is the case of Pablo Paxbolon, *cacique* of the pueblo of Tixchel south of Champotón. Born at the very beginning of Spanish domination, he was educated in the

Franciscan monastery in Campeche, returned to his people at age fourteen, and not long after became head of their ruling family. In his early twenties he entered fully upon his duties as leader, loyal to the overlord. In 1583, when he was about forty, the government executed a formal contract with him to undertake without substantial Spanish supervision the reduction of rebellious Indians in the adjacent interior, a contract that was renewed four years later. Again, in 1599 he actively rounded up fugitives, and in 1604 he was involved in negotiations that led to the submission of a number of apostate interior towns. Similar, although less discretionary, commissions are known to have been extended at about the same time to Juan Chan, *cacique* of Chancenote in the far northeast of the peninsula.[24] Other Indian groups apparently acted similarly, although most campaigns were under direct Spanish supervision and control. Apparently some of the loyal principales were awarded the title *hidalgo*, which brought with it some reduction in tribute.[25]

Although it appears that the descendants of Indians from central Mexico who had been Montejo's allies in the original conquest of the Maya continued to have certain military functions through the colonial period, by the middle seventeenth century the use of all other Indian forces, even under direct Spanish leadership, had ceased.[26] Along with this withdrawal of military trust from the Maya went a general prohibition against their possession of firearms, although it was seldom enforced. The Indians, who as a regular part of their subsistence hunted deer and other forest animals in the secondary growth of brush that surrounded their milpas, found muskets eminently useful. But in times of political instability their firearms might be subject to confiscation.[27]

Parallel to the employment of local Maya leaders in military matters during the early years after the conquest was the attempt, as has been said, to educate their offspring. Initially, priests established schools for the native nobility in which they taught Spanish or even Latin. But skill with the Spanish alphabet—only slightly adapted—also enabled the writing of the Mayan language, and from this came the limited but real tradition of literacy in Maya that resulted in the native literature that includes the books of Chilam Balam, some of which are now widely known in translation.[28] But just as the Maya militia was eliminated after the early decades, so were systematic attempts to teach Spanish to Indians. Such limited education in literacy thereafter was through the catechism classes to which all Maya youth were subjected, in which native catechists might teach selected pupils to read and write in Maya.[29]

In time, as the colonial period wore on, the separate category of *principal* or *cacique* disappeared (except as the latter came to denote the appointed pueblo *gobernador*), as the holders of these hereditary statuses tended either to rise to become accepted as *vecinos*—sometimes with adoption of a Spanish surname—or else to sink into what appeared from above to be a homogeneous mass of those deemed legally Indian. With ethnic and economic complexity came a hardening of hierarchical attitudes between *vecinos* and *indios*.

Even in the smallest towns and the most rural areas, where *vecinos* and Indians both spoke Maya and many of them might engage in almost identical subsistence pursuits, the latter deferred to the former. *Vecinos* came first, Indians second. At the rather frequent dances, for instance, *vecinos* and *indios* usually did not dance together, but the *vecinos* might dance their fill and then leave the dance floor and the rest of the night for the Indians.[30] These attitudes were also manifest in minor personal services offered without question by Indians to at least the upper classes of the *vecino* world.[31] Although only duly constituted authorities could legitimately mete out whippings for minor infractions of rules or for nondelivery of goods when due under *repartimiento*, almost any *vecino* could with impunity abuse almost any Indian by cuffs or kicks.[32] In the Yucatecan saying, "The Indians cannot hear except through their backsides."[33]

That set of attitudes continued into the twentieth century. The anthropologist Robert Redfield, from his study of communities on the peninsula, related of the town of Dzitás that the expectation was that a descendant *vecino* should carry a Spanish name, an Indian a Mayan name; any Indian was inferior to any *vecino*, regardless of how dark-skinned and poor a *vecino* might be. Although an older *indio* was addressed respectfully, only a *vecino* would be called *don*. And, of course, Indians should not put on airs: "In domestic life both classes wore the folk costume, but there were many small differences in costume associated with the difference in status. The huipils of the indias had little or very simple embroidery, while the huipils of the vecinas (*ternos*) had cross-stitch embroidery. 'If an india had worn a terno it would have been taken from her and burned at the door of the church.' "[34]

In short, the position of those legally classed as Indians was firmly at the bottom of a highly stratified social and economic structure.

As soon as the conquest had been accomplished by those independent military entrepreneurs who took the financial as well as the physical risks of warfare, the centralist Spanish government bestirred itself to eliminate the system of feudal rule that was the automatic result. But in Yucatan, attempts to centralize met successful resistance from the four well-entrenched Spanish municipalities, and it was almost two centuries before an effective system of district magistrates directly subject to the king's governor was instituted. Even then, a parallel juridical power was wielded by the Spanish *cabildos*, determined on self-rule.

Alongside the independent spirit of the Spanish centers was the decentralizing bent of the Indians, who displayed distaste for *congregación* by fading into the forest and against whom periodic campaigns of resettlement were necessary. Although the pervasive tendency to disperse caused their spiritual care and education to suffer, it did not eliminate the importance among them of the new *república de indios*, one of which was seated in each major Indian pueblo. There, Indians in elective offices patterned after those of the Spanish municipalities collected taxes and governed their subjects under the direction of a *gobernador*, who was directly accountable to the governor of Yucatan.

The separation in governance between Spaniard and Indian was paralleled by the clear legal and fiscal distinction between *vecino* and *indio*, with the latter expected to pay the entire cost of civil government, to support the *vecinos* through tribute, and to bear most of the expenses of the church. In the social realm, the Indian population was also at the bottom. As time went on, this position if anything was intensified, as recognition of the preconquest Indian nobility faded, as Indian militia units were eliminated, and as Indians were refused—officially if not always effectively—the right to use firearms.

3 / Changing with Time

However well defined the social and economic positions of the various segments of Yucatecan society may have been in theory, as time passed important changes become evident in three related areas: the relations between the people legally classed as Indians and part of those classed as *vecinos*; the size and distribution of the population; and the subsistence regime that serviced all of Yucatan.

The Merging of Civil Categories

Despite the unambiguous expectation that Indians and *vecinos* would be eternally identified by surname and despite the sense of superiority of the one over the other, through the colonial period the two social and civil categories inevitably began to overlap at the edges. The original division of the population between four incorporated Spanish municipalities on the one hand (*repúblicas de españoles*) and the large number of subsidiary but self-governing Indian pueblos on the other (*repúblicas de indios*) had been designed to keep the civil categories of *vecino* and *indio* physically separated and distinct from one another. This design was furthered by the indirect rule of Indians, in that the collection of tribute, the drafts of labor, and the conduct of *repartimientos* were administered by the Indian *gobernador* or *cacique* rather than directly by Spaniards. Nevertheless, in the long run such measures were unsuccessful. There were a number of ways in which amalgamation came about.[1]

The Urban *Criados*
The Spanish need for labor was satisfied by Indian servants, both men and women, who lived in the Spanish towns, supported and housed by their *vecino* employers, who also assumed responsibility for their tribute obligations (and to whom, of course, the servants became indebted). There, because the women served as nursemaids, these Indians had close contact with the

Spanish overlords and their children, with the result that the first language of even high-class *vecino* children became Maya rather than Spanish. The children of these *criados*, in turn, might become *criados* themselves, absorbed in the population of permanently engaged servants. Or they might drift outside the walls of the Spanish town, take up residence in the barrios or wards that sprang up around each of the four Spanish municipalities, and there join the pool of day laborers.

Unattached Servants

An Indian available for day labor, who lived immediately outside the walls of the Spanish town, might in Yucatan be referred to as *naborí*.[2] Formed into a *república de indios* exactly like those of the outlying pueblos, Indians of this category were responsible for the standard tribute but were not subject to *servicio personal* or *repartimiento*. They worked for *vecinos* and most of them were also slash-and-burn agriculturalists, some farming tracts recognized as communal property of the barrio, others paying rent in the form of labor to a *vecino*'s cattle farm.

But the presence of these extramural barrios was also an attraction to *indios de pueblo*, many of whom might be drawn from the hinterlands to the outskirts of the Spanish town without passing through the intermediate step of becoming a *vecino*'s *criado*. At the same time, individuals of the growing class of mestizos and mulattoes, also marginal to the Spanish society, tended to move into these suburban barrios, joining the pool of day laborers and—like their Indian compatriots—making slashed clearings for cornfields wherever they could. They also customarily spoke Maya and usually dressed like Maya, but as non-Indians they were not legally bound by Indian tribute requirements; they were *vecinos*. Thus, these extramural barrios came to house a population of Maya-speaking laborers and swidden farmers essentially alike in life habits but differing in legal status—some Indian, some *vecino*.

Vecino Dispersal

As the colonial period wore on, there was a dispersal of *vecinos*—chiefly mestizos, but also mulattoes and a few Spaniards—from the four Spanish municipalities to the larger of the Indian settlements. According to some estimates, by the end of the period these non-Indian residents amounted to some 30 percent of the population of the important or *cabecera* Indian towns and about 15 percent of even the smaller outlying pueblos.[3] As was the case in the extramural barrios, the language of these towns was almost entirely

Maya, which was spoken so habitually that mestizo *vecinos* of the pueblos were often, even predominantly, monolingual in that tongue. Such literacy as existed—and it was limited—was literacy in Maya.[4]

Indios Hidalgos

Indians of the special class known as *hidalgos* were exempt from tribute, and upon them other tax burdens fell lightly. In central Mexico, the people of this category were descended from the preconquest Indian nobility, especially the *principales* of those towns that had early befriended the invading Spaniards. Although some historians have accepted this situation as equally applicable to Yucatan, the position has been challenged with the suggestion that the *indios hidalgos* were descended not from native Maya nobility but from the Mexican Indian allies who accompanied Montejo on his third and final campaign.[5] Whatever their origin, as the colonial period advanced these *hidalgos* apparently tended to become identified as *vecinos*.

Racial Mixture

From the very beginning, of course, there developed a category of genetically mixed Spanish and Indian individuals, mestizos—chiefly children of Indian women by Spanish fathers, and usually illegitimate. At the same time, with the restricted but sporadic importation of black slaves and servants, there developed a category of mulattoes, some of them part Indian, some part Spanish.

All these offspring were classed as non-Indians, hence legally *vecinos*. And it seems clear that their Indian relatives saw advancement to this status as desirable. But although as *vecinos* these mixed bloods were exempt from the tribute and obventions of those who were Indians before the law, they were not any the less marginal to the Spanish society that reigned inside the one Spanish city and the three *villas*.[6]

The effect of all this—despite the feelings of difference in social rank between *vecino* and *indio*—was that by the end of the colonial period there was a decided blurring of the line between *vecino* and *indio* in a social, although not a legal or taxable, sense. As I noted earlier with regard to Redfield's study of the pueblo of Dzitás in the twentieth century, *vecinos* have been regarded as those with Spanish names and *indios* those with Indian names, between whom some corresponding class distinctions should be maintained.

But Redfield found that some part of the population of Dzitás fit these expectations with uncomfortable ambiguity: at one extreme of the 225 households, there were some Spanish-speaking families, *de vestido* (i.e., wearing Europeanized clothing), associated with specialized occupations; at the other end there was a much larger number of families in which Maya was spoken, the folk costume alone was worn, and occupations were subsistence agriculture or woodcutting. All these latter (Dzitás informants said) should have been *indios*—that is, should have had Indian names (for the legal distinction was by then eradicated)—but this was not uniformly the case. Redfield goes on to say that, "there are 38 households in which the social factors are inconsistently distributed; included are Maya-speaking mestizos who have specialized occupations, Maya-speaking *de vestido* people, and Spanish-speaking people, with the woman only *de vestido*, some of whom are simple agriculturalists and others of whom carry on specialized occupations. Of these intermediate families some have Spanish names and some Indian names. In the thinking of the old conservatives these 'mixed people' should not be there at all."[7] Obviously, the real situation departed from a conservative ideal, which in fact had eroded well before the end of the colonial period.

An indication of the nature of the overlap between civil status and ethnic origin of name is organized in table 1. This is derived from well-categorized lists of both males and females from nine separate parishes, spread from west to east in Yucatan, and dating from roughly the first decade of the nineteenth century. Of men in the legal and taxable category of Indian, 22 or four-tenths of 1 percent have Spanish names; of those legally *vecinos*, 106 or nearly 8 percent have Indian names. Put another way, of men with Indian names, nearly 1.8 percent are *vecinos*, while of men with Spanish names the same percentage are legally taxed as Indians.

In demonstrating this relatively small overlap, the figures in table 1 lend credence to the Yucatecan expectation that civil status could be predicted on the basis simply of the paternal surname. For with any given male of Indian name the chance was only about one in 55 that he would not be a legal Indian, and for a male with a Spanish name the chance is almost exactly the same that he would not be a *vecino*.

The corresponding proportions among females are nearly double those among men. Of Indian women, 46 or nearly three-fourths of 1 percent have Spanish names; of *vecinos*, 246 or more than 15 percent have Indian names. Again, among women with Indian names, 3.7 percent would be legally *vecinos*; of those with Spanish names, about 3.3 percent would be Indians.

Despite the general coincidence of name with civil status, then, a small but consistent blurring is evident.[8] The difference between the sexes in the

TABLE 1

The Coincidence of Name and Tax Status

| | Number of Tax-Liable Individuals | | |
Linguistic Origin of Surname	Indian	*Vecino*[a]	Total
Men			
Indian	5,815	106	5,921
Spanish	22	1,263	1,286
Total	5,838	1,369	7,207
Women			
Indian	6,468	246	6,654
Spanish	46	1,352	1,398
Total	6,454	1,598	8,052

Sources: Sources are name lists from nine parishes, dated 1802–11, in which civil status (*vecino, indio*) is clearly indicated and which formed the basis of information abstracted by Dumond and Dumond (1982, pt. 1) for the following documents: Abalá (1–4), Cacalchén (3–9), Chancenote (7–7), Chichimilá (10–5), Halachó (15–7), Homún (18–7), Kikil (23–5), Tixcacalcúpul (51–5), Xcan (58–3). Juveniles are omitted from the count.

Precise sources of surnames are not pursued. The category *Spanish* may include some names of non-Spanish origin, but they are clearly not Indian. Indian names include both Maya and the fairly common Yucatecan surnames derived from the Nahua language family.

[a]The few *indios hidalgos* listed for the towns of Homún and Xcan—a total of eight Spanish-named and thirty-seven Indian-named males, four Spanish-named and forty-three Indian-named females—are included here with the expectation that they would be taxed as *vecinos*. The complete elimination from consideration of this rare category changes the proportions on the table somewhat but does not alter the conclusions to be drawn from it.

degree of this concordance occurs because more Indian-named women and Spanish-named men married each other than did Spanish-named women and Indian-named men, and civil status followed the male, the wife assuming the position of her husband.[9]

But an even greater factor in the blurring of the categories can be illustrated. Although table 2 is drawn from an uncomfortably small sample—four lists from four parishes—it shows that nearly 3 percent of the Maya-

TABLE 2

Indian versus Spanish Surnames in Marriage

		Wives		
		Indian Surname	Spanish Surname	Total
Husbands	Indian Surname	1,662	33	1,695
	Spanish Surname	50	114	164
	Total Individuals	1,712	147	1,859

Sources: Based on four name lists, each from a separate parish and of differing dates between 1803 and 1840, in which conjugal units were unambiguously identified, and which formed the basis of information abstracted by Dumond and Dumond (1982, pt. 1) for the following documents: Ixil (21–6), Homún (18–7), Kimbilá (43A-3), Tixcacalcupul (51–5).

named women married Spanish-named men, while fewer than 2 percent of Maya-named men married Spanish-named women. But it shows that while 22 percent of the Spanish-named women married Maya-named men, 30 percent of Spanish-named men married Maya-named women.[10] The result here is significant in terms of the modification of at least the affective interrelationships of many individuals otherwise divided between the categories Indian and *vecino*. That is, to the extent that this sample represents rural Yucatan, one can conclude that about 30 percent of *vecinos* would have had a mother of Indian surname and hence probably Indian civil status and about 50 percent of *vecinos* would have had either a mother or grandmother of Indian surname. This points to a situation that will become of great importance in the chapters that follow: a significant number of rural Yucatecan *vecinos* must have had a preponderance of Indian relatives and must have been Indian in outlook if not Indians before the law or as perceived by the majority of urban Yucatecans.

Population

Before dealing with the economic regime, changes in population size and condition must first be addressed. Two calculations of population sizes of Indians and *vecinos* through the colonial period are summarized in table 3.

Most of the original figures on which these and similar compilations are based were recorded in terms of tributaries or other taxpayers rather than as the total of all individuals. Differences between the two calculations have

TABLE 3
Two Estimates of the Population of Yucatan, 1511–1842

Date	Estimate A			Estimate B		
	Indians	Non-Indians	Total	Indians	Non-Indians	Total
1511	1,128,000	—	1,128,000	>800,000	—	>800,000
1528				800,000	—	800,000
1549–50	265,000	1,550	266,550	240,000	insignificant	240,000
1580					2,500	
1600–1605	150,000	6,300	156,300	185,000	7,050	192,050
1609				195,000		
1639–40				209,000	10,000	219,000
1650	160,000	8,400	168,400			
1700	185,000	21,250	106,250			
1736				127,000		
1750	280,000	45,550	325,550			
1794–1800	320,000	100,000	420,000	254,000	103,000	357,000
1821	380,000	120,000	500,000			
1842				431,520	143,840	575,360

Sources: Estimate A is that of Gerhard (1979, 25), estimate B of Cook and Borah (1974, 38, 48, 75, 112, 123, and 124), who accept the 1842 estimate of Regil and Peón (1853, 289) but agree with those authors in rejecting the figures for 1845 and 1846. The 1842 totals are otherwise supported by a recently published census of 1821 (Rodríguez Losa 1985, tables 8, 9): lacking a division of the population into Indians and non-Indians, the 1821 census yields a figure of 486,931 for the total population of all jurisdictions except for Mérida, Campeche, and Bacalar, which are missing, and a total projected population for Yucatan—with the three absences corrected by regression—of 538,907.

been attributed largely to the use of different multipliers when converting tributaries or other population fractions to total population.[11] These two lists agree, certainly, in indicating a massive population loss in the century or more following the conquest—a decline by a figure that even the more conservative formulations place at 80 percent of the original population. Both of the sources of table 3 calculate the loss to be closer to 90 percent— although acknowledging a very important uncertainty regarding the loss from disease and warfare in the murky period between the shipwreck of 1511, which deposited the early castaways on the Yucatecan beach, and the completion of the conquest campaigns of the 1540s. Where the two present compilations do not agree is in the timing of the population minimum: One places it in the early seventeenth century, a time corresponding closely with the date of the population nadir in the central Mexican highlands.[12] The other places it about a century later.[13]

Whatever the precise timing, the major cause of the massive decline must have been for Yucatan, as it was for highland Mexico, devastating epidemics of newly imported diseases. Although lists of such epidemics are not in agreement regarding all dates, they do agree in general frequency. One of these counts twelve major epidemics in the 244 years from 1566 to 1810, nine of them falling before 1727; identifiable diseases are typhus, yellow fever, smallpox, and measles. To make matters worse, the epidemics were interspersed with a still greater number of famines or other demographically traumatic events.[14]

Both estimates in table 3 agree that a rebounding of the Indian population began no later than the mid-eighteenth century and by the outbreak of the insurrection in 1847 had risen to a figure approaching 450,000—probably no more than one-half, possibly no more than one-third, of the native population of Yucatan at the time Columbus made his first landfall in the Indies. Meanwhile, after the conquest the small non-Indian population grew steadily, reaching a size in the mid-nineteenth century that approximated a third of that of the Indian population.

As will be seen, these changes provided much of the basis for shifts in the nature of Yucatecan agricultural activity during the colonial period.

The Agricultural Regime

In considering the broad trends in economic activities through the time of the Spanish colony, it is possible to bring internal population movements, population decline and growth, and the subsistence system into at least fuzzy alignment.[15]

With the major drop in Indian population that continued for at least a century—possibly almost two centuries—after the conquest, the tributary income that was so basic to the Yucatecan economy decreased progressively and substantially. And here, as in highland Mexico, the depopulation of the land was balanced by the development of cattle-raising estates. Unlike those of central Mexico, however, these holdings—referred to in Yucatan as *estancias*—were of modest size with only a few regular hands to conduct the business, which was the small-scale production of beef for local consumption and hides for export and the keeping of bees for honey and wax, both of which were exported as well as consumed locally. Corn and cotton consumption in the Spanish towns continued to be produced by the Indian population, despite its shrinking size, so that these earlier ranching operations, most of which were located near the coast on the west or north of the peninsula, included almost no horticulture. Because *estancia* manpower requirements were still low, there was no significant shortage of labor and little development of debt peonage.

It was not until sometime in the eighteenth century, as the Indian population began to rebound and the non-Indian population continued its increase, that the situation began to change. The alteration was then fairly dramatic.

With tracts in the populated areas absorbed by Spanish *estancias*, the burgeoning Indian and mestizo population began to find no lands nearby for the shifting cultivation of maize. Although hopeful farmers might complain about this conversion of lands that had previously been open to them, they adjusted by renting land from *estancias*, usually by becoming *luneros*, or hands who gave one day a week (Monday or *lunes*) to the landlord.

As the growing population began to absorb the food supply, the *estancias* for the first time had found it profitable to raise crops such as rice or corn for the urban markets (the standard European grains did not grow or store well in Yucatan). By the year 1800 shortages had become chronic, and grain was being imported, paid for chiefly by exports of hides and other products of the cattle industry, which not surprisingly tended to expand in response to growth in internal and external markets. A decline in locally produced cotton was roughly balanced by the loss of foreign markets for cotton cloth that resulted from growing outside competition.

Increase in local demand—mainly for *aguardiente*, a crude rum—also helped to stimulate the beginnings of a Yucatecan sugar industry in the southwestern and southern regions, where rainfall was heavier and sugar cultivation was possible. Here, for the first time, a critical shortage of field hands was experienced in the labor-intensive cane fields, and some black slaves were imported to the region around Campeche and Champotón. This situation was not general, however.

Reforms under the Bourbons

In 1713 the Treaty of Utrecht ended a European war, permitted some British participation in the trade of Spanish America, and confirmed the Bourbon replacement of the Hapsburgs on the throne of Spain. In doing so, it presented the scepter to a line of monarchs who staunchly favored absolutism in government and efficiency in fiscal management. The reforms that served these double ends attempted simply to stave off the bankruptcy that dogged the Bourbon heels, but they worked drastic changes in the colonial world of Spanish America, Yucatan included.

The policies accomplished their goal in two major ways: by collecting tribute and taxes directly, rather than through contractors working on commission, and by freeing trade to stimulate the economy and thus to generate more personal income and more transactions subject to tax. Economically, the policies did stimulate Yucatan as a whole. Socially, there were hardships wreaked upon the Indians and their local organizations.[16]

The Stimulation of Commerce

The Spanish fleet system that had managed the trade between Cádiz and the colonies for so long never fully recovered from depredations suffered during the successional wars, and the Caribbean foothold that was allowed the English by treaty stimulated contraband as well as an increase in shipment by foreign vessels. The climax came during the Seven Years' War (1756–63) in which Spain was pitted (as usual) against England, which was able to take and hold Havana for a time. More than seven hundred English ships were said to have entered that captive Spanish port during the few years of occupation, hauling in textiles, ironware, timber, livestock, and black slaves.

When the war ended, Spain tried to combat her loss of control of Caribbean commerce by an internal policy of so-called free trade: she relaxed the traditional restrictions on intercolony commerce and on exchanges between the colonies and Spanish ports other than Cádiz, and she lowered tariffs, although trade was still not broadly permitted with foreign ports or foreign ships. This modified free trade began in newly regained Cuba and was extended to Yucatan in 1770. In 1812 the port of Sisal became commercially important, posing a threat to the dominance of Campeche. In 1814 both Yucatecan ports received authorization to trade with almost complete freedom from colonial restrictions, while continuing to collect duties at the the reduced scale introduced in 1770.[17]

A result of this was a rapid growth in Yucatecan commerce. Although the export of cloth had suffered damaging competition from developing mills in Mexico and abroad, shipments of Yucatecan cordage (from agave fiber) and other agricultural products were substantial. Duties collected on trade through Campeche increased nearly sixfold between the end of the Seven Years' War and the close of the century.

And because those items that Yucatan could supply were largely agricultural, agriculture boomed. Tithe income—which tapped growth in commercial farm and ranch production—quadrupled between 1635 and 1815, with a 100 percent increase from 1775 to 1815.[18] Thus, the royal aims of increased revenue were fairly well met, although even the lowered import and export duties did not eliminate the wholesale smuggling that had become traditional.

The Imposition of Direct Government

In the year after the close of the Seven Years' War, royal fiscal control was imposed with the intendance system, beginning—as with free trade—in Cuba. In 1786 the innovation was installed in Yucatan, the title *intendant* added to that of governor, and a highly organized fiscal management staff put in place below that functionary. Finally, direct representatives of the governor with broad administrative and judicial powers, agents such as those who had been forestalled for so long by the *cabildos* of the Spanish municipalities, were thrust upon local districts. Eleven *partidos* were created, each headed by a magistrate called a *subdelegado* or subdelegate, who was assisted by a team of *jueces españoles* or justices of the peace. A *subdelegado* or *juez español* was thus assigned to every parish seat or *cabecera* in Yucatan, with powers much more wide ranging than those of the *capitanes a guerra*.

The *repúblicas de indios* then became answerable to these local officials, rather than directly to the governor of Yucatan. The new officials also extracted directly from the Indians the tribute and other taxes that had earlier been collected by the Indian *gobernador* of the *república*. This included not only the tribute destined for the crown or the *encomendero* but the portion of the tax that was supposedly destined for local community (*república*) expenses, which from this time forward was to be held on behalf of the

Indian republics by the central government of the state. The upshot was that the *repúblicas* had much less money available for their government expenses and periodic festivals, which required both gunpowder for fireworks and alcohol for drinking.

At the same time that the amount of direct government of the Indians increased, two ancient institutions of indirect control were eliminated. In 1783, the *repartimiento* was abolished—no doubt to the Indians' relief, although the decline of the market for cotton cloth and the increase in other forms of commerce apparently had already forced most entrepreneurs in directions other than those for which the *repartimiento* was advantageous. And in 1785 the private *encomienda* was abolished, or rather phased out, with the grants being brought to an end on the death of the current incumbents.

Altogether, the new policies caused discomfort to the Indian *repúblicas* in the loss of revenues over which they had previously had independent (and usually nonaccountable) control. More particularly, they distressed the officers of those *repúblicas*, who found their powers seriously eroded.

Pressure on Land

Another set of trends coincided with the Bourbon fiscal introductions that in the long run was far more lethal to the welfare of Indians, or for that matter to all rural subsistence farmers regardless of civil status. As I noted earlier, the eighteenth century was a time of significant growth in both Indian and *vecino* population, a circumstance that underlay the trends discussed in the next two sections.

The Expansion of Commercial Agriculture
Further economic stimulation of Yucatan came with the Bourbon-encouraged export trade of the late eighteenth century, expanding the cattle and crop production of the newly commercial estates. Mixed farming on former cattle *estancias* was reflected by a change in nomenclature, the term *hacienda* coming to be used for these larger agricultural establishments. Furthermore, because of the lands available on these estates, but no longer accessible on the overcrowded tracts near pueblos or extramural barrios of western Yucatan, there was a continual exodus of Indians from the pueblos and *vecinos* from the towns to new settlements on haciendas, which were growing in population and production. By the end of the eighteenth century there were establishments with as many as two thousand head of livestock.

Although there was some grumbling by hacienda owners, the landlords began to pay the tribute owed by the Indians who lived on their lands, recording the amounts as debts to be worked off. This was the inception of a true form of debt peonage, although it never became as pervasive as in central Mexico. So it was that by the end of the eighteenth century and the colonial era a significant proportion of the Yucatecan population, both Indian and *vecino*, lived on privately held rural estates.

But this rural development was almost entirely a phenomenon of the region of the northwest and of the western coastal zone around Campeche. That is, the commercial developments were largely confined to the area with the greatest population and with the best access to the seacoast and its two active ports. The result was that in the region where there had earlier been space enough for both the small cattle *estancias* and the swidden-farming pueblo dwellers, the *estancias*-become-haciendas showed an appetite for all available lands. In this competition, the *vecino hacendado* inevitably beat out the small subsistence farmer.

To the east and south, however, the much more thinly settled but growing rural population simply expanded into unoccupied lands without significant change in modus vivendi. The turn of some of these people to feel pressure on lands would come only in the following century, as the government made free to sell what it called *terrenos baldíos* (vacant lands), which the rural people saw as *monte* in which to raise their crops. Still, such pressure sprang not from internal growth but rather from attempts by the Yucatecan government to avoid bankruptcy (see chapters 4 and 5).

The Loss of *Cofradía* Estates

At the same time, and almost perfectly coincident with the centralization of the Bourbon civil government, there was a fiscal centralization effort by the bishop of Mérida. This was a plan for the confiscation and sale of *cofradía* estates of the *repúblicas de indios*—couched in terms of the Indians' good. These estates had developed as communally operated cattle *estancias* for the maintenance of the cult of specific saints, their income directed especially toward expenses for the annual fiesta. They thus provided support for the ritual side of the *república de indios*. The bishop's aim was to sell off the estates, for which there was now a ready market, and invest the money in certain mortgages that promised a fixed income of some 5 percent per year; money and income would be managed for, rather than by, the Indians.[19]

Faced with the loss of their revenues to increasingly efficient Bourbon government tax collectors—revenues that had often been diverted from other community maintenance projects to the support of the annual fiesta—the *repúblicas* could have relied on the *cofradía* income to ease their financial shortfall. But the confiscation of the *cofradía* estates left them no source of village-controlled income at all. And sale of the estates to budding commercial enterprises heightened the pressure on now crowded lands.

Fortunately, the governor of Yucatan was both opposed to the bishop's plan and no real friend of the bishop himself, and before all the estates had been sold he was able to halt transfer of the remainder through an injunction from the *audiencia* of Mexico. This salvaged some of the *cofradía* lands, but nearly two-thirds of them had already been lost, and those sold were almost without exception located in the western and northern portions of the peninsula where the pressure of population was greatest.[20]

The upshot of these convergent circumstances was that around 1780 there were heard the first cries of anguish from the western Indians.[21] The lands they had traditionally counted on to farm, and which they considered pueblo lands, had shrunk appreciably, and those tracts remaining were inadequate for their system of farming.

This cry would continue, but it would also continue to be strongest in the west and north of Yucatan. In the much less densely populated region of the east, the shortage of lands never became great enough to seriously inconvenience the mass of subsistence farmers. For not only was less territory gobbled up by commercial interests in that region, but the population grew more slowly or in some cases even diminished. More specifically, although the population of all Yucatan approximately doubled between 1736 and 1795, that of the two districts of Valladolid and Tizimín (north of Valladolid) together decreased 20 percent or so in the same period.[22]

Thus, the imbalance in population densities between west and east that had begun with the first establishment of Spanish settlements remained throughout the colonial period. At the end of the eighteenth century the eastern fringe of lands bordering the Caribbean Sea and much of the region south of the sierra were still recorded by Yucatecans as *despoblado*, uninhabited, and in fact were populated only by thinly scattered hamlets of Indians who had eluded movements to concentrate them in pueblos. That *gran despoblado* was not included in the *partidos* by which Yucatan was governed, and to the basic economy of Spanish Yucatan the far eastern and southern lands were surplus. Although legend peopled them with wild and unchristianized Indians similar to the contemporary Lacandones of the Chiapas lowlands, when actions in the Caste War brought these people into view they would be found to bear Christian baptismal names and to derive from essentially the same colonial background as people of the pueblos remaining under close government surveillance.

The Constitution of Cádiz

Although the first blows of rebellion against Spanish rule were struck in mainland Mexico in 1810, no significant ripple of the movement reached Yucatan at the time. In Yucatan, indeed, far more noticeable waves were stirred by the activities of liberals in Spain who busied themselves with making laws while the Napoleanic War churned around them.

Although the Spanish Bourbon monarch was exiled from his country, a loyalist legislative body assembled at Cádiz with American Spanish representation. In 1811 this assembly, the Spanish *Cortes*, decreed the abolition of all colonial tribute. And because the *encomienda* had already been phased out in favor of direct payment to the Crown, this meant the abolition of the head tax Indians paid to the king.

On March 19, 1812, the assembly proclaimed a liberal constitution, one that drew upon the ideals of both the French Revolution and the more liberal of Spanish traditions and declared that the Spanish nation consisted of all Spaniards of both hemispheres and that these Spaniards included all men born free and living in Spanish dominions. Instantly, Indians were *vecinos*—citizens.

The constitution also provided for the election of *ayuntamientos* in all towns of significance, whereas until that time in Yucatan the only elected *vecino* municipal governing bodies had been those of the original Spanish settlements—Mérida, Campeche, and Valladolid especially, for Bacalar had dwindled to a half-forgotten military outpost. And it provided for the election of a central legislative body in each province, Yucatan included.

The effects were two-pronged. In the Spanish municipalities, there was surprise, even among the strongest liberals, that Indians might appear on the *cabildos*. In the pueblos, where the *repúblicas de indios* were automatically abolished, the expanding *vecino* rural population threatened to monopolize the elective positions to the exclusion of the traditional Indian leaders.

Still further, on November 9, 1812, the Cádiz *Cortes* issued a far-reaching decree declaring that among other things all "Indian Spaniards" of the American colonies should be free of mandatory personal services to any individual or to any corporate body, religious or civil, and that they should pay the same parish fees as all other classes. Where civil works were to be required, the requirements would fall equally on all citizens.

In Yucatan, knowledge of the decree engendered heated disputes between the church party and the rapidly growing and active faction of liberals. The reluctant governor was finally induced to promulgate the decree, in both Spanish and Maya, together with the specific statement that special parish fees to be eliminated included the traditional obventions of the Yucatecan Indians. This occurred on February 27, 1813, at almost the same moment that certain Yucatecan liberals, who controlled the Mérida *ayuntamiento*, had cranked up the first printing press ever to operate in Yucatan—an occurrence that may have influenced the governor's decision, for had he refused to publish the decree of the *Cortes* the liberals were obviously capable of disseminating it themselves.

The results were immediate. Indians refused to report for civil or community works that had previously used their labor alone—roadwork, logging, salt making, cotton weaving, wax harvesting. Prices for some goods rose. Corn and wax had to be imported from abroad.

Hardest hit was the church, where parish house servants, sacristans, *maestros cantores*, even the *fiscales*, who were charged with teaching the catechism to the Indian children in the pueblos, failed to report for work. Couples failed to report for marriage ceremonies. Burials had no services. Children stopped attending the daily catechism instruction, causing a severe shortage of oil for the altar lamps (oil had been a part of their tuition). And there were, of course, no obventions.[23]

Although the evidence is uneven, it appears that the disruption of church business was more severe in the east. From Izamal eastward, it was reported that Indians were leaving the pueblos to live in the bush, where they might remain for months at a time without divine service. The elimination of punishment for noncompliance with church dictates was fairly consistently claimed to be the cause of these undesirable changes.[24]

The clergy urged the promulgation of laws forcing Indians to tithe in lieu of paying obventions, although the subsistence products of customary Indian endeavors were not those on which tithes had been traditionally charged. At the same time, the priests recognized that most of the Indians had insufficient money at any one time to be able to afford the higher charges customarily made to *vecinos* for the church service for marriages, baptisms, and funerals.

On January 3, 1814, the governor issued the decree the clergy demanded, requiring that all Indian Spanish citizens must pay one-tenth of all their harvests in all products with which they had previously paid obventions. At the same time, he directed the clergy to lower their fees for the sacraments so that Indians could pay them.[25]

Roughly a month later, following liberal arguments that the governor was not empowered to issue such a decree, the proclamation was revoked, and a bipartisan meeting was called to concoct a solution to the impending bankruptcy of the Yucatecan church. But the meeting was dominated by the clerical party, and the formal decision was that the governor's interpretation of the *Cortes* decree had been wrong and that religious obventions were not covered by it. Both governor and clerics appealed the question to Spain, and matters remained unresolved.

The indecision was settled suddenly and unambiguously. A British army under the Duke of Wellington invaded Spain from Portugal, permitting Ferdinand VII to return to his country. The monarch's first stroke in the interests of absolute rule, in May 1814, was to abolish the constitution of 1812 and all other acts of the Cádiz legislative assembly. On August 26, 1814, the governor of Yucatan was able to proclaim the obventions still in effect, and in January 1815 this was confirmed by a resolution of the king, who also stated specifically that mandatory services to the church such as those of the *fiscal* and other functionaries must be resumed.

Liberals had predicted rebellious acts by the Indians if their plight were not improved. But surprisingly the Indian population accepted its disenfranchisement and the resumption of tribute and obventions with apparent docility.[26] After nearly two years of bankrupt confusion, colonial life resumed its customary pace.

Enter Independence

For some years the pace of Yucatecan life was again slow, the liberal movement quashed by a reactionary government, the most vociferous jailed, and the status quo maintained to perfection. Although independence fever was afoot in Mexico, it still failed to reach conservative Yucatan. But if liberalism was moribund in that isolated province, in Spain it was by no means dead.[27]

In 1820, a Spanish military force mobilized to suppress independence movements in the American colonies turned on the Spanish king and forced the restoration of the constitution of 1812. In Spain there emerged a period of extreme liberalism. In Yucatan liberals began to resurface, and the governor was forced to swear allegiance to the revived constitution. Dispatches from

Spain called for immediate restoration of the decree of November 9, 1812, and the equal treatment of Indians and other citizens.

But the ranks of Yucatecan liberals had now been infiltrated by churchmen who were violently opposed to the abolition of the obventions. The growing number of hacienda owners, or *hacendados*, generally supported abolition—because they were called on to pay the obventions of their Indian workers—but they could not overcome the pro-obvention stand of the church. Yucatan was hopelessly, noisily divided, and the resolution—to disseminate the new dispatches quietly and then to proceed as though the decree of 1812 did not apply to the obventions at all—was consciously ineffectual. Thus, despite the ferment in Spain, in Yucatan there was no essential change at all.

Then in October the Spanish *Cortes* decreed the suppression of the mendicant clerical orders. The priesthood in the Yucatecan pueblos was secularized, and the Franciscan convents began to be disestablished. Even the numerous liberals among the strong Franciscan clergy in Yucatan were thus forced into opposition against newly liberal Spain, while the suppression of their order went on apace.

At this point Mexico rose with the revolutionary *Plan de Iguala*, promulgated by Agustín de Iturbide, containing guarantees of complete independence under a monarch to be invited from Europe, of the supremacy of the Catholic religion with the retention of full rights and property by the clergy, and of the equality of American-born Spaniards with their Iberian cousins. This combination was beguiling indeed, for it captured the reactionary element for the independence movement.

And it had the same effect in Yucatan, which announced its support for a Mexican empire. On September 15, 1821, Yucatan proclaimed independence from Spain. The colony was dead. Would a new world arise?

Colonial Legacy

In sum, after 1659 the colony was relatively peaceful. But if the period was quiet it also witnessed slow but significant social changes in the loss of a sharp boundary between the civil categories of *vecino* and Indian and interrelated developments in population size and economy.

The first of these involved the infiltration by at least some individuals originally of Indian status into the *vecino* category and the concurrent slide of a few former *vecinos* into the Indian civil state. The legal distinctions remained substantially unambiguous, as patrilineal inheritance of civil status assured that an Indian surname almost invariably marked a legal Indian and a Spanish surname marked a *vecino*. But race mixture and intermarriage, most frequently marriage between *vecino* men and Indian women, were such that by the end of the colonial period as many as half of the rural *vecinos* would have had either a mother or a grandmother who was a legal Indian. This blurring of emotional boundaries would mean that those who were Indians before the law were not the only people who were Indian in outlook.

The second of these changes was hinged to the massive decline of the Indian population before 1700 and its rise thereafter to possibly one-half the pre-Hispanic level. In the populous west and north of the peninsula, the decline permitted the occupation of former swidden lands by *vecino*-operated cattle *estancias* that produced hides and other products for export; the subsequent growth—generating internal demand—saw the *estancias* converted to haciendas catering to local subsistence needs. The growing Indian population of the west, now without available milpa lands, became tenants of the haciendas.

A scant twenty-five years before the events that would impel her irrevocably into the Caste War, Yucatan became part of an independent Mexico. And into that union she carried with her as baggage from her colonial days the elements that would combine to bring about the fiery contest.

With a tradition of local self-government by the select few of Mérida, Campeche, and Valladolid, Yucatan would find herself ripped apart by regional factions and unable to cleave to a consistent political course because of bickering, backbiting, and even bloodbaths over divisions at the highest levels of government. And this infighting would only exacerbate her internal situation: an economy based on a poorly productive agriculture, a religious structure that could only be supported by the heaviest levies on the poorest segment of the population, and a peasantry of scarcely enfranchised Indians amounting to three-fourths of her population for whom in the west there was a growing shortage of land and an increasing burden of debt peonage and who in the east had showed themselves willing to engage in armed rebellion when leadership appeared.

And in the far southeast, like a canker, there was a growing colony of English woodcutters that the independence of Mexico and Guatemala would spur to new claims for territorial integrity and separation from Spanish control. As her colonies wrenched themselves away from her, stubborn Spain refused to renounce her colonial sovereignty. When finally driven to recognize Mexico (1836) and Guatemala (1863), she made no formal disposition of any rights to her territories that were occupied under treaty by the English. This would provide the argument on which the British based their claim to the territory.

But conflicting understandings of territorial rights would drive a wedge between Mexico and Britain and provide the circumstance from which would emerge material support for the insurgents in the rebellion soon to rip Yucatan apart. Between Guatemala and Great Britain the same misunderstanding continues to this day.[28]

Thus, although the later colonial period was placid there were tensions below the surface. And more than a hint of rural disaffection was demonstrated by the now famous events at Cisteil, in the district of Sotuta in central Yucatan.

The Cisteil Revolt and the Last Canek

As I noted earlier, leaders known by the title Canek had surfaced early in the colonial history of Yucatan. The last Canek, however, was something different. As the earlier men called Canek marked the first stages of Yucatan's colonial history, the last one predicted its end. His Cisteil insurrection provided a foretaste of the great social revolt of the nineteenth century—incorporating Spanish elements of religion and thought in a movement that, brief as it was, seemed to aim both for social redress and mystical revitalization.

So far as has been determined, the final Canek was born in a barrio of Campeche as Jacinto Uc—some years after the capitulation of the last of the independent Petén Caneks. Taken in by a Franciscan priest, he was educated in convents at Campeche and in Mérida—and unusually well for one born an Indian, gaining knowledge of Spanish and perhaps Latin. But he was finally ejected from the religious establishment for loose living, some later commentators suggesting that the root cause of his riotousness was the fact that the religious calling was not truly open to him because of his Indian birth.

In 1761 he became an instant celebrity, was marked as a rebel and committer of unspeakable sacrilege, and stood as the central actor in one of the most frightful executions ever seen in Mérida. After it was over some intellectuals suggested that the entire affair was trumped up by young military officers and that the victim had committed no significant crime. Unfortunately, the records relating to the Cisteil events are sketchy in the extreme, and a modern inquirer can read almost anything into the occurrences actually documented.

On November 20, 1761, obviously then a man of mature years, Jacinto Uc was in the pueblo of Quisteil or Cisteil[29] in the district of Sotuta in central Yucatan attending the fiesta of the patron saint and its customary drunken aftermath. He was said to have suggested that the joyful party be prolonged. Retiring to the nearby cemetery, he there began a long harangue that was quoted verbatim by one of the witnesses against him at his trial, a sort of sermon elaborating upon the evils the conquest brought to the Indians of Yucatan. He first noted, and emphasized the most, the priests' inattention to the proper care of the Christian needs of the Indians; second, he argued that the tribute required of the Indians and the use of corporal punishment against them constituted oppression. Uc's reportedly impassioned speech concluded with a call for rebellion and heightened piety. Uc was said to have worked one or more minor miracles, after which he was crowned in the same church, accepting the crown from the head of the Virgin and the mantle from her shoulders. He adopted the title *Rey Jacinto Uc de los Santos Canek Chichan Moctezuma*, or "King Jacinto Uc of the Saints Canek Small Moctezuma."[30] About this time, a *vecino* merchant visiting in the town was killed, and a priest who had come to say mass heard there was a rebellion and ran away to give warning.

Commentators who accept the account of these events differ with regard to their significance, some suggesting that the rebellion was a long held plot in which Indian leaders from many towns were involved. Others take the occurrence as the spontaneous punctuation of a drunken orgy. But there seem to have been a number of armed Indians in the immediate vicinity in very short order, as Jacinto Canek (as he has come to be commonly known) soon appointed officers to head the now-rebel pueblo. The *cacique* of nearby Tabi was to be governor, and Canek's own son the leader of the military forces.

Drunk or sober, the actors did not have to wait long to be noticed. The priest fled to Sotuta, where the *capitán a guerra* immediately assembled a hundred foot of militia and a troop of cavalry composed of between ten and twenty men. Not waiting for the infantry, the swashbuckling officer left immediately with his horsemen and galloped into the Cisteil plaza. In the firing that greeted them, he and eight or ten of his men were shot dead. The infantry pulled back.

Government forces were raised in the *partido* of Tihosuco to the east, and by November 23 patrols were capturing messengers from Canek with a general call to rebel arms. Three days later a force of five hundred or more attacked Cisteil. In the battle that followed some six hundred rebels were claimed to have been killed, with the militia loss at forty; at least a portion of Cisteil was burned. Canek and three hundred men escaped to a nearby hacienda, were dislodged the next day, and finally captured.

By December 7 the prisoners had all been removed to Mérida. Rumors of conspiracy grew. One juicy story was that Maya servants were all going to rise at one coordinated moment and murder their masters. One was reportedly found sneaking ground glass into the food of his employer. Arrests were made, as various people were supposedly implicated in pueblos east of Maní and south of Valladolid, although there were also some in pueblos around Campeche, in a pueblo northeast of Mérida, and in Mérida itself.

By December 12 Canek had been tried before the governor of Yucatan and sentenced. His public execution took place on a specially made platform on which he was placed alive, his bones broken with an iron bar, and his flesh torn off in chunks with tongs. His remains were finally burned and the ashes scattered to the winds. The whole proceeding reportedly took five hours. In the next days, eight of Canek's major accomplices were hanged and more than 600 were flogged and had an ear cut off. One account said that there would be more than 170 additional executions before the session was complete, although it is not certain that these were carried out.[31]

Proclamations by the governor ordered the surrender of all Indian firearms within two weeks' time and banned the performance of traditional native dances and the use of non-European musical instruments in Indian fiestas. The pueblo of Cisteil was ordered destroyed and the ground sowed with salt to perpetuate the memory of its treason.[32]

On the one hand, there can be no reasonable doubt that there was a real act of rebellion in Cisteil, considering the killing of a man and then the shooting of the posse from Sotuta. It seems also entirely likely that missives were dispatched inviting other towns to take part. On the other hand, there seems to be no convincing evidence that there was any advance planning for the acts of November 20, and there certainly seems to be only the most flimsy evidence of any widespread conspiracy—based as it is only on after-the-fact "confessions" of a few witnesses, most of whom were presumably put to the torture.

In all, three facts would be relevant to events in the following century: First, given the support that was rallied in a very short time, it is evident that there was a willingness for rebellion among certain Indians of Yucatan, particularly in the region east and south of the major area of population.

Second, the obvious overreaction of the white Yucatecans—manifested in the brutality of the execution of Canek and the widespread and hysterical acceptance of allegations against people and pueblos that were almost certainly not involved at all—bespeaks both expectation and fear of an Indian rebellion. This is despite the fact that there had been no real insurrection of Indians since missionizing and conquest were finally completed more than a century before. Third, there is no indication of a backward-looking "nativistic" movement that would re-create the pagan past; Canek's call is couched in entirely Christian terms (although interpreted by the Yucatecans as a call from the devil), and his major complaint is inattention to the religious needs of a Christian community.[33]

As we will see, these same conclusions will be relevant to the mid–nineteenth century and the beginning of the Caste War.

Part 2. Learning Rebellion, 1821–1848

4 / Strains of Independence

The first steps along the path of independence seemed firm. The Constitution of 1812 remained in force in Yucatan, and the officials elected under it continued to govern. But the stability was illusory, for underlying economic and social issues continued to press for resolution, and factional strife would increase amid vituperation and bloodshed.

The Land Issue

The growth in population and the arrival of independence in Yucatan combined to bolster the importance of land in two different ways: through the need to expand agricultural production and through the government's need for money. The first of these, of course, led to a partial solution of the second, but together they contributed to the circumstances that would underlie the Caste War. Although some historians hold that problems with land were the major cause of the rebellion, the view I express here is otherwise. Land issues certainly did contribute to the expansion of the uprising, but as I will show in a later chapter, they were not a crucial factor in the initial outbreak of hostilities nor in the rebel resistance that continued into the 1850s and after.

As a whole, during the colonial period pressure on broad expanses of crown land had been relatively light. The *cabildos* of the three enduring Spanish municipalities, Mérida, Campeche, and Valladolid, had tended to conduct most of the public business that concerned any of their surrounding regions. Within those regions Indian members of *república*-centered pueblos and the nonmember immigrant *vecinos* who resided in the same pueblos made use of lands largely as they pleased, so long as they respected the numerous but relatively scattered tracts under patents of private ownership.

With independence and the sudden conversion of the large number of Indian pueblos into municipalities not confined to Indian governance, however, local sovereignty of lands not under clear private ownership became an issue. Three classes of these lands were shortly recognized in various Yucatecan statutes.

Indian communal or *community lands* were patented lands that had been purchased or received as specific gifts or grants by *repúblicas de indios* in the course of the long colonial period. These included what were left of the *cofradía* estates, although these were not held without strings from the church.

Ejido lands were tracts considered by Spanish custom to serve as the commons for each organized town. With the legal recognition of mixed (i.e., not solely Indian) municipalities in the nineteenth century, there arose a need for explicit recognition of these village lands. The traditional but somewhat indefinite bounds of these were clarified in 1841, when the size of *ejidos* was limited to four square leagues (sixty-four square kilometers) measured outward in each direction from the main church of the community.[1]

Baldíos, or *terrenos baldíos* ("waste" or uncultivated lands), so called, were lands not in private ownership and not under either of the two preceding categories. They were considered by the state to be at its disposal, although rural subsistence farmers customarily made free use of them for milpas or grazing.

When the *estancias* had adapted to rising population late in the colonial period, it had been through simple diversification, and when additional lands came to be absorbed by these growing commercial establishments, it was often at the expense of nearby Indian pueblos; the title of such lands was poorly defined, and whatever the previous use had been they were acquired as though they were *baldíos*. These moves were usually gradual, however, and as the commercial estates slowly expanded they drew increasingly on landless Indians as members of the larger force of labor required for farming as opposed to cattle ranching. As I have indicated, this growth of haciendas was largely confined to the western part of the peninsula.

But as the need increased for locally produced sugar (the result of factors I will discuss shortly), this pattern was altered in two directions: because the regions of earlier hacienda development were seldom sufficiently watered for sugar cultivation, new and more humid lands were sought, and the heavy labor needs of sugar production required an immediate and sharp increase in the labor force.

The first of these requirements was met by expansion into the more southerly *partidos* of Sierra Alta and Sierra Baja and portions of the Chenes, with a lesser development north of Valladolid. By the late 1830s the triangle from Hopelchén to Tekax to Peto was the center of the industry.

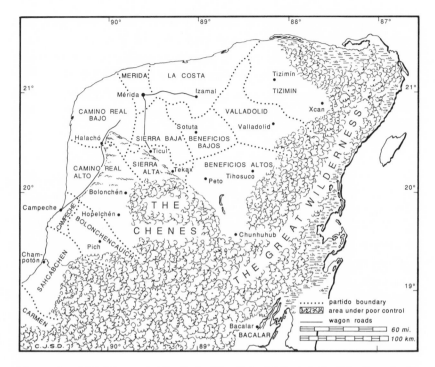

Map 3. Land Divisions near the End of the Colonial Period. Partido *Boundaries (about 1790) are based on Cook and Borah (1974, map 2), with minor adjustments. Roads are as described by Acereto (1977, 142). The wagon road south of Mérida was not completed until after 1788.*

The lands needed were acquired as *baldíos* by purchase or lease from the state, under a series of laws that made such acquisitions increasingly easy. The first important land law had been passed in 1825, only two years after independence, providing for colonization of *baldíos* by purchase. In 1833 the remaining *cofradía* lands were ordered sold, with the funds to be delivered to the bishop. After 1840 the speed with which such lands entered private hands was increased as the state used land both to repay forced loans drafted to support the government in its increasingly frequent tribulations and to pay soldiers in the absence of money.[2]

The second requirement was never really satisfied, for plantation labor was always in short supply. Debt peonage increased to the extent that it could be managed on the new sugar holdings, but the real need was for seasonal, rather than permanent, labor. Indians were paid at the rate of one *real* per day for the hard, periodic work of the fields, yet insufficient labor could be obtained and the shortage plagued the plantations. In spite of this, the sugar industry finally produced a respectable volume: between 1827 and 1833 the tax receipts from local *aguardiente* more than tripled. Thereafter, although varying in the rate and the way in which it was collected, the *aguardiente* tax provided important revenues until the Caste War virtually eliminated the industry.[3]

The Pendulum of Politics

With independence from Spain, two sets of oppositions came strongly into play. The first of these was between liberals and conservatives, who shortly emerged as the political parties called federalist and centralist, respectively. Between 1821, the year of independence, and 1840 the centralists ruled for three separate intervals and the federalists for two. Although the flip-flops from one to the other reflected pressures from Mexico, the oscillations in Yucatan were not exactly in phase with changes in the central government. Yucatan marched to her own drumbeat, and after 1840 she would proclaim two periods of independence from Mexico and would vacillate in her loyalties while war raged between Mexico and the United States.

The second of the oppositions referred to was between Mérida and Campeche. Although Mérida was more often federalist than centralist, and although Campeche often took the lead in centralist pronouncements, the fit between municipality and political party was by no means perfect. The civilian inhabitants of Campeche were predominantly liberal and federalist; it was the presence there of the major military garrison of the peninsula that often dictated otherwise. In the long run, however, it was regional antipathy that dominated the relationship of the two cities—antipathy that transcended and cut across mere political sympathies and did much to set the stage for the Caste War.[4]

The brief centralist period under Iturbide—who ruled as emperor of Mexico after 1821 in place of the imported monarch he had promised— almost toppled such financial equilibrium as Yucatan possessed. First, imperial tribute was abolished throughout Mexico. This, while not altering the Indians' religious contributions, did free them of their traditional civil payments. The Yucatecan government wisely put in place a temporary head tax euphemized as a *contribución patriótica*, payable by Indians and non-Indians alike. For the first time this spread the basic burden of taxes to *vecinos*.

Second, Mexican law set a new schedule of national customs duties running on the order of 25 percent of invoice value and forbade the importation of foreign flour. For Yucatan, which for decades had luxuriated under the low-tariff system of relatively free trade proclaimed in the late years of Spanish rule and which possessed a climate where bread wheat would not adequately mature, this measure was intolerable.[5] Yucatan protested to the central government and—apparently—simply failed to comply with the law, in a quiet display of the insubordination that would become characteristic of her relations with Mexico.

In March 1823 Iturbide abdicated in the face of pressure from Santa Anna and others, ending independent Mexico's first imperial experiment. Two months later Yucatan executed her first political about-face: her tradition of local self-government asserted itself and she declared herself part of a Mexican federal republic—an action that the interim central government of Mexico found embarrassing, inasmuch as a national constitutional convention was then meeting but had not yet agreed on any governmental form for the country as a whole.[6] By January of the following year the central government had followed suit, however, and one of its early acts was to declare war on Spain, whose forces were still occupying the fortress of San Juan de Ulúa outside Veracruz and shelling that city, proclaiming an embargo on all trade with Spain and Spanish possessions.

On February 15, 1824, the city of Campeche declared herself on the side of Mexico and in favor of war on Spain and the embargo on Spanish trade. She also called for the elimination of all Iberian-born Spaniards from their occupations in favor of American-born Creoles, a move that the central government had rejected as unlawful. But Mérida reacted negatively. Whereas Campeche traded almost exclusively with Veracruz and other Mexican ports and stood to lose little by the embargo, Mérida sustained a lucrative and—she thought—crucial commerce with Spanish Havana, which would be eliminated under the law. Thus, while Campeche disobeyed Mexico and conducted a witchhunt for foreign Spaniards, Mérida disobeyed by refusing to end trade with Spanish colonies.[7]

Faced with this double insubordination, the Mexican government dispatched a representative to negotiate—in the person of none other than Antonio López de Santa Anna, soon to assume the role of antihero for which he is famous in Mexican history. Now, however, he insinuated himself into local regard, was even appointed interim governor of Yucatan, and succeeded in bringing Yucatan back into conformance with the law before an army could be dispatched from Mexico to force the issue.[8] While the embargo now cut off the customary trade of Mérida in which cattle products had been exchanged for Cuban sugar, it worked to stimulate the development of Yucatecan sugar plantations.

Meanwhile the government of Yucatan had adopted a federalist constitution and passed several laws of importance. These replaced the *contribución patriótica* with a permanent *contribución personal* payable by all adult males at the rate of 12 *reales* per year. They reinstated the *república de indios* with its measure of independent Indian governance, recognized the continuance of Indian *cofradía* estates while encouraging their sale, and decreed the continuation of Indian obventions at the annual rate of 12.5 *reales* per adult male and 9 *reales* per adult female. Somewhat later, collection of tithes from *vecinos* was made a part of civil law, the money to be collected by the state with a portion distributed to the church.[9]

But in 1829 a strong centralist movement in Mexico was gaining strength, and by the end of that year it would replace the Mexican federalist government. In Campeche the military garrison pronounced for centralism, was seconded immediately by the garrison in Mérida, and the military bloodlessly usurped power to initiate the second period of centralism in Yucatan. A product of this second centralist period was the reduction of the local tarriff rate to three-fifths of that collected elsewhere in Mexico.[10]

The pendulum swung again in November 1832, as a faction in Mérida issued a formal pronouncement for a return to federalism. With the local military now joining this movement in large numbers, it achieved success—again bloodlessly—and the federalist constitution of Yucatan of 1825 was restored. In the following month federalism also triumphed again in Mexico.[11]

In 1834, however, the field was reversed again as Santa Anna and the centralists were elected to power in Mexico. In Yucatan, centralist forces—led as usual by the Campeche garrison—saw their chance and pronounced in support. This time they were opposed militarily by the lawful federalist government in Mérida, but in the ensuing fighting the amateurish federalist militia was routed by the seasoned regular centralist troops at Hecelchakán, where the bloodshed was substantial.[12] For the first time in nearly two centuries, except for the brief incident at Cisteil, Yucatecans faced Yucatecans over smoking guns. After another rout of the federalist force in July, centralism was reestablished in Yucatan for the third time. The preceding federalist government was declared illegal, and virtually all of its legislation was nullified.[13] During the turbulence Indian troops were said to have been raised for political ends by *vecinos* in the Valladolid region—specifically by one Agustín Acereto, of whom more will be heard in later chapters.[14]

In 1835 self-government was reduced in the Mexican states, which were redesignated "departments" under the centralist government. Santa Anna and his party were clearly in the ascendant, although his military defeat in Texas the following year would bring his fortunes into brief eclipse.

The Insurrection of Imán

Under the centralist government of Mexico, Yucatecans of both Mérida and Campeche found causes for acute discomfort. There was the imposition of a tax on internal transactions. There were, again, the customs duties. Since 1827 merchants in the state had enjoyed their special status with lowered duties, but a new schedule of 1837 removed this, with the result that their competitive commercial ability was threatened. In addition, Yucatan's income from its own customs house was assessed a substantial percentage by the central Mexican government to defray costs of the war brought on by the Texas declaration of independence.

And, finally, in order to replace the Mexican army troops lost in the Texas war the central government was taking away Yucatecans who were on active duty with the army. Normally, much of the active Yucatecan military corps was not armed but was composed of laborers and artisans who were employed in their own home regions in various public works. But now they were not only given arms, they were moved away from the peninsula—a circumstance that was entirely repugnant to the home-loving provincial people. The department governor warned the Mexican president that Yucatecans were mimicking Texas and favoring separatism.[15]

Then, in 1838, the army, centralist-oriented, uncovered a plot among members of the battalion stationed at Izamal to pronounce in favor of federalism. A number of officers were arrested and one, the captain of a local company from Tizimín, Santiago Imán, was court-martialed and jailed for ten months. But as soon as he was free he returned to Tizimín, enrolled some deserters of his old battalion and some *vecinos* of the town, and formally pronounced for federalism. Opposed by government troops, he was defeated at Espita, fled toward the coast, was attacked in a rancho he had fortified, and finally was forced to withdraw toward Chancenote. After another defeat he melted into the eastern forests and the government troops retired.

Beginning to organize anew—reportedly with the help of a young officer named José Dolores Cetina[16]—Imán's force was galvanized into hope and

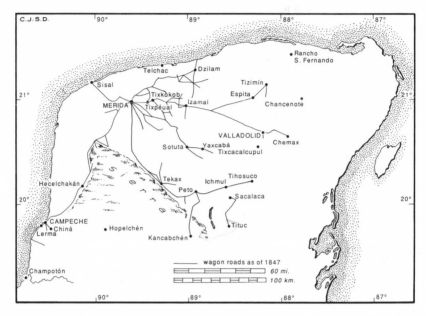

Map 4. Location of Events from 1830 to January 1847. The road network is of the 1840s (Anonymous 1848).

action when a troop of soldiers from his old battalion mutinied rather than face shipment to Mexico as replacements, and as their sole resort they joined him. In November 1839 they occupied Tizimín, Imán's hometown.

This time a large force of Mexican garrison troops faced and dispersed the *pronunciados*, and Imán retreated again to the forests with a small band. The army returned to Campeche, leaving a detachment of two hundred men in Valladolid.[17]

It was when hiding near Chemax that Imán for the first time turned to the local Indians, promising them the abolition of obventions in return for their support in his fighting force.[18]

The immediate effect was that Imán was surrounded by eager, armed Indians. Then, urged on by the federalists of Mérida and Campeche who saw their opportunity to animate the movement for a return to federalism, Imán moved to occupy Chemax. There he organized his force, now largely eastern Indians, into four sections: one at his command and three others captained by men of apparent valor but unsavory reputation—Vito Pacheco, Vicente Revilla, and Pastor Gamboa.[19] Next he occupied the predominantly Indian barrio of Sisal, immediately outside the walls of Valladolid. As the Valladolid commander attempted to dislodge the new army from his backyard many of his men deserted and he was himself shot in one of the early volleys. Valladolid fell.

On February 12, 1840, Imán issued the formal act of his revolution, with three major objectives: reestablishment of the state constitution of 1825; reinstatement of the government displaced by the centralist rebellion of 1834, which would then call new elections; abolition of the obventions charged Indian men and women, replacing them with a religious contribution of one *real* per month to be paid by Indian males alone.[20]

In the wake of the Texas war and other adventures, the centralist movement was in disarray throughout Mexico, and in Yucatan new adherents were attracted to the federalist cause. There, the party faithful worked to subvert the military officers who still supported the centralist state government. On February 18, the officers of the citadel of San Benito in Mérida and civilians of that city united to produce an act not only sustaining Imán's Act of Valladolid but going further: it declared that Yucatan would remain independent of Mexico so long as Mexico failed to return to the constitutional federalist system.

The officers who joined the anticentralist movement included many former centralists. Sebastián López de Llergo, who had commanded centralist forces in the decisive antifederalist actions of 1834, now moved with a federalist troop to occupy a number of towns between Campeche and Mérida. On the last day of February the federalist congress and governor who had been displaced in 1834 came back to work; they proclaimed the state constitution of 1825 in force and declared for independence that would last until federalism was reestablished in Mexico.

This left the sole centralist force holed up in Campeche, where the ordinary citizens, dissatisfied with the customs schedules, were also on the verge of revolt. Nevertheless, the Campeche military force was strong and was quickly reinforced by sea from Veracruz. The result was a long standoff at Campeche between the Mexican forces within the city and two separate local forces without—that of López de Llergo with the government-sponsored army and militia of independent Yucatan and that of Santiago Imán with his four sections of eastern Indian irregulars. The single real engagement occurred in March, when the Mexican commander Rivas Zayas advanced outside of Campeche and was attacked by the section of irregulars led by Pastor Gamboa. Although the easterners were repulsed after a four-hour engagement, their spirit was such that Rivas Zayas found it prudent to fall back to Campeche and stay there. After a siege of two months a negotiated settlement allowed him to withdraw by sea, and Yucatan remained free.[21]

The state congress in the summer of 1840 confirmed the promise of Imán's Act of Valladolid, abolishing the obventions and substituting a religious head tax of one *real* per month, payable only by Indian males aged fourteen to sixty, to be collected by the state in cash. This was in addition to the regular civil contribution, but the result was an annual reduction of taxes of 9.5 *reales* for each Indian married couple.[22] Nevertheless, from complaints made after hostilities began it appears that at least some of Imán's enlistees had understood him to be promising an even greater reduction.

Independent Yucatan, 1840–1843

The restored Congress busied itself revising the constitution of 1825. The result, adopted in March 1841, added to the earlier document significant liberal guaranties of freedom of religion and the abolition of special rights previously accorded the Catholic clergy.[23] The move toward religious tolerance was an attempt to encourage immigration.[24]

In the elections that followed the adoption, Santiago Méndez of Campeche was the electors' unanimous choice for governor. An upright and respected liberal and federalist of considerable political experience, he had worked actively for the defeat of the centralist military force in Campeche. The electors split on the choice of vice governor, and the election was decided by the state congress in favor of young Miguel Barbachano, a political newcomer—Campeche-born, educated in Spain, and resident at the time in Mérida.[25]

It was at this election that political events in the *partido* of Tihosuco first attracted notice. There, the generally dominant centralists, who counted Antonio Trujeque as their leader, were opposed by federalists supported by Vito Pacheco and a wealthy Indian of the vicinity, Jacinto Pat. At the moment of the election Pat appeared with more than a thousand Indian voters who, it was said, were not altogether sober. The federalists carried the day.[26]

Meanwhile, the centralist Mexican government under President Bustamante had declared the federalist-bent Yucatecan authorities to be rebels, all Yucatecan vessels pirates, and the ports of Campeche and Sisal closed. Because Mexico had no significant navy, however, the declaration had little effect on Yucatecan foreign commerce, although it temporarily inhibited direct trade with Mexican ports.

It had more effect on local feeling. The government made overtures to newly independent Texas in search of an alliance that would improve security. Although Texas rejected outright alliance—unless Yucatan declared absolute independence from Mexico, which she was not yet willing to do— Yucatan was able to contract for aid from the small Texan navy. She began to provide port facilities for the Texas squadron when it was in the vicinity.[27]

The Mexican declaration also promoted the feeling that Yucatan should— as the Texans said—become totally independent. As a result, in October 1841 a legislative committee proposed an act of permanent independence that was actually passed by the Chamber of Deputies, the lower house, and then sent on to the Senate.[28]

At this point differences began to emerge. Méndez was in favor of membership in a federalist Mexico. He was seconded in this by *Campechanos* generally, most of whose commerce had been with Mexican ports—particularly Veracruz—and who feared that independence would impair these connections permanently. Barbachano, on the other hand, favored complete independence, being generally supported by *Meridanos*, especially the younger and more adventurous among them.[29] Senate action, however, was delayed by talks with a Mexican emissary.

As the Bustamante government in Mexico had become increasingly unstable, Santa Anna again seized power and was named president of a provisional government. Incensed by the friendship between Yucatan and Texas, the scene of his earlier downfall, one of his early acts was to send a native Yucatecan, Andrés Quintana Roo, to induce the state to return to the fold.[30]

After lengthy and stubborn talks and many expostulations from the emissary regarding the concourse with Texas, a draft treaty was signed containing conditions under which Yucatan would be reincorporated into the Mexican union. The conditions, nothing short of amazing in the autonomy they granted Yucatan, attest to Yucatan's recalcitrance: She would have essentially complete control of interior government, of the army recruited and stationed in Yucatan (which would not be exposed to duty elsewhere), of the schedules of customs duties, and of the income from the customs stations. She would be guaranteed free trade with all Mexican ports. Her financial contributions to the Mexican republic would essentially be limited to those she decided herself.

It is not surprising that the Yucatecan congress ratified the treaty with Mexico in short order. It is equally unsurprising that the central government rejected the agreement out of hand, pronouncing it more suitable to an alliance of equals than to the reincorporation of Yucatan into Mexico. The next Mexican commissioner presented far different conditions: complete acceptance of the aims of the provisional and centralist Santa Anna government, acceptance of all decisions of a Mexican congress then beginning to work on a new national constitution, and the severance of all relations with Texas. Before the congress of Yucatan had finished formulating its rejection of these conditions, Santa Anna began preparing for war; Yucatan responded by raising troops, offering lands from the *baldíos* to soldiers who would remain in service through the fighting.[31]

In August 1842 a Mexican force occupied Carmen, on the Laguna de Términos, and shortly afterward an advance guard landed at Champotón to begin a very slow movement north. By early November they were reinforced from Veracruz, so that the total invading army amounted to some 6,000 men—nearly the size of the army Santa Anna had fielded against Texas. Méndez left the Mérida government in the hands of Vice Governor Barbachano and moved to Campeche to take personal charge of defense arrangements. The Yucatecan force massed there included some 4,500 men, of which only 650 were regulars; the rest were green, including units of the militia and some volunteers from the east, largely Indians, again under Gamboa, Revilla, and Pacheco. Among the latter was an Indian from Tepich named Cecilio Chi.[32]

The first action came when Pastor Gamboa and his eastern irregulars moved south to Lerma with orders to observe the invaders but took the opportunity to go still farther south and ambush the Mexican force as it neared the town, which caused the Mexicans to arrive at Lerma in a state of confusion. But as the Mexicans approached Campeche, the Yucatecan military officer in charge there, Pedro Lemus, obligingly pulled back from fortified heights near the city; the heights were immediately occupied by the invaders, who thereby partially commanded the Campeche plaza with their artillery. The Campeche city government was incensed and demanded the removal of Lemus, who was replaced by Colonel Sebastián López de Llergo. Lemus was shortly banished from the peninsula under charge of treason, after which he showed his spots by joining the Mexican forces.[33]

Yet the city of Campeche—fortified in the colonial era after repeated pirate incursions—had long been considered impregnable, and so it proved itself again. For three months the besiegers and the besieged exchanged artillery bombardments. Morale in Campeche remained high, as the city was supplied regularly by small boats that easily evaded the larger Mexican ships in the shallow waters along the Campeche strand. Meanwhile the Mexican force was finding itself unwelcome among noncombatants in the region, it was unable to obtain supplies except for those shipped in from Mexico, and its highland troops were beginning to wilt in the normal buildup of spring heat. The siege was punctuated by a single sharp and bloody engagement when the Mexicans, seeking a local supply base, moved a detachment to the pueblo of Chiná, which then was heavily attacked by the Yucatecans. With losses to both sides substantial, both vacated the area.[34]

The financial costs of the war mounted. In March 1843 the Yucatecan Congress imposed a temporary *contribución patriótica* amounting to four *reales* per month for most Yucatecan males aged sixteen and over, limited to two *reales* per month for those Indian males who were subsistence farmers. Forced loans from wealthy Yucatecans supplied immediate cash.[35] Furthermore, Barbachano declared that Indians who entered the forces and fought with their own arms would be exempted from payment of both civil and religious contributions.[36]

At about this same time the turncoat Lemus convinced the Mexican general, Matías de la Peña y Barragán, to make a thrust at Mérida, which unlike fortified Campeche was open for the taking. As General Peña loaded twenty-five hundred men in his transports and sailed north, López de Llergo marched quickly to Mérida with sixteen hundred picked men. The Mexican ships coasted up the west side of the peninsula, finally unloading at Telchac on the north shore. López de Llergo moved in that direction, his detachment augmented by other forces, including a section of eastern irregulars commanded by Vito Pacheco. After several feinting movements on both sides, the Mexicans entrenched at Tixkokob, where on April 11, 1843, the Yucatecan troops attacked them smartly, inflicted and suffered losses, and then, unable to claim victory, withdrew to Mérida.

Peña y Barragán moved closer to the city, camped at a convenient hacienda, and contacted Mérida to offer conditions. López de Llergo responded that his only aim was for the Mexicans to leave Yucatan, but he graciously consented to listen if the Mexicans would like to *ask* for conditions.[37] At this point humor enters.

According to the historian Baqueiro, just as the attack was most expected in Mérida an Indian boy from Peña's captive hacienda appeared asking to deliver to the acting governor a letter he had been charged by General Peña to carry to a certain centralist partisan in the city. When the addressee was summoned, the letter was opened and found to request intelligence from him concerning the military force of the defenders, to which at Barbachano's dictation the addressee responded that the city was defended by four thousand troops with other battalions on call, that "eleven thousand Indians of the pueblos of the East and of the Sierra . . . armed and supplied on their own account" would shortly arrive to aid in the city's defense, and that the Mexicans should withdraw to avoid annihilation.[38]

Whether this story is apocryphal or not, Peña did request immediate negotiations, and as a preliminary he withdrew from the outskirts of Mérida under harrying by guerrillas of the eastern forces. Attempting to move into Tixkokob, he found the place occupied by more eastern irregulars led by Miguel Cámara, who refused to vacate. As Peña settled at the pueblo of Tixpehual he found himself faced by three columns: one column of eastern irregulars under Pastor Gamboa, a second under Cámara, and a third consisting of the regular forces of López de Llergo, which had followed him from Mérida. He capitulated. Departing by ship for Tampico, he left hostages to ensure that he did not move his force back to Lerma and join the siege of Campeche.[39]

Peña y Barragán was replaced as supreme commander of the invasion forces by General Pedro Ampudia, who had recently arrived before Campeche with five hundred fresh Mexican troops. Ampudia found himself as ineffective against the fortifications of Campeche as Peña had, despite an increase in his firepower, and he was shortly faced as well by the active López de Llergo, who was now a brigadier general. The arrival off Campeche of the Texan naval squadron, which promptly disabled one of his steamships, further distressed Ampudia, and he entered confidential negotiations with Santiago Méndez, which culminated in a rather anticlimactic offer to withdraw his forces provided the Yucatecan would agree to send a commission to Mexico to work out mutually agreeable conditions under which Yucatan would again join the country.

Tired of the war and groaning under its expense, the commerce of their ports hampered by Mexican ships of war, and their trade with Mexico cut off, the Yucatecan congress agreed. Ampudia and all the remaining Mexican forces withdrew by early June 1843.[40] That same month, as the special "patriotic" head tax for the war expired with Ampudia's withdrawal, the congress acted to set the personal contribution permanently at four *reales* per month for males aged sixteen years and over and half that for Indian subsistence farmers. But it abolished the obventions.[41] It would not be until the following year, July 1844, that the government would act in a miserly way on Barbachano's promise of exemptions from civil taxes for Indian enlistees by granting a four-month holiday from personal contributions to those Indians who had served in the Yucatecan army during the crisis.[42]

In late July of 1843 the Yucatecan commissioners traveled to Mexico as promised. Shortly before negotiations were successfully concluded, however, a bit of political buffoonery enlivened life in eastern Yucatan.

In November Agustín Acereto proclaimed an ineffective revolt in Valladolid with the aim of reinstating the centralist government of 1839. In Tihosuco, Antonio Trujeque proclaimed support, usurped the local government, and according to one source immediately ordered the apprehension of his rivals—Vito Pacheco, Jacinto Pat, and others. But as the revolt faded before widespread opposition, Trujeque and his adherents found themselves out on a limb and were forced to flee from the restored officials of Tihosuco. One of the latter was Gregorio Pacheco, the father of Vito, who ordered that the insurrectionists be pursued and brought to justice. The Tepich Indian Cecilio Chi is said to have rounded up most of them. It is not clear how Trujeque fared, for, like Vito Pacheco, Jacinto Pat, and Cecilio Chi himself, he was ready for action a few years later.[43]

For their part, the Yucatecan commissioners were able to obtain terms from Mexico that were similar to those of the abortive treaty negotiated almost two years before by Quintana Roo. That is, although losing the liberal provisions of her own Constitution of 1841 by accepting the constitution just devised for Mexico, Yucatan was promised the power to organize her interior government and manage her treasury as she saw fit, to set the schedules of customs fees and arrange disposal of the revenues, and to trade freely with Mexican ports on the same basis as any other region of the nation; she was relieved of the obligation to furnish troops for military duty outside of Yucatan; and amnesty was guaranteed for all who had opposed Mexico. In short, Yucatecans achieved essentially what they had asked and been refused before the costly and inconclusive war began.[44]

The Second Interlude of Independence, 1845–1846

In January 1844, formal allegiance to the new Mexican government was sworn by the government in Mérida, which under the centralist system was redesignated the "Department of Yucatan." Within little more than a month President Santa Anna, the perennial double-dealer, violated the provisions of the Treaty of December 14, 1843, under which Yucatan had rejoined the union.

On February 21, 1844, Santa Anna's government issued an order recognizing those exports from Yucatan that would be accepted freely in Mexico as her native products. The effect of the list was to ban the importation into Mexico of Yucatecan *aguardiente*, sugar, cotton, tobacco including cigars and cigarettes, henequen cord, corn, and some other products. The proscriptions covered the state's most important products, except salt. In Yucatan the price of sugar, now produced in excess of local need, plummeted.[45] Although the unhappy department continued to comply with her legal obligations— sending a list of nominees from which the central government would name a governor, electing deputies to the national congress and to the department's legislative assembly, and so on—she registered vociferous protests by letter and by her representatives in the national congress. These received no satisfaction, however, other than a general statement that the measure was for protection against traffic in contraband—an evasion Yucatecans interpreted as evidence that the proscriptive order had been dictated by Santa Anna's backers among Mexico's competitive commercial interests.[46]

From the list of nominees, José Tiburcio López was appointed governor of the department of Yucatan, and routine business continued, including some attempts to fix church finances. By agreement the church would stop collecting religious fees directly but would receive an annual subsidy of one hundred thousand pesos to support the work of the bishop and the parish priests. No separate religious contribution was provided for beyond the *contribución personal*, the civil head tax due from each adult male, from which the civil authorities hoped to be able to squeeze sufficient money.[47]

Other taxes were sought. Although land used for commercial purposes had long been taxed in a variety of ways, a law of October 1844 established a fee for farming both on public lands and on *ejidos* and community holdings of the pueblos, without exemptions for subsistence milpas. The law was understandably unpopular, and a year later the tax was removed for Indians' subsistence plantings.[48]

As Yucatecan protests over her exports continued, the Mexican government fell and rose again, General Joaquín Herrera replacing Santa Anna in a coup in December 1844. Yet another year passed without the consent needed to nullify the damaging order of February 21, 1844.

Yucatecan patience wore thin. On January 1, 1846, following a revolutionary *pronunciamento* against Mexico in the military citadel in Mérida, the assembly of the department declared an end to Yucatan's obligation to recognize Mexican supremacy. Governor López refused to publish the decree, resigned the governorship, and the assembly—monopolized by the Mérida party—named its own president, Miguel Barbachano, to act in López's place. Elements in Campeche were displeased by the choice.

At almost the same moment yet another presidential coup in Mexico replaced General Herrera with General Mariano Paredes, who promptly protested Yucatan's separatist action. With General Zachary Taylor moving a U.S. army toward the Río Grande, Paredes sent a special emissary to Yucatan with a plea for patriotism. But the agent could offer no promise to nullify the offensive order of February 1844, produced only what the Yucatecans considered evasions, and quickly left in a huff. One further letter from Mexico arrived; it acknowledged that the treaty of December 1843 was in effect but declared that the order of February 1844 could not be nullified until some measures were taken in Yucatan to suppress contraband.

On July 2, as General Taylor moved from the Río Grande toward Monterrey, the Legislative Assembly of Yucatan issued a decree stating dissatisfaction with the supreme government's stand, announcing Yucatan's continued separation, and restating her intention to rejoin the union when terms of the Treaty of December 14, 1843, were recognized.[49]

Unlike the earlier declaration of independence, this statement of contingent separation did not bring unity to the peninsula. The split between partisans of Barbachano and Méndez had widened, with strong resentment among the latter at Barbachano's accession to the acting governorship. With strong centralist-federalist opposition now erased, the strife between the two relatively liberal parties was almost exclusively regional—drawing, indeed, on the old tradition of mutual distaste.[50]

Meanwhile, in May 1846 Mexican objections to the conduct of war with the United States led to a revolutionary pronouncement in Jalisco that urged Santa Anna's return, and by August it had swept the country. On August 22, from his seat of exile in Havana the habitual centralist Santa Anna decreed a new government and the restoration of the federalist constitution of 1824. Contacted by Barbachano as he passed through Sisal on his way to Veracruz, Santa Anna wrote that if Yucatan would support his movement he would recognize the treaty of 1843. The Yucatecan assembly promptly proclaimed its support for the *pronunciamento* of Jalisco and Santa Anna, pledging its return to the union as soon as the new government recognized the treaty.

In September Monterrey was taken by the U.S. forces. On October 25 fear of the U.S. war, mistrust of Santa Anna, and sectional differences led Campeche to make a revolutionary pronouncement calling for the restoration of the liberal constitution of 1841 and Yucatecan independence. It was seconded, however, only in towns in the immediate vicinity of Campeche and in Tihosuco, far to the east. There, Antonio Trujeque declared rebellion and immediately ordered the jailing of his favorite enemies, Cecilio Chi and Jacinto Pat. Pat finally secured his release by donating five hundred pesos to Trujeque's war chest; Chi obtained his more quickly by offering to raise Indians for Trujeque's cause. Within three days he reportedly reappeared with two hundred followers.

Chi was not the only recruiter, however, and the attractiveness to enlistees was said to include relief from taxes. José Castillo of Tixcacalcupul joined with one hundred, as did Juan Vázquez with a substantial force that included Bonifacio Novelo, a man who would become particularly notorious.[51] The predominantly Indian army of six hundred was organized into three sections, one under a Miguel Beitia of Tihosuco, seconded by Chi, the others under Castillo and Vázquez. They marched on Ichmul, but events quickly compelled them to pull back and wait.[52]

Word was received in the last days of October 1846 that the government of Santa Anna had recognized the treaty of December 14, 1843 and nullified the order of February 21, 1844. Immediately, the Yucatecan legislature decreed a reincorporation into Mexico and reestablishment of Yucatan's federalist constitution of 1825—the best fit with the Mexican federalist constitution of 1824—and called for elections.

Despite their disgust at the reincorporation, under the strong influence of Santiago Méndez, who had not joined his city's revolutionary movement, and after an amnesty granted by Barbachano, the Campeche rebels withdrew their pronouncement on November 26 and grudgingly went home. This included the element operating from Tihosuco.[53]

The Rape of Valladolid and the Triumph of Campeche

But in Yucatan peace was not to be. The war with the United States was spreading, with nearly all of northern Mexico now in foreign hands. Within only two weeks—on December 8, 1846—a new *pronunciamento* rang out from Campeche, this time warning that reincorporation into Mexico would propel Yucatan into war with the United States; that grave damage would be inflicted by a U.S. blockade of Yucatecan ports; and that Santa Anna's word had been consistently false. The pronouncement called for postponement of reincorporation until Mexico should recognize and sanction in its constitution the exceptional position of the peninsula; for reestablishment of the liberal constitution of 1841 of independent Yucatan; for the appointment of Domingo Barret—*jefe político* of Campeche—as provisional governor; and for the reduction of the *contribución personal* to 1.5 *reales* per month, or 18 per year.[54]

Whether it was because of the looming cloud of conflict with the United States, the thought of lowered taxes, or for some reason not apparent, the reception of this new Campechano call to rebellion was entirely different from that of the October before. Not only did Santiago Méndez lend his support, but militia units from all over the peninsula joined the call, and the movement spread like wildfire. When Barbachano stood fast against it, civil war erupted.

There were adjustments in personal alignments between the two parties, including some by leaders of irregular units with Indian adherents. Vicente Revilla stayed with the government forces. Vito Pacheco, on the other hand, pronounced in Yaxcabá in favor of the rebellion. In Tihosuco, Trujeque renewed his pronouncement and occupied Peto with the force he already had at his disposal. Regular columns from Campeche and irregulars joining with them swept the countryside. Among the declared rebels, only Pacheco was trounced by a government column, and as the victorious detachment moved on to engage Trujeque at Peto, it was ambushed by a portion of his rebels—some said by men under Cecilio Chi—and almost annihilated. By early January the south was solidly in Campechano hands, and Mérida itself was virtually surrounded.[55] It did not aid Barbachano's cause when on December 31 he had to announce that the *villa* of Carmen on the Laguna de Términos, that old gateway to Yucatan, had been occupied by the U.S. Navy.[56]

With only the northern strip between Mérida and Valladolid still in government hands, the Campeche army ordered Trujeque and Vázquez toward Valladolid with a force now consisting of nearly two thousand men, two-thirds of them Indians, but including Bonifacio Novelo and other *vecinos* from the Valladolid barrios. Engaging the Valladolid commander, Lieutenant Colonel Claudio Venegas, at Tixcacalcupul, they forced him back to the *villa*. The attackers occupied the extramural barrio of Sisal on January 13, and the short siege of Valladolid began.[57]

Among the municipalities of Yucatan, Valladolid was the most conservative, preserving the strongest vestiges of the colonial caste system, with a small and ingrown upper class. *Vecinos* from the barrios—not to mention mere Indians—were routinely excluded from many fiestas in the plaza, and the hatred they felt for the stiff-necked people in the center of town was famous even in a society in which almost impenetrable class barriers existed everywhere.[58]

The result was that *vecinos* of the outlying barrios not already in the attackers' army joined the encircling force, shouting insults at the besieged in the center of town, who were quickly squeezed into the plaza itself. Looting began on the outskirts, and the besiegers made good use of stolen *aguardiente*. By now the drunken mob obeyed their commanders only when it suited them. On January 15 it evidently suited them well, for they responded to an order for an all-out assault.

It was said later that Colonel Venegas had raised a white flag at the moment of the assault, but if he did it had no effect. Venegas was seized and dragged to captivity in Sisal. The horde poured into the center of proud Valladolid, running wild, with Trujeque and Vázquez completely losing control. Rape, pillage, and murder spread through the city. Besides combatants, eighty-four people were murdered, their corpses dragged through the streets and then piled on bonfires of furniture, government papers— anything combustible.[59] According to Baqueiro, those killed had been fingered in advance by an inside act of rebellion.[60] On January 17, Bonifacio Novelo, at the head of what—with probable exaggeration—was said to be a thousand Indians, broke into Venegas's jail and murdered him.[61]

Word of the carnage electrified the state. From Mérida Barbachano wrote in anguish to the Barret faction, lamenting that a race war could erupt and calling on them and all whites to unite for their salvation. Barret responded that a race war would be terrible but that rather than being the fault of the revolutionary movement blame would lie with earlier (unspecified) acts of the government. He called on Barbachano to surrender so peace could return.

Indeed, with the military situation as it was, Barbachano had no choice but to surrender, but he couched his resignation in a lengthy and politically conceived statement that lamented the bloodshed and rejected responsibility for the sack of Valladolid. With the governor gone, the loyal government troops were given generous and honorable terms of surrender, which they accepted on January 22, 1847, a scant six weeks after the second Campeche *pronunciamento* and a week after Trujeque ordered the final assault on the plaza of Valladolid.[62]

In the aftermath of the massacre, Bonifacio Novelo was jailed, but Valladolid was not to return to tranquility.[63]

5 / Year of Turmoil

Warfare would begin in earnest later in 1847. Before considering the complex political posturing that ushered in the fighting, however, some background factors warrant a brief reexamination.

The Condition of the Indians

The population of Yucatan may have expanded fairly rapidly in the decades leading to 1821 (see table 3), for which date a census only recently brought to light suggests a total of 538,907.[1] But it increased only slowly or not at all over the next twenty-five years. In 1846, a census yielded only 504,635 in raw figures, and corrected for presumed underenumeration, achieved only 575,351—an increment of less than 7 percent in the twenty-five year period.[2] A rounded number of 575,000 will be used here for that date, while recognizing that others are more inclined to accept the lesser figure of 500,000 for the population of the peninsula at the outbreak of the Caste War.[3]

An estimate of the division of this population between the legal categories Indian and *vecino* in the more populous *partidos*, is given in table 4.[4] As had always been the case, in the early nineteenth century the non-Indian population was proportionally greatest in the north and west, especially in the old colonial *partidos* of Sierra Alta and Sierra Baja (which are lumped together in the table), La Costa, Camino Real Bajo, and Mérida. Heavy as the Indian population was throughout the peninsula, in the *partidos* of Beneficios Altos and Valladolid it overwhelmingly dominated.

With independence, those classed legally as Indians had become full-fledged citizens, the males voting as members of the greater society and able to take part in the governance not only of pueblos having both *vecino* and Indian residents but of all Yucatan. But in 1824 the *república de indígenas* was again brought into being, with the result that there were again parallel jurisdictions in all pueblos. One was the usual *cabildo*, organized after the Spanish colonial model and pertaining to both Indians and *vecinos*. The

TABLE 4
Estimated Numbers of Indians in Eleven Partidos

Eighteenth-Century Partido[a]	a Indian Population (circa A.D. 1800)[b] (%)	b 1821 Indians	b 1821 Vecinos[c]	c 1846 Indians	c 1846 Vecinos[d]
La Sierra[e]	70.2	79,552	33,770	84,881	36,033
La Costa	78.4	59,977	16,524	63,995	17,631
Beneficios Altos	88.1	48,202	6,511	51,432	6,947
Valladolid	84.3	46,533	8,666	49,651	9,247
Camino Real Alto	83.6	38,250	7,503	40,813	8,006
Beneficios Bajos	80.8	36,580	8,692	39,031	9,274
Camino Real Bajo	64.2	27,523	15,347	29,367	16,375
Tizimín	74.0	21,815	7,665	23,277	8,179
Mérida	53.0	16,326	14,477	17,420	15,447
Campeche	61.9	11,334	6,976	12,093	7,442

[a]By 1821 the *partidos* of Sierra Alta, Sierra Baja, La Costa, Beneficios Altos, Beneficios Bajos, Camino Real Alto, and Camino Real Bajo were redesignated respectively Tekax, Mamá, Izamal, Ichmul, Sotuta, Hecelchakán, and Hunucmá. Because these new designations are also the names of towns referred to in the text, the eighteenth-century designators are retained here for purposes of clarity. By 1846, the *partidos* had been clustered into districts too large to provide meaningful information regarding population distribution.
[b]Calculated from Cook and Borah (1974, 92, table 1.8), which is based on ethnic attributions of heads of families between 1782 and 1805.
[c]Derived from proportions in column a and figures in Rodríguez Losa (1985, table 9).
[d]Derived from figures in column b, which are increased by 6.7 percent, the increment (in total population) from 538,900 to 575,000.
[e]The two Sierra *partidos* are lumped as are figures in Cook and Borah (1974, 92, table 1.8).

other was the *república*, still functioning only for legal Indians, in which only they voted, and which served as the old mechanism of indirect rule: the *cacique* or *gobernador* was again responsible for maintaining order and for collecting from Indians the civil head tax and church obventions. And as had been the case since the Bourbon reforms, the *gobernador* answered to a local civil official, the *jefe político*, who now was the chief officer of the *partido*.

The *república* also continued to organize the predominantly Indian fiestas in which the religious brotherhoods or *cofradías* took such a prominent part.

With expanding population and government-imposed restrictions, the lands available to the swidden-farming rural people, *vecinos* as well as Indians, had steadily shrunk. In addition, in the 1840s there was a short-lived tax charged subsistence farmers for making use of their customary plots. Remaining *cofradía* estates had been sold, depriving the *república* of this source of income. In the long run, of course, the major force in land matters was the growing commercialization of agriculture.

Before 1840 this pressure on land was heaviest in the west and had less effect in the southern- and easternmost occupied regions of the state. As table 5 shows,[5] the least densely populated areas were those of Beneficios Altos, Tizimín, and Bacalar in the east, and Bolonchencauich and Sahcabchén in the southwest. On the other hand, the distribution of rural income-producing properties (i.e., those devoted to anything other than subsistence maize plantings) closely follows the density distribution of the population (the strong positive correlation of columns d and g, table 5). In other words, the rural commercial establishments were where the population was centered—an unsurprising circumstance. Furthermore, these rural commercial establishments were *over*concentrated in the regions of densest population (the strong positive correlation of columns g and i, and the substantially weaker correlation of columns d and i, table 5). Thus, while there was a greater amount of land available in the least densely populated regions, there also was a greater potential pool of labor in those regions, as is shown by the ratio of population to rural properties (columns h and i, table 5).

The implication is that before 1840 there was a much higher proportion of subsistence farmers (as opposed to commercial laborers) in the east and south. This confirms that the forces that reduced the land available for subsistence farming up to that time had much less impact in the far east and south than in the other regions.[6]

In the years 1840 to 1847, alienation of so-called *terrenos baldíos* increased, as tracts continued to be sold for money needed by the struggling government or were allocated to soldiers who had served in the Yucatecan armies. One modern historian reports that nearly 750,000 hectares are documented as conveyed in the period from 1843 to 1847. Almost one-fourth of this amount was in the region around Peto and east to Tihosuco, in what had been the colonial *partido* of Beneficios Altos and an approximately equal fraction in an area made up by the two colonial *partidos* of Valladolid and Tizimín. These were regions of heavy Indian population, the latter two

TABLE 5
Population and Taxable Rural Properties by Partido, 1820–40

Eighteenth-Century Partido[a]	a Area	b Population	c Population Density	d (rank)	e No. Rural Properties	f Ratio Prop/Area (e/a)	g (rank)	h Ratio Prop/Pop (e/b)	i (rank)
	(km²)[b]	(1821)[c]	(b/a)	(rank)	(1836)[d]	(.000)	(rank)	(.0000)	(rank)
Campeche	693	18,310	26.4	—	18	26	—	98	—
Mérida	1,210	30,803	25.5	—	103	85	—	334	—
Sierra Baja	2,750	47,099	26.9	1	255	93	2	541	5
Sierra Alta	4,447	66,223	14.9	2	138	31	6	208	9
Beneficios Bajos	3,129	45,272	14.5	3	220	70	3	486	6
La Costa	5,858	76,501	13.1	4	867	148	1	1133	1
Valladolid	5,580	55,199	9.9	5	378	68	4	685	2
Camino Real Bajo	5,044	42,870	8.5	6	278	55	5	648	3
Camino Real Alto	8,590	45,753	5.3	7	99	12	8	216	8
Beneficios Altos	12,022	54,713	4.6	8	98	8	9	119	11
Tizimín	7,530	29,480	3.9	9	160	21	7	543	4
Bolonchencauich	3,447	11,100	3.2	10	23	7	10	207	10
Sahcabchén	19,100	8,712	0.5	11	29	2	11	333	7
Bacalar	14,086	2,863	0.2	12	0	0	12	0	12

Rank-order correlations, Campeche and Mérida excluded: columns (d) and (g), $\rho = 0.881$; $t = 5.89$, significant at .025 level; (d) and (i), $\rho = 0.468$; $t = 1.67$, significant at .2 level; (g) and (i), $\rho = 0.776$; $t = 3.89$, significant at .05 level.

Note: Taxable rural properties were all those other than subsistence agriculture (Regil and Peón 1853).

[a]See table 4, note a. By 1821 Bolonchencauich and Sahcabchén were redesignated Lerma and Champotón, respectively.
[b]Cook and Borah (1974, table 1.19).   [c]Rodríguez Losa (1985, 100, table 9).   [d]Regil and Peón (1853, table B).

having a higher density of nonsubsistence rural properties. With areas of the former Beneficios Altos and Tizimín both low in population density, the choice of these regions for land distribution makes intuitive sense.

Nevertheless, another one-fourth of the documented lands so transferred to private individuals was in the heavily populated regions of the northwest: in the former *partidos* of Mérida, Camino Real Bajo and Alto, the Sierras, and La Costa. In addition, the few documented examples of relatively violent Indian protests against land transfer and taxation policies occurred in the relatively densely populated areas of the old *partidos* of Sierra Baja and Beneficio Bajos.[7]

Altogether, it is reasonable to say that the residents in the more thinly populated regions in the east and south were much less affected by the land shortage owing to nineteenth-century transfers than were campesinos who lived from Valladolid westward and in the two old *partidos* of the Sierra.

With regard to customary taxes, table 6 summarizes the situation between independence and about 1840.[8] Between 1840 and 1846, as I indicated in the preceding chapter, changes in taxation for both religious and civil purposes had been both rapid and inconsistent in direction, but by the end of the latter year neither obventions nor tithes were being collected and the civil tax had been raised above the level shown in table 6, only to be reduced to eighteen *reales* annually after the triumph of the Campeche coup in early 1847.[9]

Historically, the charges for sacraments had been greater for *vecinos* than for Indians. With the elimination of obventions and tithes, however, there had also been a parallel reduction in the charges for marriages and baptisms to a uniform rate of four and three *reales* respectively, and by mid-1847 parish priests had reportedly all agreed to stop levying charges for burials.[10] The condition of church finances was considered that same year by the extraordinary Assembly of Ticul, which recognized that the expenses of the church, which would require a sum approximating twelve *reales* per year per taxpayer, were not being adequately met. Ironically, the recommended solution was not that a separate tax be levied but that the situation existing since 1844 be continued, which would include attempts to squeeze the money from the regular civil contribution and continue to impoverish the already strained civil government.[11]

In any event, by the middle of 1847 the charges reflected in table 6 had been equalized between Indians and *vecinos*, both paying what had previously been the most common Indian rate for baptism and marriage, as well as the same eighteen *reales* per year in a civil tax that was to include support of the church.

TABLE 6
Representative Taxes, 1824–40

	Indian	Vecino[a]
Annual Civil Tax:		
Males, aged 16–60	head tax, 12 *reales*	head tax, 12 *reales*
Annual Religious Tax:		
Males, aged 14–60	head tax, 12.5 *reales*	tithe
Females, aged 12–55	head tax, 9 *reales*	
Fees for Sacraments:		
Baptism	3 *reales*	7 *reales* to 1 peso
Marriage	4 to 10 *reales*	7 to 11 pesos
Burial	0 (pauper) to 18 *reales*	18 *reales* (infant) to 15 pesos

Sources: Based on Baqueiro Anduze (1943, 210–12), González Navarro (1970, 54), Pérez Martínez (1938), Sierra O'Reilly (1954); the fees for sacraments are drawn particularly from Dumond and Dumond (1982, pt. 2, documents 9-2, 11-4, 13-4, 20-5, and 58-2, dating from 1813 to 1841).
[a]Wealthy landed Indians might be charged at or near the rates for *vecinos*.

One other tax needs to be mentioned. In April 1847 the tax on *aguardiente*, hitherto reluctantly paid by producers, was shifted to consumers, who paid it upon purchase at the rate of four pesos per barrel. This was highly unpopular with the Indians, who consumed great quantities at their fiestas.[12] Other changes in taxes would be decreed before the end of 1847.

These issues would loom importantly in the troubles of the next few years.

Movement and Countermovement

Although Campeche had triumphed decisively in the short internecine war that began the year of 1847, the victory did not lead to peace. With Carmen occupied by the United States, aggression from that quarter was feared. Even before hostilities in Yucatan ended with the resignation of Barbachano, announcements of Yucatecan neutrality were sent to Commodore P. S. P. Conner, commanding the U.S. fleet in the Gulf of Mexico, and an emissary was dispatched to Washington to urge acceptance of the same status.[13]

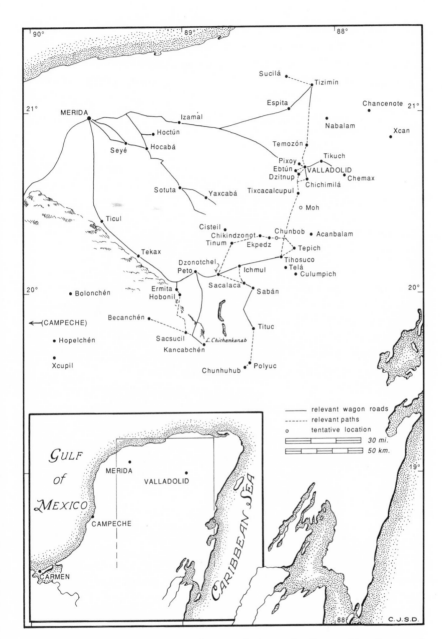

Map 5. Location of Events of 1847. Places marked tentative (here and in other maps) were not found on usable maps but are based on text descriptions only. Paths are reconstructed from appropriate maps and text sources.

In the east, Valladolid was a wasteland. In a public statement in Mérida Trujeque denied responsibility for the massacre, laid primary blame for the riot and carnage on *vecinos* of the Valladolid extramural barrios, and took credit for having captured and jailed Bonifacio Novelo for the murder of the military commander. Unfortunately, Novelo broke out of jail almost immediately and soon appeared at the head of a gang of several hundred, most of them Indians, raiding in and around the *villa*.[14]

A fresh column of troops from the capital and a new *jefe político* restored some order, forcing Novelo to hide in the countryside. In the face of regional disorganization, legal inquiry into the debacle of January 15 uncovered nothing significant. A column of Campeche troops being sent to Valladolid by way of Tekax and Peto—where activity of Barbachano partisans under one Felipe Rosado was suspected—mutinied, went wild, and sacked Peto. Attempting to turn the debacle into a *barbachanista* coup by taking charge of the mutineers, Vicente Revilla was unable to keep them from looting Tekax and other pueblos before they dissipated. He was caught, tried for leading them in insurrection, and banished. A year later he attempted to return and was shot by a military patrol, ostensibly for resisting arrest.[15] For security reasons, the government moved temporarily from Mérida to Campeche.

Inevitably there was a fresh pronouncement, this time from the junior officers of the Mérida garrison, with José Dolores Cetina taking the leadership. Their call on February 28 was for reinstatement of the legally elected government and the constitution of 1825; for permanent reduction of the annual head tax to twelve *reales* for all citizens, with a lifetime exemption from the same tax for all who took up arms in their cause; and for recognition of General López de Llergo as acting governor until the return of Barbachano. López de Llergo accepted the charge, but faced with an untenable military position, he made peace with the Barret government within two weeks. Cetina and some other officers were jailed in Campeche, then banished to Cuba.[16]

Things remained unsettled. In the east, a band of masked men entered the house of the *jefe político* of Tizimín in broad daylight and assassinated him. A political motive was suspected.

Yet the government managed to hold things together, and the situation gradually quieted. In May, word was received that Yucatecan neutrality would be respected by the United States, although at the price of ending all trade with Mexican ports, and in the same month Colonel Eulogio Rosado was named *jefe político* and military commander of Valladolid *partido*. Control was seemingly being restored in the east. But Bonifacio Novelo was still at large, and the hinterland remained in turmoil.[17]

Despite having proclaimed the constitution of 1841 in effect when their movement began, the provisional Barret government did not set dates for immediate elections. Instead, at the end of May a large selection of prominent men—with no *barbachanistas* present—was assembled in Ticul and charged to make recommendations regarding a series of matters, including taxation and church finance. The discussions lasted until late June, with little immediate result. But at their close Justo Sierra O'Reilly was sent to Washington to negotiate for the end of the occupation of Carmen and for a recognition of his government by the United States to provide a safeguard against any retaliatory pressure Mexico might exert because of the Yucatecan stand in the U.S.–Mexican War. Elections were finally set for July 18. To no one's surprise, Santiago Méndez of Campeche was elected governor and scheduled to take office in September.[18]

The Tribulations of Manuel Antonio Ay

But election day brought new drama in the east. On that day one Miguel Gerónimo Rivero, owner of the hacienda of Acanbalam, located forty kilometers south of Valladolid, reported to Colonel Eulogio Rosado that for a week he had watched large groups of Indians from six different pueblos hauling provisions of various kinds toward Culumpich, the hacienda of Jacinto Pat, *cacique* of Tihosuco. Rivero's servant, sent to Culumpich to investigate, had returned to say that the place was full of Indians from throughout the district; that there was a general conspiracy against whites that was led by Bonifacio Novelo, Jacinto Pat, and Cecilio Chi; that in the rancho Tzal they had established a magazine stocked with muskets acquired in Belize; and that they intended to attack and take Tihosuco. Rivero and his family had fled.[19]

On that same day Colonel Rosado was sought out by Antonio Rajón, justice of the peace in Chichimilá, located seven kilometers south of Valladolid, who bore a similarly disquieting report: following his customary Sunday practice, Manuel Antonio Ay, *cacique* of Chichimilá, had been drinking with friends in an establishment operated by Rajón, when in a state of drunkenness Ay dropped his hat on a table and Rajón removed from it a letter he took to be inflammatory. Despite a threat from Ay, Rajón immediately traveled the short distance into Valladolid to report the incident.

Two versions of this letter exist in the literature, one quoted by the historian Baqueiro with his assurance that it is an exact rendition of the original, the second a copy discovered much later in manuscript in the papers of Colonel Rosado. Both show the letter, dated at Tepich, July 1847, to be addressed to Ay with Cecilio Chi as author. Varying only to the extent that different interpretations of poor handwriting may be responsible, the two versions agree in the substance of three points communicated from Chi to Ay:

- Tell me how many pueblos are involved in the matter.
- I intend to attack Tihosuco.
- They are on my tail here, so give me two or three days' notice before you come to join me.[20]

However the letter was viewed in 1847, from the distance of the present it reeks of inauthenticity. The fact that it is written in Spanish raises doubts in itself, for face to face Chi and Ay would certainly have communicated in Maya, and literate Maya-speakers of the time preferred to write in Maya as well. Indeed, when questioned about it, Ay professed not to be able to read the letter at all because it was in Spanish.[21] Beyond that, the Spanish in Baqueiro's version of the letter includes misspellings that present the effect more of spoken country dialect than of orthographic misunderstanding, and accent marks (not common in any mid-nineteenth-century Yucatecan writing) are abundant.

But the letter alarmed Rosado. Ay was arrested and his house was searched, yielding a letter from him to Bonifacio Novelo—not incriminating in substance, although Novelo was a fugitive—and a list of people from whom money had been collected for an unknown purpose. Hauled before a military court, Ay was faced with testimony from Rajón regarding not only the letter found in his hat but setting out Ay's response to Chi (obtained by Rajón in a manner not specified in the histories): that as soon as Ay had raised a sufficient force he would join Chi at Tepich. On his side, Ay denied being in league with Chi or with Pat in any movement against Spanish Yucatecans. But he confessed (with what means of persuasion we are not told) that at the behest of Bonifacio Novelo he had collected money for a pronouncement aimed to reduce the annual head tax from eighteen to twelve *reales*. He stated that the money had been placed for safekeeping with one Secundino Loria of Chichimilá. Loria, for his part, denied receiving any such deposit and testified instead that he had refused to be shaken down for five pesos by Ay and three associates (in the presence of an unknown *blanco* and a force of inebriated Indians cheering for Cecilio Chi), insisting that he had suffered enough at the time of the January 15 assault on Valladolid, when his house was broken into and he was physically maltreated.

The letter, the testimony, the report from Culumpich, and Yucatecan fear over the eastern situation were enough for Ay to be convicted and sentenced to death. On July 26 Manuel Antonio Ay, aged twenty-eight to thirty years, was executed by firing squad in the plaza of Santa Ana in Valladolid, while the streets of the *villa* were guarded by closely ranked soldiers to prevent any attempt to free him. Masses of Indians are reported to have watched and waited silently.[22]

War in the East

But the execution of Ay settled and stabilized nothing. Instead, it signaled the beginning of a series of confusing and rapidly snowballing events that grew from isolated actions to widespread warfare. These would not be confined to a single rebellion by Indian campesinos against non-Indian *vecinos* but would be intermingled with partisan strife among factions in the highest circles of government.

On July 25, the day Ay was sentenced for conspiracy to rebel, José Dolores Cetina marked his surreptitious return from Cuba by appearing in the Barbachano stronghold of Tizimín to issue a call to rebellion. His official pronouncement proclaimed the same conditions that had been announced in the abortive movement he had led in February and March, to which was added the continuation of Yucatecan neutrality in the war between Mexico and the United States. On being challenged to surrender Valladolid to the movement, Colonel Rosado chose not to fight but to negotiate with Cetina on the grounds that the danger posed by the eastern Indians was immediate and greater. Baffled for the time being, Cetina agreed tentatively to join Rosado and was allowed to enter Valladolid with the military force he had raised around Tizimín and to billet in the barrio of La Candelaria without mingling his troops with Rosado's.[23]

In the meantime, word had been received by the lameduck Barret government of the suspicions raised against Jacinto Pat and Cecilio Chi, and orders were sent to the *jefe superior político* of the department of Tekax to arrest Pat and Chi for suspected conspiracy. The order was passed on to the subaltern *jefe político* of Peto *partido*, who now was none other than Antonio Trujeque. Accompanied, oddly enough, by his former enemy Vito Pacheco, Trujeque left immediately for Culumpich, Pat's hacienda near Tihosuco. It was apparently on July 26, the day of Ay's execution, that Trujeque and Pacheco arrived at Pat's establishment.

Far from finding masses of Indians and piles of supplies, they found Pat peaceably tending to his ordinary affairs, so beguilingly serene that those who had come to arrest the man who was their old acquaintance and Trujeque's favorite political enemy concluded that the government had made a mistake. They remained at Culumpich much of the day, enjoyed the wealthy Pat's hospitality, and left him as they had found him.

Their approach to Chi, the influential and experienced soldier of Tepich who was at home in his own base of power, must have seemed more touchy, for Trujeque adopted a ruse. Stopping in Tihosuco, he sent a small force under Captain Beitia on to Tepich—fourteen kilometers distant—with an invitation for Chi to come to Tihosuco with his men so that Trujeque could pay them for the military services they had rendered in January under Chi's leadership. Beitia found Chi in a drinking establishment late on the night of July 26 and received his promise to come to Tihosuco. Alone, his escort on the outskirts of town, Beitia wisely attempted no arrest.

But Ay had been shot, and Chi was apparently aware both of the execution and of his own incrimination. Rather than fall into the trap at Tihosuco, he raised two hundred men, set lookouts around Tepich, and wrote immediately to supporters in the pueblo of Telá, also thirteen or fourteen kilometers from Tihosuco and somewhat farther from Tepich, asking for men to join his force. But his letter missed its addressee, fell into the hands of the *alcalde* of Telá, and was sent immediately to Trujeque at Tihosuco.

On July 28, the day following this adventitious disclosure of Chi's action, Trujeque moved on Tepich with his own military detachment, heavily reinforced by Tihosuco *vecinos*. Chi's sentinels did their work imperfectly, for a meeting was apparently disrupted, and four men in attendance were taken—although all other adult Indian males escaped, Chi included. Dividing his force into parties, Trujeque had the town searched. And for the second time he showed himself unable to control his men, for the search led to a sack of Indian dwellings, abuse of remaining Indian families, and the rape of a ten- or twelve-year-old Indian girl.

Leaving muskets with the *vecinos* of the place for their protection, the following day Trujeque marched on Ekpedz, where he arrested one more man for association with the conspiracy. Upon interrogation—using what means we are not told—the five prisoners confessed their relationship with Chi, admitted that in meetings at Tepich they had planned with him to attack Tihosuco, and reported that Bonifacio Novelo would join and Jacinto Pat would furnish munitions as well as men. Once successful at Tihosuco, they would aim to take the entire state. They understood that as many as five hundred or six hundred men would be drawn from pueblos as far north as Chichimilá, as far south as Polyuc and Chunhuhub, and as far west as Tinum. On July 30 the five were shot.[24]

One must suppose that the *vecinos* of Tepich itself had taken some significant part in the harrying of the Indian families because on that night, July 30, as a single *vecino* sentinel kept watch, Chi and his force fell on the hapless *vecinos* of his own pueblo of Tepich and massacred all but one. The sole survivor reached Tihosuco the following day with news of the disaster.

Trujeque immediately sent word of the raid to the central government and issued pleas for reinforcements from nearby military posts. On August 1 he was joined by a company from Ichmul. More *vecinos* of Tihosuco were armed. Two columns were shortly dispatched to Tepich by different paths, one under Vito Pacheco, the other under Beitia. The way was disputed by armed rebels. Beitia was ambushed and fell back to Tihosuco, but after considerable fighting and some losses, Pacheco was able to reach Tepich on August 4, finding it deserted by all but a few women and children. He returned to Tihosuco.

Meanwhile additional reinforcements had arrived at Tihosuco, and a column of more than two hundred men moved on Tepich under Captain Diego Ongay. Forcing a number of rebel breastworks and fighting off ambushes, they reached the village on August 7 with, again, some losses. As before, the Indian men had deserted the town, but this time the Yucatecan force burned everything to the ground including the church. Some of the buildings torched were said to have had women, old people, and children trapped inside. The Yucatecans filled the wells with rubble to render the pueblo uninhabitable. As the official government newspaper in Mérida reported, "Tepich does not exist, and the name of the rebel pueblo has been erased." The parallel with the fate of Cisteil after the brief rebellion of the 1760s is unmistakable.

But these new rebels were not to be defeated by the eradication of a town, even their own. They immediately fell on Ekpedz, killed several *vecinos*, burned houses, captured a number of muskets that had been collected by the authorities from Indians, and pulled back to dig in at Rancho Chunbob. As word reached Tihosuco on August 9, Ongay moved out immediately with 250 men, ran into a series of punishing ambushes, and was forced to stop and fortify himself. On August 10 a section of reinforcements under Pacheco dislodged the attackers, and the two Yucatecan columns were able to move on Chunbob, finding it vacated. On August 11, suffering from fatigue and lack of supplies, they returned to Tihosuco.[25]

The next day the rebels struck Rancho Yaxché; looted gold, money, clothing; and killed one *vecino* boy. They then moved on to Rancho Xcanul.[26] When word reached Tihosuco, where there were now some eight hundred men, Ongay marched out again, ran into a trap, and took losses but gained Rancho Xcanul at bayonet point. It was now the middle of August.

Northward, closer to Valladolid, rebel parties that included men who had fled from Chichimilá upon Ay's execution had also been at work. Entrenched at a Rancho Xca, these rebels repulsed two hundred Yucatecan soldiers. Finally dispersed, they moved south toward Tihosuco, burned houses, and murdered everyone they found at the hacienda Acanbalam— the establishment of Miguel Gerónimo Rivero, who had carried the first allegations of the planned Indian uprising to Colonel Rosado—and then similarly devastated a second hacienda.

This force of about two hundred rebels was thought to be led by Bonifacio Novelo and Florentino Chan, the latter of Dzitnup. But it was also said to include two mestizos who had deserted from the Campeche force that had mutinied earlier at Peto—and who, it was said, were surely masterminding the Indians. Pursuers from the garrison at Valladolid overtook nothing but an insignificant party near Tihosuco, for the large rebel body had carefully doubled back and was again raiding around Valladolid. That *villa*, now almost without troops because Rosado's men were in the field, mounted a small force that drove rebels from a nearby rancho, and in the action Antonio Rajón, the man who had denounced Manuel Antonio Ay, was wounded. At about this time Bonifacio Novelo was reported to have gone to buy arms in British Honduras, where obsolete flintlock muskets from the Napoleonic War were almost certainly available commercially as surplus.[27]

And so the rebellion grew among distinct parties, by small, dispersed actions, rapid movements, attacks without sustained fighting. During August the action remained within the region between Tihosuco and Valladolid. This was home territory, for with the exception of a scattered few like the deserters from the Peto mutiny, the rebels were people of that region.

Response in the West

In the major population centers of the west, reactions to a revolt that was largely Indian came in two directions. On the one hand, a nearly pathological backlash was inspired by fear of armed Indians to whom an implacable hatred of all *vecinos* was attributed—a backlash like that after the outbreak at Cisteil nearly a century before—which led to excesses of inhumanity in legislative and juridical actions as well as in rhetoric. On the other hand, many people obviously found it impossible to believe that the rebellion was a campesino uprising but instead chose to consider it as another of the machinations of the major political factions as they struggled against each other. These two different views of the events were brought into symbolic alignment in a contemporary folktale.

This was the story of a meeting at Pat's hacienda, Culumpich, of all the major rebel leaders—Cecilio Chi, Venancio Pec, Florentino Chan, Bonifacio Novelo, and, of course, Pat himself. Pat presented the fighting as an act of partisan political strife and asked for a consensus regarding which Yucatecan party should be supported. The others, however, regarded the civil altercations as a pretext under which to launch a war of extermination against non-Indian Yucatan. That this is tradition rather than fact is suggested by the absence of any specific source for the inside intelligence and by the date assigned to it: August 7, 1847, the day Tepich was burned, probably the day rebels struck Ekpedz, and a day when Chan and Novelo were reported fighting near Valladolid—a day, in short, when it would have been impossible to unite the people mentioned, even if their aims were coordinated enough for any such planning meeting to have occurred at all. Both of the major contemporary historians, however, appear to subscribe to the notion encapsulated by the story: the original stirring of rebellion was nurtured if not created by politically partisan strife, but as it developed it became a social movement in its own right, as the abiding hatred of Maya for Spaniard found its expression.[28]

It was on August 5 that word was received in Mérida of the outbreak of fighting. Immediately, Governor Barret issued a resounding call for unity among all loyal Yucatecans, and Barbachano—returned from Cuba—had his adherents join with the Campeche government in a public show of cordiality and solidarity.[29] The next day, in the interest of the same unity, amnesty was declared for those who had pronounced in Tizimín. Cetina accepted and submitted and was shortly thereafter sent with his command to occupy Tixcacalcupul, whence he could watch the road between Valladolid and Tihosuco.[30] In Tixcacalcupul he is said to have lodged with the parish priest, Eusebio García Rejón, whose servant-protégé was a tall and very dark youth, probably half-caste although nominally Indian, named Crescencio Poot, who because of his protector's tutelage was educated—that is, was literate, fluent in Spanish, and had some knowledge of Latin. Whether the inevitable association of Cetina and Poot was responsible in any way for Poot's later career as a rebel cannot be known, although the possibility provides food for speculation.[31]

A series of other extraordinary decrees by the governor dealt with aspects of the fighting more directly. Martial law was declared, requiring all non-Indian males aged sixteen and over to take arms for the duration of hostilities. Traffic in firearms and ammunition was absolutely prohibited. Collection of all firearms remaining in the possession of Indians was ordered within twenty-four hours, on pain of stiff penalty for delay. Trial of conspirators, highwaymen, and ordinary thieves was to be conducted by military courts, in most cases councils of officers of the local militia. And the army was established in three commands, one located in Mérida, a second in Campeche, a third in Valladolid.[32]

In addition, Indians were deprived of those rights of citizenship that had been accorded them with increasing liberality since independence. They were declared incapable of managing their own affairs, although able to pay taxes. The república de indios was modified in that responsibility for the maintenance of Indian order and the supervision of Indian conduct was to be exercised by caciques appointed by the government from individuals of any class and ethnic group, not only Indians. Local alcaldes of pueblo civil governments, justices of the peace, and parish priests would also have special responsibility for tutelage of Indians and supervision of their behavior in all its aspects. A special judicial system was established for Indian matters, to be supported by a special tax on Indians of one real per year. In addition to the eighteen reales per year of ordinary civil contributions levied on all adult men, Indians would be assessed an additional one real per month per taxpayer to provide support for the church.[33] Following the outbreak of troubles, then, the major taxes charged Indians and vecinos are those shown in table 7.

The decree regarding the collection of firearms was particularly distressing to Indians all over Yucatan, for whom flintlock muskets and fowling pieces of rudimentary technology were important for hunting birds and deer in the new growth bush of fallow milpas. The natural resistance to the move was exacerbated by the hurry and by the behavior of some local alcaldes, who at high prices secretly sold back to Indians the arms they had just confiscated. All of this led to increased friction between Indians and alcaldes and, apparently in some cases, newly appointed non-Indian caciques. Arrests and charges of rebellion became frequent.[34] These troubles

TABLE 7

Some Taxes in December 1847

	Indian	*Vecino*
Annual Civil Tax:		
Males, aged 16–60	head tax, 18 *reales*	head tax, 18 *reales*
Annual Religious Tax:		
Males, aged 16–60	head tax, 12 *reales*	none
Annual Judicial Tax:		
Males, aged 16–60	head tax, 1 *real*	none

Sources: Based on Aznar Pérez (1849–51, 3:147–49; Baqueiro (1878–87, 1:249, 562–66); Cline (1950, 631–33, 637); González Navarro (1970, 79).

coincided with tales of the most vicious sort that circulated in and around Mérida. In striking parallel to events following the 1761 uprising in Cisteil, a great conspiracy was rumored, by which all Indians would rise up on August 15 in concert with the arrival at Mérida of Cecilio Chi and his army, where Chi would be crowned king among the strewn corpses of the *vecinos*.

The consequent witchhunt—again like events of 1761—brought widespread charges of a conspiracy to rebel and with them the jailing of Indian leaders all over western Yucatan. In the month following mid-August 1847, more than two hundred were said to have been tried in Mérida alone—many of the accused sent there for hearings when the military courts of the pueblos had more than they could handle—and a number were executed.

Whippings were common, with or without legal hearings. The historian Baqueiro, after quoting descriptions from newspapers and other sources, refers to one

that we saw with our own eyes in Xcupil, then our pueblo of residence. The justice of the peace made . . . a denouncement like those that were so common, an accusation . . . that the Indians of the pueblo, in concert with those of the East, were to rise en masse against the authorities and assassinate the vecinos. The justice secretly collected an armed force . . . and at midnight *fell on the conspirators who were sleeping peacefully*, pulling down the doors of their huts, cutting not only the ropes of their hammocks but also those of their sleeping wives and children. At that same hour they conducted the prisoners to the Assembly Hall, where, binding them with a musket crosswise between their hands and feet, they left them thrown on the ground for the rest of the night. . . . [In the morning] there were 36 prisoners, including old men, young men, and some almost children, all tied. There were their wives and their sons and daughters who had come with gourds of breakfast, which they had been unable to deliver. . . . A moment later, the justice of the peace arrived, ordered the drummer to beat a call, at the beat of which the armed vecinos assembled and formed at the whipping post. Then began the spectacle. . . . Untying one after another of the unfortunate prisoners, suspending each from the post, applying at once the most cruel lashes that made blood pour from the backs—in presence of their women and children whose heartfelt tears . . . were turned to blood by the pain. The detestable operation lasted about an hour, while nothing was heard but the moans of the victims punctuated by the sobs of their families. . . . After this they were led tied one with another to the chief town of the partido, where they were put at public works until, after great distress, they were able to regain their liberty.[35]

The most spectacular of these proceedings was the trial and execution of Francisco Uc, the very wealthy *cacique* of the barrio of Santiago at Mérida, accused of writing letters urging other Indian leaders to join the rebellion (letters that were not produced at his trial). As he lay in jail, cries for his death were heard from mobs in the streets, especially mobs of have-not *vecinos*. Trapped in inconsistencies in his own account of his whereabouts at certain times, he was found guilty, refused clemency by governor and legislature, and executed in September.[36]

Needless to say, it was unlikely that either the legal decrees or the hearings and punishments would quiet Indian unrest.

Rebel Triumphs

On September 1, 1847, the elected legislature was formally installed, and the following day it officially declared Santiago Méndez governor and Manuel Sales Baraona vice governor. It then proceeded to elect the governor's Council of State and in the spirit of political reconciliation chose Miguel Barbachano as First Councilor.

At about this same time, José Dolores Cetina was ordered with his command from Tixcacalcupul to Tizimín, where he was to organize the militia and improve the state of defense against rebels who were encroaching on the pueblos of Xcan and Chancenote to the east. Once in Tizimín, however,

Cetina merely turned to augmenting his own force, paying no attention to the rebel advance. When a column under Lieutenant Colonel Manuel Oliver was ordered to Tizimín to relieve him, Cetina withdrew to Sucilá, refused to deliver his men, and seemed hostile. On September 27, he and Oliver engaged, and Oliver won. Cetina, as usual, escaped and faded into the hinterlands.

But in early October Cetina reappeared with a small band in Mérida and surprised and captured the military citadel. From that position of local strength he again proclaimed his revolution. With most of the government officials in Campeche, Barbachano was induced to intercede with Cetina in the interests of unity and the war with the rebels. The result was the proclamation of a new bipartisan government, in which top executive power was to be shared by Méndez, Sales Baraona, and Barbachano. With the two Campechanos absent, the initiative was all with Barbachano.

But from Campeche the two legitimate officials objected strongly and immediately sent columns of troops north. At the same time they ordered the withdrawal of armed forces from the east and south, their destination Mérida and the quashing of still another Cetina insurrection.[37]

In the east, the result of the pullout was predictable. Rebels invaded Tixcacalcupul late in October, put it to the torch, and killed fourteen *vecinos* and two priests, one of them Eusebio García Rejón. The perpetrators were said to include workers from García Rejón's own hacienda of Moh —which had been managed for him by his protégé Crescencio Poot—in resentment for his usurpation of *terrenos baldíos* in the region. Some would blame the murder on Poot himself, although he later denied it. In any event, the success of the raid led to a swelling of insurgent ranks as many local Indians, not hitherto involved, joined the rebellion. And Crescencio Poot was among them, at the head of the ex-workers from Hacienda Moh.[38]

Next, Tihosuco was heavily threatened, surrounded by great numbers of rebels in what was then the first real siege of a plaza actively defended by a Yucatecan force. The soldiers remaining in the pueblo under the orders of Antonio Trujeque were few, however, and on November 10 Trujeque and his defenders pulled out to Ichmul. With the action at Tihosuco led by Jacinto Pat, the former *cacique* of the Tihosuco *república*, the town was not burned but preserved intact to become Pat's headquarters.[39]

As most of the state's military might lurched toward Mérida, Cetina slipped from the city to Izamal, where, apparently despairing of forceful action from Barbachano, he proclaimed himself governor of Yucatan on November 5. He then advanced on Valladolid to face Colonel Rosado.

Despite the smallness of the garrison remaining at Valladolid, on November 17 Cetina was defeated decisively by Rosado—and again escaped. There was now less support for him in the region than he had found during his previous escapades, for local worries were mounting over the Indian rebellion. Cetina faded from view.[40]

There was no letup among the eastern rebels. Following the capture of the pueblos of Tixcacalcupul and Tihosuco came those of Tinum, Sabán, and Chikindzonot. At Sacalaca fighting was heavy, and the place would have been gained by the rebels had not Captain Cirilo Baqueiro appeared in Tekax with a military force from the southern district of Chenes, moved to Peto where he found more men, and counterattacked the harrying rebels on November 24. They were dispersed from Sacalaca, and Baqueiro moved to other pueblos in the region but was finally forced by heavy action to establish himself at Ichmul.[41]

The attention of Yucatan was now focused again on the east, and its military forces were swinging in that direction when on December 4 Cetina appeared in Mérida with 170 men and—in the almost total absence of its garrison—took the city again. But it quickly became clear even to Cetina that his earlier support there had melted in the heat of the eastern rebellion. After negotiations he submitted to Méndez on the latter's promise that he would recommend that the legislature grant amnesty. At this point the "civil war," as opposed to the "race war" or "barbarians' war," was thought by most Yucatecans to be over.[42]

But there was cause for Yucatecan alarm in the east. Close to Valladolid, rebels attacked Chemax unsuccessfully on December 4 but then burned the pueblos of Xcan and Nabalam along with numerous ranchos. Then they began to encircle Valladolid.[43] On December 5 rebels attacked Ichmul and on December 19 laid siege to it. Although there were reportedly some rebel defections by this time, the attrition was much more than offset by new recruits, and rebel numbers continued to swell. *Vecinos* of the region, in contrast, began to emigrate rapidly westward. On December 24 they evacuated Ichmul, the troops leaving for Peto and taking with them the three hundred remaining *vecino* families.[44]

At the close of 1847 the secretary general of Yucatan wrote to the superintendent of British Honduras asking for an embargo on sales of arms and munitions to the rebels in that colony.[45] The government of the peninsula would have frequent occasion to reiterate that request, but it would be decades before Yucatan would receive real satisfaction.

Beginning on December 20, a special session of the Legislative Assembly met in Mérida. It passed emergency taxes to apply to individuals and business enterprises with incomes above a certain level; it granted amnesty to participants in the recent mutinies—this covered Cetina—and as it dissolved itself it gave emergency power to the governor between legislative sessions. Immediately, in January 1848, Méndez used his special powers to issue several important decrees. These decrees restricted *vecinos* from leaving their towns of residence during the rebellion and conceded rewards for those who distinguished themselves in the military campaign. They called up for support of the fighting troops those Indians who remained loyal to the government, declaring them *hidalgos* and excusing them from all taxes for life if they would remain in the forces for the duration of hostilities. They granted amnesty to those rebels who submitted to the government without further fighting and abolished the religious contribution of one *real* per month that had been levied on Indians in August of the previous year.[46]

In the same month, January 1848, an affair surfaced that raised strong suspicions of collusion between *barbachanistas* and rebels. Amid rumors that the eastern rebels were attempting to provoke an uprising among Indians of Hocabá, Seye, and Hoctún—towns frighteningly close to Mérida—a man was arrested carrying letters addressed to both José Dolores Cetina and Miguel Barbachano, potentially implicating them in a scheme to aid the rebels by easing their entry into some eastern pueblos. Cetina was arrested. Barbachano was able to extricate himself on the claim that the purported collusion was a plot by Yucatecan officials of Sotuta and Yaxcabá who wanted to use him to convince the rebels not to attack those towns. On the strength of this, Cetina was released. The major historians, however, obviously remained convinced that *barbachanistas* were in fact in concourse with rebels.[47]

Meanwhile the rebel isolation of Valladolid progressed. Chemax, so stoutly defended by Yucatecans in early December, was evacuated. On December 29 the rebels took Tikuch, a scant eight kilometers east of Valladolid, driving Vito Pacheco and three hundred men back to Valladolid. In early January rebels occupied Pixoy, on the road to Mérida, and Ebtún, and were dislodged with difficulty. On January 18 heavy rebel forces moved up from Chichimilá. They were dislodged several times from the Valladolid suburbs, but they always returned, and by January 22 they had surrounded the *villa* except for the Mérida road, which they shortly interrupted again at Pixoy. Valladolid was besieged.[48]

Following the loss of Tihosuco, Yucatecan concern had focused on the region around Peto. Eulogio Rosado was relieved at Valladolid by Colonel Agustín León and in late December took command at Peto. On orders from Governor Méndez, and with a view toward reconciling the strong *barbachanista* supporters of that region, Eulogio Rosado's staunch *barbachanista* kinsman, Felipe Rosado, was appointed commander of the Peto battalion of militia. This appointment brought the return to the Peto militia of some members who had earlier deserted for political reasons.

The rebel pressure increased. At the end of December rebels occupied Dzonotchel, only fourteen kilometers from Peto. Now able to count some sixteen hundred men under his command, Eulogio Rosado believed he could retake Ichmul and perhaps even Tihosuco. On January 24 he sent out columns to begin this movement with the reoccupation of Dzonotchel. But his men were stopped cold almost at the outskirts of Peto by an overwhelming enemy force.[49]

On the following day Felipe Rosado and most of his close associates, including much of his militia battalion, disappeared. According to the historian Baqueiro, he had the previous evening convened a meeting of *barbachanistas* who, after assuring themselves that the aim of the rebels was to restore Barbachano to power, agreed to withdraw their support from the Méndez government. Most of them moved with Felipe Rosado to his hacienda of Sacsucil south of Peto and converted it into "a great town, where the refugee families lived like the Arabs in the desert, in their curious field tents . . . amid laughter, songs, and happy predictions in favor of the cause they were supporting."[50]

While these defectors, joined by a steady trickle of Barbachano adherents, waited happily in the country for the triumph of Barbachano and the rebels, a series of events added to suspicion and the deterioration of morale in Peto. It was suspected that agents of Felipe Rosado were working to smooth an Indian takeover of Peto; one toward whom such suspicions pointed was Anselmo Duarte, who nevertheless remained in the pueblo. Juan María Novelo—of whom more will be heard later—was apprehended and accused of having been sent from Sacsucil to convey rebels to the pueblos of Hobonil and Ermita; he was tried but somehow acquitted, or at least released.[51] Inside Peto, a stock of arms and munitions was discovered that was marked "For Jacinto Pat, or for D. Felipe Rosado, in Sacsucil."[52] This last was only a month after a printed broadside appeared on Mérida streets proclaiming that Jacinto Pat had announced his support for the return of the Barbachano government that had been displaced by the Campeche coup of December

1846, and this (it went on) of course demonstrated the political nature of the supposed Indian uprising.[53] When the attacking rebels appeared before Peto they were heard to cry "¡Viva Mérida! ¡Viva don Miguel Barbachano gobernador!"[54]

The final and apparently deciding occurrence in Peto was the sudden contamination of water in the main well from which the military force was provisioned—an event in which Anselmo Duarte was suspected of involvement. On February 6 Colonel Rosado evacuated Peto with the remaining vecino families. With nearly fifteen hundred men at arms and in the absence of a heavy Indian siege, questions were inevitably raised. When they reached Tekax, Rosado was reportedly on the verge of having Anselmo Duarte shot—not only because of Rosado's suspicions but because Duarte had said he would demand a court martial of the commander and his officers for having abandoned their post without sufficient cause. Whatever occasioned the decision to evacuate, Eulogio Rosado clearly was demoralized. He requested that he be relieved of his command, although the request was not then acted upon.[55]

In the middle of February, rebels fell on Sacsucil, burned it to the ground, and killed thirty-six people; Felipe Rosado himself was at the time erroneously said to be included in that number.[56] With this event, and whether or not there was collusion between Jacinto Pat and the barbachanistas, the persistent notion that the rebellion was simply a part of the political machinations of the governing factions of the state was finally abandoned by every Yucatecan.

6 / Peace and War

That some *barbachanistas* intended to make common antigovernment cause with the rebels is not to be doubted. Whether Miguel Barbachano himself was involved is less clear (although by no means ruled out by the evidence), but it is unmistakable that factionalism among rulers and would-be rulers facilitated the growth of the rebellion. There is no guarantee that unity among politicians would have led to the immediate suppression of the revolt, but it would certainly have slowed the spread of the insurrection and thereby contained it geographically.

As it was, the rebellion began in the area extending north from Tihosuco, on the eastern edges of the old *partidos* of Beneficios Altos and Valladolid, at the easternmost rim of the region that historically had been both relatively well populated and under fairly secure government control. From there it spread west as a moving front, and by early 1848—as described in the preceding chapter—had successfully invested virtually all of Beneficios Altos and Valladolid and had made serious inroads in the *partido* of Tizimín.

Although, as this chapter will argue, a significant number of recruits to rebellion were legally *vecinos* rather than Indians, the latter made up the vast majority of rebels. Beneficios Altos and Valladolid were the *partidos* with the highest percentage of Indians among their populations (see table 4), together claiming roughly one hundred thousand Indians when hostilities began, while Tizimín could count nearly one-fourth that many. If fewer than half of those Indians were actively pursuing the revolt by the end of 1847, the total rebel population must have exceeded fifty thousand—of whom, using reasonable demographic assumptions, a maximum of one-third were males above age fourteen. With boys even younger than this said to be found regularly in the rebel army, active soldiers could already have exceeded fifteen thousand.[1]

A successful move into the heavily populated *partidos* of Beneficios Bajos and Sierra Alta would open an area in which the Indian population available for recruitment was enough to double rebel strength. And that is exactly what happened in 1848. As the active rebel front moved into these more westerly zones, its force was swelled by Indians and others who felt prompted to rise up. But there was never a concurrent, general, and peninsula-wide uprising of Indians to take the government armies from all sides at once. The rebellion began, and in an important sense was to end, as an eastern movement. The only lasting leadership began and remained in eastern hands, while recruits from the newly risen regions to the west and south acted more or less independently for as long as they were in rebellion. Like most Yucatecans, the general run of the rebels showed a determination to stay close to whatever place they called home.

The Rebel Military Machine

When the remnants of the Caste War rebels were studied in the 1930s and after,[2] their local governing organization was administered by men with military titles—corporal, sergeant, lieutenant, captain, major—who directed quasimilitary "companies" that included all able-bodied males with their female and juvenile affiliates and around which the entire society was organized. This was obviously the heritage of the nineteenth-century rebel organization, which in turn was evidently modeled on the Yucatecan militia. By early 1848 it appears this rebel military apparatus was coming into being.

As had been provided nationally by law in 1827 and in Yucatan by laws of 1828 and 1832, each of fifteen districts was required to organize one or more battalions of local militia, each battalion to be composed of eight companies and numbering eight hundred to twelve hundred men in total. The commander of each battalion (a colonel) and his staff (a lieutenant colonel, a captain, a lieutenant, sublieutenant, and some lesser functionaries) were appointed by the Yucatecan government. Companies, on the other hand, were organized by individual towns and were officered by local individuals chosen by the local members; minimally, these included a captain as commander, a lieutenant, two sublieutenants, four sergeants, eight corporals, and three drummers. No military rank was established between those of captain and lieutenant colonel.[3]

Membership in this local militia was mandatory for all able-bodied non-Indian males between the ages of sixteen and fifty. Although legal Indians were exempt from compulsory service, they could enlist as volunteers. Indians had been actively recruited for actions in the 1830s and 1840s, and, as previous chapters have made clear, a number of the rebels—most, but not all, with Indian surnames—served in early campaigns.

In May 1848—following events to be related shortly—some of the rebel officers had begun writing to the superintendent of British Honduras for a variety of reasons, in a cycle of correspondence that was to last for about a year. Among these officers were those signed as Jacinto Pat, *comandante en jefe*; Cecilio Chi, *comandante general*, or simply *general*; Venancio Pec, *comandante general del oriente*; Juan Pablo Cocom and José María Tzuc, both *comandante de Bacalar*; José Victor Reyes, *secretario general* or *comandante general*; one Espada, *comandante de armas*; Francisco Cob and Bernardino Poot, both *capitán*.[4]

The battlefront apparently was divided among generals who commanded specific sectors: Pec here designated himself "Commanding General of the East," while Pat and Chi appear to have split their primary responsibilities between the southern and central regions, respectively.[5] It is possible that at this time the term *comandante* may have been used by the rebels primarily in its functional sense—for one who commands—rather than to designate a specific rank in the military hierarchy. A decade or so later, however, the term clearly would designate a specific rank between those of captain and general. Although British translators who handled mail in Spanish or Maya in British Honduras usually rendered it as "commandant," the term is also translated as "major."[6] The ranks of *coronel* and *teniente coronel* were not employed by rebels in the early days of the revolt, although they would later be used by pacified rebels affiliated with Campeche. In the later years, at least, each of the higher military ranks among the rebels was indicated by the wearing of a distinctive earring.[7] Whether this had begun as early as 1847 is unknown.

An additional and consistently prominent position was also established in that of the secretary, literate in both Maya and Spanish, who was responsible for maintaining communication with the outside world. At times this office would achieve the formal dignity of "Secretary General"—as in the letters just mentioned.

Thus, the rebel acquisition of military titles, while fairly true to the militia models at the ranks of captain and below, involved more selective borrowing and possibly some innovation in the designations applied to the highest of the leaders. The annexation of spouses and children to the companies such as was reported in later times was, of course, to be expected in a society long under total military mobilization.[8] It also was related, however, to the method of warfare adopted as soon as the rebellion began, for anyone, male or female, armed or not, could add to the shouts and constant noise that were the hallmark of rebel battle.

Like all military organizations, that of the rebels was segmental. But the connections between segments were especially fragile: True to the prototype provided by the Yucatecan militia company, when new rebels joined the movement they almost always did so under officers of their pueblo or region who were of their own choosing. And although the companies so organized at least nominally fell under the command of a *comandante* and, ultimately, a general, they clearly operated independently when they chose to. Examples of this practice will be seen throughout the account that follows.

In the ordinary view of white Yucatecans, Indians as a class were incapable of leadership—hence, Yucatecans expected that *vecinos* when present among the rebels would naturally lead. So Baqueiro conveys a typical remark regarding the two mestizos mentioned in the previous chapter as deserters from the mutinous Campeche force who reappeared with Bonifacio Novelo and Florentino Chan in rebel action: they "were surely those who were in charge" of the party.[9]

A less characteristic, but more astute, evaluation was one that granted military genius to the Indian leaders who

> displayed tactics entirely new to the country, unknown by the whites
> —tactics that consisted of never fighting in the open, entrenching
> themselves in the impenetrability of their woods and fighting behind
> a multiplicity of parapets scattered within it: it was a war of pure sur-
> prises that they waged, of ambushes skillfully disposed and devised;
> and in this class of warfare they held an immense superiority over
> their incautious enemies, who fell into their frequent traps.[10]

When threading their way through the thorn forest, Yucatecan soldiers would come suddenly on these barricades of boulders or tangled logs and branches thrown across the road, and in the instant of recognition would come a withering fire from the barricade and either roadside.

The use of the breastwork during sieges was also developed early by the rebels. First, the surrounding countryside would be scoured for several kilometers around the target, with all buildings torched that might provide cover for the defenders. As the siege itself was established a series of boulder barricades would be thrown up by the attackers, then worked steadily forward toward the defenses of the pueblo—sometimes by men lying flat on their backs and rolling the rocks with their feet while they took advantage of the slight cover provided by the tumbling boulder, sometimes under cover of dense smoke from fires set for that purpose.[11]

A tactic reminiscent of tales of Mexican Indian warfare at the time of Cortés's invasion involved the use of ear-splitting noise. In Yucatan this was created by constant gunfire, as well as—according to the historian Baqueiro—"incessant shouting and . . . playing of wooden drums and other rustic instruments, with which the Indians almost deafened our troops."[12] And so,

> the din of a heavy, constant gunfire (albeit uncertain and not very lethal); the infernal uproar produced by the horrible yelling of that multitude of unarmed people who accompanied . . . [the rebel soldiers] only with the aim of instilling fear by their yells, and among whom even the women and children mingled; the fires; and the isolation from all communication, came to prey on the defender's mind. . . . So they ended by trying to flee from it even when they had the power to resist, preferring to find death outside rather than in that frightful . . . enclosure. And usually they found it, for in order to break the siege they had to take and then cross by main force a multitude of breastworks occupied by the Indians.[13]

Except for the antiquated fowling pieces used by those campesinos lucky enough to have them and muskets captured from Yucatecan forces (which during the rebel successes of 1847 and early 1848 amounted to a considerable quantity), guns and munitions were obtained by trading various booty to enterprising dealers from British Honduras. As I mentioned earlier, the guns available from Belize were chiefly flintlock Brown Bess muskets that began to be sold as surplus by Britain after Napoleon's defeat. These were the equal of the small arms then in use by the Mexican army, which also had acquired British surplus guns, and were undoubtedly equivalent to anything in use by Yucatecan forces. With severe limitations placed on the usefulness of both the simple Yucatecan artillery as well as the Yucatecan cavalry by the bushwhacking nature of the fighting, the two sides were roughly equal in the sophistication of their military equipage—except that a large proportion of the rebels, known as light troops or *ligeros*, carried machetes only, or in many cases had nothing except their lungs.

The arms sales from British Honduras merchants caused anguish in Yucatan. But to the request from the governor of Yucatan that such trade with the rebels be prohibited, Superintendent Fancourt had responded that

> to prohibit the exportation of powder from within the British limits would be an interference with the trade of the settlement which would I fear be felt as a great hardship by the settlers, nor do I think that such a course would be successful. . . . However . . . I beg you to believe that I am most anxious and shall not fail to employ any influence which I may properly exercise with the settlers to prevent arms or

ammunition from being furnished to men who employ them for the purposes of rapine and bloodshed.[14]
His influence in this direction was not strong, as will be seen. Nevertheless, arms were never plentiful enough among the rebels to arm all their soldiers.

Groping for Peace

Hoping to negotiate a settlement of the war, Governor Méndez in early 1848 appointed a commission headed by Miguel Barbachano to meet with Jacinto Pat. At almost the same instant the bishop of Yucatan, José María Guerra, appointed for the same purpose a commission of priests led by José Canuto Vela.[15]

On the day Barbachano announced his acceptance of the commission—February 12—Yaxcabá in the central region was evacuated. The government forces were marshaled at Sotuta.[16]

On the next day at Valladolid, where despite the investing army of rebels the action had for weeks been surprisingly quiet, those rebels on their own initiative asked for a formal discussion of peace. Captain Miguel Bolio and Padre Manuel Antonio Sierra O'Reilly, the parish priest of Valladolid, went to meet them.[17] The conditions suggested by the rebel spokesmen were as follows:

- Reduction of the civil head tax to twelve *reales* per year.
- Return of the muskets taken from Indians in accord with the newly proclaimed disarmament law.
- Reduction of church fees to a uniform ten *reales* for marriage, three for baptism.
- Punishment of Juan Vásquez and Antonio Trujeque for wrongs they had done to Indians and indemnification of the Indians for damages suffered.
- The personal presence of Miguel Barbachano to hear the conditions of the rebels and guarantee their fulfillment.

The Yucatecan emissaries asked the rebels to present the conditions in writing, and both teams withdrew, setting the date of February 15 for the delivery of the written proposal, and promising solemnly to suspend hostilities until that time. On February 14, there was a smashing rebel attack on Chancenote, which until then had been held by a sturdy force of the town's own residents. As many as fifteen hundred rebels reportedly fell on the plaza, which was defended by fewer than one hundred. Many families

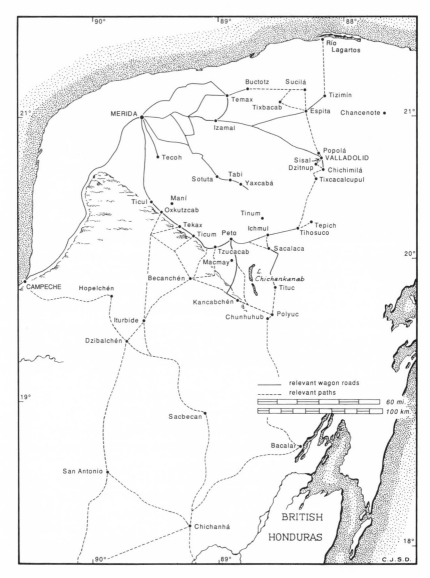

Map 6. *Location of Events of Early 1848. Route of the Valladolid evacuation is drawn from descriptions in references cited in the text.*

and defenders were massacred, some in the church, but by heroic effort a number escaped.[18]

In view of the agreed armistice, the Yucatecans saw this attack as an act of unconscionable double-dealing; nevertheless, on February 15 Colonel León was approached by rebel emissaries. They failed to provide the written conditions for peace, but they also insisted that the attack on Chancenote had been the work of a separate force over whom those besieging Valladolid had no control; they promised that on the following day, both Bonifacio Novelo and Bernardino Chan would meet with León to parley. There was, however, no such meeting. León received word that Novelo and Chan had been called to Tihosuco to confer with Jacinto Pat.[19]

Meanwhile, on February 15 Barbachano and his party, having combined forces with the clerics, left for Tekax, where on behalf of both the civil government and the diocese the groups immediately dispatched letters to rebel leaders at Sotuta, Valladolid, and Tihosuco.[20] They received the first response on February 23. Writing from headquarters in Tabi, the rebel officers of the Sotuta region had responded memorably as follows:

> One thing only I say to you and to the worshipful holy curates: Why didn't you remember or take notice when the governor began killing us? Why didn't you show yourselves in our favor when the whites were killing us?—Why didn't you rise up when one Padre Herrera did what he wanted with the Indians? This padre put his horse's saddle on a poor Indian, mounted and whipped him, and cut his belly with his spurs. Why did you not pity us when this happened?
>
> And now you remember, now you know there is a true God? . . . [W]hy didn't you think of the true God when you were hurting us? And now you don't have spirit to take the return of your whiplash. If we are killing you now, you first showed us the road. If the houses and haciendas of the whites are burning it is because you have burned the pueblo of Tepich and all the ranchos where the poor Indians were, and the whites ate their livestock. How many granaries of poor Indians' corn the whites broke open to eat! How many cornfields the same whites harvested when they went through them looking for us to kill us with gunpowder!

They recounted complaints regarding the confiscation of muskets, enumerated the rebel force available to conquer Sotuta, and pointed out that they had been induced into military service during the civil strife with the promise of a reduction of taxes—only to have the taxes doubled. They ended with a refusal to pay any sum in head tax and to the church only ten *reales* for marriage and three for baptism. The letter bore the signatures of six captains and the scribe.[21]

The response from the rebel commander or commanders encamped before Valladolid was similar in its final conditions—if the complaints in the unsigned letter could be called conditions—regarding taxes and church fees. The grievances recounted included particularly the killing and burning of old people and children at Tepich, the burning of the images and paintings of saints in the Tepich church; and an accusation that the Campeche-faction troops had used that same church building as a stable and latrine.[22] The commission could find no real hope of settlement in either of these cases.

But communications from Pat's headquarters, received on February 25, rang more reasonably. Although one letter recounted essentially the same complaints to the state government regarding taxes and the burning of Tepich, it concluded by saying that if the government were to decree the abolition of all taxes for both Indians and non-Indians, and permit the Indians to keep their arms, perhaps the war would be concluded. This was signed by Jacinto Pat, Florentino Chan, and Raimundo Chi, the latter pair identifying themselves as *comandantes*. A second letter to Padre Vela, signed only by Pat, asked on behalf of both Indians and Spaniards that fees be set at ten *reales* for marriage and three for baptisms. At the same time, Pat gave fresh evidence of the lack of any centralized direction among the insurgents. In a letter to Felipe Rosado—who had reappeared seemingly from the dead to work with the commission—he blamed some of the rebel atrocities on bands not under his control, which were raiding out of Becanchén. He said he was having them pursued.[23]

To their joy, the next day the commissioners received a letter from Manuel Ignacio Tuz, adherent of Pat and leader of a section of rebels of Macmay, inviting Governor Méndez to a conference to be held at Tzucacab. Cooperatively, on March 1 the governor issued a decree providing for the abolition of the civil head tax as soon as hostilities should end and providing also for the (necessarily accompanying) cessation of payments by the state to support the church. On March 6, Vela and a group of local Yucatecans met with Tuz at Tzucacab on behalf of the governor and laid the groundwork for a later conference with Pat himself.[24]

Nevertheless, the promising words of Pat's correspondence and the governor's response were not paralleled by encouraging acts elsewhere. Stiff fighting resumed at Valladolid. Yucatecans made one fairly successful raid on rebels at Chichimilá, seven kilometers south of the city, but their attacks on Dzitnup, even closer, produced devastating losses as the rebels sucked them into a trap. Following this punishment, León and his staff agreed to evacuate the civilians from Valladolid, a process that began in early March as the military force struggled to maintain an open track northwest to Espita, to avoid the main road west.[25]

In the region southwest of Valladolid, early rumors had it that the rebels at Tabi would negotiate and peace might be possible with the total abolition of the civil head tax. But at the beginning of March, rebels estimated at five to six thousand fell on Sotuta. To other peace demands was then added the return of the image of the Virgin of Tabi, which had been taken to the church at Sotuta when Tabi was evacuated. After four days of hand-to-hand fighting the Yucatecan force abandoned the plaza and Sotuta fell to the rebels and the torch.[26] There were no negotiations.

About this time word was received that the isolated southern pueblos of Chichanhá and San Antonio were in revolt, and at the end of February rebels besieged and took Becanchén.[27] The far south was moving into the rebel camp.

Then, on March 10 the rebel Miguel Huchim appeared at Valladolid asking for discussion of the peace terms suggested in correspondence with the commissions in Tekax. Although without faith in the results, a party led by Father Sierra and Colonel Victoriano Rivero kept the requested appointment outside Valladolid. They were immediately surrounded and escorted to the rebel camp. Moved from there to Dzitnup, on the morning of March 14 all were executed by machete except Sierra and two other priests, who remained captive.[28] So ended peace hopes in the northeast.

That same day all remaining Yucatecans evacuated Valladolid. The long caravan of one hundred or more wagons and hacks, followed by walking civilians totaling more than ten thousand, were guarded by the military forces along the road that had been cleared as far as Popolá on the way to Espita. But when the rear of the train was not yet outside the town gate, rebels began to pour into Valladolid from the undefended side toward Sisal barrio, forcing the rearguard under Colonel León to abandon the planned slow withdrawal. Attacks on the column continued heavy all the way to Popolá, with many casualties among noncombatants. At Popolá the scramble became a riot under the harrying. The column broke into panic-stricken disorder that lasted the three days to Espita and beyond as rumors of pursuing Indians flew, although the actual rebels had been left safely behind. Even at Temax order could not be established, and a Campeche military unit mutinied and raced for home. León struggled to maintain the semblance of a rearguard action, but mob panic ruled all the way into Mérida.[29]

With the flight from Valladolid, which had been the center of gravity of the Yucatecan defense of the east, the remaining government posts of the vicinity were also abandoned, including the strong-point of Tizimín. *Vecinos* fled north to the coast, where they suffered not only from harrying rebel forces but from exposure, until survivors were finally picked up by coasting vessels from Campeche, Cuba, and the United States.[30] While peace negotiations continued near Tekax, the east was in the hands of triumphant rebels.

The Abortive Treaty of Tzucacab

After the evacuation of Valladolid, hostile action ceased for a month or more. The rebels seemed more interested in agricultural matters, for the season when the milpas were burned was beginning. There was also the round of religious festivals in the eastern villages, at several of which Padre Sierra, still detained, was called to officiate.[31] Yucatecans focused attention on reports from the peace commission at Tekax.

There, on March 18 a letter bringing news of the evacuation of Valladolid was received from Governor Méndez, but it also brought an invitation to Barbachano to assume the governorship. This was a desperate bid to settle the hostilities, given constant rebel requests for Barbachano to serve as guarantor of any treaty.

On the same day, Barbachano wrote to Pat from Tekax, laying the groundwork for a treaty by announcing that he was again governor and summarizing the peace conditions he would accept:

- Tekax to be evacuated by the government, save for the priests of the bishop's peace commission and for Felipe Rosado, who would be appointed *jefe político* of the area.
- Religious taxes to remain abolished for everyone.
- Fees for baptism to be set at three *reales* for baptism, ten for marriage, a half *real* for burial.
- Firearms confiscated from Indians to be returned or, if destroyed, paid for.

He asserted that he, Barbachano, was the only person who could give the rebels justice and hear their grievances, and he promised that any transfers of personal property involving Indians not certified by the *caciques* would be investigated by the government—presumably to reduce extortion by *vecinos*. He urged Pat to deal with Felipe Rosado and with the bishop's commission. Although his appointment had not yet officially been made, he signed the letter as governor.[32]

In further desperation, the Méndez government in letters dated March 25, 1848, made simultaneous offers of the sovereignty of Yucatan to the United States, England, and Cuba, in exchange for support and protection.[33] There were no takers. Finally, on March 27, calling on the extraordinary powers accorded him by the legislature in its last session, Méndez proclaimed his own resignation and Barbachano's accession to the governorship.

Barbachano was sworn in at Tekax, proceeded to Mérida to assume direction of the government, and left Padre Vela to continue the peace negotiations. The commission immediately wrote to Tuz asking him to proceed with confidence to establish a meeting, for Barbachano could now treat as governor.[34] An exchange of letters between Vela and Tuz and between Pat and Felipe Rosado followed, while the hinterland was filling with rebels moving from Tzucacab toward Tekax.[35]

Barbachano now dispatched a mission to Cuba to attempt to induce Spain to assume sovereignty of Yucatan or at least to provide massive assistance in exchange for either a mortgage on Yucatecan public income or ownership of Cozumel Island. Still unsuccessful, the messengers returned home, then sailed for Mexico where the U.S. troops were leaving that country following the settlement of the U.S.–Mexican War. The Yucatecan commission presented a letter dated April 18 to the president of Mexico in which Barbachano outlined the Yucatecan plight and asked for aid in return for reincorporation into the union.[36]

On the date on which that letter was written, Vela and his fellow commissioner Felipe Rosado left Tekax for Tzucacab, and at their first stop met Juan Justo Yam, one of the rebel commissioners, in company with other Pat adherents said to include Pat's youngest son as well as a leader named José María Barrera, (of whom more will be heard).[37] These arranged for safe passage through throngs of armed rebel Indians, reaching Ticum at midday. A second commissioner, Francisco Cob, escorted them on to Tzucacab, where after four hours' additional travel they were greeted by Pat. Among Pat's commissioners was Manuel Meso Vales, a priest detained by the rebels for his services. Pat was guarded by twenty-five hundred armed troops.

In Pat's quarters he and Vela that same night worked out the remaining details of the treaty. The following day, April 19, it was written and signed by Vela and Felipe Rosado for the Yucatecans and by five commissioners (including Padre Meso Vales) on behalf of Pat, who then swore adherence to it. There was no armistice during the negotiation, and on that day it was learned that the masses of rebels through which Vela's party had passed on their way to Tzucacab had occupied Tekax, while the Yucatecan guard retreated to Oxkutzcab.[38]

On the evening of the signing, the Yucatecan commissioners were accompanied by Pat and his captains to Ticum. The following day—April 20—they were escorted through occupied Tekax by a company that included the priest Meso Vales and José María Barrera, to protect them against the two thousand disorderly rebel rank and file, who were nearly all drunk. At the end of the day the commission reached Yucatecan lines at Oxkutzcab. Three days later, April 23, the treaty was ratified by Barbachano in Ticul.[39]

The nine conditions of the final treaty can be paraphrased as follows.[40]

1. The civil head tax or *contribución personal* is abolished forever, for all Yucatecans, white and Indian.

2. The fee for baptism is established at three *reales* and the fee for marriage at ten *reales*, for all Yucatecans, both *vecinos* and Indians.

3. Fields and ranchos may be established in the *ejidos* of the pueblos, on community lands, and on public lands (*terrenos baldíos*) without payment of rental; from this time forward no such lands shall be alienated.

4. Through the agency of Jacinto Pat, all muskets confiscated by the last previous state government (i.e., under Méndez or Barret) shall be returned to the Indians, it being understood that those muskets remaining from the twenty-five hundred taken will be returned immediately, with the number found to be short to be purchased and delivered to Jacinto Pat so they can be distributed to their owners. All arms that the Indians now bear will remain with them; livestock and other effects that the troops of the leader Jacinto Pat have taken will be recognized as theirs and will not be reclaimed by others.

5. Inasmuch as Governor Miguel Barbachano is the only person who will ensure that the provisions of this act are carried out, he will remain established in his office for his lifetime, this being the cause of arms having been taken up.

6. From this time the *caudillo* Jacinto Pat shall be governor of all the leaders of the Indians of Yucatan, and with Governor Miguel

Barbachano he will determine the regimen under which harmony of the peoples may best be achieved.

7. All indebted workers shall be excused from their existing debts, including both workers who have gone on the campaign weapon in hand and those who have not; those who wish to contract new debts shall be responsible for them.

8. Taxes on the distillation of *aguardiente* remain abolished in all pueblos of Yucatan.

9. When Governor Miguel Barbachano has ratified this agreement, all belligerent forces shall retire to their homes save those required for the maintenance of minimal order.

Historians have predictably taken issue with the causal statement in article 5,[41] and they, like contemporary Yucatecan commentators, have noted that the provisions of articles 1, 2, 3, and 8 were already the law of the state as a result of governmental decrees of 1847 and 1848.[42] But if these and other conditions were acceptable, in desperation, to Yucatan in general, they were not acceptable at all to a large proportion of the rebel armies, including the forces led by Jacinto Pat. For upon Pat's departure from Tekax following his farewells to Vela, the captain he had placed in charge of the town was killed by unruly troops, and not long afterward Manuel Ignacio Tuz, who had acted as go-between for the commissions, was murdered by Pat adherents for having had traffic with the *blancos*.[43]

But the most dramatic reaction rose from Cecilio Chi. Upon receiving word of the treaty Chi reportedly wrote to Pat from Tinum accusing him of treason and cowardice, and he dispatched two armed columns, one for the war front and one for Tzucacab. Pat, who had received from Barbachano a silver-mounted baton of office and a shoulder band of white satin on which appeared in gold the words *Gran Cacique de Yucatán*,[44] wrote Barbachano for immediate delivery of the muskets to be channeled to him under the treaty, so that he could defend himself against Chi. But even as wagons of muskets were being dispatched, observers at the Yucatecan post at Oxkutzcab saw columns of smoke rising in the distance. This was the the destruction of Maní in Chi's smashing attack in which more than two hundred people were killed and most of the town burned. Shortly thereafter, Pat himself was confronted by Cecilio Chi's second column, a force of fifteen hundred men commanded by Pat's earlier adherent Raimundo Chi. This Chi demanded the gifts from Barbachano and destroyed them in the presence of Pat and of their two gathered armies.[45]

To the extent that they had ever stopped, hostilities resumed.[46]

Lessons from the Treaty

Before turning to the climax of rebel triumph, it is well to examine some implications of the efforts for peace. These point on the one hand toward the identity of the rebels and on the other—closely related—toward the underlying causes of the rebellion. These implications can be drawn from the conditions of the actual Treaty of Tzucacab, from those stated in preliminary correspondence between Barbachano and Pat, and from peace conditions mentioned at various times by other *caudillos*.

First of all, an implication of Article 5 of the Treaty of Tzucacab is that at least Jacinto Pat's entry into hostilities was related to political movements in the Yucatecan capital, a possibility that all investigators have considered. Article 6 adds to this the elevation of Pat to the top of a new kind of government. Although Article 6 might be passed off as a simple forecast of demands the rebels would later make for complete political independence, it can more easily be ascribed to personal ambition on the part of Pat, one of the authors of the treaty. Pat, after all, is the only known (legally ascribed) Indian of comparable wealth or standing to be important in the rebellion; although others were *caciques* in local *republicas*, Pat was the owner not only of the hacienda Culumpich but of other landed properties including a sugar rancho.[47] He was thus vastly more atypical as a rebel than were individuals bearing Spanish names, presumably *vecinos*, whom Yucatecans as a matter of course felt should not be among rebel Indians at all. One must suspect a personal agenda on Pat's part—although an agenda repudiated by the mass of rebels.

Omitting consideration of Article 9 as simply a housekeeping measure, I will discuss other conditions briefly here, for they have something to say about attitudes of the rebels generally.

The abolition of the head tax, Article 1 of the Tzucacab treaty, was a condition included in every statement except for the earliest one at Valladolid, which asked for reduction rather than total abolition of the tax. Put into effect, this measure would provide an immediate financial gain for both Indian and *vecino*, or at least for all those Indians and *vecinos* who were responsible for paying their own head tax. Not so immediately benefited would be members of the growing class of debt peons—which included both Indians and poor *vecinos*—because the major source of peonage debts lay in the landlord-creditor's assumption of the tax bills of his employees. While the measure would mean less cash outlay for *vecinos* all over Yucatan—most of whom were *not* peons, of course—among Indians it would especially benefit those of the eastern outskirts of the heavily settled regions, for as I showed earlier the largest proportion of independent, taxpaying Indian campesinos lay in the east, while debt peonage engulfed a growing number of them to the west.

The establishment of uniform fees for baptism and marriage, in Article 2 of the treaty, was also specified in all communications. These fees would be set at the level at which Indians had paid for decades or even centuries but well below the level that had been customary for *vecinos* until only a few years before the outbreak of hostilities. Although this provision would set a cap on such charges for everyone, the immediate benefit would accrue only to *vecinos* and the very few rich Indians such as Jacinto Pat, who were almost certainly taxed as *vecinos* by both state and church.

The return of confiscated muskets, Article 4 of the treaty, was the third condition specified in all communications. It would benefit only those legally classed as Indians, who had been the sole losers under the confiscation decree.

The right to free use of inalienable lands, Article 3 of the treaty, was not a condition posed anywhere except in the Tzucacab document—indeed, it does not even appear in Barbachano's letter setting out conditions understood as preliminary to the treaty. It thus appears that it was of more limited appeal. Although in theory the benefits would be for all small independent farmers, both Indian and *vecino,* it would be of clearest benefit in the eastern *partidos,* for it was in those regions that there were both a greater proportion of independent subsistence agriculturalists and a larger expanse of public lands. The subprovision of the same article that forbade further alienation of public lands would be of benefit almost exclusively in the east, for it was only there that substantial tracts of unallocated lands remained.

The cancellation of workers' debts, in Article 7 of the treaty, is also a condition mentioned only in the Treaty of Tzucacab and not in any preliminaries. It would benefit both Indian and *vecino* peons, which were concentrated in the western portion of Yucatan. That these peonage debts were an issue with certain of the rebels, despite the limited appearance of such a condition in the various statements of peace conditions, is suggested by a comment by the official Mérida newspaper to the effect that this provision of the treaty might stop the burning of landed properties by rebelling debtors who wanted to destroy the records of their indebtedness.[48]

The abolition of taxes on the distillation of aguardiente, in Article 8 of the treaty, was also mentioned nowhere except in the final treaty. This prohibition would presumably benefit all campesinos and any other poor Yucatecans—

and particularly those who took part in and were responsible for the expenses of local fiestas, which were often predominantly Indian—for any such tax would undoubtedly have been passed to the consumer. To judge from the situation known later in eastern Yucatan and British Honduras, small stills were plentiful around pueblos of any size and were operated by petty entrepreneurs both Indian and non-Indian. It may not be coincidental that Pat himself owned at least one.

Of the six conditions just discussed, the first three appeared in all statements of grievance referred to in previous sections, the last three only in the Tzucacab treaty. If one is looking for broadly recognized grievances, then, one must conclude that the capitation tax, the church fees, and the confiscation of the muskets were the most important and that the others were less compelling. Interestingly, of the three concluded to be so important, the first would have been of direct potential benefit to both *vecinos* and Indians, the second almost exclusively to *vecinos*, the third exclusively to Indians.

With regard to major underlying causes of hostilities, the evidence discussed so far is only preliminary, but two statements can be made.

First, with the strongest complaints related to civil taxation, church fees, and the rapid confiscation of muskets, and only lesser complaints related to the spread of debt peonage or the alienation of public lands, the major causes would seem not to lie in land shortage or in the manipulation of debts. (Of this, more later.)

Second, what is particularly clear is that even the totality of the complaints articulated in the Tzucacab treaty negotiations (which can be thought of as an attempt by Pat and Vela to list all possible grievances) cannot be accepted as sufficient initial cause for the rebellion, simply because the treaty—which would have satisfied all complaints except for allegations of misconduct directed against specific individuals—did not interest the majority of rebels. That is, most of them wanted most of all to fight and evidently wanted it strongly enough that one must suppose their attitude was deeply held and of long standing. I will return to this again and again in later pages as questions of cause are dealt with.[49]

With regard to rebel identity, more details can be filled in at this point in the story. To loyalist Yucatecans, the Caste War was a baldly racial conflict that pitted Indian against white and by extension those bearing Indian surnames against those with Spanish names. An extreme result was that in the first days of the war the Yucatecans identified *all* people of Indian name as the enemy and consequently hounded western Indians, which led to the execution of a number of people of Indian surname who must surely have been entirely innocent. Even when the excitement died and these excesses were corrected, the Yucatecan classification of the combatants remained: Indians—or at least *indios bárbaros*, barbarian Indians—against non-Indians. This harked directly to the traditional and legal contrast between *indios* and *vecinos* that had been enshrined in law since the conquest, and the legal categories were consistently regarded as ethnic categories, regardless of how specific individuals might conceive of their own allegiance. And so any Spanish-named rebel was considered by upper-class urban Yucatecans to be a traitor to his own "race."

But an enumeration of the rebels mentioned by name in each of the two major histories written before the end of the nineteenth century—by Serapio Baqueiro and Eligio Ancona—reveals that more than 20 percent carry Spanish surnames.[50] This is not to say that one-fifth of the mass of those who rebelled were non-Indians in the legal sense, since one cannot doubt that when *vecinos* were present they did have a greater chance of holding leadership positions than Indians. Most of the individuals named in the histories that cover the war into the 1860s were at least minor leaders, and as time went on and the rebels survived in the east, criminal defectors from Yucatan tended to end up among the rebels, often as commanders. Thus, Spanish names are almost certainly overrepresented among surnames cited in the histories.

Nevertheless, one can only suppose for the following reasons that the rebel forces from the very beginning did indeed contain a significant number of *vecinos*: the proportion of Spanish names; the evident fuzziness between the categories *indio* and *vecino* in a social (rather than legal) sense, as I discussed in chapter 3; and the fact that a few Indians carried Spanish names and some *vecinos* carried Indian names. Some of those Spanish names have been mentioned in earlier pages, and many more would have appeared if all those who signed letters and other documents as secretaries of rebel leaders had been mentioned, for with few exceptions the secretaries had Spanish names.

If one adds this discussion to the implication inherent in Article 2 of the Treaty of Tzucacab, which would irrevocably set *vecino* church fees at the level of those historically paid by Indians and thus be of immediate benefit to *vecinos* alone, one must conclude that the supposed Indian rebellion of the Caste War was not a purely Indian movement after all—if "Indian" is defined according to Yucatecan law. Although most of the rebels certainly were legally Indians, a significant if minor number were not although they may have regarded themselves as Indian in terms of ethnic allegiance.[51] But the expansion here of the term *Indian* to incorporate *vecinos* self-identified with the rebel movement would risk the danger of confusion, given the long-term Yucatecan penchant for semantically equating the legal and ethnic categories.

As a solution to the semantic problem, I therefore turn to the classification system in use at the time by those speaking Maya rather than Spanish. Like the Spanish *indio* and *vecino*, this nomenclature, too, was dichotomous, with its contrast between *masewal* (plural *masewalob*) at the lower rank of society and *dzul* (plural *dzulob*) at the upper, with certain in-between categories such as *kaz-dzul*. In practice, *masewal* has been almost always rendered in Spanish and English as *indio* or "Indian," while *dzul* is translated as *blanco* or "white." *Kaz-dzul* might be translated "part-dzul," although *kaz* may also mean "bad." Both the words and their translations are usages of long standing.[52]

But *masewal* is in origin a Nahua word (commonly written *macehual* outside of Yucatan) thought by some scholars to have been introduced to the peninsula by the Mexican Indian forces accompanying Montejo to the conquest. Its meaning in central Mexico is "peasant" or "plebe," and although its denotation is given as "Indian" in many dictionaries of Yucatec Maya, it is also given in some as it would be in central Mexico—"plebe." Maya *dzul* is translated strictly as "foreigner" or "outsider."[53] Unlike *indio* and *vecino*, of course, the Maya terms *masewal* and *dzul* carried no necessary *legal* implications.

This dichotomous Maya classification was used at the very beginning of the Caste War, and it continues in use among modern survivors of the rebels in Quintana Roo, where *masewal* refers to *us* (as opposed to *them*), whatever the linguistic source of our name, and *dzul* to the enemy, especially the Spanish-speaking Yucatecan enemy.[54] How long these last particular lexical nuances have existed in the Mayan speech of the rebels is not clear, but it nevertheless seems appropriate hereafter to use and understand *masewal* in its original and proper sense and to regard the *masewalob* of the rebellion as a group united in protest but not absolutely so in race or civil status, a group that included many individuals who were *vecinos* as well as those who were Indians before the law and many with Spanish as well as those with Indian names. Whether these groups thought of themselves collectively as "Indians" in a social sense is less important than that they conceived of themselves as underdogs, united in opposing the governing forces in Yucatan.

All of this accords well with the conception I will develop here of the Caste War as a rebellion of eastern Yucatecan campesinos—most of them Indian in origin and all of them Maya in speech, to be sure, but first of all campesinos, whatever their racial, ethnic, or civil status.[55] It is in this company that Jacinto Pat, a recognized Indian of position and means, stands out as unique, a fact that can only underscore the presumption that he harbored private political ambitions.

7 / Climax

Although at the end of May 1848 the tide was turning against the rebels, it was probably not perceptible to them and it was certainly not evident to the Yucatecans, who saw their world falling to pieces.

The Crest

With the Yucatecan withdrawal from Becanchén in the south, the emigration of *vecinos* remaining in the southeast began in earnest. A small armed camp was established by Colonel Cirilo Baqueiro at Iturbide in the Chenes region as an outpost against the spread of insurrection, but on the day the Treaty of Tzucacab was signed by Padre Vela and Jacinto Pat, Iturbide was attacked by three sections of rebels, each composed of more than one thousand belligerents,[1] most of them reportedly from southern regions. Coming on in good order, with a drum and bugle corps to set their cadence, the large number of rebels inspired heavy desertions in the Yucatecan ranks and forced Colonel Baqueiro to withdraw the following day.[2]

When he fell back on Dzibalchén, Baqueiro found to his surprise that it was already abandoned, and he then retreated to Hopelchén, headquarters of the *partido*—only to find that it too had been evacuated.[3] He and his force pulled back to Campeche with scarcely a fight, leaving the entire Chenes district in rebel hands.

But the *masewalob* did not press their advantage, having suffered heavily at Iturbide despite their triumph. Intelligence received in Campeche was that most of them had withdrawn quickly toward the east. Thus encouraged, some fugitive *vecinos* made their way back toward Dzibalchén to retrieve belongings they had abandoned in their haste—only to lose their lives.

A similar fate befell an armed detachment that moved into the region on May 6 to make contact with the attackers and open peace negotiations like those just concluded at Tzucacab. Taking a rest at Tzuctuc, some sixty kilometers east of Campeche, they were surprised by a force of rebels who seized their stacked arms, then attacked and routed them with their own guns.[4] But Tzuctuc was to be one of the closest actual rebel approaches to Campeche.

Meanwhile, in the far southeast the increasing belligerence of the Indians around Chichanhá aroused fear at Bacalar, a point desirable to the rebels because of its strategic location for trade with British merchants. In February the superintendent of British Honduras responded to the commander of the Bacalar post that the British settlement would provide asylum for both settlers and garrison in case of need. At the same time he called uneasily for increased vigilance by the small British military unit.[5]

And on April 16 a rebel force commanded by Venancio Pec appeared at Bacalar asking the Yucatecan commander for powder and muskets. Receiving a refusal, they attacked. Despite the fortified strength of the old station the rebels closed in, raising breastworks in exposed sight lines by using the trick of lying on their backs to roll boulders into place with their feet. On the third day of fighting they gained the pueblo, and the defenders barricaded themselves in the fortress, but to no avail. On the next day the rebels accepted the Yucatecan surrender, allowing all those who yielded to seek refuge on British territory.[6] As reports filtered through to the capital at Belize City, however, alarm was generated by fanciful rumors of ten thousand rebel Indians burning and then occupying Bacalar.[7]

Not long after the *masewalob* took Bacalar, the British superintendent was responding by letter to the new station commander that the rebels would be allowed to trade with residents of the British settlement on the same free basis as the *vecino* population that had been displaced.[8] Thereafter, correspondence between Belize and Bacalar became a recitation of complaints from both directions: the rebel commander complained about assassinations of *masewalob* along the Hondo by the Yucatecan refugees; the superintendent complained about violations of the British border by rebels in pursuit of Yucatecans, and he transmitted grievances from Belizean woodcutters who claimed that undelivered logs they had bought on the Yucatecan side of the river before the conquest had been sold by the rebels to third parties.

The British superintendent held that his position was one of correct neutrality that prohibited both rebel incursions into British Honduras and Yucatecan attacks from British Honduras against rebels in Yucatan. At least one rebel soldier was shot by his commander in Bacalar following a complaint from the superintendent that he had led a detachment across the Hondo, seized two Yucatecans, and hauled them across the river, killing one of them.[9] And complaints from the same Bacalar commander to the

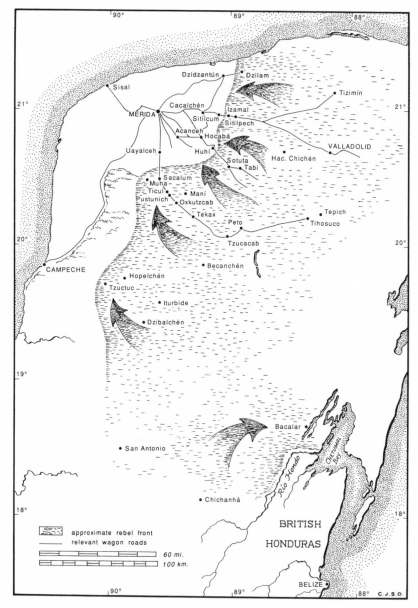

Map 7. *The Extreme Rebel Advance, May 1848. Based on dispatches cited in the text.*

superintendent led to arrest warrants against several Yucatecans for the alleged murder of Indian rebels on British territory. Two of these were tried and sentenced to death, although the superintendent commuted the sentences to life imprisonment, and at least one other—Domingo Martínez—was formally charged with similar killings, but proceedings were dropped when it turned out the act had occurred outside British territory.[10]

However, the stand was interpreted by Yucatan as siding with the rebels, and Superintendent Fancourt was accused of "persecuting our compatriot don Domingo Martínez because, using the right that he doubtless had to fight the rebels, he made war on them when he could."[11]

That the rebel position in Bacalar facilitated rebel trade in munitions as well as other commodities is beyond doubt. In British correspondence there are references to the presence of merchants from British Honduras in Bacalar, and the same intelligence was received by Yucatan.[12] But the superintendent refused to sanction the export of powder (although he did not flatly prohibit it), refused to provide protection for any residents of the British settlement who chose to carry on trade in Bacalar, and the Public Meeting (functioning as the legislature) refused to authorize the presence of a British Honduran commercial agent there.[13] Thus, it was by acts largely of omission that the British superintendent pursued his vision of neutrality.

At this point in the war, within Yucatan the situation was beginning to seem irremediable to the government forces. With the loss of Tekax and the raid on Maní, General López de Llergo pulled his force from Oxkutzcab to Ticul and prepared to defend that point, counting a total of some eighteen hundred troops. By now most of old Sierra Alta and eastern Sierra Baja were deserted by all *vecinos* except for troops at Ticul and Sacalum on the Mérida road and an advance post at Pustunich. And so they were besieged by the rebels, now led by Jacinto Pat himself, who bowed to the inevitable and again took up the sword.[14]

On May 16 a Yucatecan counterattack directed partly by José Dolores Cetina achieved some success but only barely avoided the loss of Pustunich. Two days later Sacalum was burned by the rebels, then retaken by Yucatecans, but its destruction weakened the position at Ticul, from which retreat was ordered by Yucatan on May 26. Although the withdrawal was planned to be orderly, the rebels forced entry to the Ticul plaza before it was vacated, and panic marred the flight to Uayalceh, halfway to Mérida. This left the rebels in complete control of Sierra Alta, and when Sacalum and Muna were also evacuated it gave them most of southern Sierra Baja.[15] Yet this was to be the limit of the rebel advance.

Yucatecan hope had been pinned in the north on the defense of the strong-point of Izamal, and a major share of their resources had been allocated to it. The lull that followed the evacuation of Valladolid was ruptured on May 9, when rebels attacked Sitilpech, a short distance east, and then appeared at Izamal in a force said to be under command of Bonifacio Novelo and Miguel Huchim.

Repulsed in their first strike at Sitilpech, stubborn *masewalob* returned and were given the place on May 15. First attacking outlying settlements in the region, defended with difficulty by government troops, the rebels began the siege of Izamal on May 20. Rebel soldiers threatened the supply road from Sitilcum constantly, but the worst threat was the military leadership within Izamal, torn by political antagonisms between the two colonels in command. To the amazement and chagrin of military headquarters in Mérida, on May 29 the government troops abandoned Izamal. Still farther north, rebels briefly held Dzilam in eastern La Costa.[16] These points would mark the extreme limit of rebel advance, although this was certainly not recognized at the time. The Mérida government made ready to evacuate that city for Campeche, while the bishop and his religious establishment poised to sail for Havana.

But in late May of 1848 the rebel tide had reached the pause before the ebb.

Already in early March—before the Yucatecan evacuation of Valladolid and weeks before the treaty meeting in Tzucacab—press reports received in the United States asserted that the attacking force was composed of 40,000 well-armed rebel soldiers, and by mid-May the total figure was claimed to be 250,000.[17] Both figures are impossibly high, but some estimates of the number of fighting rebels were even higher, reaching totals equivalent to three-fourths of the total Indian population of the peninsula.[18]

By the end of May the old *partidos* of Bacalar, Beneficios Altos, Valladolid, Tizimín, Beneficios Bajos, and Sierra Alta were in rebel hands, significant eastern portions of Camino Real Alto and Sierra Baja had risen, and rebels occupied the eastern fringe of La Costa. The total number of legal Indians of *all* ages in these rebellious regions probably exceeded 200,000 and may possibly have approached 250,000. Thus, the high figure claimed in newspaper accounts would have to have assumed a total rebel movement equivalent to 100 percent or more of the population of those regions who were legally classed as Indian—surely an exaggeration, for all evidence indicates that in every zone involved there was a significant fraction of the lower-class population who simply fled or, at best, followed the rebels with the greatest reluctance or under outright coercion.

The historian Baqueiro cites figures to suggest that between 1846 and 1851 the decline in the overall population of Yucatan amounted to about 100,000—which included Yucatecans who had emigrated, the dead on both sides, and the people of all ages who were still to be counted among the *masewalob*.[19] By 1851, however, a very large number of the active rebels as well as more passive sympathizers had returned to their homes under amnesty.

It is reasonable to conclude that in May 1848 the total number of people swept into the rebel movement exceeded 100,000 and that the number of males active in or directly supporting the fighting was greater than 30,000, although many of these were without firearms. It is barely possible that the numbers were closer to 150,000 and 45,000, but they could scarcely have been higher. Even so, a rebel movement of such size was short lived, as subsequent events will show.

For when the surge to the west appeared closest to success and the future darkest for the embattled Yucatecans, the assailant from the east suddenly relaxed the deathgrip. It occurred almost quietly, as a low-keyed ending to the first violent stage of the campesino rebellion.

The Rebel Withdrawal

According to local tradition, the *masewal* troops were as surprised as Mérida military headquarters at the government evacuation of Izamal. On the morning of May 30, "they entered stealthily, first in clusters, then in throngs, then they scoured the commercial establishments, taking the goods they could carry, and after making offerings to the Virgin of the church, they began their retreat, but leaving on fire all the houses of thatch, and even some of masonry."[20] And when Yucatecan commanders sent scouts into Izamal over the next two days, they found it deserted. On June 2 government forces reoccupied it, with no more resistance than could be made by a few lingering bands of looters.[21]

What happened here, at a time when masses of rebels were at the threshold of Mérida? A fetching explanation was reported in the 1930s by Edward H. Thompson, onetime consul of the United States in Mérida and sometime owner of the Hacienda Chichén, located at what was to be for a long time the western frontier of remnant rebel territory. It is not surprising that the story, told to Thompson by a son of Crescencio Poot, the young leader who joined the rebels at Tixcacalcupul, has been quoted in most English accounts of Caste War history since Thompson's book was published.[22] It attributes the end of the rebel advance and a melting away of rebel troops to the appearance of swarms of certain winged ants, harbingers of the seasonal rains and of the season for planting.

When my father's people took Acanceh [said Leandro Poot] they passed a time in fasting, preparing for the taking of T'Ho [Mérida]. The day was warm and sultry. All at once the *sh'mataneheeles* appeared in great clouds to the north, to the south, to the east and to the west, all over the world. When my father's people saw this they said to themselves and to their brothers, "Ehen! The time has come for us to make our planting, for if we do not we shall have no Grace of God [i.e., corn] to fill the bellies of our children."

In this wise they talked among themselves and argued, thinking deeply, and then, when morning came, my father's people each said to his Batab [captain], "Shickanic"—"I am going"—and in spite of the supplications and threats of the chiefs, each man rolled up his blanket and put it in his food-pouch, tightened the thongs of his sandals, and started for his home and his cornfield.

Then the *Batabes*, knowing how useless it was to attack the city with the few men that remained, went into council and resolved to go back home. Thus it can be clearly seen that Fate, and not white soldiers, kept my father's people from taking T'Ho and working their will upon it.[23]

It is true that the capture of Izamal came exactly at the time of the usual corn planting season. Taking as a model the pause in fighting that had occurred immediately before the Izamal campaign, when the rebels stopped to burn their fields, it cannot be doubted that the planting season did decimate their ranks, particularly of those soldiers who found themselves at a substantial distance from their homes. But a more basic reason for the faltering of the rebel advance surely lay in the very nature of the uprising.

As the rebellion spread westward from its beginning around Tepich, it did so by recruiting campesinos in the new regions. Like the government militiamen, the rebel soldiers fought hardest and fought most in those neighborhoods to which they were native. It should be no surprise, for instance, that when Padre José Canuto Vela wrote to the rebel leaders in search of peace he reached his addressees in their own home territories: Jacinto Pat responded from Tihosuco, and the leadership of forces that had been active around Sotuta responded from Tabi. The *masewalob* who gathered to attack Iturbide were predominantly from the region south of

Peto, and those who took Bacalar were largely people of Chichanhá and its surroundings. Although new advances involved cadres of what one can think of as the more "professional" rebels from the east, the bulk of the active army was always recruited locally. This is a standard technique of revolutionists everywhere, but it is especially understandable in nineteenth-century Yucatan, where continuity of residence and dislike of geographic dislocation had always been marked.

But at a point still to the east of the *camino real*—that long-time road connection between Mérida and Campeche—successful recruitment stopped and the rebel advance stalled. There, with most of Sierra Alta and Beneficios Bajos and much of La Costa and Sierra Baja in their hands, the rebels had reached the heartland of the original Spanish colony, the region longest under close Spanish domination, the area of the heaviest fully settled population, and also—it turned out—home of the campesinos most loyal to the status quo. And the faltering was intensified as those few rebels who were fighting at a distance from their own regions decided it was time to go home.[24] There would never be a return.

The failure of rebel recruitment in the west was made more decisive, undoubtedly, by measures taken by government. On the one hand, loyalist Indians received an immediate reward. One of the decrees of Governor Santiago Méndez in January 1848 had created the status of a newly defined *hidalgo*, which carried a lifetime exemption from taxes and was awarded to Indians who joined actively on the Yucatecan side; such awards continued under Barbachano. Most of these Indian volunteers, at least in the initial months, served not as soldiers but as porters or other laborers with the combatant force. Titles of *hidalgo* were passed out widely—more than nine thousand by July 1848[25]—no doubt increasing the sense of loyalty to the legitimate government that was already felt by the western Indians.

On the other hand, the military officers who had shown themselves so prone to evacuate pueblos and retreat were reassigned. A reorganization brought the replacement of old division commanders with new (one of whom was José Dolores Cetina) and reshuffled lesser officers, resulting in a corps of commanders in which a large proportion were staunch *barbachanistas*. The chance of mutiny for political reasons was lessened. At the same time, although fresh attempts to secure aid from the United States, England, and Cuba were unsuccessful, the confiscation of a good deal of movable wealth from the church permitted payment of immediate obligations, including those related to the maintenance of the army.[26] And so the perennial impulse to mutiny for want of supplies was also lessened.

The result was a suddenly revitalized Yucatecan army, but the illustration of that must wait until later.

Causes of the War

The beginning of the insurgents' retreat to the east provides an opportunity to offer a second word regarding the causes of the outbreak. For once driven again to eastern Yucatan and contained there, the *masewal* peace conditions would begin to differ in certain substantial ways from those they had specified earlier.

Traditionally, commentators have claimed the following circumstances to underlie the rebellion:

First, hatred of the Maya for outsiders: this has been seen by some as a trait of national or racial character that predated the conquest, after which it easily focused on whites and their adherents, those people here collectively referred to as *vecinos*.

Second, oppression of the Maya by upper classes: this, of course, must have nurtured the hatred just mentioned, and it has been alleged that this oppression was furthered by both state and church. Both imposed taxes and exacted labor, while the former facilitated the taking of land, and the latter also charged fees for administering the sacraments.

These two conditions have been well-nigh universal in discussions of the Caste War, particularly discussions by tradition-oriented Yucatecan historians, but with decided differences in emphasis from one writer to another. Early historians, those to whom the war was a series of personally experienced events, tended to emphasize the first condition—congenital Mayan hatred—while freely acknowledging the contribution of the second.[27] In the second camp, including but not limited to later historians, are those who have been more inclined to derive the hatred the Maya felt for their masters from the behavior of the latter over decades and centuries.[28]

To these two basic conditions some writers would add a third: territorial designs of Great Britain, expressed locally through expansionist proclivities in British Honduras. Although an element of this anglophobia is detectable in virtually all Yucatecan histories, some present it as more of a facilitating condition than an actual cause.[29]

In addition to these underlying and important causal factors, certain proximate circumstances have been used to explain why the rebellion happened when it did. One given universal recognition is the series of civil disorders that punctuated the period from independence to the outbreak of the rebellion. Incidental to these bellicose movements and countermovements was the arming of the Indians.

All the approaches just mentioned conceive of the rebellion in ethnic or racial terms. And all of them also have in common an emphasis on subjective feelings that add up to hatred as the motivation for rebellion by Yucatecan Indians.

A second category of writers includes chiefly—but not exclusively—those who have written within the past four decades. In a generalizing way the outlook of these may be characterized as more economic or materialist than social-psychological.

Among these, the writings of Howard F. Cline have been especially influential—if largely unpublished. It was he who first in English stressed the postindependence Yucatecan emphasis on modernization and development, with the rise of plantation industries such as sugar and, to a lesser extent, tobacco. Modernization or progressivism in this conception included the measures taken by Yucatan to extend citizenship to Indians, which led in turn to a loss of the traditional trappings of indirect rule by which the Maya had been insulated from *vecino* society (through *repúblicas de indios*, *cofradías*, and so on) and to the invasion of formerly Maya territories by new industries with new needs for land. Later writers increased the emphasis on basic economic factors, as research led to a realization that the nineteenth-century Yucatecan economy was expanding rapidly and was more complex than had been generally appreciated, and as studies underlined the expansion of new agrarian endeavors, especially sugar and tobacco. Such writers have emphasized both the shortage of labor and the need for new lands.[30]

Many of these latter authors have thus emphasized the agrarian rather than the ethnically Indian character of the rebellion. Indeed, a recent inventory of Caste War literature characterized the newer, revisionist approach as one largely stressing the agrarian nature of the struggle and the competition for land that underlay it.[31]

The Present View

In the preceding chapter, I was at some pains to suggest that the rebellion was not a strictly Indian movement, as *Indian* was commonly defined in Yucatan; that from its beginnings the grievances articulated by the rebels included some that would apply only to *vecinos*; and that although most of the agrarian rebels were Indians, the movement was at its basis at least as much agrarian as ethnic. On the surface, this would seem to place the present argument in the second class of causal discussions just mentioned. I prefer to locate it somewhere in between the two, however, for I am hesitant to see it as being so materialistically agrarian as do the others.

The evidence indicates that there was indeed an expansion of the commercial use of land in the nineteenth century that made inroads in certain territories that the peasant farmers—whether Indian or *vecino*—had traditionally considered their own, and that these agrarian people had objected, often strenuously. The question is, however, was this the condition that triggered the original rebellion? Was the war simply a struggle for subsistence resources? I think the answer must be no.

As I noted earlier, there is no good reason to think that in the area in which the revolt began there was any overpowering sense of deprivation on the part of the independent subsistence farmers because of the alienation of *baldíos* that was being permitted by the government. As I also suggested, the disposition of *baldío* lands by the government did not appear in statements of grievances until the Treaty of Tzucacab was concocted by Jacinto Pat and Padre Vela. In this regard, the provision regarding freedom of land use falls together with the requirement that peonage debts be erased. Both of these conditions must have provided impetus to some of the many rebel recruits who enlisted as the movement spread west, but there is no evidence that they were a spur to the original rebel movement around Tihosuco, where the evidence rather suggests that land was still plentiful.

Furthermore, the alienation of *baldíos* had been ended by government action before the treaty was drafted and hence was no longer an active grievance—although to the extent that it was a real irritation the *masewalob* might indeed want a treaty guarantee for the future. But—and this may be the crowning fact—despite the listing in the Treaty of Tzucacab of all the grievances that Jacinto Pat could think of, and despite the wholesale surrender on all points by the government of Yucatan, virtually none of the rebels were willing to lay down their arms in return for the treaty guarantees. This included Pat's own army to the same extent as others.

That is, once war was joined the rebels wanted more than anything else to fight. This bespeaks, I think, a deep-seated subjective feeling—as opposed to a desire simply for material well-being—that can hardly be ignored. And given the history of Yucatan, one must suppose—as I said before—that this subjective attitude was of very long standing. That is, whether or not one wants to label it *hatred*, one must nevertheless accept that there was a passive amount of pentup lower-class resentment over the conditions imposed by the rigidly stratified social system.

But two questions flow from this: If there was such a social-psychological component, why was it manifest so much more strongly in the east than in the west? And if there was longtime resentment involved, why did the rebellion occur when it did rather than much earlier?

With regard to the first of these, one may roughly divide Yucatan into three regions: the far west and portions of the north, the traditionally populated "old colonial" region in which there was no significant rebellion; the central regions of rapidly expanding nineteenth-century population—the Sierras and Beneficios Bajos—where rebellion was embraced when it appeared from the east; and the eastern borderlands, where the rebellion originated—and, indeed, where it has never entirely ended.

In the first of these, the existing social relations were of especially long standing. Although social stratification was strong, the lower elements of the hierarchy had long ago made their peace with it. The situation was stable, not threatening, and it was preferable to the disruption of war with its unimaginable outcome. The lower classes did not rebel but rather tended to join the government forces. From this area came the highest proportion of the newly appointed *hidalgos*; indeed, freedom from tax obligations obtained in this way must have seemed a most generous reward for actions to many who were classed under the old laws as legal Indians and who were not inclined toward rebellion.

In the second, central area, there was undoubtedly unrest, which was manifest as the lower orders joined the rebels when the front of hostilities approached from the east. Many of them probably drawn from the growing group of debt peons, they burned *fincas* or haciendas at which they had been employed—possibly, as the newspapers said, to erase the record of their debts.

In the third, eastern area, a question of loyalty to *vecino* landowners was almost nonexistent among independent campesinos—Indians and poor *vecinos*—who also found themselves responsible for their own taxes, unlike debt peons or hacienda servants for whom the landowner usually paid. Taxation, both church and civil, struck hard at the meager yield of their subsistence endeavors. It was the freedom from complex obligations to the Yucatecan system that also made them the most free to join the armed forces when the call went out from leaders like Santiago Imán, Pastor Gamboa, or Vito Pacheco.

It is here, then, that the subsistence or materialist element is to be found—but turned on its head, as a permissive condition rather than cause: the easterners were the least enmeshed in the highly stratified socioeconomic system of Yucatan. They were the most free to rebel.

To turn to the second of the questions—why the rebellion occurred when it did—is to allow the invocation of a relatively easy answer. This answer must indeed lie both with what Cline called "progressivism" in the attitude of Yucatecan society in the large sense, and in the political dislocations that characterized the region from independence to 1847.

Beginning in the late colonial period, particularly with the liberal reforms of the Cádiz *cortes*, and moving steadily through the period of independence, the social situation of the Indians had improved. Granted suffrage first, full citizenship arrived when taxes were equalized with those of *vecinos* and when the Indians were extended de facto the right to serve in the armed forces. The level of their expectations can only have been steadily rising. It would have been given a particular lift as they were promised—or at least as they plainly thought they were promised—a virtually complete remission of taxes in exchange for such military service. But rewards were slow in coming; taxes remained. Expectations fell.[32]

It was at this point, in January 1847, that the Campechanos and their allies attacked Valladolid, and the bloodbath that resulted so suddenly made the peninsula sit up in fear of race war. Although the mob violence, the killings and lootings, were obvious acts of resentment and rebelliousness, they were as much acts by lower-class Valladolid *vecinos* as by invading campesino soldiers, resentment locally engendered and locally expressed. The massacre was an isolated event of banditry, not of generalized revolution, just as the ensuing depredations in the Valladolid hinterlands by Bonifacio Novelo and his gang of marauders were acts of localized outlawry.

Whether or not there was subversive collusion between Manuel Antonio Ay, Cecilio Chi, and Jacinto Pat, upper-class Yucatecans now expected it or something like it, and despite recent social changes they were as prepared to find Indian treachery as their grandparents had been at Cisteil two generations before. Inevitably, they did find it, first in the alleged conspiracy, then in the local banditry that followed.

In August the muskets were confiscated from Indians all over Yucatan, martial law was proclaimed, military tribunals took over from regular courts, the special Indian religious tax was reimposed, and prominent Indians were arrested, flogged, even executed—again, all over Yucatan.

Just as Indians had begun to see themselves as partners like everyone else in Yucatan's irregular political movements, they were disenfranchised, jailed, and tortured. Measures could not have been better contrived to turn local banditry into general rebellion.

As de Tocqueville put it, "evils which are patiently endured when they seem inevitable become intolerable when once the idea of escape from them is suggested."[33] And when Jacinto Pat and his friends, many of them with experience gained under Imán and other Yucatecan military leaders, plotted aid to Barbachano, it was to a movement that would have furthered their continued expectations. But it was triggered into violence at Tepich, the Yucatecan response brought their expectations to an end, and war was the inevitable result.

In earlier decades and centuries, changes in lower-class patterns of expectations had not been sufficient to raise high hopes, and as they began to rise they were not so abruptly dashed. But in 1847 both material and psychological conditions were perfect for the social revolution that Yucatan had never before experienced. There *was* deep-seated hatred, and there were also agrarian conditions that on the one hand exacerbated the hostility of campesinos and on the other provided their freedom to act. From the standpoint of upper-class Yucatan, the combination was well-nigh unbeatable.

Part 3. Dividing the Realm, 1848–1853

8 / The Screw Tightens

The first of many severe reverses to the rebels came in the southwest, although with little immediate effect on the war as a whole. Following the withdrawal of all local government forces to the walls of Campeche on May 20, 1848, a company of volunteers under Pantaleón Barrera—a journalist, but the only leader available—left those walls to attack *masewal* headquarters at Hopelchén. The rebels gave way, but immediately reoccupied as Barrera pulled back to Hecelchakán for reinforcement by local *vecinos* and *hidalgos*. In mid-June the renewed column again attacked, forcing a rebel retreat from Bolonchenticul. But then the *masewalob* drove past Barrera toward Campeche and were only narrowly repulsed. Barrera and his force fell back to the city, leaving the Chenes again in rebel possession.[1]

From Mérida, General López de Llergo was orchestrating a dramatic turnabout in Yucatecan fortunes. Even while Izamal was being abandoned to the rebels, Yucatecans reoccupied burned-out Sacalum, beginning a series of triumphs that the citizens still clinging to the western littoral would hear with a resurgence of pride and relief. From Sacalum Cetina attacked and regained Ticul on June 7, and three days later a combination of Yucatecan columns routed the rebels from Maní. Active throughout the region south of Mérida,[2] Cetina's division finally dislodged Jacinto Pat's besieging army from Muna. Rebel thrusts directed by Pat and his commanders, who included José María Barrera, Pablo Encalada, and Pat's favorite son Marcelo, were unable to stem the Yucatecan advance, which on July 24 forced them to evacuate their headquarters at Pustunich.[3]

From Hocabá and Huhí still farther north—points the Yucatecans had held against the nearest rebel advances—the government launched a push on June 17 that carried its troops to Sotuta, but then they were forced back to clean up remnant rebels attacking past them toward Mérida. Still, in early July the *masewal* force at Sotuta—estimated by the Yucatecan attackers to be nine thousand strong—was again dislodged,[4] and by mid-August the vicinity was firmly in Yucatecan hands. On August 24 government troops drove the *masewalob* from Yaxcabá. At almost the same time, Cetina was

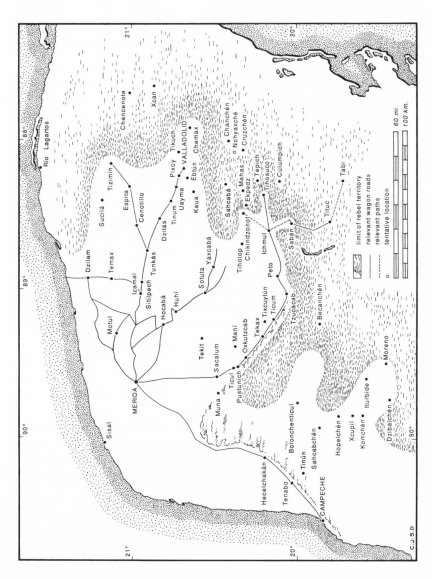

Map 8. Rebel and Yucatecan Positions, Late 1848. Based on dispatches cited in the text.

advancing his division headquarters from Sacalum to Ticul, his thrusts from there driving the rebels from Oxkutzcab and finally, on August 19, from Tekax itself.[5]

Meanwhile, *masewal* losses were great east of Izamal, as on June 9 a substantial Yucatecan force plowed toward Tunkás, to take it after stiff action. Government troops established an advanced military outpost or *cantón* there. Shortly after, large groups of unarmed Indians came in, claiming to have had no part in the hostilities, and were allowed to return to their pueblos in the region. Rebels massing at Cenotillo were dispersed by a Yucatecan attack, and a *masewal* force of size that attacked Tunkás on June 26 was harshly repelled. The Yucatecans moved on Dzitás, which they regained on July 19 after occupying Cenotillo.[6]

Thus, by late August government forces directed from Mérida controlled the region northwest of a line extending roughly from Tekax through Yaxcabá to Dzitás. In three months they had recaptured nearly half of the territory they had lost in the northern parts of the peninsula. At least partly responsible for their new success was a recognition of the feasibility of bypassing the inevitable rebel breastworks; Yucatecan columns began regularly to move forward with flanking parties deployed well to both sides of the main body, prepared to hit the rebel rear whenever their barricades appeared. A second change, however, was simply one of spirit. As the rebel Francisco Puc reported to captive Padre Sierra when he returned from one disastrous campaign,

These are not, Señor Vicario, those who abandoned Valladolid: if they were it's impossible that they should have triumphed [as they did]. When we besiege these people, they counter-besiege us quickly; when we think to surprise them with our ambushes, we ourselves are surprised from the rear.[7]

In Campeche, on the other hand, substantially all of the Chenes region was still in *masewal* hands.

By this same time assistance in money and arms began to flow in. Although the United States, Britain, and Spain had rejected Yucatecan annexation proposals, the turn toward Mexico was immediately successful. Even before the commissioners who were appointed to conduct negotiations landed in Veracruz, letters from Yucatan and her supporters in Mexico had induced the Mexican cabinet—newly freed from its concern with war against the United States—to propose a special program of aid, which was voted by the congress in early June. It was some weeks later before material assistance found its way to Yucatan, however, and by that time the gains just described had been accomplished. On August 17 Barbachano decreed Yucatan again a part of Mexico.[8] Although this would have some significant impacts on the rebels, they would not feel the full effect for decades. An immediate result of the infusion of Mexican money was the first payday for the Yucatecan army since the beginning of the war.[9]

As 1848 wore on, the government turned attention again to the Chenes. An offensive underway from Campeche in late August moved successfully to Bolonchenticul, Sahcabchén, Xcupil, and Komchén. But in late September at Dzibalchén a large body of rebels hit them and forced them back to Hecelchakán. One section halted at Tinum to ready a fresh campaign, when homesick troops mutinied and deserted; the reduced force was recalled to Campeche. Within a month a detachment from Hecelchakán had to battle cross-country to join the government division fighting around Tekax. The Chenes had reverted again to rebel control.[10]

The day after his decree of reunification with Mexico, Governor Barbachano declared amnesty for rebels who would lay down their arms immediately.[11] In September the decree began to be disseminated in the zone of hostilities, and when a government detachment swept the northern coast at Sucilá, they met a large number of Indians who had come to take advantage of the amnesty and return to their homes. As Yucatecans took Ebtún and Espita, former rebels and rebel sympathizers presented themselves for surrender in such large numbers that the rebel leadership retaliated by slaughtering Yucatecan captives.[12]

Still moving, the Yucatecan force attacked and dislodged rebels at Tinum and Kaua west of Valladolid, and then on September 20 gained Uayma, chasing the rebels as far as Pixoy, only four kilometers from Valladolid.[13]

But in the broad east-central region the rebels were more successful in slowing the government advance. There, few *masewalob* defected in response to the decree of amnesty. Beginning on September 8, fighting was heavy around Yucatecan-held Yaxcabá, which was attacked by rebels gathered from Ekpedz, Tepich, Tihosuco, and Chikindzonot, under the leadership of Cecilio Chi, Venancio Pec, Florentino Chan, Crescencio Poot, Cosme Damián Pech, and others of local note, who formed in military fashion and marched openly to the cadence of drum, fife, and bugle. Surrounding Yaxcabá, they repulsed counterattack after counterattack, forming and retiring to their drum beats and bugle calls. Although the government forces obtained reinforcements from all the garrisons within reach, the *masewalob* breached their lines within the pueblo itself on September 21. The Yucatecans fell back to Sotuta. Once entrenched there, although dogged by rebels, the government troops were more successful. Under Eulogio Rosado, newly appointed to the command, they threw the *masewalob* back and even regained Yaxcabá, which they then held.[14]

This fighting and the continued threat to Yaxcabá and Sotuta led the northern division to pull back toward Temax in October, yielding the ground they had just won. But the retreat was short lived, and on October 28 the Yucatecan division dislodged the rebels again from Sucilá, successfully attacked and took Tizimín on November 3 and stiffened against a large force of rebels that counterattacked on November 5 but which they finally forced to disperse after almost a week of heavy fighting.[15]

With Yucatecan success, a new problem forced itself on them: where to dispose of those captured rebels who for one reason or other had not been shot out of hand. On November 6, 1848, Governor Barbachano decreed that rebels who failed to heed the offer of amnesty and surrender would be subject to confinement and to expulsion from Yucatan for a period of ten years.[16] It was this decree that would authorize the beginning of a persistent traffic in *masewalob* sold as indentured labor to Cuba.

In the south, as in the far north, the proclamation of amnesty had its effect. But despite rebel defections, the adherents of Jacinto Pat, directed by his son Marcelo Pat and José María Barrera from headquarters at Ticum, continued to pressure the Yucatecans headquartered at Tekax. Beginning October 6 with as many as five thousand *masewal* troops recruited in the immediate environs, the rebel siege lasted until late November, amid complex shifts in the fighting and while several outlying pueblos changed hands repeatedly.[17] But when Marcelo Pat was shot through the spine, the rebel thrusts ended abruptly.

The *masewal* army pulled back to Tzucacab, where Marcelo, dead of his wounds, was the center of a drunken wake that lasted all day and night of November 26 and into the afternoon of the next day, when he was given a lengthy funeral in which two priests—one of them Manuel Meso Vales—prayed in marathon fashion at the command of Jacinto Pat while thousands of *masewal* troops thronged the plaza firing their muskets. At nighttime Marcelo Pat was buried before an altar in the parish church.[18]

At that, a Yucatecan column under Cetina left Tekax and dislodged José María Barrera and the demoralized *masewalob* from Tzucacab. Two days later the column converged with others and took Peto. Pat and his family and close adherents fell back to Tihosuco.[19]

December 1848 was decisive. Early that month Yucatecan forays around Peto dispersed most of the harrying *masewalob* and produced surrenders of former rebels as well as the appearance of *vecinos* who, believing a year earlier that Jacinto Pat had only been engaged in a partisan movement on behalf of Barbachano, had failed to emigrate and had waited out the war either in hiding or in captivity somewhere around Peto.[20] José María Barrera was active in the field here and again barely escaped capture. On December 12 a government march on Tihosuco found that the rebels had evacuated that pueblo so dear to Jacinto Pat, leaving it in perfect condition.[21]

Similar government action farther north was also successful, and *masewal* morale must have been seriously damaged. The government occupied Espita and other centers in mid-month and on December 24 launched the final push to retake Valladolid. It succeeded easily on Christmas day.[22]

Now the rebel leaders and their major forces had been pushed east of Tihosuco: Jacinto Pat at Rancho Tabi, another of his properties; Bonifacio Novelo at Mahas; Venancio Pec at Nohyaxché; and Cecilio Chi at a nearby settlement called Chanchén.[23] Thus, by the end of December 1848, nearly eighteen months after the first uprising in Tepich, the government had pushed the frontier substantially to its prewar position save for the territory of the Chenes still serenely in rebel hands.

But having moved this far east, the Yucatecans would find themselves stymied. Most of the remaining territory from Tihosuco and Valladolid to the Caribbean was ground that had always been so marginal to the Yucatecan economic system that it was in fact surplus. This was to prove the ultimate base of rebel power, into which government forces would make few permanent advances in the next half century.

The Approaching Stalemate

With the recapture of Valladolid and Tihosuco and the expulsion of the rebels to the eastern wilderness, or "desert" as the Yucatecans referred to it, the government military action took on a different character. Now it was confined to short thrusts into surrounding areas to permit disaffected rebels to take advantage of the offer of amnesty, to liberate *vecino* prisoners who might have remained in rebel hands, and above all to forage for food, for the Yucatecan army lived entirely off the land.[24] But rebel strength prevented them from making significant advances farther east.

In January 1849 the government established advance *cantones* at Tikuch and Chemax east of Valladolid. Skirmishes with rebel forces continued in that region, in which Bonifacio Novelo was particularly active. In March a longer expedition of Yucatecan troops battled as far as Chancenote, while others established posts at Tizimín and Espita. From Tihosuco the government launched successful raids against Ekpedz and made a sally toward Jacinto Pat's property at Culumpich, which found substantial resistance but not its owner.[25] They dispersed rebels at Chikindzonot and took the pueblo for a new *canton*; a number of rebels yielded there to the amnesty. The government gained Sabán but was then besieged by a *masewal* force under José María Barrera, Atanacio Espadas, and Pablo Encalada. Meanwhile, rebels harried Tihosuco, beginning a determined siege in late January. Action continued into the spring, with the Yucatecan forces winning skirmishes but actually controlling no more than the restricted areas around their fortified camps.[26]

That year the major Yucatecan progress was in the far south—in the Chenes region, finally, and at Bacalar. In the Chenes, government forces reoccupied the territory as far east as Hopelchén in February, although fighting there remained heavy for a time, and it was June before most of the dispersed refugee families had been resettled. In May, June, and July the government advanced toward Iturbide. In August they were finally thrusting successfully to Dzibalchén, and at the end of September they hit Moreno. Although most of these moves did not lead to permanent occupation, an effective *cantón* was established at Iturbide.

By fall 1849, then, the Yucatecan line extended raggedly, with strongpoints at Iturbide, Peto, Sabán, Tihosuco, Valladolid, and Tizimín. But government troops were spread thinly in much of this territory.[27]

Then sometime before fall one of the strongest of the rebel leaders met his unexpected death.

The Murder of Cecilio Chi

Cecilio Chi, accompanied in his campaigns by his mistress—or possibly wife—had been cuckolded by his secretary, one Atanacio Flores, whose own reaction to the illicit affair was to throw himself into religious devotions. Embarrassingly questioned by Chi about his endless telling of the rosary, Flores resolved the affair by arming himself with Chi's own machete, secreting himself behind the door of the thatched hut that served as barracks, and splitting Chi's head as he entered. Chi's soldiers instantly attacked. Grabbing the ready guns in the barracks to put up a valiant fight in which he is said to have killed seven men and wounded fourteen, Flores finally was downed in a volley fired by reinforcements from Pec's camp at nearby Nohyaxché. With great veneration Chi's body was carefully dressed, decked out with a red sash to hold his machete, treated to its wake, and finally buried at the parish church at Tepich, his own birthplace and that of the rebellion itself. With dawn of the day following his death, the body of the unfaithful woman was found hanging from a tree at Chanchén.[28]

So ended Cecilio Chi, the rebel reputed by the Yucatecans to be the most implacable in his hatred, the most determined to exterminate the race of the Spanish conquerors of Yucatan. Despite the graphic description of his end, the date of the occurrence is in question. The account given here is said to have come from the rebel Atanacio Espadas, who claimed to the historian Baqueiro to have led the avenging detachment from the camp of Venancio Pec. Espadas dated the occurrence in December 1848, and the historian Ancona points out that Chi was not mentioned in connection with any fighting after that time. Nevertheless, on the basis of other evidence both Ancona and Baqueiro date the death in the spring of 1849. Chi's name appears as that of signatory on copies of correspondence to Belize as late as March 22, 1849, which is in keeping with such a conclusion, although a document issued by Venancio Pec and Florentino Chan in September of that year (to be mentioned later) speaks of Chi as though he were still alive.[29]

Thus, at one extreme Chi may have died in December 1848 and had his name used for a time thereafter as a matter of policy by his successors;[30] at the other, he may have been militarily inactive in 1849 and died as late as September of that year. If it was the latter, before his death he had joined in an about-face with other rebels equally committed to the struggle, indicating that there were conditions under which peace could be made after all.

The Contraband Capital of Bacalar

With the rebels maintaining a lively resistance around Valladolid and Tihosuco, the major source of their supplies for warfare on the relatively stable front was now seen even more clearly to be the British settlement of Honduras, rather than plundered Yucatecan military columns. Even before the rebels had captured Bacalar an official agent of Yucatan had called at Belize to deliver correspondence from Governor Barbachano requesting assistance in shutting off the supply of powder to *masewal* forces, to which— as I noted in an earlier chapter—the superintendent had replied that while he would do all within his power to discourage such traffic, he feared his ability to dampen free trade was limited.[31] After Bacalar was captured by forces of Venancio Pec, the Yucatecans received intelligence that British tradesmen were selling munitions within Bacalar itself and that ships were sent from British Honduras to New Orleans specifically to haul powder for trade with the rebels.[32]

Following the reincorporation of Yucatan into Mexico, Yucatecan complaints channeled to the British representative in Mexico alleged that British Honduras was supplying arms to the rebels and that British Honduras officials had mistreated Yucatecan refugees. When Superintendent Fancourt was called on to explain the situation to Her Britannic Majesty's representative, he responded that he knew that munitions were being exported from the colony, that he had done all in his power to discourage it, but that with his limited means for enforcing the law he was unable to prevent it, in large measure because the people of British Honduras in general felt more sympathy for the rebels than for the Yucatecans. He added that he had been as evenhanded as possible in dealing with Yucatecan refugees and that he had been instrumental in preserving a great deal of the property of former residents of Bacalar by obtaining its peaceful removal following the rebel capture of the place. He pointed out that he had commuted to life imprisonment the sentences of death handed to the two Yucatecans tried for killing alleged rebels in British Honduras, that charges against a third had been dropped because the event had apparently occurred outside the limits of British territory, and that an Indian rebel had been executed by his own commander upon receipt of the superintendent's complaint that he had murdered a Yucatecan refugee on the British side of the Hondo.[33]

But concern over the rebel occupation of Bacalar and the powder trade brought continued attacks on the rebels by loyal Yucatecans, some of them refugees living in the British settlement, others apparently lurking in Yucatecan territory around the Bay of Chetumal. At least one such raid, in December 1848, ended unfavorably for the Yucatecan attackers.[34]

In early 1849 Vito Pacheco showed up among these irregulars. Some information indicates that during the early summer of 1848 he had been living on Isla Mujeres, although another account relates that when Barbachano assumed power Pacheco, a known Méndez partisan, feared for his well-being and fled to the Caribbean coast where, with a small boat, he occupied himself by fishing around Ascension Bay, his former haunt as a smuggler.[35] In January 1849, however, he was on the eastern shore of Chetumal Bay near Punta Calentura with a body of four hundred Yucatecans reportedly recruited from refugees along the east coast of Yucatan, in the company of a

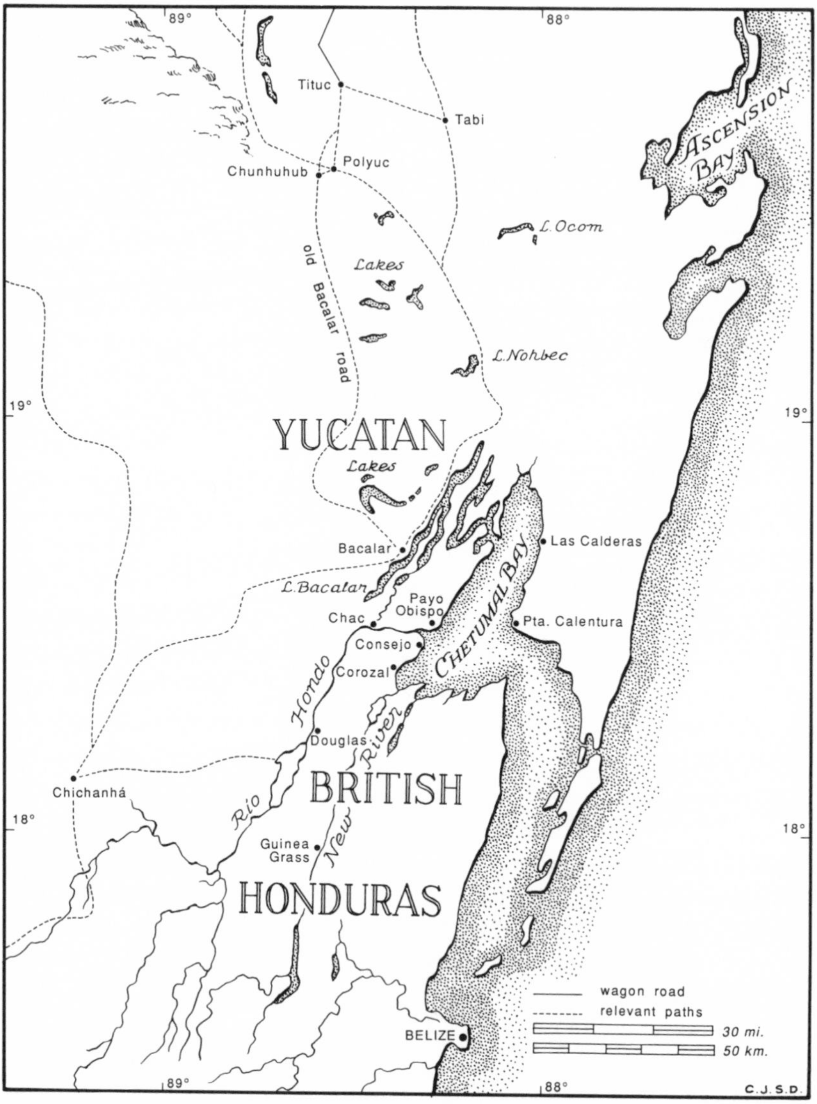

Map 9. Location of Events in the South, 1849. Points in the south are based on Anonymous (1848), Heller (1847), Faber and Rhys (1867), Miller (1888), and Usher (1888), with comparative reference to Berendt (1878).

Yucatecan sailor who operated a small schooner that had been designated a coast guard by the Mérida government. On January 18, Pacheco circulated a proclamation among Yucatecan refugees in British Honduras, calling upon them to join his force for the liberation of Bacalar.[36] And shortly thereafter he made a formal call on the British magistrate at Punta Consejo, exhibiting his commission as a lieutenant colonel in the Yucatecan army, signed by Governor Barbachano. He announced that he would attack Bacalar by water.[37]

What happened next is unclear. Later that same month a Campeche newspaper reported that Pacheco's force was fighting around Payo Obispo, on Chetumal Bay, and early the following month it was said to have taken and held Las Calderas, a point on the east side of the bay. At the same time, however, an officer named Solís was said to have moved with seventy-two men against Chac, on the creek draining Lake Bacalar into the Río Hondo, when he was fired upon from the Hondo by two boatloads of British Hondurans. While defending himself against these he was attacked from the rear by rebel Indians, and his force was annihilated.[38] It is possible that this was the event alluded to by the historian Baqueiro, who, writing of Vito Pacheco, said it was "of public voice and fame, that seizing the opportunity of defeat . . . suffered at Payo Obispo, he made off with the supplies and sold everything to the enemy."[39] So much for local effort.

But the next month, at great sacrifice of money and matériel the poverty-stricken government of Yucatan created a new military division, designated the Seventh, and dispatched it by sea to Bacalar in a heroic attempt to interdict the powder trade. On April 20 the force of eight hundred men under Colonel José Dolores Cetina left Sisal. Nine days later they landed on Chetumal Bay, moved up the Hondo, and began initial skirmishes with the rebels. Dividing into two sections, one on land under an officer named Ongay and a second on water under Cetina himself,[40] they began a painful movement toward the old *villa*. Their progress upriver was punctuated by the attempts of some Belizeans to warn the rebels of the approaching flotilla by firing off their guns from the British side of the Hondo.[41] The Yucatecans fought a sharp battle at the mouth of Chac Creek in which, according to a prisoner, the rebels were led by a black man from the Belize colony named Jorge Yach, who was assisted by a Frenchman[42]—evidently a reference to one George Fantesie and his French partner Silvestre Lanabit, who were known powder brokers.[43] On May 2 the general attack on Bacalar itself began, and, flanking the town to attack from both sides, Cetina's division took the place two days later.[44]

Quickly, a number of the displaced residents of Bacalar returned with their families from British Honduras, as Cetina hastily improved the fortifications. But the rebels were not to be shunted aside. In mid-May Bacalar was attacked by an army said to number more than four thousand under the command of José María Tzuc. It included not only people of the region of Chichanhá, where Tzuc was leader, but others from farther north under Isac Pat and Cosme Damián Pech, and for a time José María Barrera was possibly present. The heavy rebel siege would continue throughout much of the remainder of 1849, and although a number of successful Yucatecan sorties would be made in the vicinity, the garrison and civilian occupants would face distress for lack of provisions.[45]

At the end of June, the third in command of the Yucatecan expedition, Angel Rosado—who, like his older brother, Colonel Eulogio Rosado, was a native of Bacalar, and furthermore the darling of the local Yucatecans— was seriously wounded. He died in early July. There followed a rash of defections by the Bacalar refugees who had so quickly joined the force, reducing its strength to the point where Cetina ordered that any others attempting desertion were to be shot out of hand.[46]

The summer of 1849 also saw the end of Vito Pacheco. After the capture of Bacalar, Cetina had enlisted Pacheco with a boat to serve as a coast guard at Chac, in order to prevent the rebels from harvesting milpas in the area. Among the small force assigned to Pacheco was a sergeant who was to keep him under surveillance. The man denounced him, charging that Pacheco harvested the milpas himself and sold the produce to the rebels. Taken to Bacalar, Pacheco was court-martialed and sentenced to death. He died calmly, cautioning the firing squad to aim well and saying airily to Colonel Isidro Gonzales, the second in command, *"Adiós, compañero,* I'm ahead of you."[47]

So died Vito Pacheco in the *villa* founded by Gaspar Pacheco three centuries before.

Dealing for Powder

But the Yucatecan recapture of Bacalar did not interrupt the powder trade along the frontier between British Honduras and Yucatan. Traders simply shifted their route to the old pueblo of Chichanhá. Reports of this reached Yucatan almost immediately,[48] and in September of that year Governor Barbachano could provide specific allegations, not only that powder, arms, and lead were being introduced to the rebels through Chichanhá, but that two Belizean schooners, *Dart* and *Dream*—property of one Austin Cox, a merchant of British Honduras—had sailed for Ascension Bay under the pretext of hauling salt and turtle though in reality carrying munitions.[49] Similar information was furnished by the British Honduras magistrate of the northern district, who reported that a trade road from Chichanhá struck the Hondo and the colony border at a point some twelve miles above the village of Douglas, and that another led from Chichanhá to Guinea Grass on the New River in the British Honduras interior.[50] By the end of the year other individuals active in the powder trade were identified by the Yucatecans— one a man called Yach and the second a Frenchman.[51]

Still under heavy pressure from the rebels, the Bacalar garrison established a post at the mouth of Chac Creek; here they stopped and searched all boats moving along the river. This aroused irritation among British Hondurans, law-abiding and otherwise, and to complaints from the superintendent to Yucatan.[52] Yucatan continued to remonstrate about the powder trade through Mexico and the British representative there, citing Article 14 of the convention of 1786 between England and Spain in which it was stated that "His Britannic Majesty . . . will strictly prohibit all his subjects from furnishing arms or warlike stores to the Indians in general situated upon the frontiers of the Spanish possessions."[53] But the superintendent took no stringent measures until embarrassment reached a point where something obviously had to be done.

On September 13, 1849, the vessel *Four Sisters*, another owned by the merchant Cox, was halted by the Yucatecan force at Chac and found to be carrying, not only nearly a ton of gunpowder (seventy-nine *arrobas*, or kegs of twenty-five pounds' weight) and four hundred pounds of lead, but also an Indian agent of Jacinto Pat and a letter by which Cox consigned the cargo to the rebel leader.[54] On September 28, Superintendent Fancourt circulated a decree that strictly banned residents of the British settlement from selling munitions to the rebels, and early the next month he appointed a second magistrate for the northern district of British Honduras and ordered that boat traffic should be searched as necessary to enforce the decree.[55] This did not stop either trade or irritation.

The importance to the rebels of the southern supply of munitions meant that Bacalar continued to draw their attention, which of necessity limited their ability to fight in the north, where a trickle of rebels continued to surrender. Nevertheless, the dead Chi was replaced by Venancio Pec and Florentino Chan, both of them totally committed to the rebel cause and, in

Yucatecan eyes, both of a ferocity rivaling that attributed to Chi himself. Although their headquarters at Cruzchén was successfully attacked by Yucatecan troops at least once, the rebels were strong enough to retain control.[56]

From Tihosuco, Pat had drawn off some of his forces to swell the ranks of the attackers at Bacalar, but the siege of his favored pueblo went on. And when the government tried to move troops from Sabán to Tituc, to strike at the rear of the rebels near Bacalar, Pat's army was able to hit them so hard they retreated in a rout that the historian Baqueiro described as one of the worst of the war. José María Barrera was said to be partly involved.[57]

But by August the rebels had learned that they could bypass Bacalar and still contact Belizean merchants willing to evade Superintendent Fancourt's decree. Rebel pressure on the southern *villa* began to relax. The newly strengthened *masewal* army at Tihosuco was now able to drive its soldiers inside the old pueblo. Only emergency reinforcements dispatched by Eulogio Rosado from his headquarters at Ichmul preserved the *cantón*. And Sabán continued under siege by Atanacio Espadas and José María Barrera, the latter of whom Baqueiro now characterized as "the whites' most terrible enemy."[58]

Yet it must have been about this time that a rupture among *masewal* leaders reached a point at which internal fighting was inevitable. It brought the death of the second of the original generals of the rebellion.

The Factional Killing of Jacinto Pat

Neither antecedents nor actual events are clear. But it seems apparent that by September 3, 1849, a warrant for Pat's death had been issued by Venancio Pec and Florentino Chan—the so-called eastern faction from around Valladolid—and expressed in a circular bearing that date and the signatures of Pec and Chan, which was addressed to "the *Señores Capitanes* in their respective Domains."

> We inform you that don Jacinto Pat is no longer our commander for having failed in our mandate, for which reason wherever he may be found he will be killed. Our *Padre, Señor General, Señor* D. Cecilio [Chi] rose for freedom and whatever he may say is what will be done. D. Jacinto Pat inflicted much pain . . . establishing the punishment of flogging and the practice of labor drafts [*servicio de semaneros*] doing to us that for which we rose against the whites. . . . Another of his

crimes is the despoiling of his subordinates . . . in union with other Captains who follow him, for which cause . . . D. Baltazar Che, D. José Isac Pat and D. Pantaleón Uh are no longer in authority . . . for having scorned our mandate. We inform you also . . . that the same D. Jacinto Pat established a war tax on the *Señores* of the pueblos and *Señores Capitanes*. . . . That is not what we desire; freedom is what we want. . . . From now on there will be no mandate other than that which *Señor Comandante General Señor* D. Cecilio [Chi] may establish with *Señor* D. Venancio Pec and *Señor* D. Florentino Chan. There will be no taxes, no beatings, no purchases of woodlands to cultivate, no collecting of money among the poor, nor will things the troops have gotten from the enemy in warfare be taken. Whoever opposes . . . will be killed just like Jacinto Pat, because there is no double mandate.[59]

Five days later Pec entered Rancho Tabi, Pat's headquarters, and seized Pantaleón Uh but found that Pat had fled for Bacalar the day before. Several days later—the exact date is not indicated—Pat was overtaken by Pec's party at Rancho Holchén, fifteen to twenty kilometers from Bacalar. There Jacinto Pat was killed. Members of his family also died together with Baltazar Che (his second in command) and some other captains, among whom Barrera was conspicuously absent. The fugitives were found to be carrying a substantial sum of money—five thousand to twelve thousand pesos by various accounts—and were reportedly on their way to seek sanctuary at Bacalar or British Honduras.[60] According to Pablo Encalada, an avowed eyewitness, Pec then proclaimed himself governor and commander in chief of all the rebels. José María Barrera was left as de facto leader of Pat's remaining forces.[61]

Although the murder of Pat brought no lasting internecine warfare in its train, it seems to have been followed by a period of some instability. For while Pec and Chan could immediately claim the supreme command, it was not long before rumors arose of the presence of rivals, and it is clear from later events that José María Barrera continued to operate as an independent agent. After a time his faction would triumph and for more than a decade would hold the supreme position among the *masewalob*.

The Front after 1849

The brilliant Yucatecan drives to the east and south marked the beginning of a second stage of the war of rebellion. For as the rebels had reached the geographical limit of their effectiveness somewhere to the east of Mérida, so the government troops reached their own limit at the eastern edge of the region that Yucatan had effectively controlled at the outbreak of the war—and bogged down. The limits for rebels and government were controlled by different factors, however.

The rebels had been able to expand their rebellion territorially only so long as they were able to raise to their cause within each area a substantial proportion of the predominantly Indian lower classes resident there. The Yucatecans, on the other hand, were forced to stop when they reached the farthermost of the developed towns that provided adequate bases for their military apparatus. Beyond this they were unable to support the new garrison centers that would be necessary for further definitive conquests. Indeed, the government was unable to feed or pay its troops wherever they were found.

The pattern of the war in 1849 and after, therefore, was one in which government garrison strong-points were located at preestablished pueblos of a size adequate to provide minimal accommodation for several hundred troops. Radiating from each of these was a series of smaller *cantones*—advance posts or cantonments—that provided both military cover and, most importantly, bases from which foraging parties moved out constantly to harvest rebel grainfields, to loot rebel corncribs, and—almost incidentally—to round up noncombatant families and herd them through the Yucatecan lines. The rebels for their part spread widely, headquartered in dispersed hamlets, planted their milpas, and harried Yucatecan outposts and towns.

As one area was exhausted of food for both Yucatecans and rebels, the government *cantones* were moved to new, greener fields, the rebels shifted as they could, and the process began again. Although this sapped rebel strength to the point of exhaustion and near starvation, it was for the Yucatecans a hand-to-mouth existence they could maintain for only so long. Eventually the rebels must be conquered, cajoled into peace, or simply ignored.

A stalemate had been reached. But it would be some time before the fact came home fully to either Yucatecans or *masewalob*.

9 / Olive Branches with Thorns

In 1849 the government campaign for peace moved on several fronts, with stimulus from Mexico and British Honduras.

On March 6, 1849, Superintendent Fancourt of the British settlement was approached by a group of Belizeans who had resided in Bacalar during the period of rebel occupation, foremost among them a Baptist clergyman, John Kingdon, but including also men who could be described as traders and loggers. The party furnished copies of correspondence with the rebels in which the Belizeans suggested mediation by an outside power such as Britain, in order possibly to resolve the conflict "on the principle of a just division of the country." To this, Jacinto Pat had responded that his people were fighting for liberty and that it "would be indeed well if a division were made of the territories of Yucatan as you suggest."[1]

The theme was reiterated by Kingdon in a letter to Fancourt of March 8, in which he alleged that the notion of dividing the territory came first in correspondence between Governor Barbachano and Jacinto Pat. Fancourt responded that he could not mediate without the authorization of his government, to whom he would submit the matter, "and if, as I learn from your letter of this date, the Authorities of Mérida should have already expressed the same desire for a partition of territory," an amicable arrangement might be worked out.[2]

Later that month, the suggestion of British mediation was taken up by the other major faction of rebels, as Cecilio Chi, Atanacio Espadas, and Venancio Pec wrote to Fancourt to request specifically that the Belize government supervise a division of territory.[3] On August 10, Fancourt received word from the British minister in Mexico that the Mexican government had approved his tentative offer to mediate, with the proviso that although limited self-government for the rebel Indians might be acceptable, they would have to remain obedient to the central government. Two days earlier the same information from Mexico was received in Yucatan, but with it no special instructions.[4]

Very shortly after this, Yucatan was taking her own measures, the governor appointing three peace commissions to act under the overall direction of José Canuto Vela—one for the east, under Padre José Antonio García; one for the region around Tekax, under Padre Vela himself; and one for the Chenes region, under Padre Manuel Antonio Sierra.[5] In October, Barbachano published a renewed decree of amnesty for any rebels who would lay down their arms and surrender.[6]

Response to the offer of amnesty was not encouraging. On October 9 Florentino Chan and Venancio Pec notified Barbachano that the conditions were not acceptable. They stated that they would not submit to the government for the government was to blame for prolonging a war that had begun simply to abolish taxes and other burdens; they would not lay down their arms. But, they said, when the government removed its troops from *masewal* territory the war would simply end. "And then you will consent to the division of the land so that we shall have peace and love each other as God loves us. . . . The Government of Mérida shall bring together the pueblos that are subject to it; and the Government of the East shall bring together in the same way those that are subject to it."[7]

Almost immediately, Barbachano sent a protest against British involvement to the minister of exterior relations of the Mexican government, enclosing correspondence from *masewal* leaders (of which the letter from Chan and Pec just cited was a part), which, he said,

> gives to understand, without fear of error, that the rebels are directed by the English of Belize, insisting upon the refusal to return to the obedience of the Government, proposing to be governed by themselves without dependence upon the State, and to be absolute owners of the territory of the East, that is to say of a considerable part of Yucatan. . . . It is not mediation between the rebels and the State that the British Government offers, but an intervention that carries with it long-range aims that are not hidden from the least perceptive eye.[8]

Meanwhile, the Yucatecan peace commissions reached their destinations. In the Chenes, there was scarcely any response by rank-and-file rebels to the commission's offer of amnesty. This was true despite a relative lack of authority or harmony among those rebels, where each captain was said to act independently, and in a region where the *masewal* population was growing steadily through the immigration of northerners who wanted to get farther from the most active hostilities. The rebel commandant José María Cocom bluntly advised the commission and government troops to go back where they came from.[9]

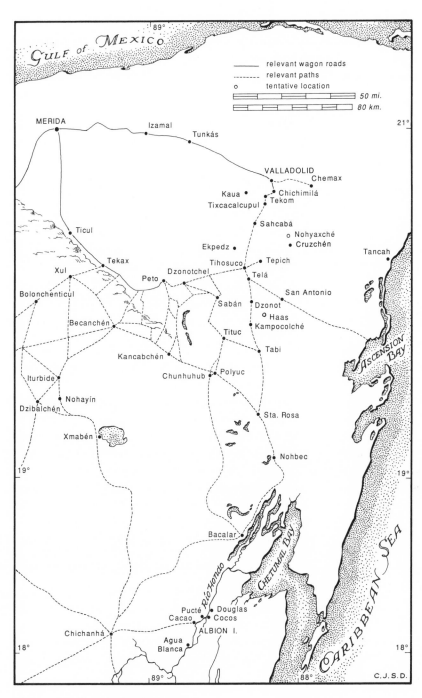

Map 10. The Frontier Region, 1849–50.

In the region around Tekax, Vela also was unsuccessful. One of his messengers was murdered almost immediately.[10] Although large numbers of supposed rebels were scattered with their families through the bush, most of them without arms and actually simply waiting for a chance to surrender, it was not possible to contact and reassure them because of the interminable foraging patrols of the government troops. The limited supplies available to the Yucatecans meant that as one military party returned with their booty of food another must go,

> and with them [said Vela in correspondence to a friend who was also a deputy of the state congress] an equal or larger number of women and men called *botineros* [plunderers]; who when they arrive at the ranchos and milpas, without distinction soldiers and non-soldiers hurl themselves on the inhabitants, whom they insult, harass, and hurt— and woe to the women they catch! This done they proceed to plunder everything that comes in view, and then the harvest is undertaken: . . . this finished, the good ears are shelled, . . . the poor without shelling are carried in sacks and in convoy with the horses of the *botineros*. . . . I leave you to calculate the days the short provision will last . . . the troops, who are not fewer than 500 in number. . . . I leave to your prudent judgement the result achieved with the excursions now being to a distance of 8 or 10 leagues [thirty to forty kilometers] from the post, because the milpas in the vicinity have been used up.[11]

No wonder that the prisoners taken were dying of starvation in jail and that those who surrendered did so more from hunger than a change in heart.[12]

Only in the vicinity of Valladolid was there marked success, where surrender-inclined rebels could elude the vigilance of their officers and approach Yucatecan strong-points to give themselves up. Surrenders resulted in the rapid repopulation of Chichimilá, Tixcacalcupul, and Tekom, but did not involve the famous and intransigent leaders—Venancio Pec, Florentino Chan, Miguel Huchim, Crescencio Poot, and Bonifacio Novelo.[13] Presumably, the efforts would have had broader effect if Padre García and his commissioners had been able to make still wider contact with the unhappy *masewalob*—at least that is what the good father reported.

Military sweeps in the vicinity regularly brought in families, some of them no doubt the women and children of active rebels who were either hiding or fighting. In February 1850 Padre García accompanied one of these forces on such a march that culminated in a sharp raid on the headquarters of Pec and Chan at Cruzchén and that rounded up altogether some 150 people, apparently including a few active men as well as the plentiful women, children, and old people. In a letter to Justo Sierra, García expressed his surprise at the number and size of the scattered ranchos encountered. There were, he said,

> groups of 70 or 80 houses arranged in their fashion, with their little plantings and other forms of settledness and stability. The families found in this condition . . . will not abandon their hut and way of living on any invitation, especially if . . . [they have] news that the house they had in their [home] pueblo has been burned and the place where they were born destroyed.
>
> If there were some way to convert these ranchos into pueblos, introducing into them some police, putting in their little churches, you can believe that it would be one of the best means of pacifying this region, but the ill luck is that there is no one who would dare this, at the immense distance they are from quick assistance.[14]

But even some of the intransigent rebel leaders appeared to soften. In a letter of November 18, 1849, Pec and Chan said they would be willing to treat but that they were unable to do so because of the misfortunes suffered as the government troops continued to round up and carry off their wives and children, destroy their fields, and burn their houses. After this response, and with some pressure from the bishop in Mérida, a short field armistice was engineered to allow talks.[15] It was at this same time that Superintendent Fancourt's efforts also reached their climax.

As Fancourt attempted to contact the rebel leadership to inform them of his authorization to mediate, he learned that Pat was dead, but by October he had made alternate arrangements to meet Florentino Chan and Venancio Pec at Ascension Bay. He also heard from Barbachano that Yucatan would comply with the directions of the central government.[16] But this did not mean that Yucatecans had lost their suspicion of British intentions.

On November 22, in a schooner anchored in Ascension Bay, Superintendent Fancourt had his interview with Venancio Pec and, apparently, other rebel leaders. The Yucatecan historian Baqueiro reports that the shore of the Bay "presented the appearance of a place in which a great fair was being held," with families and abundant food—ducks, chickens, pigs—brought to present to Fancourt,[17] although Fancourt himself mentions only that he had to wait for a week before the rebel leaders appeared. The substance of the talks, as reported to Governor Barbachano, has relevance both to the genesis of the hostilities and to the state of rebel demands in late 1849.

Introducing himself to the rebels as a friend of the Mexican government as well as of themselves, Fancourt asked the nature of their complaints.

They replied [Fancourt reported] that the origin of the quarrel was that the contributions which the Indians were required to pay were too heavy for them and that they bore upon them unequally and unjustly. . . . They said they had no faith in the promises of the government, that the government had never kept faith with them and that they had once before taken up arms for the purpose of aiding the government in Mérida . . . and that promises were then held out to them which had been subsequently broken. . . . They finally declared that no arrangement would be satisfactory that did not secure to them an independent government, that they desired to have a portion of the country relinquished to them—a line drawn northward from Bacalar to the Gulf of Mexico—and to be relieved from all contributions to the government of the state. They added that they had no objection to Spaniards residing within the territory which they sought to obtain but that they would never consent to their exercising authority.[18]

Thus, although taxation continued to be stressed, in contrast to the early stage of the war there was the addition of a desire for territory in which they would be independent. Fancourt reported that he did not encourage their hopes in this regard.

On my part [Fancourt continued] I made them distinctly understand that the supreme government would not concede them any right of sovereignty or relieve them of their allegiance, that they were disposed I thought to allow them a certain portion of territory for their separate occupation, and that it appeared to me not improbable that they would concede to them local self government, and that I did not apprehend any difficulty would arise with respect to their contributions.

Unfortunately for relations between British Honduras and Yucatan, the conversation then took its turn toward the rebels' high regard for the British.

On my asking them how they proposed to govern the portion of territory the cession of which they demanded, they replied that they knew that they could not govern it themselves but that they wished the "Governor of Belize" to be their governor. I informed them that such an arrangement was absolutely impossible, that the Government of Mexico was on friendly relations with the Government of Great Britain, and that Her Majesty would not afford any countenance to such a project. . . . Benancio [sic] Pec then stated . . . that if they could not enjoy that which was to be apportioned to them free from the control and interference of the general government, they would one and all migrate to the British settlement of Honduras.

Fancourt concluded his letter to Barbachano by suggesting that a Yucatecan commission be appointed to meet the rebel leaders at Belize and by urging a truce in preparation for talks.[19] Although the Mexican government seemed to approve of Superintendent Fancourt's progress, there was to be no meeting.[20]

Whatever the central government in Mexico felt, Yucatecans remained wary of British involvement. In Mexico City the Yucatecan patriot Manuel Crescencio Rejón published a series of articles claiming that a pact had been made at the highest levels of the Mexican and British governments to cede Yucatan to the English in payment of the Mexican national debt.[21] In Yucatan, newspapers asserted their lack of trust in the British and reported that rebel prisoners were saying that by the next Easter the English would come to divide the territory on their behalf.[22] Flames were fanned higher when Yucatecans who had escaped from the *masewalob* reported that censuses were being made in all the rebel pueblos, presumably by order of the English.[23]

As evidence in support of Yucatecan skepticism, in May 1850 copies of captured rebel letters were transmitted by the Mexican government to the British minister in Mexico, who sent them on to Belize.[24] The earliest was from Paulino Pech to another officer, dated October 26, 1849—a time after Fancourt had completed arrangements to meet the rebels but before the actual talks. In it, Pech, who styled himself *comandante general*, said that "the paper of the English Queen arrived. She is going to divide this land of Yucatan, and for this it is necessary that you alert your captains so that they will talk to their soldiers to strengthen the war with the enemy. . . . The English Señor says that we have everything, that we lack nothing. . . . This includes powder, shot. We have all."

The second, dated December 2, followed the meeting with Fancourt, and was from Venancio Pec to a rebel captain, directing that "each pueblo has to be counted without exception, in order to form the census of all the pueblos, to the end that their names appear written, because that is how the Sr. Governor of Belize wants it." Two others, both dated December 29, related specifically to censuses of rebel settlements in progress or just completed, said to be "on order of the *Señores Ingleses.*" In the last, dated January 25, 1850, José María Tzuc, writing from near Bacalar, reported to "*Sr. Comandante General* D. Paulino Pech" that he had received a letter from "the *Señor Inglés* in which he advises me that he has powder and lead, and he is going to see if he can bring more" and quotes a price in case the rebels want to order.

The letter from the queen cited by Paulino Pech was presumably simply Fancourt's communication in which he confirmed the date of his meeting. The identity of the "English Señor" in the first and last letters is more questionable. Fancourt himself made no mention of a census, although it is not impossible that he asked Pec to ascertain how many rebels would be affected by negotiations. On the other hand, it will become clear that certain elements in British Honduras were interested in continuing the division between rebels and government in Yucatan, and it is not outlandish to think that some of them with designs on the territory had actively connived at such a census. Indeed, one must suppose that it was in large part personal interest that had led Kingdon and his collaborators to suggest a division of territory in their original approach to Superintendent Fancourt, and one must also be suspicious in that some rebels reported after the Fancourt talks that D. *Jorge* was to represent them in peace negotiations.[25] Thus, the "English Señor" may have been none other than George Fantesie—a free agent who was certainly not acting for the British government.

Other Yucatecan press reports alleged that British Honduras was urging the rebels not to submit and was promising to obtain the concession of territory for them; that Venancio Pec and Florentino Chan were at odds, the former wanting to join the English while the latter was opposed; that D. *Jorge* and a Mister Lanzot (Lanabit?) were among the rebels as agents of some kind; and that Pec wanted to recapture Bacalar in order to trade it to the English in return for rebel sovereignty over eastern Yucatan.[26]

That Pec's imputed regard for the British was not all Yucatecan imagination is confirmed by events. He apparently intended to follow up his conversations with Fancourt by meeting with Queen Victoria, and to that end was attempting to arrange the charter of a ship to England when a series of attacks by the Yucatecan colonel Pablo Antonio González disrupted the intended embarkation. In one action González took Pec's horse and *bastón* or staff of office. In another, apparently with the connivance of Atanacio Espadas, who surrendered to amnesty immediately afterward, González seized both a British flag and Pec's travel fund of twenty-five hundred pesos.[27]

Upon reporting the text of Superintendent Fancourt's interview with Venancio Pec in November, Justo Sierra O'Reilly, who now was editing the Campeche newspaper *El Fénix*, expressed mistrust of British intentions and advised against sending any commissioners to Belize. This was clearly the feeling of Yucatecans in general and of the Yucatecan government in particular.

Although on February 1, 1850, Governor Barbachano acknowledged Fancourt's letter, he pointed out that the rebels were not of one mind and that a truce would therefore be difficult to engineer.[28] Thus, he did not allow Fancourt to pursue his efforts—"judging the intervention of such astute neighbors [as the British] to be dangerous."[29] No commissioners were appointed. Thereafter, as Fancourt reported, his own position deteriorated because the delay "enabled persons here [in Belize] through the press, which is in the hands of Indian partisans, to excite distrust in the minds of the chiefs and induce them to believe that I sought to betray them."[30]

Meanwhile, direct negotiation attempts by the Yucatecans elicited letters from the rebels but achieved few concrete results. When a brief armistice was arranged with the bishop's help in early 1850, Venancio Pec, Florentino Chan, and Bonifacio Novelo quickly presented their list of thirteen rebel conditions, dated January 24, 1850.[31] These can be abbreviated as follows.

1. We shall retain our arms.
2. The lands we now occupy shall be ours.
3. Our people shall be collected into pueblos by our own leaders.
4. Officials governing our pueblos shall be appointed by ourselves.
5. Priests shall be welcome among us.
6. Spaniards in general, government troops in particular, shall not force themselves in any way upon us.
7. Spaniards shall be free to come and go peacefully among us for trade.
8. Pueblos shall have their lands; rights to private property shall be respected.
9. *Terrenos baldíos* in the east and north shall not be subject to sale but shall be freely available for milpas farmed by the poor.
10. Jailed rebels and the families collected by Yucatecans shall be freed.
11. Families shall be free to reconstitute themselves.
12. There shall be a general amnesty for all.
13. Indian and Spaniard shall be free to reside where they wish, in the territory of either.

In addition, there was an added, unnumbered proviso that the clerical fee for baptism would be three *reales*, for marriage ten.

But the Yucatecan commissioners were embarrassed and impotent for the rebel provisions violated the specific orders issued when the commissions were formed: that any rebels given amnesty must be disarmed and that those who submitted should then be settled in towns under the control of Yucatecans.[32]

So ended negotiations with Pec and Chan, although as late as the middle of that year, 1850, rebel leaders were writing to say that they were still willing to negotiate.

The Conduct of War

As rebel milpas within reach of the government garrisons were exhausted by the foraging expeditions, the posts were shifted to new and richer territory. This was, indeed, the primary reason for the establishment of new *cantones*, taking precedence over mere military necessity.[33] As noted earlier, actual government control of the war-torn territory was limited to those places under direct Yucatecan occupation—the major garrisons located in old established towns, plus the scattered *cantones*, most of which were in Indian pueblos. From these, their periodic sweeping missions through the territory were directed both to locating unharvested milpas and to apprehending *masewalob*. But no matter how cleanly they swept, when they returned to their posts the hinterlands reverted to the rebels.

In these wide-ranging patrols the government troops were inevitably successful, partly because of what seems to have been a loss in rebel morale but in part because of the nature of the rebel military tactics. Their method was to allow attacking government troops free entrance into a settlement and then to attack, with themselves as the besiegers. On the few occasions when they found themselves besieged or encircled, they panicked and were inevitably defeated soundly.[34]

And so the swift, sweeping campaigns came one after another, and the roundup of rural families continued. The ultimate fate of internees, whether or not they were actually rebel soldiers, was unpredictable. Some were, in effect, sold to Cuba.

Slaveholding had been abolished in the former Spanish colonies as they gained their independence, but it remained in practice in Spanish Cuba. Nevertheless, legal strictures against importing new slaves and especially the heavy interdiction of slave shipments by tireless British patrols in the Atlantic had resulted in a heavy demand for labor on the island.[35] Thus, pursuant to Governor Barbachano's decree permitting banishment of active rebels, at the beginning of 1849 the first lot, 135 captives, was shipped by government enterprise to Cuba. Dispersed among planters, they brought ten ounces of gold per head with indentures of ten years. When protests by the Mexican consul in Havana and the foreign minister in Mexico City brought the Cuban retort that the immigrants had come of their own volition as servants indentured for a specific term, nobody was fooled. A second shipment in May raised Yucatan's financial gain to more than eight thousand pesos. Enough noise was made in Mexico that this practice by the Yucatecan government was either interrupted or moved underground after the first shipments,[36] but the notion of exchanging prisoners for cash would continue to be attractive to Yucatecan officials and, indeed, to some private citizens.

This was by no means the limit of the brutality visited on captives and internees, and in early 1850 General López de Llergo could report that an official policy, ameliorative in intent, was well established: Indians with or without arms who were taken while actually harrying Yucatecan troops were considered prisoners; those collected in the bush without resistance were not prisoners but would be moved to the Yucatecan lines where they were free to collect in pueblos giving obedience to the government; children up to the age of twelve or thirteen years were not to be separated from their parents; women and children were to be treated humanely.[37]

In practice, the relatively humanitarian rules were not often followed. Commonly, captured *masewalob* identified as officers were shot out of hand, while those rank and file not shot might be taken prisoner—although some Yucatecan commanders were reputed to take no prisoners under any circumstance. However charitable the Llergo principles sounded, for the mere noncombatant internees their realization was often perverted.[38] Some adults, and orphaned children in particular, were apt to be sold off as servants to townsmen and others. Whether some of these ended up on the Cuban market, by private rather than government channels, is not certain, but given practices that would come to light only a few years later it seems likely.

As provisions available to troops at Tihosuco grew short in February and March of 1850, new areas were reconnoitered. In February some of the force was shifted to Tepich. On March 1, a column of five hundred Yucatecan troops cut a huge swath south of Tihosuco, searching for rebels and grain. Covering some twenty-eight settlements up to 120 kilometers from Tihosuco, the detachment ended by falling on the rear of Rancho Kampocolché, which for some time had been the major headquarters of José María Barrera. This massive sweep resulted in the deaths of two important rebel field commanders and the rounding up of three hundred *masewalob*, among whom were the daughter of Venancio Pec and the wife of Pantaleón Uh.[39]

One result of this successful Yucatecan maneuver was an uncharacteristic loss of morale among many of the rebel leaders. As Francisco Cob wrote to his superior, Calixto Yam, "You must know, *mi señor*, that the enemy has taken all the powder that I was storing. . . . *El señor comandante* D. José Isac Pat has disappeared from us and we have only found his hat and his horse. . . . Tell me, *señor*, if there is a force in pursuit of those who have caused us so many damages, because if there is not, I'm going to go off and die in the bush because no other hope now remains to me."[40]

But those less troubled by the setbacks, such as Venancio Pec, issued strong statements. Pec warned that the Yucatecans wanted to cut the rebel passage to Santa Rosa, which was their gateway to Bacalar and Chichanhá and the crucial powder supplied by Belizean merchants.[41]

A second result was the establishment of a government *cantón* at Kampocolché, which the Yucatecans had found to be surrounded in all directions by milpas and other plantings, and another at Dzonot, between Kampocolché and Tihosuco. This led to the embarrassment of Barrera, ousted from his headquarters, who then threw his army vigorously against Kampocolché, Dzonot, and the Tihosuco road.[42] Efforts to regain Kampocolché would become important in rebel military action of the following year.

Peace Efforts Again

The Yucatecan military campaign intensified with the arrival in February 1850 of the Mexican general Manuel Micheltorena, a veteran of wars against the Comanche Indians in the northern state of Chihuahua, who was sent by the central government to take charge of the government army and to relieve General López de Llergo. Diagnosing the problem as one of a highly decentralized foe who kept up numerous small actions only loosely coordinated with one another, Micheltorena increased the centralization of the Yucatecan forces, reasoning that their ability to respond locally would be heightened. The result was that Eulogio Rosado was placed in command of essentially the entire zone of hostilities and charged with unremitting pursuit of the dispersed *masewalob*.[43]

Even so, the peace-seeking and indefatigable Padre Vela did not give up. On March 31 he wrote from Tihosuco to José María Barrera with proposals for peace and repeated them in another letter written from Kampocolché. In response to the latter, Barrera and one José María Vázquez wrote on April 16, just as a Yucatecan force based at Sabán was returning from a damaging strike at Rancho Santa Rosa. Barrera and Vázquez complained of the Yucatecan raid, arguing that a parley for peace was out of the question while such fighting continued. Both Vela and the Kampocolché commander, Colonel Juan María Novelo, replied by letter. The latter, reminding both Barrera and Vázquez of a former acquaintanceship when they had all been partisans of the federalist party and of Barbachano, assured them that the same party would extend its protection to them now. The former, arguing that the Kampocolché garrison had orders to fire only when fired upon, also sent an especially affectionate greeting to Vázquez on the ground that he, Vela, was an intimate friend of Vázquez's brother.

Barrera's written response to this—of April 20—asked Novelo to put up or shut up, saying that if peace were to be discussed a truce of two weeks was necessary. A letter from Cosme Damián Pech, José Isac Pat, Francisco Cob, and Calixto Yam made the same requests, and Colonel Novelo agreed on his own authority to call a truce. May 4 was agreed on for a general parley at Kampocolché.[44]

Neither Venancio Pec nor Florentino Chan was a party to these negotiations. Whether Pec, who was occupied in the south with the establishment of regular channels for the flow of war matériel, was consulted at all is not indicated. Chan, however, wrote to the rebel signatories from Cruzchén on April 24, saying that he had dealt with *dzulob* even as highly placed as the bishop of Yucatan but that he had become convinced that the only thing they wanted was for "the poor *masewalob* to hand over their arms in order afterward to do with them as they wished," and because he did not want to be a lamb led to slaughter he was determined to cut off dealing with the priests and to push the war to the bitter end. He reported having captured a letter sent from one *dzul* to another between Valladolid and Chemax, which said that "the commissioners had left to deceive the caudillos of the Indians, and that if God permitted that this was successful, those who submitted would soon die of flogging."[45]

The rebels did not keep the appointment at Kampocolché. And Colonel Rosado, who had come to that *cantón* especially for the parley, was furious over what he deemed a trick to gain time to reorganize the rebel forces. He ordered an immediate strike on Barrera's new headquarters at Haas. Meanwhile, Vela wrote a friendly letter to Barrera, saying he had hoped to mediate and counseling "patience, patience, patience. I tell you, however, that if you or any of your friends come here, I will wait for you to protect you. I expect to remain here three days. . . . Don't be afraid. . . . *Adiós amigo.*"[46]

Needless to say, there was no meeting.

Friction on the Hondo

After Superintendent Fancourt's decree banning the export of powder from British Honduras, the munitions dealers apparently decreased in number, at least for a while. By the end of April, 1850, Yucatecans reported intelligence that the only powder merchants remaining were a José Ayala and a "Mister Gelas" who were said to have places of business at Chichanhá, "as well as the Negro Yach who has one at Rancho Cacao [on the Río Hondo]."[47] By this time, too, the stability of the war front had served to reduce the amount of plunder taken by the rebels and, since booty had been the major source of goods they traded for powder, the reduction hampered their ability to buy. When Florentino Chan and Venancio Pec assumed control, they divided the command between north and south,[48] and Pec took personal charge of the acquisition of powder.

The resolution of the cash shortage seems to have lain with a suggestion from José María Ayala who was reportedly selling munitions at Chichanhá. He urged the *masewalob* to turn to the cutting of logwood in the southern forests, the production to be sold in British Honduras for money to buy powder. As a result, around the end of March Ayala himself was put in charge at Chichanhá by Pec, who then sent out a call both for soldiers to increase the size of the force assigned to harry the garrison at Bacalar and for laborers to cut dyewood.[49]

In April, a Yucatecan military force arrived at Bacalar to relieve the survivors of Cetina's Seventh Division, exhausted and weakened after their year of grueling duty in the face of constant attack by rebels under José María Tzuc. With the garrison temporarily reinforced, Cetina took the opportunity to send a large body of fresh troops up the Hondo toward Agua Blanca, where he understood the Chichanhá rebels were engaged in their woodcutting for profit and powder. On April 29 the expedition, consisting of sixteen boats and 250 to 300 men under the command of Lieutenant Colonel Ongay, moved up the Hondo past the British post at Douglas. Immediately, J. H. Faber, the British magistrate there, gave chase in his launch in order— he said—to see that the rights of bona fide British Honduras residents were protected.

At Cocos, as Faber reported, he learned that Ongay's force had seized two Yucatecan residents of British territory, and a short distance upstream (apparently at Pucté where the Yucatecan detachment had just finished a noisy skirmish with a party of rebels) he caught up with Ongay and secured the release of those in custody. Thereafter, he moved quickly upstream toward Agua Blanca to give notice of the Yucatecan excursion to Belizean woodcutters whom he believed to be there. While passing Cacao he sighted the two known gunrunners Fantesie and Lanabit on Albion Island on the British side of the river—presumably at their usual residence. Finally reaching Agua Blanca, he made sure that most of the cutters and ninety-five head of their work oxen were crossed to British territory from mahogany works on the Mexican side. Returning downriver, Faber met Ongay still on his way upstream and was told that some of the Yucatecan officers had seen four kegs of powder and some guns at the establishment of Fantesie and Lanabit. Faber paused there on his way downstream, saw some goods but no munitions, and then went on.

The story told by a Yucatecan participant in the Ongay expedition is somewhat different. According to him, the noise of their first action with the rebels would have warned anyone near Cacao, some eight kilometers farther upstream, of their advance, and when they reached that place they saw at an establishment on the British shore [i.e., Fantesie's] "an immense number of kegs of powder," which were heaped in disorder with other goods, as though just hauled back across the river. Faber was said to have met the Yucatecans and begun to accompany them upstream from there; although he indicated that he would stay abreast of them, when it was dark he gave them the slip and beat them to Agua Blanca. When the Yucatecan detachment arrived at that point they found on the Mexican side of the river fourteen Belizean laborers—Faber reported twelve—who said they had spent the night in the brush. The Yucatecans took the laborers into custody together with seven yoke of oxen, and over protests raised by the British foreman from the British side of the stream they set fire to a substantial store of logs. There is no indication that they found any rebel woodcutters.

According to Fantesie and Lanabit, the force stopped on its way downstream and its officers looted their stock of goods, which included one double-barreled gun but no powder.[50]

This action led to complaints on both sides. For their part, the Yucatecans protested Faber's action, accusing him of purposely warning rebel forces at Agua Blanca of their moves. On the other side, the British protested the arrest of the woodcutters whom they insisted were legitimately cutting mahogany under the terms of a contract with a Yucatecan to whom the concession belonged, while the woodcutters themselves were taken to Sisal and Mérida and held for trial.[51] The complaints of Fantesie and Lanabit were also transmitted to the Mexican government, although with what must have been little enthusiasm:

It is very doubtful [wrote Superintendent Fancourt to the Governor of Jamaica] whether . . . Albion Island in the River Hondo is properly speaking within the limits of the settlement of British Honduras, but I have felt bound to consider it as British territory as I find my predecessor, Col. Cockburn, made a grant of the island on the 25th July 1831. . . .

I may add that there can be no difficulty in proving that the complainants Lanabit and Fantesie have both aided the Indians with munitions of war and fought in the ranks of the Indians against the Mexican authorities. In any other state of society than that of British Honduras these parties must have been prosecuted before the legal tribunal.[52]

Hunger in the North

By mid-year of 1850 resettlement of the older pueblos and *villas* behind the advanced Yucatecan lines was a fact from Izamal to Valladolid, Ticul to Kampocolché, and Iturbide to Kancabchén. The life of former days was slowly reestablished, although hampered both by the presence of the Yucatecan military establishment and by recurrent *masewal* raids. For despite the impression of general demoralization that went with the rebel dispersal in much of the zone of hostilities, they repeatedly raided important points. In July they hit Kaua, penetrating to the plaza in a hit-and-run attack. In June, while a major Yucatecan campaign was under way to the east, they surprised Ekpedz with a night raid. In August they struck Dzonotchel and held possession for a time.[53] And their trade in munitions with southern smugglers tended if anything to increase, for on his return to Mérida from Bacalar Colonel Cetina named seven people as regular dealers in such contraband, four of them Yucatecans in origin—one of whom, Juan Trujillo, was a priest.[54]

But the rebel triumphs were ripples against the major current, which was still running in favor of the government troops. In June Lieutenant Colonel Patricio O'Horan with a force of seven hundred began a month-long drive to the south that took them overland to Bacalar, moving through Polyuc, Santa Rosa, and south by way of Nohbec, and returning by a route farther west, where on different occasions they caught José María Vázquez and Pedro Pech, the former accused of being a rebel, the latter certainly one. At

Kancabchén the prisoners were hanged, their bodies dragged out behind officers' horses and dumped alongside a road.[55]

Although by late summer new *cantones* had been established at San Antonio and Nohyaxché in an attempt to cut off rebel access to Ascension Bay, the system by which rebel plantings were used to support Yucatecan troops was beginning to collapse, particularly in the north. Repeatedly, even long-distance foraging raids from posts around Valladolid produced no foodstuffs because there simply were no milpas. In September a sweep by Colonel Novelo visited advanced *cantones* and many settlements and collected more than two hundred people. He found plantings extending from Kampocolché southward but none to the north.[56] Those rebels who remained in the north had been harried to the verge of starvation, and many were moving out because of it.[57]

The *cantones* were also suffering, as Rosado reported to General Micheltorena: "In the present season chills and fevers reign in them, and because of this it is only with great effort that each *cantón* can cover its line with a corporal and four soldiers, while the hospitals are full. . . . In the . . . *cantones* there is no aguardiente to cheer the soldiers, sandals are very scarce, and with the corn of the last harvest already consumed, they must forage day and night in the deepest part of the bush, and when they do not find [ripe grain] they lay hands on green cobs."[58]

Micheltorena's response was to order greater effort in the south to keep pressure on the rebels. In the worst of the seasonal rain, parties from Tekax, Iturbide, and Dzibalchén were detached to set up posts as far south as Nohayín and Xmabén, floundering through mud, dislodging the rebel defenders, and then starting the inevitable search for food.[59]

The local *masewal* reaction was to raid towns weakened by troop withdrawals: In November they hit Tekax as it was preparing to hold its annual fiesta; the *masewalob* burned houses, looted military stores of clothing and armament, and then disappeared. They struck Bolonchenticul and with difficulty were repulsed. Xul they burned completely, but most of the rebel attackers were caught and killed.[60]

In the north, a three-week Yucatecan thrust from Tixcacalcupul under Lieutenant Colonel Ruz hit Cruzchén, now the major garrison of Florentino Chan and Bonifacio Novelo, and then chased Novelo and Crescencio Poot all the way to Tancah on the coast of the Caribbean, never catching them but capturing their supplies and personal possessions. Escorted back to Valladolid were more than two hundred *masewalob*, nearly eighty of them said to have been taken with weapon in hand.[61]

Thus, as 1850 pushed toward its close, *masewal* and *dzul* troops were performing as they knew how—both suffering, both hungering, neither victorious.

The Rebels in 1850

The return of the war to the east in 1848 had been accompanied by wholesale defections of rebels and their sympathizers, and this continued as hostilities became localized at the former eastern frontier of colonial Yucatan. Around Valladolid surrenders had been especially heavy and were increasing.[62]

There are no trustworthy population figures for the rebels. A list of April 4, 1850, reportedly from the military archives in Mexico, gives names of two *comandantes* and 102 captains "according to information it has been possible to collect up to the 22nd of the past March, with . . . the pueblos to which each one corresponds, and the force they respectively command," the latter summing to more than 85,000 men.[63] This is clearly unbelievable, indicating a total rebel population of more than 250,000—half the population of the entire peninsula in 1845. More conservatively, one contemporary historian believed that in the mid-1850s the total of *masewalob* (men, women, children) not under government control ran to 70,000 people[64]—but even that figure is high.

One must suppose, rather, that by no later than 1850 the original 100,000 or more who had joined or at least trailed the rebel movement had decreased by at least half. It is unlikely that more than 60,000 men, women, and children were to be counted as rebels as the 1850s began, and the figure may well have been considerably lower. Capitulations to Yucatecan authorities would continue.

Other inferences may also be drawn from conditions in 1850, a time when the rebel organization was on the brink of significant and sudden change. The Yucatecan histories suggest that with the deaths of Cecilio Chi and Jacinto Pat came a period of confusion; as authority disappeared, the remaining leaders vied for position. It was this, they propose, that resulted in the demoralization that allowed Yucatecan detachments to move almost at will through rebel territory.[65]

Indeed, not long after the assertion of authority by Venancio Pec and Florentino Chan, there were rumors of their overthrow. In the region around Dzibalchén in the south, prisoners repeatedly claimed that Pec, Chan, and Bonifacio Novelo had been deposed by the British, who had given the government to José Isac Pat and to Pablo Encalada, and they also said that because of dissatisfaction many rebels were moving south toward the Petén district of Guatemala. At about the same time in British Honduras, George Fantesie reported to J. H. Faber that Pec was out of favor because after his interview with Superintendent Fancourt at Ascension Bay he had agreed to a truce for peace talks, and that Pec was being replaced by Jacinto Pat's brother.[66]

In view of the later history of the *masewalob*, it would not be surprising if there were successional struggles among the leaders, but there is no clear evidence that Venancio Pec and Florentino Chan were effectively challenged. It was Chan who wrote the apparently deciding letter to Barrera and other leaders when they were on the verge of peace talks with Padre Vela, and at the same moment Pec was in the south actively working to obtain munitions and calling for recruits to supplement the siege of Bacalar and for workers to cut logwood. It should also be remarked that both Pec and Chan had been adherents of Chi and that their continued exercise of authority seems to say that Chi's faction had emerged supreme.

But perhaps the seeming demoralization of the rebels was not an effect primarily of the death of the two most important leaders. Rather, the new stability of the war front simply brought into clearer view the decentralized and chronically uncoordinated aspects of the *masewal* leadership. While the front was moving and the Yucatecans were either retreating or advancing rapidly, the lack of coordination among rebel military maneuvers had not been apparent. But when rebel behavior could be viewed from a stable location, it became evident that the major *comandantes* acted with almost absolute independence, drawing upon their own adherents for their own maneuvers, cooperating or not as they saw fit, although usually honoring requests from other commanders for assistance where it was necessary.

In any arrangement based on personal allegiance through face-to-face contact there is a limit to the breadth of control that can be maintained. Between this and the independent stance of the leaders, it is not surprising that when J. H. Faber was sent by Superintendent Fancourt in late 1848 to interview the leaders of the rebels who had just taken Bacalar, he was driven to remark that "the Indians seem to have no regular form of government—it appears to be a kind of military dictatorship, under which the authority of the Chiefs is not always respected, in fact the Indians appear to be runaway schoolboys who try to do the most with their momentary liberty."[67]

But whatever the degree of coherence of the rebel organization, the leadership had notions of its grandeur. Thus, with the change in the conditions of peace that were proffered by the *masewalob*, with the introduction of demands for independence and territorial separation, the commanding generals—Pec and Chan—each assumed the title of governor.

Whatever increase in self-pride this may reflect, the pressure on *masewal* families by foraging and pillaging *dzulob* engendered the response that had been customary since Yucatecan history began: the erstwhile rebels retreated farther and farther into the bush to reestablish their scattered, irregularly formed pueblos and farmsteads, where they could hope to live in peace and isolation. So it was that by 1850 a great migratory movement to the well-watered forests of the south began, to the region less immediately accessible to the *dzul* enemy. In time, this relocation would bring an arm's-length accommodation to the Yucatecan government through an unratified but effective treaty of peace.

Meanwhile, however, the militant rebels farther north would be buoyed up by a divine visitation that was to revitalize their movement and change their world.

10 / A Parting of Ways

In 1851 rebel disunity manifested itself in an irrevocable divergence. One part of them resolved to remain in rebellion and received strength from God himself. The other portion wavered, and took the first steps toward a return to their old-time allegiance.

The Descent of God

In late 1850 a divine visitation galvanized the rebel world into hope. At the place of the miraculous appearance a pueblo sprang up in the wilderness. It would grow, and grow famous, as the rebel capital, and it would provide a psychological as well as political center around which the most recalcitrant of the rebels would group themselves for half a century.

The miracle came when it was most needed. As the historian Baqueiro describes it,

in the midst of all of the triumphs . . . [of the Yucatecans], when the Indians were often found dead of starvation in their huts; when rather than humans those who were led prisoner to the *cantones* appeared to be corpses; . . . when the line of advanced garrisons had left them almost without territory, . . . then is when they unexpectedly form a new settlement, a new fort a short distance from Kampocolché, where they join together with so much confidence that . . . no effort of the whites could overcome, because a mysterious divinity has come from heaven to strengthen them.[1]

The first public notice of events related to this visitation came after a furious rebel attack on the Yucatecan garrison at Kampocolché on January 4, 1851, beaten off with difficulty from the central plaza itself and with heavy *masewal* losses.[2] Captives reported they had come from a new pueblo in the east, from a region not populated before. José María Barrera had new headquarters.

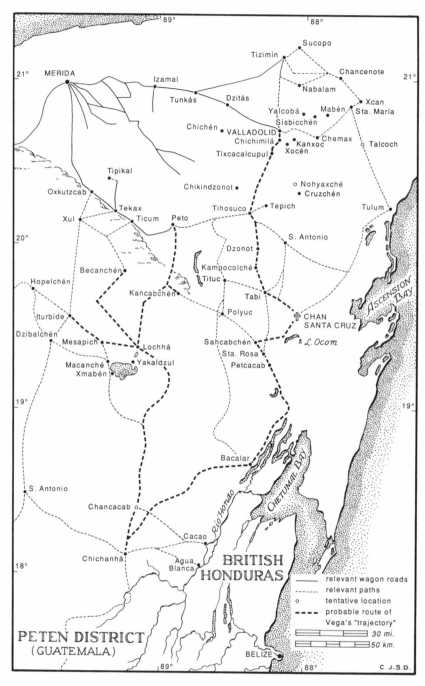

Map 11. Location of Actions of 1851–53. Based on dispatches cited in the text, accounts in Baqueiro (1878–87), and Hernández (1854–55).

On March 21 a Yucatecan column under Juan María Novelo left Kampocolché to search out the new town—referred to as *Chan Santa Cruz*, "Little Holy Cross"—and reached it on the second day, after a march of about fifty kilometers. Because of the large number of families now living around the new center, surprise was impossible, and the fight was sharp. As Colonel Novelo reported,

> the two crosses that they worship . . . fell into my power, . . . [and were] conveyed here to Kampocolché in their own tabernacle. The patron of these, Manuel Nauat, native of Kanxoc of the partido of Valladolid, made a vigorous resistance, giving a machete cut to . . . Captain D. José Antonio Carrillo, paying in the act . . . with his life.

In addition to Nauat, the rebels lost seventeen others, but Barrera, as always, escaped. In and around the settlement were so many families that Novelo was unable to round up all the thousands. He attributed this presence and the new cult to a conscious plan of Barrera, saying that

> by the communications taken from Barrera which I transmit, one is informed of the degree of superstition in which . . . he maintains the Indians with respect to the adoration of the crosses, having made them believe that these appeared at a well [i.e., cenote] of the same hamlet, that they speak in the name of God and assure them of the triumph of their cause, provided that they occupy Kampocolché. From all parts of the interior families come to Chan Santa Cruz with the aim of knowing and adoring the crosses, burning candles and presenting them with money, maize, and other things.[3]

The crosses were described by another witness as wearing *"hipiles* and *fustanes,* embroidered in the manner of those used by the *mestizas* of the country."[4] Novelo also reported capture of documents regarding the powder trade through Chichanhá.[5]

More than twenty-five years later, the historian Baqueiro presented what he called a tradition of the time. While admitting that for lack of witnesses it was neither as detailed nor as accurate as might be desired, all his sources agreed that both the divine visitation and the new pueblo were owed to the efforts of José María Barrera.

As Baqueiro reconstructed events, Barrera had sometime earlier come across a cenote of promise and had marked the place by carving three small crosses (although a later description by Baqueiro himself mentions only one) in the bark of a tree growing near it. Indians had begun to come to the cenote, and they burned candles to the cross or crosses as a matter of course. Barrera then had three standing crosses (although Novelo's dispatch mentions only two) erected at the spot, which increased both the devotional display and the tendency of rebel families to settle nearby when they had lost their milpas elsewhere to the government troops. Barrera invented the story that the crosses had descended from heaven. Calling the folk together, he made use of Manuel Nauat, a ventriloquist, to give well-meditated discourses ostensibly emanating from the crosses, thus inspiring the *masewalob* and urging them on to assault Kampocolché, Barrera's favorite strong point that had been wrenched from him.[6]

Like Colonel Novelo, the historian Baqueiro rationalized events as an urban Yucatecan, viewing the rising cult of the cross as arrant superstition. Indeed, most Yucatecans were shocked at what they regarded blatant sacrilege, characteristic—as one was to remark—of "these Indians whose small understanding never could be illuminated by the sublime torch of the Catholic religion, still less permit them to comprehend its holy dogmas."[7] The Spanish-named Barrera, they asserted, could only have been exploiting that small understanding with great cynicism.

That someone was privy to the means of making the crosses speak is not to be doubted, but whether it was José María Barrera will never be known. To the limited extent that it is possible to draw directly upon Barrera's known words, one is not driven necessarily to believe that the visitation of God through the crosses occurred by his devious machinations. The single known letter received by the government in British Honduras over his name (known in English translation only) can be interpreted as an anguished cry for help and also a sincerely uttered call to religious ecstasy. Dateline Santa Cruz, January 1851, and addressed to the superintendent of Belize, it bears the purported signature of Barrera and the secretary José Victor Reyes.

Respectable Sir:

I put you and the Magistrates of Belize in knowledge that the Holy Cross Three Persons speaks to his Secretary General and says that at this date you must be informed that the Holy Cross begs of you to give them powder, shot and all the implements of war. My beloved Sirs come and receive a holy benediction and enjoy the benefit of speaking with the True Christ who spilt his Blood for your sakes. Do not fail to come for the real Christ says that only you believe in him [sic] as we do poor Indians that we are.[8]

But there were communications from the cross less ephemeral than speech, for it entered an active campaign of writing proclamations and letters. A document carrying 1850 dates within its text is presumably the earliest example of the lengthy sermons, proclamations, or exhortations putatively emanating from the cross and bearing the signature Juan de la Cruz. Speaking at once as the cross, as Christ, and as God, it announces the divinity of the cross, laments the hardships suffered by the *masewalob*, issues a set of commandments to them, and promises them grace, all interspersed with passages glorifying the cross itself. The document is closed, in signature position, with the names "Juan de la Cruz of Balam Na" and "Juan de la Cruz of Xocén." A date near the end—read as February 10, 1850—is in error, however, for the text makes it clear that when the document was written Kampocolché was already in the hands of the Yucatecans, and they took it only in March 1850:

> And another of my commandments for you, ye my beloved, is that it is necessary that there be brought one thousand weapons and one thousand bearers for liberating this Rancho Kampocolché. This is the hour for them to liberate it, this Rancho Kampocolché, for once and for all![9]

The document also states that "it was on the fifteenth . . . of October that I began to speak . . . in the year 1850."[10] On the other hand, it makes no reference to the death of Manuel Nauat, unlike the introductory sections of later versions of similar documents.

It is not unlikely, therefore, that this earliest exhortation was among the "communications" that Novelo reported taking on the first Chan Santa Cruz raid of late March 1851, and which he said would provide intelligence "of the degree of superstition in which . . . [Barrera] maintains the Indians with respect to the adoration of the crosses." A date in February of 1851, rather than 1850, would be entirely reasonable and would place the document before the death of Manuel Nauat.[11]

The more common conception, however, has been that all of the written exhortations and other communications were authored by the successor of Nauat after the latter's death. This new mouthpiece of God is referred to by Baqueiro as Juan de la Cruz Puc, because he is said to have so signed a letter in which he announced to the *masewalob* that the crosses had not truly vanished after the Yucatecan raid on Chan Santa Cruz.

Baqueiro reports that he obtained a description of this letter with much effort and that it stated that after refusing to speak to their Yucatecan captors and tormentors the crosses had reappeared in the church of the rancho of Yalcobá. There were references to "a governor who is to be found in the ruins of Chichén," advice that the people should have no fear because they would be succored by not one but three holy personages, and the statement that "the hour had struck in which the hawk was going to perch on the high towers of the Cathedral of Mérida." At the foot of the letter, by the signature, were said to be three crosses.[12]

Unfortunately, the original letter is not known. In structure, however, it seems to have paralleled a series of five extant letters dated in August and September 1851, which were addressed to Governor Miguel Barbachano and the Yucatecan commander at Valladolid. These latter speak as the cross to complain that on March 23 its patron (i.e., Manuel Nauat) was killed and the cross itself carried captive to Kampocolché, mistreated, and robbed of money and other goods and valuables. The cross calls for the return of its property, asserts its divinity, and decries the hostilities. There are references to Chichén and to the Cathedral of Mérida—but the latter regard only masses to be said, rather than a mystical hawk. It directs the governor to withdraw his troops and release his prisoners, commanding everything on its own behalf as well as in the names of Jesus, Mary, and the three personages of the Trinity—God the Father, God the Son, and God the Holy Spirit. In the harangue, the voice of the cross and the voice of God are intermingled and become one. With the two signatures that appear on all of the letters of the series—"Juan de la Cruz of Balam Na" and "Juan de la Cruz of Cenil"—there appear drawings of two crosses.[13]

Without having for comparison the earlier missive described by Baqueiro, one is free to wonder if perhaps that letter too was signed by two persons named "Juan de la Cruz," without surname—if perhaps the name Puc was unconsciously glossed by witnesses or by Baqueiro as a result of common belief; if there was a place-name indicated; and if perhaps there were two rather than three crosses at the close, although there might be references in the text to "Juan de la Cruz Three Persons" and certainly to the Christian Trinity. That is, one may be inclined to suspect that the letter referred to by Baqueiro was closely similar in its entire form to those addressed to the *dzul* governor.[14]

While the rebels were thus being reassured and encouraged by the spoken and written word of the crosses of Chan Santa Cruz, Bonifacio Novelo was reportedly moving around the countryside, carrying from place to place the image of a saint that he claimed appeared miraculously.[15] Perhaps this manifestation was intended to further animate the spirits of the people now settling so heavily around Chan Santa Cruz, but if instead it was an attempt to install somewhere a rival to the attraction of the crosses, it was a lure that was stillborn.

Now convinced of the need to establish an independently governed territory in eastern Yucatan, the rebel leadership must have seen that the concentration of *masewalob* at Chan Santa Cruz provided the one thing that their realm had hitherto lacked: a capital, a focus of sentiment and government. But when this miraculous capital appeared, it came not to the seat of any of those rebels of highest prestige, who had been of the eastern party of Cecilio Chi—leaders such as Florentino Chan and Venancio Pec, the two designated *gobernador*, or Paulino Pech, called *comandante general*. It came rather within the territory of the *comandante* José María Barrera, heir to the forces of the south once led by Jacinto Pat and to some extent a rival of the eastern faction. It is not unlikely, then, that Bonifacio Novelo's perambulations with a putatively miraculous saint were an indication of disappointed factionalism.

Whatever was Novelo's aim, immigration to Chan Santa Cruz swelled. The next Yucatecan raid on the new capital began on May 3, 1851, the day of the Festival of the Holy Cross. Colonel Pablo Antonio González left from the advance *cantón* of San Antonio with the intention of marching through Chan Santa Cruz and on to Chichanhá, but despite the festivities in full swing at the new capital it was well defended by an estimated fourteen hundred rebel troops. The Yucatecan force—one-tenth the size of the defense—fought its way with difficulty to the plaza, finding the place to have "the aspect of an entirely new settlement, . . . the houses dispersed through a thick wood, . . . the terrain composed of . . . hills and ancient trees that intertwined their branches and formed an immense vault." Water came from the cenote of the mysterious crosses, where "the trees . . . were blackened with the smoke of candles. . . . The fanaticism they held toward the crosses was inconceivable."

González held the place overnight, then was forced out by the enemy and the moans of his own wounded. Despite rebel harassment, his withdrawal was orderly. Because of losses and the eighty-one prisoners they herded along, the Yucatecans returned to San Antonio, foregoing Chichanhá.[16]

Yet these able defenders of Chan Santa Cruz were the same rebels who had been the target of repeated Yucatecan thrusts in the area from Tihosuco to Valladolid and who had lost their morale to the point that government patrols could move through their midst almost at will. It was clear to everyone that they were stiffening.

Trudging toward Peace

As I noted earlier, however, well before the crosses appeared miraculously at Chan Santa Cruz, distress from the war and the shortage of food had stimulated a movement of *masewal* families southward, in a repetition of their age-old strategy of disengaging to seek the solitude of the wilderness. By the beginning of 1851 traders moving up the long road from the settlements of the Petén District of Guatemala to the pueblo of Dzibalchén in the Chenes had brought word that the region was strangely full of Indian families making milpa in the bush. Although peaceful, these immigrants clearly were not attuned to Yucatecan desires, for they had declined to return to their earlier status within the social and economic world of Yucatan.[17]

This new situation along the common border with Guatemala, together with the still-exasperating status of Chichanhá as a focal point in the rebel arms trade, prompted communications from the government of Yucatan to Modesto Méndez, Guatemalan governor of Petén District. By letter dated April 1, 1851, Méndez agreed that with the Petén curate Juan de la Cruz Hoil he would travel through the border area as far as Chichanhá and that he would render whatever service he could toward ending hostilities there.[18]

Leaving the Petén capital of Flores on July 15, the two emissaries expected to visit a series of towns along the way and to arrive at Chichanhá where they would join José Canuto Vela, who had been reappointed to head the eternal Yucatecan peace commission.[19] But when they arrived at Chichanhá on August 19, Vela had not appeared. Méndez and Padre Hoil began negotiations assisted by Padre Felipe de Jesús Rodríguez, whom they found had been ministering in Chichanhá since the outbreak of the war. Although the Chichanhá rebels were strongly inclined to treat with Guatemala rather than Yucatan, Méndez dissuaded them, and on the basis of his guarantees induced them to make peace by means of a simple statement dated August 21, 1851. The five provisions amounted to an announcement of their submission to Governor Barbachano, of their expectation of continued spiritual care from Rodríguez, of their receipt of full amnesty from the government, and of guarantees of their protection by the local military commanders and the governors of Yucatan and Petén. The signatories were Méndez, Hoil, and Rodríguez; Angelino Itzá, titled first *comandante* of Chichanhá; Romualdo Santos, second *comandante*; and twenty-five to thirty lesser rebel officials. Méndez and Hoil then departed.[20]

After this agreement made at the hands of a representative of the government of Guatemala, other rebels of the south quickly expressed interest. On

August 28 José María Tzuc addressed a letter to Méndez from his position besieging Bacalar, asking for negotiations on behalf of both himself and José María Barrera.[21] A month later José María Cocom, rebel commandant in the Chenes region, contacted the priest Manuel Antonio Sierra, a member of the peace commission, and indicated at least a grudging willingness for talks.[22] But at about the time of Cocom's suggestion, word was received in Yucatan that José María Barrera—presumably now informed that the Chichanhá surrender was to hated Yucatan rather than Guatemala—had fallen on Chichanhá with a force of more than four hundred, taking possession of the territory and dragging the peaceably inclined leaders away.[23] This effectively dampened the enthusiasm of other southern commanders for precipitate surrender, but seeds had been sown that would bear fruit before even a handful of years had passed.

Worsening Trials

Despite the new and divine support of the cross and the explosive growth of their capital at Chan Santa Cruz, times of great trouble were in store for the northern rebels. The origins of trouble, however, were to be found in earlier events in Mérida.

Although aid to the state government had been promised by Mexico, payments were arriving several months late. With sixteen thousand Yucatecans under arms, not only were there no extra supplies for the troops, there were no reserves of manpower that could be called up for relief. And again political infighting had developed in Mérida between the party of Barbachano and certain Yucatecan delegates to the national congress. Their struggles had enlisted more and more of the active military as participants in the political drama.[24]

Colonel José Dolores Cetina, still in Mérida after his triumphal if hungry return from Bacalar, joined with others in late 1850 to publish a newspaper that targeted Eulogio Rosado and his supporters, now partisans of the anti-Barbachano faction. A contrary sheet promptly emerged from that faction; between the two papers there was editorial wrangling over the conduct of the war.

Although Mexican General Micheltorena ignored all this, avoided local politics, and concentrated on running his determined campaign to end the eastern rebellion, politics would not leave his forces alone. In November 1850 Agustín Acereto and the garrison troops of the Fourth Division in

Valladolid mutinied against their commanders, Colonel Méndez and Lieutenant Colonel Ruz, both *barbachanistas*, and imprisoned them in order to proclaim revolution with the goal of separating Yucatan from Mexico. Colonel Eulogio Rosado moved a column from Tihosuco to restore order, Colonel Cetina was sent from Mérida to take command of the disrupted Fourth Division, and the two erstwhile enemies, meeting perforce in Valladolid, were able to claim a personal and political reconciliation.

In the calm after the meeting of Rosado and Cetina, Barbachano won a third and uncontested term as governor to begin in January 1851. After a year of this seesaw experience, however, Micheltorena was fed up. He resigned, announcing to Mexico that because of inadequate resources and the divisiveness of the Yucatecan leaders he could not pursue the war. In May 1851 he was relieved by General Rómulo Díaz de la Vega, a man of vigor, talent, and ego, the second Mexican general to take command of the Yucatecan army.[25]

Immediately, Vega reorganized the military to cut the active force to a level in keeping with Yucatecan resources. Although this reduced the total number of men on the line, it provided for forces in reserve, called "sedentaries," who were to relieve troops of active units every four months. Medical facilities were improved, and a commissariat was established— indeed, appropriation of private property and forced lodging were expressly forbidden, although the ban was obviously not always enforced and certainly was not meant to the apply to food and shelters of the rebel enemy.

As a result, some active troops went home after three years in service, most of that time without pay. But the initial by-products of the rotation were the mutinies of those ordered to remain on active status, great unwillingness of sedentaries to be called back, and a slump in Yucatecan military pressure during much of the rest of 1851.[26] The end result was a force from which short but violent and effective campaigns could be demanded.

One of Vega's first plans was to relieve the detachment at Bacalar now commanded by Colonel Isidro González. Not since June 1850, when O'Horan made his brief overland visit, had there been direct contact with the Bacalar garrison. In February 1851, González had reported by letter that his food was essentially gone and that his force was not strong enough to take grain from the enemy. The next month, in broad daylight, Venancio Pec made a direct assault on Bacalar with eight hundred rebels and penetrated the plaza, only to be dislodged by the superhuman efforts of González and his sickly detachment. The *masewalob* were reported to have suffered 130 dead by the time they withdrew.[27] In late May, González reported that he had pledged his own credit to buy supplies in Belize, but because he had been unable to make a payment that avenue was closed for the future. The detachment was in dire need.[28] Yet almost another year passed before any relief was delivered.

By late 1851 Vega's plans were complete, and his energy prevailed despite the difficulty in recalling the sedentaries to active duty after their four-month rest and problems stemming from the lack of morale in those frontier pueblos subject to the rebel attacks (which had increased as the government troops paused in their steady harassment).[29] The plan was ambitious, involving what the commander called a "grand trajectory" through enemy territory.

Yucatecan military sections now stationed at Kancabchén, Becanchén, and Iturbide in the Chenes pushed out to rendezvous at Lochhá. Simultaneously, a section from Valladolid struck east to the Caribbean coast to hit the rebels from the rear. And at the same time, on February 19, 1852, Vega himself left Tihosuco with three sections, bound for Bacalar by way of Chan Santa Cruz.

Vega's march went swimmingly. Musket fire from ambush was heavy as his men neared the rebel capital, and warning bombs (*bombas de aviso*) boomed to announce their approach, but they met no resistance as they occupied the town.

The Chan Santa Cruz they entered now was centered on a church and three barracks of thatch. Three hundred to four hundred houses, also thatched with palm, were scattered over the uneven ground in groups of eight or ten, spaced broadly apart. Paths crossed in all directions through deep woods, while freshly chopped trees marked only a few formal streets. A cenote near the center of the settlement yielded water. But each house group had its private cemetery, some with fifty or sixty graves marked by piles of rocks and wooden crosses. Other graves were scattered without order; here and there exposed pieces of corpses protruded. Corpses also lay unburied, some stretched out in hammocks as though resting. The forty prisoners taken were walking skeletons, starving rather than surrendering. Nevertheless, some maize was located and appropriated by the Yucatecans.

In the hollow that surrounded the cenote was a mahogany tree blackened with the smoke of many candles. The crosses of worship had fallen prisoner to Yucatecans at least twice, but each time they had reappeared miraculously at the foot of that tree. On the tree itself was a small cross three or four inches high, cut into the bark, with the inscription "*Santa Cruz 2 de noviembre*"—presumed by the historian Baqueiro to be the traditional date for the miraculous founding of the place. The little cross was referred to as the "mother of the crosses." It was said that no power could cut the tree for all instruments would lose their edge. Vega therefore had the tree cut down and asked the prisoners if they did not see it fall. They were said to have responded simply: "The crosses cannot be wrong."[30]

The crosses of regular worship were no longer at the cenote but within the church, where, in the "large and obscure gallery there was in one end an altar to which no one could approach except the functionary in charge of the three crosses. These were on the altar, dressed in *hipil* and *fustán*; behind the altar was an excavation in which was placed a barrel that served as sounding board, . . . [giving to the voice] a sound hollow and cavernous. All of that was hidden from the view of those in the chapel: within the excavation the functionary placed himself to say whatever Barrera wanted."[31]

In the early days of March, the last of Vega's force vacated Chan Santa Cruz, pressing south. Touching at several isolated settlements where a number of supposed rebels were rounded up, they scoured the countryside for grain for the garrison at Bacalar. In one of these actions the wife of rebel commander José María Tzuc was captured. The joyous arrival of the entire force at Bacalar was completed by March 13, including a mule train laden with maize.

On April 3 Vega's hard-marching column was at Chichanhá, where it rendezvoused with two of the Yucatecan sections that had advanced through Lochhá. Chichanhá was described as having had two hundred houses and seven hundred to eight hundred inhabitants, but it had been largely destroyed by the force from Chan Santa Cruz that attacked it after its surrender the previous year.[32]

His grand trajectory at last swinging north, Vega and his men marched through Lochhá and by the end of the month were enjoying whatever comforts were available in the garrison at Peto. At Chichanhá Vega had left the powder traders a reminder of his military presence: during succeeding weeks two Yucatecan commands ranged the area west of the Río Hondo, and detachments were stationed at Agua Blanca and Cacao to intercept movements in the major route of the powder trade.[33] They would also contribute to peace, as I will show later.

State of the War

In the north, things were relatively quiet. In May 1851, Eulogio Rosado had taken the rebel headquarters of Cruzchén and made it his own *cantón*, forcing out Bonifacio Novelo and Florentino Chan. The result was that a number of Cruzchén rebels or their families presented themselves for surrender.[34] And when Rosado inspected all the *cantones* of the surrounding area late the following year, he reported the region essentially pacified, with only repopulation remaining to be accomplished.

He was seconded in this opinion by Padre José Antonio García. Between December 12, 1849 and May 1850, García stated in a report to José Canuto Vela that there had been 5,680 surrenders at Valladolid; since that time presentations had increased, but they were taking place so fast in so many pueblos in the region, that no count was possible. Thus, by late 1852 not only the immediate environs of Valladolid were repopulated, but the village of Chemax a short distance to the east counted eight hundred male *vecinos*, with two hundred to three hundred each in Santa María, Xcan, Chancenote, Sucopo, Sisbicchén, Nabalam, and Yalcobá, as well as all the towns from Valladolid west to Izamal.[35]

But there were still pockets of rebels in the northeast who would make themselves known over the next few years. Indeed, in late 1852 there were rumors of attacks plotted on newly repopulated Xcan, from which *masewalob* reportedly intended to drive against Tizimín.[36] In April 1853 activity erupted northeast of Valladolid, when the discovery of a rebel presence provoked a Yucatecan attack on Mabén[37]—one that would prove to be the first of a series.

But the evidently deteriorating state of *masewalob* health in the south had not ruled out a bellicose reaction there, as Vega's expedition sapped the strength of the regular garrisons. During Vega's absence in the southeast, José María Cocom invaded Dzibalchén, burned it, and carried off families. Zacarías May invaded Tekax, almost taking one of the barracks before being driven back; unfortunately for him, two months later portions of Vega's force briefly occupied his own headquarters at Macanché.[38] But this did not end the fighting in the south. Lochhá was reoccupied by a Yucatecan detachment in late June 1852, while the following month Zacarías May attacked Oxkutzcab with a rebel force of four hundred men from Macanché.[39] From Tepich south, engagements continued throughout that year, in some of which Claudio Novelo, son of Bonifacio Novelo, was reported to be fighting alongside his father.[40]

Yucatecan retaliation for these raids, as well as more commonplace causes of mortality, brought the *masewalob* a series of painful losses in those years. In mid-1852, Colonel Novelo, galvanized by the sounds of Yucatecan *bombas de aviso*, indicating *cantones* were under rebel attack, had immediately launched a counterthrust at Chan Santa Cruz, surprising it in a blinding rainstorm on June 18. The charge—limited to bayonet and machete because rains had saturated all gunpowder—brought death at last to the veteran Venancio Pec, who styled himself governor. Also killed was a rebel commander identified erroneously as Juan Bautista Yam, while a number of Yucatecan prisoners were liberated. When Novelo left two days later, Chan Santa Cruz was leveled and burned; only the thatched church still stood, which Yucatecans could use as a billet when they passed through again.[41] Novelo reached Bacalar on June 28, having touched half a dozen rebel settlements, and once there attacked José María Tzuc, who was still harrying the Bacalar garrison. After scouring the area for grain for the Bacalar post, Novelo turned north again, arriving at Kampocolché in late July.[42]

On December 31, the seemingly indestructible José María Barrera, battle heir of Jacinto Pat and reputed founder of Chan Santa Cruz, died at a place called Yokdzadz or Yokdzonot—not from wounds but from "illnesses and ailments." The *comandantes* Crescencio Poot and Atanacio Puc wrote feelingly to inform Paulino Pech and other high commanders, lamenting the leader they would "no more see at our side . . . fighting for our sacred freedom."[43]

Skirmishes continued into 1853, although as will become clear later the Yucatecan forces would increasingly be involved with affairs other than war with the *masewalob*. In February, Chan Santa Cruz—rebuilt after Colonel Novelo's destruction—was attacked in a Yucatecan hit-and-run raid. And in May a Yucatecan force passed through the rebel capital again, this time moving to Ascension Bay, where on the twenty-seventh a surprise fight killed Paulino Pech, rebel *comandante general*, other officers, and José Victor Reyes, an interpreter.[44]

As 1853 wore on, deeper divisions would plague both the rebels and the Yucatecans.

Peace in the South

On December 26, 1851, *masewalob* under José Isac Pat and Cosme Damián Pech had attacked José María Tzuc at or near Chichanhá, reportedly because Tzuc and his followers had refused to submit to the dictates of the miraculous cross. Tzuc, however, was victorious in a battle in which, according to one source, "the streets of Chichanhá ran with blood and corpses."[45] Pech was killed, and Pat was forced to retreat toward the coast.[46] This was the first decisive step toward permanent division.

On April 22, 1852, while patrolling the Río Hondo after General Vega's departure from Bacalar, Colonel Juan María Novelo had a friendly meeting with rebel *comandante* Andrés Zima, who led a force composed of a captain, three lesser officers, and fifty-three men of Chancacab, a place said to be some sixty kilometers southwest of Bacalar. After only a brief parley, Zima signed a peace agreement for his people. The conditions were straightforward: The former rebels submit to the laws of the legitimate government; they ask for military support in case of attack by the remaining rebels; they announce their intention to remain at Rancho Chancacab, which they regard as their home; they agree that copies of the act be transmitted to the governor of Yucatan.[47]

This was the first formal agreement for peace between active rebels and Yucatecan officers. Although its terms violated the desires of Yucatan, which called for those who surrendered to give up their arms and move to the settled portions of Yucatan, it forecast what would come in the much more important agreement to be made with pacified *masewalob* in 1853. In May of that year, the superintendent of British Honduras was contacted by José María Tzuc, who told him of the desire of the rebels of the far south to conclude a treaty of peace with Yucatan.[48]

No such peace movement included the rebels from farther north, however. At Chan Santa Cruz, Bonifacio Novelo was reported in June to have had one rebel leader executed and others assaulted—including José Isac Pat, now titled governor—after hearing that they were considering surrender.[49]

And in July, while southern rebel leaders were coming together to prepare for peace negotiations,[50] Crescencio Poot made one of his periodic attacks on Tixcacalcupul, although he was quickly forced to turn tail.[51] It was also rumored that in July or August Bonifacio Novelo had marched south to do battle with Tzuc for offering peace, but instead had been attacked and severely beaten, and then was pursued so hard by Tzuc that he was forced to take to a boat on the coast—from whence his whereabouts were unknown.[52]

Despite these hostilities in the north, the Yucatecans appointed a peace commission composed of Gregorio Cantón as its head; Lieutenant Colonel Eduardo López, of General Vega's staff; Lorenzo Zavala, as interpreter; and the priest Manuel Antonio Peralta. These were dispatched to Belize by sea, while Colonel Juan María Novelo moved his command to Bacalar to provide support.

Arriving in the British colony and meeting with Superintendent P. S. Wodehouse, the commissioners were disheartened to be told that the most basic of the rebel conditions was the geographical division of Yucatan. Despite that unacceptable stipulation, on September 13 talks began in Belize City with commissioners José María Tzuc and Andrés Zima. These two spoke for ten additional leaders, who by 1853 represented a number of the growing centers of the far south (see table 8).

Surprisingly, the condition that Yucatan be divided was given up with relative ease by these rebels, and three days later—on September 16—an agreement was signed by Cantón, López, Tzuc, and Zima. Its fifteen articles appear to be the result of mature negotiation in which both sides made concessions. The provisions can be summarized as follows:[53]

1. The followers of those commanders represented by Tzuc and Zima submitted themselves to obey the government of Yucatan, who in turn granted amnesty for wartime acts.

2. The submitting commanders would provide four hundred armed men who would join with government troops to do battle with those rebels who did not accept the peace.

3. The submitting rebels would retain their arms as long as the war should last, thereafter retaining only fowling pieces, which they would obtain in exchange for military muskets at the Yucatecan military stores.

4. Those submitting could return to their original homes and take possession of their properties there, subject to their ability to establish their earlier ownership.

5. A commission would be named by the government to oversee the rearrangement of property implied in Article 4.

6. Submitting Indians could, if they chose, continue to reside in settlements formed during the war, establishing them as new pueblos of the State of Yucatan, provided they met the ordinary conditions set by law for the recognition of pueblos; those that did not so qualify would continue as ranchos subject to the new pueblos.

7. Non-Indians who submitted would be able to remain in the settlements formed by the Indians and would be subject to the ordinary laws of the state.

8. No Indian could be compelled to work without recompense and would be obligated only for such civil duties as were owed by whites (i.e., *vecinos*).

TABLE 8
Rebel Commanders Party to the Treaty of 1853

Commander	Area with which Associated or Mentioned[a]	Reference
Pablo Balam	Kancabchén	Baqueiro (1878–87, 2: 316)
Raimundo Chi	Tixcacalcupul	Baqueiro (1878–87, 2: 286)
José María Cocom	Mesapich	Vega dispatch, Mar. 18, 1853 (ER, Mar. 23, 1853)
Pedro Regalado Ek	Tipikal	List of Apr. 4, 1850 (Reina 1980, 402–4)
	Yakaldzul	Ruiz dispatch, Dec. 30, 1855 (GS, Jan. 2, 1856)
Pablo Encalada	Chikindzonot	Rosado dispatch, Jan. 18, 1850 (BO, Jan. 23, 1850, 2–3)
	Lochhá	Encalada declaration, Aug. 12, 1867 (EP, Sept. 27, 1867)
José María Hernández	Chichanhá	Letter of J. Galaz, Mar. 20, 1852 (BCP)
Pedro José Ix	Oxkutzcab	List of Apr. 4, 1850 (Reina 1980, 402–4)
	Macanché	Vega dispatch, Mar. 18, 1853 (ER, Mar. 23, 1853)
José Leocadio Lira	Rancho Teul	T. Fajarda to M. Barbachano, Mar. 23, 1852 (SD, May 5, 1852)
Felipe Puc	Chichimilá	Baqueiro (1878–87, 1: 228, 230)
José María Tzuc	Chichanhá	Present chapter, passim
Juan Bautista Yam	Polyuc	List of Apr. 4, 1850 (Reina 1980, 402–4)
Andrés Zima	Chancacab	Vega to Exmo. Sr., May 5, 1852 (SD extra, May 12, 1852)

[a]Of these, Tixcacalcupul, Chichimilá, Chikindzonot, Oxkutzcab, and Tipikal are north of the sierra. Thus, somewhat more than half of the total appear to have been southerners in origin.

9. No government authority or private person would be permitted to compel Indians to labor for wages, and if the latter agreed to work willingly the wage arrangements would be subject to approval by pueblo *alcaldes*.

10. Indians would be at liberty to move as they wished for purposes of commerce and to dedicate themselves freely to the work they desired, in the same manner as whites.

11. An Indian recognizing wives or children in the power of another could reclaim them freely upon presenting reasonable proof of the relationship.

12. Indians accepting the peace would remain exempt from both civil personal taxes and religious taxes but for the support of the church would pay six *reales* for baptism and two pesos (i.e., sixteen *reales*) for marriage.

13. The *vecinos* who had taken part in the rebellion and were among the Indians would have the same guarantees conceded to the Indians and could return to their original residences under complete amnesty.

14. Those *masewalob* submitting would be required to present themselves in Chichanhá to be entered on a list of those who were pacified. Those who failed to do this would be considered still in rebellion.

15. When the treaty was ratified by the governor of Yucatan, such Indian prisoners as pertained to the forces of the leaders on whose behalf the treaty was signed would be released.

Immediately after the signing, Commissioner Cantón sent a long letter to Díaz de la Vega, explaining in detail the reasoning that led to certain Yucatecan concessions. Indeed, these included—compared with previous Yucatecan positions—allowing the pacified rebels to retain arms, permitting them to remain settled well away from centers under government control, and exempting them from all taxes. On the other hand, Cantón could point out that the rebels had given up all talk of territorial division, that they had agreed that firearms retained on a permanent basis would be limited to fowling pieces for hunting, and that they had agreed to a doubling of the fees for baptism and marriage that they had first insisted on (three *reales* for baptism, eight for marriage), which would partially offset the loss of religious taxes. Almost immediately thereafter, Yucatecan commission members paid a visit to Chichanhá.[54]

The governor of British Honduras reported the proceedings to the British minister in Mexico, sending a copy of the agreement. To this the minister shortly responded that Mexico would refuse to ratify the accord with the rebels, which was regarded as violating Mexican sovereignty, although they would agree to a full pardon for former combatants.[55] Although the *masewalob* were at once informed of this refusal,[56] the news apparently had no observable effect. And so the *pacíficos del Sur* came to receive de facto recognition by Yucatan, although without the support of any agreement accepted formally at the highest levels of government.[57]

In December, José María Cocom and thirty men from Mesapich went into Hopelchén and traded peacefully.[58] Other provisions of the unratified agreement were followed as the pacified rebels amassed a force to make war on the still active rebels at Chan Santa Cruz. By November, a captain operating under the orders of Tzuc was poised to attack Chan Santa Cruz itself, and forces from that center were deployed for defense.[59] But cholera raged in Santa Cruz and the *pacíficos* wisely desisted in their advance. Although armed clashes between *pacíficos* and rebels were frequent in ensuing years and although there were periodic reports that the *pacíficos* were mustering forces as specified by the treaty, there is no indication that any such force was ever again actually raised and moved into a tactically aggressive position.

Not surprisingly, the signing of the agreement prompted at least some population realignments both to the north and the south. Certain of the southern leaders who were not signatories—such as the active Zacarías May—began to appear in action against the Yucatecans in the vicinity of Chan Santa Cruz. And some of those rebels who were represented in the peace negotiations were apparently not originally southerners—that is, they had not hitherto appeared in action in the far south (see table 8).

With regard to this period, a contemporary Yucatecan asserted that the pacified rebels or *sublevados pacíficos* totaled about fifty thousand, whereas the still active rebels, the *sublevados bravos* could count fewer than half as many adherents, or around twenty thousand.[60] In view of the ensuing histories of both groups and of some censuses that were attempted later in the southern *pacífico* area, it seems more likely that the dissident *masewalob* divided themselves between camps approximately equal in size—possibly twenty thousand to twenty-five thousand in each one, allowing each side to field five thousand to six thousand soldiers, boys and men, under total mobilization.

Whatever the precise figures, the "treaty" of 1853 confirmed the most massive and definitive split to ever rend the dispersed ranks of the *masewalob*. Although there would be other defections and even pacifications supported by formal written agreements, the numbers of people rejecting the rebel cause on any other single occasion would be modest, and the impacts on the rebel movement much less significant. Thus, the defection of 1853 marks the end of the initial and only relatively pervasive stage of the rebellion.

Even so, the pacification in the south would not be permanent, for as pressures on the *masewalob* would change with time and circumstance, so would their strategy for dealing with their world. But it would be more than a dozen years before events initiated in the centers of government in western Yucatan would drive masses of southern *pacíficos* back into the arms of the active rebels.

Part 4. Finding Foe and Friend, 1853–1869

11 / Tribulations, Triumphs, Miraculous Crosses

Although 1853 brought to the south a peace that would last with some perturbations for nearly a decade and a half, it brought immediate troubles to the cities of Yucatan. It also brought the death of a tried and favorite Yucatecan commander as well as renewed attention to the sale of captive *masewalob*—a canker that would eventually spell difficulty not only for relations between Yucatan and Mexico but would worsen ties between Yucatan and England. An account of this traffic in people, however, must await the next chapter.

The Slide to Civil Strife

For the most part, Yucatan in 1853 was busy with insurrections that had little relation to the *masewalob*, either slave or free, *pacífico* or *bravo*. In Mexico, a conservative revolution began in Jalisco and spread to the Mexican capital, and the flag of Santa Anna was again raised. On January 19, 1853, in sympathy with this movement and in opposition now to Miguel Barbachano, José Dolores Cetina—that practiced revolutionary—proclaimed the Plan of Jalisco for Yucatan and called for the dictatorship of Santa Anna. The complicated upshot of this was that in February Barbachano was deposed at the same time that centralist rule was established throughout Mexico. All states then became departments, their former military commanders now their appointed governors. On August 7 Rómulo Díaz de la Vega assumed the governorship of Yucatan.

But Miguel Barbachano also was adept at revolutionary politics. In September his plotting came to a head with a *pronunciamento* in Tizimín, where a new revolutionary force was headed by Colonel Sebastián Molas, seconded by Manuel Cepeda Peraza, and shortly counted a force of two thousand. Sweeping west, these federalists joined battle in late September with the centralist government troops at Mérida. Eulogio Rosado, loyal to that new government, stripped the *cantones* of the east to gather an army and marched to Mérida. He was followed by a straggling mass of eastern civilians who, left without protection, rushed to evacuate most of the frontier pueblos.

But as Rosado's troops began the final onslaught against the revolutionaries, now holed up in parts of Mérida, they recoiled on finding their foes dead or sick in their makeshift barracks, for the insurrectionists had brought cholera from somewhere in the east. The combination of government arms and disease brought quietus to the revolution, as the remaining revolutionaries were dispersed and some executed, including Colonel Molas.[1] The doughty Rosado, arriving at Izamal on his way back to the east, found his force grappling with the sickness; he contracted it himself, worsened, and quickly died. Like José María Barrera, he met his death in bed.[2]

Meanwhile, the *masewalob* concentrated at Chan Santa Cruz were not idle. With the government troops and the civilians having almost entirely abandoned the east, they struck at the pueblos where they had been so often repulsed, destroying and looting at will. Tihosuco, Ichmul, Chikindzonot, Sabán, Sacalaca, Dzonotchel, Tahdzibichén, Tixcacaltuyú, Yaxcabá, all temporarily disappeared under the rebel torch, and lesser *cantones* were inundated, some of them never to reappear as Yucatecan outposts for the remainder of the war. Families who had tarried were carried away to *masewal* territory, and many were hacked up by machete.

Then, as the loyal troops who had survived the pestilence straggled back from the west, the *masewalob* withdrew again east of Tihosuco. Despite their burst of energy, the rebels were in sorry shape: "horribly emaciated, almost without blood in their bodies, and with unkempt hair that fell down their backs to their shoulders, they seemed more spectres fled from a cemetery than warriors."[3]

Capping all events, however, was the last and greatest massacre of the Yucatecan year. As the federalist revolt deteriorated, a handful of its leaders drifted into hiding east of Tizimín. A group led by Captain Narciso Virgilio moved quickly to recoup their fortunes. On the advice of three of them—one of whom was Baltazar Moguel—they sought aid from the Indian rebel commander Clemente Uch of Mabén, who joined them with four hundred men to strike a blow against the government. The combined force occupied Tizimín on December 8, drawing additional recruits from the *vecino* militia there. But these were vastly outnumbered by the Indians who flocked to the banner of the rebel *comandante* from Mabén.

The presence of so many Indians so near the rebel frontier was unsettling enough; then Uch unwisely suggested that Virgilio, thoroughly

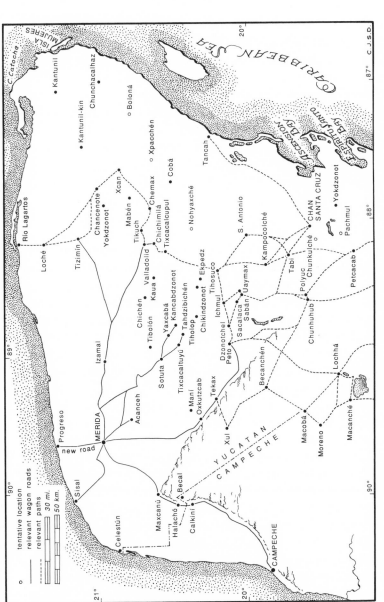

Map 12. Location of Events of 1853–58. The boundary between Yucatan and Campeche is the current one, which varies only slightly from those of earlier accords (Fremont 1861). The relationship of the boundary to the southern pacifico settlements was undetermined in this period.

outnumbered, should yield command to him. Virgilio bugled the entire force into formation on December 11, using the ruse that the new, combined army should return to Mabén to face the approaching government troops and that in preparation for the march there should be a muster for instruction in the use of arms.

Without warning, Virgilio's massed *vecino* troops opened fire on the Indian formation beside them. More than three hundred corpses, including that of Clemente Uch, marked the site of this last stroke of the Yucatecan civil revolt of 1853.[4]

Virgilio and some of his compatriots were pardoned by the government, reportedly because they claimed their action was a stratagem to trap the Mabén rebels.[5] Those most closely involved with luring the Indians into complicity, however, were sent to prison—save for Moguel, who escaped to be heard from again.

Trials of the Faithful

The reestablishment of government troops in their old strong-points coincided with efforts to further the progress made by General Vega's "Grand Trajectory" to finally smash the rebel resistance. In November 1853, troops led by Pedro Cantón drove toward Chan Santa Cruz, but they pulled back at the last minute when they saw that cholera was wreaking havoc in the region.[6] It may well have been cholera that caused the rebels themselves to disperse from Santa Cruz, for in December the *masewalob* were reported to be scattered in small groups between their capital and Tancah, on the Caribbean coast.[7] Not long after, however, Chan Santa Cruz was the base for five hundred armed men, some of whom were deployed to Pachmul and other points south of the capital to await the *pacífico* forces of José María Tzuc, from whom they feared the attack promised in the 1853 peace agreement.[8] But Tzuc's army held back, and cholera saved the rebels again.

By April of the following year, the rebel capital was not so well protected. On the first of that month a column of three hundred Yucatecans under Lieutenant Colonels Lázaro Ruz and José María Vergara left Tihosuco and in four days marched to the vicinity of Chan Santa Cruz. When about sixteen kilometers away, they were brought up by a spirited defense and moved only half the remaining distance in another four days. On April 10 they penetrated the plaza and dispersed the rebels, claimed by prisoners to number more than eight hundred and led by *gobernador* Calixto Yam and a *comandante* named Moguel. That night the *masewalob* returned to battle to the sound of trumpets. Besieging the Yucatecans in the town, the rebels pinned them there until the fourteenth, preventing them from foraging for food. They then attacked hard, only to be repulsed with losses and chased for several kilometers. The government troops, low on powder and very hungry, conducted an orderly but necessary withdrawal.[9]

The following month, the government floated a plan to raise seven hundred men and establish permanent *cantones* at Chan Santa Cruz, Pachmul, and other pueblos nearby. But when they were able to muster little more than half the necessary force, they resolved simply to march on the rebel capital once more. This drive was again spearheaded by colonels Ruz and Vergara. Leaving Tihosuco on May 22, they occupied Chan Santa Cruz on May 26 after inflicting punishment on the strong force of defenders. Near a recently opened well, the soldiers found two large troughs of water from which they drank thirstily. A few hours later many of them were sick, their symptoms suggesting cholera. Some died the same day. It is said that when the rebels attacked they asked the newcomers how they liked the water. Ruz thought it was poisoned.[10]

Retiring a short distance from Chan Santa Cruz for a healthier billet, the Yucatecans suffered from shortage of water, and the sickness continued to reduce them. By June 2 only about 90 of the original 375 men were still healthy. As they finally began to withdraw, the rebels fell on them. Both Ruz and Vergara died. A few demoralized survivors reached Tihosuco.[11]

The rebels followed this victory with raids around Tihosuco and Peto, both of which were repulsed, and a successful one into Sotuta *partido*, in which they took prisoners and booty.[12] The Yucatecan response was a renewal of the attempt to field a force large enough to occupy and hold the rebel headquarters, at least for a time. To this end they organized a pair of so-called flying columns, to be led by Juan María Novelo and Pablo Antonio González.

Leaving Mérida on November 14, 1854, González marched by way of Tihosuco directly to Chan Santa Cruz. His descriptions suggest that the primary seat of worship there had been shifted from the hollow around the cenote to higher ground. As Baquerio paraphrases him,

> the Indians had completely transformed the place. On the beautiful terrace of its plaza stood a church 30 *varas* [twenty-five meters] long and 12 [ten meters] wide, built of very good wood and covered with carefully selected palm, and further with some gratings on the sides that embellished it. Everywhere there were erected numerous

private houses, ample chambers that served as barracks, and strong fortifications.

Gonzales had wanted to establish his own headquarters there, but changed his mind on discovering

> an atmosphere poisoned with the putrid stench given off by more than 200 skeletons that were found at the entrance of the town [remains of the Ruz-Vergara party], and at the other end an equal number of more recent corpses that belonged to the prisoners taken in the partido of Sotuta, who had been killed a few days before.

He settled therefore at a place called Yokdzonot, reportedly south of Chan Santa Cruz.[13]

Meanwhile, Juan María Novelo, who left Peto on November 28, stationed himself at Pachmul. From there he raided more than forty ranchos and a multitude of scattered dwellings, taking prisoners and foodstuffs. One party caught and scattered a large rebel force on its return from the Río Hondo, where they had gone to trade booty taken in the productive raids of the preceding few months.[14] Of the reported six hundred *masewalob* making up the traders, there were plenty of survivors to swell the forces that harried both Novelo and González with ever increasing effect.

Exhausting the food at Yokdzonot, González shifted his headquarters to a pueblo called Chunkulché, reportedly also south of Santa Cruz. But during the ensuing month rebel pressure grew increasingly severe, both because reinforcements were being called in from more and more of the outlying ranchos and because Chunkulché was not located so as to share support with Novelo at Pachmul—a situation that appears to have been worsened by petty rivalry between the two colonels. Heavy attacks on Pachmul in late February caused high Yucatecan losses that, coupled with a large number of sick, forced Novelo's withdrawal on February 28, 1855. In the last stages of this retreat rebel attacks caused further heavy damage and the loss of a number of both wounded and prisoners. González withdrew on March 10.[15]

After this three-month invasion, the *masewalob* were again left in relative peace. Although in July troops under Captain Onofre Bacelis had left Tihosuco destined for the *masewal* capital, they returned to their base ten days later; having found no cornfields in the eighty to ninety kilometers they had covered, they were without supplies. This was taken to indicate that the rebels were hiding their families and concentrating their strength around Chan Santa Cruz itself.[16] There was no further Yucatecan campaign into rebel territory in 1855.

Yucatecan Politics and Its Repercussions

As the flying columns under colonels Novelo and González were leaving on the campaign just described, Rómulo Díaz de la Vega was recalled to Mexico by Santa Anna, to be replaced, by the Mexican General Pedro de Ampudia in late 1854. The rule of neither Ampudia nor Santa Anna was to last long, however. The preceding March had seen the first revolutionary pronouncement against Santa Anna's current government, this time in the state of Guerrero. Gaining adherents and military advantage, the dissidents succeeded in stimulating Santa Anna's renunciation of leadership in August 1855. After some minor hesitations, Yucatan followed. Santiago Méndez was appointed interim governor of Yucatan by the new, more liberal Mexican government, his term beginning the following November.[17] He was to hold office until a regular governor was elected under terms of the Mexican reform constitution of 1857. But friction between followers of Méndez and Barbachano was far from extinguished, and the outcome of the Méndez government would be a rivalry that intensified and resulted finally in the separation of Campeche from the state of Yucatan—a move with important repercussions in the Caste War.

The Yucatecan military campaign languished when Vega departed. Although the advance *cantones* were maintained, strength was lowered and morale followed.[18] This was a turning point. Although military campaigns against the rebels would continue, the people of the settled portions of Yucatan began to find other compelling interests.

But for their part, the rebels kept their spirit. On December 20, 1855, a force of two hundred under the former southern leader Zacarías May moved through the northern fringe of *pacífico* territory, killing a number of the pacified former rebels and concluding with a hit-and-run attack on Becanchén. On retiring, they captured firearms and two *pacífico comandantes* from Macanché—one of them Pedro José Ix (see table 8)—and carried them away.[19]

In April 1856 a movement of two Yucatecan military sections from Valladolid and Tihosuco was planned to converge at Nohyaxché and then strike Chan Santa Cruz with their combined force. But it miscarried when the first to arrive was attacked by rebels and virtually annihilated. The survivors limped away, while their successful rebel attackers once more went on to the Sotuta region, where they attacked and largely razed such important places as Yaxcabá, Tibolón, Tiholop, Hacienda Xul, and Kancabdzonot, leaving more than 160 dead. On their return they hit Tihosuco, although without success, for it was strongly defended.[20]

In October, a large rebel force assaulted Tixcacalcupul and destroyed Kaua, where the last dozen inhabitants were killed. At almost the same time a party attacked Tihosuco and was again repulsed, only to return with heavy rebel reinforcements in late November, when they were estimated to number two thousand. This time they were beaten off with help from Valladolid.[21]

In early August of the next year, 1857, rebels said to number only a few less than one thousand attacked Chikindzonot, killed 61, and removed all the saints' images from the church.[22] At about the same time they seriously hurt Ekpedz. In reporting this last attack, Colonel Novelo complained that the force the Yucatecan garrisons then could field was inferior to that of the rebels and that more such attacks must be expected because the *masewalob* had become convinced that the Yucatecan detachments were too weak to chase them. He remarked that only Peto and Tihosuco were strong enough to withstand raids. Desertion by militia members was continuing. Morale was terrible.[23] So the trials of the rebels changed slowly to triumphs.

About this time, rebel prisoners reported that at Chan Santa Cruz construction had begun on a chapel of stone for the miraculous crosses, while the *masewalob* were receiving clothing, guns, and ammunition from Belize.[24] But they also said there were internal divisions at the rebel capital that had led to the imprisonment and possible assassination of rebel leaders Juan Chable and Pedro Dzul, called *gobernador* and second commandant, respectively. This was at the hands of Claudio Novelo, the ranking military commander, who had nevertheless lost prestige by these actions.[25]

While the *masewalob* of Chan Santa Cruz were active against the dwindling strength of the Yucatecan lines, they also expanded southward at the expense of the southern *pacíficos*. In May 1857 the superintendent of British Honduras reported that Indian residents of British territory in the northwest of the colony informed him that "several bodies of Indians of another tribe—the Chichanhas—numbering in the aggregate, according to my informants, 8,000 individuals" had crossed into the colony because of rebel pressure, were cutting brush and timber for their cornfields, and intended to settle.[26] As these new settlers were indicating their willingness to abide by British demands that they spare mahogany trees when slashing their fields, rebels of Santa Cruz allegiance appeared on the lower Río Hondo. In mid-June of 1857 they forcibly occupied a mahogany logging works operated on both sides of the river by the British Honduras firm of Young, Toledo, and Company. Seizing work cattle, people, and property, they refused to leave until they were paid a substantial sum of money, and while there they reportedly crossed the river, violating British territory.[27] The result was that Young, Toledo vacated the Yucatecan shore, despite their claim to be there with legitimate leases, and their work on the British side was only carried on under threat of the levy of further monetary "rents" by the rebels.[28] Such Santa Cruz presence in the area, however, was seasonal rather than continuous.

Massacre at Tekax

As usual, the machinations of Yucatecan politics had repercussions for the Caste War. On July 26 Pantaleón Barrera took office as the first governor elected under provisions of the national constitution of 1857 after an acrimonious session of the legislature in which the voting results were assessed and certified and indications of chicanery were counted against an opposition candidate, Liborio Irigoyen.[29]

Those defeated were not satisfied. On July 4 pronouncements of insurrection came from Maxcanú, Acanceh, Maní, and elsewhere, declaring the election null, proclaiming José María Vargas interim governor pending new elections and Colonel José Dolores Cetina "Commander in Chief of the Army of Restoration of Liberty and the Laws." Although little in the way of strength was behind the revolution in most places, in Tekax the movement took an ugly turn when local people and militia members mutinied against both their commander and an order that he move some of his garrison to the front against the *masewalob*. A rebellious force of five hundred was raised, the deputy commander of local troops was killed, and the commander was forced to run for help. From Mérida troops were dispatched against Tekax under Colonel Manuel Cepeda Peraza. But, hoping to steal the advantage, the Tekax revolutionists attacked Cepeda as he was overnighting at Oxkutzcab, commandeering a dozen captive rebel Indians from the Tekax jail to carry their ammunition. After a four-hour battle the Tekax men were dispersed, but in the meantime Tekax had been occupied by troops dispatched by Colonel Novelo from Peto, leaving the scattered revolutionists no alternative but to melt into the landscape.

But revolution had also reared its head in Campeche, where on August 6 the young firebrand Pablo García spearheaded a movement that by military action and negotiation gained control of the city's powerful defenses. The ensuing proclamation named José María Vargas provisional governor of Yucatan, reduced taxes, changed some requirements of the military conscription law, and named Pablo García as political and military chief of the district of Campeche. The Mérida government had no recourse but to call troops from their regular posts and send them under Cepeda Peraza against Campeche in early September. When they came together, the opposing forces held their attack, hoping for talks, while tying up a substantial proportion of Yucatecan military strength. It was evident that Pablo García felt Campeche could no longer submit to Mérida as a part of the state of Yucatan.[30]

So it came about that on September 13 the rumor flew through Tekax that a force of Campeche insurrectionists had appeared nearby. The small garrison still on duty in the pueblo counted many *campechanos* in its ranks, and it seemed wise to Captain Onofre Bacelis and *jefe político* José María Avila to defuse further revolution by disarming most of their soldiers. On the following morning a formation of three hundred to four hundred armed men with Campeche ribbons on their hats marched into town led by three or four shouting in Spanish, "Don't move! Don't be afraid! We are *pronunciados* of Campeche! *Viva* Campeche! *Muera* Mérida! *Viva* Irigoyen! *Muera* Barrera!"[31] Rather than oppose them, most of the local garrison—disarmed or otherwise—moved to join and mingle in their ranks.

Now mistrustful and unable to get his remaining force to open fire, Captain Bacelis muscled his way from the plaza, leaving pieces of his jacket in the hands of some of the newcomers who tried to stop him, and with a few loyal soldiers fought a retreat down a side street. A group of twenty-two of his men, whom he had sent to the second floor of a stone barracks under Sublieutenant Ramírez, finally opened fire. About this time the invaders turned and cut down the soldiers who had defected to them, making it clear they were no detachment of *campechanos*.[32]

The carnage began. Machetes banged against door fastenings. Old, young, male, and female were dragged from their corners and the machetes swung. Doors opened, stores were sacked and houses plundered, save for a few within musket range of the marksmen on the barracks balcony. The old priest Bartolomé Marín broke his leg jumping fences to escape and was then caught and set in the plaza with a big hat on his head, unable to move, presumably waiting to be hauled away prisoner. By 3:00 PM the streets were colored with blood. Attempts to negotiate with the soldiers in the upstairs barracks brought only continued firing, while members of Ramírez's family were dragged up and butchered in his view.[33] When night came bonfires flared. The wooden supports for the defenders' balcony were torched, but the only immediate effect was to drive the soldiers indoors. The predominantly Indian invaders, now largely drunk on the *aguardiente* manufactured in Tekax, took out guitars and sang little songs around the fires, while the few *vecinos* who remained alive listened from whatever hiding places they had found.

Meanwhile, Bacelis and Avila scoured the settlements in the vicinity, looking for help without success, still not sure who the attackers were. Finally, in Oxkutzcab Bacelis scraped up a force of eighty to one hundred, armed them however he could though finding almost no powder, then raced back toward Tekax. Along the way they met a fleeing, seriously wounded refugee who said the invaders were many and that they were rebel *masewalob*. At the Tekax cemetery in the morning, Bacelis divided his small force to form two flanking parties, while he led a central body. The operation was quick. After one brief volley that used up their ammunition, the rescuers fixed bayonets and charged the plaza from three directions. The invaders, now the worse for a night of debauchery, put up little resistance but fled from the plaza and town to pause briefly on the hills above Tekax, where they could look back at the devastation. With a final yell they departed.

Survivors began to creep from hiding places, some hideously wounded with machete strokes, many having been left for dead by the attackers. The second floor of the barracks had still not collapsed from the fire. The local merchant Anselmo Duarte, whose store and house on the plaza was one of the few entirely untouched buildings, opened his stock of merchandise as charity to those in need. The death toll has been said to exceed one thousand, including many entire families.[34]

Although there was little doubt as the massacre concluded that it was the work of the rebels of Chan Santa Cruz, there is apparent uncertainty in the sources about the identity of the leader of the raid—an incursion that quickly achieved legendary status for its display of rebel cunning and depravity.[35] Not long after the event, however, prisoners taken during other skirmishes provided what seems to be specific intelligence. In one case, a prisoner indicated that the Indian rebels who a month earlier had been taken from prison in Tekax to labor for the local insurrectionists were able to make their way to Chan Santa Cruz with word that Tekax was barely guarded; he also stated that the attackers were not more than four hundred in number— which the Yucatecan officers found unbelievable. A second prisoner, taken very shortly thereafter, testified that he had been part of the Tekax raiding party, confirmed that the strength had not exceeded four hundred, and stated that the leader was the rebel commander Dionisio Zapata,[36] of whom much more will shortly be heard.

Despite the rapidity of their withdrawal from Tekax, the rebels returned to their own region with considerable booty. In early November they were reported on their way south to trade their plunder across the Río Hondo. Although this commerce was delayed because of a record flooding of the river, it was apparently concluded in January 1858, in transactions from which the *masewalob* received a large quantity of gunpowder smuggled out of Belize, most of it by Yucatecan refugees living in the British colony.[37]

Strife in the Cities

Although Yucatecans paused to express horror over Tekax, the dispute between Campeche and the state government was not ironed out. Cepeda Peraza remained camped before the southern port city for a time, and as negotiations led to no resolution the government troops finally occupied some of the outlying sections of Campeche. Artillery duels between the besieging government forces and the defenders in the walled defenses demolished parts of the city. In November the *campechano* insurrectionists resorted to the sea, sending a force of five hundred north under Colonel Andrés Cepeda and accompanied by Liborio Irigoyen, which took the port of Sisal. It then launched a drive against Mérida itself but was soundly trounced. The *campechanos* fled back to Campeche, and the stalemate continued.[38]

Fortunately for eastern Yucatan, the Santa Cruz rebels seemed to have their attention on something besides the outposts weakened by the concentration of Yucatecan military power in the west. On their withdrawal from Tekax the raiders had struck Ichmul and then Sacalaca, where they were fought off, and a month later *masewalob* staged a substantial raid on Chichimilá with three hundred to four hundred men, where they were again repulsed. But besides these, the raids in the region were small. East of Valladolid, the Yucatecan banner was carried chiefly by Onofre Xuluc and a band of *hidalgos* from Tikuch, who attacked rebels east of Mabén.[39]

Meanwhile, Governor Barrera, aware that the insurrections were protesting his election, conceived a plan to mitigate the dispute by yielding the governorship to the military commander of the state. On December 10, 1857, General Martín F. Peraza assumed the powers of the governorship.[40]

And a week later in Mexico, General Félix Zuloaga pronounced against the constitution of 1857, proclaiming the presiding president, Ignacio

Comonfort, dictator. The national congress was dissolved, and Zuloaga arrested Benito Juárez, who held the office of president of the supreme court and vice president. Campeche pronounced for the Comonfort movement and proclaimed a Campeche-dominated junta to rule Yucatan. As Governor Peraza moved to Campeche to talk things over, Mérida also joined the Comonfort movement but came out in support of Peraza for governor and commander in Yucatan. As an aid to negotiations, Peraza withdrew the military force besieging Campeche—this was January 1858—but talks still made no progress.

Then, in that same month in Mexico, Comonfort was forced out and fled to the United States, to be replaced as head of an increasingly reactionary government by General Zuloaga. Juárez, freed from jail by Comonfort before the latter's departure, was declared president under the constitution of 1857 by fugitive members of the elected but dissolved congress. There were then two governments claiming rule; some Mexican states went for Zuloaga, others for Juárez.

Mérida elected to follow Zuloaga. Campeche chose to wait for Mexican matters to stabilize before making a commitment. But the upshot was an agreement to divide the state—not with the eastern rebels, but between Mérida and Campeche.

On May 3, 1858, representatives of Mérida-dominated Yucatan and separatist Campeche signed articles of division, the latter to receive the southwestern part of the peninsula. The mutual frontier was delimited carefully in the west but not so specifically in the east, leaving room for future bickering. Campeche agreed to carry part of the load of the Caste War by paying each month a portion of its state income. Thereafter, Yucatan and Campeche functioned as two de facto states, although the division would ultimately require approval by the central Mexican government.[41]

A New Cross in the East

The cross cult proved too attractive to be confined to a single center. As early as 1851 a Campeche newspaper gave a tantalizing hint of the presence of more than a single such oracle, although the lone account must remain less than definitive. It remarks that

in days past, the forces . . . took prisoner, in one of the lengthy thrusts that are made from the advance camps of the Chenes, a famous Indian impostor who has been passing among the rebels as the son of God, and has directed many ridiculous and extravagant communications to the government of the State . . . and with this artifice has been able to hoodwink the Indians. . . . The new Messiah preached nonsense to them, profaned the sacred ceremonies and rituals of the Church, heard confessions of all the penitents, baptized, blessed marriages, and said masses, for all of which he charged very dearly, since we have seen him in his letter lament that our soldiers in one of their raids have relieved him of those offerings.[42]

Unfortunately, the absence of any sequel that further identifies the supposed captive, reportedly taken in the Chenes district far from Chan Santa Cruz, suggests that this account may be more editorial enthusiasm than truth.

Nevertheless, the possible hint of another messiah of the cross was prophetic. In 1853, while the southernmost dissidents were occupied with thoughts of peace, those *masewalob* holding the region north of Chan Santa Cruz and east of Valladolid had centered themselves at Mabén—presumably the pueblo of that name located only some forty kilometers northeast of Valladolid—where they became the target of government attacks.[43] It was to Mabén that embarrassed revolutionaries under Narciso Virgilio had turned for the troop of four hundred that was then so treacherously gunned down in Tizimín. And, as I noted earlier, among these messengers of enticement had been Baltazar Moguel.

At or near Mabén was a place becoming known as Rancho Santa Cruz, and here in late February of 1854 one Moguel, further identified only as a Yucatecan deserter, was said to be heading the rebel force.[44] In late March, "Chan Mabén, also called *Chan Santa Cruz del Oriente*," or Chan Santa Cruz of the East, was reported burned by Yucatecan troops for the seventh time.[45]

But rebel activity in the area did not flag, for on October 12, 1855, the same rebels attacked Tikuch, only sixteen kilometers from Valladolid, and were driven off with difficulty. This time they were said to be led by "Juan de la Cruz, the major leader of the rebels." And they left pinned to the door of the church a lengthy proclamation of the cross paralleling those earlier written exhortations emanating from *Chan Santa Cruz del Sur*, the Chan Santa Cruz of the South.

Beginning "Jesus Mary, in the name of God the Father, God the Son, and God the Holy Spirit," this proclamation called on all Yucatecans to believe and to obey and announced that the cross would come with its soldiers to repair the world. It closed with the signatory names "Juan de la Cruz of Cobá," "Juan de la Cruz of Chichén," and "Juan de la Cruz of Maní." One must suppose that there were also three drawn crosses, one by each signature, although the published version—a Spanish translation of the Maya original—gives no such indication.[46]

Then in December, far to the east, Yucatecans waylaid a force of *masewalob* reportedly on their way to attack Loché. Among the dead was "Victor Xuluc, patron of the crosses, to whom the rebels pay blind obedience, . . . the evil person who attacked Tikuch"—that is, the Juan de la Cruz of Santa Cruz of the East.

By this time the headquarters of these rebels had been driven by Yucatecan pressure to a place called Chanchén still some thirty-two kilometers farther east—a location that places it essentially on the shore of the Caribbean.[47] Nevertheless, through the next two years harassment closer to Valladolid provoked Yucatecan campaigns, several led by Captain Pedro Acereto, each of which apparently inflicted some damage. In March 1856, Acereto was finding corn to be scarce in the region, although the *masewalob* had plenty of edible root crops. And soon afterward, Loché was attacked and burned, prompting Acereto to undertake a two-month campaign that reached the eastern tip of the peninsula. There in one engagement he fought with a group that he nevertheless presumed from the quality of their armament and spirit to be from Chan Santa Cruz in the south.[48] From February through May of 1857, the garrisons of Tizimín and Valladolid were both active in response to rebel raids, maintaining pressure on the east.[49] In May 1857 Pedro Acereto reported that among the rebels killed on one of his forays was a Nicolás Batún, claimed to be a patron of the crosses, although his seat of cross worship was not identified.[50]

Peace in the North

On December 18, 1858, Governor Irigoyen of the diminished state of Yucatan proclaimed a new amnesty as an inducement to *masewal* surrender. Active rebels would be given until January 20, 1859, to accept the offer; rebel prisoners held by the government were to be released upon their promise to carry copies of the decree to their active compatriots.[51] Although the offer reaped no harvest among the *bravos* of Chan Santa Cruz, it did belatedly bear fruit in the far northeast of the peninsula.

After repeated drubbings administered by Yucatecan patrols to the rebels centered at Mabén, that headquarters had shifted closer to the Caribbean shore. In the years 1856 through 1858, the official newspaper reports fifteen different Yucatecan thrusts from Valladolid or Tizimín into the region extending from Xcan to the coast and northward.[52] Nor were these the only ones.

After the heavy rebel raid on Tikuch of 1855, in which the exhortation of the cross was pinned to the church door, it is evident that the loyal Indian residents were angered enough to take an active part in harrying the rebel enemy. Their indefatigable leader in this was the *cacique* of the pueblo, Onofre Xuluc, who first appears leading a detachment of his *hidalgos* in late 1856[53] and who was thereafter a regular participant in campaigns to the east of Valladolid, reinforcing Yucatecan columns and also leading a number of patrols without Yucatecan supervision.[54]

January 20, 1859, came and went, and the amnesty might as well not have been offered. Much of the fighting was in the vicinity of the again-deserted Yucatecan pueblos of Xcan and Chancenote. But during a long march extending from June 8 to July 23 of that year, and after battling at several points in the area, a force from Tizimín then fought at a place called Nuevo Santa Cruz-Kantunil. This was apparently somewhat farther east and presumably at or in the immediate vicinity of a pueblo called Kantunil that had been first encountered in a sally of September 1856.[55] In this entire region, the rebel forces met were small, with enemies killed and captured being fewer than half a dozen in most engagements. It thus appears that the rebels of the northeast were scattered and relatively weak, although tenacious and obstreperous enough to have caused the abandonment of towns resettled in the early 1850s.

And it was in that region that the amnesty of late 1858 at last brought results. On June 7, 1859, two Indians arrived at Tizimín from the vicinity of Xcan carrying letters datelined Xpacchén and Montaña del Oriente, stating that they wanted to take advantage of the amnesty. Although the period allowed by the original decree had passed, they were told they could proceed if they moved to appoint their peace commissioners quickly.[56] Then on July 4 a delegation of five rebels from Chunchacalhaz, located far to the east near the Caribbean coast, arrived in Tizimín to make a similar plea. They explained that their delay had been caused by the death of their secretary, killed in a Yucatecan raid, for they had no one else who could write. They were given a similar period of grace.[57]

Yet it was only on October 2 that a treaty was finally executed. On that date commissioners representing the state of Yucatan and the *masewalob* concluded their agreement. The rebel commissioners signed as represen-tatives of Kantunil, this evidently after relocating westward to a place of that name and closer to Valladolid, for their signing was authorized by leaders previously identified as being from Xpacchén and Montaña del Oriente.[58]

There were nine articles. The government granted the other side amnesty, freedom from contributions and taxes for three years, the right to reclaim family members within the Yucatecan lines, and aid in moving its people from Kantunil to other established pueblos if requested. For their part the *masewal* parties promised to remain settled at Kantunil for at least a year; to recognize the bishop; to assist in returning servants fleeing from Yucatecan-controlled territory; to both repel and induce the surrender of as many rebels as possible; and to send a list of their own numbers within fifteen days.[59]

This treaty did not embrace all the dispersed rebels of the northeast, but that area was peaceful over the next year almost as far south on the Caribbean coast as Tancah. And additional towns—such as Yokdzonot and Boloná—continued to ask for formal peace, until by 1861 the entire northeast could be declared pacified, and the rebel Santa Cruz del Oriente had ceased to be.[60]

The Condition of the *Masewalob*

The nadir in rebel power had been reached in late 1852, when Colonel Eulogio Rosado could refer to much of the eastern peninsula as pacified, and when even small detachments of government soldiers could move with impunity through rebel territory to round up families and disperse scattered groups of combatants. But rebel recovery was swift. In 1853 and 1854 there were signs of their stiffening resistance in the trouble they gave Yucatecan columns that invaded Chan Santa Cruz. This strength was complemented by Yucatan's withdrawal from an all-out commitment to the war.

It was in these years that the rebel cross cult and war center in Mabén gained prominence. Even though hit repeatedly by Yucatecans in 1853 and 1854, the *masewalob* of Mabén had been able in late 1855 to carry out the spectacular strike against Tikuch, sixteen kilometers from Valladolid. Although the ensuing government attacks forced them to shift their position farther and farther toward the east coast, they continued to draw fire from the garrisons of Valladolid and Tizimín.

By 1857 the swell in rebel strength and morale at Chan Santa Cruz was especially marked: Santa Cruz *masewalob* appeared along the Río Hondo, they displaced *pacíficos* southward into British Honduras, and—most spectacularly—they sacked Tekax. This was to be followed in natural progression by more daring raids. By 1858 most of the towns northeast of Valladolid that had been mentioned by Rosado as repopulated—Chemax, Xcan, Chancenote—were once again abandoned by their *vecino* populations because of rebels raiding from the cult centers in Mabén and elsewhere. Before long the Yucatecan evacuation would extend southward to centers that had been in government hands since late 1848.

During this period there were frequent changes in the titular rebel leadership at Chan Santa Cruz, although the nature of the historical sources does not permit absolute certainty regarding many of the transitions. Those it is possible to reconstruct with at least modest confidence are shown in table 9.

As I noted earlier, the title of governor of the *masewalob* had been assumed by Venancio Pec and Florentino Chan as they took over the place of the assassinated Cecilio Chi, and it was they who were apparently responsible for the killing of Jacinto Pat. But as early as February 1850 there were rumors that Pec and Chan were in disfavor, one apocryphal story being that the British had replaced them with José Isac Pat and Pablo Encalada, another that Pec was thrown out by his own people because he had shown himself willing to make peace under English sponsorship.[61] The death of Venancio Pec was reported in a Yucatecan raid in June 1852, and there is no reason to doubt it. That of Florentino Chan was not similarly reported, but there seems to be no mention of him after mid-1851. Although there is no evidence that the emergence of José Isac Pat was accompanied by any renunciation of positions by Pec or Chan, Pat obviously outlasted them both and in June 1853 was said specifically to carry the title of governor.[62]

While Pec and Chan claimed the dual governorship, Paulino Pech was titled *comandante general*; this is clear in numerous letters addressed to him with that title.[63] His death is reported specifically for May of 1853.

The remaining leaders are less well documented in the positions shown in table 9. Those of Calixto Yam and Juan Chable are based essentially on single testimonies. Claudio Novelo, Bonifacio's son, was reportedly "first commandant" in March 1856, and in December 1857 was said to be the Chan Santa Cruz general, but this last appears in a source based on rumor and containing some obvious misinformation of other kinds.[64] There is also a disappointing hiatus in reports of any sort from 1853 to 1856. Given the information available, however, one must conclude that in these years there was considerable instability in the highest military positions, despite the increase in overall rebel strength. With 1858 and the appearance of Dionisio Zapata, however, the situation stabilized and would remain so for some six years, through 1863.

TABLE 9

Ranking Civil and Military Leaders of the Major Group of Rebels to 1858, with Dates of Appearance in the Literature

Gobernador (month/year)	General or *Comandante General* (month/year)
	Cecilio Chi (7/47–5/49)
	Jacinto Pat (7/47–9/49)
Florentino Chan (7/49–6/51)	Paulino Pech (10/49–5/53)
Venancio Pec (7/49–6/52)	
José Isac Pat (2/50–6/53)	
Calixto Yam (4/54)	
Juan Chable (3/56)	Claudio Novelo (3/56–12/57)
	Dionisio Zapata (1/58)

Note: Dates are those of specific references cited in preceding sections of the text.

Less instability is evident in leaders of the religious cult. Manuel Nauat was succeeded in March 1851 by someone with the surname Puc. In January 1858 the leader of the cult was still a man named Puc,[65] his given name now clearly indicated as Venancio—or Benancio, as it was commonly written in the nineteenth century. As will be seen, this increasing clarity of identification and the stability that would characterize the entire hierarchy of Chan Santa Cruz for the next six years can be attributed to the triumph of the cult in the political arena. It is thus no accident that no *gobernador* was referred to for a lengthy period after early 1856, and there would be none while the cult maintained its political preeminence.

And, finally, after the breakdown of peace talks between the Santa Cruz rebels and the government, after the defection of the southerners and the slackening of the Yucatecans' aggressive effort in the region south of Valladolid, the attitude of the bellicose *masewalob* holding allegiance to Chan Santa Cruz was changing radically. Earlier, they had been rebels fighting a government to whom submission was somehow conceivable, even if totally unacceptable. Now those campesino soldiers carried themselves as warriors locked in steady battle with a mortal enemy who might be vanquished or at least permanently repulsed. The former rebellion had become a war between two opposing forces representing separate governments and roughly equal in strength—at least so long as hostilities remained at the eastern frontier near the *masewal* heartland.

The attitude that the warfare was between equals was not shared by the rebels of the north—those who had paid allegiance to the cross at Mabén and then at derivative centers as the seat of worship was pushed farther and farther toward the Caribbean. To them submission was still something that could be seriously considered. Only those rebels who would not or could not submit remained active, still defying their former world but now committed to separation and independence.

As the people of western Yucatan turned away from the east toward new enterprizes, and as *bravos* and *pacíficos* settled into stable territories and embraced commitments to separate paths of action, a period began during which the instability of *masewal* leadership—an outline of which has just been suggested for Chan Santa Cruz—would be demonstrated unmistakably. Rather than shifts among leaders scarcely perceptible even to friendly outsiders such as some of those in the British colony, there would be changes in factional alignments as wrenching and dramatic in their way as any of those experienced in *dzul* Yucatan since independence.

Nevertheless, despite these changes to come, Chan Santa Cruz was entering a period of autonomy that marked the apex of its power. It is fortunate that for the early years of this period there is the greatest amount of information regarding the internal organization and operation of the separatist *masewalob*, as the next few chapters will show.

Plate 1. The Church in Tepich, 1990. Ruined and reoccupied, the part now in use is roofed with tin. Photograph by the author.

Plate 2. Ruin of the Massive Franciscan Church at Tihosuco, 1990. Half of the original facade stands separately at the right. The rear portion has been returned to service within the past fifteen years. Photograph by the author.

(Opposite top) Plate 3. The Hollow and
Cenote of the Miraculous Cross, 1990.
Now within a park in the modern
municipality of Felipe Carrillo Puerto,
Quintana Roo. Photograph by the
author.

(Opposite bottom) Plate 4. A Clothed
Cross in Eastern Yucatan, 1990.
Photograph by the author.

(Above) Plate 5. Altar Remnant of
the Early Church of the Cross, 1990.
Located by the cenote of the original
miraculous cross in the park at Felipe
Carrillo Puerto, the crosses have been
freshly renewed (or introduced) in blue
paint. A small museum occupies the
building at the right. Photograph by
the author.

(Opposite top) Plate 6. The *Masewal*
Church at Santa Cruz, 1901. Copied
from a deteriorated print in Anonymous
(1901).

(Opposite bottom) Plate 7. North Face of
the Former *Masewal* Church, 1990. Felipe
Carrillo Puerto. Photograph by the
author.

(Above) Plate 8. A *Masewal* Barracks at
Santa Cruz, 1901. Upon General Bravo's
conquest the structure became a field
hospital. Copied from Anonymous
(1901).

Plate 9. Negotiators of the Unsuccessful
Peace Agreement of 1884, Belize. Left to
right, seated, General Teodosio Canto,
masewal General Juan B. Chuc; standing,
Captain Esteban Núñez, unnamed aid to
General Canto, Comandante Crescencio
Dzib, Comandante Aniceto Dzul, Captain
Luis Naal, and trader José Domingo
Andrade. Enclosure to H. Fowler dispatch
No. 2, January 15, 1884 (CO123/172, British
Public Record Office, Kew, Richmond,
Surrey).

Plate 10. General Santiago Pech of Icaiché.
Enclosed with H. Fowler dispatch No. 2,
January 15, 1884 (CO123/172, British
Public Record Office, Kew, Richmond,
Surrey).

Plate 11. General Gabriel Tamay of Icaiché. Enclosed with H. Fowler dispatch No. 2, January 15, 1884 (CO123/172, British Public Record Office, Kew, Richmond, Surrey).

Plate 12. Belize Officials and the Santa Cruz Delegation, January 1892. Most individuals are not identified. Left to right, standing, first is Carlos Melhado of Belize; third Colonial Secretary M. O. Melville; fourth, General José Crescencio Puc; sixth, Governor Sir Alfred Maloney; seventh, an interpreter named López. Seated, center, "a demarara boy who came to Belize as servant to one of the W. I. R. [West India Regiment] officers, and ran away to the S. C. Indians. A saucy ruffian, travelling as Puc's interperter." Enclosed with A. Maloney dispatch No. 20, January 20, 1892 (CO123/198, British Public Record Office, Kew, Richmond, Surrey).

Plate 13. Juan Peón Contreras, on Campaign. His standard is over his left shoulder, while his assistant Dorada cranks the hand organ. Copied from a photo captioned "Juan Bautista, precursor II del Mesías . . . y su discípulo el mestizo Dorada, en su misíon Cívico-Religiosa al territorio de los Indios bárbaros de Tulum, Yucatan, 16 de Marzo de 1887" (Peón Contreras de Elizalde 1888).

(*Opposite*) Plate 14. Military Garrison
at the Ruined Church in Ichmul, 1901.
From this point the final advance on
Noh Cah Santa Cruz began in 1900.
Copied from Anonymous (1901).

(*Above*) Plate 15. The Church and Plaza
at Santa Cruz, 1901. The structure in
right background is a former *masewal*
barracks; behind the tree is the house
attributed to F. Ake. The thatched
structure immediately beyond the
church was described as a dance
pavilion. Copied from a deteriorated
photograph in Anonymous (1901).

(*Opposite top*) Plate 16. Barracks and Plaza at Santa Cruz, 1901. A thatched *masewal* barracks is on the left, the north wing of the church on the right. Both housed units of Bravo's Mexican army. The house in the left background was that of *masewal* governors of Santa Cruz, taken over as quarters by General Bravo. Copied from Anonymous (1901).

(*Opposite bottom*) Plate 17. House of the *Masewal* Governors, then of General Bravo, Santa Cruz, 1901. Before the house are Governor Cantón, General Bravo, and their officers. Copied from Anonymous (1901).

(*Above*) Plate 18. South Side of the Former *Masewal* Church, Felipe Carrillo Puerto, 1977. The small chapel immediately south of the main church was built in the twentieth century by General Francisco May. South of it is a monument to both May and Juan Bautista Vega, erected in 1970. Photograph by the author.

Plate 19. Statue of Cecilio Chi, Tepich, 1990. Photograph by the author.

Plate 20. Sign of Welcome to the Maya Zone near Felipe Carrillo Puerto, 1977. Thatched Mayan houses are across the road on the left. Photograph by the author.

12 / Massacres and Machinations

Although the garrison at Bacalar was progressively weakened through unfailing inattention from Mérida, by January 1858 the commander was able to increase the size of detachments at Chac and Santa Elena on the Río Hondo. This move was apparently in expectation of increased trade in munitions as the dry season brought the reappearance of Santa Cruz representatives at the borders of the British colony, bent on trading the spoils of their raids on Tekax and elsewhere. By now the Yucatecan guards at those posts had set a quota of two kegs of powder per person as the maximum that could pass along the river, regardless of the vessel or the citizenship of its crew, and were stopping and searching all boats.[1] But their efforts to halt the rebel acquisition of gunpowder were futile.

Terror in the South

In January 1858 the Santa Cruz rebels, in greater strength than usual, camped at Pucté (on the Yucatecan side of the Hondo at the lower end of Albion Island) in a well-guarded camp beyond the reach of the Bacalar garrison. This time they brought the miraculous cross with them. Considerable numbers of them crossed the river into British territory but obediently left their arms behind. The leaders were said to be "Benancio Puc . . . the Patron or Headman, also the Padre . . . [in] charge of the Santa Cruz," as well as the generals Dionisio Zapata and Leandro Santos and *comandante* Zacarías May. That they were peacefully inclined toward the British was made clear when one of these leaders traveled downstream to Douglas to apologize to the magistrate for the Santa Cruz troops who had extorted money from British logging works the year before.

At the behest of the colony superintendent, Captain W. Anderson of the Second West India Regiment paid a visit to the Pucté camp on February 9 but found it already abandoned. Based on the size of the encampment and, apparently, interviews with Belizeans across the river, he estimated the

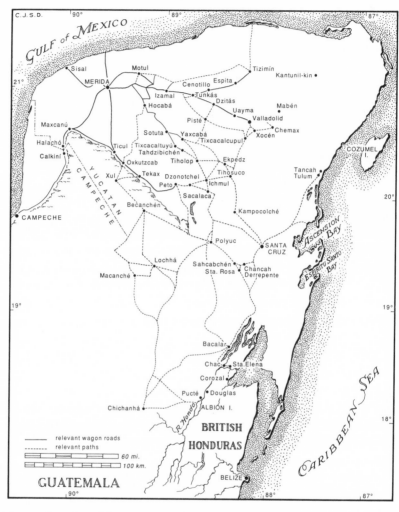

Map 13. Location of Some Events of 1858–64.

force to have been not less than fifteen hundred men, most of them armed. Although sometimes interested in cloth, this time the *masewalob* traded only for powder, giving horses, mules, poultry, hammocks, and other unspecified articles. Anderson was also able to judge the amount of powder they had been able to obtain, for "on examining that part of their Chapel at Pucté which served as a store for Powder and judging from the Marks on the uprights of the Building which were said to indicate the quantity stored, I should estimate it at about 150 kegs or more." The rebels were said to intend a return in May to trade for more powder, and he presumed that they had returned to Chan Santa Cruz for the interim season.[2]

But the *masewalob* had not left the southern region, as Captain Anderson believed. By one account they had been observed by outposts of the Bacalar garrison to be traveling north on the usual track to Chan Santa Cruz. A Yucatecan party followed for a certain distance, and then the garrison relaxed its vigilance.[3]

This was a fatal mistake. In the heavy darkness of the night of February 21 the rebels attacked from all directions and in great number, and Bacalar was gained within less than an hour. Part of the garrison and families managed to escape—some by swimming, a few in a very small canoe, and some by good luck having gone to outlying agricultural properties before the raid.[4] The leader of the attack was reputedly the general Leandro Santos.[5]

Reports flew of atrocities inflicted on the captives, particularly the men, and refugees and relatives of Bacalar residents sent impassioned requests for intercession to the superintendent. Immediately, Superintendent Seymour penned a letter entreating Venancio Puc to spare lives and dispatched it to Bacalar by Captain Anderson.

But this effort was too late—owing to the difficulties of communication between the Río Hondo and Belize City—for Captain Anderson was preceded by James Hume Blake, a magistrate in the northern district and the chief landowner of the town and region of Corozal. On hearing of the plight of the captives, Blake hurried to Bacalar and found that there were around fifty persons still held who might be ransomed. The rebels asked eight thousand dollars for their release, but Blake consented to raise four thousand and—apparently—some gunpowder as well, which seemed to be acceptable. As he retraced his steps to Corozal to raise the money, he left three companions, two Belizeans and an interpreter, as hostages for his return.

Captain Anderson and a small Belizean delegation joined forces with Blake for the latter's second trip to Bacalar, which they reached at about 3:00 P.M. on March 1. When Blake arrived he was asked if he had brought the money and the powder; he indicated the powder would follow. Anderson delivered the superintendent's letter. Given freedom to roam the town, the two negotiators found a stench that came "from the side streets where bodies, stark naked, male and female, in every state of decomposition were being devoured by the dogs and 'John Crows' (turkey buzzards)."[6] Because of the different stages of decay, they concluded that there had been a succession of killings and "that many had been murdered when incapable of resistance [as] the marks of rope around the arms showed."

No rapid answer came to Superintendent Seymour's letter, which had to be placed under consideration by "the Santa Cruz; the idol and oracle of the tribe, consulted in every matter of importance, never seen by laymen and which . . . goes up to Heaven for instructions."[7] Early that night there was a service in which all the *masewalob* assembled in front of the house holding the cross. Two boy attendants—referred to as "angels"—sang before the house, and drums and bugles sounded at certain parts of the song. And then, with Venancio Puc and the angels inside the house with the cross through which God would speak, "the subordinate Chiefs and soldiers knelt outside, and did not rise until the service was over when they crossed themselves and rubbed their foreheads in the dust."

But this was not the end of the cross's performance. Not long before midnight, amid much hurry and bustle, the prisoners were called out, followed by Captain Anderson, who saw them placed in a line before the house of the cross, where *masewal* troops were kneeling in the road. "There were about 40 female prisoners . . . and 12 or 16 men. . . . Cap[tn] Anderson . . . heard a 'squeaking whistling noise' and when it ceased it was announced that the Santa Cruz had demanded a higher ransom for the prisoners."

The new demand was four thousand dollars for the women, three thousand for the men. Blake could not produce so much on the spot but offered to bring the money later. As the sentence of death was pronounced on the prisoners, Anderson raised the matter of the superintendent's letter. After some time, the cross indicated willingness to trade the prisoners for Manuel Perdomo, commander of the Bacalar garrison who had successfully escaped to British territory. Anderson refused, despite pleadings from his own party.

Five or six females were then selected by some younger officers and removed from the prisoners; some men who were goldsmiths or other artisans were taken aside (Anderson reported two, Blake four); and the children were separated and divided among the officers. Of the rest,

a procession was formed, and marched off toward the East gate. First came a strong body of troops then, alternately in Indian file a male prisoner and his executioner, driving with his machete . . . and holding by the rope which confined his arms. Next the women, 35 in number, driven and held in a similar manner passed on, and another body of soldiers closed the rear. The Englishmen . . . saw the white dresses of the women . . . pass through the gate and halt under a clump of trees 150 yards off. . . . Shrieks were heard, but in 10 minutes all was quiet again. . . . The Indians always strip the clothes from themselves and victims during these massacres so there was no blood on their shirts next day.

Soon there appeared a deputation from Venancio Puc who told Anderson he hoped "the Superintendent would not be offended by what had happened. The Spaniards always treated their prisoners in this way. The Indians merely followed a lesson taught them."[8]

The next morning Anderson and his companions were free to go and did so, Blake receiving the return of the cash he had deposited for the ransom but not some merchandise he had included as a part of the total. The *masewal* attitude as they left was described as subdued and somewhat aloof, as rebel soldiers washed their machetes in the lake. Although steady comings and goings had made estimation difficult, Captain Anderson concluded that there had been as many as sixteen hundred soldiers in the place at the same time, but of these about one-third were mere boys. And "one or two of the officers . . . [were] Mexican Spaniards. One a negro."[9]

At that time, the *jefe político* of Bacalar, who was also among those who escaped, could list 123 persons known to be dead. Adding the missing, he estimated the total of those killed to be around 250.[10]

Uneasy Aftermath

In the weeks after the massacre, Bacalar was almost deserted by its rebel captors, presumably because their attention was turned farther north: In the early morning of April 1, 1858, a force of about eight hundred of them invaded Valladolid. Led by Claudio Novelo, Crescencio Poot, Pedro Dzul, and Juan Balam, and guided by two deserters from the local government battalion, they penetrated into the barracks itself. Repulsed with the greatest difficulty and considerable Yucatecan losses, the *masewalob* entrenched themselves at the pueblo Xocén, over which desultory fighting occurred for the next day or so.[11] Finally burning Xocén, they harried the region around Chemax for several days, while the weakened Valladolid garrison struggled to field a force capable of clearing even the city's outskirts.[12]

Not until late August was there another major incursion from Chan Santa Cruz. Then, early one morning all of Peto's outposts were passed successfully by *masewalob* who reached the corners of the plaza before they were discovered. After three hours' fighting they were driven off with a reported loss of at least forty men. Pursuing government patrols found forty-eight or forty-nine corpses left from the massacre of a nearby pueblo. The few *masewalob* who were taken testified that this raid had been led by Crescencio Poot, Claudio Novelo, and four other commanders.[13]

Nor did civil disturbances within Yucatan cease. Liborio Irigoyen had given his support to Juárez, rather than Zuloaga, for president, in opposition to the line taken by Governor Peraza. True to form, insurrection followed. On September 10, Pedro Acereto proclaimed in Uayma and marched on Valladolid with a small force—an act reportedly not so much from political bent as from anger at having been removed from his command because of complaints that as interim commander at Valladolid he had misappropriated six hundred pesos intended to pay his troops. But when he took Valladolid two days later, his force augmented by deserters and malcontents, he issued a statement proclaiming Liborio Irigoyen governor in place of Martín Peraza. Immediately three colonels—two of whom were the Bacalar heroes José Dolores Cetina and Isidro González—pronounced in support of Irigoyen and took control of Maxcanú. A similar pronouncement followed in Tizimín, and insurrectionist troops moved on Izamal. Other pronouncements then were issued in Ticul, Tekax, Peto, and various other points in the south. On October 1, Peraza renounced the governorship and two days later Irigoyen took possession of it.[14]

Fortunately for the Yucatecans, the *masewalob* took little immediate advantage of this altercation despite the weakening of the frontier posts by Acereto's movement, although they did direct some disruptive effort toward the *pacíficos* in the south and made minor incursions over much of the frontier. But on December 20 a party raided past Tixcacaltuyú to Sotuta, taking and holding that town for five hours during which there was much looting but, surprisingly, no dead or wounded among Yucatecans. In the same raid, however, more than one hundred people were killed around Tahdzibichén, Tixcacal, and Tiholop.[15]

By now, ten years of warfare had passed, and pueblos even a short distance east of the old colonial heartland of Yucatan still could not relax into the security of former days.

Insights of 1858

Despite an estrangement from the British that followed the uncomfortable events at Bacalar, the *masewalob* were not ill disposed toward them.[16] Indeed, in a humanitarian vein the rebels allowed two of the children taken in their raid on Bacalar to be ransomed.

This benevolence followed upon considerable effort by James Hume Blake and upon repeated visits to Chan Santa Cruz by two British Honduran traders to the rebels. The two boys ransomed were a son of Leonardo Canto and the young José María Rosado, aged ten and eight, respectively, the latter of whom more than fifty years later was to write his remembrance of his stay. Reports generated by the negotiations—which of necessity passed through Bacalar—indicated that the now partially demolished town had been converted into a purely military post, without resident families but with a rebel garrison of about four hundred, where the victims of the February capture still lay unburied in the places they were killed.

The rebels had selected eight-year-old José María Rosado and five others from among children of the Bacalar prisoners because they could read and write at least minimally. They were apportioned among Venancio Puc, who was patron of the cross—or *tatich*, as he was called—and four generals. José María was taken to the rancho of General Leandro Santos and later to *Santo Cah*, "Holy Town," as Chan Santa Cruz was termed, where he gave two of the Santos children daily lessons over the next five months.

The Santos rancho, apparently a perquisite of generalship, was cared for by some twenty-five rebel men with their families, although it was implied that the general also worked in the fields at times of heavy labor, such as when the slash was burned. The young Rosado reported that the Santos house at *Santo Cah* was a large stone structure with a thatched roof, enclosed by a covered veranda, and surrounded by a yard and orchard, with a constructed well nearby. During his stay, he said, a large masonry church was being built, chiefly by prisoner stone masons who were fed by the generals, each of whom provided rations for a week's time in rotation. Rosado reported that the church was finished by the time of his release and was quoted as saying that "the people . . . have formally renounced the religion of their conquerors."[17]

Of the cult and its functioning, José María Rosado said many years later that

an old Indian called Tata Naz (Nazareo) was in charge, and as a priest (under the Tatich) he led the prayers and rosary. The four Generals and all the Officers met once a week . . . to hear the word and command of the Santa Cruz, who spoke through the mouth of Tata Naz' son in a fine thin whistle, always at midnight behind a curtain near the Altar, all in darkness. Only the Generals and Officers were allowed in, the soldiers and women outside waiting to hear through one of the Generals what the orders were from the Cross. A Captain from General Santos once related to me what took place at one of these meetings: after closing doors and extinguishing the lights, the Tatich called out the names of the Generals and Officers who were present. Any absentees from the previous meeting had to give a satisfactory reason; if the reason was not approved by the Tatich, the offender was ordered to send a quantity of corn to headquarters (the Tatich's house) next day.—Then a small brass bugle sounded, a loud noise like the flopping of a huge bird was heard. The congregation all went flat on their faces striking their breasts saying "We believe in the Santa Cruz who will talk to us." Then the cross, or rather Tata Naz's son, started in a sharp whistling voice saying: "My people and beloved chiefs. I have just now returned from a long excursion in the Capital and principal military guarded towns of Yucatan.[18]

The voice of the cross then proposed a raid on Valladolid, and all dispersed after a rousing cheer for the cross and the *tatich*.

The next day a grand meeting of all the officers and soldiers took place at the plaza of "Chi Qui Whi" in front of the first General's (Don Pantaleón Zapata) house and arranged that the second General Don Crescencio Poot would take command of the expedition, assisted by the third General Don Leandro Santos, and the fourth General Don Bonifacio Novelo to follow as reserves, leaving the first General to guard the Santo Kah. . . . All the women were ordered to prepare a certain amount of *totopostes*, baked thin round corn cakes about seven inches in diameter, strung in rolls of 200 each, and a quantity of baked dry ground red pepper, wrapped in corn thrash, rolls of about 2 ounces each. This is their army rations and if kept dry can be used at all times.[19]

That raid was a fiasco. The army spent its time at a large rancho where anis was being distilled into liquor and were caught by the Yucatecans. The officers responsible for the loss were whipped. Not long afterward a captain was executed by machete for taking another man's wife.

All Baptisms and marriages are performed by Tata Naz, the former to infants using the prescribed words and pouring water on the head, the latter simply saying in Maya "I marry you in the name of the Holy Cross Amen." The greatest crimes punishable by death were blaspheming against the Santa Cruz and meddling with another man's wife. Once a prisoner musician was killed for telling some of the Indians not to take the Cross for God. . . . At another meeting my

Gral. Leandro Santos was drunk and when the cross was talking, shouted "Stop talking Braulio (Tata Naz's son who acted for the cross) we have enough of sorcery." He was immediately whipped and put under arrest, tried the next day by the Tatich and the other 3 Grals, and made to pay 25 barrels of corn, cautioning him if such offence was made [again] immediate death would follow.[20]

Yet even with the tyranny of the cross, decision making was not entirely centralized. Traders came frequently from British Honduras, selling "salt, gunpowder, shot, and other goods . . . to the chiefs. The soldiers were not allowed to buy anything direct but only through the chiefs." One of these traders, José María Trejo, had worked quietly to obtain the release by ransom of the two boys, and the second, Lorenzo Lara, completed the negotiations, only to find that not only the approval of the Tatich and Santos was required but that of all the generals. A more homely diffusion of power is illustrated by the fact that Santos, in order to obtain agreement from the other generals, whom he regarded basically as enemies, had his wife work through their spouses to apply domestic pressure.

Once acquiescence was obtained, there was a formal session with the cross in which young Rosado was taken into the church and interrogated.

The lights were put out and in the darkness I heard a sound as if a storm was nearing; the thin, loud whistling voice started . . . saying: "You young . . . white face prisoner listen to me. Our beloved general Don Leandro Santos in whose custody you are has pleaded for your freedom, asking us to allow you to return to your father. . . . Now tell me with all truth, do you wish to go? or do you wish to remain with us?" My reply through the General who was then holding my hand, was as he had instructed me, "I wish to remain with you. I do not wish to go, as I am well treated by Gral. Don Leandro Santos." Then the cross said in a very loud and angry voice, "You have not told me the truth, I know the sentiments of your heart, that you are anxious to go to your father. I will let you go but you will now be punished for telling a lie and trying to deceive me." I . . . received 10 switches, during which I screamed for mercy.[21]

On November 20, 1858, his lacerated back soothed with warm pig lard applied by Leandro Santos's wife, he and the trader Lara left Santo Cah—or *Noh Cah* (great town, i.e., city), as it was also called—for home. Upon his safe arrival José María's hair was cut to remove the lice, he was washed well, and a doctor treated him for malaria and possibly hepatitis, for his "complexion was yellow, . . . stomach puffed up and . . . liver swollen."[22]

The Sale of Rebel Prisoners

Despite success in pacifying the rebels of the extreme northeast, for Yucatan the year 1859 was troubled. Revolts against the Irigoyen government began in February with a pronouncement in Mérida, which was quashed, and continued with a movement in Peto, also beaten, and then in Cenotillo, in Espita, in Motul, in Izamal—not all inspired by the same dissidents, but all put down. Yet Irigoyen's enemies—many of whom he had banished to Havana when he took office—continued to plot. There is an indication, albeit not entirely unambiguous, that some of these enemies were maintaining themselves and funding their revolutionary actions by contracting for rebel prisoners to be shipped to Cuba.[23]

As I noted earlier, the shipment of captured rebels to Havana had been first attempted in 1849 while Miguel Barbachano was governor, a time when the war was in full swing and prisoners, often starving, filled the jails. By shipping these captives to Cuba where they were forced to serve a certain number of years as indentured labor, some Yucatecans saw a chance to clear their jails and provide funds desperately needed by their government. But the humanitarian outcry had been loud both at home and abroad, and the sales were aborted almost as soon as they were begun. Nevertheless, other attempts followed.

In July 1853 the Mexican consul in Havana advised Mexico that the Cuban government had received a request for permission to import Yucatecan Indians in the same way that Asian workers were being imported. The Mexican government protested this vigorously, declaring that any such importation to Cuba amounted to slavery. Although the exchange of legalistic arguments appeared to go nowhere, the captain general of Cuba apparently agreed reluctantly not to approve the importation.

Whatever this refusal might amount to, it came a little late, for already in June a Belizean Creole had reported to British Honduran authorities that he had just returned from a voyage as crew member of the *Jenny Lind*, a small vessel that at the behest of a resident of the island of St. Thomas named Juan Bautista Anduce (or Anduze or Andruze, all of which appear in documents) had sailed from Belize in early May. At the bays of Espíritu Santo and Ascención, rebels were enticed on board to trade, then seized and taken to Isla Mujeres, where they were transferred to Cuban fishing boats and hauled to Havana. When Anduce was arrested in Belize he was found to be carrying a letter from his Havana contact, one Francisco Martí y Torrens, in which Martí offered twenty-five dollars for adult males, seventeen dollars for adult females and adolescent males, and eight dollars for boys under twelve and girls under sixteen. Anduce was tried in British Honduras for violation of antislavery laws and sentenced to four years' hard labor. Mexico, once informed, joined Britain in complaints that finally led to some action in Cuba in early 1854. Of the thirty-six persons kidnapped, five had died by then, twenty-seven were returned to Yucatan at Martí's expense, three elected to remain in Cuba as free laborers, and one went to Spain as a paid servant. Martí was never prosecuted, however.[24]

Nevertheless, President Santa Anna, whose own government had protested the kidnappings by Anduce so strongly, approved in early 1854 a request by the Bavarian consul in Havana, acting as representative of a local firm, for the importation of Yucatecan Indians to Cuba as indentured laborers under conditions that included the following: that the agreement should be freely contracted by the laborers for a period of five years; that they should be properly passported by Mexico or Yucatan; that they be allowed (with some further conditions attached) to take wives and children with them; and that the Mexican consul in Cuba should have free access to them.[25]

The traffic in rebel prisoners evidently then resumed, although details are scarce.[26] Following the fall of the Santa Anna government in 1855, various Yucatecan administrations continued to be attracted to the idea, and whereas information remains relatively scanty, such traffic seems to have been increasingly engaged in for gain by private Yucatecans. During the governorship of Pantaleón Barrera a contractor offered to provide the government with both cash for expenses and muskets for the war— promising forty pesos per adult male, twenty-five per female. The contract was completed under Governor Martín Peraza, when Yucatan received altogether twenty-five thousand pesos and some muskets. By the same time, the traffic in orphaned children—rebel or otherwise, both Indian and mestizo— had become extensive, with some members of principal Mérida families assuming guardianship of orphans ostensibly to better their condition but in reality to market them in Cuba.[27] Indeed, under Peraza some of the adults shipped off were reportedly not Yucatecans at all, but Mexicans who were found on the peninsula, even including a few Mexican soldiers assigned there.[28]

Other contractors increased the offer to Governor Irigoyen, who finally agreed to accept money in return for prisoners at a price three times as high as contracted by Peraza, but he also submitted the arrangement to the Mexican government of President Juárez for its response. That response was stingingly negative and was accompanied by a threat to have the British patrol the Yucatecan coast to prevent the practice.[29] But when the letter arrived Irigoyen was no longer governor, and an administration shortly to come to power was willing to ignore the Juárez stand.

It was fortunate for Yucatan that Irigoyen had acted so successfully to put down the rash of insurrections of early 1859, for in July of that year the Chan Santa Cruz rebels—choosing what this time was for them the absolutely wrong moment, a moment when Yucatecan frontier garrisons were again on duty—struck hard at Yaxcabá, Tiholop, Ichmul, and Tihosuco and were soundly defeated at all four.[30] But the following month, civil disruption resumed, as José Dolores Cetina and Pedro Acereto—commanders of the southern and eastern sectors of the Yucatecan front, respectively—pronounced against the government and in favor of a ruling junta to consist of Pablo Castellanos (president of the supreme court), Agustín Acereto (Pedro's father), and one other, all of whom would yield to Castellanos as interim governor. He would then observe the federal constitution of 1857. Cetina was designated commander in chief of the campaign against the rebels. Rather than confront the substantial military force involved, Irigoyen left the government to Castellanos on August 24.[31]

One of the strongest stands of Castellanos was to comply with the Mexican government's refusal to countenance the sale of indentured laborers: he imposed severe penalties on those who engineered such contracts, he prohibited the issue of passports that could be used to transport orphans and other children, and he wrote to the governor of Campeche to ask him also to refuse such passports.[32] But Castellanos had not long to rule. On October 1, the Mérida garrison pronounced in general support of the liberal Irigoyen, called for the removal of Castellanos and Cetina from their positions, and committed the mistake of naming Agustín Acereto as interim holder of both the governorship and the military command. On October 15, Castellanos stepped down and Acereto took over the government. The sale of rebel captives was not only resumed but was stepped up, despite the stand of the national government.[33]

A Campaign to Chan Santa Cruz

With a native of eastern Yucatan as governor, hope for some decisive action against the rebels was high, and in fact one of Governor Acereto's first acts was to amass a force to strike a decisive blow at Chan Santa Cruz—a move that lost some popular enthusiasm, however, as rumors circulated that his main object was to obtain prisoners for the Cuban trade.[34] In any event, Agustín Acereto moved his government temporarily to Valladolid for the campaign, and his son Pedro organized the force that would be commanded by himself and staffed by young officers, almost none of whom had experience handling large forces against the *masewalob*.

Whatever the situation, efforts to collect troops were the most successful in years. In the first days of January 1860, a column of 2,211 Yucatecan soldiers and 650 *hidalgos* left Valladolid, moved to Tihosuco, the most advanced post still held by the government. Moving on to Kampocolché, where they arrived January 7, they then plunged into the wilderness. It was only when they had advanced to within six kilometers of the rebel capital that they heard the explosions of warning bombs and received their first fire. Efficiently enough, they thrust into the *masewal* capital with their main force and two flanking sections, gaining the plaza on January 11 after only light resistance. Those who knew the rebel capital found it had changed since the times of earlier Yucatecan occupations, the last of which had been in 1855.

> What the rebels have made of this town is admirable, for there is a fine church, almost finished, of masonry, two fine houses with arcades inside and out, 29 houses of rubble masonry, many of thatch, and seven open wells, with the streets being very well delineated.[35]

But the ease of their entry should have put the Yucatecans on their guard, for the rebels were up to their old tricks. As the plaza was secured a cavalry unit of one hundred men dashed through the town and out the other side in hot pursuit of retreating rebels, only to be ambushed and cut off. They barely fought their way back to safety. Two days later Colonel Narciso Virgilio—he of the massacre of Mabén rebels at Tizimín—moved out with a force of five hundred on a foraging run to the south and had to cut his way back. Other thrusts brought the same story: easy out, tough return. Although on one of these maneuvers Yucatecans gleefully, if fancifully, reported the death of the rebel general Dionisio Zapata,[36] morale suffered as they found themselves boxed up in Chan Santa Cruz. A single terse, noncommittal message that Pedro Acereto managed to dispatch—dated January 23—was all the news that arrived in Mérida while the expedition was in the field. A personal letter from Virgilio, dated the same day and presumably sent out at the same time, reported that since the occupation they had suffered eighty-seven casualties, "and the Indians are still in front of us, that is to say we are half besieged, [with] our soldiers intimidated and the Indians very strong in their breastworks, we have not been able to disperse them. Pray to God for us because who knows if we shall return. . . . Goodbye everyone."[37]

On February 15 some six hundred survivors, their commander among them, began to limp into Tihosuco. The remnant army was immediately demobilized and dispersed.[38] There was never an official report.

What had happened? As the historian Baqueiro reconstructed events, and as a survivor would later report, Acereto had tried first to withdraw toward Ascension Bay but found the way impassable against rebel strength. Next, moving out toward Tihosuco at dawn, the Yucatecans traveled without trouble until 10:00 A.M., and then were hit hard, and hard again.

The vanguard, unable to hear bugled commands over the din of rebel shouts and gunfire, broke and scattered, and the rearguard soon did the same. The center, around Acereto himself, held longest, but Acereto's horse bolted and so, finally, did everyone else. The rout surged west toward Kampocolché—roadblocks and ambushes met, arms thrown aside, troops scattered in panic, men captured or cut down by machete. The few survivors straggled into Yucatecan territory.

Losses were more than two thousand muskets, nearly as many men, with powder and shot, artillery, horses, and—one must add—the deserving Narciso Virgilio. In the opinion of the historian Baqueiro, "this was the most ignominious and bloody defeat of Yucatecan arms."[39] According to information received in British Honduras, the captives who were marched off to Chan Santa Cruz included an entire "military band, bandmaster and all, . . . and the young Indians are taught the bugle and drum."[40]

Peninsular Rivalries

After the downplayed defeat there was no halt in the sale of rebels—or at least of captives passed off as rebels. Governor Agustín Acereto promptly entered into a new agreement to deliver prisoners to Ascension Bay or other points along the east coast, where they would be picked up by Cubans, in return for 170 pesos for males aged sixteen to fifty, 120 pesos for females the same age, and 80 pesos for girls aged ten to fifteen. People were actually delivered, although where they came from was never made clear. One estimate held that during Acereto's administration one hundred Yucatecans were sold each month.[41]

In large part it was this canker that led to scurrilous newspaper stories and to resistance against Governor Acereto and his obviously tyrannical leanings, which in turn brought the imprisonment or exile of most of his opponents. Because his antagonists were welcomed in Campeche by the liberal and hotheaded Governor Pablo García, Acereto in August signed a decree refusing admission at Sisal of imports from that state, and soon after the Yucatecan Council of State refused to call elections on the ground that to do so without including the people of Campeche within the electorate would imply a negation of the opinion always held in Yucatan that separation of the state of Campeche had been unconstitutional.

Governor García deployed troops at his border and armed some vessels to patrol the Yucatecan coast, almost immediately capturing a boat with thirty Indians bound to Cuba for sale.[42] When Yucatan seized a Campeche vessel in retaliation, Campeche occupied the Yucatecan port of Sisal. At the same time, the Yucatecan Lorenzo Vargas pronounced against Acereto, and war was on. But while Pedro Acereto's troops were being called in from the east to put down the insurrection around Ticul, one of Agustín Acereto's military guard defected and released Acereto's political prisoners, who then took over the Mérida citadel and imprisoned Acereto and most of his supporters—except for José Dolores Cetina, who, as usual, made himself scarce. As an interim government formed to support Vargas for governor, Pedro Acereto retreated first to Izamal, where in talks he declined an offer of safe passage to Cuba. He slipped home to Valladolid, hid his arms, dispersed his men, and faded into the northeastern countryside.

Not more than a month after his triumph, Vargas called constitutional elections. The candidates who emerged were himself and Irigoyen. Interestingly enough, however, Irigoyen and Pedro Acereto had been in negotiations—despite the fact that the liberal Irigoyen had been jailed by Pedro's reactionary father for a year and more—and before the election could be held, in January 1861, Pedro Acereto surprised and captured Valladolid and pronounced, apparently with the aim of making Irigoyen governor.[43] He was initially successful, gained Izamal, and then modified his unpublished plan so as to proclaim himself, rather than Irigoyen, governor and commander in chief. A government attack was turned into a smashing victory for Acereto, and Vargas fled to Campeche while his supporters scattered in various directions, leaving Mérida without government. The void was filled when Manuel Cepeda Peraza, commanding the Mérida garrison in the citadel, released Agustín Acereto from jail and proclaimed him governor. Son Pedro's pronouncement was immediately nullified.

To give the impression that he was at heart a republican—which he was not—Agustín Acereto this time called for immediate elections in which he ran essentially unopposed and was elected to the office he had twice gained by coup. This was in April 1861, at which time despite the landslide for Acereto the new state congress was heavy with elected liberals, and the stage was set for continued strife.[44] To cap it all for Agustín, on May 6, after Yucatecans had taken the matter to the national congress, President Juárez decreed an end to the export of rebel captives from Yucatan under any pretext, with guilty parties subject to the penalty of death, the seizure of their ships, and the imprisonment of their accomplices for one to ten years. The British were asked to give assistance with maritime patrols.[45]

Dzul World of the 1850s

The economy of the peninsula had been virtually annihilated by the war. Hostilities wreaked physical destruction on the growing agricultural industry that lay in the path of the spreading battlefield, especially the sugar plantations concentrated both north and south of the Sierra and north of Valladolid. A less direct, although equally devastating, effect was wrought by the total military mobilization, which sucked up productive labor. Between 1848 and 1851 all able-bodied *vecino* males over age sixteen were required to enlist in active military units, which accounted for sixteen thousand to seventeen thousand men—11 percent and more of the *vecino* population as enumerated in the 1840s. In addition, the grant of *hidalgo* status and permanent remission of taxes to Indians who served attracted more than two thousand,[46] most of them from western Yucatan, the location of the most stable and productive haciendas. Agricultural production dropped, and imports of maize climbed. As these effects became unmistakable, recruitment of *hidalgos* was curtailed, and soon decrees specifically exempted all hacienda workers, *vecino* or Indian, from most war-related service.[47]

Despite these efforts to restore production, the war and the political machinations accompanying it resulted in a political economy that was tottering on the brink of a dissolution barely staved off by forced loans and imposts collected from Yucatecans who could pay, modest aid begged from Mexico, and a de facto moratorium on payment of public debts. The armed forces served almost always without pay, and officers frequently resorted to personal credit to feed their troops.

It is hardly surprising that desertion from the army, including its *hidalgo* auxiliary, became a chronic problem, as men went home simply to eat. It was because of this economic stress that General Vega had reorganized the army in 1851, expecting that the "sedentaries"—those troops temporarily excused from active military duty—would provide badly needed services in the economic sphere. The amount of corn imported did drop. There was no appreciable decline in the pressure to desert, however.[48]

As I noted, the demographic impact of the war made itself felt in the shortage of manpower. Although some figures adduced for losses are too high to be credible,[49] there is somewhat wider agreement that the loss was at least approximately equivalent to the difference between the figure of slightly more than the 500,000 population enumerated in the 1840s and the figure announced in a census in 1862.[50] These census results are recapitulated in table 10, which also summarizes the unequal loss by region—the east (around Valladolid) and south (the Sierra) suffering the most. Altogether, the figures bespeak a reduction in population of no less than 180,000 persons—more than one-third of those who had been counted in 1846.

The population loss was owed to a number of factors. There were, first of all, the *masewalob* who had defected, which in 1862 included both rebels still active around Chan Santa Cruz and the *pacíficos* who, according to the terms of their peace agreements, were outside both the economy and the limits of the census of that year. This *masewal* total was estimated earlier at about 50,000 people, perhaps slightly more. To it must be added campesino emigration, including both those who had been shipped to Cuba—a figure estimated at about 2,000 in total[51]—and those who fled south into British Honduras or Guatemala. This latter total, including many former rebels, must reach at least 10,000 and was perhaps considerably higher.

The remainder of those unaccounted for is still more than 100,000 persons, and unfortunately this figure cannot be broken down further with any precision. Heavy emigration began in 1848, primarily *vecinos* who headed for Carmen, Tabasco, Cuba, and elsewhere; a few moved also to the islands such as Cozumel and Isla Mujeres off the northeast coast of the peninsula. There is evidently no way to estimate the total number of these emigrants, just as it is not reasonably possible to assess the number still remaining to be mentioned—that is, the casualties both of the war with the *masewalob* and the hostilities between factions of *dzules*, a figure that certainly totaled many thousands.

Yet in spite of the loss of productive capacity and the massive reduction in population, the 1850s was a decade in which economic regrowth of the peninsula began. Although in 1851 the area that had been replanted in sugarcane was less than thirty hectares, by the end of the decade it had

TABLE 10

Loss of Registered Peninsula Population, 1846–62

Region	Population 1846	1862	Numerical Loss	Percentage Loss
State of Yucatan				
Northwest	92,200	82,900	9,300	9.9
Central	104,900	76,000	28,900	27.6
South	127,800	52,100	75,700	59.2
East	97,500	35,500	62,000	63.6
Offshore Islands	—	1,700	(1,700)	—
State of Yucatan, total	422,400	248,200	174,200	41.2
State of Campeche	82,200	72,000	10,200	12.4
Total, peninsula	504,600	320,200	184,400	36.5

Sources: Figures are rounded from Rodríguez Losa (1978) and Suárez Molina (1977a, 1: 44–50), who use the 1846 population figures without correction. Use of 575,000 for the total population in 1847 (see chap. 5) increases the total loss to about 255,000, or 44 percent. On the other hand, there is no real certainty of the accuracy of the 1862 total (see Rodríguez Losa 1978).

grown to two thousand—half the area that had been in production when the war began.[52]

But the long-term importance would lie with the growth of henequen cultivation. Since pre-Columbian times the production of cordage from the agave plant known as henequen had been a regular, if minor, Yucatecan industry, providing through the colonial era a small export of products of fiber rasped by hand from the fleshy matrix of the leaves. Henequen export was encouraged after independence. And despite the labor-intensive means of production, by the mid-1840s it was the second most important agricultural product—after sugar—and accounted for about 14 percent of the monetary value of exports.[53] As environmental luck had it, the region left most securely to the Yucatecans by the Caste War was the dry northwestern corner of the peninsula where the henequen plant did particularly well. In 1851, there were already more than a thousand hectares in henequen production, and the outlook for export of henequen fiber was promising.

Despite the burden of military adventures in the 1850s, during that decade local inventors devised the first successful means for removing the henequen fiber mechanically and in 1859 had hooked one of the decorticators to a steam engine. By 1860 there were twenty-six hundred hectares in henequen, and the area would increase sixfold in the next decade, to literally explode after the 1870s—following the development in the United States of the mechanical harvester that needed twine to bind bundles of grain and with the sudden availability of foreign capital to spur the growth of a monocrop economy.[54]

This was an economic development unaffected by the separation of Campeche and the southwest of the peninsula that occurred in 1858. Campeche, with its new boundary largely removing it from immediate contact with active rebels, began an independent life on the coast and in the forests of the southwest. Mérida was left free to concentrate on the northwest. In 1860 both states found themselves able to face away from the *masewalob*, who had successfully defended the forests of eastern Yucatan and were determined to maintain their separation from the *dzul* world.

13 / Cross Triumphant, Cross Deposed

The early 1860s brought an increase in knowledge of the internal workings of the cross-dominated society of Noh Cah Santa Cruz (as the *masewalob* called their capital) but only while events were changing those workings significantly. The period also brought political connivance that threw Yucatan directly into the arms of the French military force that would seat Maximilian on the throne of Mexico.

The Cross Speaks to the English

In January of 1860, a force of several hundred Santa Cruz soldiers had appeared on the lower Río Hondo to collect rents but then left suddenly— apparently upon hearing that Pedro Acereto was invading their capital.[1] Strangely enough, during the months of Yucatecan political confusion that followed Acereto's defeat the *masewalob* were not especially active.

In June a party appeared again on the Hondo, this time in strength of one thousand or more. While a portion went on to attack the *pacíficos* at Chichanhá, taking prisoners, others took the opportunity to claim rents from residents of British Honduras who farmed or otherwise worked on the Yucatecan side.

In the course of these bill-collecting operations, armed rebel soldiers crossed the Hondo into British territory at least three times. At one occasion some twenty took a prisoner and dragged him to their side of the river where he was held until he made arrangements to pay the claimed rent. On another, an estimated one hundred, including the *patrón* of the cross and the officers Dionisio Zapata, Leandro Santos, and Zacarías May, crossed and appropriated the boat and goods of a Belizean trader. And, again, a group of twenty-two crossed and forced a Belizean boatman to provide them passage along the river and to Bacalar, although they did pay him for the trip.[2]

Incensed, the British superintendent immediately dispatched an officer to Bacalar to convey a letter addressed to Venancio Puc, the *patrón* at Noh Cah Santa Cruz, strongly protesting the crossings of armed men into the colony.[3] Although this occurred in early summer, no response was received until the following February, when a bland apology from Puc admitted that his men had gone "to the English side armed, . . . but committed no disturbance," and professed friendship.[4] According to information received from a Belize resident who had recently traded in Chan Santa Cruz, the decision to apologize was made on the strength of an order of the cross to do so. Three of the four generals, he said—Dionisio Zapata, Leandro Santos, and one Bernardino Chi—acquiesced and signed the letter, but the fourth— Bonifacio Novelo—objected strenuously and was sentenced by the cross to fifty lashes for insubordination.[5]

But scarcely was the weak apology received when the British limits were again violated. Five *pacíficos* crossed the Hondo with cattle and a horse they claimed as their property bound for sale in Corozal, but which a Santa Cruz rebel commander asserted had been stolen from him. As the *pacíficos* fled, twenty-five armed rebel soldiers crossed the Hondo and captured five of the animals, which they returned across the river. The men then turned and fired their muskets helter-skelter at the British side.[6] This also brought a prompt remonstrance from the superintendent, Captain Thomas Price,[7] whose letter to Venancio Puc was direct and demanded an apology. It ended, "You will excuse me, in presence of your recent delay in answering my despatches, in now stating to you, on behalf of Her Majesty the Queen of Great Britain, that I require a written reply within one month from this day—and further that, if delayed beyond that day, or if not satisfactory, I shall take the most effectual measures to obtain complete redress."[8]

Furthermore, the letter would be delivered by hand by a pair of British officers, who would await a reply. Two lieutenants, James J. Plumridge, Third West India Regiment, and John Thomas Twigge, Royal Engineers, were deputed, leaving Belize City on March 17. At Corozal they hired as interpreter one Arcadio Orío—the only suitable person who could be induced to go with them, despite lucrative pay. In rebel-held Bacalar they were able to hire a second interpreter, the professional trader José María Trejo,[9] who claimed familiarity with the road, with Chan Santa Cruz, and with Venancio Puc. Sending the superintendent's letter ahead by a *masewal* messenger detailed by the Bacalar commandant, the party of Plumridge,

Twigge, two orderlies, and the two interpreters, left Bacalar on March 26 or 27 with a rebel guard of eight.[10]

On March 30 or 31 they arrived near Santa Cruz, where they were stopped by an armed party who cocked their muskets in a threatening way and then escorted them into town. By one account,

> as the party passed through the streets great excitement prevailed, and crowds of Indians came forward to gape at the white strangers, yelling savagely or flourishing their macheats. On arriving at the Plaza, in front of a church-like building, the officers were taken into an open shed and ushered into the presence of . . . Puc himself, who reclined in his hammock. . . . They at once explained the nature of their mission and asked . . . for a written reply to Capt. Price's despatch. Puc, however, did not appear to recognize their presence, as he did not condescend to open his lips. The commissioners[,] having waited patiently, at length remarked that they had but a short time to remain, and requested an immediate answer. Without raising his head, Puc addressed the interpreter to the effect that he could not give an answer just then; that the officers must wait till "god came."[11]

The visitors were disarmed and confined to a shed. Although the trader-interpreter Trejo was apparently soon given his liberty,[12] the others were held without food or drink from the morning of their arrival until past midnight, when they were awakened by the beating of drums, the firing of muskets, and a guard of soldiers who informed them that God had come and called for them.

> The church or temple to which they were now hurried was built for the reception of the cross, and consisted of a high central building with an arched roof, with low flat-roofed wings supported by a series of arches and stone pillars. . . . After some delay they were taken by the hand and led to an interior entrance . . . [and] ushered into a spacious and lofty aisle, utterly dark. Here again their invisible guide led them by hand over the prostrate forms of such favoured Indians as were admitted into the presence of God. Then they were ordered to kneel down. A soft chanting music which had hitherto pervaded the building now ceased, and amid the deep silence that ensued a still small voice was heard, as it were, in mid-air, speaking in the Maya dialect.[13]

It is here that the interpreter Trejo claimed to have saved the lives of the party. By his account,

> The voice said . . . ["]Have you come about the letter that was sent me? That letter was a very insulting letter. . . . The captain and the soldiers

who crossed over [the Hondo] . . . have already been flogged. . . . You have come to pick a quarrel with me, the letter says that the Queen will send troops against me, if the English want to fight, let them come in thousands if they like, if this be the case say so—and I will dispose of you at once.["] I was very frightened, . . . our lives were in great danger. . . . I told the voice we have not come about what is mentioned in the letter, but to make trade and make peace. The voice replied ["]Very well, if the English wish to make peace and trade with us today and sell, we are very well satisfied, you can go to Belize and tell your General to send me a thousand arrobas [i.e., twenty-five-pound kegs] of powder, and I will pay for them in gold or in mules. . . . We expect the powder in four weeks.["] I said we will tell the Governor so. We were then dismissed and sent again to the guard room.[14]

The next morning they were fed, and Puc, apparently already the worse for drink, called on them and gave them liberty to walk around the town. But he also forced Twigge to swallow a spoonful of chile peppers and follow it with a glass of anis liquor. Puc continued to tipple, parading "the streets surrounded by a guard and followed by an Indian Ganymede, who carried a bottle of aniseed [i.e., anis liquor] and a calabash as a drinking vessel. He frequently stopped to take a draught . . . until finally he sank to the ground incapable, his guard the while standing around their prostrate chief, unmoved by the exhibition."[15]

Puc was drunk for four days, while the commission waited his permission to leave. He had told them they could do so after God spoke again, but they learned that God never spoke while Puc was drunk. And yet the drunkenness did not mean they had no further contact with the patrón and his officers. As Trejo described it, Puc "made Mr. Plumridge swallow aniseed until he vomited," and when he "had Mr. Plumridge and Mr. Twigge several times before him, he hauled and pulled them about, slapped them on the head, gave them aniseed, made them kiss him, and hug him up, and made them dance and sing."[16] On Trejo's advice they accepted the treatment as impassively as possible.

The Belize superintendent suspected that Trejo's twisting of information to Puc was not simply an attempt to save everyone from execution but rather was directed toward some personal aim.[17] But much in his account was later confirmed by a Belize resident who had been a prisoner in Santa Cruz and was acting as Puc's personal servant during the time of the commissioners' visit. This man reported that Trejo's successful efforts at salvation began even earlier than the midnight interrogation of Plumridge and Twigge in the blackness of the church.

I was in Santa Cruz . . . when a letter was received there by Puc from the Superintendent of Belize. . . . The same night . . . the cross was consulted. It stated that it did not like the letter sent by the English, that it was insulting, and it gave orders that on their arrival in Santa Cruz the two English Officers and the two Spaniards should be . . . killed. [When] the officers with two English soldiers and two Spanish interpreters arrived . . . the Indians ordered them to halt. The bugle was immediately sounded to assemble the troops and take them out to the execution. Trejo, one of the interpreters who came with the officers then began to speak and told Puc and the commandant that the letter did not convey the sentiments of the superintendent, that the English did not understand Spanish properly, and that no doubt some mistake had been made in translating it. They believed Trejo.

He also added, in contradiction to the midnight words of the cross itself, that "no order was given by the cross to punish any of the Indians who carried away the cattle from the English side. Without the order of the cross Puc could not chastise anyone, although he is patron of the cross. The cross said with reference to . . . carrying off the cattle that it was well done and that if it had been a greater thing it would have been all right."[18]

On the evening of the fourth day of the enforced visit, Plumridge and Twigge visited Puc as he was sleeping off his debauch in the church and finally got permission to leave. Puc cautioned the interpreter to have the powder sent as promised.

And so ended the face-to-face encounter of the queen's representatives with the chief agent of the speaking cross, which gained little except firsthand confirmation of the way in which the cross dictated commands through the *patrón* or *tatich*. One small and humane by-product of the visit was that one of the interpreters was given a piece of music written in Santa Cruz by a captive Yucatecan musician, Gerardo Castillo, which was then sent on to Castillo's family in Mérida.

Despite their embarrassment, the British felt themselves powerless to take effective action. The powder promised by Trejo was not delivered. Instead, the superintendent ordered a detachment of British troops to the northern border and issued a ban on the export of munitions to Yucatan.[19] A number of Yucatecan residents of northern British Honduras fled their homes for a time in fear of a retaliatory rebel raid, but no such action occurred, and the customary unsteady but peaceable relations with the rebels were soon reestablished.[20]

A Map of Santa Cruz

Further confirmation of the organization of the *masewal* capital, albeit indirect, is encapsulated in a sketch map of the Santa Cruz area. Although no date is written on it, it was obviously made sometime during the reign of Venancio Puc. A drawing from a photograph of the original map is shown in figure 1.[21]

On the map, the church is indicated on the customary east side of the plaza and as described by Plumridge and Twigge is flanked by attached, arcaded buildings—the one on the south marked clearly *casa de Puc*, that on the north with a deteriorated identification that is probably the same. Behind the church are various buildings attributed to artisans, and also a well.

The entire west side of the plaza is occupied by buildings of Dionisio Zapata—his house on the north, barracks of his men on the south—as would be appropriate for the ranking general. A second house north of there, drawn with four entrances, is also attributed to him. Other barracks are located both north and south of the plaza, those to the north not associated with a particular commander and at least some of the four barracks on the south pertaining to Marcelino Castillo. Castillo had been in charge at Bacalar during the cattle-stealing incident protested by Plumridge and Twigge and had signed himself grandiosely as "Commander of Brigade."[22] As a part of the same southern edge of the plaza is a house attributed to José María Canché. East of that house and south of the church with only one corner on the plaza the map shows a dwelling of two entries attributed to Zacarías May. Corresponding to that same position, but north of the church, is the house of four doors labeled as belonging to Leandro Santos.[23]

In Yucatecan towns of the period, individuals of highest status tended to live closest to the plaza, and the presumption that the same characterized the rebel capital is supported by the plaza location of houses of Puc, Zapata, and Santos. But what then of the other individuals identified as rebel generals in that period? The map shows no houses anywhere assigned to Crescencio Poot or Bonifacio Novelo, both of whom were said by young Rosado to be among the four generals in 1858, and both of whom would achieve still higher station later. Neither is there a house of Bernardino Chi, said by

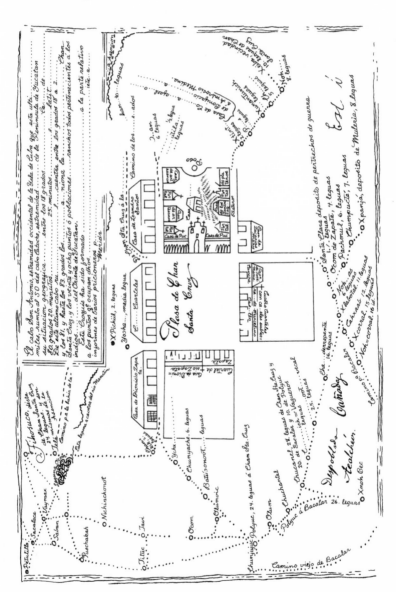

Figure 1. Noh Cah Santa Cruz and Vicinity, about 1860. Drawn from a photograph (courtesy of the late Alfredo Barrera Vásquez). The present whereabouts of the deteriorated original was unknown to the owner of the photograph and is unknown to the author.

Superintendent Price's informant to be one of the four generals in 1861 but whose name was probably a misrendering of Bernardino Cen (important later but not represented around the plaza) nor a house of Claudio Novelo, son of Bonifacio, who had been reported to be the commanding general in 1856 and 1857 and of whom more will be heard. Considering that Zapata and Santos were Puc's companions on each of his known visits to the Río Hondo and that May was along on at least one of these, one may suppose that some of the generals while holding high military rank and commanding considerable power were of a faction not close to Venancio Puc himself. Although speculative, this suspicion is not unreasonable in view of the map, and it will not be ruled out by the later history.

But we turn now to more concrete events, for the *masewal* armies were busy, whether or not accompanied in their campaigns by their miraculous cross.

The Abduction of Tunkás

A memorable expedition in late June and early July of 1861, shortly after Agustín Acereto's election as governor of Yucatan, carried *masewal* forces in raids on Tixcacalcupul, Dzonotchel, and Ekpedz. In Sacalaca, they killed great numbers by locking them in the curate's house and collapsing roof and walls on them.[24] Nevertheless, although Pedro Acereto retained his nominal position as commander of the eastern front, he and many of his soldiers removed to Mérida to support his father. There Agustín declared war on the liberal state congress, assumed its powers, and governed as a tyrant. His opponents were now concentrated in neighboring Campeche, where they had taken refuge en masse.[25]

It was this political altercation that fostered the spectacular raid on Tunkás, similar in manner to the attack on Tekax four years earlier. Rumors had been flying around Valladolid that Acereto's enemies in Campeche were attempting to enlist Indians in their cause, and so at 9:30 on the morning of September 7, 1861, it was with no particular anxiety that the people of Tunkás watched three parties of armed men march openly and in formation into their town from the Mérida road. But these were certainly no militiamen.

The first company was led by Claudio Novelo, who with calm assurance greeted by name some of the well-known *vecinos* of the place. The second was captained by Crescencio Poot, the third by a rebel named Lorenzo

Briseño. The combined force of about three hundred men secured the town barracks essentially without resistance, blocked the roads from the pueblo, and began rounding up all inhabitants, shutting them up in three buildings. The scene belonged to Crescencio Poot, appearing in a purloined black frock coat worn over his white cotton trousers—uncommonly tall, almost black of skin, his stentorian voice carrying his orders to all ears as he maintained a discipline unusual among *masewal* attackers. The town was systematically sacked.

At this point, proceedings departed from those of the raid on Tekax, for there was no massacre; only two people were killed. Instead, around 5:00 P.M., as soon as the loot was amassed and the hundred or so mules of the town were rounded up and loaded, the captives were hitched together and made to march off in a long caravan, herded along by guards. More than seven hundred people were taken. A fortunate few of the prisoners escaped en route, while the others who could not keep up were killed as they dropped out. By September 9, forty-seven corpses of these unfortunate laggards had been recovered by pursuing Yucatecans.[26]

Yucatecan action was limited. Governor Acereto rushed no aid at first because he could not believe the attackers were anyone other than his political rivals, and then he sent two hundred men from Valladolid and one hundred from Mérida, all of whom arrived far too late. The only pursuit that was even slightly effective was led by a Tunkás *vecino* and sometime military officer, Manuel Rodríguez Solís, who had been at his rural property when the raid captured his wife and child. Raising what force he could in the vicinity, he chased after the rebel rearguard but after being thrown back two or three times was forced to withdraw. Again, as was the case after the raid on Tekax, when the realization of what had happened finally sank in, all Yucatan was stunned.[27]

Once arrived at Noh Cah Santa Cruz, the prisoners were far from secure. According to Baqueiro, a week after their arrival they were called out and placed in open formation, where all had their heads lopped off except for the wife and daughter of Rodríguez Solís. But this was an exaggeration: firsthand reports indicate that whereas nearly all males who could not pass themselves off as lower class—that is, proper *masewalob*—were killed, many of the females were not.[28] In August of 1862 three escaped male prisoners (two of them with Spanish names)—one a native of Oaxaca, captured when Pedro Acereto was defeated, the other two of Tunkás—reported that they had saved themselves by asserting that they were "Indians," that is, *masewalob*. They were then put to work as agricultural laborers at the rancho San Lorenzo, a property of General José Leandro Santos, located some six leagues (twenty-four kilometers) from the rebel capital. Among other captives they were able to name eleven surviving males (nine with Spanish names, four of them musicians, including Gerardo Castillo), none of whom had been captured at Tunkás, and forty-six females (forty-two of them with Spanish names), all except one of them kidnapped from Tunkás. These women included the sisters Encarnación and Josefa Rodríguez—the latter the wife of Manuel Rodríguez Solís—and young Pastora Rean, all of whom will be mentioned again. It is significant that whereas all but one of the females named were from Tunkás, none of the males was. The escaped captives indicated that there were also prisoners from Sacalaca, although they did not know their names.[29]

From Acereto to Empire

Even the ineffectual pursuit of the rebels was now to backfire on Agustín Acereto and his supporters. With Acereto's resentment of Campeche growing as it became a sanctuary for his enemies, he arranged for one of the officers who had been dispatched to follow the cold trail of the Tunkás raiders, to lead some men into the Campeche hinterlands as part of a plot to unseat Governor Pablo García. But in the Chenes region this unlucky officer was caught by an unexpectedly rapid Campeche response to his attempt to foment revolution and was routed in a battle. Governor García demanded that the leaders of the movement sent against him be turned over to him for justice; Acereto brusquely refused. Campeche once again moved troops to the common border and dispatched vessels toward the Yucatecan port of Sisal.

In the meantime, on September 29 most of the members of the Yucatecan congress dismissed by Agustín Acereto gathered at Halachó in extraordinary session. They declared Acereto suspended from the governorship and named Liborio Irigoyen to fill the office provisionally, then closed their session and quickly fled into Campeche. Pedro Acereto and his troops moved to Halachó and the Campeche border. In late October, when an anti-Acereto force popped up at Oxkutzcab, Pedro's troops promptly attacked from two directions. But the Oxkutzcab defenders won, the few troops obedient to the congress advanced from Campeche, and Pedro retreated to Izamal. Additional pronouncements supported the congressional decree of September 29, and in early November Irigoyen again took over the government in Mérida.

There remained, however, the Acereto stronghold in the east. As a force of more than a thousand men under Francisco Remírez marched on the Aceretos in Izamal, father and son were forced to Valladolid where discussions of armistice brought no result. And then through shrewd generalship and unusual aggressiveness Remírez and his soldiers forced the Aceretos to flee Valladolid for the hinterlands. But on December 23 Agustín Acereto's concealment was discovered, and he was wounded so gravely on capture that he died before he could be carried to Valladolid. Pedro, however, was not to be found; he had doubled back to Mérida and into hiding.[30]

The next year, 1862, found Irigoyen working to repair the damaged ship of state. In April a new constitution was adopted, and in August duly elected officials took office, Irigoyen the elected governor. To his credit, it appears that with his accession—and, of course, the Juárez decree of 1861—the export of indentured servants finally came to an end.[31]

The new officeholders were confronted immediately with *masewal* activity in the east. In late July there had been a heavy raid on Pisté, with prisoners taken and a few killed; Rodríguez Solís sallied from Tunkás with a force he had gathered for his personal revenge but missed the action. And before the end of August rebels under Crescencio Poot took Dzitás, killing more than thirty people. Only after a small party of local men holed themselves up in the church and defended it successfully for several hours did the rebels tire of the game and begin to withdraw. When troops from Valladolid finally arrived they were soundly defeated and dispersed by the retiring *masewalob*.[32]

But the submerged Pedro Acereto, still plotting revolt, and the active eastern rebels, still following the dictates of their cross, were but two of three impending dangers. In December 1861 a Spanish squadron had occupied Veracruz on behalf of three nations intervening in Mexican affairs with the avowed purpose of collecting debts—Spain, England, and France. With the first two of these quickly abandoning the effort, France was left to send her troops inland where she would finally place the emperor Maximilian upon a throne in Mexico. But before that came about, the invading French were handed a defeat by the Mexican army at Puebla on May 5, 1862. Thus, for the time being, Yucatan was able to ignore the intervention in Mexico. Home was bad enough.

In September Pedro Acereto surfaced again, although now sick of a debilitating disease. Gaining adherents in the east, in October he and his second, Colonel Francisco Cantón, issued an official pronouncement from Tizimín, declaring Irigoyen deposed and replaced by a five-man junta.[33]

Pursued by Manuel Cepeda Peraza and a substantial government army, on November 1 Acereto found himself besieged in Motul, threw off the attackers, and withdrew to Tunkás. He was besieged again in mid-month, this time defeated and his forces dispersed, himself hustled away on a litter. By the end of the month he was dead. The Acereto movement had finally collapsed.[34]

But this did not bring calm. The short peace of winter 1862–63 gave way to yet another revolutionary pronouncement, as colonels Felipe Navarrete and Francisco Cantón rose to unseat Irigoyen with the support of Manuel Rodríguez Solís, whose attention was now turned from his hatred of *masewalob* to political intrigue. This time, despite the help Irigoyen obtained from Campeche, the insurrection was successful. Navarrete became interim governor in July, his program largely limited to promises to fight the *masewal* rebels in the east. And he made some attempt to do this, organizing troops and stockpiling supplies—but most of his planned attacks were never made, and the few that were, failed.[35]

The power to be reckoned with now was the French. In Mexico, a regency government had been established to rule until a monarch arrived, and in Yucatan republican feeling ran high, although the entire Mexican situation seems to have been almost ignored by Navarrete, who talked only of the eastern rebels.

But Campeche, now just as republican, raised loud objections: the French presence in the Gulf of Mexico interfered with her shipping. Governor García asked permission to use the port at Sisal to bypass the French; Navarrete refused. Now, with García's help, Manuel Cepeda Peraza raised men in Campeche and marched north in November 1863 to declare against the Navarrete government. But Yucatecan citizens gave him and his Campechanos little support, jumped instead to join the defending army of Navarrete, and Cepeda Peraza was forced to disband. The next month Navarrete turned the card around by marching on Campeche.

A French squadron now lay close off the coast, and its blockade of the Campeche port was of direct assistance to Yucatan. By early January Navarrete had the upper hand, although the strong city did not yield. A three-way flurry of letters between Pablo García in Campeche, Navarrete on its outskirts, and the French commander offshore led finally to a capitulation on January 22, 1864, in which García yielded to the French rather than to Yucatan. Two days before the settlement was signed, one of Navarrete's brigades proclaimed for the French-backed regency and was shortly seconded by the others. The upshot was that as Navarrete's forces triumphed at Campeche the entire peninsula was surrendered to the empire.[36]

For a time peace prevailed in the cities of the western peninsula. It did not do so in the east, however, where the *masewalob* could be as active as they chose.

The *Masewal* Threat

Early in 1863 much of the energy of the Santa Cruz *masewalob* had been directed to the south, where Crescencio Poot led parties totaling several hundred in successful raids on Becanchén, now largely depopulated, and then farther south against *pacíficos* of Macanché and Lochhá, the latter of which he attacked during a fiesta on January 3. Many prisoners were taken.[37]

Masewalob struck again in that direction in April and chased some of the *pacíficos* as far south as the upper Río Hondo, where a rebel column estimated at six hundred under Venancio Puc touched at a logging works operated by a British Honduran company on the Mexican side of the river, and where Puc sternly ordered his men to commit no depredations.[38] The *masewalob* turned to the annual demand for rents from those residents of the British colony who farmed in Yucatecan territory.

At this point there emerged a hint of collusion between the rebels and certain residents of Albion Island in the Río Hondo, which was administered as part of the British territory. According to witnesses, Manuel Jesús Castillo, a man of property on the island who was engaged in trade in logwood and other enterprises, was aided by his clerk, José de los Santos López, in conniving with Puc and his men to make prisoners of five local residents against whom Castillo had a grudge and to chase away *pacíficos* to whom he did not wish to pay rent. One of the residents he had fingered was caught by Puc's party on the Yucatecan side of the river, while López was present. Made to pole López and six armed rebels across the river, the prisoner jumped into the water and escaped. The remaining four of the intended victims, warned by the escapee, refused to cross the river to the Yucatecan side to pay their rents but said they would send the money across instead. They were then visited on British territory by armed groups of the rebels, still accompanied by José de los Santos López. One of the delinquent renters, Isidro Méndez, was dragged across the river by the party, which was led by Puc, Leandro Santos, and Dionisio Zapata. There Méndez managed to escape—with, he said, the connivance of Zapata.[39]

Although the inevitable British protest followed, Puc, Santos, and Zapata pointed out in a letter to the British magistrate that they had caused no disturbance in British Honduras and asserted that their sole traffic with Castillo was to sell him the corn they had forcibly harvested from the plantings of those farming the Yucatecan side from whom they were unable to collect cash rents. Although the affair ended peaceably between rebels and British, López was deported from the colony and Castillo evidently remained under a cloud that later would serve him ill.[40]

Farther north, the jabbing and looting raids of the rebels, their killings and kidnappings, continued all the time that the pronouncement-devoted Yucatecans in the west were expressing their rivalries. Only a few of the raids of this period have been mentioned here for they were all very much the same—a band of *masewalob* struck a town, burned, captured, left, and was seldom interfered with. These went on month after month, year by year, as more and more towns were abandoned. What had been an active frontier became an empty no-man's-land.

In late 1863 Baqueiro himself visited this region.

I saw the families, at nightfall, climb to the top of the hills where they formed small garrisons in order to be covered from the surprises of the enemy. I saw military detachments where there was nothing to the view but the sky and the trees of abandoned houseyards; unhappy Indians, pressed into service in the encampments, locked in the choir of the churches so they couldn't desert; roads dangerous within a very short distance of the principal military barracks; and everywhere destroyed churches, images smashed, and buildings whose owners either whitened the desolate fields with their bones, or had been carried captive. . . . I saw the isolation, the desolation, and the misery; everywhere traces of blood and of pain attested by trenches and fortified squares; scattered human remains.

He went on to say that

from the height of the church of Ichmul [he had contemplated] the immense desert that the barbarians had formed. . . . [N]othing lived; the church had been horribly profaned; the houses had fallen; plants and lofty trees covered with their bowers and desolate leaves what in other times were streets and plazas; and within that limitless horizon, how many towns equally deserted present themselves to view![41]

And yet life was not going smoothly for those in power in the *masewal* capital, as information reaching British Honduras would soon testify.

Revolt in Noh Cah Santa Cruz

In January 1864, rumors floated around Corozal of convulsions within the rebel body of Santa Cruz. Toward the end of the month, "His Excellency the Superintendent of Belize" received a letter datelined Santa Cruz, January 1, 1864, over the signatures of Leandro Santos and Dionisio Zapata, with Gerardo del Castillo signing as secretary. They provided a glimpse of their history.

> We have much pleasure in giving Your Excellency a slight sketch of all that has taken place for the last sixteen years during which a voice has been heard among us which we were given to understand was God himself. It as such was venerated. It administered justice and as there was not the least enlightenment among us we became stupified when we heard and saw what was taking place; after the lapse of some time however, it was the cause of much evil. . . . We even feared that we might commit crimes through simplicity. Seeing that during so many years such numbers[,] certainly not less than 6,000 souls, have been constantly killed for no offense whatever, the day at length arrived in which Divine Providence enlightened our minds.

By what means this enlightenment came to them they did not say. Merely that,

> at the risk of our own lives we have removed out of the way the originators of all these crimes. They were first, the man who styled himself patron of the church, an old man who acted as his secretary, and a boy or rather a youth, who was in reality the person who used to speak and was called God and who administered justice with such energy. This was done in the obscurity of night, but we gradually discovered that he was no saint but a christian.[42]

Their uprising, they said, was stimulated by

> the plan of these ringleaders [which] was to assemble 5,000 troops, to make a general list of all the prisoners . . . and to have them butchered on the 30th of last month in the presence of the assembled troops in the square. After this the troops were to march against Ticul or Kuzcab [Oxkutzcab] and against the people of Xul. They had strict orders that every person they took should be killed for it had been decreed by God that not a single white person should be left alive. After taking Xul they were to pass on and take Tekax and this achieved, they were then to proceed to the Capital.

But, they continued, the plan "moved our weak hearts." And so we conspired to . . . prevent these misfortunes. It was agreed upon and carried out on the 23d December in the following manner. We first locked the boy up in prison in the evening. At night two of us went about shouting and in the middle of the night we called together the still doubting *comandantes*. We commenced operations with a very small escort. We caused the reveille to be sounded, but the troops would not act according to our wishes until they had seen the ringleaders executed. They were then satisfied and commenced to shout in triumph and to rejoice over the deed which had just been done.

The motive they alleged was beyond reproach: "Our poor country has been too long oppressed through the wickedness of bad men."

Finally, they asked that the letter be kept secret, hinting at factional strife: "Everything can be arranged, but one must take time lest our bright prospects should be blighted. . . . [W]ith much secrecy all that we long for will be achieved."[43]

At about the same time there were credible accounts of new rebel intentions toward Yucatan. Becoming "disgusted with the constant slaughter of prisoners taken in their various raids," Zapata and others were said to be ready to make peace, the prisoners were reportedly liberated, and Puc's wealth was divided among the *masewalob*.[44]

In February word of the upset at Chan Santa Cruz was received in Yucatan and Campeche. Despite the business of reforming the government to conform with the dictates of the regency, under which the states of Campeche and Mérida were combined as a single department of the again centralist nation, Navarrete made plans to capitalize on Zapata's inclinations for peace. Within a month a commission of five men—Manuel Antonio Sierra and two other priests, with Pantaleón Barrera and Juan José Méndez—was appointed to go to Belize to work out a treaty.[45]

The commission did not move as fast as did a free agent named José María Martínez de Arredondo, who took it on himself for reasons of his own (which will emerge in the next chapter) to go to Chan Santa Cruz to scout out the state of affairs. On March 14 he penned a letter to the editor of the official Mérida newspaper in which he reported his return from the rebel capital and provided a list of ten Spanish-named males and fourteen Spanish-named women (again including the Rodríguez sisters and Pastora Rean), many with children, whom he knew to be alive as prisoners in the town, and he stated that additional prisoners whose names he did not know were also to be found there.[46] But whatever the conditions Arredondo had encountered, by the time the official commission arrived in northern British Honduras in mid-April the situation at Noh Cah Santa Cruz had changed dramatically.

On April 4, the British magistrate at Corozal confirmed reports that Zapata along with some Corozal traders had been assassinated when on the way "to escape to the English side of the Hondo, and it is supposed that he would have succeeded but for a quarrel with his wife, who immediately after his flight conveyed intelligence of it to the Indians." The new leaders were named as Bonifacio Novelo, Bernabel [otherwise Bernardino] Ken [or Cen], and Crescencio Poot.[47] There was also a less certain report received in Yucatan from an escaped rebel prisoner that Zapata had earlier killed Santos over the latter's pretensions to power.[48]

The work of the Yucatecan commission, therefore, was confined to attempts to contact the new rulers of the rebel territory, which yielded no results at all, and to collect intelligence of a general nature. This came out somewhat better.

They reported that the actual killers of Zapata had been partisans of Venancio Puc from the settlement of Chancah Derrepente, located south of Chan Santa Cruz, who had attacked Zapata at his rancho of Sahcabchén. They also stated the new rulers—that is, Novelo, Poot, and Cen—had executed eight of the murdering party but had not put a stop to the killing of *dzul* prisoners who had been under Zapata's protection. The new hierarchy they found to consist of, in addition to Novelo, Cen, and Poot, the *comandantes* Miguel Uc, Pedro Dzul, Tomás Canche, Lusiano Canul, Juan Balam, Balbino Ake, Claudio Novelo, and Victoriano Villorín. The total number of the rebel population they placed at about four thousand.

The principal town that they call Chan Santa Cruz is irregular, in that although it includes some 200 houses, these form groups without order or symmetry, and in them live the most influential and those that have the character of commanders or authorities; the permanent garrison is commonly of 400 men distributed in nine barracks, who are relieved each two weeks, since . . . each one has his musket that he keeps in his quarters in the town or in the bush. When there is reason for alarm they are advised by means of rockets or bombs, at the report of which they come together armed from all the rancherías. . . .

When the triumverate composed of Venancio Puc, Apolinar Sánchez and José Oa [or Na], was alive, it appeared as an interpretive oracle of the will of heaven, on whose voice hung men's life or death. With these assassinated because Zapata discovered their hoaxes, there were glimpsed hopes of order and individual security, but with Zapata's murder all is back to barbarism. Today an Indian, it is not known with what motive, discharges the priestly functions, lives in the church praying and singing all day, makes baptisms, and discharges other functions assisted by sixteen children, eight boys and eight girls, who serve him like a chorus in his superstitious and outlandish canticles.

The intelligence-gathering commissioners touched also on internal dissention, saying that the *masewalob*

have a distillery that belongs in common to all the commanders, and the aguardiente that they produce they distribute among themselves, or they sell it to those that they call the troops, very dear, at six reales the bottle; for this reason and because of the successive deaths of some of the commanders, the mass of the Indians are not entirely in agreement, because the death of Venancio Puc has left partisans; Leandro Santos also had many, and Dionisio Zapata is wept for by his, who threaten death to Bernabe Cen, who is in immediate danger. One of the *comandantes* named Marcelino Castillo has just died of natural causes, by which means the number of the caudillos is diminishing from day to day, a circumstance that is a powerful element to foment anarchy in Chan Santa Cruz.

They went on to recommend military and economic measures.[49]

There is not much doubt that their report provided a great deal of the information contained in the well-known description of the rebel governing hierarchy that was published by the Austrian F. Aldherre, who accompanied Empress Carlota to Yucatan in 1865.[50] Some of his description, however, appears also to have been drawn from a novelized account of Chan Santa Cruz published in 1864 by Pantaleón Barrera, one of the commissioners, under the pseudonym Napoleón Trebarra.[51]

Aldherre provides no complete personal names for the patron's assistants in the manipulation of the cult, but he indicates that besides the supreme priest, the *patrón* or *tatich*—who was also the political head—there was a second titled "Interpreter of the Cross" or "Interpreter of God"; this was *tata* Polin. And there was a third titled "Organ of the Divine Word." For services, which were always at night, the time when God descended, the *tatich* was said to bring the population together by having a bugle sounded, and when God had descended the *tatich* would conduct the interrogation of the cross. The questions were answered by a whistle sounded by the Organ of the Divine Word, representing the voice of God. The will of the cross was then communicated to the public by *tata* Polin.

Besides the church and its attached structure, there was a stone building referred to as a palace, which was

> that of the general in chief of the army, who is called tata Chikiuic, and his habitation has the name Chikiuic. This general is under the orders of the Tatich. . . .

> The women who fall prisoner remain closed in a kind of redoubt formed in the yard of the so-called palace of the Tatich and are subject to a heavy servitude, worse than slavery. They work without ceasing; they prepare food, not only for the owner of the house but for all of his Indian servants, sew the clothes, water the plantings, take care of the corrals, clean chickens and pigs, and perform, finally, the hardest tasks. The men whose lives are spared are dedicated in the ranches of the commanders to the hardest and heaviest of labors, and many die of overwork.

Finally, Aldherre stressed—as did Barrera in his novel—the mutual distrust and constant spying on one another. "Espionage is recognized as a system, and there is formed in this way a kind of secret police. The triumvirs spy among themselves; the generals do the same. One of them is chief of the spies. The Indians call him "tata Nohoch Dzul." There are in Chan Santa Cruz a guard of 400 men. From nightfall, sentinels are placed everywhere, but they are not evident, they are squatting, supported on their weapons, behind the walls and behind the trees."[52]

The Power of the Cross

In the foregoing pages I have quoted extensively from accounts of the operation of the cult of the cross to put on accessible record such relatively primary information as exists. The political aspects of the cult and its manipulation can now be summarized more succinctly.

The brief history of the manipulations by Venancio Puc that is given in the letter of Zapata and Santos in which they announced his death suggests that the organization of the cult had been stable for more than a decade—that is, presumably from the time that Juan de la Cruz Puc succeeded Manuel Nauat as *patrón*. Until the second half of the decade of the 1850s, the political power appears to have been with an individual termed *gobernador* or governor, but after about 1857 there was no such office, and the speaking cross itself seems to have directed everything. This included military matters as well as affairs of internal justice, with the cross masterminding attacks and meting out whippings and capital punishment to rebels and captives alike. The cross was also fairly regularly taken into the field, as was the case at Bacalar in 1858 and on at least one other—and probably more—of the routine visits to the border of British Honduras. In these cases, Venancio Puc served as a field commander as well as religious factotum.

The identifications of the persons who filled the three important functional positions in the cult are ambiguous. Although at first glance there seems to be no reason to question that Juan de la Cruz Puc of 1851 and Venancio Puc of 1858 were the same person, on closer inspection such a reason does appear. The later versions of the basic exhortation or proclamation of Juan de la Cruz include a genealogy of the early *patrones* of the cross (to be discussed again later), in which Venancio Puc is specifically said to have been the second patron, following Manual Nauat, and then behind him and without specified numerical order occur a woman and one Atanacio Puc.[53] But according to Baqueiro's biography of Crescencio Poot, when on the last day of 1852 Poot and Atanacio Puc announced the death of José María Barrera, Atanacio Puc was "chief priest of the crosses."[54] This would mean that Venancio Puc followed Atanacio Puc in the priesthood, although it also means that one or the other of the sources is in at least minor error and that the correct sequence is not immediately certain.

It is also possible that incumbents of the office of Organ of the Divine Word had not changed in this time. The Zapata-Santos letter just referred to appears to indicate that this person, who began his work as a boy, was now a young man. As of 1858 Rosado reported his name as Braulio, whereas at his death in 1864 his name is given in at least two sources as José Na (perhaps better written Nah). However, in view of the very high proportion of nineteenth-century Yucatecans of all classes who carried José as their first given name (e.g., José Venancio Puc, José Dionisio Zapata, José Leandro Santos, José Dolores Cetina, José Eulogio Rosado, to mention only a few), it is probable that Braulio's name was also José and thus entirely possible that this person was José Braulio Nah. Finally, with regard to the Interpreter of the Divine Word, it is entirely likely that there was a change between late 1858 and late 1863. That is, José María Rosado reported a *tata* Naz (Nazareo or Nazario) as holder of that position, but by late 1863 that incumbent had apparently been replaced by *tata* Polin—possibly as the result of death by natural causes. Because *tata* Naz was said by Rosado to be Braulio's father, one is left to suppose that the predecessor of Apolinar Sánchez was one Nazario Nah.[55]

The achievement of power by the cult of the cross was apparently, it must be reiterated, at the expense of the original politico-military leadership, which had earlier included Venancio Pec, Florentino Chan, and Calixto Yam, and in which commanders of long standing such as Bonifacio Novelo and Crescencio Poot should clearly have been in line to succeed. Zapata and Santos, on the other hand, appeared as major leaders only as the cross cult achieved the apex of political power. Thus, the traditional leadership must have been sidetracked through the activities of Venancio Puc and the prestige he gained for the cross. And so it appears not at all surprising that with Puc dead and the cross cult in a situation of at least temporary embarrassment, both Zapata and Santos were shortly done away with, and the heirs of the old guard emerged.[56]

Finally, one must say something about the society that was marshaled by Puc and the cross. I have made references to ranchos of both Santos and Zapata.[57] Their existence, together with José María Rosado's description of the Santos rancho that was cared for by people who seem to be retainers and the Aldherre account of the assignment of prisoners to work the ranchos for the commanders, underlines both the fact that the population tended to live as dispersed as ever, despite the attraction of the cult at Noh Cah Santa Cruz, and the fact that the perquisites of the highest leaders included something that smacks of the private estate worked by vassals. In the same vein, the leaders also apparently had the proceeds from their monopoly on the distillation of liquor.

Estimates of the rebel population obtained by the Yucatecan commissioners Barrera and Sierra were in the vicinity of four thousand. This number seems modest, almost certainly too modest—unless the figure related only to the immediate vicinity of the *masewal* capital—but it is not entirely out of scale with the size of the military force that the rebels were known to command. On more than one occasion British informants estimated the total force under arms in one place at about fifteen hundred. One fugitive from Chan Santa Cruz, on the other hand, remarked that "when all have been called up for any reason, with inclusion of servants, they made a thousand men."[58] Given heavy natural mortality, which the general state of rebel health seems to imply, and a relatively high birthrate, one could expect the male population between the ages of twelve or thirteen and fifty-five or sixty to amount to about two-thirds of all males or roughly one-third of the total population. Thus, a fighting force of between one thousand and fifteen hundred, of which many were boys, could relate to a complete population of between four thousand and five thousand. This assumes, of course, that the one thousand to fifteen hundred represents *total* mobilization, which in view of the dispersed pattern of settlement may well have occurred only rarely, if indeed at all. As will be seen, other estimates placed the total rebel population much higher than this.

Voice of the Future

And what of the cult of the speaking cross after the death of Puc? Pantaleón Barrera and the Yucatecan commissioners had reported continuation of the "priestly functions," with continual singing, praying, performance of baptisms, and so on, by an unnamed "Indian" who lived in the church. But the major oracle seems to have moved.

At the close of his novelized description of Chan Santa Cruz, Barrera reported recent word (i.e., in 1864) that Bernardino Cen was attempting at Tulum to engineer "the resurrection of the famous Tatich."[59] Precisely what this might have been intended to mean is not thoroughly clear, but in June of 1864 some prisoners fled Santa Cruz by "taking advantage of the departure of the Indians who headed to *Santa Cruz Xtulmul* with the object of consulting their oracles that they say exist in that place."[60] This seems to have been a miswriting of *Santa Cruz Xtulum* or *xTulum* (i.e., Tulum). And in October of that same year, when the government of British Honduras requested the return of more than one hundred fugitive Chinese indentured laborers who had taken refuge at or near rebel Santa Cruz (as will be recounted later), the matter was referred by the *masewal* leaders to the cross at Tulum, which rendered the final negative decision.

That is, although some devotions focused upon a powerful cross seem to have continued actively at Noh Cah Santa Cruz, the major cross oracle was at Tulum. Thus, while dual centers of cross worship earlier had come to an apparent end in 1859, when the Kantunil rebels surrendered and returned to the orthodox fold, no more than five years later there were again at least two major centers of the cross in operation—Noh Cah Santa Cruz and Santa Cruz Tulum. There would never again be fewer.

14 / Unsteady Peace in the South

The rebel leaders who accepted the treaty of September 16, 1853, represented settlements that were scattered in the bush from the Río Hondo, at the border of British Honduras, to the town of Iturbide located in what in 1858 would become eastern Campeche. For the first year the treaty was in effect, José María Tzuc, leader at Chichanhá and the chief rebel signatory of the treaty, apparently acted to some extent as head of the entire collection of *sublevados pacíficos*—or, at least, the government of Yucatan chose to think he did.[1] It was apparently Tzuc, for instance, who was responsible for marshaling the armed force that had marched against Chan Santa Cruz according to provisions of the treaty, only to halt for fear of the cholera that raged in the rebel capital.

But on October 12 of the next year, 1854, José María Tzuc died, apparently of natural causes. Although reportedly the *pacíficos* had applied to Rómulo Díaz de la Vega as governor of Yucatan for the selection of a successor from among their nominees, Vega insisted that they elect their own leader.[2]

Before this could be effected—indeed, before Vega's response reached them—it became plain that no transition in leadership would be entirely smooth. In early November 1854, Andrés Zima, the second signatory of the treaty of 1853 and the interim leader at Chichanhá, notified the Yucatecan commander of Bacalar that he was at the Río Hondo, where he had retreated rather than do battle with partisans of the son of José María Tzuc. Although Zima claimed sufficient force to withstand the pressure, he preferred to settle the matter peaceably. With the intercession of a priest from Bacalar, the Chichanhá leaders did meet to elect Tzuc's successor as directed by Vega, and they chose the same Zima—who reportedly also received the vote of Tzuc's errant son Luciano.[3]

But this solution was not to last. Within two years Luciano Tzuc was commander at Chichanhá, and Andrés Zima had emigrated to British Honduras, where he established a settlement in English territory across from Chunabá on the Río Hondo, and where he would become a man of some property.[4]

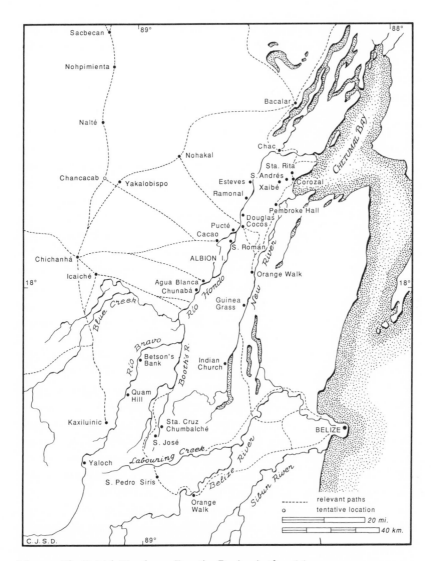

Map 14. The British Honduran Frontier Region in the 1860s.

As will be seen later, however, there is no indication that Luciano Tzuc's influence—unlike that of his father—ever extended farther than the immediate vicinity of the settlement of Chichanhá, while other and more populous pueblos gained prominence and power farther to the northwest. Indeed, from the evidence available it appears that much of Luciano's effort was expended on the collection of extortionate rents from Belizean logging enterprises and farmers who exploited lands on the Yucatecan side of the frontier.

Extortion on the Hondo

As official British thinking evolved in the nineteenth century, it included a claim to be Spain's lawful successor in British Honduras, a point of view made manifest in early 1862 when the former British settlement (a classification recognizing that the ultimate sovereignty was not British) was declared a British colony (which asserted British ownership).[5] This brought with it government by a lieutenant governor rather than a mere superintendent, although that official continued to report to the Colonial Office through the governor general of Jamaica.

It also emphasized the importance of a precise determination of the British boundary, for questions could legitimately be raised as to whether the limits of the actual British settlement in the 1850s were within the boundaries that had been conferred by treaty with Spain.[6] Such questions came to focus on the region of the upper Río Hondo. Whatever a close reading of historical events might suggest to others, England's official position would be developed around the claim that the northernmost major tributary of the Río Hondo—a stream known as Blue Creek—constituted the upper course of that river, which she could claim as the frontier. As the boundary question assumed importance, Yucatan voted for a more easterly boundary than did England, asserting that the real headwater of the Río Hondo was the tributary complex formed by Booth's River and the Río Bravo.[7]

But although the location of the British Honduran boundary would become a subject of contention with both Mexico and the southern *pacíficos*, it was not exclusively germane to the first extortionate appearance on the Hondo of Luciano Tzuc and his Chichanhá soldiers. In September 1856 the logging establishment of Young, Toledo, and Company on Blue Creek was occupied by men under Tzuc, who threatened to destroy the mahogany then amassed at the stream unless more than five thousand dollars in rent was paid. Although the tract being logged included not only lands located in disputed territory south of Blue Creek but also some on the north of that stream that were clearly in Yucatan, the company could demonstrate that their right to work the area had been purchased by advance payment to the Mexican government.[8] But that claim was of no moment to Tzuc, whose occupying force was called off only after he was satisfied by cash in the amount of six hundred dollars, with the promise of two hundard dollars annually.

The company sought redress from the Yucatecan government through its garrison still at Bacalar, but it was unsuccessful either in its claims for money damages or in having Tzuc controlled.[9] And although Tzuc's occasional sorties bordered on banditry, his basic approach contained an obvious logic: as de facto ruler of southern Yucatecan territory and holder of an implied or actual irregular commission as *pacífico* commander from the Yucatecan government, he was entitled to the perquisites of rule. As I noted earlier, this view was also taken by the rebels of Santa Cruz, who in 1857 occupied a works by the same company on the lower Hondo, extorting a money rent of three hundred dollars and the promise of nine hundred per year thereafter. The combination of these pressures from both *pacíficos* and *bravos* forced Young, Toledo to consider withdrawing from all territory claimed by Yucatan, whether or not they held a lease from the Mexican government. They did not do so immediately, however, but continued to pay "rent."[10]

After 1858, as the Santa Cruz rebels extended their control southward through the capture of Bacalar, they also appointed local governing functionaries in their territory. Where their grounds impinged on those claimed by Chichanhá, the two vied for control, and in some cases both were successful in collecting annual "rents" from the same British enterprises.

Tzuc's move to levy charges for use of lands on the Yucatecan side of what he believed to be the frontier established the leitmotif of Chichanhá policy for ensuing years, in which collection of fees from various residents of British Honduras evidently provided the major source of income of the former rebel center. But in this first case it appears to have backfired on Luciano Tzuc.

By the middle of the following year, 1857, Tzuc had been deposed by his own people, "it is said on account of an unfair distribution of the money extorted from Messrs. Young and Toledo. He now wanders about harmlessly within the [British] settlement."[11] He was replaced by one Feliciano Ya.[12] But in 1861 Tzuc was said to have visited Campeche, where he announced a plan to campaign against Santa Cruz and received government support of some kind. He also must have improved his image, for when Ya was succeeded by José Uluac in 1861 or early 1862, Tzuc was named second in command, and by mid-1863—presumably after Uluac died—he had assumed command with the title of general. His force, however, was dwindling.[13]

During this time the regular windfall of "rents" from logging works was enhanced by smaller charges levied on the steadily increasing number of petty agriculturalists, as Santa Cruz pressure encouraged the southward migration of campesinos trying to avoid hostilities. The threats that accompanied these various monetary charges were an unsettling factor along the frontier.

The Unclear Lines of *Pacífico* Power

Somewhat farther north, meanwhile, separate and more populous centers had taken shape. As I mentioned in an earlier chapter, it was not long after the outbreak of the Caste War that peace-seeking campesinos had begun to gravitate to the broad and bucolic expanses of the southern bush. An early rebel pueblo in the region was Macanché, where an important commander was José María Cocom. In the days before the peace Cocom had spent much of his time harrying the Yucatecans around Iturbide, and he exercised a certain hegemony over much of the southern region.

Another southern commander, who was to achieve even wider notoriety, was Pablo Encalada. According to Baqueiro, Encalada passed most of the first half of 1849 in command of forces from the Macanché region, taking part in the long rebel siege of Sabán, while Cocom with forces from the same area figured in the concurrent siege of Tihosuco. According to Encalada himself, however, he had spent this time in the direct service of Jacinto Pat, first as a personal servant, then as manager of one of Pat's properties, Rancho Hotomop, whence he accompanied Pat on the latter's fatal trip toward Bacalar in 1849 and witnessed his murder by Venancio Pec. He claimed that he spent about two years as a prisoner of Venancio Pec, then was put at liberty and moved to Lochhá, where he remained. At his arrival, Lochhá was unsettled, but within a year counted some three hundred families, at which time Encalada was elected commander and his appointment confirmed by Cocom. Not long after, peace was made between the southern rebels and the government.[14] Both Cocom and Encalada were listed as parties to the treaty (see table 8).

Although he may have been outranked by José María Cocom, Pablo Encalada was also a multisettlement commander important in his own right. When in July 1857 Luciano Tzuc was deposed at Chichanhá and replaced by Feliciano Ya, the latter was represented as under the higher-level direction of Encalada at Lochhá.[15] And Encalada's reputation was underscored that same year as Campeche squared off against the rest of Yucatan in the separatist maneuver that led to the successful rebel massacre

Map 15. Location of Some Events of 1854–69.

of Tekax, as described in an earlier chapter: at the moment the port city found itself confronted by a superior Yucatecan government force under Manuel Cepeda Peraza, allegations appeared that the sometime Campeche partisan and political hopeful Liborio Irigoyen had written to Encalada to offer him second place in a new state government, if only he would lead fifteen hundred *pacífico* soldiers against the Yucatecan army.[16] Whether the allegations were true or not, that they were made at all bespeaks Encalada's stature. Indeed, his reputatión belies his own claims to a distinctly unwarlike role in the rebellion.

As I noted previously, after the pacification of the southern region the trade in powder between some residents of British Honduras and the rebels of Santa Cruz had continued through the expanse of thinly populated country between Chichanhá and Bacalar—a country that the small and isolated Yucatecan garrison at Bacalar and the shrinking *pacífico* cadre at Chichanhá were unable to police. When the rebels recaptured Bacalar in early 1858 and converted the site into an outpost for unhampered contact with the merchants of British Honduras, pressure on the *pacíficos* of Chichanhá increased.

But at the end of April of that year, *pacífico* stability was threatened when José María Cocom and two other leaders were assassinated. Reports conflict. Encalada claimed that it was the result of a rebellion in the *pacífico* settlement of Mesapich.[17] Tiburcio Briceño, *pacífico* commander of Chansut, reported that the insurrection involved *pacíficos* of Xcopoil and Macanché, as well as Mesapich, who wished to rejoin the rebels of Santa Cruz, feeling that any Yucatecan triumph over the *masewalob* of the east would result in a general reinstitution of taxes on all former rebels.[18] A contemporary newspaper editorial, however, reported that the presumed revolt was more accurately described as a drunken brawl in which, unfortunately, Cocom was a casualty.[19]

Whatever the case, a Yucatecan force was dispatched under Captain Onofre Bacelis, the hero of Tekax, which made prisoners of fourteen men and dragged them to Mérida for trial.[20] The Bacelis occupation of *pacífico* towns began in June and lasted several weeks, generating complaints from at least one Indian resident. These reached Pablo García, the feisty head of government in newly independent Campeche, who complained loudly that Yucatecan troops had violated Campeche territory. To this, Governor Peraza of Yucatan responded that no evidence had been presented to show that the rebelling settlements were within the limits of Campeche, and that furthermore the *pacíficos* had made their original surrender to Yucatan and so were Yucatecan subjects.[21]

In evident confirmation of ties with Mérida, Encalada claimed that after Cocom's death he was elected commandant in chief by a vote of all the southern *pacífico* settlements and that it was Yucatan that confirmed him in that position.[22] And it was also to Yucatan that Tiburcio Briceño of Chansut pledged support in October 1858, when Liborio Irigoyen was installed as governor of that state.

But while indicating a tie with Mérida, Briceño's letter raises a question regarding the real sphere of Encalada's authority at the time, for Briceño was signed as commandant in chief, seconded as signatories by twenty-nine named officers: one *mayor general* or major, five *comandantes*, thirteen captains, and ten lieutenants, as well as representatives of the lower ranks[23]—a group that must have represented settlements over a substantial region.

But not all *pacífico* allegiance remained with the state of Yucatan. By 1860 Campeche could claim to have appointed a *pacífico* military commander of her own—one Andrés Arana, headquartered at the western settlement of Mesapich. In December, when Arana reported an attack presumably (although not certainly) by Santa Cruz rebels, it was a Campechano military force that responded.[24] And three years later the letter-writing Briceño had moved west from Chansut to Nohayin, a dependency of Mesapich, from where he too reported to the governor of Campeche.[25] It is probable that for the next few years there were at least two major headquarters among the more northerly of the southern *pacíficos*—with Mesapich and its surrounding settlements giving allegiance to Campeche, and Lochhá and its dependent hamlets leaning toward Mérida.

Even so, the new state of Campeche was eager to claim the territory pertaining to both these centers, as was reflected in a census presented to the Mexican congress in 1861 among documents supporting Campeche's claim to separate statehood (table 11).[26]

Despite the numerical strength of the *pacíficos* evident in the figures of table 11, the people were dispersed over a wide region, where individual settlements remained a frequent target of the Santa Cruz rebels. Some years later, for instance, Encalada could say that his pueblo of Lochhá had been invaded and burned on four separate occasions between 1853, the date of the pacification, and 1867.[27]

One of the better attested of those attacks was described briefly in an earlier chapter. This was the raid of January 1863, led by Crescencio Poot, which began with depredations at the Yucatecan town of Becanchén, where the rebels took prisoners, then moved to *pacífico* territory. At Macanché they tried unsuccessfully to convince the commander that they came in peace;

TABLE 11

Pacífico *Settlements Listed in the Campeche Census of 1861*, Partido *of Hopelchén*

Administrative Unit	Settlement	Population	Total
Lochhá Pueblo	Lochhá (*cabecera*)	1,047	
	Rancho Cacabcastro	48	
	Rancho Chankantemo	223	
	Rancho Champich	146	
	Rancho Chanxpuhil	80	
	Rancho Chansut	41	
	Rancho Chanxucchil	121	
	Rancho Chanyakaldzul	161	
	Rancho Holkax	27	
	Rancho Nohkantemo	168	
	Rancho Xarauco	234	
	Rancho Xhalal	131	
	Rancho Xcalotacal	143	
	Rancho Xkancabacal	79	
	Rancho Xkanhal	94	
	Rancho Xpoxoyokal	128	
	Rancho Xyaxché	198	3,069
Mesapich Pueblo	Mesapich (*cabecera*)	921	
	Rancho Elecib	868	
	Rancho Yakalcab	2,576	
	Rancho Nohayín	904	
	Rancho Xkanhá	870	
	Rancho Xmabén	387	
	Rancho Xmakanché	2,793	
	Rancho Xchumpil	1,309	
	Rancho Yacasú	703	11,331
			14,400

Sources: Data are rearranged from information in Aznar Barbachano and Carbó (1861, document 44). The *partido* of Hopelchén then included much of the old colonial *partido* of Camino Real Alto (Rodríguez Losa 1989).

and on the morning of January 5 they moved away only to run into a brief firefight with men of the pueblo under *comandante* Paulino Martín, then attacked Yakaldzul where they took some munitions and livestock. Late in the evening they attacked Lochhá in the midst of its fiesta, taking prisoners and more livestock.[28]

By July of 1863, the title of *comandante general de los pacíficos del Sur* was being claimed by one Manuel Barbosa, an appointee of the governor of Campeche, residing at Mesapich, the evident successor there of Andrés Arana.[29] But there is evidence that Lochhá was not under his thumb, for at the end of October of the same year the official Campeche newspaper reported that "one Encalada has promoted sedition in some of the *cantones* [of the *pacíficos*] inciting them to disobedience, asking their separation from Campeche."[30] No further details are given, but it seems that Encalada and Lochhá did not lean toward Campeche.

But with the triumph in early 1864 of the Maximilian monarchists, the states of Campeche and Yucatan were again united in a single department of Yucatan as part of a centralist organization modeled on that of the Santa Anna era. Indeed, the guidelines for the conduct of government under the new regime were promulgated simply by declaring that Governor Díaz de la Vega's proclamation of November 23, 1853, was again the law. This established local districts and *partidos* of the department and also reaffirmed the existence "in all cities, *villas*, and pueblos" of *repúblicas de indígenas*, which would be administered by a *cacique* appointed from among *hidalgos*.[31]

There was evidently no attempt to impose that *república* organization on the *pacíficos del Sur*. But the absence of such attempt and the elimination of the division between the two former states did not mean that the *pacíficos* were subjected to fewer crosscurrents of influence nor that there were fewer ulterior reasons for peninsular politicians to meddle in their affairs. Beneath a surface calm there was as much friction now between republicans and imperialists as there had ever been between republicans and centralists or between Mérida and Campeche.

Within less than three months of the acceptance of the French-backed regency government, the *pacíficos* were reported on the verge of rebellion. An investigation initiated by the political prefect of the district of Tekax (as the *jefe político* was to be called under the empire) revealed that the excitement was generated by a proclamation circulating over the purported signature of Felipe Navarrete, interim chief of the new department. It announced that the *pacíficos* would be subjected to the standard head tax, that *caciques* would be appointed for them by the government, and that they would be disarmed. The response of the former rebels was, of course, that they would see themselves torn to pieces first.[32]

With the smoothness of the diplomat—and, possibly, of a long-term Mérida partisan—Pablo Encalada wrote to the Tekax prefect, Jacinto Escalante, with professions of faith in the government and certainty that the troublesome proclamation was a hoax. Escalante responded with an embassy of two men who carried conciliatory letters addressed to all the influential *comandantes* of the *pacíficos*; these leaders then met in formal assembly to affix their signatures to a document announcing their recognition of the falsity of the proclamation and their continued fealty to the government. The document, with fifteen signatures, also announced their understanding that those responsible for the hoax were Tiburcio Briceño and one Fernando Medina. Unfortunately, no further details are known.[33]

Despite the ease with which this near rupture was healed, the greatest crisis of the *pacíficos* would erupt under meddling of government officials.

British Honduras against Icaiché

By June 1863, correspondence from Luciano Tzuc carried the dateline "Santa Clara" or "Icaiché," indicating the abandonment of the old settlement of Chichanhá—presumably because of its exposure to raids by the rebels of Santa Cruz—and the establishment of Santa Clara Icaiché.[34] Although only a short distance away and even closer to the upper Hondo, the new site was on a hill surrounded by heavy thickets of cane. For the next decade the people of Icaiché would prove more exasperating to the British than would the active *bravos* to the north, despite the modest size of this southernmost *pacífico* settlement. In 1866, the village was said to have about one hundred houses and a population of some four hundred, of these "fighting men being about one hundred fifty in number, . . . formed of scum of all the surrounding communities, unrecognized by and outlaws from the other border Indians, savage and lazy, ruled only by their wants and desire of ardent spirits."[35]

The first Icaiché-inspired teapot tempest, complete with territorial violation, occurred in 1864. One Susano Canul—Luciano Tzuc's brother-in-law, as it turned out—was accused of killing his son on British ground, and he fled to the Yucatecan side of the frontier, leaving three other children and some livestock at San Román, on Albion Island; San Román was a settlement belonging to Basilio Grajales, a Yucatecan immigrant and naturalized citizen in British Honduras, and the former employer of Susano Canul. Tzuc punctiliously wrote to British Honduras asking to be allowed to take his relative's children and property under his care. Before the requests could be responded to, Tzuc on other business sent his second in command, *comandante* Marcos Canul (who may or may not have been related to Susano) to a settlement in Yucatecan territory near Albion Island with orders to apprehend one Inez Carrillo, who was accused both of stealing some mules from the estate of his own deceased father and of trafficking in powder with the Santa Cruz rebels. But when Canul and his fifteen soldiers had Carrillo and the mules in custody and were on their way to Icaiché, they were attacked by a band of fifty or sixty men, among whom they claimed to recognize Basilio Grajales and other people of San Román. Carrillo and the mules were liberated.

Tzuc next issued a written threat to the settlement of San Román and shortly entered British territory and raided the village. Grajales said Tzuc was accompanied by both Susano Canul and Marcos Canul. Tzuc did not catch Grajales but took his son and more than twenty other hostages, who were dragged to Icaiché to be finally released for ransom. Meanwhile, Grajales was arrested by a British magistrate on suspicion of having led the earlier raid into Yucatan on Marcos Canul; he denied having had anything to do with the raid and then escaped from the magistrate, who had become suddenly very sick.[36]

Exactly where the truth lay was never revealed. On the one hand a respectable British Honduras logging entrepreneur claimed to have learned that Grajales and his San Román men were not involved in the raid on Marcos Canul. On the other, the lieutenant governor of the British colony clearly believed Grajales led the raid and the same reported that he had taken refuge with the Santa Cruz rebels at Bacalar, for whom he was an agent and supplier of munitions.[37] From the British point of view, the real exasperation was that although Tzuc claimed a Campeche appointment as general, datelined his letters *"Imperio Mexicano Icaiché,"* and signed as *"Comandante General de los Pacíficos,"* the central Mexican government refused to take any responsibility for his actions or to attempt to control him, reporting of Icaiché that "if their Principal Chief has any appointment from Campeche or from Yucatan it is certain that he does not derive his authority more than from the personal influence which he exercises over the Indians."[38]

Although the British Honduras officials gave no sign they were aware of it, the local government in Mérida did take some action. In July, one

Dionisio Valencia, a lieutenant colonel of the Yucatecan National Guard, was dispatched to Icaiché to obtain the release of the prisoners. Arriving en route at Lochhá, he found that Encalada had already heard of the matter and was awaiting a report from a Lochhá man who was in Icaiché at the moment. On July 28, the traveler returned with a letter from Tzuc reporting that the British magistrate had demanded the release of the prisoners and that he had complied with the demand. Both Encalada and Valencia were thus able to wash their hands of the affair,[39] while Luciano Tzuc remained to enjoy the ransom.

Later that same year Luciano Tzuc died. But that did not relieve the British of a belligerent neighbor, for he was succeeded as general in command at Icaiché by his former *comandante* Marcos Canul[40]—a man who would show himself even less willing than Luciano to be guided by British inclinations.

It was under Canul that disagreements regarding the sovereignty over territory between the tributaries Blue Creek and Río Bravo, or even between the Hondo and Belize rivers, reached their peak. This was first exacerbated by a decree of the new Imperial Commissary of Yucatan of September 19, 1864, in which that functionary laid claim as part of the Mexican Empire to the entire province of Petén in Guatemala as well as to all of British Honduras.[41] In February 1865, Canul and his second in command, Rafael Chan, wrote to the British Honduras Company to demand a current rental of $250 per year for lands where the company cut mahogany along the Río Bravo—well within British territory by British reckoning—plus back rent of $2,000 for the eight years in which the works had been located there.[42] The company refused to pay rent on the grounds that the works were entirely within British territory. But to sidestep trouble and follow the precedent established by other British concerns on the frontier, they offered to pay $250 per year "subject to your protecting our Gangs from any molestation from other parties"—that is, not as rent, but as "protection."[43]

If Canul was satisfied by this arrangement it was only for a short time. On April 27, 1866, he and a force said to number somewhere between 80 and 125 raided two works on the Río Bravo, logging settlements called Betson's Bank and Quam Hill, where they killed two men, looted stores, drove off cattle, and abducted more than 60 people.[44] Canul's version of the occurrence was that he had gone peaceably to Betson's Bank to arrange for the payment of the "rent," when he was fired upon by the storekeeper, whom his men then killed, and with this changed complexion to the situation he moved on to raid Quam Hill and take hostages. He demanded $12,000 for their release.[45]

When the manager of the British Honduras Company failed to bring off negotiations with Canul, who had dragged the hostages to Icaiché, the lieutenant governor appointed a commission that was able to reach an agreement—paying (partly with public funds) $3,000 directly in ransom, with additional bribes and commissions totaling about $4,000.[46] Canul's acts led, finally, to complaints from Lieutenant Governor Austin in Belize to Pablo Encalada in Lochhá; Encalada replied noncommittally but with thanks for having been informed and appointed a commission of two men to go to the British Honduras frontier to investigate.[47] This appointment was delayed until November, however, so that by the time the commissioners arrived on the Río Hondo events had taken a far more serious turn.

To the discomfiture both of Icaiché and Santa Cruz, one upshot of the Canul operation was a ban on all trade in powder across the frontier except by specific license of the lieutenant governor. A second was the stationing of a British military detachment at Orange Walk on the New River.[48] Nevertheless, Canul's success served to encourage him in his aggressive approach—which would shortly lead to something like real warfare.

Asunción Ek and the San Pedro Skirmishes

It was in May of 1857 that the superintendent of British Honduras had heard the first reports of substantial numbers of Yucatecan Indian fugitives moving into forests of the British settlement.[49] The region of their choice was along the border with Guatemala, south of the Hondo in the upper drainage of the Belize or Old River.

And it was in mid-1860 that the *pacífico* officer José Asunción Ek first came to the notice of the English, when he wrote from the Río Hondo to the magistrate of the northern district asking for assistance in collecting rents from Andrés Zima and other emigrants, said to be owed to the pacified rebels at Chichanhá. He signed himself "Asunción Ek, General."[50] But by 1862 Ek and some followers had left Chichanhá or its environs—possibly out of fear that they would be forced to take up active arms against the rebels of Santa Cruz—and moved deeply south through the region where territory claimed by the British met that of the Petén District of Guatemala. Ek was said to be respected and obeyed on both sides of this "frontier,"[51] the precise location of which was still to be determined.

These new villagers themselves apparently first broached the desirability of having government appointments to confirm locally elected *alcaldes* and other officers, as was the practice in Yucatan and Guatemala. The British Honduras lieutenant governor acceded, appointing village *alcaldes* and sub-*alcaldes*, and giving Asunción Ek the special title of *comandante* with authority over all the villages around his own, San Pedro Siris, "in consideration of his having been a General amongst them."[52] That Ek took his appointment seriously was made clear when he asked for a list of his duties, requested munitions with which to defend British territory, asked for the installation of a school at San Pedro, and complained about damage to the cornfields of his people caused by cattle of the British Honduras Company.[53]

And so things stood until after the Icaiché raids on Quam Hill and Betson's Bank of 1866. At the resolution of that affair, the British commissioner responsible for negotiations recommended that some arms and ammunition be supplied to Ek as a deterrent to further depredations by Canul. They were delivered that same summer.[54]

But in October Captain Peter Delamere, commander of the British military detachment at Orange Walk, New River, also serving there as magistrate, received word from a laborer employed at a logging works near San Pedro Siris that Marcos Canul of Icaiché intended to come to San Pedro in early November, his purpose being to raid logging establishments in the area.[55] Making a grueling two-hundred-kilometer round-trip march to visit settlements and logging works, Delamere arrived at San Pedro to find that Canul had not appeared, although he was daily expected. And where Delamere had anticipated a handful of armed men under Ek's command, he saw about two hundred, who with their commander were obviously mistrustful. His conclusion was that "Ek and his Indians are traitors and are only awaiting Canul's arrival at San Pedro to join him in a raid on English settlements."[56] During his return journey to Orange Walk he took depositions from people familiar with the San Pedro region that strengthened him in this conclusion.

Soon the lieutenant governor received letters from Ek written shortly after Delamere's visit, in which he expressed fear of Icaiché but also fear and distrust of the motives that had occasioned the visit of Delamere's detachment. To these the British official responded by giving Ek permission to resist a force from Icaiché in the event of an attack.[57] But when Canul and his men arrived at San Pedro, Ek's welcome was not belligerent, for on December 4 he wrote to the *alcaldes* of his villages that the Icaiché leaders were present in San Pedro and that they had come in friendship for the purpose of collecting rents from logging works.[58]

Whether this friendship was entirely voluntary on his part is not so certain; some reports, at least, suggested that two of his subordinate officers, Santiago Pech and Juan Balam, were subversively working to unseat Ek and join Icaiché.[59] In any event, Ek's letter followed by a day letters from General Canul and *comandante* Chan datelined San Pedro, demanding money from two logging foremen—six hundred dollars from one for the rent of land logged for nine years and one thousand dollars from the other for land exploited through twelve years. A few days later Canul and Chan wrote to the lieutenant governor of British Honduras stating that the purpose of their visit to San Pedro was to determine whether the British troops had molested the people of that region, which they asserted to be Yucatecan territory.[60] According to priests serving the area, Canul was convinced that the treaty of peace with Yucatan of 1853 gave to the *pacíficos* all lands west of the Belize River.[61]

On the day that Ek had written to his villages, the foreman of one mahogany operation on Labouring Creek, unable to pay immediately the eight hundred dollars in back rent demanded, was taken by a group of armed men to San Pedro. He was held for a week before release.[62] Upon receipt of information of this abduction, of the demands for rents, and of Canul's presence at San Pedro Siris, Lieutenant Governor Austin commissioned a civilian, Edwin Rhys, to deal with Canul and Ek, and he directed Major Angus Mackay of the Fourth West India Regiment to move with Rhys and 140 men by way of the Belize River to San Pedro. At the same time, the Legislative Assembly formally established a militia, and a second, smaller force of these volunteers was sent to move up the Hondo to approach Canul from his flank.[63] The operation was not accomplished swiftly, but Canul's force was still in or around San Pedro when the British arrived.

Traveling by water to the old settlement of Orange Walk on the upper Belize River, located less than twenty kilometers from San Pedro, the main government force marched out on the evening of December 20 along a path cut for trucking mahogany, arriving at 10:00 A.M. the next day within a kilometer of San Pedro. There they suddenly met a band of Canul's men. Both groups began to fire, each later claiming the other had shot first. The skirmish lasted about fifteen minutes, with some casualties on both sides, when retreat was blown by the British bugle. A number of the British soldiers continued to fire for some minutes longer, until Canul's men ran low on powder and began to disperse. Those more pugnacious soldiers then joined the retreat where—as one British historian put it—"the three combatant officers, the gallant major at their head, nobly led the strategic movement to the rear."[64] Equipment and munitions were dropped along the way in what witnesses interpreted as a rout. Commissioner Rhys was never seen again, alive or dead, and was supposed to have been either shot or to have perished later in the bush. The lieutenant governor was furious and blamed Mackay for cowardice, although the official inquiry exonerated him sufficiently that he could sell his commission and leave the service more or less gracefully.[65]

Within a few days there had been a reorganization at San Pedro that drew its people closer to Icaiché. Juan Balam wrote to announce his appointment by Canul as *comandante* of San Pedro and to say that he would be collecting rents.[66]

It was only after this—the beginning of February—that the commissioners of Pablo Encalada arrived at the British Honduran frontier to investigate Canul's behavior and to report ineffectually that Encalada had written to Canul to demand both that he desist from aggressive acts and that he present himself at Lochhá.[67] Ironically, the visit of the commission occurred precisely as some party attacked the settlement of Indian Church, plundered the place, killed two men, and burned three buildings; men of San Pedro and of the associated village of San José, located on a tributary of Booth's River and the Río Bravo, were suspected.[68] And by now British machinery had been set in motion that, although it did not reduce the predominantly Indian population of Icaiché or San Pedro to submission, served partially to assuage British feelings.

In January 1867 the military garrison of the colony had been enlarged by three hundred men of the Third West India Regiment under Lieutenant Colonel Robert Harley. On January 30, Harley, brevetted Brigadier General, sailed from Belize City with a substantial force of the Third and Fourth West India Regiments, to move up the Sibun River and thence to Orange Walk, Belize River, where he arrived on February 3—the very day of the Indian Church raid. The detachment moved against various settlements in the region, burning San Pedro Siris on February 9 and nearby San José on February 12, only in the latter place receiving even token resistance. In the fiesta hall at San Pedro was found hanging a letter from Ek to the governor claiming that by treaty the entire region west of the Belize River belonged to the *pacíficos*.[69]

This did not settle things. Less than two weeks after the destruction, Juan Balam was reported to have rounded up dispersed campesino families at the settlement of Guinea Grass, located on the New River not far from Orange Walk, and moved them to areas under his control. Fears were expressed that the New River town of Orange Walk itself was in danger.[70] As demands for rents also continued, Lieutenant Governor Austin dispatched a body of militia under Captain John Carmichael Jr. (of whom much will be heard later) to move through the region of the earlier disturbances "to arrest traitors and recover plunder." Carmichael set out at the end of March 1867 and took the opportunity to destroy San José (which was being rebuilt by its occupants) and nearby Santa Cruz Chumbalché—acts that Harley branded as ill advised.[71] Most of the people of the villages that had been struck abandoned the region and moved westward into Guatemala. Ek was known to be in league with Canul and for at least a time was with other refugees at Santa Rita, Petén. Some of the fugitives would be slowly induced to return.[72]

By April of that year, 1867, Lieutenant Governor Austin could report that he had received word from Encalada that he had Canul in custody and that Ek and Balam had been chased out of the region. Although Canul was not in Encalada's hands for long—if, indeed, he ever was—the beefed-up British military detachment maintained in British Honduras over the next three years was enough to deter most acts of aggressive extortion.[73]

The Arredondo Affair

As I noted earlier, with the assumption of authority in Mexico first by the regency and then by Emperor Maximilian, the government was reorganized along centralist lines. As imperial commissary appointed to govern the peninsula of Yucatan, José Salazar Ilarregui arrived in Mérida in September 1864 to replace Felipe Navarrete, who had served as interim head since early that year.[74]

Salazar quickly turned his attention to the embarrassing existence of the eastern rebellion, which some observers believed he did not at first take seriously, attributing its continuation to the machinations of certain Yucatecans who found personal gain in it.[75] In October, he appointed a *defensor de indios*, "Defender of Indians," to provide counsel in the legal system, and the next month he issued the predictable call to the active rebels to make peace, which of course they ignored.[76]

He also found the de facto independence of the southern *pacíficos* to be an insult to the imperial dignity. He promptly set about to appoint an official representative of the emperor to govern the southerners and bring them back into the national society. His choice for this office, however, left something to be desired.

José María Martínez de Arredondo—the name often appearing simply as José María Arredondo—was from a distinguished Mérida family. Born in 1837 as one of the younger sons of Francisco Martínez de Arredondo, lawyer, legislator, and political friend and sometime secretary of Governor Miguel Barbachano, José María was the younger brother of a second Francisco Martínez de Arredondo, whose distinguished legal career would take him to the supreme court of Mexico.[77] José María, however, was of different stuff.

Criminally indicted in 1862 for "abuses committed while holding a commission as inspector of maritime customs in Sisal,"[78] he was evidently at liberty in December of 1863 while the case was pending, for then José María had managed to enter Chan Santa Cruz and apparently remain there for a number of days—either immediately before or immediately after the assassination of Venancio Puc—and he evidently also made contact with Luciano Tzuc, then general at Icaiché. On his return to Mérida, in a gesture obviously designed to attract attention and build public sympathy, he wrote to the editor of the official newspaper the letter described in an earlier chapter, in which he listed by name a number of prisoners he knew to be alive in rebel hands.[79]

Despite public appreciation of Arredondo's gesture,[80] by the following fall he was in jail.[81] When it seemed in October 1864 that the proceeding was going against him, he wrote a flowery plea for his release to Salazar Ilarregui. He enclosed a letter to himself from Luciano Tzuc dated September 18, 1864, in which among many other protestations of friendship and respect Tzuc waxed indignant over José María's incarceration and possible deportation to Cuba "after so many services you alone . . . contributed by entering among those *malditos* of Santa Cruz and urging revolution among them, now they repay you like this." Tzuc also offered to furnish men for the reconquest of Bacalar.[82]

With this evidence of his standing with Tzuc, as well as what must have been a persuasive manner, Arredondo was not only released from jail but was appointed political prefect to the southern *pacíficos*.[83] He went to the south in November 1864.

He was in the news again the following January, for on the sixth of that month he appeared in Mérida shepherding fifty-seven representatives of twelve settlements of the southern *pacíficos* who pledged their loyalty to the imperial government and stated that they accepted the emperor's plan of organization. It was announced that a dozen of the delegates would go to the capital to pledge their allegiance to Maximilian in person.[84] This audience with the emperor occurred on January 28, 1865, as Arredondo was lauded by the Mexican press for his efforts directed toward smoothing relations with the "Indians."[85]

For the next nine months Arredondo lived with the *pacíficos*, establishing his seat at Mesapich. By decree of Salazar, Pablo Encalada served as subprefect—that is, as Arredondo's second in command, while still living at Lochhá.

It is not clear just when friction developed between Arredondo and his charges. In the early months he sent a string of letters to Salazar in Mérida, giving detailed reports of his activities. He called a great conclave to explain the new order; he opened water wells; he instituted the collection of taxes on goods imported into the region, appointing Tiburcio Briceño tax collector and striving to place the tax collection point so that it could control all access roads; and he prepared accommodations for circuit priests. He reported that his relations with Encalada and the Indians were excellent but that his association with mestizos of the region—especially the traveling merchants—was not pleasant, and he asked repeatedly for a small force of armed men to keep—he said—the traders in line.[86]

But his administration was unhappy for people other than the traders, who of course objected to the new taxes. By September, complaints against him were lodged with the *defensor de indios*, alleging dictatorial behavior and minor financial extortion. According to Encalada, José María had the poor judgment to beat and injure the Mesapich *comandante*.[87] Whatever the total base of complaints, by the middle of October 1865 Arredondo had evidently been informed that his removal was pending.[88] But it was never carried out, for on October 24 he was murdered.

The official publications are entirely silent with regard to the assassination and its immediate aftermath, although various rumors flew at the time.[89] Fortunately, there are manuscript documents that bear directly on the events.

What is clear is that on October 24 a substantial body of people had collected at Mesapich. According to one account the meeting was to appoint a new *comandante* for that settlement. Encalada asserted that he and an armed guard had gone there at Arredondo's request to deal with trouble between the latter and the existing *comandante*—apparently the one José María was accused of beating—and that on his arrival he found that Arredondo had mustered his own armed force from Nohayín. There ensued a confrontation between Arredondo's party and men of other settlements, who had apparently been stirred up by the Mesapich *comandante*. The size of this second group prevented anyone from intervening to save the political prefect.[90]

The most detailed of the eyewitness reports said that at the gathering Encalada was actually hearing and attempting to deal with various complaints against Arredondo when the proceeding was disrupted by the sudden appearance of "more than one hundred men" from around Xmabén. They surrounded the plaza in sufficient numbers to intimidate everyone else, some of them entering Arredondo's house and dragging him from his hammock to the center of the plaza. There they slapped him, beat him with gun butts, and finally hacked him with machetes. They ended by mutilating the corpse.[91]

After the killing, and on the same day, multiple copies of a document signed by Encalada and thirty-five other commanders were sent to nearby *vecino* towns and to Mérida. These circulars announced that the pacified rebels would stand together, that they intended to remain where they were, and that "against him who would hurt the soldiers or their commanders we will raise our hand" but that they were enemies of no one except the rebels of the east.[92]

No government response followed the assassination or the circular. Whether this was because of embarrassing aspects of the Arredondo appointment, which has the earmarks of a local scandal, or because of the wider situation of the empire in Yucatan is not certain. For things were becoming unstable: in the same month, October, the government of Tabasco, never brought under imperial control, had furnished troops to Pablo García for the reconquest of Campeche, and his little army was in action under Colonel Celestino Brito.

On November 10, having had no reaction to their broadly circulated announcement, the *pacíficos* gathered at the settlement of Xmabén and issued a formal act of independence. The seven articles declared the south separated from Yucatan, recognized Encalada as *gobernador* and José Antonio Uc as *comandante general*, asserted the maintenance of open trade and travel with Yucatan, promised peaceful relations with the government and towns of Yucatan, and called for the services of priests. The act was signed by twenty-two men of high rank, presumably *comandantes*, and eighty captains. A week later a copy of the act was sent by Encalada to the imperial officer in Tekax for transmittal to Mérida.[93]

There was still no overt government reaction, and the *pacíficos* pursued their usual course, now more than ever convinced of their ability to go their own way. Events of the following year, however, would cause the declaration of independence to be forgotten by those of them who did not want to resume the war.

The Subversion of Lochhá

The relationship of the death of Arredondo to the ensuing disruption of the *pacíficos* of 1866 and 1867 is obscure, although contemporaries asserted that there was some connection.[94] One apparently surreptitious government observer, however, reported no outstanding harbingers of revolution in the *pacífico* region but instead detailed a situation of inherent instability such as had been characteristic of all the *masewalob* since the rebellion first began.

Among the heavily Indian population of pacified rebels, this observer said, there had gathered a substantial number of army deserters and fugitives from justice, who were in large part mestizos. Although nominally ruled again by the politically adept Encalada with the title of governor, now with the support of Antonio Uc, of Xmabén, as general, each pueblo was governed in practical independence by its commanders, among whom there were factional divisions. One party was led by Uc and his commanders of Xmabén, who were under the influence of two sometime merchants of Iturbide, the brothers Andrés and Manuel Barbosa, the latter having held the Campeche appointment as commandant in chief. Encalada and his assistants of Lochhá led a second party; Buenaventura Cruz and Paulino Martín of Macanché, a third; and the brothers Eugenio and Andrés Arana, now of Yakalcab, still another.[95]

This instability was tipped decisively as some of these factions gravitated toward the rebels of Santa Cruz, and the fragile balance broke. Actual hostilities were not opened until late June of 1867—a year and a half after Arredondo's death and the declaration of independence—but there had been a number of preliminary signs of increased contact with the Santa Cruz rebels.

In September 1866, Andrés Arana had visited Albion Island on the Río Hondo, representing himself as a merchant of Lochhá in quest of powder not for the *pacíficos* but for Santa Cruz. As the story was obtained by the British, Santa Cruz and Lochhá had combined their interests, and during the ban on powder sales from British Honduras that had followed the Icaiché attack on Quam Hill, Arana had been commissioned by Noh Cah Santa Cruz in the hope that, being from Lochhá, he might have better luck buying powder than they did.[96]

The following month, on October 20, 1866, what amounted to a commission as general under Noh Cah Santa Cruz was issued to *comandante* Paulino Martín of Macanché: this was in the form of a written exhortation to him and all *masewalob* by the cross speaking as the son of God, issued from the "grand and populous city of Santa Cruz," and urging them to unite against the enemy. It was signed "Juan de la Cruz three persons."[97] In May of 1867 Martín and five other *pacífico* officers sought a passport from Encalada to go to Corozal in British Honduras, but actually they went to Noh Cah Santa Cruz where they agreed to induce their people to join the active rebel camp.[98] In retrospect, at least one observer opined that the underlying reason for the defection was fear that the central government might still take active steps to punish the killers of Arredondo.[99]

The subversion of some factions, however, did not signal a change in allegiance for all. And when the revolt came it was with armed assistance from soldiers of Santa Cruz under Crescencio Poot.

In January 1867 the anti-imperialist Manuel Cepeda Peraza, who had been ordered to stay within the limits of Mérida by the Salazar government, managed to get out of the city and join the republican forces besieging the imperial remnants in Campeche, while much of the outlying area of the former state was already under Pablo García's control.[100] In February García appointed Manuel Barbosa as *jefe político* of the Chenes district—an appointment that raised eyebrows.[101] And late in the same month Salazar Ilarregui declared that Mérida was at military risk, although the city was not invested by forces under Cepeda Peraza until April. On May 15, Maximilian was captured by republicans at Queretaro; on June 1, Campeche fell to Brito and García; on June 15 Mérida fell to Cepeda Peraza; and on June 16, 1867, Maximilian was executed. And the end of the Mexican Empire coincided almost perfectly with the end of peace in the south.

On June 18 a *pacífico* soldier ran to tell *gobernador* Encalada in Lochhá that the Santa Cruz rebels were coming. Encalada's first act was to warn a visiting priest, who left the pueblo immediately, and within minutes a rebel force that Encalada reported to be around a thousand strong (others estimated four hundred to six hundred) was led into the plaza by Crescencio Poot, guided by Paulino Martín and four of the *comandantes* who had been with him in Santa Cruz that spring.

Encalada was upbraided by the newcomers for his poor relations with the eastern rebels and was imprisoned, while some Yucatecan merchants were seized, robbed, and killed. Paulino Martín was named general, and one Pablo Kuyoc of Lochhá took the office of governor. Then the eastern army departed, ostensibly to raid the Yucatecan lines to the north. Encalada was held prisoner by the *pacífico* turncoats until June 27, when their new leaders appeared before him with a small armed squad, intent on putting him to the machete. But the common soldiers refused to execute Governor

Encalada, and in the confusion that resulted he was able to send a call for help to General José Antonio Uc in Xmabén. Uc arrived promptly the next day with three hundred of his soldiers and clapped Kuyoc and three other ringleaders in jail, while at the same time the loyal commandant of Nohayín, Andrés Huchim, imprisoned Paulino Martín of nearby Macanché. The sixth defector, Asunción Cab, who was second commandant of Macanché, made his escape, and Encalada believed he fled to Chan Santa Cruz with word that would bring another rebel force upon them.

With the agreement of loyal *comandantes* Huchim and Juan Crisóstomo Chable of Nohayín, Uc ordered the execution by machete of the five captured conspirators. The sentence was carried out formally on July 4 in Mesapich, with representatives of each *pacífico cantón* in attendance.[102]

The prompt action of Uc did not end the rebellion or the involvement with the Santa Cruz rebels, however. Wisely, Encalada chose to leave Lochhá immediately with his family.[103]

In late July word was received in Iturbide that Lochhá and Macanché had been occupied by forces of Chan Santa Cruz, apparently without a struggle, and the following day Nohayín was taken against only light resistance. General Uc reported that forces from Xmabén had left for the fray.[104]

Although the imperial government had ignored the earlier declaration of independence, republican Campeche called up militia and raced double time to the scene. Governor García himself went to Hopelchén for the operation, with Colonel José Luis Santini in charge at Iturbide. Santini moved to occupy Nohayín, while Encalada and *comandante* Juan Chable retreated to Dzibalchén, and Uc held firm at Xmabén.[105] A few days later Santini reported that all of the "so-called *pacíficos del Sur*, with the exception of some two hundred men at most, under Uc, Huchim, and Chable, have made common cause with the rebels of Santa Cruz, and are found today arms in hand." A firsthand, if probably exaggerated, report was that the combined southern and Santa Cruz force in the region totaled two thousand.[106] Most of the newly rebellious were from the eastern *pacífico* sector— Lochhá, Chunxán, Kantemo, Yakalcab, Chunupil, Mesapich, and Macanché, while the booty taken in their raids was said to be accumulated at Mesapich. The western centers of Xmabén and Nohayín, as well as some of the people of Mesapich and Xkanhá, remained loyal. But the rebels did move briefly into the western sector for Xmabén was burned when Uc was temporarily dislodged.[107]

But the tenacious defense by Uc and the Campeche forces under Santini had their effect and something of a line was held. Before the middle of

TABLE 12

Major Southern Pacífico *Commanders, 1853–68*

Chichanhá/Icaiché[a]	Mesapich	Lochhá
José María Tzuc, 1853–54	José María Cocom, 1853–58	Pablo Encalada, 1853–67
Andrés Zima, 1854–56		
Luciano Tzuc, 1856–57		
Feliciano Ya, 1857–61	Andrés Arana, 1860-?63	
José Uluac, 1861–63		
Luciano Tzuc, 1863–64	Manuel Barbosa, ?1863–67	
Marcos Canul, 1864–		
	fragmentation and warfare, 1867–68	

Sources: See text.

[a]Removal from Chichanhá to Icaiché occurred in 1863 under Luciano Tzuc.

August the Santa Cruz rebels pulled out for their city. According to the account of a spy sent by General Uc to rebel-held Mesapich, Crescencio Poot bade farewell to the southerners, saying "I have the bull cinched; play him with the cape if you want to, but I'm going home."[108]

The defecting southerners then shifted their people eastward, abandoning the more westerly of the *cantones* while retaining control of Lochhá and Yakaldzul, and word was received that they would move most of their population still farther east into former Santa Cruz territory, to be concentrated around Santa Rosa, Polyuc, and Chunhuhub. On September 8 Colonel Santini attacked and took Yakalcab, holding it for three days before retreating again to Xmabén,[109] after which relative calm descended.

Meanwhile even farther to the south most of Icaiché territory had remained loyal to the government, although people in the easternmost sector —at Ramonal and Los Cocos on the Río Hondo—did defect to Santa Cruz.[110] Whether they actually engaged in fighting at the time of the Lochhá insurrection is not evident, but later that year Icaiché attacked Ramonal, claiming to defeat the defectors under Juan Bautista Yam—the only principal of the peace agreement of 1853 who appears among the newly rebellious southerners of 1867.[111]

Between 1853 and the close of the 1860s, shifts in power alignments and leadership among the *pacíficos* occurred with confusing frequency; the sole exception was the lengthy tenure of Pablo Encalada at Lochhá (see table 12). But the relative peace that settled in the south after 1868 coincided with the beginning of the last and most quiescent stage of the continuing war of rebellion, as will be seen in later chapters. Although in that time *pacífico* tranquility was punctuated by sporadic if minor raids by the *bravos*, leadership was stable. But the extent and population of the important region formerly subservient to Mesapich and Lochha were much diminished by the defections of 1866–67. They would remain so for almost two decades.

15 / Rebels and Friends

In the decade of the 1860s, after palace revolts convulsed Noh Cah Santa Cruz and while the southern *pacíficos* rended themselves between east and west, not only colonists but officials of British Honduras gravitated toward the overt paternalism that would characterize their dealings with the Santa Cruz rebels for the rest of the century. This attitude was intensified late in the decade, when elimination of Maximilian's empire was followed by a decisive rupture in diplomatic relations between Mexico and Britain, making cooperation between the Mexican states of the peninsula and the British settlement-turned-colony even less likely than before.

For their part, as the new leaders of Noh Cah Santa Cruz consolidated their power their steps included new gestures of friendship toward their useful British neighbors. In these, the John Carmichaels, father and son, new aristocrats of the British frontier, were inextricably involved.

A Change of Landlords

The figure of John Carmichael the elder strides onto the scene at Corozal in 1859, when he succeeded James Hume Blake as chief property owner of the district. Indeed, there would be two John Carmichaels, father and son, and for the elder this was by no means a first appearance in Central America.

A merchant of Liverpool, in 1845 Carmichael had extended his dealings to the Mosquito Coast of Nicaragua and Honduras, exporting British manufactures to Central America and returning his ships with cargos of mahogany cut by his own crews on lands granted by the British-supported royal government of Mosquitia. Some of his affairs at this time were apparently handled by an agent in Belize, and he must have already been familiar with British Honduras. But Central America was politically unstable, and the Mosquito Kingdom was the subject of hearty dispute over sovereignty. In the early 1850s the Carmichael logging works in northwestern Mosquitia was destroyed in hostile military actions by the government of Honduras (the nation called Spanish Honduras by the British) and in depredations by desperados. As was customary, Carmichael submitted claims for monetary reparations to the British government, which transmitted them to Honduras. The result was a lengthy set of pleas that by October 1858 had obtained no result; John Carmichael was adjudged bankrupt, and the claims were assumed by his creditors.[1]

The bankruptcy did not depress Carmichael's entrepreneurial talents nor, obviously, did it destroy the faith of his backers. The same year in which his Mosquitia enterprise ended on the rocks he was licensed to cut mahogany in British Honduras for ninety-nine years in the name of Carmichael Vidal & Company. Less than six months after the bankruptcy judgment itself, he announced to the superintendent of British Honduras that he had taken possession of the properties of the ailing Mr. Blake in the north of the British settlement and so was now landlord and *patrón* at Corozal. To cater to his new Yucatecan and Indian tenants—who were in the majority on his property—he suggested the initiation of a Sunday market, which in fact was forbidden by the settlement's blue law. With characteristic presumptuousness he also proposed a number of administrative changes in the government of the district.[2]

The following year, 1860, he obtained a ninety-nine-year lease on five thousand acres of crown lands in the vicinity of Corozal. But by 1864 the assets of Carmichael Vidal & Company were in the hands of liquidators in bankruptcy, and his license to cut mahogany was sold.[3] Thereafter, Carmichael concentrated on agriculture, creating one of the first sugar plantations in British Honduras by developing the estate of San Andrés, located a short distance west of Corozal. On the New River south of Corozal he built the local version of a manor house, which he grandly christened Pembroke Hall.

In the spring of 1865, Carmichael—now holding an appointment as justice of the peace—came headfirst against the major local representative of government, when as *patrón* he announced that a form of bullfighting would be permitted during a fiesta to be held in the Maya town of Xaibé, located on his lands. He was challenged in this proposed violation of the law by the newly appointed (and very young) magistrate of the northern district, Edwin Adolphus, but Carmichael permitted it anyway, while constables watched. Adolphus brought charges against all the bully boys—Yucatecan and English—who had taken part in the bull teasing. These were defended by Carmichael's lawyer.

Although all were found guilty and fined, Adolphus was subjected to rough verbal treatment by the lawyer and Carmichael, who followed the trial with a petition to the British Honduras Legislative Assembly, for which Carmichael collected signatures from his Mayan and Yucatecan tenants. The document accused Adolphus of misuse of authority and harassment of the populace, and asked for redress. James Hume Blake, still in the region, reported to the lieutenant governor that the signatures had been obtained by extortion, and the assembly disallowed the petition.[4] The occurrence can be interpreted in various ways, but it is clear both that Carmichael used it to impress the new magistrate with his stature and that he felt free to use coercion against his dependents to achieve his ends.

Flight of the Chinese

As operator of an important sugarcane plantation, Carmichael received an allotment of Chinese immigrants in 1865, when British Honduras imported 474 indentured laborers from Amoy.[5] This attempt to overcome the shortage of agricultural hands brought forth complaints from Carmichael to the lieutenant governor in February 1866 about the quality of Chinese labor and an oblique request for the transfer of his own laborers to someone else. By July he found them working better and did not give them up.[6]

In August, however, Lieutenant Governor Austin reported that about one hundred of the Chinese had "absconded from the estates of the British Honduras Co. on the New River" to cross the Hondo and join the Santa Cruz rebels. They were said to have been "goaded into desertion by injudicious and unjust if not cruel neglect or treatment on the part of the manager."[7] Although Austin blamed the affair entirely on the British Honduras Company, a later administrator of the colony reported that most of the trouble had taken place on Carmichael's San Andrés estate, where the gangfighting Chinese had killed a foreman.[8] When in September the Corozal magistrate received a report from a trader to Santa Cruz regarding efforts to return the Chinese to the colony, it contained a reference to one who had worked for Carmichael:

> The Chinese, the chiefs say, are Indians like themselves, and . . . the cross at Tulum has ordered that they are to be well treated and taught to work and to be distributed among the officers for that purpose. One of them who speaks Spanish well, undoubtedly the Pembroke Hall interpreter, told him, Mr. A. [i.e., Domingo Andrade,

the trader, brother-in-law of James Hume Blake], that they deeply regretted having gone to Santa Cruz. . . . There are 108 of them at present. . . . Four in all have died. The General Bel [Bernardino] Cen killed one himself for having left his rancho without his permission.[9]

Whatever the motive for Santa Cruz's refusal to return them to the British in 1866, its leaders would be sorry later, for the retention of the enterprising Chinese had an unforeseen economic effect on rebel society.[10] Meanwhile, the active rebels of Noh Cah Santa Cruz had other enterprises at hand.

Action in the North

In his short reign at Santa Cruz, Dionisio Zapata had declared an end to the chronic raiding of the Yucatecan lines, but there was no comparably pacific policy adopted by the triumvirate of Bonifacio Novelo, Bernardino Cen, and Crescencio Poot, which succeeded him. Although the three spent 1864 largely consolidating their power at Santa Cruz itself, by late November they were ready for new adventures. These first took the form of a weeklong thrust into the region between Tepich and Tzucacab, where they raided nearly twenty settlements, left fifty-five citizens dead and others wounded, and took booty. Counterattacking Yucatecans did the rebels no serious harm.[11]

The attacks stimulated a letter to the official newspaper of Yucatan from the historian Serapio Baqueiro, in which he pointed out that the *sublevados bravos*—the fighting rebels—were better officered and better equipped than before and that even if their total number did not exceed four thousand (the estimate made by the futile Yucatecan peace commission of that year) they were more dangerous than ever.[12] There is little doubt that the improvement in equipment was owed to trade into British Honduras. Descriptions of the rebel soldiers only a few years later seem to indicate that at least some of them were using percussion muskets rather than the older and less efficient flintlocks. These were almost certainly surplus British army guns available through civilian traders, providing a great improvement in reliability, particularly in wet weather. If these were standard rebel equipment it is doubtful that the Yucatecan militia or even regular Mexican troops who came to Yucatan were significantly better armed.[13]

After 1864 Maximilian's government moved to improve the military forces on the peninsula. In February 1865 the Mexican general José María Gálvez arrived at the head of a battalion of regular Mexican troops and was dispatched to Valladolid where he assumed command of the lines facing the rebels. And at the end of April General Severo del Castillo arrived to command the entire active military force of the department, now designated the Seventh Imperial Division. He let no time pass before he put into effect a plan that was a modest forerunner of the strategy that would be used in the final conquest of the *masewalob* nearly forty years later. Rather than content himself with slashing forays through the woods to Chan Santa Cruz (as the Yucatecans persisted in calling the rebel capital), he would cut a broad road to tie that center firmly to Tihosuco so it could be occupied permanently.

Work on the road was begun by six hundred Yucatecan soldiers under Colonel Francisco Cantón. But at Dzonot they were attacked and put under siege by a very large enemy force. To relieve them, Gálvez moved from Valladolid with 250 Mexican regulars, half a dozen cannon, munitions, and rations. Augmenting these with 150 Yucatecans, he moved through Tihosuco on June 17 and approached within six kilometers of Dzonot without resistance. Then he was hit from all sides and brought to a halt. With great difficulty, his disciplined section moved slowly and finally gained Dzonot—in the process losing many men, his cannon, his mules, and his baggage.

In Dzonot without supplies, the only recourse for the now combined force was to return over the broad track to Tihosuco. The withdrawal began on June 19. The regulars behaved well but the rest of the force broke and ran, leaving wounded, guns, personal equipment, and corpses scattered all the way to safety. Securely back and with evident reference to tendencies in the Mexican capital to belittle the intensity of the Caste War, Gálvez said something that can be roughly rendered (for accounts differ regarding his exact wording), "The next man who tells me there is no Indian war in Yucatan I'll blow his head off!"[14]

No further attempt was made to put the brave plan into operation.

The following year, Severo del Castillo was reassigned to Mexico, to be replaced as commander of the Seventh Division by another Mexican, General Francisco G. Casanova, who within a few months—perhaps with the ambitious view of taking the offensive again—dispatched Lieutenant Colonel Daniel Traconis and a battalion of men from Valladolid to Tihosuco. Almost immediately, on August 3, 1866, the force was invested by the rebels, who were able to penetrate the outskirts of the town and pin the government troops within the plaza. Unlike the year before at Dzonot, no relief came. Even though substantial detachments from Valladolid and Peto moved to within striking distance, they simply stopped and waited. Inside

Tihosuco hunger grew, and although messengers were able occasionally to slip through the lines and call for help, none came. At long last, on September 15 a column under Teodosio Canto and Feliciano Padilla hacked their way through the besiegers to strengthen the garrison, but they brought no supplies and their presence made things worse. About this time a report was put out by the inactive "reinforcements," still parked a safe distance away, that Tihosuco had fallen. Mérida lamented. Nevertheless, with a desperate set of coordinated frontal and flanking attacks, the Tihosuco defenders were able to dislodge many of the besiegers and burn their camps. On September 23 they saw the *masewalob* lift their siege and disengage—after fifty-three hungry days.[15]

It was in the month following the Tihosuco siege that the cross of Santa Cruz sent its written commission to Paulino Martín appointing him general among the *pacíficos* of the south, as described in the last chapter. Yet while Yucatecan patriots busied themselves with the campaigns against the sagging remnants of the empire in Campeche and Mérida, leaving the eastern front exposed, the usually active rebels made no major aggressive moves against the *dzules*.

It may be that the ban on powder sales declared by Governor Austin in July 1866 was having its effect. At any rate, the *masewalob* showed themselves particularly anxious to buy British powder in early 1867. But it would be several months before they were finally able to do so, and then it was only owing to the efforts of their good friend John Carmichael.

Cultivating the Rebels: The Great Powder Heist

Just when John Carmichael the younger joined his father in British Honduras is not clear, but it was not later than 1861. By 1866 he could claim to speak both Maya and Spanish, and late that year he served as interpreter and commissioner to the Indians when Captain Delamere made his advance on San Pedro.[16] With the creation of the British Honduras militia, John Jr. was named captain and commander of the detachment at Corozal, in which capacity he undertook the destruction of the villages of San José and Chunbalché in early 1867. This act alienated him from the *pacíficos* of Icaiché but did nothing to hurt the standing of the Carmichaels at Noh Cah Santa Cruz.

While John the younger was still preparing his strike against San José, John the elder was courting Santa Cruz favor by promoting a meeting with rebel representatives in order to smooth future commerce and especially by negotiating a shipment of powder to them under a special permit from Lieutenant Governor Austin. Although Austin's Executive Council agreed that Carmichael should pursue trade agreements, it firmly opposed any sale of powder. Despite its negative recommendation, in early February Austin promised Carmichael he would issue a permit for him to ship powder to Bacalar, the governor's reasoning being that his ban on powder sales was meant to apply only to those people hostile to the British, which included Canul and Icaiché but not at the time the *masewalob* of Santa Cruz.

And so forty kegs of powder were loaded on a boat at Belize and—over the separate protest of the Legislative Assembly[17]—were sent to the neighborhood of Corozal. On February 15 the kegs and other merchandise were embarked under care of one Francisco Moreno and two hands. On the lower Hondo a dory intercepted Moreno. Six men boarded his boat, demanded the powder, and scuffled with the crewmen. Moreno jumped overboard and while in the water was shot twice, but he reached the British shore and escaped, as did his two men. The attackers with the powder then headed for Yucatecan territory, reportedly intending to make their way to Mérida by boat. A vessel dispatched from Corozal did not find them, nor did a rebel force from Bacalar.[18]

The attackers were Francisco Meneses, the brothers Miguel and Encarnación Mena, and three others. Meneses, the Menas, and one of the others were Yucatecans who had lived in Corozal for some time; the other two were from elsewhere, apparently Central America. Subsequent inquiry showed that Meneses claimed a commission as captain in the Yucatecan army, was said to have been absent from Corozal while he served with his military unit in besieged Tihosuco, and carried written authorization from Maximilian's government in Yucatan to interdict traffic with the Santa Cruz rebels. Encarnación Mena held the Yucatecan rank of sergeant.[19]

In later years the affair would probably have seemed more amusing than serious, if Moreno had not died within several days of the attack. Eight years later, Miguel Mena was finally tried in Corozal for murder and was convicted and hanged.[20]

After the hijacking, the rebel triumvirate continued to importune the lieutenant governor for permission to buy powder—for a fiesta, they insisted—and John Carmichael continued to urge the sale.[21] Arrangements for another transaction went forward, although now in secret. Yet in early May the *masewalob* were forced to go into their major fiesta of the Holy Cross without their powder.[22]

Public objections to the suspected shipment continued to be raised in Belize.[23] But the arrangements—now for 220 kegs, to be shipped under rebel guard but in a British vessel—were completed so quietly that when two rebel *comandantes* arrived in Belize City in June to receive their license from the hand of the lieutenant governor himself, they were forced to cool their heels until he came home from a trip, for not even the colonial secretary knew what was going on.[24]

They finally received the shipment and had powder for the raid on Lochhá in June and July 1867, when their army under Crescencio Poot spearheaded the fight against Campeche and her few remaining *pacífico* allies (see chapter 14). As the *masewalob* left Lochhá, they promised to attack Icaiché, which unlike other *pacífico* settlements had failed to heed their invitation to join again in rebellion.[25] They may well have made use of some of the powder in action farther north, too, for sometime that year they apparently fell on Tihosuco, once so dearly defended but left essentially unguarded as Yucatecan republicans struggled in the west to unseat the imperial government and then settle differences among themselves. By late 1867 the *masewalob* had reportedly destroyed Tihosuco "to the foundations,"[26] and it was finally abandoned by the government.

A Tourist in Noh Cah Santa Cruz

John Carmichael the elder did not drop his role as advocate for the rebels of Santa Cruz with the successful shipment of powder. In August, at about the time that the Santa Cruz army ended its campaign against the Campeche forces in the formerly pacified south and left that fight to the newly rebellious *masewalob* of Lochhá, Carmichael wrote to the lieutenant governor that one Diego Ake, an important rebel, was in Corozal with a number of his followers to trade. Carmichael took the opportunity to complain about the duties charged these deserving if belligerent friends, and his statement gives an idea of their major exports to British territory. "They understood and so did I that all their produce except Horses and Cattle, would be admitted free. Such is not the case. The magistrate exacts a trifling Duty on Swine, and they are liable to pay Duty on Rice, Beans or Frijoles, Straw Hats, Rubbing Stones, Heniquen and Henniquen Ropes, Dryd Peppers."[27] This brought no concessions but only a memorandum from the colony treasurer to the lieutenant governor, stating that the law required those duties.[28] Despite the tax, the Santa Cruz men conducted commerce as usual.

Although clearly sympathetic to the rebels, it is not clear that Carmichael had at this point any direct hand in trading with Noh Cah Santa Cruz. His son soon would have, however.

In September and October 1867, John Carmichael the younger made what seems to have been his first trip to Noh Cah Santa Cruz, one that may not yet have involved trade, although that would follow. And if his account of that trip was written with an ulterior interest that he made no real attempt to hide, it is certainly one of the most succinctly complete descriptions of the place and the organization of its people that has survived.

The trading outpost of Bacalar young John found largely tumbled down, the camp of a garrison of two hundred or more rebel soldiers, surrounded by sentry posts. There Carmichael was housed for the night on the plaza, then furnished with horses for his train and with six rebel soldiers for escort. It took five days to traverse the road from Bacalar to Santa Cruz, during the first four of which there no settlements were seen. On the fifth day the party passed a number of villages and a series of guard posts, until they reached the city itself, where at the outskirts Carmichael was asked to dismount and wait. He was then met by Crescencio Poot with an honor guard of two hundred men and a band of thirty-two musicians and escorted to the plaza, where he was again well housed.

The following day he visited Bonifacio Novelo, "the Patron or Head Chief," who lived in a fine house across the square from the stone church. Novelo said he was head of the church, which possessed more than two hundred thousand dollars (as Carmichael expressed it) in currency as well as jewels and ornaments. He was also the administrator of civil justice, lauded by Carmichael as "firm yet impartial." Novelo made clear that his people could be counted on to aid the English against the pugnacious soldiers of Icaiché, should they be asked to.

Carmichael visited Bernabel [sic] Cen, the second chief and commander of the army, who claimed his force consisted of eleven thousand men, to which the defectors of Lochhá and Macanché contributed four thousand. Each soldier performed fifteen days of military service every month without pay, his musket and ammunition supplied by the leadership, his rations provided by himself. He was allowed, however, to keep any booty he might take, save for a share given to the church. When his tour called for duty at Bacalar, he was free to take his gain with him and trade it to British Hondurans.

Carmichael found the city of Santa Cruz altogether inviting, with a plaza formed by houses of masonry and, especially, the great church:

Tis here the celebrated Cross is kept, which when the Government of Santa Cruz was in the hands of unscrupulous men, was made the instrument by means of ventriloquism of inciting the ever credulous Indian to commit deeds of unparalleled barbarity and ferocity. Now, the Indians are not imposed upon by those mockeries, but taught to worship the Divine Being through the Cross alone. With the exception of their belief in the efficacy of Saints and the absence of priests, their religion is Roman Catholicism, but all prayers are addressed through the Santa Cruz.

A school was attached to the church where children were taught both Spanish and Maya, and the plaza was further enclosed by barracks, a prison, and a council house. In the center of the square was the place of execution.

Carmichael estimated the total population at about seven thousand and said he learned there was another town of about the same size some sixty miles away and near the ruins of "Tulun" (i.e., Tulum). Although cultivation in the region was little developed, he represented the soil as being most productive for maize, tobacco, sugarcane, rice, and cotton, with forest products also available.

Finally, he reported a council meeting of "the three principal chiefs," in which he was asked whether, if peace with Yucatan should be made by division of the state, England would "be willing to take over this territory and make it part of British Honduras, they . . . becoming British subjects?"

Without reporting the answer he had made to this question, Carmichael closed his attractive glimpse of Santa Cruz by remarking that benefits of acquiring the territory would include "fresh Capital, . . . an addition of some 15,000 labourers, a fresh impetus to trade, and above all a state of security conducive to immigrations which would cause the Colony to become one of the more flourishing and prosperous of Her Majestys settlements in the West Indies." Below his signature he placed his rank, "Captain B. H. Militia."[29]

The pretty picture of the place did not incline Lieutenant Governor Longden to a policy of acquisition. In his acknowledgment of the report he remarked that "the boundaries of British Honduras are clearly defined and . . . Her Majesty's Government have no desire to alter those boundaries." For his part the lieutenant governor—even though new to British Honduras—was inclined to lower the estimate of rebel size toward that made earlier by Plumridge and Twigge (five thousand soldiers) and was relieved to say he found no evidence that the trip had been made under any sort of commission from the British Honduras government. A minute added to his dispatch in the Colonial Office in London directed dryly that "the Santa Cruz people should be made distinctly aware that the British Government would not annex them, and Mr. Carmichael forbidden to excite hopes."[30]

Could the attitude expressed by these officials have been recognized by those in power in Yucatan, the latter might have rested somewhat easier regarding British territorial intentions. But they still would have ample reason to complain of the traffic in munitions between British Honduras and Noh Cah Santa Cruz, which would continue for another thirty years and more.

A Soldier's Duty

Among the *pacíficos* defecting to Santa Cruz after the death of José María Arredondo was Juan Bautista Yam, signatory of the peace agreement of 1853, who turned again to the blandishments of the cross in the 1860s. Early in 1867 he was Santa Cruz *comandante* at the settlement of Esteves on the Río Hondo.[31] As proof of good faith in the effort to control Canul and his men of Icaiché, the rebel leadership had then sent a party to post notices in all settlements on Yucatecan territory along the Hondo, inviting allegiance to Noh Cah Santa Cruz. They threatened any who might take up arms against the British, and called on Canul to submit—an invitation he of course declined.[32]

The rebel *masewalob* also set up a line of *bombas de aviso*, or warning bombs, along the Yucatecan side of the Hondo from Esteves upstream almost to Albion Island, to warn themselves of incursions from Icaiché—an indication that this extent of the river was under regular Santa Cruz control. In May they caught a small party of Icaiché men who had crossed the river to trade, killed a number, and seized their goods.[33]

The success of the Santa Cruz detachments in their fight with Icaiché along the Río Hondo was not unmarred. In late fall of 1867 Canul and his men hit the area around Esteves and Ramonal, reportedly defeating the Santa Cruz *masewalob* under Yam and capturing what they and Pablo García could claim to be "documentary proof" of ties between rebels and the English.[34] It is possible that the heretofore indestructible Juan Bautista Yam was killed in that raid; in any event, he does not appear again.

In the eyes of the Santa Cruz leaders that attack underlined the need for them to maintain an armed force along the Río Hondo. Their continuing efforts to maintain a detachment there had repercussions uncomfortable for some of the participants, however.

In very late 1867 the *comandante* at Ramonal, Isidro Ake, began to round up Maya-speaking people living on the British side of the frontier and move them across to his own territory. This was in the guise of returning "deserters" to their proper places. But some of the "deserters" had resided on British territory for years—although it is possible that many had moved briefly across the Hondo to Yucatan to take refuge when British military units had marched against the San Pedro communities.

On December 25 Edwin Adolphus, the young magistrate at Corozal, received word that an armed group of Santa Cruz rebels had taken such a prisoner on British territory, and the following day he was notified that a party of the same rebels had seized a man in Corozal itself. He immediately dispatched an army patrol that was joined by John Carmichael the elder. About halfway to the Hondo they came in view of an armed group of rebel soldiers from Ramonal with their *comandante* Ake, escorting four other men. The matter grew complicated when Carmichael insisted that the soldiers were friendly, denying that they had taken prisoners—a representation he made even as the British party overtook the *masewal* soldiers whose four escortees agreed with alacrity that they were being marched off against their will.[35]

The entire group was then paraded back to Corozal, the rebels' prisoners released, and the rebel soldiers thrown in jail. Witnesses said that these *masewalob* had visited Carmichael the elder while they were in Corozal, that he was aware they were on British territory with their arms in violation of conditions that had been set out for their visits, and that most of the rebels thought him—Carmichael—the magistrate in Corozal. Some witnesses alleged that as supposed magistrate he had given permission for Ake to repatriate his prisoners.

Naturally, this affair served to increase the friction between Carmichael and Adolphus. Carmichael insisted he had been commissioned by the previous lieutenant governor, J. G. Austin, to meet with Santa Cruz representatives to discuss matters pertaining to the local peace and that Ake was merely such a representative. He denied again that there were prisoners involved, at least that any prisoners had been with Ake when he called at Carmichael's house and store in Corozal. Lieutenant Governor Longden and his council examined Carmichael's "commission" and concluded that he had been empowered to do no more than consult regarding problems created with the Santa Cruz rebels when the sale of powder was banned more than a year before—and that ban had now been lifted. Longden reprimanded Carmichael for having exceeded his authority, indicated that he believed that both Carmichael and his son had overly encouraged the Santa Cruz *masewalob*, and formally revoked his commission. Carmichael wrote indignant letters of self-justification, in which he implied that the real fault lay with Adolphus, whom he claimed to be roundly hated by nearly everybody.[36]

Notification of the state of Ake's intrusion brought a friendly letter of apology from the three rulers of Noh Cah Santa Cruz, who took full responsibility for Ake's action. They explained that he had been directed to cross the river and, with Carmichael's permission, collect any rebel soldiers who had deserted in order to pose them against the men of Icaiché, who had recently attacked their post at Esteves. They promised to allow no such entries into British territory in the future. At virtually the same time they asked for another two hundred kegs of powder and twelve thousand gun flints.[37]

Meanwhile, Adolphus turned up the names of seventy-eight persons who had been forcibly taken across the Hondo by Santa Cruz troops since the previous October, of whom forty-nine were said to have escaped back to British territory, and of these, thirty-six were hiding in the bush for fear of being "repatriated" again. Adolphus also learned that immediately after being released Ake threatened to continue his captures and had sent at least one armed force across the Hondo for that purpose.[38]

Thoroughly miffed, Carmichael the elder attempted to resign as justice of the peace, although there is no indication the resignation was accepted.[39] As the affair finally blew over, Lieutenant Governor Longden received word—believable but of uncertain reliability—that all in Noh Cah Santa Cruz had not been as sweetly yielding as the letters to him had indicated. For when the news of the capture of Ake and his prisoners had first reached the rebel capital, "Novelo and Bel Cen, the two principal chiefs were for answering with cold steel, but . . . Crescencio Poot . . . set his face against it saying that if they are going to quarrel with the English they must make up their mind to submit to the Spaniards."[40]

In February 1868, John Carmichael Jr. announced his intention to make another trip to Santa Cruz. This time it was clearly for trade, for he mentioned carrying "specie or produce," and he also asked if he could ship powder to Bacalar.[41]

Pacíficos and *Bravos*

Armed disruptions along the Hondo dismayed British Honduras residents, who were in terror that Canul and his Icaiché men would be tempted to attack them, both as easy targets and for what he might think was complicity with his enemies.[42] Partial solace came to them with the establishment in 1868 of the Frontier Police, a force of twenty-four mounted men charged with the maintenance of order along the Hondo, of which Captain James Plumridge was named inspector.[43]

Even more encouragingly, on his return from a trip to Campeche early that same year Canul appeared to have turned over a peaceful leaf. He had been well received by Governor García and given encouragement in his fight against the rebels of Santa Cruz, but he had been given none for extorting rent from British companies.

Not long after Canul's visit, García explained to the owner of a British Honduras logging works that Canul was commissioned by the Campeche government as chief of the Icaiché district, a position in which he was formally addressed as General Marcos Canul, commander of the *cantón* of Icaiché. He received no pay from the government and he paid no taxes, but he was permitted to make use of rents he collected in his district. He was provided with munitions when they could be spared, and in return he assisted in checking the advance of the rebels of Santa Cruz. García assured his visitor that he would restrain Canul from extorting rents in those areas in which there was a legitimate question regarding the boundary of the colony, and he indicated he would not enter into any dispute regarding that boundary but would leave it to be settled by the central Mexican government in negotiations with Britain. He urged a halt to the powder trade with the rebels.[44]

He repeated his words regarding Canul and his extortionate rents in correspondence to the lieutenant governor of British Honduras, for whose information he enclosed a copy of his letter addressed to Canul in which he ordered him to desist. He asked the governor also, of course, to restrain the sale of munitions to the rebels.[45]

So it was not surprising that Canul informed the British that he wanted peace, and the next months witnessed a number of very civil exchanges of visits and letters between Canul and British officials.[46] When rents were suddenly demanded from logging operators in presumed British territory by one Domingo Tzuc of the Guatemalan settlement of Yaloch—a village nevertheless considered subject to Icaiché—Canul and his second in command, Rafael Chan, disavowed the act. They removed Tzuc as captain and took him into custody at Icaiché; his successor expected he would be shot.[47]

While Icaiché was professing friendship with British Honduras and trade restrictions were relaxed, the rebels of Noh Cah Santa Cruz resumed buying military supplies from residents of the colony. And at the end of the annual burning and maize planting in the spring of 1868, major attention was again turned to their new allies around Lochhá. After the upheavals of 1866 and 1867, the main headquarters of these renewed rebels had been established at Chunxán, an existing but hitherto unimportant settlement at the eastern edge of the former *pacífico* region. The disturbance involved in this, however, had generated a good deal of emigration, as many of the remnant *pacíficos*, not happy with the newly rebellious turn of events, took almost any opportunity to present themselves to officials of nearby pueblos in both Yucatan and Campeche.[48] One Campeche estimate in March 1868 was that more than thirteen hundred had relocated outside their former region in order to distance themselves from the troubles.[49]

In May, with Santa Cruz assistance, the Chunxán and Lochhá rebels attacked the still pacified settlements to their west. Once again a Campeche detachment was sent from Hopelchén to join a group of *pacíficos* under Francisco Mian and Eugenio and Andrés Arana—the latter who only the year before had been counted among the rebels. On May 10 and 11 the combined force moved out from Yakalcab to take Chunxán successfully, only to retreat immediately in what became a rout.[50] By the close of that season the rebels and loyal *pacíficos* were divided between the new centers of *bravo* Chunxán on the east and *pacífico* Xkanhá on the west. One may suppose that the former, given its new hardihood, was the seat of a cult of the miraculous cross, but unfortunately no description of the place seems to exist. The latter was under command of Eugenio Arana. These two opposing centers would endure.

While some of the Santa Cruz soldiers were carrying this fight to eastern Campeche, others were more peaceably employed. On August 16, 1868, about two hundred of them entered British Honduras under arms, stopping at Santa Rita, about a half mile from Corozal. Their *comandante*, Albino Ake, and his three captains then visited magistrate Adolphus to obtain permission to trade. Leaving their guns at Santa Rita, they passed three days at commerce. When they left, Ake told the magistrate that they had spent about three thousand dollars. They promised to return in November or December to trade again.

Adolphus reported that in his four years at Corozal he had never seen so many of the Santa Cruz people there and that until early 1867—about the time Carmichael began to negotiate with them—he had seen no armed Santa Cruz soldiers in Corozal. But from that time on the number of rebels under arms increased steadily with each visit they made.[51]

Sometime not long before this latest peaceful visit to British Honduras there must have been upheavals at Noh Cah Santa Cruz, although ripples did not reach as far as the British colony. In May 1868 the governing triumvirate had written a friendly letter to the lieutenant governor; as usual, Bonifacio Novelo was a signatory and presumably the ranking leader. At the end of the same month, an account given Yucatecans by a man who had just escaped from Noh Cah Santa Cruz, where he had been a prisoner, listed the principal leaders as Crescencio Poot, Pedro Dzul, José María Canche, and José María Méndez, without mention of either Novelo or Cen.[52] Novelo's name appears on no further correspondence, nor is it ever encountered again in an active context.[53]

A year later a letter from the rebel leadership lists Poot alone as "Governor and Commander in Chief." This particular letter is related to the brief ascendancy among the rebels of a Yucatecan colonel known familiarly as *El Chelo* ("The Blond"), which again illustrates the interplay of Yucatecan politics and *masewal* affairs.

The Greater World Intrudes—Again

As I remarked earlier, the stumbling end of the empire did not bring tranquility to Yucatan. Both conservatives and the liberal followers of Liborio Irigoyen (*"liboristas"*)—the latter of whom insisted that as legitimately elected governor at the time the empire took over Irigoyen was still in office—plotted against the de facto postempire government of Cepeda Peraza. In December 1867 an armed insurrection in Mérida from which Cepeda Peraza escaped to Campeche, then to Mexico, introduced a conservative government. But Cepeda showed up again, now with fifteen hundred Mexican soldiers and Campeche volunteers, and retook Mérida during the first week of February 1868. The conservative army under Colonel Francisco Cantón retreated to Valladolid then—as had so many armed forces before—faded into the forests of the northeast.

In April, Cepeda Peraza's position as governor was confirmed by a legitimate election, but his health was deteriorating rapidly (he died the next year), and he resigned in favor of the vice governor. A conservative-*liborista* axis was now in motion, and on January 31, 1869, it brought off another military insurrection, this one under José Antonio Muñoz, "El Chelo," who seized the Mérida citadel only to be promptly besieged there by the government. While El Chelo's mutineers and the besiegers eyed each other, sympathizers of the mutiny outside the citadel were arrested and executed, until one night the mutineers slipped out of the citadel and stole away. And the insurrection was over.[54]

El Chelo the fugitive had gone southeast, suspected of joining the eastern rebels. And so it turned out. From a military base at abandoned Tihosuco, which was now open to them whenever they chose to occupy it, the *masewalob* drove into the center of the state. On July 1, 1869, from a pueblo of the Sotuta region Muñoz and the rebel leadership issued a kind of ultimatum. After a statement saying that Muñoz had joined them three months before, they closed with the announcement that,

> We are soldiers of Our Holy Cross and of the three Persons, whom we respect and venerate.

And they signed,

As governor and commander in chief,	José Crescencio Poot
As general,	José Asunción Coba
As *comandante* of the *gran guardia*,	Antonio Ek
As *comandantes*,	Claudio Novelo, Teodoro Moreno
	Antonio Chable, Juan Aguilar

And added below the rest:

> The time has come when you will pay for what you have done to me.
>
> José Antonio Muñoz[55]

They burned Yaxcabá. Within a week they attacked Tzucacab, which they also burned and largely destroyed, and returned to Tihosuco. Colonel Traconis reconnoitered the territory with a force from Valladolid, and there was minor action. But the *masewalob* pulled back from their advance base in early August into their eastern fastness.[56]

Muñoz's union with the rebels was short lived. In September Eugenio Arana, commander in chief of the remaining southern *pacíficos*, reported that El Chelo had been executed publicly at Noh Cah Santa Cruz—at ten one morning and his corpse thrown outside the city amid much outcry, his crime that of conniving to take as wife a general's widow to whom the people were said to pay great respect.[57] So ended this particular intrusion from Yucatan.

An action of the Mexican, rather than Yucatecan, government, however, was of far greater impact on the rebels—and in the long run certainly in their favor. Upon his resumption of the presidency, Benito Juárez abruptly severed relations with all countries that had recognized Maximilian.[58] This included Britain, and so from 1867 to 1884 communication between the two countries was limited drastically, rendering impossible a final resolution of issues important to both: placement of the boundaries of British Honduras and termination of the unrestricted trade in arms to the rebels in Yucatan. Until these two issues could be reconciled, there would be no end to the long-standing rebellion, and the *masewalob* would be left undisturbed in their eastern forests. But by the end of the 1860s the Yucatecans had ceased to care very much, for their attention was drawn more and more exclusively to the northwest corner of the peninsula, where the henequen industry was nearing its boom, and riches were beginning to flow.

Rulers of Noh Cah Santa Cruz

Much of the 1860s was dominated by the three-part rule of Novelo, Cen, and Poot—a rule that must have involved a delicate balance of strength between them: almost without exception, when the name of one was affixed to a letter, the names of all appeared, although at the time of their accession to power in 1864 they had not been partners for long.

Bonifacio Novelo was a charter member of the rebel movement, having figured in its very first acts. Indeed, if the sack of Valladolid in January 1847 can be considered the first real event of the war, then Novelo was active in it even earlier than Cecilio Chi and Jacinto Pat. More than twenty years later, in 1867, he was described by young John Carmichael as "a man of about 60 years of age[,] immensely stout and . . . of a lighter shade of colour than the generality of the Indians, . . . dressed in a many colored blouse, . . . white loose cotton drawers terminated from the knee downward with rich lace." John Carmichael called him "Patron or Head Chief."[59]

Bernardino (or Bernabel or Bel) Cen, the second chief, was considerably younger, and his name does not appear in accounts of the early days of the war. Carmichael described him as "pure Indian, short, somewhat stout, with a frank open countenance, and an eye indicative of courage and resolution." A former prisoner said he was "respected above all the others and . . .

distinguished by the two earrings he uses always, and the decoration on the front of his shirt, which is of gold coins." He was said to command the entire army.[60]

Crescencio Poot had been mentioned in reports of the war almost as long as Novelo, with much of his early action focused around his home area of Tixcacalcupul. As mentioned earlier, he was extremely dark, whether or not of African admixture, and unusually tall. Carmichael simply referred to him as third chief.

John Carmichael's reference to Novelo as "Patron" can be taken to mean that he was *patrón* of the cross or *tatich*—that is, high priest.[61] One Santa Cruz escapee in 1864 reported that Novelo had replaced the "Interpreter of the Crosses" after the sacred triumvirate were killed the December before, and a governor of British Honduras called him "the spiritual chief . . . at Santa Cruz, . . . seeking to rule in the cloister through superstitions rather than openly with his colleagues in the field"[62]—a statement that seems in keeping with Novelo's much earlier attempt to promote a saint's image as miraculous. But Domingo Andrade, a regular trader from Corozal to Santa Cruz and a personal friend of many of the rebels, on more than one occasion referred to Novelo as *presidente*—implying an office more civil than religious.[63] Thus, Novelo's actual role in cult matters is not clear, and it may be significant that he is not listed in the well-known genealogy of the early *patrones* to which passing reference has earlier been made.

Included as preamble to at least three extant versions of the basic proclamation of Juan de la Cruz that date from the late nineteenth century or after, the short list of the patrons of the cross includes four individuals. As Victoria Bricker translates one document,

> The very first leader was my patron, Don Manuel Nauat;
> The second one was my patron, Don Venancio Puc,
> And Doña Hilaria Nauat, and Don Atanasio Puc.[64]

All readings of these versions agree in the identity of the first, second, and fourth: Manuel Nauat, Venancio Puc, and Atanasio Puc. All vary in the name of the third.[65] Although the first two of these names are of people easily identifiable historically as high priests of the cross, the third and fourth are not. Atanasio Puc, the fourth, was a rebel and contemporary of Venancio Puc whose close association with the cult rests on two pieces of evidence—the genealogy just quoted and Baqueiro's reference to him as "chief priest of the crosses" in 1852.[66] As I noted in an earlier chapter, it is not impossible that Atanasio Puc was the "Juan de la Cruz Puc" referred to as having assumed the role of mouthpiece of God in 1851.[67]

No woman named Nauat appears in relevant historical accounts at all, although by the end of the 1860s there was a female *patrón*—a *patrona*—of the oracular cross located at Tulum, a woman repeatedly identified as María Uicab (who will appear in the next chapter). Given the evident importance of María Uicab, it may be that on historical grounds the best explanation of the variation in the female name lies in poor handwriting and miscopying by one or more scribes.

The upshot of this is that there is no unambiguous statement regarding the identity of a high priest at Noh Cah Santa Cruz in the late 1860s. Indeed, either Bonifacio Novelo or Atanasio Puc could have been that "Indian" who "discharges the priestly functions, lives in the church praying and singing all day" as described by the unsuccessful Yucatecan peace commission in the aftermath of Venancio Puc's death.[68] It is not until considerably later in the century that there will again be an unambiguous identification of the high priest at Noh Cah Santa Cruz.

That a cult of the cross was still vital at the city, however, is suggested by numerous references to church functions there, and not least by the written message that was sent by the cross in 1866 to name as its general the turncoat *pacífico* Paulino Martín and thus to bring the southern defectors back to the rebel fold: this letter (in the existing Spanish translation) was datelined "my great and populous city of Santa Cruz,"[69] which could only be Noh Cah Santa Cruz. Nevertheless, following the death of Venancio Puc in late 1863 the major oracle had been transferred from Santa Cruz to Tulum—from where, as I indicated earlier, it pronounced its refusal to return the absconded Chinese to British Honduras. At Tulum it was apparently regularly consulted on important matters, although, as John Carmichael the elder put it when referring to one pending transaction, "there is the oracle to consult which is only a form to satisfy the common people."[70]

There was weight in the oracle, nevertheless. And this weight was thrown to Crescencio Poot's advantage not long after the withdrawal and presumed death of Bonifacio Novelo in 1868. For Poot was selected over the popular but sanguinary Bel Cen to become *gobernador*, political head of Noh Cah Santa Cruz (where, incidentally, he was never said to be *patrón*). According to an apparently knowledgeable former captive, Poot's rise was specifically because the *patrona* willed it and assigned Cen instead to command the armies (table 13).[71]

Who was the *patrona*? It was that María Uicab just mentioned, who will shortly appear again as the division between the most respected (although not the only) rebel religious center at Tulum and the strongest (but not the

Table 13

Leadership at Noh Cah Santa Cruz, 1858–68

Year of Appearance	Governor or General-in-Chief	Important Commanders	High Priest
1858	Venancio Puc	Dionisio Zapata	Venancio Puc
1864	Dionisio Zapata		Bonifacio Novelo? María Uicab? (oracle moves to Tulum)
1864	Bonifacio Novelo	Bernardino Cen Crescencio Poot	Bonifacio Novelo? Atanacio Puc?[a]
1868	Crescencio Poot	Bernardino Cen	?

Sources: See notes to text.

[a]As indicated, Atanacio Puc may have preceded Venancio Puc as high priest.

sole) rebel military base at Noh Cah Santa Cruz becomes unmistakable. This division and the rise of Crescencio Poot to the highest secular position in the major rebel center of Noh Cah Santa Cruz marks the beginning of a period of stability and quiescence for the *bravos*, during which they grew ever closer to the British colony south of them and flirted again with the idea of peace with Yucatan.

Part 5. Keeping the Faith, 1869–1903

16 / *Bravo* Enterprises

With the return of Mexico to republican government, the situations in what were again the separate states of Yucatan and Campeche varied significantly. One of the few common elements was the mutual abolition of the *república de indígenas*. Although in Campeche it had been eliminated almost immediately upon separation from Yucatan—when Governor Pablo García decreed the *republicas* replaced by companies of the national guard captained by the former *caciques*—it was reinstated soon after under the empire. But with García's resumption of office his earlier decree was again in force, and a little more than a year later Yucatan also proclaimed abolition of the *república*, effective January 1, 1869.[1] Thenceforth, Indians of both states of the peninsula were once again fully citizens.

Otherwise, there were strong surface differences. In smaller and more homogeneous Campeche a period of relative stability ensued, with Governor García holding his office for another three years. In Yucatan, however, between June 1867, when Cepeda Peraza reconquered Mérida, and the end of December 1876, when the faction supporting Porfirio Díaz siezed power, there were more than twenty changes in the individuals who exercised supreme power in the state. Seven of these changes were to commanders of the Mexican military force on the peninsula who stepped in when the instability became too much for them or the central Mexican government to tolerate.[2] Needless to say, these shifts, most of which related to individual personalities rather than to doctrine or philosophy, did nothing to stabilize the military situation on the eastern frontier.

By the end of the 1860s the *masewalob*—both *bravo* and *pacífico*—had formed the alliances that would characterize them for the rest of the century. In the south, those who had made peace in 1853 and then resisted the temptation to fall away during the internal troubles of 1866–67 had divided themselves into two groups. The group directly headquartered at Xkanha, including subsidiary settlements paying allegiance to Campeche, was served by priests of the Mérida diocese and itinerant traders from Campeche and would lean gradually toward the centers of Europeanized

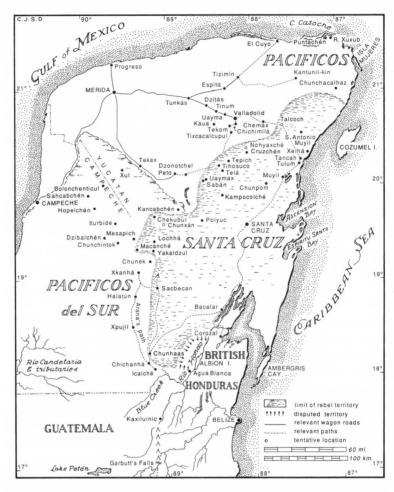

Map 16. Location of Events of 1869–95. The limit of bravo territory is from Allen (1888) and Anonymous (1884). Arana's route is derived from his account (see text) and by reference to Mexico, Instituto Geológico (1895) and Sapper (1895).

civilization. In the far south, the much smaller group centered around Icaiché would pay at least nominal allegiance to Xkanha, to Campeche, and to Mexico; but its people would be served by churchmen only seldom (later by priests from Belize), would trade as much as possible in the British colony, and would in fact derive a major reason for their existence from the opportunity to exploit the activities of British Honduran colonists. That opportunity would be lucrative so long as there was no boundary agreement between England and Mexico.

In the east, the piecemeal withdrawal of Yucatecan troops from their far advanced posts had left a no-man's-land between the rebels and their mortal enemies, a buffer that added to the *masewal* sense of security. Peacefully inclined rebels were beginning to make annual visits to Corozal or even Belize to trade or work as laborers. Both government officials and commercial interests of the British colony would display an increasing paternalism toward them. The result was that the recalcitrant rebels of the cross, even those of belligerent Noh Cah Santa Cruz, would mellow in the direction of coexistence—truceful, if not peaceful—although one in which a hatred of *dzules* would still be nurtured. This relative mellowing characterized the last stages of the continuing rebellion.

Such a change of attitude was in part a result of the simple passage of time. By now, no more than a third of the *masewalob* had been as old as ten years when hostilities began in 1847. That is, by the year 1870 nearly two-thirds of all *rebels* had been born after 1840, and this would have included essentially half of the active *bravo* soldiers.[3] Among the aging but still effective leaders this was not the case, but it was true of the rank-and-file cannon fodder, a majority of whom would never have known any existence other than war against *dzulob*. And these *dzulob* were now truly foreign to them; save for a few captives still alive in Noh Cah Santa Cruz, *dzules* were entirely outside of their daily experience.

With the inevitable forgetfulness it engenders among older people and the naivete natural to the younger, the passage of time would also have been erasing the vestiges of the old legal distinction between *indio* and *vecino*. In the early days of the war that distinction was always present in conditions of peace that were proposed but almost never achieved. By now, however, the *masewalob* surely thought of themselves as a homogeneous whole, with less and less attention paid to the ethnic origin of surnames—as is the case among the remnant rebels of the present century.[4]

But the tendencies just described are those perceptible only over the long term. To an observer on the ground in 1870, business must have seemed to be going on much as it always had.

Patrons to the Rebels

In 1869, two bodies of Santa Cruz soldiers had visited Corozal, one of them led by the general Bel Cen, who came to trade for powder but promised to return around Christmas for varied purchases. The influx of these parties—armed with machetes or even muskets, despite the remonstrance of the magistrate—caused jitters among the residents of Corozal, and the impact was heightened when it was rumored that on Cen's return he intended to drag away from British territory the entire populations of the predominantly Indian villages near Corozal. In November of that year a rebel detachment crossed to the colony settlement of Consejo, seized a Yucatecan and his wife, and hauled them back across the river, where the woman was flogged and the man killed. The jitters became panic. To calm fears, Lieutenant Governor Longden ordered Captain Plumridge to move the entire small force of border police to Corozal, even though this left the upper Hondo unpatrolled[5]—and would have untoward consequences, as will be seen in the next chapter.

Whether or not the concentration of this minute force at Corozal was responsible, Bernardino Cen and his rebels elected not to visit as promised. As an alternative, the Santa Cruz leaders named John Carmichael the elder as their agent in Corozal, to collect debts owed them at year end and transact other business. Carmichael was given informal approval in this office by the lieutenant governor, in the hope that "the appointment may be the means of preventing the recurrence of such confusion and alarm" as prevailed each time the *masewalob* presented themselves in force, no matter how peaceably.[6]

But there were other factors that would continue to draw the rebels closer to the colony. In June 1870 the indentures of the Chinese laborers expired. At the same time, railway construction was pending in Costa Rica, where a line to link the country's Caribbean coast with its capital threatened a labor boom in which the princely wage of one dollar per day would draw off much of the pool of workers that existed in the English colony.[7] With a labor shortage looming, local Indian manpower was seen to offer the best solution. Indeed, Mayan laborers—when obtainable—were preferred by a number of the Corozal planters,[8] and by 1871 at least one of the estates in the north depended entirely on Indian hands.[9]

By 1870 some of this labor on plantations in northern British Honduras was being provided not only by Indians normally resident in the colony but by Santa Cruz soldiers who were excused to work for a time while stationed at Bacalar. Although excellent workers, these latter had the drawback that they were "not allowed by their chiefs to remain more than a month or two at a time" in the colony.[10] John Carmichael was said to work his San Andrés estate to a considerable extent with these off-duty rebel soldiers. And despite their limited work periods, in 1872 Carmichael apparently expected the largest sugar crop since he had begun his planting.[11]

Thus, the *masewal* labor pool that had been so alluringly articulated by the younger John Carmichael after his trip to Noh Cah Santa Cruz in 1867 was tapped by Corozal planters, although without the British political domination of the rebel region that young Carmichael obviously envisioned. In this way, the attraction of the British colony to the rebels would expand well beyond the *masewal* leadership to the rank and file. As the military adventures of the common soldier and his chance of sharing booty were more and more curtailed, individual financial dependence on British colonists would assume greater and greater importance.

Action in the North

Secularization of rule in Noh Cah Santa Cruz had already softened the trend toward militant and dictatorial government that had been so strong in the days of Venancio Puc. Nevertheless, in the early 1870s aggressive action had not yet stopped. Indeed, military successes came more easily than ever.

Whereas twenty years earlier the advance Yucatecan military stations or *cantones* had formed a line to the east of their major frontier settlements—a line as far east as Kampocolché and Cruzchén—by 1870 the forward stations of the Yucatecan army were the remaining population centers themselves— Tizimín, Espita, Tunkás, Dzitás, Tinum, Tixcacalcupul, Chemax, and Valladolid.[12] East of that irregular line lay no-man's-land, a fringe zone now virtually without inhabitants. Farther east of there was secure rebel territory. It had been ten years since the capital of Santa Cruz was occupied even briefly by a Yucatecan force, and then it was the decisively defeated Acereto army. Gradually, a dispersed rebel population had been spreading north toward the *pacíficos* around Kantunil-kin.

The *bravos* now seemed to attack Yucatecan towns at will. In August of 1870 a Santa Cruz force under Crescencio Poot raided Chichimilá with the aid of seven turncoats, expecting to subvert and carry away the entire population of that town only four kilometers from Valladolid. But when the subversion misfired, the infiltrating force was fought off by only thirty-two men—eighteen valiant *hidalgos*, several soldiers, and miscellaneous Chichimilá residents—who barricaded themselves in the church. The defenders were quickly reinforced by *hidalgos* from Tekom, and the rebels then were hit by Traconis with 150 men from Valladolid. But the *bravos* left with booty and some prisoners, and a dozen more men and women followed them voluntarily.[13]

Later in the year, in December, a rebel force estimated at four hundred to five hundred, made up of men from Santa Cruz as well as former *pacíficos* of the south, raided half a dozen settlements around Tekax. Although they were chased away, it was without a decisive engagement, and they succeeded in destroying hamlets and in discouraging resettlement in an area that had been depopulated because of the war.[14]

The buildup of pressures of this sort led in early 1871 to a new but brief Yucatecan campaign.

Expedition to Tulum

The expedition of 1871 was reportedly launched to explore that far eastern zone once so often crossed by Yucatecan patrols and now so little known by them. The aim was to thrust into the northward-expanding rebel population and at the same time to lift flagging Yucatecan morale by showing militiamen of the day that they could still track the rebels to their haunts.

On January 21 or 22, 1871, a thousand men consisting of militia of the eastern *partidos* left Valladolid under command of Colonel Daniel Traconis.[15] Moving through Chemax, they turned east–southeast for Tulum—Santa Cruz Tulum, or Santo Cah Tulum, as it was known by then. A week later they found heavy signs of rebel occupation in trails, abandoned houses, and cleared fields. They captured a *masewal* as a guide. That night, January 29, they were near Tancah and the coast. The next day they moved south almost to the limits of Tulum without the alarm being given, then jumped several hunters who eluded them and raised the cry. Advancing smartly into Santa Cruz Tulum, located some four kilometers from the coast and the ancient ruins of that name, they took the town against the sound of rebel trumpets and drums. Their patrols returned with seven prisoners.

Tulum was found to be the "center of all that series of settlements that are being formed," and one of the prisoners was the son of María Uicab "to whom is given homage as far as Chan Santa Cruz." According to Traconis, from confiscated documents it was known that

all the rebel Indians are subordinated to that woman whom they call *Santa Patrona* or *Reina*, and it is not daring to suppose that, she having much less power than the people of Chan Santa Cruz, [the latter] maintain or perpetuate the farce of rendering her a kind of cult, whether to sustain the prestige of their ridiculous idolatry—she being the one who stands forth interpreting the will of the crosses that they force [all] to believe [can] speak—or to exploit by such means her prestige or influence in that region far from the principal center of the barbarians.[16]

Advancing a dozen kilometers south to take the important settlement of Muyil, Traconis then turned southwest an equal distance and struck Chunpom. There he found a functioning forge with iron rods that had been fashioned in the diameter of a musket bore, evidently for use as projectiles. As to the place itself, "Its inhabitants are provisioned in Chan Santa Cruz, that is 12 leagues [forty-eight kilometers] distant, whence come to them monthly a detachment of 25 men to garrison it."[17]

Suddenly, the Yucatecans began to hear warning bombs from the direction of Noh Cah Santa Cruz, indicating preparations by the rebels. Having set out with no avowed intent to attack that strong-point, they hastened toward Valladolid, where they arrived triumphantly on February 7. The march of little more than two weeks had taken them to the eastern edge of the peninsula, where they subdued three important enemy towns— however briefly—and gained new information regarding rebel strength and disposition.[18]

They had learned that Tulum was the seat of a cross cult in its own right, while hearing that Chunpom was within the politico-religious sphere of Noh Cah Santa Cruz. No statement is made that a separate and active cult center was operating then at Chunpom, but the fact that it was later known to be such a center and that some kind of regular guard duty, or *guardia*, was already being held there says that it was also an important center of the cross worship by the early 1870s.

A New Center in the Far North

The successful traverse by Traconis and his militiamen did not still rebel activity. On July 5, 1872, the pacified settlement of Kantunil-kin was attacked by a *masewal* army of about three hundred strong, men that later information indicated had come from a pueblo called San Antonio Muyil. The leader of the attackers was reportedly one Juan de la Cruz Pomol, *comandante* of the pueblo. The *bravos* looted the church and burned much of the village. On their retreat they moved east to the coast and abducted virtually the entire population of pacified Chunchacalhaz, herding the people back to San Antonio.[19]

This new danger posed to the northeastern campesinos and to Yucatecan plantations recently established in the region led the owner of one of these, Nicolás Urcelay, to organize a reprisal. On July 31 a command of about three hundred men again drawn from the militia of the eastern *partidos* left Tizimín under Urcelay's direction and moved east to Kantunil-kin, where they incorporated a force of *pacíficos*. The dim trace of the attackers led east. At six of the rebel campsites they noted that "in the center . . . [the *bravos* had] formed some frameworks, with roof of palms in triangular form, in which they placed the Cross that they were accustomed to carry on their incursions."[20]

Passing through abandoned Chunchacalhaz, a place of thirty-three houses and a church, they reached the coast, where they kept a scheduled rendezvous with boats from Isla Mujeres, then coasted south. Although now hampered by cases of cholera, they nevertheless disembarked at Xelhá, where they found a man and his wife made prisoner at Kantunil-kin but abandoned by their captors because of the man's bad leg. Guided by the wife, the Yucatecans moved inland toward San Antonio Muyil, twenty kilometers distant. The next morning, August 14, they captured three men and learned that the day was one of fiesta at their destination, with a large crowd attending. Marching another two kilometers, they heard a warning bomb go off, and two kilometers farther on they were attacked. Yucatecan flankers moved out and took the town in short order. Juan de la Cruz Pomol, the San Antonio commander, was killed with the first volley.

This hitherto unknown village was found to consist of about eighty houses and a church building twenty meters long, "over the principal altar of which there were 39 crosses, with dustcovers of cloth; at one and the other side of the church there were two houses about 20 *varas* [sixteen meters] long, with a railing of poles around them on which could be counted about 60 hammocks, both being . . . their barracks."[21]

According to prisoners, San Antonio was a daughter village of the settlement of Muyil in the south. It had been hidden not only from the government but from the *bravos* of Noh Cah Santa Cruz until two years before, when it was discovered and forced to contribute men to the rebel army. The raid on Kantunil-kin had been organized by Pomol, at whose request María Uicab had also sent one hundred men from Chunpom to add to the raiding party.[22]

The Yucatecans immediately burned the town and marched away before they could be trapped by a reinforced enemy. On August 15 they reembarked in their boats for Isla Mujeres.

And so this expedition too brought new information: The hitherto unknown San Antonio Muyil was a power that threatened danger to its pacified neighbors. The practice of carrying a miraculous cross on its forays marked it as an active participant in the cross cult. Above all, its cross-adorned church and its barracks for holding *guardia* bespoke a place of religious importance, a regional center in its own right.

Continuing Skirmishes

Small actions continued around the rebel frontier over the next two years. In January 1873 a sustained series of *masewal* raids toward Kaua and Uayma brought the sack of a dozen settlements and the capture of more than 150 people, who were dragged back to Noh Cah Santa Cruz.[23] This was evidently the result of a policy of forcible recruitment of prisoner labor for the estates of rebel leaders, for among ranchos mentioned as those where abductees were put to labor were two properties of Crescencio Poot;[24] one of Vitorio Vitorín; and one of Baltazar Moguel, now a *bravo comandante*.[25] On July 26, 1874, *bravos* under Crescencio Poot raided a settlement within six kilometers of Peto, taking a dozen prisoners and burning nearly twenty houses.[26] This incursion was apparently the only major one of that year.

By this time *bravos* of the far southern settlements of Macanché and Lochhá had tended to withdraw toward Chunxán and the east, leaving the two formerly important settlements as mere rebel military outposts. The southern rebels were estimated to be able to field about nine hundred men, some six hundred of them armed with flintlock firearms.[27]

Although in 1873 President Lerdo de Tejada of Mexico had sent additional federal troops to Yucatan with the specific aim of ending the everlasting *masewal* rebellion, his reinforcements were occupied not with the rebels but with the maintenance of a modicum of order among the constantly contending political factions of urban Yucatan. For a time, Mexican General Ignacio Alatorre was provisional governor, but when elections led to shootings and a number of deaths—one of them the assassination of Manuel Rodríguez Solís, whose wife Josefa had been languishing as a prisoner in Noh Cah Santa Cruz since the capture of Tunkás in 1861—Alatorre resigned in a huff. He issued a public denunciation of the "blind spirit of partisanship" that seemed the guiding light of Yucatan.[28]

These troubles were followed a short time later by the insurrection of Colonel Pedro Rosado Levalle, which brought a declaration of martial law and the administration of government by another federal general. As a part of the revolt, pacified *masewalob* around Chichimilá had been armed, and when it fizzled they refused to give up their guns. They were immediately wooed by yet another insurrectionist, one José Coronado, but his followers were defeated by Colonel Francisco Cantón at the end of July 1873.[29] Coronado tried to keep his movement going, but by early the following year the pacified rebels had almost entirely deserted him. Many finally surrendered their arms.[30]

The leaders in Noh Cah Santa Cruz were reported in both 1873 and 1874 to be Crescencio Poot, Bernardino Cen, and Tomás Canché. In 1874, the earlier (but undated) deaths of both Bonifacio and Claudio Novelo were confirmed by escaping prisoners.[31] But despite the continuity in leadership, not all relationships among the powerful were smooth, as will shortly be seen.

Masewalob in 1874

In the years after the death of Venancio Puc in late 1863, political decentralization of the rebel world had increased. First of all, Tulum assumed religious primacy with possession of the oracular cross that was consulted on political matters. Next, although many of the southerners had been subverted into partnership with Santa Cruz, they were clearly at least semiautonomous. Then, from the Traconis and Urcelay campaigns there emerged indications that not only Tulum but Muyil and Chunpom were important in their own right. Finally, the existence of San Antonio Muyil, a separate cult center that had functioned for several years without significant contact with the major *bravo* settlements farther south, underscores the fact of local autonomy, even though San Antonio was ultimately forced into concourse with Santa Cruz.

Nonetheless, to observers at the time and some distance away, like those of both Yucatan and British Honduras, the rebel polity still seemed monolithic. As one acting governor of the British colony wrote, the rebel presence north of them "is kept in a state of perfect discipline by leaders who combine the functions of Chief and of Priests, who work upon the superstition of their Indian subjects by mystic rites which . . . blend certain of the forms of Christianity with others of a pagan character, also by the oracular utterances . . . of an ancient cross for which they have a peculiar veneration."[32]

To be sure, the rebels for the most part worked with a common purpose in opposition to Yucatan, and all apparently still paid obeisance to the cross (or crosses) and gave respect to the might and reputation of Noh Cah Santa Cruz. But consistent with their earliest history the reality fell short of centralized organization or direction. An example is offered by the San Antonio Muyil raid on Kantunil-kin, in which a local commander planned a raid, organized it, and then went for approval and support to the oracle.

The size of the population among the still rebellious union of settlements was a subject of perennial interest to outside observers. In 1874, it was reported from British Honduras that the people of Noh Cah Santa Cruz held

the frontier line of the Hondo and the whole country for one hundred miles aback of it, from the river mouth to Albion Island. . . . [The group] also holds and garrisons with a large guard changed every two or three months, the old Spanish fortified town of Bacalar.

Further,

the number of available fighting men in this tribe has been variously computed at from 500 to 4,000. I should judge [said an acting governor of the colony] that 1,000 would be as large a number as they could bring into the field at any one time.[33]

This may be overly conservative; in 1875 an escapee from Santa Cruz reported that some sixteen hundred men were on duty at all times—nine hundred at Noh Cah Santa Cruz, four hundred at Bacalar, and one hundred each at three other *cantones*.[34] This would indicate a total military resource closer to the estimate of four thousand that was rejected by the governor just quoted. And there were other relevant observations: only a few years earlier John Carmichael the younger had indicated his understanding that the population around Tulum was approximately equal to that of Santa Cruz.[35] In 1872, the northernmost of the rebel towns, San Antonio Muyil, had fielded a force of two hundred men for their raid on Kantunil-kin— presumably all the fighters they could muster—to which were added one hundred more from Chunpom.[36] And in 1873 the maximum field force of the turncoat rebels active in the south had been estimated by Campeche officials at nine hundred men.[37]

Putting these together, and discounting somewhat the highest estimate for Santa Cruz, one must suppose that all rebels combined could field at least twenty-five hundred and possibly closer to five thousand men. If one assumes that the active military counted all males aged twelve and over and if one uses the same demographic assumptions as those employed earlier, these males could represent as much as one-third of the total population, more likely about one-fourth. The breakdown of resultant estimates by area are shown in table 14. Although there is great possibility for error in the estimates, it seems not unreasonable to think that the total rebel population in 1874 reached at least twelve thousand but may not have been more than sixteen thousand.

With regard to those former rebels who in the 1870s were still observing the agreement of 1853, the same acting governor of British Honduras observed that "higher up the Hondo, above Albion Island the Ycaiche tribe, which is under Mexican rule, can muster from 300 to 400 men, not so well armed or nearly as well disciplined as the Santa Cruz, with which tribe they are at feud."[38] But in 1877 a messenger to Icaiché from British Honduras placed the figure considerably higher: "there are about 200 houses and 216 men living in the town [Icaiché], but in the neighboring villages . . . there may be reckoned 1,000 men or more."[39] In Campeche, government officials in 1870 believed that their jurisdiction might include a total population of twelve thousand pacified former rebels subject to Xkanhá but not including Icaiché.[40] Thus, the total population of the southern pacíficos—Icaiché and Xkanhá combined—must have approximated and perhaps slightly exceeded that of the bravos as a whole. In addition, there were scattered pueblos of pacíficos north of rebel country. Their numbers were not spoken of in the literature, however, perhaps because they were not seen as a problem.

The Return of Josefa Rodríguez

Mentioned frequently among the prisoners still held at Noh Cah Santa Cruz were three women, Pastora Rean and the sisters Encarnación and Josefa Rodríguez, all captured at Tunkás in 1861. The first of these, Pastora Rean, was said to have become the wife of Crescencio Poot to whom she bore at least two children.[41] The third was the wife of Manuel Rodríguez Solís.[42] According to one account, both captive sisters worked as domestic servants to the widow of Dionisio Zapata. According to a second, Josefa had been given as wife to a ranking rebel (whose name was not mentioned) in a union that had issue, although no children were identified.[43]

On December 23, 1874, Josefa Rodríguez was conducted to Corozal by a party of eight rebels—three of them women—led by comandante Vitorio Vitorín. Upon their arrival, an English trader named Trumbach contacted the Corozal magistrate, Edwin Adolphus, to report that he had been in

TABLE 14

Conservative Estimates of Masewal Population in the Early 1870s

Division	Soldiers	Total Population	Source
bravos			
Noh Cah Santa Cruz	1,000[a]	(3,000 – 4,000)	British Administrator (1874)
Tulum, Muyil, Chunpom	(1,000)	(3,000 – 4,000)	J. Carmichael Jr. (1867)
San Antonio Muyil	200	(600 – 800)	Yucatecan commander (1872)
Chunxán	900	(2,700 – 3,600)	Campeche commander (1873)
Total rebels	3,100	9,300 – 12,400	
pacíficos			
Icaiché	300 – 400	(900 – 1,600)	British Administrator (1874)
Xkanhá	(3,000 – 4,000)	12,000	Campeche Governor (1870)
Total southern *pacíficos*	3,300 – 4,400	12,900 – 14,000	

Sources: For specific sources, see text.

Note: Parentheses indicate projections from a stated estimate. Total population is taken as three to four times the number of soldiers. [a]If a less conservative estimate of Noh Cah Santa Cruz is used, and if Tulum and associated settlements are still taken as equivalent, the *bravo* population ascends to about nine thousand soldiers, or twenty-seven thousand to thirty-six thousand total.

negotiations regarding the release of Doña Josefa, that he had with him two thousand dollars intended as her ransom but that now Vitorín refused to give her up, saying he understood the money to be her inheritance rather than a ransom and that he expected to take both money and woman back with him to Noh Cah Santa Cruz.[44]

With some difficulty, Adolphus and Trumbach were able to talk to the woman privately. "I . . . inquired of Doña Josefa [said Adolphus] if she were a prisoner. She replied that she had been so for many years at Santa Cruz. I thereupon asked her if she wished to stay on British territory or to return to Santa Cruz. The unhappy creature, who appeared almost afraid to speak, answered that she would like to remain but could not, as her sister, who had been her fellow prisoner for so many years and to whom she was greatly attached, would surely be killed if she did."[45]

But fear for herself conquered fear for her sister. That same afternoon while the rebels were making purchases at a store she approached Adolphus and "implored me to rescue her from her keepers who were shortly about to take her back to Santa Cruz a prisoner." She was then removed from rebel custody by the Corozal police and sent to Belize, although not without some worry that disappointed rebels might try to seize her by force.[46]

Immediately, Adolphus wrote to Noh Cah Santa Cruz to inform the leadership of what he had done and to advise them that he had received and was holding the two thousand dollars, which *comandante* Vitorín had refused to accept because he said he was not authorized to take it as ransom. Adolphus stated he would deliver the money to any person who might be properly empowered to receive it.[47] Although Bel Cen, of whom Vitorín had indicated he was particularly fearful, was in Bacalar not long after and sent for the money, his messenger was refused, apparently because he did not carry authorization from Noh Cah Santa Cruz itself.

Only in early February 1875 did Adolphus receive a letter from Poot asking him to hand the money to Domingo Andrade (a trader to Santa Cruz and now also a commercial logcutter in rebel territory) for transmission to the proper persons. According to Andrade—who had carried Adolphus's original letter to Noh Cah Santa Cruz—Cen had made trouble when the letter was read and threatened to kill the messenger (Andrade) but was quieted by counterthreats from the other leaders, who agreed to use the money to buy gunpowder.[48]

For her part, Doña Josefa was returned to Yucatan by ship to a homecoming that, possibly out of tact, was scarcely mentioned in the newspapers.[49] In Noh Cah Santa Cruz, the aftermath was more dramatic. The split between

Poot and Cen widened. Cen reportedly heard that Poot had ordered his death and fled to Tulum with about a hundred loyal followers; from there he made his way with a dwindling group of thirty retainers to San Antonio Muyil, where he arrived in June 1875.

To San Antonio also came a servant who had fled from Rancho Xuxub, an establishment at the northern tip of the peninsula that was being developed by an American named Robert Stephens. The servant's story must have involved a promise of booty, for Cen bedeviled the *comandante* of San Antonio, now one Juan de la Cruz Pat, until Pat agreed to furnish men for a sally. On October 12, Cen and Pat, with around seventy men, raided Rancho Xuxub and various settlements in its vicinity. At Xuxub they murdered Stephens and three others.

But the smoke from the raids drew a force of irregulars led by the appointed military chief of the settlement of Puntachén, Baltazar Montillo. While half of the *masewal* force tried to flee with prisoners and booty, the other half stopped to fight the Puntachén party. In the action thirteen rebels were killed. They included both Cen and Pat. The remainder dispersed, with most of their prisoners escaping in the confusion. One of three captives taken by the Yucatecans was Encarnación Cahum, a rebel leader at the raid on Kantunil-kin three years before. He was subsequently executed.[50]

In Yucatan, the result was a flurry of correspondence between the U.S. consul and Mérida officials regarding the Stephens murder.[51] For the rebels, the result was the loss of a leader of great prestige. Had Bernardino Cen lived, he might well have fomented rebellion against Crescencio Poot and Noh Cah Santa Cruz. As it was, rebellion in the *bravo* capital was to wait another decade.

The Flickering Light of Peace

After that last fateful raid by Cen, the people of Noh Cah Santa Cruz and their allies of the Tulum region finally lapsed into relatively peaceable behavior, with only occasional reversions to their old bellicosity. There was one minor strike near Peto in October 1875, and although the affiliation of the hundred or fewer raiders was not determined at the time by the Yucatecan military,[52] at least one captive taken by the rebels in that raid was led off to Noh Cah Santa Cruz. There he was interrogated by Crescencio Poot himself regarding military armament around Peto. The prisoner escaped when he was sent to Poot's Rancho San Felipe to work. When he reappeared behind the Yucatecan lines he reported that while en route to the rancho shortly after All Saints' Day, he had passed a party carrying 370 firearms, ammunition, seven bugles, and other equipment, all new and all being sent to Poot by the Corozal traders Trejo and Andrade. He also said that Santa Cruz was planning a raid to test the new armament.[53]

So the apparent turn toward truce by the rebels of Santa Cruz did not mean the city would be found without its guard. In January 1876, the *masewalob* in a visit to British Honduras were reported by Lieutenant Governor Mundy to "have traded very freely, purchasing large quantities of guns, powder and some hundreds of Enfield rifles, besides large quantities of silks and other sorts of clothing."[54] Even if the shipment of arms seen by the captive Yucatecan in November 1875 was somehow related to the same order mentioned by Governor Mundy, it appears that Noh Cah Santa Cruz was intent on rearming with firearms of improved design.[55]

In December of 1876, a Santa Cruz soldier and his wife who had lived at Noh Cah Santa Cruz since the rebellion among the southern *pacíficos* nearly ten years earlier, deserted to British Honduras because the man believed he would be executed for accidentally causing the death of his captain. He confirmed that the rebels were commanded by Crescencio Poot and Tomás Canché but added that they had been ordered by Tulum to undertake no attacks on Yucatan without authorization from the cross and to dedicate themselves to farming. He claimed that Tulum, Noh Cah Santa Cruz, and Bacalar were the only places having regular garrisons—Tulum with one hundred men, the others with only fifty each, all of them relieved every two weeks. As a result of these commands of the cross, he said, the men of Santa Cruz were keeping in reserve all the arms received from traders over the past months.[56]

Whatever the cause of the military inactivity of the rebels, the Yucatecan government in 1877 took advantage of it to introduce a feeler for peace negotiations. One of the regular traders from British Honduras to Noh Cah Santa Cruz (who is not named in the records) agreed to carry to the rebel capital a list of points for discussion, with the aim of getting the *masewalob* to meet commissioners from Yucatan or Mexico to discuss a formal treaty. Such a treaty, the trader was to say, would include guarantees of personal safety, promises of a money payment to the rebel leaders and to soldiers of Santa Cruz and Tulum, and an agreement regarding territorial rights: Bacalar, Santa Cruz, and Tulum would belong to the pacified rebels, while some points—including Ascension Bay—would be under control of the regular government.

Assuming that this information as it reached British Honduras was accurate, the apparent willingness of Yucatan to consider territorial concessions represents a significant change in attitude. Nevertheless, Poot reportedly responded to the trader "in very plain terms and advised him never again to approach him with such proposals if he wished to return alive to his own country."[57] For his part, Lieutenant Governor Barlee of British Honduras proposed to court the favor of the four ranking leaders of the rebels with the gift to each of them of a new Martini-Henry rifle, and he remarked at the same time that the rebels had lately deposited money to purchase ammunition and some four hundred additional rifles, presumably Enfields, from British Honduras traders.[58]

Despite the new armament, still no raids by the rebels were reported. Then, in February 1879 a substantial party suddenly struck a hamlet south of Tekax, and two weeks later hit two villages north of Peto. Total Yucatecan dead were four, and five children were dragged away captive—paltry action compared to attacks in the past.[59] Activity lapsed again.

As Crescencio Poot grew older he had not only acquiesced in the calls from both the cross and the British to halt raids by his soldiers on Yucatan, he himself became increasingly sedentary. At Noh Cah Santa Cruz he lived in the solid house at the northeast corner of the plaza—the house that once had belonged to Leandro Santos and that thereafter would be the regular abode of the *gobernador* when in the capital—and he now gave himself heavily to drink.[60] He was seldom if ever as far from home as Corozal but sent lesser commanders to represent him in the British colony. His emissary was most often Juan Bautista Chuc, who rose to be second in command, who carried the title of general, and who may have played an active part in the cult of the cross. Although there is no direct evidence of the nature of any such involvement, Chuc is one of the few people to be mentioned by name in late manuscripts of the proclamation of the cross, where his death is lamented.[61]

Yet rebel strength in these quiet years was never allowed to slack. In 1880, the general commanding British forces in the West Indies belatedly inspected British Honduras for its military preparedness in the face of unpredictable neighbors. From local sources he transmitted an estimate of about four thousand armed men who could be fielded by the Santa Cruz *masewalob*—presumably including both Tulum and Noh Cah Santa Cruz; this was twenty times the number he gave for Icaiché.[62]

But there would be no reason for the British to fear attack by their neighbors to the north. At the beginning of 1880, *bravo* leaders began to make their annual trading trip not to Corozal but to Belize City itself. There they conducted their business through an appointed agent in a regular Belize trading firm, and they paid a ritual visit to the lieutenant governor or his representative.[63] Their feelings toward the British were becoming ever more friendly. Although rebel leaders had periodically (if sporadically) shown their regard for their southern neighbors and had at various times indicated a willingness to become British subjects, the increasing warmth of the relationship provided a foretaste of the affection for the English that remnant rebels would carry into the twentieth century and to the present day.[64]

Although Lieutenant Governor Barlee of British Honduras had what seemed reliable word of an impending Yucatecan raid on the rebels, it never materialized.[65] Instead, in 1882 the same official received information that the Yucatecans were again undertaking negotiations in order to "induce the Santa Cruz Indians to open . . . the territory they occupy, to general trade. . . . The Indians decline this overture unless the territory they have occupied and held so long (some 30 years) be absolutely recognized as their own; if this be done they are willing. . . . [But] Mexico is not likely to surrender . . . territory she views as her own."[66]

By the following year, a recognized Yucatecan agent, Francisco Avila, was living in the rebel capital and was known to the lieutenant governor in British Honduras as "having been employed as a mediator between Mexico and . . . Santa Cruz."[67] The rebels, too, were softening. In 1883 Avila accompanied Juan Bautista Chuc on the annual *masewal* shopping trip to Belize in which their party called on the lieutenant governor.[68] That Avila's position was also known by the people of Noh Cah Santa Cruz among whom he lived seems clear from events of the succeeding year.

In January 1884, General Teodosio Canto, vice governor of Yucatan, arrived in Belize City with the avowed intention of making peace with the Santa Cruz rebels. For the administrator of British Honduras (the lieutenant governor himself was on leave) he produced as credentials a letter from the governor of Yucatan addressed to Avila—who was described as "agent of the Yucatecan government amongst the Indians"—which introduced Canto as the governor's representative seeking peace.[69]

Avila's status was reiterated by Administrator Henry Fowler, who remarked that he "has been living amongst the Indians for some time, with the view of winning back their allegiance to Mexico, and he prepared the chiefs for the present negotiations."[70] Although because of illness Avila was not a member of the annual rebel delegation in 1884, those rebels who came to Belize City were evidently prepared for some discussion of peace. On January 10, 1884, substantive talks were held in the presence of Fowler.

Yucatan was represented by General Canto. José Crescencio Poot, described as governor and general of Santa Cruz, was represented by a party that included his second in command, General Juan Bautista Chuc; *comandantes* Aniceto Dzul and Crescencio Dzib; captains Luis Naal, José Chan, and Esteban Nuñez; and by Poot's personal friend, the trader José Domingo Andrade. The following day the agreement in both Spanish and English was signed by all those mentioned above, with the following provisions.

- José Crescencio Poot shall continue to be governor of Chan Santa Cruz until his death.
- At the death of José Crescencio Poot the right of electing their new governor is conceded to the inhabitants of Chan Santa Cruz subject to the approval of the government of the State of Yucatan.
- The government of Yucatan pledges not to send any official to govern the inhabitants of Chan Santa Cruz without the previous consent of such inhabitants.
- There shall be mutual extradition of criminals.
- Under the preceding conditions the chiefs and other inhabitants of Chan Santa Cruz acknowledge the Mexican government.
- The commissioners on each side shall take a copy of this treaty for the ratification of their respective governments.

Finally, the British administrator, Henry Fowler, signed as witness.[71]

But the move to peace again went nowhere. Events of the next evening were described later in a letter from Crescencio Poot to Fowler.

Mr. Canto took too many glasses of Brandy and had a quarrel with General Aniceto Dzul in which he ill treated the latter, tearing even the shirt he had on and using very insulting language affecting even myself who am here; if he did this before being certain of having gained his object, being still in the Colony, what would he not do in his own country if the said treaty were ever to come into force? It is true that the day after it occurred he was sorry and sent them [i.e., Chuc and Dzul] a letter in which he asked pardon; . . . that is worth nothing, Sir, for one who did not as yet know whether he had gained his object ought to have been careful.

So now I can accept no kind of treaty and should they wish to go to war again it is very well and I will be here to await them although I do not intend to begin it myself.

If this occurrence had not taken place I might have accepted the . . . treaty.[72]

Probably significantly, Poot made no mention of any consultation with the oracular cross as he considered the possibility of an agreement with Yucatan.

In 1884, Mexico and Britain also resumed diplomatic relations. And that year Porfirio Díaz, who had served one term as president of Mexico and ruled for another through a surrogate, was voted to his second term, after which he would rule without interruption for more than a quarter century. Both events were portentous for the rebels. Plantations of henequen were growing in northwestern Yucatan by leaps and bounds in response to North American demand for twine—with labor short and the state's economy booming. This, too, would have its effect.

The Violent End of an Era

Not only did formal peace with Yucatan fail to follow the attempt at treaty making, there were other repercussions. Late in 1884, Francisco Avila was put to death. According to a brief Yucatecan press account this occurred at Chunpom; according to a Belize newspaper it happened at Tulum. No details were given that led up to the event, nor the reason Avila was in Chunpom or Tulum. He was said to have been garroted, hanged from a tree, and burned.[73]

Successful rebellion against Crescencio Poot finally came. During or before April 1885 Aniceto Dzul, the officer assaulted by the tipsy General Canto, broke with Poot. With some 150 men and his own chief lieutenant, *comandante* Román Pec, Dzul fled to Tulum, saying he would never return to Santa Cruz. From Tulum and Chunpom he was able to attract about four hundred additional soldiers. Reputedly, the altercation arose from Dzul's belief that Poot intended to conclude peace, while his support by Tulum soldiers came from rumors that Poot would open Tulum to trade with Yucatan.[74]

The shortness of the interval between the violent death of Avila and Dzul's break with Poot suggests the two events were related. And the fact that the former occurred at Chunpom or Tulum, both of which then provided troops to support Dzul, seems to say also that it was the faction closest to the oracular cross that was in special opposition to the whole notion of surrender. Clearly, there was a break between Noh Cah Santa Cruz and the Tulum-Chunpom axis, and one may suspect that it was in essence a break between the secular and religious governing institutions of the *masewalob*.

In any event, upon learning that Dzul was trying to buy arms and ammunition from a seagoing Belizean trader, Poot moved against him, and the battle was on. There ensued a summer of confused reports, one being that Poot was dead, another that he had fled to Lochhá for reinforcements, yet another that he would throw himself on the mercy of the Yucatecan government "pleading his nine years of pacific policy and his recent attempts to come to some amicable understanding with them."[75]

But for the aged Poot there was no hope: his star had fallen and Dzul's, with that of his Tulum and Chunpom allies, was ascendant. In late August or early September, Poot was killed along with Juan Bautista Chuc and his entire family and seventy-one other officers and soldiers. Also among the dead was Poot's friend and supporter from British Honduras, the brother-in-law of James Hume Blake, trader and logger José Domingo Andrade.[76]

And so ended an era. Although the rebels would continue to be commanded by men old enough to have been members of the movement since its beginnings in the 1840s, gone were those who had begun the war as commanders of the highest rank.

17 / *Pacífico* Affairs

Settlements of the pacified *masewalob* of the south were scattered from the hinterlands of Iturbide and Dzibalchén in Campeche to the edge of settled British Honduras, skirting west of points that professed allegiance to Noh Cah Santa Cruz. Although the supposed headquarters of all *pacíficos del Sur* was located at Xkanhá, where General Eugenio Arana ruled in his nominally official capacity under the government of Campeche, the detached group around Icaiché in the south operated with even more independence than appears to have characterized the secondary settlements closer to Xkanhá. The attention of this southernmost center continued to be fixed on the "rents" extracted along the borders of the British colony.

The advantage taken of this opportunity of location, of course, depended a good deal on the character of the leader at Icaiché. General Marcos Canul was certainly not behindhand. With his men he even perpetrated a visit of extortion to Corozal, one the British government declared an invasion. When that happened, it revealed to British officials that certain Yucatecan immigrants to the colony looked on Canul's sudden presence with good cheer.

The "invasion" occurred while the upper Hondo was unpoliced, the border police transferred to Corozal as a weak bulwark against the *masewalob* of Santa Cruz. On April 14, 1870, Canul and more than one hundred men approached unseen to within five miles of Orange Walk, on New River. Here they stopped and sent a message to R. J. Downer, the local magistrate, announcing their pending arrival, which they assured him should cause no alarm. But it did cause alarm, and nearly all of the townspeople deserted before Canul arrived.

The first of Canul's men reached town around 6:30 the following morning, and soon thereafter the general and his second in command, Rafael Chan, presented themselves at Downer's house with a troop of 115 that was augmented as its stragglers drifted in. Canul demanded boats to move down the New River toward Corozal, refusing to take no for an answer. In the early afternoon he and his men embarked.[1]

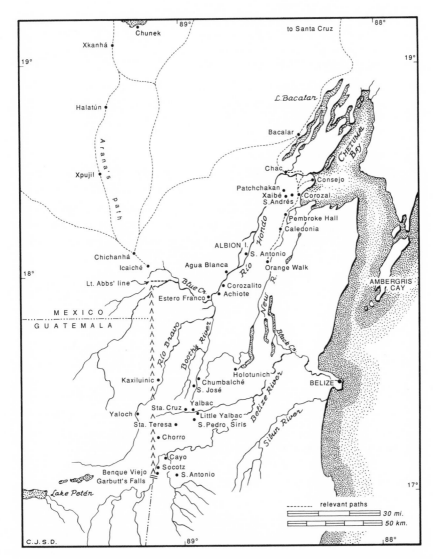

Map 17. *The British Honduran Frontier Region in the 1870s and 1880s. The western boundary is as marked by the British after 1884 (see text).*

Sometime after midnight the little army arrived at Caledonia estate on the lower New River, where they reportedly behaved well, and then they marched out to Corozal on the morning of April 16. Not far outside town they were met by Captain Plumridge, Magistrate Adolphus, and some others, all now forewarned. At first the visitors agreed to leave their arms outside the town and were shown buildings they could use for that purpose, but about that time several Yucatecan residents of the area showed up sporting ribbons with the Mexican colors on their hats. One Laureano Flores, the foreman of a nearby plantation, greeted the Icaiché men warmly in Maya and began a harangue in the same language, waving his arms and saying words to the effect that "I join you now and all of us are one! What have you come here to do? For some years you have meant to go to Corozal and now let us see if you will do it or not! Death or life! *Viva! Viva* México! *Viva* Don Pablo García!"[2] And the combined company marched armed into Corozal.

While an advance guard of Icaiché men moved carefully through the town in skirmish formation, weapons at ready—supposedly to look for Santa Cruz soldiers—the few Corozal officials and English residents who had not fled the town joined the frontier police in a protective stockade hastily thrown up. The Icaiché force occupied the plaza and not long afterward Canul sent a demand for three thousand dollars—a sum the people in the stockade construed as a ransom for the town but which Canul later insisted was to mollify his men for attempting to make them stay at the edge of town rather than in its center.

But already two cries for help had been sent. A messenger from Plumridge managed to pass the Icaiché scouts and rode thirty-four hours to reach Belize, where the lieutenant governor immediately declared martial law in the north and dispatched a military party. Possibly even before Plumridge's messenger was able to get away, a Corozal resident and regular trader to the Santa Cruz rebels mounted his horse and spurred for the Hondo, where he issued a call to the rebel garrison at Bacalar.

But Canul did not wait around. When he was refused first the three thousand dollars and then a scaled-down demand of one-third that amount, Laureano Flores was rumored to have urged him to torch the town and seize Carmichael and others for ransom. But the prudent Canul evacuated Corozal at nightfall for an estate outside its limits. After breakfast the next morning, he began a slow move to the Hondo and then upriver, apparently taking with him objects looted from the church in the Maya settlement of Xaibé.[3] At Albion Island he waited a day or two before finally crossing out of British territory.

On April 17, the day of his departure, a party of fifteen Santa Cruz soldiers passed through Corozal in watchful pursuit. On April 18, sixty more crossed the Hondo from Bacalar, of whom twenty-five moved into the town itself. On April 19, some sixty more arrived. And this was the guard—almost one hundred armed Santa Cruz rebels—who met Major McAuley when he arrived from Belize at the head of his soldiers. With difficulty, the major persuaded the friendly but heavily armed Santa Cruz men, many now bent on getting drunk, to go back to Bacalar. Although disgruntled at the rejection of their guardianship, they withdrew. A few days later the English residents of Corozal subscribed to a gift of appreciation for the rebel soldiers.[4]

A first consequence of the adventure was the jailing of eight Corozal residents of Yucatecan origin, whose behavior in proclaiming a Mexican invasion was deemed treasonable. Laureano Flores, however, had wisely retreated with Canul. A slightly later result was the capture and trial of Canul's secretary José Dolores Sarmiento, who had taken advantage of his presence in British Honduras by stealing a horse. He was given a year in jail.[5]

And a third consequence was a claim from Corozal against the Belize government for damages from the raid. Although the Icaiché soldiers were well behaved despite their threatening demeanor, the English residents asked the cost of the construction of their hurriedly built stockade, as well as the sum they subscribed and sent to Bacalar as their gift of thanks to the rebels. After a long delay, the Belize government paid $675—half the cost of the stockade—but disallowed the gift. As one might expect, the largest individual reimbursement was claimed by John Carmichael.[6]

Canul also sent a claim to the lieutenant governor, a demand for the three thousand dollars he had not received at Corozal.[7] It was, of course, refused.

This sequential occupation of the British town by *pacíficos* and then by *bravos* brought the reestablishment of military posts both at Corozal and Orange Walk. And with this protection again came a feeling of security along the British Honduras frontier, although as will be seen it would not end trouble from Icaiché.[8]

Pacíficos of Campeche, 1870–1872

Although as many as twelve thousand of the *masewalob* in southern Campeche were thought to be peaceful, the whole area was exposed to the rebellious turncoats of Chunxán, who were sporadically active. In 1870, Governor García made a plea for aid to the Mexican government.[9] Rather than succor him, in May of that year the national congress heard a suit against García's conduct in office—which included the alleged misuse of the labor of rebels captured in the 1867 rebellion in the south—and removed him from office in early June. There was a brief flurry of resistance to this action in Campeche, but federal troops were there to keep urban peace, if not to protect Campeche's exposed southern flank; and so Pablo García left office.[10] That his pleas for assistance had substance was shown later that year when the rebels of Santa Cruz combined with southerners to attack south of Tekax toward Iturbide, where they burned a settlement.[11]

But the *bravos* were not the only cause of uneasiness in the region. The people of the ordinary *vecino* villages continued to be suspicious of the bush-loving *pacíficos*. In 1871, residents around Dzibalchén claimed that "the so-called general" Arana "bribes the field hands . . . and hides them in his forests, without obeying the orders of the authorities that they are to be delivered. . . . Agriculture suffers terribly from this."[12]

A similar but even broader complaint was given in the annual report on the Chenes *partido* for the following year. Agriculture was said to suffer because of continuing hostilities, the presence of the *pacíficos del Sur*, and from the lack of field hands. Commerce was stagnant because of not being participated in by the most numerous potential consumers, the pacified *masewalob*.[13]

Still, the *pacíficos* were not without peaceful ambition. In early 1871, a delegation from General Arana requested that the Campeche government establish a school at the *pacífico* headquarters settlement.[14] In response, on March 8 Governor Joaquín Baranda decreed the expenditure of thirty pesos per month for a teacher.[15]

The first school did not go to the capital Xkanhá, however. The *pacíficos* had established a new settlement, Chunchintok, closer to the mestizo towns of Iturbide and Dzibalchén, and it was here that the government intended for the first school for the *pacíficos* to be placed.[16] Money was included in the regular state budget for 1872; indeed, the specified sum continued at a high $360 per year, this at a time when the four other schools in the *partido*—at Bolonchenticul, Hopelchén, Iturbide, and Sahcabchén—were each budgeted at $180 or less.[17] And as 1872 arrived, the Chunchintok school was declared in fact to be open.[18] By late 1872 primary schools were planned for the settlements of Chunek and Xkanhá as well, although no money was yet budgeted.[19]

Action across the Hondo

In April of 1871, a party of Santa Cruz soldiers fell on and killed two men from Icaiché at Achiote in British territory on the upper Hondo. A remonstrance to Noh Cah Santa Cruz brought the response that the attack was not authorized, and the rebel officer in charge was immediately recalled from the border.[20] But the attack also raised complaints from Icaiché about the British insistence that *pacíficos* be unarmed when entering the colony, for it was obvious that their lives were not safe when their Santa Cruz enemies were anywhere in the vicinity.[21]

This and other incidents led at last from grumbling to direct action by Canul and his followers. Whereas their compatriots of Xkanhá were moving to assume the trappings of civilization—albeit unsteadily—the Icaiché *pacíficos* turned again to the machete.

It began with a case tried by R. J. Downer in his capacity as magistrate at Orange Walk (New River) on August 12, 1872. An Icaiché soldier, Pedro Mansinero, had gone on orders of his captain into a settlement a few miles downstream from Orange Walk to find a woman who had left Icaiché five months before and refused to return. Mansinero entered the house of José Eugenio González, owner of a property on which Mansinero believed the woman was hiding. In the absence of González, Mansinero demanded the woman be handed over, used a knife to threaten a laborer as well as González's wife, and ransacked the dwelling in his search. Mansinero was sentenced by Downer to two months in jail.[22]

On August 31, Canul and about 150 men crossed the Hondo in the vicinity of Corozalito and marched to González's house, robbed it, dragged González away, and chopped him to pieces.[23] The following day they marched to Orange Walk, where they arrived about 8:30 in the morning. As I noted earlier, after Canul's "invasion" of Corozal in 1870 a detachment of soldiers had been placed permanently at Orange Walk. On this date, it consisted of an officer, two sergeants, and thirty-eight men.

The belligerent *pacíficos* entered the town from two points. One party immediately broke into Downer's house and made to cut him down in his bedroom but were stalled when his wife threw herself in the way. After a tussle, Downer was seized and tied up with his hammock while his house was sacked. His resourceful wife, gaining time, offered the raiders three thousand dollars for his life, but when she could not produce the money on short order three of them again charged Downer with upraised machetes.

At that moment, the elderly townsman Henry Oswald and two policemen boldly rushed the house with fixed bayonets. The startled attackers, then numbering about a dozen, tumbled out through the backdoor, leaving only their leader trying to drag Downer from the house. He was bayoneted by a policeman.[24]

Oswald, Downer, the police, and the soldiers retreated under fire to the police station and the military barracks. The fight was kept up most of the day. The Icaiché men, barricaded behind a pile of recently cut logwood and in various dwellings, finally forced the defenders to evacuate the police station, but they were unable to dislodge them from the barracks even by burning them out. Canul and his men finally slackened their fire at about 2:30 in the afternoon, and sorties from the defenders drove the last of them from town.

By the end of the fighting, much of Orange Walk had been burned, two soldiers were killed, and about twenty-five soldiers and civilians were wounded. On their side, Icaiché lost five men and suffered a number wounded—one of them Canul, who was believed to be dying. Nevertheless, on their retreat, they plundered Corozalito.[25]

Shortly thereafter Canul did die.[26] But Orange Walk was demoralized. It fell immediately in population from one thousand to fifty and only slowly recovered.[27]

There were no direct diplomatic channels between Britain and Mexico in 1872, but a written complaint regarding the Orange Walk raid was delivered to Veracruz in February 1873 by an English vessel.[28] The answer from the Mexican foreign minister essentially reiterated the earlier responses from that government to similar claims: that Mexico would not be held responsible for the behavior of Canul or other "savages"; that British Honduras had cultivated her own trouble through her involvement in the powder trade; that "since the year 1867 the lawful government of Mexico has not given any military appointment to Canul nor any authority whatever."[29] Britain responded that she would take whatever local steps were necessary, including pursuit across the border.[30]

Although on the diplomatic level the matter remained at an impasse, the British were certain that the problem of Icaiché would be solved only with the resolution of the boundary question between British Honduras and Yucatan.[31] But their threat to cross the disputed border in hot pursuit of errant *pacíficos* did not help to speed the resumption of diplomatic relations, and it would be years before any boundary settlement could be reached.

The raid on Orange Walk also inspired a proposal from the younger John Carmichael for a sweeping reorganization of the government of the northern district of British Honduras—one that would, he said, "remedy this growing evil" of hostile attacks on the colony. Claiming twelve years' experience there, he recommended that "the regular troops should be entirely withdrawn from the Northern District"; that he, John Carmichael, "should be permitted to re-embody . . . my old company of militia to the number of 70 rank and file"; and that the office of magistrate of the northern district as well as the small force of police there should be abolished, with himself acting for the former and his men in place of the latter. His proposal was not, of course, adopted.[32]

And that was the local swan song of the Carmichaels. John the elder died in August 1873, and his son apparently did not appear in the colony thereafter. Carmichael's British Honduras holdings seem to have been sold or otherwise transferred. Despite his history of financial problems, there is no indication that he died insolvent.[33]

Pacific *Pacíficos* Again

Rafael Chan, elevated to command at Icaiché with the death of Canul, was immediately conciliatory in his relations with British Honduras. He presented an apology and asked for peace.[34] On the other hand, Chan complained to Campeche that the British were displeased with him and with Icaiché; that they continued in friendly relations with the rebels of Santa Cruz; and that those rebels were intent on murdering him. He implied— and the Campechanos so believed—that Canul had been killed by the *bravos* rather than while leading a freewheeling attack on the English.[35]

In any event, Lieutenant Governor Cairns responded to Chan with four conditions for the reestablishment of good relations: That he, Chan, should formally apologize for Icaiché behavior in person at Belize or at Orange Walk; that he should agree in writing to submit any complaint against British Honduras residents through the officials of the colony; that he should furnish a party of about twenty people to work on the reconstruction of heavily damaged Orange Walk; and that he should restore such looted property as he could trace.[36]

To this Chan simply wrote again of his desire for peace and asserted his lack of responsibility for the Orange Walk raid. On the same date General Arana of Xkanhá wrote to Cairns in a comparably friendly vein, saying that upon hearing of the affair he at once acted to relieve Canul of his command, only to learn that he was dead.[37] Despite Chan's failure to deliver on the demands of Cairns, after the death of Canul the Hondo was more peaceful.[38]

Before long Arana wrote again, now of an interest in strengthening his ties with the British colony. Like Chan, Arana urged a "treaty" with British Honduras, and he kept urging it despite the lieutenant governor's reiteration that no treaty was necessary for Arana's people to trade in the colony and that a colony governor was not authorized to enter into formal treaties anyway.[39] The upshot was that Arana visited Orange Walk in early November, 1874, and conducted talks with the magistrate. Arana stated that he had departed Xkanhá with a force of 450 men, scattering them in detachments along the way to safeguard his route. He declined to go on to Belize City. He asked that his *pacíficos* might have free entry to the colony for trade and to seek employment; that the "ill-advised events of past years" be forgotten; and that all *pacíficos* should be protected by English law while in English territory. In return, he promised that he would ensure that no armed party of his people should cross the British boundary; that any *pacífico* crossing the border would carry a formal passport, issued at his headquarters or at Icaiché; that any person entering British Honduras should be subject to her laws; that any question regarding debts or commercial relations between individuals would be submitted to legitimate English authorities; and that criminals or other fugitives from British Honduras would not be harbored in *pacífico* territory but if apprehended would be returned.

The lieutenant governor in a written response repeated once more that he had no power to make treaties, and he then assured Arana that *pacíficos* coming to trade or to work would be given the full benefit of English laws. Arana was reportedly satisfied with this, and he and his party left British territory on November 19 for their return journey.[40]

Although the meeting went well, there was one aspect of it that should have served as a warning for the future: Arana complained that residents of San Pedro Siris were farming lands in Yucatan without paying rent, but in thus declaring these lands to be Yucatecan he evidently considered the boundary of British Honduras to lie well to the east of the point favored by the English. No real issue was made of it at the time,[41] but it would become important later.

Who Governs in the South?

Clearly, a lack of agreement on the common boundary between the British colony and Mexico had formed the base of the British trouble with people of Icaiché and Xkanhá. In the period after the fall of Maximilian, boundary negotiations were ruled out by the absence of diplomatic relations between England and Mexico, and through the 1870s communication was desultory. Near the end of that decade, the Mexican minister of foreign affairs would argue again that in Central America England possessed no more than the territorial privileges granted her by Spain.[42] Those Spanish concessions had specified the Río Hondo as the British northern boundary, a line acceptable to the colony. But they gave the southern boundary as the Sibun River, which was not acceptable to the settlers, and the western frontier of the settlement had been described only vaguely as around the source of the Sibun—a point at which the British settlement impinged on Guatemala rather than Mexico. Here, however, the situation was complicated because the boundary between the Petén district and Yucatan had never been agreed upon by Guatemala and Mexico.

In 1859, Britain and Guatemala had signed an accord in which the boundary of the British holding was recognized not as the Sibun River but as the more southerly Sarstoon, the line extending from the coast upstream along that stream to Gracias a Dios Falls, then roughly northward to Garbutt's Falls on the Belize River, and from there due north to a junction with the east-west line separating Mexico and Guatemala—wherever that line might be found to lie. When this accord with Guatemala was signed, a beginning had been made at marking the common boundary, but as the surveying party moved north of Garbutt's Falls, vociferous objections to further demarcation were voiced by British Honduras logging interests, who feared (without grounds, it would turn out) that a clear definition of the boundary there might show them trespassing on Guatemalan territory. Finally, the "demarcation" was limited to boundary pyramids set up at the two falls, Gracias a Dios and Garbutt's, and a line chopped a very short distance south, rather than north, of the latter.[43]

Following the proclamation of the Maximilian government in which claim was laid both to the Petén region of Guatemala and to British Honduras, the British ambassador in Mexico had attempted to reach some specific boundary agreement with that country, without success. But after the troubles at San Pedro Siris, the resulting declaration of martial law in British Honduras, and the reprisal expedition under Colonel Harley in 1867, British work on the boundary was taken up unilaterally. As a step toward delineating the northern frontier, a line was cut by Lieutenant Abbs of the Royal Navy due west from a point on Blue Creek—which the British construed as the upper Hondo and hence the boundary with Mexico—to the longitude of Garbutt's Falls. Although the intention was then to carry the project south from that point, neither the British government nor the colony was willing to pay for the work, and after 1867 the project lapsed.

With this lapse, the colony government had also turned its attention away from the Mayan villages around remote San Pedro Siris, and for nearly a decade that area was allowed to go its own way. The result was reoccupation of the zone by many of the inhabitants who had fled in 1867, including the former *comandante* Asunción Ek. By 1875, Ek was again functioning as commander of his area but now openly under orders from Icaiché, and by then or soon thereafter Icaiché had appointed *alcaldes* in Holotunich, San José, Yalbac, Little Yalbac, Santa Cruz, Santa Teresa, and Chorro, as well as in San Pedro and in some settlements nearby that were located within what the British regarded as Guatemala. The backwoods residents considered themselves liable to be called to military service at Icaiché and, of course, acknowledged no fealty to the British government.[44] With this occupation there was an attendant claim by Xkanhá, through Icaiché, that the territory was Mexican. Rents were levied on Belizean loggers, most of whom paid— following their established custom—rather than suffer trouble; those who did were issued an annual license in the name of Arana, stamped with the official seal of Xkanhá.

This erosion of British control in the southwest came to the attention of the lieutenant governor of the British colony in 1875, when the colony surveyor as well as recalcitrant loggers reported that Icaiché was claiming the entire region west of the Belize River and as far downstream as the mouth of Black Creek and, of more immediate moment, the Icaiché-appointed *comandante* at Holotunich, one Bayote, was threatening to take a logger into custody until he paid his "rent."[45] This led to the dispatch of the Orange Walk magistrate and a few frontier policemen to the area for a careful but effective show of force, as a result of which Bayote agreed to make no more levies.[46]

But General Arana in his written response to the lieutenant governor's complaint reiterated his belief that the lands around Holotunich were Mexican. By the following summer, the rent claims resumed, again from Holotunich but now from a new *comandante*, Sico Figuero (or Figueroa, as it is sometimes written). This time, a warrant of banishment from the colony was passed against the *comandante* by the British Honduras executive council.[47] Although Figuero left Holotunich, he moved only to the vicinity of San José and Chumbalché, still in the colony. There he appeared in company of some renegade mestizos, including two García brothers originally from Honduras, opposing entry into San José by two constables of the frontier scouts; they all were then charged by the colony government with the offense of treason-felony. Both Figuero and the Garcías were unsuccessfully chased, but one of the latter was finally captured in June of 1877 and thrown in jail in Orange Walk.[48] The next month, General Arana visited Albion Island with Rafael Chan, the Icaiché commander, but declined to go on to see either the Orange Walk magistrate or the lieutenant governor. His presence was suspected to have something to do with the jailing of García, who was quickly moved from Orange Walk to Belize to forestall any rescue attempt, and then tried and sentenced to seven years in prison.[49]

In letters of September and November of that year Arana complained about the arrest of García and other matters and restated his certainty that Holotunich and its vicinity were Mexican territory.[50] In January he wrote to inform the lieutenant governor that Rafael Chan had been removed as commanding general at Icaiché, for causes unspecified.[51] Chan was replaced, Arana said, by Santiago Pech—a man who shortly before the skirmish with the British under Major Mackay in 1866 had been mentioned as a sub-*alcalde* of San Pedro Siris under Asunción Ek and as no friend of the English.[52] Now, Arana continued to state his claim to Holotunich as Mexican.[53]

Whatever Pech's attitude may have been earlier, as the new commander at Icaiché he was circumspect in his dealings with the British. On April 4, 1879, he wrote to the magistrate at Orange Walk to ask whether the sugar establishment and distillery of one Felipe Novelo, located near Benque Viejo, was within British territory. For although Novelo had four years earlier obtained a license from the Icaiché-appointed *comandante* Asunción Ek of San Pedro, he had paid his tax only to the colonial treasury after learning it was on territory claimed for the colony. When, that same April, Pech renewed the Icaiché claim for rents to Novelo, Lieutenant Governor Barlee sent an inspector of police and a British army lieutenant to the area to investigate. This visit again yielded the information that the predominantly Indian inhabitants of the western region had embraced Icaiché and that they considered themselves liable to military service under Pech's command.[54]

Before steps could be taken to open further negotiations with General Pech, the lieutenant governor received word that a party of Pech's men had entered the colony, seized a native family from the vicinity of Holotunich and taken them away. Immediately, he wrote to Pech and informed him that he had ordered soldiers and police to forbid the entry of all Icaiché people to the colony; that they were to stop all traffic in pigs, corn, cattle, and other goods commonly traded across the border, and that the order would be in force until Pech returned the kidnapped parties.[55]

Word was then received that there had been no actual intrusion by Pech's Icaiché soldiers but that the apprehension had been made by men from San Pedro and San Jose acting under Pech's orders; that the affair arose when a man shot his brother and then reported that he died of snake bite; and that Pech had ordered the murderer arrested and brought to justice. Pech himself came to Orange Walk to discuss the matter and also, apparently, to trade. But on a summary order from Governor Barlee he was jailed and held until the governor himself could arrive at the town.[56] Six days later, on November 25, Barlee administered a long-winded lecture to Pech and told him he would stay in jail until the people taken from the colony were returned. When they were brought back—on December 4—Pech was released and the border ban lifted. Ironically, and despite his show of hardness, the lieutenant governor then suggested that if Pech would nominate *alcaldes* for those villages of the colony that were peopled with his adherents, he, Barlee, would formally appoint them to the positions to serve under authority of the colony.[57] But although Barlee and Pech agreed on *alcaldes*, they did not reach agreement on the boundary.

When the next two years brought an interlude in border troubles with Icaiché, however, Lieutenant Governor Barlee was quick to credit his own decisive "proceedings . . . and subsequent dealings with general Pech." And, indeed, the extension of British control was partially successful. At Benque Viejo and Socotz, on British-claimed lands within a mile or so of the presumed boundary, British-appointed *alcaldes* were induced to lay out their villages with the aid of a government surveyor, and the lots the residents inhabited were sold to them for two dollars apiece and duly registered in colony records, all with the apparent cooperation of the villagers.[58]

But the lull may also have been because Pech had gone to Mexico—in order, he said, that the "government of which I am a subject should inform me . . . as to the limits of . . . this *cantón*." He returned in early 1882 with selected articles from the treaties between Great Britain and Spain of 1762, 1763, 1783, and 1786, as well as an article of the treaty between Britain and Mexico of 1826. With these as a basis, Pech renewed his claim to have been operating legitimately in areas erroneously claimed by the British.[59]

Barlee's response, of course, was to deny Pech's claims and to stress that only the governments of Mexico and Britain could come to a final boundary agreement. To this a stiffer letter came purportedly from Pech—although this authorship was doubted by Barlee—repeating the claim and offering a month for residents of the disputed territory to move out if they desired, after which

I shall take possession and hoist the Mexican standard, assuring the Lieutenant Governor and other inhabitants of that colony that I will respect as sacred all the divisory lines without trespassing on a single line, excepting that by force you should like to appropriate what does not belong to you nor never was granted.[60]

In his response, Barlee suggested a round of talks and closed with a counterthreat.[61]

When Governor Barlee arrived in Orange Walk a short time later, his suspicions regarding the authorship of Pech's ultimatum were confirmed to his satisfaction, for he found that the magistrate had just received a letter from Celestino Peña, secretary to General Pech, in which he alleged that he, as regular scribe for the illiterate Pech, had nothing to do with the truculent letter but that it had been written while Pech was visiting San Antonio on Albion Island in May. At the same time, witnesses stated that Manuel Castillo of San Antonio, with his employees José Santos López, José María Sevilla, and Paulino Cortez, had been circulating copies of portions of the treaty of 1826, and one witness indicated his belief that Castillo and his men wanted to obstruct British claims in the hope of forcing the abandonment of Orange Walk by its inhabitants, and thus to have a chance of cornering the trade with the Icaiché people that was normally focused on that British town on the New River.[62]

This intelligence brought on an executive council meeting at Orange Walk on June 8, 1882, that advised the arrest of Castillo and the other three and a ban on all trade with Icaiché. Both measures were put into effect the next day, and the new prisoners were sent to Belize to await trial. The search of Castillo's office revealed official paper bearing the stamped seal of the *cantón* of Icaiché, and in the house of López, Castillo's secretary, were found copies of the correspondence between Pech and Barlee.[63] Apparently, the sudden arrests induced Pech to make a hurried trip to Campeche, as events will show.

Local sympathy, however, was with the elderly Castillo; there were reports that witnesses had been threatened and some of them disappeared. Castillo, López, and Sevilla were tried on July 12 and found guilty of treason-felony (the fourth man, Cortez, had died in jail in the interim); Castillo was sentenced to seven years, each of the others to ten.[64]

A British Outpost in the West

While the trial was pending, the lieutenant governor found that his attempt to neutralize Pech's claims to territory for Mexico had not stopped assessment of rents by Icaiché in the remote western zone. Reportedly, a party from the settlement of Yaloch, just across the presumed border in Guatemala, had visited settlers in British Honduras and made the familiar money demands. This time, an expedition of paramilitary volunteers marched from Belize City under the command of Henry Fowler, the colonial secretary and major of volunteers.[65] Upon his arrival in early July 1882, Fowler reported "parties of Indians . . . prowling about, visiting the various mahogany works, demanding rents and threatening to tie people up with the object of inducing people to run away and then go in for plunder."[66] It was here that he learned and reported to Governor Barlee that Santiago Pech and a son of Manuel Castillo had gone to Campeche for orders. Fowler turned his effort to constructing a temporary fort.

In order to test the allegiance of the people, he made an example of the campesinos of the little local village of Santa Cruz, who had told mahogany cutters in no uncertain terms that they intended to give their allegiance to Mexico. But when Fowler offered them the option of remaining and recognizing the territory as English or of moving out, the *alcalde* and people of Santa Cruz elected to stay; and they were then allowed to trade with British Honduras rather than be excluded by the ban applied to Icaiché.

Meetings with Chorro and Yaloch followed. These involved some confusion and a show of force on Fowler's part, but the upshot was that the people of the region elected to remain where they were and consider themselves under British rule. As encouragement for their allegiance, a magistrate was placed temporarily at the fort constructed by Fowler at Cayo.[67]

Meanwhile, when Pech returned from Campeche, apparently shortly after Castillo was sentenced, he wasted no time in contacting the British governor. On July 18, 1882, he wrote to say that the entire affair for which Castillo was tried had been falsified by his (Pech's) secretary Peña, who was he said "now in custody and is to be forwarded to the Government of Campeche or to the President of Mexico." Further, Pech said he himself was responsible for the documents found in Castillo's possession, for he had insisted that Castillo have them copied or translated for him.[68]

The uncertainty and countermoves led to another conference with Pech, who was finally induced to come to Belize under promise that he would not be clapped into jail. In that meeting, recorded by a memorandum of agreement signed by Colonel Robert Harley—military commander in the colony in 1867, now its lieutenant governor—and for Pech by his interpreter, Pech denied any knowledge of the letter in which he purportedly threatened to raise the Mexican standard over western portions of the colony. He reported he had learned that his secretary, Peña, was carrying on a surreptitious correspondence, by finding in Peña's possession a letter to the magistrate at Orange Walk. Pech stated he had then had Peña arrested pursuant to orders from Campeche, and was sending him to the state capital when he tried to escape and was shot. Pech freely indicated he had appointed *alcaldes* at Holotunich, San Jose, and San Pedro because he had believed the region was his to govern. Shown a map of the limits of the colony as understood by the British, he agreed to respect those boundaries provided he received a signed copy of the memorandum of agreement to forward to his government in order to make his position clear to his superiors. This was done, and in return Harley withdrew the proclamation prohibiting trade and intercourse between the colony and Icaiché.[69]

By early 1883 a magistrate was stationed permanently at Cayo and had placed himself in contact with British-appointed (or British-confirmed) *alcaldes* of Benque Viejo, Socotz, San Antonio, Santa Cruz, Chorro, San Pedro, and San José.[70] This sign of British control would, of course, significantly change the balance of power in that region.

In May of 1883, José Santos López, José María Sevilla, and three other prisoners escaped from the Common Gaol in Belize. López and Sevilla took refuge at Icaiché, where the former became secretary and the latter schoolmaster at a nearby village. This event led, in addition to an investigation of jail discipline, to renewed discussion of the entire trial. Upon the recommendation of Governor, now Sir Robert, Harley, and in consideration both of his health and advanced age, Manuel Castillo was released on August 23, 1883, by order of the Colonial Office.[71]

So peace and stability should have reigned. But in June of 1883 Santiago Pech died—of a fever, according to his second in command, Gabriel Tamay. In August, Tamay was elected general and promptly went to the capitals of the western peninsula to present himself and receive his orders.[72]

New Leader, Old Policy

Tamay, José Santos López, and eight Icaiché soldiers left Icaiché on September 1, in the company of one Andrés Ongay of Orange Walk, a young man who happened to be on his way to visit relatives in Yucatan. At Dzibalchén, Ongay reported, they fell in with General Arana—whether by accident or design is not clear—who accompanied them. Despite the fact that Tamay and Arana allegedly made the trip to seek arms for their forces, they went to Mérida rather than Campeche.[73]

On the road López said they were going to get arms to attack Orange Walk, where they would seize the magistrate as hostage for Manuel Castillo—evidently being unaware that he had just been released—and they would sieze two solid citizens of Orange Walk to hold for a ransom of five thousand dollars apiece; and they would burn the town. "Gabriel Tamay agreed to this. . . . Arana also heard, but I did not hear him say anything on the subject." But at Mérida they were told they were subject to Campeche and would have to look for aid there.[74]

Meanwhile, according to another resident of British Honduras who had been in Yucatan on business when the party arrived, Tamay got drunk and "disclosed his intentions to the Commandant of Chunchintok, . . . and . . . the latter reported to the Jefe Político at Dzibalchén, who informed the [Campeche] Governor." However it came about, at Hopelchén on the return journey the plan clearly backfired, for López and Tamay were arrested and sent to Campeche. Reportedly, López in particular was not only suspected of intending to burn Orange Walk but of having been offered two hundred dollars by Manuel Castillo's son to do so. Although he and Tamay were allowed to go back to Icaiché, it was on the strength of a guarantee of good behavior by Tamay, who was told that if he molested the English colony he not only would have to deal with the British, he would have to face the Campeche army under Colonel Santini.[75]

By September of 1884 Tamay appears to have become reconciled to peaceful coexistence along the western boundary of the colony, for he then paid the new lieutenant governor, R. T. Goldsworthy, a visit of welcome, during which he indicated his recognition that Chorro and the other western district settlements were in British territory.[76] This left the locus of dispute confined to the land between two tributaries of the Río Hondo, with the British claiming Blue Creek, the westernmost, as the upper Hondo, hence their boundary, and Mexico asserting that the Río Bravo was the beginning of the Hondo and the frontier.

And in that disputed area Tamay still collected rents. In May 1884 a case arose in which a small logging operator from Belize, contracting for the firm of B. Cramer and Company to work on lands granted to them at Blue Creek by the British Honduras government, had paid his usual sum of eighty dollars to Tamay for a license so "that he might not be molested during the present year." Unfortunately, the logger mistook his boundaries and cut on lands granted to a different company, Belize Estate and Produce. In the resulting altercation the cynical view of at least some of the British Honduras administrators was exposed when the colonial secretary remarked that the Belize Estate and Produce Company

> pay $400 annually to the Indians for the same purpose, viz. for protection against molestation. . . . This system has been going on for years and as far as I can ascertain, troubles have only arisen where parties either refuse to avail themselves of the protection offered by the Indians or where the Indians have been defrauded in the payments promised. . . . As long as the boundaries of the colony remain undefined, it is difficult to suggest any solution for such questions, but it seems to me the practice of making small payments to an Indian Chief for protection against marauding bands of Indians . . . is more satisfactory than to run the risk of a raid or scare which entails not only a heavy loss on the merchant, but considerable cost and trouble to the Government, for an Indian Chief can afford such protection at much less cost than the local Government.[77]

And payments to Icaiché were not the only tax on doing business along the colony's frontier, for the same erring contractor, no doubt like others, was accustomed to pay "to the Indians of Chan Santa Cruz $100 per annum for permission . . . to pass unmolested up and down the Hondo River, the outpost of the Santa Cruz Indians on that river is at Chaques [i.e., Chac] at which point they stop all vessels that pass."[78]

With diplomatic relations continuing broken as they were after the demise of the Maximilian government, Britain had made no progress in boundary discussions with Mexico. But in 1882 Mexico and Guatemala finally achieved an agreement on their mutual frontier, with the northern border of Guatemalan Petén stated to lie at 17°49′ north latitude and to extend "indefinitely towards the east," without any mention that British Honduras was in that direction.[79]

As a joint Mexican-Guatemalan commission began marking their frontier, administrators of the British colony began agitation with their government for permission to flag the boundary they claimed—or at least that portion of it extending north from Garbutt's Falls to a point where it could interrupt the Guatemala-Mexico boundary in its course "indefinitely towards the east." With concurrence from the Colonial Office, this work was at last taken up at Garbutt's Falls in late 1884. Meanwhile, in August of that year diplomatic relations had finally been resumed between Mexico and Britain, with the British government now insisting on negotiations to fix the boundary. In May 1886 preliminary discussions began.[80]

As the actual demarcation of the colony's frontier proceeded north from Garbutt's Falls, however, immediate remonstrance was drawn from General Tamay at Icaiché. He described the resulting line as "running with a direction from South to North West," which, he said, would include within the colony his own "peaceful and subject" *cantón* of Kaxiluinic. Nevertheless, he indicated he would take no action until receiving specific directions from Campeche. The settlement of Kaxiluinic had harbored several felons escaped from British Honduras, who—as the line advanced inexorably northward and it became clear the village would indeed lie a few kilometers within British Honduras—finally decamped for other parts.[81]

And so the closing phases of the campesino rebellion were marked by steps toward international agreements that would serve permanently to curtail the actions of the *masewal* governments, *pacífico* and *bravo* alike. To these actions of global significance both rebels and former rebels could only acquiesce, although with little immediate understanding of the inevitable consequences.

18 / The World Moves Closer

As I have stated repeatedly, the portion of the peninsula held by the rebels after their expulsion from the west in 1848 was the region over which Spanish Yucatan had never exercised effective control and which economically had been essentially surplus to them. Although the peninsula population would not recover its prewar size until the twentieth century, by 1880 it was well on the increase, with an annual increment approaching 1 percent.[1] Unlike the closing years of the colonial period, in the late nineteenth century the vital stimulus to the economy was not local demand but the international market for cordage.

In 1878, a knotting device was developed to enable the McCormick mechanical reaping machine to use string for binding bundles of grain. When the binder twine boom erupted, Yucatecan producers and their North American partners achieved a near corner on the market that they would hold for the rest of the century. In Yucatan the result was the explosive growth in henequen plantations—from a total of about twenty-six hundred hectares in 1860, to forty thousand in 1883 and one hundred thousand in the 1890s. Annual production increased even more, from thirty thousand bales of fiber (of 160 kilograms each) in 1870 to three hundred thousand in 1890 to five hundred thousand by the end of the century.[2]

This growth also involved expansion of the region of production from its heartland in the northwest. In the 1880s plantations appeared as far east as Valladolid and as far south as Tekax. Land was drawn from tracts formerly devoted to locally marketed foodstuffs, leading to increasingly large imports of staples such as maize and beef.[3] Labor, too, was siphoned off, for henequen production required a permanent, nonseasonal workforce, which was secured to the expanding plantations by debt peonage. In the 1880s the shortage led to the importation of indentured Asians and later to the enforced labor of transplanted Yaqui Indians.[4]

Despite the boom-and-bust cycles inherent in the volatile world price of fiber, for the first time in postconquest history upper-class Yucatan grew rich. Although the burgeoning henequen industry remained concentrated in the northwest, its stimulus to peninsula commerce was felt widely. In the east and south, this took the form of expanded agriculture and exploitation of forest products, much of it aided by the new availability of both Mexican and foreign capital.

Campeche was not outside the effects of the general prosperity, and Campechano woodcutters moved inland along the Río Candelaria, encroaching on some regions watched over by General Arana and his *pacíficos del Sur*.[5] In the east, relatively modest agricultural establishments and dyewood works expanded along the northeast coastal strip, one of which was the property of Robert Stephens, who was killed in the raid that led to the death of Bernardino Cen described earlier. Far more extensive was the establishment in 1876 of the Compañía Agrícola El Cuyo y Anexas at the site of El Cuyo on the coast northeast of Tizimín and safely outside the area then threatened by the rebels. A Yucatecan concern with German backing, the company concentrated first on dyewood for the German market but expanded into other commercial woods, chicle, salt, and the production of cattle, sugar, rubber, vanilla, and tobacco. By the end of the century, the labor force on their numerous productive stations reached fifteen hundred people, joined by more than one hundred kilometers of narrow-gauge tramways and nearly two hundred kilometers of telephone line.[6]

The expanding interests of Yucatan and Mexico would shortly collide with those of the remaining rebels of eastern Yucatan, stimulating unrest and the dissolution of the active rebel camp that marks the final stage of the rebellion.

Bravo Postures

The overthrow of Crescencio Poot in Noh Cah Santa Cruz had two immediate effects. The first of these was the alienation of southern turncoat *masewalob* in Chunxán and Lochhá. In October and November 1885, several hundred of these people with 327 firearms surrendered to the *pacíficos* at Xkanhá. A month later, about one hundred more presented themselves with sixty arms at Icaiché,[7] where they and other fugitives from Santa Cruz territory would form a separate barrio of the town.[8]

The second effect was a limited resumption of hostilities against Yucatan. In February 1886 Dzul and his lieutenant, Román Pec, with a force estimated at one thousand or more raided north of Peto and held Dzonotchel until dislodged with some losses.[9] In Yucatan, this unaccustomed strike brought talk of reestablishing the abandoned frontier cantonments, but nothing was done.[10]

As usual, *masewal* aggressiveness did not extend to British Honduras. In May of that same year Dzul took solicitous care in laying out the boundaries of logging works to be exploited by English companies in rebel territory near the northern end of Bacalar Lagoon. Not only was he friendly, but he tried to explain away the raid of February, saying that he had sent some of his subordinates toward Peto to arrange the treaty with Mexico that had been desired by General Canto, but that they were fired on by the Yucatecans and so retired immediately without causing damage.[11]

After the commercial courting of the Santa Cruz rebels by the John Carmichaels in the late 1860s, traveling traders from British Honduras had been largely supplanted by the regular trading trips of the *bravos* themselves to Corozal—trips undertaken at least annually, and often in considerable force, although the visitors had learned to leave their guns at the border. And as noted earlier, after 1880 a delegation of the highest ranking of the rebels journeyed yearly to Belize City, where they called formally on the governor, traded, and collected rents from the growing number of Belizean loggers who were exploiting forest resources in Santa Cruz territory. When in the city, the visitors were housed and regaled at the Cramer and Company mercantile establishment by its resident manager, Carlos Melhado, who also acted as their regular agent.[12]

Despite the killing of some British Honduran partisans of Poot incidental to Aniceto Dzul's coup, the operation of logging interests was not impaired by Dzul's accession to leadership at Noh Cah Santa Cruz. Indeed, he was said to embark on "a policy of effusive overtures to the English," promising that British Hondurans working in his domain would be warned should he have intelligence of pending Yucatecan raids.[13] But his efforts on this score were not entirely effective, as we will see.

In 1885, the first of several succeeding seasons of short maize harvests distressed eastern Yucatan. Suddenly and inexplicably, as it seemed to the newspapers, in March of 1886 two rebel leaders from Tulum, neither of them named but one of them said to be titled *gobernador*, arrived by boat at the port of Progreso. In serious need of corn and unable to find any for sale at Cozumel, they had simply gone on to western Yucatan. In Mérida they had a long interview with the governor, General Guillermo Palomino, regarding conditions in the eastern peninsula. Presumably they obtained grain, although that was not reported as news.[14] It is also not certain that intelligence obtained from this visit was crucial to later events. But with the increasing economic interest of Yucatan in the eastern forests and the emphasis of the Díaz government on eliminating pockets of campesino resistence throughout Mexico, it is likely that information from the visitors contributed to the voyage of the following month.

On April 20, 1886, the Mexican steam gunboat *Independencia* suddenly appeared off Ambergris Cay, the northernmost of the string of islands lying along the east coast of British Honduras. The captain asserted to its disbelieving inhabitants that the island was Mexican, not British, then turned northward along the Yucatecan coast and chugged as far north as the bay of Espíritu Santo. There he surprised and took into custody all the loggers who were working under permit from the Santa Cruz rebels, burning their camps as he did so. Some thirty-eight prisoners—a minority of them actually British subjects—were hauled off to jail in Mérida, where they were tried for cutting timber without a license and for complicity with the rebels. By the time the loggers were sentenced—to eighty days in jail— they had already been held for six months. Those who survived the ordeal returned home around the end of the year.[15] Although Dzul offered to attack Yucatan in reprisal, nothing came of it.[16]

Belize and Santa Cruz

In February 1887, when the acting governor of the British colony was at Corozal he received a formal visit from both Aniceto Dzul, representing Noh Cah Santa Cruz, and one Cruz Ciau, representing Tulum. The two asked three things: that they be told the meaning of rumors of a pending expedition against them by Mexico; that British traders locate at Bacalar to carry on commerce in preference to the Chinese who had cornered trade among the rebels; and that the *masewalob* be taken under the protection of the Queen of England and allowed to annex their territory to that of the British colony.[17]

After apparently receiving some answer to the first request, they were told that British traders would not settle in rebel territory because there were no guarantees for their safety. The third request would have to be relayed to the queen.

When the queen's answer came, messengers of the rebels were invited to the colony to hear it. Upon learning that the queen declined the honor of annexing them and had recommended instead that they make peace with

Mexico, the messengers—two *comandantes*—stated that they "did not want any flag unless they could have the English one. They would interfere with no one, if no one interfered with them."[18]

At the end of January 1887, frustrated by government actions inhibiting rebel commerce with the British colony, Aniceto Dzul had asked the governor of British Honduras if the Queen of England would be so good as to arrange the removal of a Mexican coast guard vessel that often hovered in front of Tulum.[19] Three months later, the crew of this patrol boat seized a Tulum sentry who approached them while they were cooking fish on the beach. Although the captive was shipped off to Mérida and imprisoned for a short time, a new Mexican policy of dealing with the rebels by persuasion sent him sent back in May to Tulum.[20] Nevertheless, Mexican coastal patrols continued, and the *Independencia*, a small vessel of three hundred tons, steamed regularly between Veracruz and Belize.[21]

This seaborne campaign caused British Honduran forest workers to shy away from the coast, but it by no means eliminated their activity in rebel territory. In late 1886 when Dzul made his customary trip to Bacalar and points south, it was partly to arrange for additional British logging works in his domain.[22]

But logging entrepreneurs were also infiltrating the region from Yucatan. In 1887 Nicolás Urcelay, the guiding spirit of the Yucatecan attack on San Antonio Muyil in 1872, was cutting dyewood at the northeast corner of the peninsula. The same year one Felipe Ibarra Ortoll obtained a Yucatecan concession to cut wood in large areas of the east coast, by some accounts over the entire coastline from Cape Catoche to the British boundary. Other speculators were becoming interested in eastern tracts classified by Yucatan as government land, as commercial interests finally awoke to the possibilities of the eastern coast, despite problems with the rebels.[23] Some observers placed among these hopeful operators Juan Peón Contreras, of Mérida, although if logging was one of his aims, he also had another and higher calling—for he obviously marched to the beat of a drum from another world.

Proclaiming the Messiah at Tulum

Juan Peón Contreras de Elizalde, as he came to name himself, was of a prominent Mérida family, and had given valuable service to Yucatan as the first director of its first public museum of antiquities. By 1880 he was evidently suffering an impairment of his mental faculties, and sometime in the middle of that decade he came under the sway of a Honduran named Rosales, who represented himself as the Messiah. It was to proclaim the Second Coming and through it to establish peace among the eastern rebels that Peón resigned his post at the museum and embarked for the east, accompanied by a mestizo named Dorada or Dorado—a disciple according to Peón, a hired keeper according to Peón's family.[24] In February 1887 he and the disciple arrived in Belize, where they outfitted themselves.[25]

It was as *Juan Bautista Precursor II del Mesías*, "John the Baptist Forerunner II of the Messiah," that he with seven others—two Hondurans and five Yucatecans, including his disciple and one Gumesindo Arjonilla—made his way by small boat north along the coast to Tancah, a short distance past Tulum. Stepping out on the beach there, he raised his "Standard of the Redemption," apparently a flag with a crosslike design on it, and began to sing in Maya to an accompaniment his assistant cranked out on a hand organ.

Mindful of the recent kidnapping of a Tulum man, the Tancah people, who were counted among the rebels of Tulum, approached with weapons at ready, threatening, then stopped to listen as Peón preached, and finally prostrated themselves to kiss his insignia of the cross. He told them he was Juan Xiu, come to save them. As the people placed themselves at his orders he erected a small prefabricated chapel, distributed gifts, and dispatched a present to the sacred oracular cross of Tulum, where most of his new adherents also repaired, leaving only a small detachment as honor guard of the new preceptor.

In four days, a large crowd presented itself at *Tancah del Redentor*, "Tancah of the Redeemer," as Peón was now calling it. The *gobernador* of Tulum, the high priest of the Tulum cross (now a man, evidently the successor of María Uicab), their wives and assistants, all came, reportedly authorized by the miraculous speaking cross to pay homage to the new preacher. For it was said that the cross had predicted the arrival of a foreign savior. There was a great dance.

The next day all walked for two hours on the path to Tulum, stopping at a special amphitheater where the sacred cross itself appeared for a ceremony. After another, shorter walk of an hour or so they arrived at Tulum pueblo for another ceremony in the cross's own temple. This launched a three-day public festival during which Peón's earlobe was pierced by the wife of the high priest—apparently to fit him for the earring that would mark him as an officer among the *masewalob*. It closed with more gifts from Peón, one of them to a cross said to reside in the "Castillo"—presumably the building so called within the precolumbian ruins of Tulum.[26]

At the end of March, Peón made a trip back to Belize with the blessings of the cross, returning three weeks later with maize and other supplies much in need around Tulum and San Antonio Muyil, where food was scarce. His return inspired another fiesta at Tulum, with singing, dancing, fireworks, and a nighttime descent by God to speak through the cross. A witness reported this last event as "taking place in the deepest darkness, in the apartment, separated from the rest of the church, called *gloria*, the entrance to which is defended by double sentinels; the governor, the high priest, and his wife enter that place; the humble folk prostrate themselves through the rest of the church, and at intervals stimulated by a kind of whistle that the Cross emits, break out in blows of contrition to the chest and ardent kisses to the air, signs of reverence and approval."[27] After two hours of this, a new round of music and bells signaled the distribution of *balche*, a beverage fermented from the bark of a tree. At the finale Peón was married to a woman of the place, Isabel Xuluc, widow of a leader and a person of evident prestige, in a ceremony in which the governor, the high priest, and their wives served as godparents. Also present were the chief priest of San Antonio Muyil and three leaders of that establishment. The formal title of "Governor of the Castle and Port of Tancah" was conferred on Peón by the cross.

Reportedly, men of the region had begun to cut dyewood for him, when Peón obtained the cross's permission to sail to Progreso, ostensibly to obtain the release of the Tulum man taken by the coast guard. He and his disciple arrived there in mid-May—luckily for them. For while they were in western Yucatan, Peón's promising mission in the east came to a violent end.

Exactly what brought on the catastrophe is not entirely clear. Newspapers in Mérida alleged that Aniceto Dzul had learned from Belize that the Forerunner II was not Juan Xiu but a Yucatecan from Mérida. The newspaper in Belize, professing to quote a survivor of the expedition, reported that Peón had fallen out with Gumesindo Arjonilla (who it seems had once been among the Santa Cruz rebels), who then wrote to Dzul to report Peón's hoax, claiming it was preparation for a Yucatecan invasion. Whatever the case, a combined force from Chunpom, Muyil, and Santa Cruz moved against Tulum and seized the principal chiefs there, then advanced on Tancah where they laid hold of Arjonilla—despite his attempts to distance himself from Peón—and at least one other man. Two or three of the Peón party were allowed to depart on foot when they thoughtfully claimed to be English, but the other prisoners were killed. These were said to include Arjonilla and others of Peón's men, the *gobernador* of Tulum, and the Tulum high priest and his wife.[28]

A Gentler Touch

In early April 1888, as an aftermath of Peón's abortive mission of salvation, rebels from Tulum attacked the works of Nicolás Urcelay on the mainland coast between Cozumel and Isla Mujeres, chased away the loggers, almost caught Urcelay himself, and burned fifty tons of cut dyewood. Little wonder, then, that by 1889 Ibarra Ortoll had assigned at least part of his unexploited interest in the eastern coast to a resident of Belize, who as agent for a British firm called the Mexican Exploration Company, Ltd., first took care of the Santa Cruz rebels by paying rent to them, then turned to peddling Mexican concessions for logging to his countrymen—thus offering safety both from rebels and from the Mexican gunboats haunting the coast.[29]

Meanwhile, the Mérida press kept up verbal attacks on British Honduran loggers, accusing them of flying their flag over Yucatecan territory as a British province and expressing satisfaction that their activities were partly curtailed by the Mexican coast guard.[30] To these the Belize press responded in kind, denying that the British flag ever flew over any part of rebel territory unless during bouts of rebel drunkenness.[31]

In spite of all, after the unpleasant visit of the *Independencia* in 1886, the Mexican military attitude softened considerably as representatives of the central Mexican government intruded more and more into relations between the British and the rebel *masewalob*. On March 2, 1887, the *Independencia* returned to British waters bearing the Mexican general Octavio Rosado, who was at pains to call formally on the acting governor of British Honduras and explain his special mission from the president of Mexico. He was there, he said, to reconnoiter before Mexico took an active hand in subjugating the rebels. The acting governor took his opportunity to refute reports in the Yucatecan press, saying that despite requests from the Santa Cruz rebels there were no British settlers at Bacalar, for the government of British Honduras refused to guarantee protection outside its boundaries. On his part Rosado opined that the best move would be to make Tulum, rather than Bacalar, the base of Mexican operations, because friendly contact with the rebels at a protected trading station near their heartland might well bring about their capitulation without bloodshed, a result the central government very much desired.[32]

Playing for Peace

These chats at Belize had more important counterparts in the diplomatic drawing rooms of Mexico. As treaty talks between Britain and Mexico continued, the possibility of a ban on the sale of arms was prominent enough that word of it reached the *masewalob* at Noh Cah Santa Cruz. In a letter to the governor of British Honduras dated January 8, 1888, the rebel leadership— Aniceto Dzul, Román Pec, and Anacleto Chi—set out their position clearly enough that it warrants lengthy quotation:

> We the chiefs of the Santa Cruz Indians residing in the country north of the Río Hondo beg to lay a statement of our troubles with the Spanish population of Yucatan before you and we pray that you will represent our case to Her Majesty the Queen of England in order that our actions may not be misrepresented to her by any prejudiced parties.
>
> At one time the Spanish people and ourselves lived together and we were subjected to all manner of bad treatment by them. It was a common thing for a Santa Cruz Indian [*sic*] to be tied to a tree and lashed and our women were treated in a most inhuman manner. Under this treatment the spirit of our people was aroused and about 50 years ago we successfully struggled for our independence and drove the Spaniards from our country.
>
> At various times since then they have invaded us, but under God's protection we have not yet been beaten. We are now a people living under our own laws and are peacefully governed by men of our own race. We cultivate the land and raise animals for our own domestic use.
>
> We wish to point out to Your Excellency and beg that you will represent to Her Majesty the Queen of England that we live as close to the British Colony of Honduras as we do to the Spanish people of Yucatan, but never on any occasion have we given any trouble to the people of that Colony. We promise that on no account will we first attack the people of Yucatan, but if they invade us we shall be compelled to fight for our country and our liberty.
>
> Living in the bush as we do where wild beasts and game exist, firearms are necessary to our existence. We therefore pray that

notwithstanding any representations which may be made by the Spanish people of Yucatan we may always be allowed, as heretofore, to purchase arms and ammunition through the Colony of British Honduras as we do not require them for the purpose of making war but solely for our own protection.[33]

On the next state visit from Noh Cah Santa Cruz, in early July 1888, Governor Goldsworthy took pains to urge the rebel leaders to reach an amicable agreement with Mexico, stressing their advantage in dealing with the central government, which could guarantee them protection against possible enemies in Yucatan. He argued that it would be folly for them to fight a nation so much more powerful than they were, one whose friendship with Britain would, in case of hostilities, inevitably cause the colony to cut off all sale of ammunition, thus rendering the rebels unable even to defend themselves.[34]

It was apparently agreed that on their return to Santa Cruz the rebel leaders would write a formal request for Governor Goldworthy's assistance in bringing about friendly relations with Mexico. And on that very afternoon—by a scarcely credible coincidence—the Mexican gunboat *Libertad* dropped anchor at Belize City. Although the captain assured the governor that the timing was sheer accident, there emerged from the boat one Enrique Sardaneta, said to be of the Mexican Ministry of Public Works and Agriculture and who had served as a member of the commission to settle the boundary between Mexico and Guatemala.

Sardaneta interviewed Aniceto Dzul and the other *masewal* leaders at Cramer's store and then had them visit the gunboat. According to witnesses the meeting was amiable, and it resulted in a bland, written statement in which those present simply affirmed that they had met on July 6 as a preliminary to arranging a treaty of peace. Verbally, Sardaneta advised the colony's colonial secretary that somewhat more definite agreements had been reached: that the rebels should not be molested by Yucatan; that they were to write to the president of the Republic of Mexico through the governor of British Honduras to ask for the protection of the president; and that when this was done, more definite arrangements would be made.[35]

Whatever Dzul's response to Sardaneta's overtures when face to face, first hand, his later, considered reaction was negative. In a letter of August 30 to the British colony's governor he alleged that Sardaneta had threatened to send troops to take Bacalar and destroy Santa Cruz, charged that Sardaneta had asked for rebel cooperation in fighting the British, and reaffirmed his affection for and support of the colony.[36] These accusations against Sardaneta were denied by witnesses to the meetings, but Dzul's attitude toward the Mexicans was clear.

To Make a Treaty

As the strength and stability of the Porfirio Díaz government in Mexico increased, it sought the settlement of boundary questions with both Guatemala and Great Britain—questions that in southern Yucatan were interrelated. As already described, the Mexican negotiations with Guatemala had inspired Britain to order the demarcation of the western boundary claimed for British Honduras, a task still not completed.

When the second set of negotiations was undertaken, conditions were laid out quickly by both Britain and Mexico: the boundary would consist of the Río Hondo to its headwaters, trade in arms with Indian tribes would be strictly prohibited by both Mexican and British Honduran governments in the region of their frontier, and each government would attempt to prevent Indian incursions from its own territory into that of the other.[37] These points would form the substantive provisions of the final treaty.

There were minor problems. The demarcation of the western boundary of the British colony crept on through the dry season of 1886, but as the surveyors prepared to resume in 1887—with only some eight kilometers of the northern end left to survey—General Tamay again raised objection and threatened to stop the work by force. This time he was brought to pause by a letter from the governor of Campeche. While not endorsing the British survey, which Mexico took to be informal rather than legal, the governor directed Tamay to avoid hostile steps, although permitting him to issue written protests.[38]

Tamay did keep up his protests and also was rumored to have built a barracks at Kaxiluinic (in British territory) to house his troops in case there was trouble. The Colonial Office responded to Tamay's representations by directing that the boundary survey be suspended. But William Miller, the assistant surveyor general in charge of the actual party, had reached the expected position on the east-west line cut by Abbs in 1867—17°59'27"— before his orders caught up with him. He found the crucial point to be more than twenty kilometers from Icaiché.[39] When the surveying stopped, Tamay subsided, although he did not leave off his claim to the area surrounding Kaxiluinic.

In Mexico City, agreement was reached speedily that the tributary Blue Creek would form the upper Hondo watercourse.[40] In January 1889, following a recommendation of the British minister in Mexico, Spenser St. John, and on orders of the colonial secretary, Miller started for Blue Creek to determine which tributary formed the main channel. Not long after, a messenger from Tamay told him to stop. Early the next month his government told him to go on, so long as he was certain of his geographical position. He continued, but reported that the Icaiché people insisted that the Río Bravo formed the boundary of British territory, and as evidence of this they claimed—with absolute truth—that they had regularly received rents from loggers working between the Bravo and Blue Creek. On March 8, the governor of British Honduras cabled the British minister in Mexico that Tamay was again threatening to stop progress.

And he did. Miller's quarters were surrounded by Icaiché soldiers, and his workers decamped. The enterprising Miller, left with nothing to do and having a letter that had meanwhile come to his camp from the colony government addressed to Tamay, simply walked to Icaiché to deliver the letter. While there he was shown a Mexican map of 1787, in which Blue Creek was clearly not the colony boundary. He also viewed Tamay's commission as general and *jefe político* of Icaiché, bearing the signature of the governor of Campeche.

But the cable to Spenser St. John had its effect, and Governor Goldsworthy was able to write again to Tamay to inform him that Mexican approval had been obtained for the survey. Whether Tamay himself received word of this from Mexico is unknown, but he acquiesced.[41] The work was completed in November, when the main course of Blue Creek was determined to cross the meridian of the colony's western border at a point a little more than ten miles north of the frontier between Mexico and Guatemala, which had been agreed to lie at latitude 17°49′.[42]

But it was not these minor hurdles that held up signing of a treaty. Neither was it diplomatic quibbling, of which there was little as goodwill reigned.[43]

Rather, the stumbling block was the repeated insistence by Ignacio Mariscal, the Mexican foreign minister, that the boundary treaty should be linked to a military expedition against Santa Cruz and that Mexico was not ready for that.[44] Without such a campaign to emphasize the immediate need for a treaty, the minister asserted, the settlement would be claimed by political enemies as a needless cession by Díaz of Mexican territory. But even after Díaz's reelection in July 1888, fear of such repercussions continued, and the

British were told again that they must wait until a military campaign could actually be undertaken.[45]

While the early discussions were in progress, St. John had suggested to his government that an immediate ban on arms sales to the rebels would be helpful. But as delays accumulated, British Honduras was specifically ordered by London to avoid any ban for the present, in the belief that the arms trade was the primary means to pressure Mexico to sign the convention.[46] In the colony itself, officials were beginning to entertain serious reservations about the ban: Related to their own well-being was the very real possibility that if the Santa Cruz rebels were forbidden the source of supply that had been open to them for so long, they might simply cross the Hondo and take what they wanted—an act the small constabulary of about one hundred men could scarcely prevent. In a more humanitarian vein, their uneasiness dealt with the question of whether the proper British position would be to ban supplies just as the rebels were pushed by Mexico, for it would appear that "while professing to be in friendly relation with them, we were conniving at their extinction."[47] Both of these considerations would trouble them for a decade.

Foot-dragging continued in Mexico until the legislature of Yucatan grew restive under the delays and on September 28, 1892, petitioned the president to get on with the business.[48] The long-awaited signing finally occurred July 8, 1893. On September 18 of that year the treaty was published in the British Honduras gazette and five days later by the Belize public press. On October 4 a letter was dispatched by the colony administrator to Noh Cah Santa Cruz, informing the supreme rebel commander—now Crescencio Puc—of the treaty, warning him that a ban on arms sales would be involved, but advising him that no such ban could take effect until necessary legislation had been passed in the colony.[49]

The treaty would not be ratified for another four years, but in British Honduras there was immediate panic. Within weeks of publication of the agreement, two hundred families fled the Corozal region for fear of Santa Cruz reprisals when powder was cut off.[50] This led to a decision by the British government to go slow in pushing for ratification, but the treaty was nevertheless formally accepted by the queen, and Mariscal was so informed in October of that year, when he finally delivered it to the Mexican senate.[51]

There it roused patriotic fervor and questions, leading to demands that Mexico be allowed to sail through British waters to gain the mouth of the Hondo. Further negotiations ensued, and the unratified treaty languished again.[52] Meanwhile, in British Honduras word was received of the continued good faith of the Santa Cruz neighbors, and panic lessened to worry, while rumors flew of an impending Mexican invasion of rebel territory.[53]

These jitters in the north, however, were in contrast to placid relations between British Honduras and her other *masewal* neighbors.

Peace, Pestilence, and Perfidy at Icaiché

It is from the period around 1890 that more detailed descriptions of Icaiché come. In 1889 the settlement was visited—apparently for the first time—by a Maya-speaking priest from Belize and again in 1895 by the same priest and a companion; each sojourn produced a description published in the Belizean Roman Catholic newspaper.[54] In 1894, the German scholar Karl Sapper also stopped some days and reported his visit in detail.[55] Other less complete accounts are approximately contemporary and relate to an incident described later in this section.[56] Together, they richly portray the southeastern *pacífico* seat as it existed in the later years of the nineteenth century.

The Icaiché settlement included the capital town and four or five surrounding hamlets. Many of the buildings were atop mounds that attested to the presence of ancient ruins. Estimates of total population ran from five hundred to more than three thousand.[57]

Surrounded by a wet plain where ponds abounded, the town lay upon a hill several hundred feet high, with flanks made secure by an almost solid grove of bamboo penetrated by only two pathways. Two plazas served four barrios—designated Icaiché, Noh-Icaiché, and San Román, the fourth being that occupied by the recent immigrants from Chunxán.

The church, dedicated to Santa Clara, was said by one priest to lack the multiple crosses of the Santa Cruz rebels but had plenty of *santos* ranged around the walls, one of them a painting of the Virgin of Guadalupe, a gift of the president of Mexico made presumably at the time Santiago Pech had visited the capital. But according to one of the priests, "the famous cross taken by Canul from Xaibe" occupied the main altar.[58]

Organization was along the usual military lines. Gabriel Tamay was both general and *jefe político*, seconded by a *comandante*.[59] His appointment was presumed to be for life, with succession through election by a council of officers; the general, however, could apparently be required to justify his actions to the entire population in council, on pain of dismissal from office.

In a small open building fenced against pigs, a guard of five or six armed men was constantly at the call of the general, while all males aged fifteen and over were soldiers, caring for their own arms and reporting for duty upon summons.

Justice was usually swift and was administered by Tamay, who at the end of each day following his usual work in the milpa would settle himself to hear pleas. Decisions might consist of restitution for wrongs, whippings or, in serious cases, execution. Those judged guilty of murder were shot and thrown into the grave of the victim. Drinking was discouraged, but teetotalling was evidently not achieved for Tamay was said to have ordered that when he was drinking his subjects should not expect him to hold court.

The taxes on mahogany and logwood collected from residents of British Honduras took care of public expenses, including the cost of some arms and ammunition and the salary of the clerk or secretary, who could both converse and was literate in Spanish. Any surplus over these requirements, apparently, was at the disposal of the general.

But all, including Tamay himself, lived by hunting and farming, raising their own maize and pigs. Along with other products, such as animal skins and hammocks, the pigs were for sale to the British colony, and individuals frequently hired out there to labor for short periods. Dress was the standard Maya fashion of the time: white trousers and shirts for the men and a white *hipil* for women. The *hipiles* were often embroidered, and the women were addicted to gold jewelry and fine shawls; visitors were particularly taken by their dainty—and very urban—silk slippers.

Tamay himself, a man of "average size" and by now elderly, was described as of only the most modest means, living in a humble house on one of the plazas with his wife and three daughters. When his subjects approached him, they kissed his hands; when these were people of rank he reciprocated by kissing theirs. He was accounted an honest and good man, even by his detractors. But some would say that when he carried out his duty in managing the exploitation of Icaiché forests, he was capable of great cruelty.

In 1891 smallpox raged through the southern *pacífico* regions as well as western and northern British Honduras. In the latter place it was attributed to a colony resident's visit to Xkanhá, where the disease was prevalent by April of that year and where it caused numerous deaths.[60] In November, the governor of the colony wrote to Tamay to recommend that his people avoid Orange Walk, where the disease was worst, but he received the response that although smallpox was decreasing at Icaiché, it had already carried away more than 150.[61] According to one of the priests who visited in 1895, there had been three hundred deaths there. Sapper seems to suggest an even greater decline, estimating the population at only five hundred in 1894.[62]

The ravages of disease were followed at Icaiché by a temporarily successful attempt to depose Tamay. In late March 1892, his position was taken from him, apparently by popular action, and given formally to one Cono, his *comandante* and second in command. Tamay's secretary, who had fled to Orange Walk, claimed the rebellious action was instigated by one Felipe Flores, a logger with an establishment at Estero Franco, located on the Mexican side of the Hondo. Flores was at odds with Tamay and had also written threatening letters to Manuel Castillo and his family on Albion Island.[63]

The upset caused consternation along the western colony border, where a number of residents had interests on both sides of the line, and prompted Eustaquio Avila, who had a logging operation near Estero Franco as well as a small sugar plantation near Icaiché itself, to rush from Orange Walk to Icaiché to protect his property. Avila claimed to have found Tamay deposed indeed and refusing to accept official mail addressed to him from the colony. Avila had with him the threatening letters written by Flores to the Castillos, and he reported that he quietly talked to a number of Icaiché corporals— for of all the officers of higher rank only Tamay and Cono had survived the smallpox—and urged them to call a public meeting at which Flores's letters were read and translated into Maya. The upshot was the immediate restoration of Tamay, the imprisonment of Cono, and the dispatch of an armed party to Estero Franco. Flores and three others were killed outright, the Flores goods confiscated and distributed among the Icaiché people, and his buildings burned. So on April 10, 1892, Tamay was able to write to the district commissioner in British Honduras to say that he was again in charge and that he had moved decisively against Felipe Flores.[64]

Stability at Xkanhá

Eugenio Arana had no dealings with the British colony for some years after his involvement with the claims of British trespass on Icaiché lands in 1877 and 1878, when he had clearly acted as the superior of the Icaiché leader. In the interim, he appears to have been living in serene peace with his neighbors of regularly governed Campeche. Then suddenly in 1893, the governor of British Honduras was informed that General Arana had arrived at San Antonio on Albion Island with about a hundred of his followers and that he had just opened a road as far as the old village of Chichanhá from his own capital of Xkanhá.

Arana himself did not come into Orange Walk, but a number of his subordinates made purchases there amounting to about eight hundred dollars before returning to Albion Island. On the island, Arana was overtaken by the commandant of the British constabulary, who described him as "an old man of about 72 years. He seemed very pleased to meet us, stating it was some 16 years since he had visited the Colony. . . . Their chief object in opening the road . . . is to trade with this Colony instead of Yucatan." With only a short section of the road remaining to be opened, trade was expected to continue. Mindful of English policy, arms had been left on the Yucatan side of the Río Hondo.[65]

The traveler Karl Sapper passed through Xkanhá following his stay at Icaiché. In general, the way of life there was similar to that in the more southerly settlement, although living in a less well-watered area the people were not so rich in the fruits of the chase. Sapper was unaware of the source of funds for the public treasury at Xkanhá, for the territory seemed to provide few marketable products. Rich in dyewood, it yet was so far from avenues of transportation—coast or rivers—that there could be no immediate market; on the other hand, the people did bleed chicle and sell a substantial quantity. Sapper doubted that trade along the new bridle path that had been cut from Xkanhá toward Orange Walk would ever be heavy, because the road passed near territory of the Santa Cruz rebels. He estimated the population at eight thousand.[66]

Whatever Arana's inclination toward increased relations with the British, he shortly received attention from the other direction. In October of 1895 General Teodosio Canto—he of the unhappy affair with Aniceto Dzul a decade before and now general in chief of the military zone that included Campeche—arrived in Xkanhá. It was apparently this Canto expedition that resulted in the population figures for the region that were incorporated in the Mexican national census of 1895. The supposed enumeration included no breakdown by community but simply a total for the entire *pacífico* region of 6,763 males and 8,237 females, occupying 2,777 houses, their zone graced by one barracks, one parish church, thirty-two jails, and thirty-one chapels or oratories. As will be noted later, this was almost certainly an overestimate of population and less accurate than Sapper's; that it was indeed an estimate, rather than an enumeration, is suggested by the population total, where men and women sum to exactly fifteen thousand. But perhaps Canto did the best he could: a Mexican news report claimed that at least some Campeche *pacíficos* declined to be registered on the grounds that they were an independent nation.[67]

Arana was at first mistrustful of Canto. But as his suspicions were allayed he indicated that his people continued in their state of de facto independence in large part because Campeche provided no significant support for them: they asked for arms but got none; they asked for a school and raised a building for it, but no school teacher came. They did receive spiritual ministrations from Campeche-based priests, although day-to-day matters were tended to by a native *maestro cantor*, who conducted regular services in Maya at the Xkanhá church.[68]

At this time the major *pacífico* functionaries were Arana, as general, who made use of the official seal with the Mexican eagle; Colonel Felipe Briceño, who served officially as commander of the local national guard; and *comandante* Anselmo Tun. A total of thirty-two settlements were under their nominal sway, including Icaiché.[69]

There is no indication that Canto's visit had any lasting effect in the way of either firearms or schools at Xkanhá; and he fell sick before he could extend his trip to Icaiché, which remained unvisited. But it was clearly a tour designed in part to pave the way for a Mexican move against Santa Cruz.[70] Other contacts between Arana and the regular government—this time in Mérida—would follow.

19 / Determination and Dissolution

The flight of Lochhá and Chunxán people at the death of Crescencio Poot marked the beginning of a steady stream of defections from the rebel cause, many of them stemming from the despotism of the leaders, including Aniceto Dzul. He and others often issued tyrannical orders to subordinates on pain of death and, of course, insisted on absolute obedience to the cult of the cross. It was Dzul, reportedly, who in 1888 decreed the killing of all remaining prisoners, regardless of ethnic affiliation, because their presence made him uneasy.[1]

But with the growing expectation of a major Mexican campaign into the eastern forests, defections stepped up. Leaving individually or in small groups, a large number of these fugitives entered British Honduras, others moved toward the frontier with Yucatan or southwest to the southern *pacíficos* and Campeche. Santa Cruz officers were detailed to stop the flight by killing those apprehended; one claimed to have butchered more than thirty in a single night.[2] But the exodus continued. In one month of 1895, 150 refugees arrived at Corozal.[3]

One major defection, possibly equaling the loss of people of Chunxán and Lochhá, entailed the almost complete depopulation of Tulum. Although Tulum had provided the military force to tip the balance when Dzul struggled with Poot, and although that center maintained the major oracular cross of the rebels, it was never the military equal of Noh Cah Santa Cruz—which had been able to act with impunity in the Peón Contreras affair. Nevertheless, Tulum had operated with essential independence of Santa Cruz at least since the beginning of the Dzul regime and probably before.[4]

At the beginning of 1892, the inhabitants of Tulum suddenly dispersed in fear of an attack from Santa Cruz. Some apparently managed to move to the southwest toward Xkanhá, but about forty families arrived safely at Ambergris Cay in northern British Honduras. There the man described in news accounts as their *gobernador* still felt unsafe from attack, and he left his people to move farther south to Cay Corker.[5] This man was Juan de la Cruz Ciau, presumably the same Cruz Ciau who had visited British Honduras

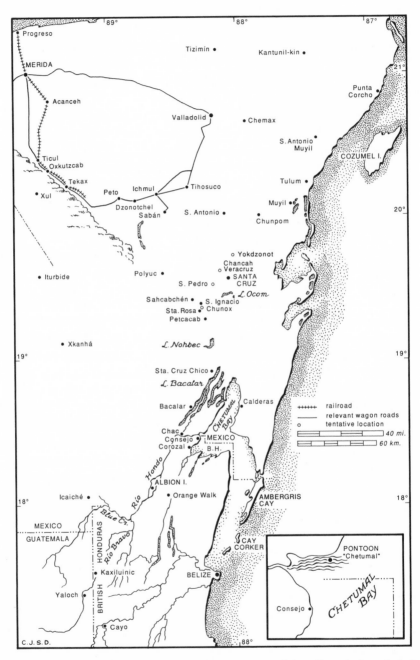

Map 18. Location of Events of 1888–98. The position of the railway is that of 1898 (Ferrer de Mendiolea 1977).

in early 1887 with Aniceto Dzul. But his supposed given name—Juan de la Cruz—suggests that he had served as Tulum high priest rather than temporal ruler, as does his rumored possession of the jewels and treasure of the sacred Tulum cross, although not the cross itself. One therefore suspects that the cause of the sudden emigration from Tulum was a serious altercation involving the cult, probably the result of continued deterioration of relations between the major secular and major sacred centers. Ciau died only a few months later under suspicious circumstances, with robbery a possible motive.[6]

There may have been enough people left at Tulum after this hegira to keep the cult somewhat alive, for cross worship was active there into the twentieth century. But the major center of worship in that region in the 1890s evidently shifted to Chunpom.[7]

How much the Tulum emigration shrank the rebel military force is hard to determine, given the extreme variation in population estimates—when, indeed, one suspects that even the rebel leadership had only a hazy notion of their strength. In 1886, Dzul had claimed eight thousand men under arms, with the administrator of British Honduras estimating seven thousand only a year later, but in that same year—1887—Dzul had revised his claim downward to five thousand soldiers.[8] At the same time he said his total population was fifteen thousand, which is roughly appropriate for the number of men he claimed under arms, given the demographic assumptions I used earlier. He did not indicate whether this included Tulum, although one may suppose that it did. In 1894, Karl Sapper heard the rebel population estimated at eight thousand to ten thousand. This was after the Tulum and other defections, and in that same year one former Santa Cruz sergeant gave six thousand as a figure that appears to have applied to total population serving Noh Cah Santa Cruz; in 1895 a refugee *comandante* placed the number of *bravo* soldiers at around two thousand. These last two figures are also in keeping with one another.[9] A figure of six thousand or slightly above for total population seems reasonable, although some other claims both at the time and later would place it higher.[10]

During this period of rebel dissolution, commercial activity from British Honduras increased around Bacalar Lagoon. As described earlier, both Noh Cah Santa Cruz and Tulum had openly requested that British traders establish stations within rebel territory. Despite official belief that the security afforded colony merchants was inadequate to make such expansion attractive, by 1892 Cramer and Company had a branch of their store at Bacalar, and three years later Carlos Melhado, long the Cramer manager, was reported to be running eight logwood operations in the vicinity.[11] In 1894 about one-third of the dyewood exported from British Honduras was cut outside the colony borders—probably all of it from rebel-controlled lands—and in 1895 it was estimated that somewhat more, ten thousand tons, would be taken that year from territory claimed by Yucatan.[12]

The defection of rebels in the face of Mexican pressure and the influx of money from British logging interests combined to have a serious effect on Santa Cruz leadership. On the one hand, there was disagreement among the leaders over whether to fight or make peace when the long expected Mexican campaign finally materialized. On the other hand, there was growing rivalry and mistrust over the allocation of money collected from the proliferating logging establishments.

In August 1888, both Belize and Mérida papers reported rumors that Aniceto Dzul had been assassinated upon his return to Santa Cruz after his unexpected interview with Colonel Sardaneta at Belize City, and these were believable enough to the Mexican government that plans to invite Dzul to Mexico for a conciliatory visit with President Díaz were cancelled.[13] But the next January the governor of British Honduras received two letters from Dzul, naming agents to represent him on the annual visit to Belize, repeating his unwillingness to negotiate with Mexico, and asserting his continued good health. Politely, the governor's answer stressed again the need for the rebels to aim for amicable relations with Mexico.[14] To this Dzul and his fellow commanders responded in favor of independence:

> Let us remain in our lands here at Santa Cruz. . . . Let each govern his own territory and let us be independent here.
>
> We shall trade with the Englishmen only and buy from them what we require. We shall not interfere with the Mexicans: neither must they interfere with us. . . . I desire that there be an end to war and to the killing of human beings.

The letter was signed by Dzul, José Crescencio Puc, José Román Pec, Felipe Canche, and Felipe Yama, who asked that the letter be forwarded to the queen.[15]

Whatever the state of Dzul's health in January 1889, a year earlier the English surveyor William Miller had found him suffering from loss of sight in one eye,[16] and little more than a year later, in early 1890, he was dead. There is no indication that he died violently.[17] His successor, José Crescencio Puc, was not so fortunate, however, for Puc and some of his adherents were killed by fellow chiefs in 1894, probably in September. The perpetrators asserted that Puc had tried to do violence to some of them and that they had acted to stop him, but a British logging operator supposed Puc was murdered because he had invited the Catholic bishop of Belize to Noh Cah Santa Cruz, had made a present of a ring to Father Silvin Gillet of the colony—and also failed to account for all the dyewood money he collected.[18]

Puc was succeeded by Román Pec, avowed leader of the most warlike faction of Noh Cah Santa Cruz. But internal trouble did not end with his assumption, for by the next year Pec was said to be actively opposed by José Ake and a peace party.[19] The strife would continue.

Whether similar friction contributed to shifts in the priesthood at Noh Cah Santa Cruz is less clear, but possible. In 1890, a fugitive couple reported that they had been married in Noh Cah Santa Cruz—at a date not specified but presumably not many years before—by the high priest, who was then Juan Canche. Only four years later, in 1894, a defecting rebel sergeant reported that the high priest had recently been Agustín Barrera, at whose death the position was assumed by his son, Pedro Barrera (see table 15).[20]

British Visitors to Noh Cah Santa Cruz

Between 1888 and 1895 three visits to the very heart of rebel territory yielded English-language descriptions. That such trips had not been common up to that time is indicated by the first of these travelers, William Miller, the colony surveyor, who stated he knew of only two other Englishmen who had seen the capital before his visit of January 1888,[21] although with the trading relationship active between the colony and Santa Cruz it is likely that there were others who failed to leave a record. The private secretary of the British governor made the same trip in 1893, expressly to give formal notification to the rebels of the signing of the boundary convention with Mexico and the expected arms embargo. And in 1895 a logging entrepreneur called on the Santa Cruz leaders on his own behalf, although he was not permitted to go to Noh Cah Santa Cruz itself.[22] Together, these provide a picture of the *masewal* region during the dissolution of rebel society that was underway.

Miller found the masonry town of Bacalar to be in fair shape, although with cannon of the fort tumbled about and the bells of the church removed—some of them to be seen at Noh Cah Santa Cruz. The Bacalar guard of sixty men, changed each two months, lived in Mayan-style thatched huts built in open spaces between the old Spanish houses. Miller mentioned no British presence anywhere on Bacalar Lagoon. But when the secretary Strange made the trip five years later, James Anderson, the Cramer logging

TABLE 15
Leadership at Noh Cah Santa Cruz, 1868–1900

Year of Appearance	Governor or General-in-Chief	Important Commanders	High Priest
1868	Crescencio Poot	Bernardino Cen	
1883		Juan Bautista Chuc	Juan Bautista Chuc?
1885	Aniceto Dzul	Román Pec José Crescencio Puc	
Before 1890			Juan Canche
1890	José Crescencio Puc	Román Pec	
Before 1894			Agustín Barrera
1894	Román Pec	José María Ake León Pat Felipe Yama	Pedro Pascual Barrera
1896	Felipe Yama	León Pat	

Sources: See text.

foreman, was headquartered at the village then called Chan Santa Cruz or Santa Cruz Chico,[23] located at the extreme north of Bacalar Lagoon. And when the timberman Beattie traveled, two years after that, his own logging establishment was in place on the west side of the lake, apparently between Bacalar and Santa Cruz Chico.

Miller's first two nights north of Santa Cruz Chico were spent in the bush, and thereafter there were hamlets where lodging could be had in the chapels—each a palm-leafed structure, with a table serving as altar and supporting a dozen or more crosses. Beattie reported that the houses in these settlements were dispersed, each in its clearing, communicating by narrow trails. For water, each hamlet had a hand-dug well, fifty to one hundred feet deep. The people, Beattie said, were

> timid and evidently unused to seeing strangers. Whenever my party (of four) emerged from the bush path into view from the houses, the women and children at once ran away and disappeared into the forest, the men hesitating between running and fighting. The Indians live almost entirely upon maize and seem to eat very little meat. Men and women are small and weakly.[24]

He reported the people to be constantly fearful of spies and wary of providing information of any kind.

> Some very simple questions which I asked were answered, but were always supplemented by the counter-question "Why do you wish to know?" On one occasion wishing to hear of ancient Indian ruins, I was questioning several Indians, . . . and getting unsatisfactory answers, pressed the question, when they turned down their hat brims and peeped at me from under them, and simply answered in monosyllables. This so frightened my interpreter that he refused to go on with the questions.[25]

Miller and Strange both described Noh Cah Santa Cruz as being almost without permanent inhabitants, although with a guard of about 150 men armed with Enfield rifles and carrying machetes of their own special pattern and manufacture. The town was used for important assemblies of the leaders. Aniceto Dzul was *gobernador* at the time of Miller's visit, and Miller found him at his settlement of San Pedro, whereas Román Pec lived at the settlement of Chunox; both places were south of Noh Cah Santa Cruz and are shown on Miller's map of his route. Strange visited Governor José Crescencio Puc at his village six miles from the capital town, which he did not further name or locate. Román Pec, governor at Beattie's visit, was found at a settlement called Chan Cah Vera Cruz—which Beattie said lay to the north of the capital an undisclosed distance—where Pec was attending the principal religious festival of the year.[26] Beattie asked to visit Noh Cah Santa Cruz but was refused on the grounds that preparations for defense against the expected Mexican campaign were underway there.

For his part, the intrepid Miller had wanted to go on to visit Tulum, where he heard there was "a particular cross, from which the Indians say the voice of God issues, and on all grave occasions this cross is consulted and they act in accordance with the directions given. . . . All the chiefs of the nation are appointed by it."[27] His timorous guides, however, refused to take him, saying that all visitors were interrogated by the cross and that this was a privilege they did not wish to share.

In general, the changes at Noh Cah Santa Cruz since Carmichael's visit of 1867 are those that would be expected under conditions of shrinking population, with one glaring exception. From the earliest period of rebel settlement in their eastern territory, individual leaders had been associated closely with certain villages in which they functioned as village headmen and—at least during the heyday of Santa Cruz—as landlords, with captives working their lands. Nevertheless, all of them evidently spent long periods in residence at the capital, probably at the time the soldiers under their particular command fulfilled their term of rotating guard duty there.[28] Now their periodic residence at Noh Cah Santa Cruz seems to have diminished, so that while still guarded, the center was otherwise vacant much of the time. And the fact that the major annual religious festival was taking place not at Noh Cah Santa Cruz but rather at a village with the provocative name of Chan Cah Vera Cruz—"Small Settlement [i.e., Village] of the True Cross"—suggests that the great masonry church at the capital was no longer the seat of the Santa Cruz branch of the cross cult. Just when the cult center may have been moved is nowhere indicated, but that it had been elsewhere for some time would be confirmed when the Mexican army finally reached the rebel capital—only to capture an empty town.[29]

The Storm Gathers

Negotiations for the boundary convention and the accompanying preparation for a ban on arms sales seem to have tempered British Honduran willingness to export weaponry to the Santa Cruz rebels, despite the Foreign Office recommendation against ending the trade too quickly. If so, it marked a definite change in the local attitude. Colony traders had sold Enfield rifles in large numbers to the rebels since the mid-1870s,[30] and by 1890 that firearm must have been in the hands of a large proportion of the *bravo* army.

But in 1894 queries from a new governor in British Honduras caused the collector of customs to respond that arms for warlike purposes were not being imported into the colony for sale to the rebels. Any traffic with them in firearms, he said, was confined to cheap fowling pieces.[31]

A new hesitation to wink at the export of military arms may well have been related to reports trickling in from Yucatan. In the mid-1890s Mexican troops were sent to the peninsula to strengthen appropriate frontiers while Mexico and Guatemala squabbled anew over their boundary. With the question settled, the Mexican troops in 1895 were said to be massing at Peto. It was also reported in Belize that Mexican or Yucatecan detachments were occupying old abandoned frontier military posts dating from the active phases of the Caste War and that these were being linked by a network of telegraph lines. The presumption was that Mexico intended an active campaign; indeed, that year the governor of British Honduras supposed that Bacalar would be occupied almost immediately by an overland force.[32]

This did not turn out to be the case. At the end of 1895 Foreign Minister Mariscal advised the British that nothing would happen soon, despite the fact that eight hundred federal troops were scheduled to join the five hundred already in Yucatan.[33] More years would pass without military action.

On the economic front, however, Mexico and Yucatan continued to advance to the east. By the decade of the 1890s, there were a series of companies engaged in, or committed to engage in, both agriculture and exploitation of forest products at the northeastern tip of the peninsula, some of which by the latter part of the decade involved actual colonization.[34] Thus, even with the Mexican army at parade rest, pressure was building on the rebel world.

In the summer of 1895, as though in a last defiant gesture against British claims to sovereignty, a Mexican coast guard vessel had eased south along the outer coast of Ambergris Cay and took aboard a colony resident who—according to his account—was forced to pilot the ship around the island into British waters on the inward side, and then northward into the Mexican portion of the Bay of Chetumal. There at the station known as Calderas, the location of British Honduran woodcutting works paying rent to the rebels rather than to Yucatan, the Mexican force seized two English boats engaged in loading dyewood, some mules and other provisions, and seven loggers. The prisoners were sailed again through British waters to the open sea and then to Mérida, where the men were sentenced to a year in jail.[35]

Although the acting governor of the colony expressed fear that such actions might cause a serious reduction in British logging in the region,[36] it did not. It did, however, encourage the loggers to pay royalties both to the rebels and to the Belizean representative of the Mexican concession holder.[37]

But, presumably because the boundary settlement with Mexico was in a delicate stage, there was no protest of the violation of what Britain considered her territorial waters. Powerless, the British Honduran government could only eye the situation to the north of them with continued unease.

Critical Commitments

The boundary treaty was stalled by the Mexican senate until Foreign Minister Mariscal proposed a further provision that would guarantee Mexican rights to navigation through British waters to Chetumal Bay and the mouth of the Río Hondo. With the British-imposed condition that this would apply only to merchant vessels, the logjam was broken, the additional article was signed on April 7, 1897, and ratifications of the final treaty and addendum were exchanged in July. A copy reached Belize in October and was immediately published in the gazette. In November, the governor decreed a two-year prohibition on the export of arms, ammunition, and gunpowder without a license from himself.[38]

In Mexico, completion of the critical agreement revivified two immediate interests: peaceful enticement of the rebels to submit, and control of the growing illicit export of logs from Mexican territory. The first of these led to the novel expedient of sending Mexican troops to hang notices in trees and other visible places along the western *masewal* frontier, notices offering amnesty and grants of lands to those who surrendered and threats if they did not. In addition, efforts were also made to encourage trade between rebels and Mexicans on the east coast and to increase trade between *bravos* and the British in the south, with a view toward accustoming the recalcitrant *masewalob* to regular, peaceful contacts.[39]

The second interest produced an equally novel floating customs station on the Río Hondo. Preparations for this had begun nearly a year before the boundary convention was ratified, when the Mexican navy sent Lieutenant Othon P. Blanco to New Orleans to oversee the building of a special vessel of shallow draft that could be anchored at the river mouth. It was to be sixty-five feet long, with a twenty-four-foot beam, and built of cyprus planks. Drawing less than three feet, it would provide headquarters for smaller launches and be manned by fifteen marines and their officers.[40] On December 24, 1897, the sixty-four ton pontoon *Chetumal*, armed with a Hotchkiss cannon and a Metralliuse machine gun and carrying Winchester repeating rifles as small arms for its crew, was towed into harbor at Belize. Lieutenant Blanco announced publicly that the purpose of the vessel was fiscal only, in that it was designed to ensure the collection of legally imposed duties on items crossing the Mexican border.[41]

On January 22 the pontoon was again under tow, this time headed out of Belize, and within a week was anchored at a point at the mouth of the Hondo immediately off the Mexican shore. There the main channel and only entrance to the river lay north of the newly determined international boundary, running close under the Mexican shore, thus forcing all boats entering or leaving the river to pass through Mexican waters beside the new Mexican customs station.[42] There the pontoon sat, headquarters to a small sailboat and a steam launch, collecting duties and ensuring that any export of wood products was under a legal permit from the Mexican holder of the logging concession or his agent.

Rebel Reticence

In quick succession the rebels were forced to adjust both to a ban on their customary source of gunpowder, which they used heavily in fiestas as well as in war, and to the presence of the Mexican government at the very mouth of their river. Even before these events occurred, however, the pressures of impending hostilities and a troubled financial horizon had taken their toll.

In January of 1896 the delegation of rebels had arrived as usual in Belize to collect rents and make purchases, and on January 14 they had their customary meeting with the British governor. Although the advance letter from Noh Cah Santa Cruz had indicated that the delegation would be led by the important *comandante* Felipe Yama, when it arrived in Belize it was composed of men of lesser rank. And when the delegates were urged by the governor to consider peace with Mexico, they responded that they did not have the responsibility that would allow them to entertain any such decision on their own.[43] Not appreciated by the British at the time, Yama had heard on reaching Corozal that the delegation would be strongly urged to make peace with Mexico and had feigned sickness and then returned to Noh Cah Santa Cruz, advising his subordinates to remain noncommittal to the governor and above all to refrain from mentioning peace when they returned to the rebel capital.[44] Later events would demonstrate the wisdom of his course.

Not long after this visit, the governor of British Honduras received a letter from rebel *gobernador* Román Pec, who signed with José María Ake, Hilario Cab, José María Canul, and León Pat. They announced that Mexican troops had advanced as far as Sabán and that the *masewalob* would fight if pressed, although they had no intention of being the ones to begin hostilities.[45] The heightened rebel uneasiness and mistrust generated an incident most unusual for that period in which they felt such evident friendship for the British. In late February, some drunken *masewal* soldiers at Santa Cruz Chico accused three of James Anderson's British Honduran loggers of being Mexicans and attempted to beat them, then striking Anderson himself when he intervened. *Gobernador* Pec apologized, asserting the miscreants had acted without authority.[46]

And in September of that year, 1896, the colony governor received another letter from Noh Cah Santa Cruz bearing the names of Pec, Ake, Cab, Canul, and Yama, in which they begged to remind the governor that he should give them twenty-five thousand pounds of powder, one thousand guns, one thousand percussion nipples, and two million percussion caps, as well as lead and shot—a letter the governor concluded "would indicate the excessive indulgence in anise seed, which . . . is the favorite drink." He responded that he could recall no such request and that he could not fill it if he did.[47]

That same month Román Pec died. There were the usual rumors in Yucatan that he had been murdered, but his death seems to have resulted from sickness.[48] General José María Ake appeared to be the likely successor, but when the choice was made it elevated Felipe Yama to the governorship— the fourth *gobernador* within a decade (table 15). José Maria Aguilar was named one of the generals and Remigio Pol a *comandante*.[49]

In October, *gobernador* Yama, seconded by generals José María Ake and José María Canul, wrote to renew the request for munitions, but mindful of the governor's earlier refusal they dissembled, saying that "to celebrate the feasts of the saints who have worked miracles for us, without intending to do harm to anyone, we beg once more, sir, for the following: 400 rifles; 10,000 lbs. of powder; 50 bags of big shot; 2,500 lbs. of sheet lead; 1 million gun caps; 1 million nipples; 100 reams of brown paper. These are the only things we need in this city."[50] Again the order went unfilled.

The rebel delegation to Belize at the end of 1896 was headed by generals Ake and Canul and the *comandante* Hilario Cab and included their interpreter, a former Belize resident named George Pennington. This time the aftermath was not so tame. The next April three rebel officers defecting to the colony reported that Ake, Canul, and Cab, with Pennington and more than fifty others, had been killed by León Pat on Yama's orders and that they themselves were fleeing persecution. Other reports shortly indicated that among the dead was a colony-born British citizen, Gabriel Rodríguez, who had been teaching the rebels to bleed sapodilla trees for chicle, for which the chewing gum market was beginning to call, and who at the time of the killings had been on a drinking spree at the rebel capital.

Some said the bloodbath resulted from suspicion that Ake and the others had sold out to the English. A letter from Yama, Pat, J. M. Aguilar, and Dario Noh announced that the executions were because the errant officers had allowed themselves to be deceived by Mexicans when in the colony. Robert Pickwoad, district commissioner in Corozal, passed on information to the effect that the delegation leaders had not adequately accounted for the money they were sent to collect, a story later confirmed by other fugitive officers. Pickwoad formally protested the killing of Rodríguez.[51]

The killings certainly did nothing to settle unrest in Noh Cah Santa Cruz. In late April the new general José María Aguilar was murdered along with a rebel captain and six Chinese said to be Aguilar's friends. Yama, Pat, and Noh now alleged that Aguilar, *comandante* Pol, and three captains (of whom one was killed) had been responsible without authority for the earlier killings and then had conspired to rebel against Yama. Governor Wilson of British Honduras would not accept this explanation of the Rodríguez death and protested again.[52]

Pol and the two surviving captains escaped, Pol and Captain Romualdo Cab arriving in Corozal not long after. Despite letters from the Santa Cruz leaders coaxing them to return with promises they would not be harmed, the defectors went on to Mérida to submit themselves to the government. To these and related upheavals, Yucatan attributed the defection of some six hundred people to the *pacífico* settlements governed by General Arana as well as a further increase in emigration to British Honduras.[53]

The ill-fated junket to Belize by Ake and his party was the last formal visit to be made by the rebel leadership to British officials. In January 1898, a delegation set out from Noh Cah Santa Cruz as usual, this time intending to protest the refusal to allow them to buy gunpowder from British logging stations at Bacalar. But as they reached the border they learned that the Mexican pontoon had arrived in Belize City on its way to the Hondo, and so they returned immediately to their capital.[54] From there they addressed plaintive protests to Queen Victoria and to the British governor, asking why the Mexicans had been allowed to "close . . . the roads to us, . . . so as to prevent the English from providing . . . our wants."[55] This was followed by more pointed letters from the *bravo* leaders both to the British governor and to the Mexicans, insisting to Governor Wilson that he should remove the Mexican presence from British waters, to the Mexicans that the customs post was on territory that was properly the rebels', to which they added scarcely veiled threats of what they would do if the customs men attempted to land and a refusal to consider any treaty of peace with Mexico.[56]

Nevertheless, a general council of all males of the Santa Cruz *masewalob* was called later that year of 1898 to consider relations with Mexico. Yama and the majority were said to favor peace and submission, while a powerful minority under Pat disagreed. But there was no compelling evidence of an open break among the leaders, and rumors of the assassination of the aged Yama failed to be confirmed.[57] Meanwhile, defections from rebel jurisdiction continued, and reports from elsewhere in their territory indicated that not only Tulum but also Muyil had been almost entirely abandoned, with only a dozen families remaining at the former and even fewer at the latter. A village named San Antonio, some sixty kilometers from Tulum, was said to be able to field about 150 men, and the force under arms directly subject to Yama was reported to be three thousand[58]—very possibly an inflated estimate.

Pacífico Attitudes

Although the approaching settlement between Mexico and England reduced Icaiché's complaints of encroachments on Mexican territory, it did not silence them entirely. In December 1895 General Tamay voiced distress that falsehoods spread regarding his intentions had caused Eustaquio Avila to give up logging on the Mexican side of the Hondo. Yet in May of the next year he let loose a real blast: misunderstanding a visit of surveyors to the Cayo district of the colony to examine possible railroad routes, he issued a blunt threat to the local magistrate that if the British attempted to survey around either Yaloch or Kaxiluinic, he would "send a troop of 200 or 300 men to settle the question with you." Kaxiluinic was now known to be within the proposed boundary of the colony, and presumably the threat would not have been tolerated by the British, except that they had no plans to survey there anyway.[59]

In 1898, after the boundary convention was ratified, the colony government learned (probably not for the first time) that logging entrepreneurs had been regularly paying "rent" to Tamay for colony lands worked south of Blue Creek and along the Hondo above its confluence with the Río Bravo. And a man who expected to bleed chicle in that region had been issued a written threat. Tamay obviously intended to continue his lucrative practice, and through 1898 he billed a series of British Honduran works along the Hondo between Blue Creek and Albion Island. But the area was now clearly British and rather than pay they objected strenuously to the colony government.

With the treaty to support him, Governor Wilson asked his government to arrange for Mexico to compel Tamay to observe its terms;[60] his suggested solution was that the Mexican government pay Tamay a salary equivalent to the sum he was accustomed to collecting from loggers. In Belize, Mexican Consul Angel Ortiz Monasterio said he would do what he could to restrain Tamay, whom he contacted through Lieutenant Othon Blanco, stationed at the pontoon *Chetumal.* Whatever the measures, they seemed to be effective, for so far as the governor could ascertain, no payments were made by British companies for work on British territory anytime in 1898.[61]

In spite of the reduction in income, the otherwise amicable attitude of Tamay and Icaiché toward the colony did not sour. On one occasion in 1897, six drunken residents of Albion Island were arrested by British Honduran constables for ransacking a constable's station on the island. While they were being escorted to jail, an armed party of fifteen or sixteen men from the Mexican side of the Hondo crossed to chase after the escort but lost their spirit when Icaiché soldiers warned them that if they created any disturbance in the colony they would not be allowed to reenter Mexico.[62] On another occasion in 1898, colony territory was violated when three men from Icaiché crossed the Río Hondo to seek the estranged mistress of one of them, caught her and her new lover, and dragged them both back into Mexico. Tamay agreed that the men responsible would be punished and the woman allowed to return to the colony if she chose to.[63]

The other *pacífico* units were, of course, less directly affected by the boundary settlement. Far to the north, the reformed rebels of Kantunil-kin had become more and more integrated into the Yucatecan social and political system, although they had never relocated physically close to settled centers, as they had promised when they submitted in the 1850s. At their request a school had been established in the settlement in 1890.[64] In 1897, however, a project was announced to open a road from Chemax to the east coast of the peninsula at Punta Corcho for the benefit of the East Coast of Yucatan Colonization Company and its dyewood cutters. At Kantunil-kin—as well as at Chemax—fear arose that the open road, planned to pass in the vicinity of San Antonio Muyil, would invite rebel attacks. An earlier suggestion to open a road from Kantunil-kin to the coast had been resisted on the same grounds. This time, Kantunil-kin requested military assistance from the government of Yucatan, to consist of both arms and musical instruments.[65] Evidently, the plans for the road were carried no further.

The cause of a decrease in trading between the Xkanhá region and British Honduras may have been the expectation of impending hostilities. On the other hand, a railway to link Mérida and Peto, begun in 1879, reached Oxkutzcab in 1891 and Tekax in 1893,[66] both of which were closer to Xkanhá than Orange Walk. By 1897, trade was apparently carried on fairly regularly between the *pacífico* region and Oxkutzcab, and in July of that year Arana himself made a trip to Mérida. After several days of horseback travel to reach Oxkutzcab, he and his party of five met formally with the military commander of the district. They were then whisked by steam train to Mérida, where they were met by the commander of that military zone, General Lorenzo García.

Arana was described as understanding Spanish but unwilling or unable to speak it. The motive of the trip was friendly, having followed a warm exchange of greetings by way of a commission earlier sent to Mérida from Xkanhá. But Arana also conferred at some length with General García, presumably regarding the forthcoming campaign of pacification in the eastern peninsula.

In an interview with the press he listed the major towns he ruled, with such commanders as he could recall (table 16). His own center of Xkanhá he said counted more than one hundred houses. By this time, too, a number of rebel defectors had moved into his territory, although he gave no number. He would probably continue to trade with Oxkutzcab, he said, although his own visits there would be infrequent, simply because there were in the *pacífico* region a number of small trading establishments, and it was also visited by traveling peddlers. His region was served by a priest from Campeche.

Arana's party must have cut an unusual figure, for it was followed by the curious as they walked the streets of Mérida. The general himself was described as about seventy years of age, and—like the rest of his party—was

TABLE 16
Important Pacífico *Settlements and Commanders according to Eugenio Arana,*
1897

Settlement	Rank and Name of Commander
Xkanha	General Eugenio Arana, *Gobernador*
Xmaben	Captain Eusebio López
Xchun-ek	Colonel Felipe Briceño
Patzuitz	*Comandante* José Guadalupe May
Chan-cheen	Sergeant, name not recalled
Yokkat	Captain, name not recalled
Sahcabcheen	(none, subject to Xmaben)
Ukum	Captain Apolonio Pech
Mexia	Captain Catalino Anchevida
Keken	Lieutenant Cristobal Chan
Castro Akas	Sergeant Rudesindo May
Chan-yaxche	Sergeant Gertrudis May
Schun-habin	Sergeant Perfecto Góngora

Source: From "La llegada del gobernador de Xkanha" (RM, Aug. 5, 1897, 2). Spelling of settlements as in the original.
Note: There were said to be other *rancherías* of less importance.

dressed in the white shirt and drawers of the customary Indian costume. All carried shoulder bags of canvas, that of Arana sporting the painted phrase *Te Amo,* "I love you."[67] Perhaps in reciprocation, in April and May of 1898 General García and the governor of Yucatan, General Francisco Cantón, extended a trip of inspection to Peto and the eastern *partidos* by paying a visit to the Xkanhá *cantón*.[68]

An element serving to bring the southern *pacíficos* more firmly into the orbits of the governing powers of the peninsula was the creation in 1895 of the bishopric of Campeche, to which were assigned both Xkanhá and Icaiché—formerly under the care of Mérida and Belize, respectively. A resident priest was assigned to Xkanhá, and the energetic first bishop, Francisco Plancarte, made pastoral visits to both Xkanhá and Icaiché during his early years in the office. The first of these came in January 1898, with a three-week visit to Xkanhá and surrounding settlements.

More noteworthy was his trip that spring by ship to Belize and overland to Icaiché. His party arrived in early May for a week's stay—the first time a bishop had set foot in that *pacífico* settlement. Initially, it was rumored that he was followed by government troops who would subjugate the town, but he and his party overcame suspicion to baptize forty-nine and confirm three hundred. And after some difficulty in surmounting the local view that remarriage of widowed individuals was not permissible, they then married fifty couples, uniting both General Tamay and his second in command with their current consorts.[69]

Pressure Builds

Nearly fifty years after the terrible rebellion first tore Yucatan asunder, the Mexican campaign to crush the faded rebel remnants and capture their long-held territory finally got underway. But it started at less than a snail's pace. In early 1896, as noted earlier, Mexican and Yucatecan forces had reoccupied abandoned Sabán; the rebel leadership declared they would fight, while the British governor, Sir Alfred Maloney, cautioned peace.[70] In 1897, the boundary treaty was ratified that brought the British ban cutting off rebel munitions. Meanwhile, the railroad from Mérida to Peto, a critical part of the Mexican military plan, advanced with scarcely perceptible speed. In February 1898, the tracks finally were within thirty-two kilometers of Peto—close enough to be relied on for transportation, although it would be more than two years before the line reached its destination.

And in 1898 things began to move more visibly, if still slowly. In November, a Yucatecan militia detachment of one hundred men took over abandoned Ichmul—fifty-one years after it had first been captured by rebels. They began chopping roads toward Dzonotchel and Tihosuco. By the end of the year Dzonotchel was connected with Peto by a new road ten meters wide and flanked by telegraph poles.[71] In June 1899, Tihosuco—that pueblo so favored by Jacinto Pat and so valiantly defended by Yucatan only to then be abandoned—was reoccupied, and a road was opened from there to Valladolid, where it was expected to link with a proposed roadway and telegraph line to Punta Corcho on the east coast.[72]

The rebels watched these slow advances with apprehension. On the coast of what they regarded as their territory, in the vicinity of the same Punta Corcho, they had seen the successful establishment of colonies of Cuban and other settler-employees by the British-financed East Coast of Yucatan Colonization Company.[73]

Although there was still no general fighting, suspicion and unease led to isolated bloody incidents. One of these brought an unwilling recruit to the rebel cause—a boy who would one day be a *masewal* leader.

Juan Bautista Vega

In late July or early August of 1897, the boat of Rudolfo Loria left Cozumel under charter for the coast of Yucatan at Tulum. The paying passenger was one Juan Fábregas, to whom was applied the title doctor and who was believed to be in search of buried treasure in the archaeological ruins. Riding along was Loria's eleven-year-old stepson Juan Bautista Vega, then in the second or third grade in school, who carried his schoolbook. They landed without incident, but while brunching on the beach they were suddenly surrounded by rebel soldiers from the village of Tulum. Fábregas, Loria, and a sailor were killed.

Juan Vega was dragged to Tulum where he was kept tied to a post for some days, his state not improved by the fact that he could speak no Maya and his captors no Spanish. Next, he was marched through Muyil and Chunpom to a place then called San José, later Yokdzonot, where he was confronted by *gobernador* Felipe Yama who ordered him killed. But an expatriate Belizean black man named "Mr. Dyo," or Joe, insisted Juan would be useful because he could read and write, and he pled for him. Yama relented. Juan then lived near Chunpom with Mr. Joe for some months while learning to speak Maya, when he was taken into service as secretary of the high priest at Chunpom, one Florentino Cituk. Chunpom is the only site of major cross worship mentioned in the available accounts of Vega's capture, and one must suppose that the cult at Tulum itself was by then moribund.

Young Juan quickly proved his value. As the Mexicans advanced from the west, tying bottled messages to the trees, Juan Vega was the only one at Chunpom who could read them. He remained in the rebel camp, and perforce would devote his entire life to the *masewalob*.[74]

The capture of young Vega and the killing of his companions was followed by other scattered attacks on Yucatecan fishermen who approached the mainland shore south of Cozumel Island, and in early 1899 a formal delegation of twenty-two *masewalob* claiming to represent the leadership of Tulum, Noh Cah Santa Cruz, and other centers appeared at the headquarters of the East Coast of Yucatan Colonization Company at Punta Corcho, where they forbade the administrator to continue to open roads between that point and the interior.[75]

Unfortunately for the rebels, their ban had no effect. Punta Corcho— or Puerto Morelos, as its name became—would soon be the Caribbean terminus of a telegraph line of strategic importance to Mexico and Yucatan. In the slow but steady progress of the final campaign of conquest the noose was drawing tight.

20 / The End of Independence

President Díaz originally intended a peaceful and orderly settlement of the rebellion and the "civilizing" of the rebels; this is implicit in directives formulated by his government in 1895 and sent to local authorities. Anticipating success, the policy included the reestablishment of old pueblos and the recognition of newer ones, with the formal registration of village boundaries, the allocation of commons, and the distribution of lands to each capitulating family. Rebels without fixed residence would be settled. Indians would be given preference over non-Indians in the choice of lands to be allocated, with the provision that ground under cultivation would not be taken from the cultivators. Local governing authorities would be named by the state government in accord with its own established governing principles.[1] But things were not to turn out this way.

The year 1899 saw correspondence between Mexico and Britain to the end that representatives of the two should meet with rebel leaders to work out a peaceful solution.[2] But a suggestion that they go together into rebel territory was opposed as dangerous by the governor of British Honduras, who argued for a meeting at or very near his border.[3] The northern district commissioner, Robert W. Pickwoad, was dispatched to the settlement of Santa Cruz Chico to consult with *masewal* leaders. With much difficulty, he finally met León Pat and other commanders in early October, although *gobernador* Felipe Yama begged off on the excuse of illness. Hesitantly, the rebels agreed that they would talk to a combined Mexican-British party, although their attitude was negative: "What do the Mexicans want our territory for? We are content with our small homes and our forest. They have their fine homes and cities. Why do they . . . trouble us?" And the plaints were interspersed with implied threats: "If the Mexicans want to come, well, let them come." Pickwoad's view was that Yama refused the meeting in order to avoid later blame from the war party of León Pat, which would almost certainly never agree to a submission and had enough strength to prevent it.[4]

Although Pickwoad was quickly chosen as British representative for such a meeting, no Mexican choice was announced. Indeed, Mexican actions seemed designed to wreck any possibility of a meeting with the rebels.

In mid-1899, word had been received in Yucatan that General Ignacio A. Bravo was ordered there with three federal battalions to strengthen the campaign, which had finally been scheduled to become active on September 15. When Bravo arrived it was as the new commander of the military district of Yucatan. By October his men were entraining in Mérida for the east, their announced strategy to lay roads and telegraph lines from Sabán to penetrate the *masewal* heartland, establishing fortified strong-points at regular intervals.[5]

Furthermore, in October the former consul of Mexico in Belize, Angel Ortiz Monasterio, turned up again at the city, revealing himself to have been all along a general in the Mexican army and now chief of military staff to President Díaz and commander of a fleet of six Mexican vessels. The general observed that the appointment of a Mexican representative to the rebels should await the equipping of the military depot planned for the Bay of Chetumal, so that policies other than peaceful could be adopted immediately, should negotiations fail.[6] Although it is doubtful that a meeting aimed at convincing the rebels to surrender their independence to Mexico would have been successful under any circumstances, the military buildups at their very doors could hardly be thought conducive.

The new Mexican station of Sombrerete—later to be called Zaragoza—was established only a short distance north of the shallow strait of Boca Bacalar Chico, which separates British Ambergris Cay from the tip of the Mexican mainland. There wood-framed barracks of galvanized iron began to spring up, and troops and matériel were unloaded. In January 1900, the force was estimated at about one thousand men, General Ortiz Monasterio was replaced as commander of the expedition by General Rosalino Martínez, and Martínez was named Mexican representative to treat with the rebels in concert with Pickwoad.[7]

But it was clearly too late. On the one hand, the British government had concluded that any negotiations should be on British soil, because Britain would be neutral in any impending hostilities; Governor Wilson prepared a letter to so inform the rebels, although he no longer had serious hope of a meeting anywhere: not in rebel territory, when one of the delegates was commander of a threatening Mexican force; not at Corozal, where no rebel would come to treat for fear of being executed for treason on his return.[8] On the other hand, the Mexican government was expressing strong reservations

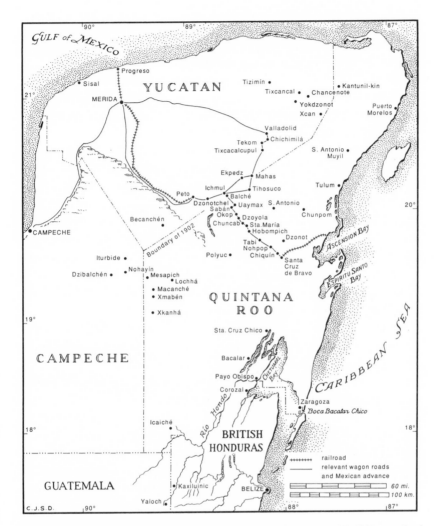

Map 19. Location of Actions of 1899–1911. General Bravo's road-building path of conquest was from Ichmul and Saban to Santa Cruz (MM 1901, 1: 410, 507–8), and he also had the road to Valladolid improved (MM 1901, 2: 288). In June 1901 Noh Cah Santa Cruz became Santa Cruz de Bravo.

about negotiations because of what it considered an unprovoked rebel attack on General Bravo's army.

For in the closing days of 1899 the rebels at last had moved. Their attack in force was directed at newly completed Mexican entrenchments at Okop, southeast of Sabán, striking first the evening of December 27 and returning

December 28 to keep up the engagement into the afternoon. Although there were *masewal* casualties from return fire, there was no effect on the defenders save to call up Mexican reinforcements from Bravo's field headquarters at Sabán.[9] And the following month the Mexican government informed the English that they would take no initiative in peace negotiations because of the rebel-initiated hostilities. The Mexican road continued to crawl toward Noh Cah Santa Cruz.[10]

Two months later an estimated six hundred rebels tried to cut the new road between Sabán and Okop by entrenching themselves across it, only to be dislodged by two hundred Mexican troops, this time losing a dozen men and precious Enfields but killing and wounding more than twenty of their enemy. Three days later they tried a similar tactic at the end of the road as it approached Santa María and again were forced off with loss of powder and lead. Here it was found that the telephone and telegraph wires were being cut by the rebels and reduced to small pieces, which could be fired as shot in their muzzle-loaders.[11] Rebels were dislodged from Santa María itself in early April, and that point became another Mexican fort.[12]

Communications from British Honduras to the rebel leaders became virtually impossible. By late 1899 the numerous British logging works along the western side of Bacalar Lagoon had shut down in preparation for hostilities, although they continued to work along the trunk of the Río Hondo throughout the campaign. James Anderson held out at Santa Cruz Chico throughout that year, but by early 1900 he, too, had pulled back. In February 1900, Anderson was induced to carry to Bacalar a letter addressed by the British governor to the *masewal* leaders. But he found that the rebel commander there had positive orders not to receive any letter that was not opened and read to him, and it appeared to Anderson that he was under orders not to forward any missive suggesting peace, opened or not.[13]

Still, some rank-and-file *masewalob* continued to cross to and from the colony throughout 1900, although in fewer numbers than before; now they were selling large quantities of cattle, sheep, pigs, and chickens.[14] By means of these crossings, in early April of that year the governor received rebel letters addressed both to himself and the queen. To the latter, Felipe Yama and León Pat sent a plea to have the Mexicans removed from their territory and asserted that it was the Mexicans who had begun the hostilities. To the former, these two leaders plus others announced their refusal to negotiate, saying "I won't send a commission because they have to speak to Mexicans, and I cannot do that."[15] The door was closed.

The Final Push

In 1900 military conditions were much changed from those existing when rebels and Yucatecans had first engaged in combat. In mid-century both had fought with flintlock muskets, which in the rains were silenced completely, and killing was left to the bayonet and machete. Although Yucatan had some cavalry, the thorny bush of the east was not the place for it, and accounts of the speed of *masewal* movements along the narrow trails make it clear that horses were no asset. Neither side had a commissariat, and even the Yucatecans—whose supply line would have been longer if they had had one—lived off the country.

But in the ensuing years there had been a revolution in technology, and the rebels had kept pace with no more than its earlier stages. As Britain followed the evolution of firearms through the nineteenth century, her outmoded models one after another became available on the world market, and the *masewalob*—as has been indicated throughout this book—upgraded their weaponry. But when breech-loading arms with their specialized ammunition came into wide use, the rebels fell behind. Dependence on such sophisticated arms was impractical for them, and they stopped with the muzzle-loading, single-shot rifled weapon in which the ball-and-powder technology was more appropriate to their condition.

The American and French invasions of the nineteenth century, however, had handed Mexico a harsh lesson in the value of advanced military technology, and by the time its army went into action against the *masewalob* it was thoroughly modern, its soldiers carrying repeating rifles that had already shown their superior power in the Yaqui wars of the Mexican northwest.[16]

The government strategy also stressed communication. From headquarters at the Peto railhead a roadway as much as three hundred meters wide was hacked, with flanking telegraph and telephone lines, and entrenched fortifications for permanent guard posts at intervals of about ten kilometers. Even though the troops were required to pay for their food, a commissariat sent rations regularly along the road.[17] At Camp Zaragoza, the garrison was supplied by civilians of British Honduras, who were allowed to approach the station by boat each Sunday to sell groceries and other goods.[18] And so the Mexican troops moved steadily but slowly onward, until the summer rains of 1900 mired them to a halt and brought the rebels brief respite. In October, the road building began again.

But if the pressure caused many rebels to flee to Guatemala or British Honduras, it evidently inflamed belligerent ardor among former rebels in the north. The pueblo of Yokdzonot and some sympathizers from Chancenote, two of the four *pacífico* towns east of Tizimín that housed remnants of people pacified in the late 1850s, returned to rebellion.

At Yokdzonot, the regular *comandante*, who held his appointment from Tizimín, had without authority appointed a second *comandante* and two junior officers, all three antigovernment and strongly sympathetic to the rebels of San Antonio Muyil, with whom Yokdzonot was having regular dealings. These four leaders, in union with an officer from San Antonio Muyil, incited an altercation in Tixcancal, the third of the pacified towns, in which a merchant was shot. They next carried the fight to Yokdzonot, where five more were killed. The new rebels and their adherents then fled for San Antonio Muyil, while the population of Tixcancal, not in general rebellion, dispersed for safety. At Kantunil-kin, the fourth town, staunchly loyal and not on speaking terms with those of either Yokdzonot or San Antonio Muyil, the men were called in frantically from outlying ranchos to prepare for defense. Rumors flew, some to the effect that Yokdzonot had become a northern bastion of the *bravos*.[19]

Thus, the force at rebel San Antonio Muyil, rather than being weakened by flight, was strengthened by sympathizers. But the events also attracted the attention of the government forces and marked San Antonio Muyil for later attention.

The Campaign Quickens

Speeding up road construction at the beginning of 1901, General Bravo pushed toward the climax of the campaign. In January he occupied Hobompich and another town of the many called Yokdzonot. In early March he was eight kilometers east of Tabi.[20] Progressing about two kilometers per day and staging the moves from his periodic entrenchments, his advance was led by patrol dogs trained to sniff the thickets and warn of human presence. These were followed by regular advance patrols, then skirmish lines of troops, laborers to cut the road, and finally by the main body of troops and the battery of artillery in formation. By now Bravo was fending off harrying attacks regularly but with ease, for his command not only was vastly better equipped but also outnumbered the poorly disciplined and—after decades of peace—unpracticed *masewalob* who came against it. The entire rebel body he estimated could field about twenty-two hundred men, a third of them stationed as guards at strategic points and a maximum of fifteen hundred available for use in the fighting line.[21] His own command, including the detachments guarding his supply line and communications to Valladolid and a telegraph line being opened from Puerto Morelos, consisted of at least three thousand.

In February 1901 yet another general, Jose María de la Vega, was delivered by a Mexican ship of war to command the southern thrust from Camp Zaragoza. As overall commander, Bravo in March declared all traffic across the Río Hondo temporarily suspended except under permit from himself.[22]

Without loss of time, Vega moved with about five hundred soldiers in twin thrusts along the Hondo and overland from Chetumal Bay. By now the rebel guard at Bacalar had been withdrawn, and at the end of March Vega's section occupied Bacalar without opposition and began to clean up the deteriorated town. Vega then shifted his base from Zaragoza to Payo Obispo, next to the anchorage of the doughty pontoon *Chetumal*, and began a methodical but slow movement north toward Noh Cah Santa Cruz, cutting a road and stringing telegraph lines as he went. At the same time, he sent a company of men and a detachment of artillery northward by boat to make a landing at Ascension Bay. There they dug in.[23]

In early April, Bravo reached Nohpop, sixteen kilometers from Noh Cah Santa Cruz.[24] There he made his last entrenchment and slowed his advance again. It was a month before he covered the remaining distance.

In the meantime, rebel soldiers were reported trying to desert to British Honduras in large numbers, while the active ranking generals—León Pat, Teres Cob, and Prudencio May—killed many to restrain them. And about the same time they murdered old, half-blind Felipe Yama, who with the Mexican army at his very door was certain the *masewalob* must sue for peace. He was succeeded as *gobernador* by Pat.[25]

Well before the invaders reached the rebel capital, there were reports from Mexican patrols that the town was deserted.[26] So on May 4 Bravo and his army were not surprised as they entered Noh Cah Santa Cruz— the miraculous village founded under José María Barrera in 1850, the rebel capital built of stone under Venancio Puc ten years later—to find the place undefended and abandoned. One must suppose that the slow pace of Bravo's final advance had been designed to allow his telegraph line to accompany him to the finish, for he immediately wired Governor Francisco Cantón of Yucatan his succinct message, filled with a consciousness of destiny:

Today at seven a.m., I have occupied this historic town, capital of the rebels.[27]

Congratulations flowed in, some of them actually telegraphed in advance. General Bravo was officially declared a citizen of Yucatan.[28]

After a rapid drive east to clear the road to Ascension Bay and link up with the Mexican force entrenched there, Bravo turned to establish his permanent headquarters at the old rebel capital. He himself moved into the house on the corner of the plaza that had been occupied by most of the *gobernadores* of the *masewalob*. A little more than a month later Noh Cah Santa Cruz was visited by Governor Cantón, who decreed that the town be renamed Santa Cruz de Bravo, and its southern outpost Bacalar de Cetina.[29] The occupations of these points did not end the campaign, however, for although the remaining rebels refused to stand, they did not refuse to fight in their own way.

Resuming his slow advance, this time southward toward General Vega, Bravo became aware that *masewalob* were still active in the bush to his north and pulled back. Several mop-up columns were sent out, although only one succeeded in engaging any substantial force, taking forty prisoners from a reported party of two hundred. And from Ascension Bay naval captain Manuel Azueta sailed north with 250 men, to land near the ruins of Tulum on June 28. Two days later, he entered Tulum pueblo, which he found to consist "of a small group of houses and arbors formed of sticks, bamboos, etc., with roofs of palm, fifteen in number. Of these houses it was evident that only four had been occupied recently. . . . In the central *plazoleta* is the house dedicated to the cult, where we saw some pictures of saints and a great number of small crosses."[30] His party took thirteen prisoners—apparently the total remaining population—who offered no resistance.

In July, San Antonio Muyil finally received attention. Mexican troops and Yucatecan militia totaling three hundred rendezvoused first at Xcan, then marched south toward that northernmost rebel strong-point. On July 29, they entered San Antonio to find it largely abandoned, then drove toward the coast where they captured a group making salt. Of the sixty captives, however, almost all were from Yokdzonot rather than the main rebel center. In the days that followed, more than a hundred additional people surrendered to the government force now at Xcan, again most from Yokdzonot but including a few from San Antonio Muyil. Word from various sources was that the bulk of the San Antonio population had moved southeast into deeper forest, locating at pueblos called San Pedro Chen and Santa Teresa Chen, which with two subject hamlets could count a force of more than one hundred men. This San Pedro was described as a pueblo of importance, with a new barracks and a chapel with many crosses that were the object of regional devotion—another cross center. But if these fugitives were pursued, no special report was made of it.[31]

In the same month, July, more than forty rebels were taken—only five of them men—at Dzonot, fourteen kilometers from Noh Cah Santa Cruz and reputedly the home of the late *gobernador* Yama.[32] But rains set in unusually heavy, and late in the summer both Bravo and Vega fell sick and returned to Mexico. The rains lasted day after day, week upon week, bogged all transportation, left the army short of supplies—a difficulty solved at the eleventh hour by five hundred mules secured by Governor Cantón. Such Mexican sallies as were possible found few of the pesky *masewalob*, whose warning bombs could be heard for several kilometers, allowing them to fade into the bush. And so the rebels sniped on, isolated soldiers and laborers their victims.[33]

To aid in bottling up the remaining combatants as the rains came toward an end, in late September Brigadier General Victoriano Huerta was dispatched from Veracruz to Tulum with an additional five hundred men. He marched to the major stronghold of Chunpom and captured a large stock of maize left by the fleeing rebels. From Chunpom he moved to Santa Cruz and then drove north again. One detachment found and destroyed a crude rebel armory, where lead, paper, caps, and 120 kegs of powder were ready for use in assembling cartridges. In late November, Huerta's column reached San Antonio,[34] returning to Santa Cruz and Ascension Bay with forty-five captives, of whom, however, only eighteen were men. In December, he sailed for Veracruz, transporting ninety-two prisoners, presumably of both sexes.

General Vega returned to Yucatan and assumed field command. He erected a permanent station on Ascension Bay, began assembly of a tramway to connect the bay and Santa Cruz de Bravo, and evacuated the numerous Mexican sick.

In Mexico, in November, the executive branch of the Mexican government sent to the congress a measure to establish the federal territory of Quintana Roo, arguing that federal officials were in control there and that without them there was no governmental mechanism operative. Congress voted approval the following April. Yucatan was left to lament the loss of territory over which she had never had real control but for which she had fought with varying degrees of intensity for more than half a century.[35]

Meanwhile, mopping up continued under General Vega, with Huerta returning to act as his second in command. In early 1902, the road and telegraph line from Bacalar finally reached Santa Cruz de Bravo, scheduled to be the new territorial capital. The railway to Ascension Bay was completed, and Mexican patrols turned to cutting pathways through the bush between Ascension and Espíritu Santo bays, taking a few prisoners, forcing *masewalob* to abandon fields cleared for planting, capturing some arms, but achieving no real engagement, as the still rebellious *bravos* showed again and again their ability to melt into the forest. The policy now was to collect all foodstuffs encountered, not as supplies for the government troops—as for so long had been the case—but to force the rebels into surrender.[36]

There were a few rebel responses in force. An engagement with Mexican troops stationed at Bacalar was claimed to have occurred early in the year, and in late March some fifty *masewalob* armed with percussion muskets hit a village near Puerto Morelos, killing some colonists.[37] Major *bravo* leaders through that year were León Pat, Vitorio Vitorín, and one Canuto Baró. Also mentioned in one news report was a "governor" with a guard of fifty men, which appears to be a reference to the high priest, presumably Pedro Pascual Barrera, with the guard of the major cross. Although in five months of 1902 more than one hundred settlements, additional isolated houses, and about one thousand separate milpas were reportedly destroyed by the government, attempts to damage the rebel leadership failed.[38] Government harassment of the *masewalob* continued throughout the year, with exploratory military columns dispatched from Santa Cruz, from Tulum, and from Bacalar.[39]

At the end of the year Vega could announce that only scattered parties remained, parties who would bushwhack isolated groups of Mexicans but who would scatter at any show of force. In February of 1903 he formally notified the secretary of war that eastern Yucatan was pacified.[40] This did not mean that hostilities were completely ended. For in that same month an encounter south of the new capital reportedly left León Pat dead, and a month later Vitorín was said to be seriously wounded.[41]

Some of the rebels accepted the surrender terms offered by General Vega, which gave capitulating *masewalob* the ability to name their own local officials and the choice of a place to establish settlements. This must have been the course accepted by most of the people of Chunpom, for there is no reference to prolonged fighting in the various reports of interviews with Juan Bautista Vega.[42]

But some of the rebels refused. They retreated into the fastness of the forest, dwindling in number but still stubbornly guarding their sacred crosses.

Meanwhile, in Santa Cruz de Bravo and in the settlements linked to it by what passed for roads—now largely populated by immigrants that included Mexican prisoners sentenced to serve in the new federal penal colony—the twentieth century slowly began to dawn.[43]

The Last Days of Noh Cah Santa Cruz

The month following Bravo's occupation of the rebel capital produced detailed descriptions of the town—descriptions that combine to be in fair agreement with the map of the early 1860s (see figure 1). A series of photographs taken when Governor Cantón visited were made into an album in honor of the occasion, and by that time news reporters provided additional grist for the public mill.

Within a week of the formal occupation, Noh Cah Santa Cruz was described as having five "magnificent edifices" of masonry, eight large private houses also of masonry but in ruins, and forty-eight houses with roofs of palm thatch and overgrown by encroaching bush. Each house had its cemetery. Fruit trees were plentiful, but all showed the disorder of neglect.[44]

High grass was everywhere, bespeaking a period of abandonment—perhaps lengthy—before the entry of the Mexicans. From the small number of houses in repair it was doubtful that more than twenty-five families had recently lived there. All settlement had ended, and the bush began less than one hundred meters from the plaza. The apparent rebel intention of creating a large masonry town on the Yucatecan pattern, a capital worthy of the name, was never realized. Yet there were features both impressive and a little oppressive.

At the entrance [from the Peto road] there is an immense and rough rock. . . . On the left rises a construction of masonry with a wide niche that serves for a cross. . . . On the altar of the cross, there are . . . human skulls.[45]

To one side of the rock there is a depression in the land and in the base is seen the beginning of a cenote. . . . Is this the famous one? There is no other in town that could be it. Some meters away are seen the first houses of the town.

On the Plaza are three nice buildings of masonry with roofs of round logs and galleries on the street and the side opposite. On the east side is the Church. Our flag now flies from it.[46]

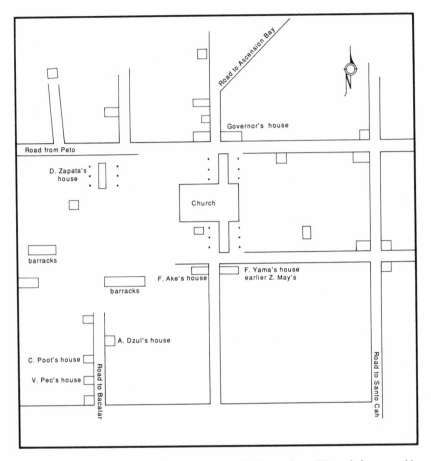

Figure 2. Plan of Santa Cruz de Bravo, 1901. Redrawn from "Ecos de la excursión a Sta. Cruz de Bravo" (RM, July 3, 1901).

Two of the three masonry buildings referred to were actually constructed as wings of the church. The third faced the church across the plaza (see figure 2); this was the onetime residence of Dionisio Zapata. The rest of the houses of the town were masonry and thatch or simply constructed of pole and thatch.

On the northeast corner of the plaza were three thatched masonry houses, one of which became General Bravo's quarters. There, "the room on the corner has the interior walls decorated with grand pictures of coconut groves, in one of which appears an Indian climbing, without more clothes than his rolled-up pants. In the main east room is painted a ship in gaudy colors, and next to this a group representing two angels and two cherubim adoring a monstrance."[47] This had evidently been the residence of the Santa Cruz *gobernador*—León Pat had held it most recently, but earlier it had housed Crescencio Poot and Aniceto Dzul.

At the southeast corner of the plaza stood two large houses of rubble masonry, one with a stairway, the other with stairs and a parapet and railing on the roof. The first of these, east of the street entering the plaza from the south, had been the house of Felipe Yama. Originally, it had been the home of Zacarías May, after which it was used by Chinese blacksmiths. Across the street to the west was the house abandoned by *comandante* Felipe Ake, who had safely defected to Corozal some years before Bravo entered the capital.[48] Other houses of known ownership were south of the plaza: one belonging to Aniceto Dzul before he became *gobernador*; another to Crescencio Poot before he assumed supreme power; still another to Venancio Pec. Closer to the plaza and near its southwest corner were pole and thatch buildings that had served as barracks for the rotating rebel guard of the town. Under Bravo, these were pressed into service as hospitals.

The massive church, measuring forty-eight by twenty meters on the inside, was thought unfinished—towers, at least, were lacking—and even more evidently had not seen recent use. The three niches on the back wall were empty. Immediately south of the church building were two rough structures of wattle and thatch, one of them said to be used for the religious services—marriages and baptisms had been recently performed—and the other for dances. The town was no longer crucial to the cult; instead, the major site of local worship was about sixteen kilometers away—at the settlement known as Santo Cah, where there was a simple church full of images of saints and crucifixes.[49]

As the remnant *masewalob* melted away before General Bravo's advance, so they had even earlier melted away from their onetime metropolis, Noh Cah Santa Cruz.

Absorption of the *Pacíficos*

For the *pacíficos*, 1901 did not mark a dramatic watershed. By that time, it was clear that there were really fewer of them than the Campeche government had been wont to suppose, or than had been estimated in the preliminary national census of 1895. When the more careful enumeration dated October 28,

1900, was finished, it listed 6,235 people for the *municipio* of Xkanhá (consisting of twenty-nine settlements, in which were 2,078 households). It enumerated 2,088 for Icaiché (in eleven settlements of 572 households),[50] although two of the eleven Icaiché villages were outside Mexican territory—Kaxiluinic in British Honduras and Yaloch in Guatemala, with a total of 370 people between them. Altogether, this was little more than half the population that Campeche had earlier claimed for the *pacíficos*, and while as an enumeration it very likely underreported the actual population, the real total could hardly have been more than ten thousand.

Contacts between Tamay and Othon Blanco representing the Mexican command on Chetumal Bay resulted in a visit by Tamay to General Vega at Bacalar in mid-May of 1901, immediately after the taking of Noh Cah Santa Cruz. The newsworthy event of his visit, however, was not the conference but Tamay's near demise on his return. Following a stop for a shopping spree in Corozal, Tamay left to cruise up the Hondo on a steamer—one that had earlier taken Blanco toward Icaiché. On May 22, the steamer hit a sunken log and sank in eighteen feet of water. For some time afterward there was no news of Tamay and his escort of thirty men.[51]

But he survived, and despite Mexican attempts to dampen his enthusiasm for extortionate levies of money upon Belizean loggers, his spirit did not flag. In 1902 his territorial claims to Guatemalan Yaloch and his attempts to wrench money from British Hondurans came together in a curious affair. Alonzo Lewis, a resident of Cayo in British territory, reported to colony officials that he had complained to Tamay that his Icaiché-issued license to bleed chicle at Yaloch was being trespassed upon by another man. Tamay's commission of officers sent to Yaloch to investigate found that Lewis's foreman was being held by soldiers of Tamay's resident garrison there, for reasons never made clear, and then they promptly got drunk, took Lewis himself into custody, and demanded several hundred dollars from him. The claims that followed, pressed by Britain against Mexico, were apparently without success for Lewis. But their transmission to Guatemala led to the Guatemalan assertion of hegemony over Yaloch.[52]

And so after 1900, with Guatemala and British Honduras both taking measures to control communities within their borders, Icaiché was finally contained. The southernmost *pacífico* center endured only another three decades, for in the early 1930s it was abandoned when the government forced the remaining inhabitants to move closer to the Río Hondo where there were schools.[53]

After the close of the active Mexican military campaign in the new Terri-tory of Quintana Roo, the end of independence was not long in reaching the rest of the southern *pacífico* region. In the years through 1900, the Campeche budgets still usually included salary for a single teacher of a school for boys in Xkanhá, but it is doubtful that the post had ever been filled.[54]

At the end of 1902, General Arana traveled to Iturbide with his staff to visit the military commander there. He announced that he was old and sick and that he was troubled by holdout eastern rebels who, pushed by the Mexican troops, were infiltrating his territory. He asked for arms and ammunition but received only a promise that the request would be sent on to General Vega, now military chief of the zone.[55] Then, beginning this same year the Campeche government claimed it was enforcing a provision of the state constitution that forbade the holding of concurrent offices in more than a single branch of government by any one person.[56] This would eliminate the single-handed administration of the government of Xkanhá by General Arana, although Arana's specific fate under the law is not clear.

When reorganization of the interior administration of Campeche took effect in January 1904, Xkanhá was again named *cabecera* of a *municipio*, with jurisdiction now over the settlements that had been subject to Icaiché. It was announced that, as in all *municipios*, there would be annual elections for its *ayuntamiento*—the offices to consist of a *presidente*, a *regidor*, and a *síndico*, together with alternates.[57] These officers were those prescribed for a *municipio* in which the *cabecera* had a population not exceeding one thousand.

But although elections were held statewide in November 1903, no results were announced for Xkanhá, and it is to be doubted that any election took place there. The same pattern of announced elections without announced results continued the following year. By 1905, it was implied that elections were actually held in Xkanhá, although results were not announced in timely fashion simply because of "difficulty of communication" with the isolated *municipio*.[58] But by 1908 communications had apparently been improved, and results for Xkanhá were reported with the others, three officers and a justice of the peace having been elected. This was repeated the following year,[59] and it is noteworthy both that Eugenio Arana was nowhere referred to and that elected position holders changed from one year to the next in proper fashion.

But the governmental functions of Xkanhá were shortly to be reduced. Internal state administration of Campeche was again modified by law, and effective January 1, 1911, Xkanhá was reduced to the status of a simple *población* in the *municipio* of Dzibalchén, as were also the other *pacífico* settlements of Nohayín, Xmabén, and Icaiché.[60] From that time on there were no local elections, for there was no longer a local government in the *pacífico* settlements, save for justices of the peace who were appointive.

The merger into the governmental units of the modern peninsula of all *masewalob*—*pacífico* as well as *bravo*—was finally complete. Ironically, and despite the trouble taken by the Campeche government to incorporate the pacific ex-rebels, in the late 1930s almost all the old *pacífico* settlements were found to lie outside the limits of that state, in the Territory of Quintana Roo.[61]

The Death of Rebellion

In the first decade of the twentieth century, the last stage of the campesino rebellion finally came to an end—if, that is, the end is signaled by government triumph, by the reestablishment of significant government control over disputed territory. But the formal end of the rebellion did not mean the end of rebellious behavior, nor did it spell the demise of practical self-rule by recalcitrant *masewalob*. Indeed, when northeastern Yucatan was visited by the British travelers Arnold and Frost in 1907, they reported that de facto Mexican control was confined within a short radius around Santa Cruz de Bravo and to the small area stretching north from Puerto Morelos that was occupied by the East Coast of Yucatan Colonization Company—which, because of danger from the "independent Indians," was able to exploit only 15 square miles of its four-thousand-square-mile concession.[62]

As independence from Spain had come to Yucatan scarcely rippling the calm waters of colonial rule, so the Mexican social and military revolution of the twentieth century entered Yucatan barely disturbing the placidness that characterized the Díaz dictatorship. This is not to say that the rule of Díaz or the domination of Yucatan by the increasingly wealthy class of henequen planters did not excite some opposition. Indeed, opposition to the Díaz government illustrates that the *masewal* spirit did not die overnight.

In early summer of 1910, only a few weeks after Francisco Madero was nominated for the presidency of Mexico on an anti-reelectionist platform, insurrection broke out in Valladolid. The poorly armed force killed the *jefe político* and the chief of police, took and held the city for a few days, and were finally routed by a combined force of Mexican soldiers and Yucatecan national guardsmen. Three of the leaders were shot and others were imprisoned, but three escaped and fled toward Quintana Roo, aiming to join the remnant *masewalob*. Pursued, suffering, finally lost in trackless forests, they were found on the verge of collapse by hunters from Chunpom. Because the three spoke Maya they were not killed outright.

Taken to Chunpom, by the skin of their teeth they avoided death on the grounds that they had fought the *dzules* and on the condition that they become soldiers of the miraculous cross. In time they were joined there by six of their fellow insurrectionists who had been sent to the prison camp that Noh Cah Santa Cruz had become under General Bravo. In February, five of the nine fled Chunpom. The four who stayed, who were of course identified with those who fled, were immediately chopped up.

With excellent if accidental timing, the fugitives reached Valladolid in early June of 1911—less than two weeks after Díaz had resigned and fled Mexico.

They were hailed as heroes.[63]

Retrospect

With the course of the rebellion now visible over its entire active life, a number of conclusions can be placed in broader perspective.

Causes of the Rebellion

I have been at pains to argue that the major cause of the revolt did not lie in the displacement of Indian campesinos from their lands by white Yucatecans, as so many recent interpretations would have it. To the real charter members of the rebellion such loss of lands was no more than a peripheral irritation, incorporated almost as an afterthought into some of the later rebel statements of grievances. Instead, the initial and most important causal elements were less immediately related to land for subsistence but were owed especially to the concurrence of other factors: the longtime subjugation and exploitation of the lower classes within the highly stratified Yucatecan socioeconomic system; the rise in lower-class expectations following independence; and the abrupt reversal of these expectations by Yucatecan action. The rebel ability to specify grievances was relatively fuzzy in the first months of fighting, and the lack of clear focus was responsible for their refusal to stop fighting when everything was going their way and all the demands they could articulate had been agreed to by the government.

That the expectations of lower-class people, particularly Indians, were cut short and that the rebellion began just when it did was related to the overall political situation of the peninsula, including a distasteful distribution of taxes, extreme rivalries between factions of Mérida and Campeche, and the machinations of individual politicians. These combined to bring on very localized hostilities and acts of banditry in the region between Tihosuco and Valladolid. These acts, in turn, were interpreted by edgy white Yucatecans as the Indian revolt that had been feared for centuries, and they brought on a characteristic overreaction of repression. For the now ambitious lower classes of the eastern regions—many of whom had visited Mérida or Campeche as irregular soldiers of the political factions— Yucatecan response was too much to stand. And so, the war.

There were sharp contrasts in the reactions of campesinos to the rebellion. The insurrection first caught fire in the east, in territory where lands had been least subject to alienation and where campesinos were most independent economically, then spread west through the new sugar region of the old Sierra *partidos*, where it apparently found willing recruits for whom the alienation of *baldío* lands and growing debt peonage were issues; but that region was never its heart. On the other hand, its spread came to an abrupt halt at the edge of old colonial Yucatan, where the heavily Indian lower classes were most completely integrated into the traditional agrarian economic system and where their relationships to that system were most complex. There they refused to rebel. It was from that edge of the real colonial realm that the *masewalob* were swept to the east again by the rejuvenated Yucatecan forces, to be confined after 1849 in the far eastern zone that had never really been an effective part of the Yucatecan political economy. So ended the initial phase of the rebellion.

By the time this had taken place there had also been a firming of rebel desires and a solidification of their demands. When they met with Superintendent Fancourt at Ascension Bay in 1849, their primary condition for peace was independence from Yucatan. They were never after to deviate from this, although they would, they said, accept annexation to British Honduras.

With these conditions not acceptable to Mexico and Yucatan—or for that matter to England—the war continued, although confined indecisively within the eastern wilderness. A part of the reason this eastern fringe had never been under close Yucatecan control may have been related to shortcomings of scale and organization within the colonial system of governance, but another part must have been more directly connected to characteristics of the environment of that eastern region as it came to be after the conquest.

The Rebel Population

I have also argued that from the beginning the rebels included a significant number of individuals who were legally *vecinos* rather than Indians, even if their proportion of the rebel total was relatively small. Although the patrilineal inheritance of legal status could cause the illusion of an unambiguous separation between Indian and European, under the marriage pattern that had prevailed since the conquest, with European men so commonly mating with Indian women, there could be no such lasting distinction. With the borderlines muddied between "Indian" and "Spaniard" in a social sense if not a legal one; with half or more of all *vecinos* able to count a mother, a grandmother, or both, who had been legally Indian before marriage; with affective relations thus made ambiguous; and with Maya the real native language of all campesinos, inclusion of *vecinos* among the rebels was inevitable. That is, many *vecinos* were "Indian" in outlook. And so they joined the fight.

Table 17 summarizes various estimates of total rebel population size that have been presented or developed in the text. In brief, the maximum strength of the total rebel population of all ages and both sexes at the height of their advance to the western portions of the colonial *partidos* of the Sierras could scarcely have exceeded 150,000—a figure equivalent to two-thirds or three-fourths of the entire Indian population of the region that finally rose in the war. Although an important component of the rebels were *vecinos*, there is no doubt that the vast majority were Indians before the law, and for the purpose of the estimate the legally designated Indians can be taken as the obvious raw material for the insurgence. My own feeling is that 100,000 is a more reasonable figure for maximum rebel population, despite some Yucatecan estimates that have run three times that number—to three-fourths of all people on the peninsula who were legally classified as Indians.

Between the farthest *masewal* advance in early 1848 and their hammering by the Yucatecans following the retreat to the east, their total strength was reduced by at least half, possibly more. The remaining active rebels, still under heavy Yucatecan punishment, were again reduced by half with the defection of the southerners in the peace of 1853.

The period from 1853 to about 1870 was that of the greatest rebel coherence and unity, and yet, ironically, while the territorial situation was relatively stable the rebels also revealed their inherent social and political instability by dramatic factional reverses in allegiance. The first years of this period saw the continued rise of the religious cult under Venancio Puc to a position of political dominance. Despite the spawning of at least one comparable cult movement in the northeast—brought to a rapid end with the capitulation of adherents who could not have numbered many more than a thousand—the Santa Cruz movement grew in strength and spirit, and a permanent capital with masonry buildings was established.

Although the overthrow of Puc at the end of 1863 displaced the speaking cross from the apex of political power in a violent alteration of leadership, the Santa Cruz capital and its power did not decline—this even in the face of the growth of a vital cross cult at Tulum. And in the late 1860s, abetted by disruptions of the southern *pacífico* area through political intrusion from urbanized Yucatan, it was Noh Cah Santa Cruz that attracted the redefection

TABLE 17
Summary of Estimates of Total Rebel Population

Date	Southern Pacíficos	Bravos	Source
1848		100,000 – 150,000	Chapter 7: two-thirds or more of total Indian population of the rebellious region.
1850		50,000 – 70,000	Chapter 9: estimate.
1853	20,000 – 25,000	20,000 – 25,000	Chapter 10: estimate.
1861	16,000	15,000 – 20,000	Chapter 14: Campeche census plus estimate for Chichanhá; the Plumridge and Twigge estimate of *bravo* strength.[a]
1864		4,000	Chapter 13: Yucatecan peace commissioners.
1867		33,000	Chapter 15: B. Cen's claim;
		15,000	Carmichael's estimate;
		30,000	Berendt's report.
1875		12,000 – 16,000	Chapter 16: Table 14.
1880		12,000	Chapter 16: British general's estimate.
1887	?20,000	15,000	Chapter 19: A. Dzul's claim.
1894–95	9,000 – 15,000	6,000 – 10,000	Chapters 18, 19: Sapper's reports; Mexico census; *bravo* refugees.
1898		9,000	Chapter 19: *bravo* refugees.
1900	10,000	6,600	Chapter 20: Mexico census; General Bravo's estimate.
1901	10,000	5,000	Present chapter: estimate.

Note: Ratio of total population to number of soldiers is assumed to be about three to one.

[a] Plumridge and Twigge's estimate is from J. R. Longden dispatch No. 6, Nov. 28, 1867, and minute to J. Carmichael's report of Nov. 15, 1867 (co123/130).

of half or more of the southerners—in another traumatic realignment of commanders and their followers.

In table 17 the wide variation in the estimates of *bravo* strength in the 1860s makes it clear that precise information for this period was not available to either Yucatecans or British. I see no reason to suppose that the active rebels numbered more than 25,000 for much of this stage of the revolt, although in 1867 following the reenlistment of the southerners in rebel rolls the active strength may have risen above 30,000—in keeping with the claim Bel Cen made to young John Carmichael in 1867 that he could field 11,000 soldiers. But it appears that a large number of those southerners who had rejoined the *bravos* after the Arredondo affair returned to the *pacíficos* before many years passed: accounts from the 1870s of the people under Arana suggest a fairly substantial population again in the *pacífico* area, and in 1885 the killing of Crescencio Poot drove the rest of the former *pacíficos* to desert the rebel camp.

Thereafter, the rebel decline in the final stages of the rebellion was steady and rapid. In 1887, Dzul claimed only 15,000 total people under his rule. This was the year in which trouble between Santa Cruz and Tulum, essentially independent of one another since the 1870s, surfaced over the Peón Contreras visit to the coast, and in 1892 the split was made permanent when nearly all of the people of Tulum and presumably of Muyil fled to British Honduras and elsewhere. The decline picked up speed as Mexico took an interest in acquiring control over eastern Yucatan. By the time of General Bravo's active advance into the rebel heartland in 1900 it is more than likely—despite his estimate in table 17—that the total rebel population was below 5,000.[1]

Yucatan as a whole experienced a drastic decline in population between the beginning of the Caste War and the 1860s. There had been a total population of 500,000 and more in 1846, from which the number of those loyal to Yucatan has been concluded to have dropped to some 300,000 in 1850 then to around 260,000 in 1854—although the censuses producing figures of these last two years have been felt by many historians to be flawed.[2] Even in the case of the few commentators who have attempted to estimate the number of Yucatecans uncountable because they were with the rebels, reconciliation of the numbers of Yucatecan defenders and of rebels led in most cases to what are surely inflated numbers of people believed killed or chased from Yucatan by the hostilities.[3] Whatever the actual numbers, there is uncertainty in accounting closely for the apparent drop.

A parallel situation exists with regard to the rebels considered alone, as their population is estimated for various years (see table 17). That is, the decline in the number of *masewalob* must be at least as great as from 50,000 in 1850 to 15,000 (both *pacíficos* and *bravos*) in 1900. That leaves a whopping 35,000, or 70 percent unaccounted for.

One significant proportion of this total can be found in the emigration southward from Yucatan. In 1861, the census of British Honduras reported that nearly 10,000 of the colony residents (40 percent of the total population of British Honduras) had been born in Yucatan.[4] Of this number, people of predominantly Spanish descent, many of them remnants of the Bacalar emigrations more than a decade earlier, were far fewer than Indians: the former had formed little more than one-fourth of the small prewar Bacalar population. An additional very substantial emigration of former rebels, again predominantly Indian, was southward along the Guatemalan-British border, where in 1857 they were rumored to number 8,000, although miscellaneous accounts of the villages they established may not support so large a number.[5]

Even regarding this an overstatement, it is not unreasonable to suppose that at least 10,000 and possibly 15,000 one-time rebels moved south into British Honduras and Guatemala at one time or another. Thus, there remain some 20,000 to 25,000 rebels lost between 1850 and 1900 still unaccounted for. Put another way, one can suppose the original rebel population declined from at least 50,000 in 1850 to no more than 30,000 (half of whom were south of the Mexican border) in 1900. That many of those lost had been killed and others had actually returned to regions under government control in Yucatan or Campeche is not to be doubted. What has received little consideration in the past, however, is the overall state of rebel health and its impact on vital processes, which must also be responsible for a significant part of the loss.

Demographic Processes

Since the arrival of Europeans in the sixteenth century, the reputation of eastern Yucatan had been one of unhealthfulness. Indeed, there were some health hazards all over Yucatan. In the nineteenth century, "intermittent fever" was said to be a problem when unusually heavy rains created widespread swamps, especially in the south, and "the mortality of those years, which are not rare, is considerable, especially among children."[6] In some country towns of the twentieth century, "fever"—presumably including, although possibly not limited to, malaria—was the chief cause of disease deaths, followed by dysentery.[7]

But the perennially swampy east coast was worse. It was there that the original conqueror Francisco de Montejo had made his first landings, only to be forced out in part by sickness that plagued his army. That the situation had not changed by 1900 is clear from the record of the Mexican campaign of subjugation, in which disease was more of a threat than enemy guns, with references to "sickness reigning on the inhospitable coasts." It necessitated the establishment of a special hospital in Jalapa, in the state of Veracruz, to care for the campaign casualties, especially the sick, although specific diseases are little mentioned.[8]

Some fairly widespread epidemic diseases that afflicted both rebels and *pacíficos* have been mentioned from time to time in the text—diseases such as cholera and smallpox—but mosquito-borne disease seems to have been endemic. It may be remembered that when young José María Rosado was ransomed from Noh Cah Santa Cruz in late 1858 he returned home to be treated for malaria and hepatitis. And in the 1890s an assessment of vital statistics pronounced malaria the single most important killer in British Honduras, responsible for about one-third of all disease deaths, in which it was followed by dysentery.[9] Indeed, one may suspect that a major reason that European settlement in colonial Yucatan remained strung out around the northern and western coasts was that the far lower incidence of groundwater—because of both porous limestone and lower rainfall—reduced significantly the incidence of insect-borne disease.[10]

Although there are no acceptable statistics on mortality and related demographic analyses available for eastern Yucatan in the nineteenth century, British Honduras officials calculated a life table from data they collected in the first half of the 1890s in the northern districts of the colony—a region from Corozal to Orange Walk occupied almost exclusively by people of Yucatecan origin, most of them Indian.

It is clear from table 18 that more than a third of all children born died during their first year and that well over half died without reaching age ten. For the older ages, it is probable that survivorship figures in the table are too high because the Maya were not accustomed to counting birthdays, with the result that the ages of older people were almost invariably skewed toward overstatement.[11] If this is so, the true life expectancy at birth would have been even less than 18.32 years.

The indications of the life table are reflected in crude death and crude birth rates for the same period, varying somewhat between different sources, but similarly dismal: For Corozal district, birthrates of 42.7 to 47.8 per thousand and death rates of 52.6 to 55.3 per thousand created an annual

TABLE 18

Abridged Life Table, Corozal and Orange Walk Districts of British Honduras, 1894

Age (x)	Mortality at Age x (Percentage of Mean Population)	Survivorship to Age x	Life Expectancy at Age x
0	34.56	10,000	18.32
1	11.67	7,053	25.02
5	3.27	5,510	28.94
10	1.46	4,627	28.15
20	3.89	3,939	22.39
30	11.85	2,918	18.98
40	10.54	2,047	15.98
50	6.98	1,464	11.47
60	14.78	788	8.05
70	17.51	326	7.16
80	25.24	65	5.41

Source: Statistics: Colony of British Honduras, 1894, table T-2 (HG, 1984).

Note: Data are presumably based on experience of both sexes for the period 1891 through 1894.

loss of population of from 0.5 to more than 1.0 percent per year. For Orange Walk district, the birthrate of 35.0 to 37.3 per thousand, as against death rates of 36.3 to 47.5, indicates a population that at best is approximately stationary, at worst losing more than 1.0 percent per year.[12] Unfortunately, the twentieth-century studies based on data collected before the days of modern health care in rural Yucatan do not include life tables, and in at least some of the studies the combinations of birth and death rates are difficult to reconcile in any way with demographic reality.[13]

A situation of high endemic insect-borne disease appears descriptive of the eastern littoral. But it is not necessarily applicable to the entire region occupied by those southern *pacíficos* who were subject first to Lochhá and then to Xkanhá, for parts of that area have been characterized as drier than real rain forest.[14] Fortunately, there are two censuses for the *pacíficos* that have been claimed as enumerations by age categories; less fortunately, while one of them appears tentatively credible in its age distribution, the second does not.

In the census published by Campeche in 1861 when in pursuit of state-hood,[15] 34 percent of the *pacífico* population of 1,440 (see table 12 for totals by town) was below age fifteen—a proportion roughly characteristic of those populations that have a life expectancy at birth of around twenty years and are declining at a rate of about 0.5 percent per year. Thus, the age distribution is at least believable, although it is also not unlikely that the ages below five years were underrepresented, as they so often are even in modern censuses. To the extent that they can be accepted, these figures mirror a population that was not reproducing itself.

But the 1900 census, which by rights should be superior, is not similarly believable. There, only 20 percent of the registered total are below age fifteen—a condition essentially impossible in any stable population with low life expectancy at birth.[16] Even at a stable rate of loss of 1 percent per year, a population with life expectancy at birth of around twenty years (which the rural *pacíficos* probably exceeded by very little) and numbering somewhat less than ten thousand individuals in total, would require almost one thousand additional living individuals below age fifteen to make the figures of the 1900 census credible. One must conclude, therefore, that the underregistration of the young in 1900 was so extensive that the entire census is questionable, certainly insofar as precisely indicating stable trends. But the general direction indicated—few children relative to adults—is in keeping with a suspicion that the population was not replacing itself.[17]

At this point it can be suggested that among the *masewalob*, the *bravo* population in particular was almost certainly failing to maintain itself through natural reproduction, and the *pacífico* population was very possibly failing to reproduce itself, or if doing so was at least not increasing. In the *bravo* east, this could be largely because of a high level of endemic, insect-borne disease, but in both east and south the level of health was otherwise marginal at best. If the demography is factored into the discussion of the decrease of the *masewalob* between 1850 and 1900, one must be struck by the fact that a decline from fifty thousand to thirty thousand over fifty years represents an annual long-term decline at a rate of almost exactly 1 percent a year—a rate that would not be unbelievable in a population that was viable in the short run but failing to reproduce itself over the longer term.

This is not to say that any such decline would be actually stable, for the periodic occurrences of epidemics argues for sporadic periods of heavy loss. It is not to say, either, that failure to reproduce was responsible for the entire decline in numbers, for there was also a more or less continual defection to controlled regions of Yucatan and southward, as well as much killing.

But in view of the evidence suggesting long-term population loss through failure to reproduce, the decrease in the rebel population between 1850 and 1900 becomes not at all surprising. There is no need to blame all of it—or even most of it—on war casualties, executions, or murders.

The Rebel Organization

As I have indicated, the rebel military organization was modeled after the Yucatecan militia, with which many of the original rebel leaders had gained experience. By this system, a local settlement or several adjacent settlements organized themselves into a company, the officers of which—corporals, sergeants, lieutenants, and a captain—were elected, the captain holding the command.[18] In the militia, officers above these ranks were appointed by the government, but among the *masewalob* the higher officers—*comandantes*, generals, very occasionally colonels or "general majors" (the latter two were more often found among the *pacíficos*, who had frequent contact with Campeche or Yucatan)—were evidently also elected from officers holding only slightly lower ranks, while new officers were elected at the bottom to take the vacated positions. Among the *pacíficos*, those elected to the highest ranks were confirmed by formal appointment from Campeche or Mérida, or at least by a local state official (as shown, for instance, by the procedural violations of the original *comandante* of Yokdzonot, whose unauthorized appointments contributed to the rebellion described in the last chapter).

Despite the hierarchy, the highest rebel officers were subject to some controls in later years, and presumably in earlier periods as well, as a council of all officers met to consider important questions, and extremely serious matters were ruled on by a grand council of all adult males, that is, of all soldiers. Thus, in 1892 General Tamay of Icaiché was removed from his command briefly and then restored by such a general council, and in 1898 *gobernador* Felipe Yama called a grand council at Noh Cah Santa Cruz to consider the advisability of making peace with Yucatan.[19]

While the captain was normally the direct commander of men from his own local region, the *comandante* was more completely autonomous and in charge of a region of varied size—sometimes with only one captain and company at his orders, but commonly with several companies, each led by officers such as captains. *Comandantes* were always relatively few in number, and it was these men whose names were most often affixed to correspondence, usually with more than one appearing as signatories, as if to guarantee broad authority for any matter discussed. There were even fewer generals—one at Icaiché, one at Xkanhá, probably one at Tulum, and no more than two or three at Noh Cah Santa Cruz.

As time went on, and as parts of companies hived off to establish new settlements, sometimes subject to others, sometimes independent, the ranks became mixed, the commanders varied. Separate companies might be led by lieutenants or sergeants—as, for instance, among the towns of the *pacíficos* under General Arana in the 1890s (see table 16) or among the remnant rebels studied by Villa Rojas in the twentieth century.[20]

Among the *masewalob*, the military organization was also the civil governing agency. Although at Noh Cah Santa Cruz, at Lochhá, and at Tulum the highest civil authority was given the title *gobernador*, he evidently achieved that rank by promotion through the military hierarchy, which retained the practical authority to organize religious festivities and remained the guardian of the sanctity and safety of the religious cult. With companies originally formed by people from localized settlements, it is not surprising that there was a strong tendency for young men to join the companies of their fathers and for their spouses and children of both sexes to give allegiance to it. For this reason, some commentators have pointed out the similarity of the rebel military companies to corporate kin groups.[21] One cannot push the kinship orientation too far, however, for it is clear that the choice of the company for membership was still largely voluntary, with individual soldiers able to shift allegiance when they saw compelling reason to do so.[22]

Factionalism and Fragmentation

Within the company, leadership was personal and direct, and this personal relationship was extended upward to *comandantes* and at times to generals. Within each unit, furthermore, the chain of command was followed strictly, with captains not attempting to control soldiers who were not of their company and *comandantes* not exercising control over members of other commands. Thus, each command and each subdivision of a command was a distinct unit, segmental and self-contained. Officers signed letters and made agreements as representatives of their subordinates and committed their followers to courses of political action (or at least intended to so commit them, and often did, although there were sometimes defections). When disagreements occurred between leaders, their commands supported them, and fission of varying degrees of seriousness was likely.

These fissions between segments were, in fact, a chronic and salient characteristic of *masewal* society from the beginning of the rebellion. The examples given in the text are far too numerous to recapitulate—from Jacinto Pat and Cecilio Chi commanding different armies to the altercation between Crescencio Poot and Aniceto Dzul. And so on, through case after case.

Despite the ease of fission, the tendency for segments to break apart was mitigated by several factors. One of these must have been the central ownership of armament, as was the case after Enfield rifles were purchased by the Santa Cruz leadership for use by all the soldiers; a major reason to keep soldiers in line was to discourage them from absconding with their issued weapons, and, certainly, it was harder to mutiny if you didn't control your own gun. A second was the opportunity for enrichment presented to the highest officers, as opposed to the rank and file. Although they never collected taxes, during the rebel heyday the major commanders held landed estates that were largely worked for them by their own followers and by prisoners. They also as a group had monopoly rights to the distillation of spirits and a share of profits from it. They had evident rights also to share in income from farm and forest lands rented out to residents of British Honduras. All of these would tend to weld the leadership into a single unit as against their followers. But, conversely, misuse of revenue and failure to divide it—or suspicion of such failure—was a fertile cause of dispute, fragmentation, and murder.

And as a powerful force against segmentation there was always the religious cult of the sacred crosses. To the support of the cult all military units were consistently devoted, and from the cult might issue sanctions on any of them or any of their individual members. Clearly, this was the strongest deterrent to segmentation—at least as long as the cult was centralized. That it was not enough to prevent all emigration by individuals and family groups, however, is abundantly clear from the rebel history.

The Fluid Campesino Population

From the very foundation of the Spanish colony, a problem to administrators was the tendency for subsistence farmers and their families to melt away from the settlements, a tendency not eliminated by their parallel and sometimes conflicting desire to stay close to the place where they had been nurtured. This urge to move into the forest was at work even during the most spirited stages of the rebellion, as rebel soldiers forsook the fray to drift southward.

This drive for individuals or families to secrete themselves must be distinguished from the tendency of segmental military units to hive off as wholes, leaders and all. The major southern capitulation of 1853 can be seen as a movement of segments. But these other, more individually drifting emigrations are plentiful in the history described here. At the same time, such movements by individuals were not always into the peaceful hinterlands. There are numerous examples of immigration to the *bravos*, some of which have been referred to—for example, the people who voluntarily defected to follow Crescencio Poot to Noh Cah Santa Cruz after his largely unsuccessful raid on Chichimilá in 1870 or the defection of the former servant of Rancho Xuxub to rebel San Antonio Muyil. The evidence says that anyone who spoke Maya and could pass as a campesino was acceptable to the *bravos*.

These individual movements by *masewalob* were generally of the rank and file rather than officers. But even a few of the *masewal* leaders seem to have managed peaceful transitions away from the active rebels—as in, for example, the apparent case of Baltazar Moguel, the army deserter who became a *bravo comandante*, married the daughter of Bonifacio Novelo, and moved safely with his wife to British Honduras. But most officers who left the rebel establishment did so only when they had reason to fear death at the hands of their compatriots. Most of them evidently identified strongly enough with the *bravo* cause to actively try to prevent the drifting emigration of their soldiers.

All in all, it is hard to escape the conclusion that below the level of the active leaders, the *pacífico* and *bravo* populations were to a certain extent fluid, with many common people moving quietly into one camp, then into the other (albeit somewhat surreptitiously), as their private interests dictated.

The Religious Cult

The growth of the cult of the miraculous cross after its sudden appearance at the end of 1850 marks the success of a faction new to power among the rebels, and as a means of achieving influence it was too attractive to be limited to one place. Within little more than two years after the appearance of the first cross at Chan Santa Cruz there was a similar cult practiced at Mabén, east of Valladolid.[23] The distance between these two religious centers—some 150 kilometers as the crow flies—was great enough that with the limited means of communication available, the political independence of the two centers was predictable. What might have happened if both had continued to develop is anybody's guess, but the northern center was quickly hammered to death by the Yucatecan military force garrisoned at Valladolid, and pacification resulted.

By the time this happened, the cult at Chan Santa Cruz had oracularly pronounced itself into supreme political power—with Venancio Puc, the manipulator of the cult, and his two generals, Dionisio Zapata and Leandro Santos, representing a faction that had not hitherto appeared in any high positions of command. Their rise was marked by spectacular rebel successes: the raid and massacre at Tekax in 1857; the invasion of southern *pacífico* realms in the same year; and the capture and massacre of Bacalar. As these successes were achieved, the building of an ambitious masonry capital was launched at Chan Santa Cruz, and captured artisans were kept alive to provide services in the new, even grandly conceived, *masewal* capital. And that miraculous capital progressed from Chan Santa Cruz to Noh Cah Santa Cruz, from village to nominal city. Within three years the leadership—that is, Puc—had shown itself willing to thumb its nose at the British in its treatment of the English lieutenants Plumridge and Twigge and had pulled off the spectacular kidnapping raid on Tunkás.

There can be no doubt that the great majority of the active rebels believed absolutely in the cross as the verbal organ of God. Despite the cynical opinions of Yucatecans and Belizeans who averred that the the real nature of the cross was a secret known to the officers as a whole, one through which they worked their will on the gullible populace, belief in the cross seems to have been as true for most of the officers as for the rank and file. Thus, during the palace revolt of Zapata and Santos at the end of 1863, other officers refused to raise arms against Puc until the young man who was the voice of the cross was locked up, and it was shown that God could not speak without his help. There were, of course, some inevitable disbelievers, but open indications of disbelief in the cross were punishable by death; this is evident in stories told by young José María Rosado after his captivity at Noh Cah Santa Cruz.[24]

During the period of iron rule by Venancio Puc and the cross there is no sign of the factionalism otherwise so chronic, and with the elimination of the rebel center in the northeast there was no cult center in evidence anywhere in rebel-controlled territory except at Noh Cah Santa Cruz. There can be no question that it was the cult that was very largely responsible for the rejuvenation of the rebels, and in anthropological terms the new religion can certainly be classed among what have been called revitalization movements—that is, movements in which a new code is spread widely among converts, leading to the formation of a new and integrated society.[25]

It appears, then, that Venancio Puc had carried all before him in his rise through the manipulation of the original cult of the miraculous crosses. It is also the shape of his personal staff of religious functionaries that we have been made familiar with by previous accounts of the Caste War: Puc himself as *patrón*, aided by an "interpreter of the cross," and an "organ of the divine word." It has been common for historians to presume that this same organization persisted to the end of the century.[26] But the evidence is against it. By the beginning of 1864 Puc was dead as a result of the revolt of his own generals, whose apparent intention to turn the rebels toward peace was cut short by a counterrevolution masterminded by the old faction of warriors led by Bonifacio Novelo, Crescencio Poot, and Bel Cen. Nevertheless, a new organization did emerge.

At the Santa Cruz capital the oracular cult was displaced from its central political position, although the evidence makes it clear that the settlement continued as one of multiple centers of worship. The major oracle appeared almost immediately at Tulum. Unfortunately, I know of no descriptions of the way in which the Tulum cross was actually manipulated, and no functionaries such as the "interpreter" or the "organ" are mentioned. In any event, Tulum and its cult, even with less military and political strength then Noh Cah Santa Cruz, rose to a position of prestige under the able priestess María Uicab.

Despite the great prestige of Crescencio Poot as a leader, and despite the religious attraction of Tulum, in 1872 a new cult and military center had sprung up well to the north at San Antonio Muyil. San Antonio Muyil then continued as a center in its own right, becoming important enough that its high priest was invited to festivities at Tulum when Peón Contreras was honored there in 1889.

By the 1880s, Tulum itself had become essentially independent of Noh Cah Santa Cruz, and in 1885 it provided support for Aniceto Dzul in his rebellion against Poot. This suggests that the split was in fact largely between Poot and the avid supporters of the cross, now centered around Tulum.

Thus, with important cult activity still conducted at Santa Cruz, there were in the 1880s three important religious centers—Noh Cah Santa Cruz, Tulum, and San Antonio Muyil. And all were also political centers. Santa

Cruz was undoubtedly the most powerful, and it maintained the important garrison at Bacalar, but none of the three was superordinate. One suspects that this was the result of the divisions between the major centers of religious and secular power after the fall of Venancio Puc. That is, although evicting the major oracle from Noh Cah Santa Cruz may have made things more comfortable for the civil rulers, it also sowed again the seeds of fragmentation.

The Peón Contreras affair rejuvenated the Santa Cruz-Tulum rivalry, but this time Noh Cah Santa Cruz was to win. Three years later, in 1892, the relations between the two centers had deteriorated to the point that the population of Tulum—and apparently also of nearby Muyil—emigrated en masse, all but a paltry remnant going to British Honduras or to the southern *pacífico* region. The major focus of cross worship in the vicinity must have passed to Chunpom, where none had been clearly indicated before. At any rate, the seat of the cult was at that settlement in 1897 when Juan Bautista Vega was placed in the rebel service. By this time—possibly even by 1890— the massive stone church at Noh Cah Santa Cruz had been retired from use in the Santa Cruz cult, and the center of worship moved outside the pueblo—perhaps to the north, to judge by the description of the location of the major annual festival at the time of the visit of one British Honduran; perhaps to the south, to judge by the location of the road leading to *Santo Cah*, "Holy Town," when the region was occupied by the Mexican army in 1901.

Thus, at the time the rebel territory was definitively penetrated and partly occupied in 1901, there were three fairly vital centers and a lesser one: one in the vicinity of Noh Cah Santa Cruz; one at Chunpom; one at San Antonio Muyil; and a remnant at Tulum. The first three of these were also political and military centers, essentially independent although leagued in their opposition to Mexico and Yucatan. And with Mexican occupation of the region the first two of those would be maintained, while the center at San Antonio Muyil disappeared into the forest, its fate not presently known. A cross at Tulum continued its reputation of sanctity, and although the actual strength of that cult in 1901 was evidently so weak as to be almost nonexistent, it seems to have grown thereafter.

In any event, the cult that once had served to unite, now simply marked the ultimate fragmentation of the rebel polity.

The Rebellion and the Larger World

A recurring theme of this work, if not the major one, has been the repercussion of national and international relationships on the *masewalob* and their rebellion. It was Mexican independence that brought the major change in the outlook of the lower classes, particularly those classed by law as Indians, who were accorded citizenship for the first time. It was strife between Yucatan and Mexico, between federalist and centralist, between Mérida and Campeche that disrupted the peninsula and provided the practical military experience and the confidence that made widespread warfare thinkable for important segments of those newly hopeful and heavily Indian lower classes. And when rebellion rose and persisted it molded Yucatecan history for half a century.

Once the fight began, it was the attitudes of the British in their settlement at the southeastern corner of the peninsula that made continuation of the war possible for the rebels. It was these attitudes that set the Yucatecans so firmly against the English—although Yucatan had lost little love on the British interlopers before 1847—particularly because in many important respects the Yucatecans understood the British position poorly or not at all.

In the first place, there was the matter of the relative numbers of British settlers compared to rebels. When the hostilities exploded, the population of British Honduras was less than twenty thousand, and with visions of hordes of frontier savages much larger than this sweeping across the Río Hondo to take what they wanted, the British colony-to-be was far more inclined to appease than oppose. They were scared to death of invasion and not equipped to defend against it. Despite Yucatan's own terror of the rebels, there is no indication in Yucatecan comments of the time that this aspect of the British Honduran position was ever comprehended—if it was, it received no sympathy.

Second, there were the British attitudes toward territory, which bore strongly on Britain's relations with Yucatan and later with Mexico. On the one hand, British Honduras was an insecure possession with no local agreement regarding boundaries. The Mexican position, as noted several times in this book, was that Spain's sovereignty over the British-occupied territory had devolved upon Mexico. The British position recognized the earlier rights of Spain but argued that with Spain's de facto withdrawal from the New World the ownership of territory passed to the power in possession at the time, which was clearly Britain. It was this disagreement that the more-or-less reformed rebels of Icaiché were to exploit so successfully.

On the other hand, the British government was not interested in further territorial expansion. Despite the obvious desires of some individual British Honduras residents, despite the inclinations even of a few of the British government officers in Belize, London had neither the intention nor desire to add rebel-controlled eastern Yucatan to a worldwide empire that was already too big and too expensive to handle. Again, there is no indication in Yucatecan comments that this was appreciated. Indeed, the assistance toward peace that Superintendent Fancourt attempted through his meeting with Venancio Pec at Ascension Bay in 1849 was viewed by Yucatan as an outright attempt to persuade the rebels to unite their territory with British Honduras—apparently simply because Fancourt gave a forthright account of the words of the rebels on the question (see chapter 9).

Third—but this very certainly *was* understood with great clarity by Yucatan—was the official British attitude toward commerce and the unwillingness to place any real barrier in the way of what London and Belize called "free trade" with the rebels by British merchants.[27] This attitude on the part of the governing officials on both sides of the Atlantic emerges against a background of strong resentment of Yucatan built up in British Honduras through a history of withstanding Spanish attempts to dislodge them from their toehold on the Caribbean coast. This resulted in sympathy for the rebel cause, despite frequent fears of what the "Indians" to the north might perpetrate in the way of raids on the British settlement.[28] Whatever the roots of policy, the trade in powder—which before 1897 was interrupted by British officialdom only when British Honduras herself was threatened by it—is what allowed the rebel war against Yucatan to continue. In British Honduras and London, government officials were well aware of this, as the text and notes of this book have made clear. It is no wonder that Yucatecans were—and still are—resentful.

Although the *masewalob* had early recognized their absolute dependence on British Honduras merchants for their ability to fight, during the period of the truculent Venancio Puc and his tyrannical cross the rebel officialdom gave little evidence of appreciation. But after Puc's overthrow and the establishment of stability under later leaders, relations became closer and closer. Sometimes daring efforts by Belizean entrepreneurs like the Carmichaels led to ever tighter commercial ties, including not only trade but the employment of rank-and-file rebels, in time creating close bonds of friendship. When the Mexican advance threatened, the rebels repeated their pleas to become British subjects and were again refused.

Finally, with the exchange of conditions between Mexico and Britain—recognition of British Honduran boundaries traded for a decisive ban on trade with the rebels—the campesino rebellion and *masewal* freedom came to a final official conclusion. At the end, as at the beginning, the rebellion was pawn to international politics.

But the rebellion also had its impact on the world. In the early years, any value of rebel trade to British Honduras was more than offset by the costs of maintaining special military forces. But as time went on the British settlement received immigration by Yucatecan fugitives, Indian and mestizo, in numbers large enough to drastically change the complexion of its northern districts. After about 1880, growing trust and friendship with both *bravos* of Noh Cah Santa Cruz and *pacíficos* of Icaiché presented the colonists not only with trade in livestock and other products but with forest tracts for exploitation—despite the "rents"—that served them well and profitably as the colony grew in manpower and capital and as logwood and mahogany were depleted within its own territory.

In Yucatan and Campeche, the impacts were more extreme. Most obvious was the total ruination of the economy in the first year of the rebellion. Less direct, but equally depressing on the long-term economy, was the reduction in population from all causes. Aside from manpower and resources wasted in actual warfare, rebel defections amounted to a significant loss not only of labor but of potential markets. As an example, after the peace agreement of 1853, the Chenes region enjoyed a certain prosperity as the *pacíficos* were trading hogs, lard, maize, beans, and forest products for salt, *aguardiente*, and other merchandise. The redefection in 1867 of half or more of the pacified rebels wrecked that trade and threw the district again into depression.[29]

Actively disputed today is the relationship between the rebellion and the development of the monocrop henequen economy. Many commentators have taken the purely ecological view that the henequen plantations developed in the northwest of the peninsula because henequen grows best there. Others have disagreed, arguing that henequen, a native plant, will grow throughout the peninsula. They maintain instead that the major plantations were located in the northwest because of the danger posed by the war in the eastern and central regions.

Both of these views are extreme. The henequen plantations developed in almost all cases on already existent haciendas. Their establishment required significant amounts of labor throughout the year, capital to support the enterprise for the near decade necessary for plants to begin producing after planting, and transportation. All of these were present in larger quantity in the northwest as a result of historical factors that well predate the beginning of the 1847 rebellion.[30]

Nevertheless, the impact of the devastating war on the broader economy did eliminate potential product competitors of henequen, such as sugar or tobacco. This circumstance combined with the continuing unsettled conditions in the east, the presence of a certain infrastructure in the Mérida region, and the explosion of the fiber market to spur the development of the henequen industry in the far northwest of the peninsula.

The interrelationships are obvious. As national and international events conditioned the occurrence, maintenance, and official end of the rebellion, so the rebellion combined with other factors to mold the development of the peninsular economies and histories.

The Aftermath in Brief

With the forced end of active rebellion and of at least nominal independence of *masewal* territory, the narrative offered here is substantially complete. The briefest of comments will suffice to characterize the course of later history.

Although General de la Vega had completed the "pacification" of the new Territory of Quintana Roo, Ignacio Bravo returned as its governing official and supervisor of the Mexican penal colony it became. While a few of the remaining rebels came to terms with the new government, most of them still refused. Some carried on limited acts of sabotage, one of which was the dynamiting of the railway between Santa Cruz and Ascension Bay.[31] By about 1905 the centers of the cult and of remnant rebel forces were apparently limited to Chunpom, Tulum, and a place called Yokdzonot or Dzonot-Guardia, possibly the Yokdzonot that had been the seat of Felipe Yama when young Juan Vega was dragged to him for judgment in 1897. But despite the triumph of General Bravo, in the first decade of the twentieth century the *masewal* settlements scattered through the eastern forests were apparently in de facto control of much of Quintana Roo.

In 1912, after the initial success of the revolutionary movement against Porfirio Díaz, Bravo was removed as governor, and the following year President Carranza decreed Quintana Roo dissolved as an entity and reintegrated into Yucatan. A series of Mexican military commanders had charge of the former territory until one of them—in spite of having repaired the trains and instituted a number of other advances in Santa Cruz—ran afoul of Carranza when he did not act to put down a revolt that was fomenting in nearby Yucatan and was arrested and shot. In 1915 the territory was reestablished, and the then governor of Yucatan in a formal ceremony delivered control—presumably in a fit of socialist generosity—directly to the Mayan leaders Guadalupe Tun and Sil May, ordering non-*masewal* residents to move to Payo Obispo (now Chetumal), which became the new capital. The *masewalob* responded by dynamiting the Santa Cruz waterworks, burning the rolling stock of the railway, and tearing up the telephone and telegraph lines in order to assure their isolation.

With heavy losses in the leadership by a major epidemic of some sickness, possibly smallpox, in 1917, some *masewalob* began slowly to move nearer to the former rebel capital. These were led by Francisco May, stepson of Felipe Yama, who as a mere boy had reportedly taken part in the fighting against the Mexican advance of 1900–1901 and had been involved in the later resistance. Under his influence the cult center of Yokdzonot, of which he was now apparently commander, was transferred to Chancah, south of Santa Cruz and nearer to it. In the old capital itself May was responsible for the construction of the small chapel that stands today immediately south of the massive church built by Venancio Puc, the latter of which remained unused.

In 1918, May's position as general was confirmed by President Carranza himself, and during the chewing gum boom of the 1920s he controlled chicle collection in a region from Bacalar to Muyil. The zone between Chunpom and Tulum was controlled from the former settlement, especially by Juan Bautista Vega, who operated as secretary of the religious cult there. Remnant rebels became heavily involved in the chicle industry, of necessity associating more and more with outsiders, and lost some of their belligerence.

The publicly accessible stance now assumed by May, however, was opposed by a number of adherents of the cross, and in 1929 the Chancah group split, with the more conservative stealing the sacred cross and moving north of Santa Cruz to Xcacal, where they established the center of the group studied by Alfonso Villa Rojas in the 1930s.[32]

After that time, the cult still at Chancah was shifted to nearby Chancah Veracruz, and the cross remaining at Tulum moved with its priest to join that at Xcacal to avoid outside visitors. Otherwise there has been no major change in the positions of the remnant centers. In the 1970s, the three maintaining regular guard duty by military companies were Xcacal, Chancah Veracruz, and Chunpom, with a combined population of about five thousand. All have been organized into *ejidos*.[33]

Through these adjustments both the cult of the cross and the abstract affection for the English have continued. Not only did *masewalob* of Quintana Roo send representatives to Belize to pay respects to the British Princess Margaret in the 1950s, but interviews with Juan Bautista Vega in 1962 were gained at the price of a framed photograph of Queen Elizabeth II, presented to him as the official representative of Chunpom.[34]

The most drastic impact of the later years has come with the opening of Quintana Roo and its attractive coast to tourism. Now the old archaeological site of Tulum, once among the most remote of the Mayan jewels, can claim the highest visitation of any site on the peninsula, as buses and cars pour southward from Cancún and the string of resorts that pockmark the coastline. The old village of Santo Cah Tulum, with one of the few gasoline stations of the coast, has been transformed into an ugly strip development on the north-south highway.

The *masewalob* are subjected not to military coercion but to cooptation. Highway signs proclaim in blatant Spanish "Welcome to the Maya Zone." Since 1987 the cenote of the miraculous cross at Noh Cah Santa Cruz has been a public park where signs proclaim the memory of José María Barrera and Juan de la Cruz and where a small museum glorifies the rebel role in the Caste War. Near the polluted water hole of the cenote stands the little stone chapel, a remnant of the apse of the first important church at the site. Fifteen years ago, the faded marks of painted crosses were barely visible within it. Today, they stare out starkly in garish blue paint.

Trees throw somber shade on the little hollow, but the great mahogany trunk with the cross carved on it was cut more than a century ago by command of General de la Vega. Now children play there.

How many still hear the voice of God?

Notes

1. Beginnings

1. This is the standard and dramatic story, based on the first-person account of Bernal Díaz del Castillo, written many years after the conquest (Díaz del Castillo [1632] 1956). The so-called First Letter of Cortés, written at a time much closer to the events described, says rather that all but the two "survivors" had been so widely dispersed into the interior that it would be impossible to contact them (Cortés 1928, 8).

2. Chamberlain (1948, 11–14); Bernal Díaz del Castillo ([1632] 1956, book 1); a lengthy discussion is in the copious notes of Tozzer (1941, 7–11). López de Gómara ([1552] 1964, 15–18) lists items traded for by Grijalva.

3. Chamberlain (1948, 14–16); Díaz del Castillo ([1632] 1956, book 2, chap. 1); López de Gómara (1964, chaps. 7–15); Tozzer (1941, 12–15). None indicates that Cortés was aware that Cozumel was the focus of pilgrimage to a shrine of the Maya goddess Ix Chel, whose hollow pottery image was reputed to conceal a priest responsible for her oracular verbal powers (López de Cogolludo, [1688] 1954, 1:360), and which some have suggested was the prototype for the oracles nurtured by the Caste War rebels in the nineteenth century.

4. For environmental characterizations, see articles in West (1964). The nineteenth-century traveler Stephens (1963, vol. 2, chap. 3) describes the great cavern at Bolon-chén, in the district of Chenes, where he descended through dark vaults, down seven different ladders, sometimes crawling through constricted passages, for a distance he estimated to be 1,450 feet and a depth below surface of 450 feet, to reach water. This was the regular dry season source for the pueblo.

5. Population distribution overall is treated by Cook and Borah (1974); that around Chetumal Bay at the time of conquest (to be discussed later) by Scholes and Thompson (1977) and Jones (1982a). For organization and named political groups see Eggan (1934), Roys (1940, 1957).

6. The story can be gleaned from notes in Tozzer (1941, 251). Chamberlain (1948, 104, 171–72) seems to attribute many of the early difficulties of the Montejo campaign (described in the next section) to Guerrero, accepting Guerrero's identification with a presumably European corpse, accoutred in Indian fashion, that was found in 1534 after an Indian raid far to the southeast in the Ulúa Valley of Honduras. But it is unlikely that Gonzalo Guerrero was the only Spaniard to go native as the conquest unfolded.

7. Chamberlain (1948). The southeastern campaign was headed by Gaspar Pacheco with son Mélchor and nephew Alonso, bearers of a name that would recur in events of the nineteenth century. See also Jones (1989).

8. It is not clear how Montejo's term "the Son of God" (Chamberlain 1948, 239) accorded with what the Maya priest said of himself.

9. Montejo applied the name of his Spanish birthplace to a series of settlements. Bacalar was the seventh of his Salamancas, although the only one to carry the name to modern times. Jones (1989) details its early history.

10. Although gold objects were reported in Yucatan by several early Spaniards, and gold may actually have been worked in the Maya region in preconquest times, the source was elsewhere. See, for instance, Bray (1977).

11. The lineage in the male line as recognized by the Maya was apparently that of Can (Scholes and Thompson 1977, 57), the designation meaning *snake* or *serpent*, Can Ek meaning *black serpent* or possibly *four stars* (Bartolomé 1978, 17 n. 8).

12. Bricker (1981, 21); López de Cogolludo (1954, vol. 3, bk. 9, esp. chaps. 8–15). Jones (1989, 132–33) cites evidence that the Itzá visit to Mérida was the result of earlier work with them by Father Orbita. The prophecies would apparently have specified a Mayan calendrical date for the Itzá to return to northern Yucatan.

13. In his passage, Cortés had left with Canek's people a horse that was lamed, asking them to care for it (Cortés 1928, 314). Given a house of its own, it was offered game and other delicate meats to eat until it languished and died. When Fuensalida and Orbita saw the temple of idols in 1618, there was "standing out among them that of *Tizimín Chac*, which was represented as a horse, seated on its haunches . . . [and] raised on its front feet" (Ancona 1889, 2:207)—permanent tribute to Cortés's steed. Orbita, outraged, leaped on it and smashed the masonry figure to bits with a rock he tore from the temple.

14. Sacalum is suggested to have been in what is now southern Quintana Roo near its boundary with Campeche. See Scholes and Roys (1948, map 4); J. E. S. Thompson (1977, 11). Jones (1989, 175) suggests it may have been at what later was known as Chichanhá.

15. Jones (1989, chap. 6).

16. Jones (1989, 186).

17. In fact, between the 1630s and 1650s virtually all of the Indians in the Bacalar vicinity ran away. See Jones (1982a, 1989) and Scholes and Thompson (1977).

18. Ancona (1889, 2:204–16); Scholes and Thompson (1977); additional material in Means (1917) and Villagutierre Soto-Mayor (1983). Scholes and Adams (1936) treat the massacre at Sacalum. The entire series of episodes is in Jones (1989, chaps. 5–7).

19. Among these pueblos was one Chanchanhá, which has been taken by a number of students to be the later Santa Clara Chichanhá (e.g., Gerhard 1979, 71; Jones

1989, 329, n. 31). Although Gerhard (1979, 71) refers to the settlement as Santa Rosa Chanchanhá, Jones (1989, 254), citing a *matrícula* of 1687, specifies it as Santa Clara Chanchanhá. By 1696 it was abandoned (e.g., Avendaño 1987, 56; Means 1917, 254), possibly as the population scattered in the aftermath of a native uprising quashed sometime in the 1690s (Molina Solís 1904–13, 2:349, referring to Chichanhá); but see Jones (1989, 331, n. 68), who states the population was moved to Dzibalchén. In any event, early in the eighteenth century Santa Clara Chichanhá was established or reestablished as a reduction of Maya southwest of Bacalar (e.g., Molina Solís 1904–13, 3:8–9). Whether or not the site was identical to that of Chanchanhá, the general region was clearly the same.

20. Ancona (1889, vol. 2, bk. 4, chaps. 8–10).

21. Jones (1989, chaps. 9, 10); Means (1917).

22. Spectacularly portrayed at Classic Palenque in the temples of the Cross and the Foliated Cross and on the sarcophagus beneath the Temple of the Inscriptions. The first two of these are illustrated clearly by J. E. S. Thompson (1970, 208–9). For early opinions regarding the preconquest significance of the cross, see López de Cogolludo (1954, 1:355–59). Most modern opinion holds these cross forms of the pre-Hispanic past to have represented conventionalized trees, associated with the four directions and with abundance and related to the rain gods or Chacs, which in some cases were shown perched in them. That the preconquest cross was as important symbolically in Yucatan as the Christian cross came to be, however, is doubtful. Aspects of preconquest religion are summarized by D. E. Thompson (1954, 7–10); J. E. S. Thompson (1970). In addition to directional trees that look like crosses, Mayan religious elements of formal similarity to Christianity included confession, baptism, fasting, the use of incense and sanctified water, and the presence of a complex and organized priesthood.

23. Carrillo y Ancona (1895, 41, 79, 88–90, 286).

24. Carrillo y Ancona (1895, 119).

25. Baqueiro Anduze (1943, 47–48).

26. Heavy use of the cross is not confined to either Yucatan or to the Maya. See Lyon (1971, 1:79).

27. For Inquisition cases conducted by Diego de Landa, see Scholes and Adams (1938, vol. 1); Scholes and Roys (1938); and D. E. Thompson (1954). Although the accounts reported have been questioned because of Landa's enthusiastic employment of torture in extracting them, Scholes and Roys (1938) conclude that they are substantially true.

28. For example, Redfield and Villa Rojas (1962, 110–11).

29. Gerhard (1979, 57–61).

30. Ferrer de Mendiolea (1977, 599–606).

31. Gerhard (1979, map 4; 70); Liss (1983, 7, 26).

32. Dobson (1973, 59, 69); Ferrer de Mendiolea (1977, 517); Gerhard (1979, 70).

33. Dobson (1973, 69–79). The folklore with regard to the name *Belize* is that it was a corruption of the surname of the freebooter Peter Wallace (a person of whom there is apparently no historical record), and the Yucatecans have often written the name as Wallix (see Dobson 1973, 51). J. E. S. Thompson (1963, 71–72) suggests that the origin lay with the Yucatec Maya word *beliz*, signifying muddy. An attractive possibility, however, is the French *balise*, beacon (e.g., Fowler 1879, 38). One cannot but be struck by the similarities in conformation between the protruding, silt-constructed mouth of the Belize River at Belize City and the Mississippi delta with its ancient Fort Balise or Balize. The fact that a substantial proportion of the Baymen apparently originated in the English colonies of North America (Liss 1983, 26) does not detract from this last possibility.

34. Liss (1983, 5).

35. Liss (1983, 26–28), who also reports that logwood, transshipped to England, was second in value only to tobacco as an export commodity of the English North American colonies (Liss 1983, 257, n. 16, with references).

36. Suárez Molina (1977a, 2:31–33); see also Ancona (1889, 4:221–22, 379); Anonymous (1866); Simpson (1966, 199).

2. Governing for God and King

1. Indian slavery under the Montejos in Yucatan is discussed by Chamberlain (1948, 22, 161–62, 250–51).

2. Shifting cultivation in the Maya region is referred to all too consistently in the literature as *milpa* agriculture, with *milpa* used as a synonym for a field cleared by burning, that is, a swidden. This is semantically unfortunate: milpa, from Nahuatl *milli* (cultivated field) plus a postposition (signifying "on"), has come in Mexican Spanish to signify simply *cornfield*, particularly that of an individual subsistence farmer. Thus, it is any cornfield of such a farmer, no matter how farmed, whether burned from the forest, permanently cultivated by rainfall, or irrigated (e.g., Santamaría 1959, s.v. "milpa").

3. Morley (1947, 142–50) provides a classic description.

4. For instance, Harrison and Turner (1978); Flannery (1982).

5. After the conquest, the designations of these lineages were used as the individual surnames, allowing the Maya to resist the wholesale adoption of Spanish family names.

6. This congregation policy was chiefly for religious reasons, whereas *encomenderos* opposed it, fearing the loss of agricultural efficiency and thus income (Farriss 1984, 159–63).

7. See Farriss (1978).

8. Gerhard (1979, 29).

9. See, for instance, Roys (1933, 201–3).

10. Scholes and Roys (1938).

11. D. E. Thompson (1954, 23–30).

12. Roys (1933, 201–3), citing López de Cogolludo.

13. *Encomenderos* were prohibited from living in their *encomienda* pueblos; *encomiendas* could be held within a single family no more than three generations, when they would be reassigned to other *encomenderos* or to the crown; and all tribute was collected by impersonal government agents who remitted the proceeds to the holder of the *encomienda* (Chamberlain 1948, 287–307, 337–43). Much the same ground is covered succinctly by Gerhard (1979).

14. For the Indian *república* organization see, especially, Farriss (1984, 231–37), who argues for the de facto local selection of the *gobernador*, and Roys (1943, 134). Gerhard (1972, 10–17) describes the Spanish organization. Patch (1993, 137) cogently recognizes the two as estates.

15. Roys (1972, 134).

16. Farris (1984) argues that the Yucatec Maya drew on behavior patterns of pre-Spanish times to approach survival under colonial rule as a "collective enterprise" to a greater degree than did, say, people of highland central Mexico. Without contesting this, I must still remark that the Spanish colonial institution of the autonomous *república de indígenas*—its members segregated socially, administratively, and often spatially from *vecino* society for centuries—could hardly have been more perfectly designed to create and maintain a sense of collectivity, whether or not one had existed before. Patch (1993, 25–26) stresses the persistence of native social stratification.

17. These developments are discussed succinctly by Gerhard (1979, 17–20).

18. The often confusing information regarding tribute and taxes is set out most coherently for the Indian population by Farriss (1984, 39–42, table 1.1). See also García Bernal (1972, 100–103, 1978, 184–85), Patch (1993, 25–29, 231), Pérez Martinez (1938), Sierra O'Reilly (1954). The overall total per family was apparently higher in Yucatan than in many parts of Mexico (Bracamonte y Sosa 1993, 20).

19. Baqueiro Anduze (1943, 210–12).

20. Farriss (1984, 47–49).

21. Farriss (1984, 44); Patch (1993, 31).

22. Such attempts were said to be responsible for many of the defections from pueblos in western and southwestern Yucatan in the seventeenth century that I referred to earlier (Scholes and Roys 1948, 305–10).

23. Gibson (1964, 154–57) describes the situation in central Mexico. Although it has been commonly presumed that the same obtained in Yucatan (e.g., Roys 1972,

chap. 15), Farriss (1984, chap. 8) suggests that members of the native nobility in Yucatan did not fare as well as those in Mexico.

24. Treated at length in Scholes and Roys (1948, 175–76, 230–33, 256–58).

25. Baqueiro Anduze (1943, 77).

26. Farriss (1984, 174, 439, n. 44; 467, n. 24).

27. Farriss (1984, 70; 429, n. 45).

28. For example, Roys (1933). Early literacy in Maya is referred to by Cantón Rosado (1943, 17–18), Farriss (1984, 97), and Martínez Parédez (1967, 32).

29. Farriss (1984, 111).

30. See, for example, the dance at Nohcacab described by Stephens (1963, 1:231).

31. For instance, Stephens (1963, 1:137) describes an incident in which Indians who were not hacienda servants respectfully and automatically approached to pick the burrs from D. Simón Peón's feet when he threw himself into a hammock and extended his legs.

32. Farriss (1984, 44). One of the whippings is described by Stephens (1963, 1:82).

33. *Los indios no oigan si no por las nalgas*, the translation corrected slightly from Stephens (1963, 1:82).

34. Redfield (1938); the selection quoted is from page 521.

3. Changing with Time

1. This section largely follows Farriss (1984, 104–11), who beautifully documents the blurring of the line between *indio* and *vecino*.

2. Santamaría (1959, s.v. "naborí").

3. Cook and Borah (1974, 86).

4. Farriss (1984, 111–12) discusses the failure of Spanish to supplant the Maya language. Stephens (1963, 1:231) describes a rural, Maya-speaking *vecino* society in the mid-nineteenth century. Regarding literacy, it is significant that the printing press was not introduced into Yucatan until 1813.

5. Gibson (1964, 154, 197) describes the situation in Mexico. Chamberlain (1948, 339), Patch (1993, 230), and Roys (1972, 148–49) take this to apply to Yucatan. Farriss (1984, 229, 443, n. 87) argues from records of persons who claimed this status and the very sporadic occurrence of *hidalgos* in Yucatecan pueblos that the origin of the *indios hidalgos* lay with Mexican Indians, such as those who accompanied Montejo in his final triumph (Chamberlain 1948, 184). But in the two colonial period Yucatecan name lists available to me in which *hidalgos* are clearly identified forty-five males of only nine names are enumerated—six of them of Maya (not Mexican) origin and three of Spanish. Although one of the pueblos is in western Yucatan, the other is far to the east, a place that seems unlikely as a settlement for Indian allies of the conquerers; the lists are those abstracted by Dumond and Dumond

(1982: 95, 301) for the following unpublished documents: Homún in 1803 (document 18–7) and Xcan in 1805 (document 58–3). Baqueiro Anduze (1943, 77) mentions that eastern *caciques* who helped the Spanish quell an Indian rebellion in 1559 or 1560 were designated *hidalgos conquistadores de la tierra*, although he provides no references.

6. Patch (1993, 137) provides a succinct statement of the situation.

7. Redfield (1938, 522).

8. Mixing has been traditionally recognized. Ancona (1889, 4:13, n. 3) points out that the common mixed offspring of whites were classed as "white" and asserts that as a class the Indians had maintained greater racial purity. Much more recently, Farriss (1984, 485, n. 9) reports having "seen no one designated as an Indian in a colonial document who did not bear a Maya surname, except among indios hidalgos," who should be classed with *vecinos* if not otherwise set apart from Indians. This is surprising, given the other information regarding the blurring of the ethnic boundary that is drawn from her work and used in this section.

9. Strict patrilineal inheritance alone would maintain a perfect coincidence of Indian name and Indian civil status, regardless of the amount of intermarriage. Thus, either inheritance rules were violated or, at least as probable, some landed Indians tended with time to gravitate into the *vecino* category, while poor mestizos tended to move downward. That the upwardly mobile Indian-named persons of table 2 were not all descended from the Mexican Indian allies of the original conquistadors is indicated by the fact that seventeen of the nineteen different Indian names among male *vecinos* are Maya in origin, the most common and most widespread (eighteen individuals in five parishes) being Pech, followed by Chan, Cupul, and Tun. Only three individuals hold the two names of probable Nahua origin, and one of these (Miz, probably cognate to Nahuatl *miztli*, of two individuals in one parish) is said by Roys (1940) to be well integrated as a Maya word and hence may be a borrowing from long before the conquest.

10. Caution is necessary, for the two samples (relating name to civil status and comparing names of spouses) are not entirely comparable. In the first, the proportion of Indian names for both men and women is about 82 percent of the total sample. This is probably generally representative of rural areas; the Indian population of all Yucatan around 1800 is said to have constituted three-fourths of the total but 85 percent in more rural areas (Cook and Borah 1974, table 1.8). In the second sample, the Indian-named individuals amount to about 91 percent of the total and may be less representative. The effect of the differences is impossible to assess, although it must be observed with regard to the second that a reduction of the Indian population to 80 percent of the total should serve to *increase* the percentage of Maya-named individuals with Spanish-named spouses.

11. Gerhard 1979, 62–63. There are other compilations, as, for instance, in Farriss (1984, table 2.1, with references), but the two shown here are adequate for present purposes.

12. For single compilations covering comparable spans of time in central Mexico see, for example, Dumond (1976); Gibson (1964, 136–44); Sanders (1970). Works by Sherburne Cook and Woodrow Borah, which many accept as standard, generally focus upon shorter periods (e.g., Cook and Borah 1960).

13. Patch (1993, 42–43) points out that recovery in Yucatan was delayed by the introduction of yellow fever in the mid-seventeenth century.

14. Farriss (1984, 61–62) presents these data, accepting a population minimum in the eighteenth century.

15. This section draws on the excellent summaries by Patch (1985, 1993).

16. This section follows Farris (1984, chap. 12) and Liss (1983, chaps. 3, 4).

17. Ancona (1889, 3:129, 228–29).

18. Farriss (1984, 368–70).

19. Patch (1993, 187–88) discusses the reasoning behind the bishop's efforts.

20. Farriss (1984, table 12.2).

21. Farriss (1984, 279–84).

22. For example, Cook and Borah (1974, table 1.14).

23. This series of events is set out by Ancona (1889, vol. 3, bk. 6, chaps. 2–4) and Sierra O'Reilly (1954, vol. 2); both reproduce the decree of November 9, 1812.

24. Based on twelve reports from nine parishes, dated between February 5 and June 15, 1814, evidently written in response to a request from the bishop for information regarding the impacts of the decree of November 1812. All parishes but one reported virtually no attendance at catechism class. All parishes except for three—and all parishes located from Izamal eastward—reported significant decreases in attendance at Mass, as well as some emigration to the *monte* or bush. All reported that if the services of the supporting staff of Indian workers in the churches were retained at all, it was only by excusing the functionaries and their families from all church fees. Only one parish reported relatively normal church services, and it was located the farthest west. The most consistently reported impact in addition to loss of catechism students was the absence of any personal service in the priest's quarters. There were also reports of Indians leaving the haciendas and moving into the pueblos or wherever else they wished (Dumond and Dumond 1982, pt. 2, document nos. 3-6, 14-5, 20-5, 22-1, 27-3, 47-4, 52-2, 54-1, 59-4).

25. Ancona (1889, 3:70); the decree is quoted in full by Sierra O'Reilly (1954, 2:105–6).

26. Ancona (1889, 3:75–102).

27. This section follows Ancona (1889, vol. 3).

28. The arguments are spelled out by Humphreys (1961).

29. In the Yucatec orthography devised by the Spanish, the letter *c* is pronounced hard like the English *k*, hence the two writings yield the same pronunciation.

30. Although *de los Santos* is positioned like a maternal surname, it could scarcely be that here: in the 1760s such maternal names were seldom used anywhere in Mexico except by the highest of nobles, and they were even less common in Yucatan and essentially nonexistent among its Indians. Such a maternal name would indicate a Spanish-named mother, which is most unlikely; its meaning accords perfectly with that of the rest of the string of titles.

31. Sierra O'Reilly (1954, 2:28) reports that "more than 100" were flogged. He adds that except for the eight who were hanged, the real coconspirators were put to the sword as they were captured and that the mass of captives who were flogged were innocents who were dragged in through the malevolence of the military force. Patch (1993, 228) states that 258 people were sentenced, although their precise relationships to events at Cisteil are unclear.

32. The best single compilation of various sources of information on the Cisteil revolt and its aftermath is Bartolomé (1978). A straightforward account is in Huerta and Palacios (1976, 174–90), based largely on Ríos (1940). Additional discussion is in Sierra O'Reilly (1954, 2). All of these were taken into account here, together with the treatments by Farriss (1984, 68–72) and Patch (1993, 228–29), which draw upon other material in Spanish archives. The punishment meted out to Canek himself was apparently not unheard of for unrepentant witches tried by the Inquisition. Although the intent was evidently to eradicate the village of Cisteil from the world, it has been occupied in modern times (see Pacheco Cruz 1959, 70).

33. When on my way to London to examine records of the British Colonial Office, I was asked by a Yucatecan acquaintance of historical bent if I would look up material relating to the 1760s because he was sure the genesis of the Cisteil revolt must somehow lie with the colonists of British Honduras. I can say categorically, however, that there is no indication in those records that anyone in eighteenth-century British Honduras ever heard of Cisteil, of Canek, or of his rebellious actions.

4. Strains of Independence

1. Cline (1950, 572).

2. Cline (1950, 565–68, 571–86); for the location of sugarcane plantations, see Suárez Molina (1977a, 1:169).

3. Cline (1950, 515, 519–22).

4. Ancona (1889, 3:128–31).

5. Ancona (1889, 3:259); González Navarro (1970, 54–56).

6. Baqueiro (1878–87, 1:20–21).

7. Ancona (1889, 3:283–86).

8. Ancona (1889, 3: chap. 3).

9. Ancona (1889, 3:303–7); Cline (1950, 568, 602, n. 54); González Navarro (1970, 54–55).

10. Ancona (1889, 3:318–20, 358).

11. Ancona (1889, 3:335).

12. Ancona (1889, 3:346–47).

13. Ancona (1889, 3:350–52). Apparently one of the measures negated was an act of 1832 in which forced labor had been abolished as a part of the obventions (Cline 1950, 602–3, n. 54).

14. Baqueiro (1978–87, 1:35, n. 1).

15. Ancona (1889, 3:358–62).

16. F. Cámara Zavala (1975, 50).

17. Ancona (1889, 3:363–67). Among those arrested with Imán at Izamal were Eulogio Rosado and Felipe de la Cámara Zavala, although they were not imprisoned (Baqueiro Anduze 1943, 228–29).

18. Ancona (1889, 3:367). Baqueiro (1878–87, 1:31) indicates that he also promised diminution of civil contributions and some distribution of land.

19. According to a contemporary who later achieved military fame, Vito Pacheco was a professional smuggler, wanted for murder, who joined Imán (to escape punishment, of which more later) at the head of a band of men as depraved as himself; Vicente Revilla was a military deserter who was "as active and brave as he was vicious, thievish, and bad," who led other deserters (F. Cámara Zavala 1975, 50). Pastor Gamboa was alleged to have an undeserved reputation for valor, with "under his orders 300 Indians . . . of pure race" (F. Cámara Zavala 1975, 51). Baqueiro (1878–87, 1:26–27) confirms these opinions and adds that Gamboa, too, was a military deserter.

20. Ancona (1889, 3:368–69).

21. Ancona (1889, 3:371–79).

22. Ancona (1889, 3:383); Aznar Pérez (1849–51, 1:316–17); Baqueiro Anduze (1943, 238).

23. Ancona (1889, 3:388).

24. Cline (1950, 571).

25. Ancona (1889, 3:383).

26. Anonymous (1866, 74–76). Rugeley (1992, 370–72) provides background information regarding the family of Jacinto Pat and his position at Tihosuco.

27. Ancona (1889, 3:397).

28. Ancona (1889, 3:390–92).

29. Ancona (1889, 3:393).

30. Andrés Quintana Roo (1787–1851), born in Mérida; educated in Mexico; fled to the insurgents of the war of independence as did his sweetheart, Leona Vicario, among whom they married; held posts under Iturbide and President Guadalupe Victoria; was elected to congress to represent the State of Mexico and was appointed to the cabinet of Santa Anna. The ashes of Quintana Roo and Leona Vicario are among those now preserved beneath the Monument to Independence ("La Angelita") on the Paseo de la Reforma in Mexico DF. (Rubio Mañé 1977). The account of negotiations with Quintana Roo and his successor is from Ancona (1889, 3:402–9).

31. For offers of land, see Cline (1950, 574); González Navarro (1970, 71–72).

32. Ancona (1889, 3:412–16); Baqueiro (1978–87, 1:85).

33. Ancona (1889, 3:417–18).

34. Ancona (1889, 3:421–23).

35. Aznar Pérez (1849–51, 2:238); Cline (1950, 573).

36. Aznar Pérez (1849–51, 2:240–42).

37. Ancona (1889, 3:430–33).

38. Baqueiro (1878–87, 1:111–12); see also Ancona (1889, 3:433, n. 2). The nameless boy was said to have been given a tip.

39. Ancona (1889, 3:433–37).

40. Ancona (1889, 3:438–40).

41. Aznar Pérez (1849–51, 2:245–49); Cline (1954, 605, n. 57; 633, n. 86).

42. Aznar Pérez (1849–1851, 2:499); González Navarro (1970, 72).

43. Anonymous (1866, 77–86).

44. Ancona (1889, 3:441); Baqueiro (1878–87, 1:125).

45. Cline (1950, 522).

46. Ancona (1889, 3:442–45). That contraband was involved in some of these products can hardly be doubted, given Yucatan's still booming trade with English merchants in the Caribbean; nevertheless, all of the products questioned were also produced in some quantity in Yucatan.

47. Aznar Pérez (1849–51, 2:352–53); Cline (1950, 605).

48. Aznar Pérez (1849–51, 2:484); Cline (1950, 576–86).

49. Ancona (1889, 3:445–52).

50. Baqueiro (1878–87, 1:122–23) states emphatically that this went beyond competitiveness to involve "savage hate and barbarous rancor." In his sketch of the normal characters of the two, northern Mérida is represented as more relaxed and genteel, southern Campeche as more aggressive—reversing exactly the regional stereotypes of northerners and southerners of eastern North America. Baqueiro himself was a son of the Campeche hinterland.

51. Juan Vázquez would serve long enough with the Yucatecan army in the developing Caste War to gain (with Trujeque) the special enmity of the rebels, only

to be shot by a Yucatecan force in questionable circumstances (Baqueiro 1978–87, 1:437). Bonifacio Novelo would live, though not peacefully, much longer as a rebel commander. His Spanish name marking him as a probable *vecino*, he was reputedly a mestizo or mulatto (Rugeley 1992, 385). A young Englishman who met him in his later years described him as "of a lighter shade of color than the generality of the Indians" (J. Carmichael to Supt. of British Honduras, Nov. 15, 1867, ABH, R93).

52. Anonymous (1866, 87–93); see also Baqueiro (1878–87, 1:163–64).

53. Ancona (1889, 3:457–58); Baqueiro (1878–87, 1:154).

54. Ancona (1889, 3:460); Baqueiro (1878–87, 1:155–56).

55. Ancona (1889, 3:461–66); Anonymous (1866, 94–95).

56. Baqueiro (1878–87, 1:164).

57. Ancona (1889, 3:466).

58. Baqueiro (1978–87, 1:122–23, 179). A nineteenth-century writer and observer of his time put his observations into fiction set nearly two centuries earlier (Sierra O'Reilly 1950, 1:160):

In the villa de Valladolid there gathered a short time after the conquest the . . . cream of the adventurers who carried out that labor; and although they were . . . simple soldier-folk and not very well bred as we say, . . . finding themselves suddenly with vast productive lands and many slaves, seeing themselves as great lords, they forgot their humble origin. . . . Each *regidor* of the cabildo considers himself as noble and high as the King, speaks with an air of authority to everyone, disdaining any type of honest and productive employment and believes that he was born only to govern the rest, to fritter away the revenues of his encomiendas, to order Indians flogged at the stake, to train cocks.

59. Ancona (1889, 3:467–69); Baqueiro (1878–87, 1:167–69). A letter from an unnamed witness is quoted by Baqueiro, describing Indians among the attackers as dancing around the bonfires and occasionally eating the burning flesh. There are several accounts of very early events in the Caste War in which Indian raiders reportedly sacrificed victims in ancient ways or engaged in cannibalism. Otherwise, in the mass of descriptions dating from throughout the war, there are no verifiable stories of either pre-Spanish-style sacrificial killings or of cannibalism by the rebels (although there were atrocities aplenty on both sides). One concludes that anecdotes of such happenings are simply an indication of the nineteenth-century Yucatecan view that if Indians rebelled they must be barbarians. Although perhaps in fact descriptive, Ancona's repeated use of the word *chusma*, rabble, to describe Trujeque's force, smacks of the same.

60. Baqueiro (1878–87, 1:180).

61. Ancona (1889, 3:469); Baqueiro (1878–87, 1:169).

62. Ancona (1889, 3:469–71).

63. Baqueiro (1878–87, 1:182).

5. Year of Turmoil

1. Rodríguez Losa (1985, tables 8, 9). Figures are missing for Mérida, Campeche, and Bacalar, and are projected from other years to achieve the total given; the actual 1821 figure without the three missing *villas* is 486,931.

2. Regil and Peón (1853, 289–93, table C), who point out that between 1826 and 1833 smallpox and cholera epidemics carried off more than one hundred thousand people.

3. Cook and Borah (1974, table 1.16) for the higher figure; Baqueiro (1881, 143–44) and Rodríguez Losa (1978, 161) accept the lower.

4. Ideally, rather than a projection from figures for 1821 the actual figures of 1846 (Regil and Peón 1853, table C) should be used in table 4. Unfortunately, the base areas for the 1846 presentation of Regil and Peón are large districts that combine the older *partidos* in such a way that the east, for instance, is lumped with the very densely populated Sierra and makes questionable any separation of figures by smaller areas.

5. The reservations expressed with respect to the use of the actual 1846 figures in table 4 also apply here. The present result is not changed if the figures in column b are increased by 6.77 percent, as was done in the projection for table 4.

6. See also Patch (1993, 118, 152).

7. Patch (1991, 69–74, table 3.3), who concludes that if recording omissions are corrected the total should reach at least eight hundred thousand hectares. Because of recurrent changes in both names and limits of administrative subdivisions after the end of the colonial period, it is awkward to correlate those of 1800 with those of 1847. For simplicity, I use only the designations current at about 1800, which involve a conversion from those used by Patch.

8. For similar taxes on Indians before independence, see Farriss (1984, table 1.1 and related text).

9. Obventions had been abolished in 1843 (Aznar Perez 1849–51, 2:249; Cline 1950, 605, n. 57); although the situation is less clear with regard to tithes, they were apparently not being collected after about 1840 (see Cline 1950, 603, n. 54).

10. Cline (1950, 608).

11. Cline (1950, 606–7).

12. Cline (1950, 524).

13. Ancona (1889, 3:472–73).

14. See Baqueiro (1878–87, 1:181–82, 186), who also reports that when the *barbachanistas* regained power in 1848 Trujeque was jailed and then exiled.

15. Baqueiro (1878–87, 1:190–99, 332–33), who adds simply "that's the way things were done in those days."

16. Ancona (1889, 3:478–80); Baqueiro (1878–87, 1:201–11). Reportedly signing his name *Zetina*—possibly so it would be pronounced properly in Yucatan, where *c* was so often sounded as *k*—his official documents are said to have spelled his surname *Cetina*, and so is it entered in most of the histories (F. Cámara Zavala 1975, 47, n. 11). At the time of the *pronunciamento* he was *primer ayudante*, a staff rank equivalent to major, the ranking officer in the insurrection.

17. Baqueiro (1878–87, 1:212–13).

18. Ancona (1889, 3:481–83); Baqueiro (1878–87, 1:214–26). For further discussion of the Sierra mission, see Pérez Martínez (1938, xvii–l).

19. Baqueiro (1878–87, 1:226–27).

20. The letter quoted by Baqueiro (1878–87, 1:228) is as follows:

*Tepich, Julio de 1847.—Sr. D. Manuel Antonio Ay.—*Muy Señor mi amigo, hágame Usté favor de decirme gatos pueblos hay avisados para el caso, para que usté me diga gando—Item quiero que usté me diga si es mejoro mi intento es atracar á Tihosuco para que tengamos toda provision, hasí aguardo la respuesta para mi gobierno, me dice usté ó me señala usté el dia en que usté ha de venir aca conmigo, porque aca me están siguiendo el bulto, por eso se lo digo á usté, me arusté el favor deavisarme dos ó tres dias ántes, no dejuste de contestarme no soy yo mas que su amigo que lestima—*Cecilio Chi.*

The copy reportedly found among Rosado's papers (Asociación Cívica Yucatán 1956, 11) differs in punctuation, in its correction of apparent illiteracies (e.g., *usté* is written *usted*, etc.), and particularly in that *avisado* of the Baqueiro account is rendered *aviado*, *provisión* is *población*, and *atracar* is given as *atacar*. Bricker (1981, 96) makes a point of this last discrepancy, raising the possibility that Rosado may have altered the letter for his own ends, as she renders *atracar* as "to approach" and contrasts it with *atacar* "to attack." But the same word (by a different etymology) means also "to waylay, to hold up, to attack" (Real Academia Española 1956, s.v. "atracar"; see also the same entry in Smith, Bermejo Marcos, and Chang-Rodriguez 1971). This second usage is much closer to that common in Mexico, where *atracar* simply means "to fight hand to hand" (Santamaría 1959, s.v. "atracar"). It is clear that both Baqueiro and Rosado understood the letter in evidence to mean that Chi meant to raid Tihosuco.

21. Asociación Cívica Yucatán (1956, 17).

22. The most complete account of Ay's treatment is Asociación Cívica Yucatán (1956). There is also a tradition set out in the histories that while he was held in prison before his death Ay acknowledged his guilt and foretold the horrors of the Caste War in a poetic speech to his son. The speech, ostensibly quoted verbatim by Baqueiro (1878–87, 1:231–32) but not mentioned in the papers of the time (Asociación Cívica

Yucatán 1956), smacks of journalistic creation. As of the 1990s, the Plaza of Santa Ana supports a monument to the *Niños Héroes*, those Mexican military cadets who fought to the death at the Castle of Chapultepec against invading North Americans during the war with the United States and with which the Yucatecan youths among them are immortalized. There is no remembrance in the plaza of Manuel Antonio Ay, who is banished from history.

23. Baqueiro (1878–87, 1:225–26); there is a mispagination in the volume; these are the second pages numbered 225–26.

24. Baqueiro (1878–87, 1:235–39) is followed for most details. A record of the testimony of the five prisoners (C. Carrillo, "Sumario de los cinco cabesillas fusilados el 30 de julio," Aug. 14, 1847, Archivo General del Estado de Yucatan, Gobierno), for which I am indebted to Victoria R. Bricker, modified some aspects (see also Bricker 1981, 97). One is inclined to be suspicious of the prisoners' accounts because of their extremely detailed agreement with one another and because four of the five stated that as a byproduct of their raids they would kill all white men, preserve the white women and "marry" them, and keep any female issue from such unions as their servants.

25. The account and dates are from Baqueiro (1878–87, 1:252–57), who also reports that the description of Ongay's treatment of Tepich is from an eyewitness.

26. The attackers were said to have cut out the victim's heart in the ancient manner, to have eaten it, and to have drunk his blood. This tradition (Baqueiro 1878–79, 1:257–58; see also Ancona 1889, 4:41–42) is based on words of the proprietress and mother of the boy when quoted in a newspaper. As I noted earlier, reports of behavior harking to pre-Hispanic days are so limited as to render suspect the very few that exist. The majority of Yucatecans were convinced of the barbarity of Indians, particularly of the eastern Indians, and most particularly of Indians who illustrated their savagery by the act of rebelling.

27. Ancona (1889, 4:34–36); Baqueiro (1878–87, 1:258–62). As will be seen, such arms as were not captured by the rebels from the Yucatecan forces were indeed acquired from dealers who operated from British territory, although not at this date with the sanction of the Belize government—despite Yucatecan accusations to the contrary. After the defeat of Napoleon, surplus British flintlock muskets of the "Brown Bess" pattern were made widely available, with many of them sold to Mexico (e.g., Caravaglia and Worman 1984, 73; Fuentes 1983, 208), and were probably an important if not the major small arm of the Yucatecan constabulary. Sale of these was presumably intensified sometime after 1840, as the British army completed its conversion to muskets ignited by the metal percussion cap (H. Rogers 1960, 172–75).

28. Ancona (1889, 4:5–15, 32–33); Baqueiro (1878–87, 1:263–64).

29. Baqueiro (1878–87, 1:241–42).

30. Baqueiro (1878–87, 1:245, 252).

31. Poot's biographer (Baqueiro 1887) reports that Poot's mother was widowed before his birth and that the son took her surname, and he also indicates that Poot was handsome, exceptionally tall and well built, and unusually dark even for a sunburned Indian. In the course of Poot's career a Belizean of color reported him to be "a black man" (J. H. Faber to F. Seymour, Dec. 10, 1857, ABH, R58), and an Indian woman described him as heavy in body and "in color almost black" (statement of Monica May, J. Carbó dispatch, Aug. 1, RP, Aug. 5, 1874, 1). I presume him to have been mulatto.

32. Ancona (1889, 4:36–37); Baqueiro (1878–87, 1:244–46).

33. Baqueiro (1878–87, 1:247–50).

34. Baqueiro (1978–87, 1:271).

35. Baqueiro (1978–87, 1:275–76, emphasis his).

36. Baqueiro (1878–87, 1:264–72); see also Ancona (1889, 1:37–45).

37. Ancona (1889, 4:46–50). The date is mentioned by Baqueiro (1978–87, 1:281).

38. Ancona (1889, 4:51); for Poot's involvement see Baqueiro (1887).

39. Ancona (1989, 4:51; Baqueiro (1878–87, 1:292).

40. Ancona (1889, 4:52–55).

41. Ancona (1889, 4:55–56).

42. Ancona (1889, 4:57). Cetina's actions served to further Indian successes in the east, whatever may have been his intention. One of his youthful companions in liberal politics described him as "a young man of exalted passions, of strong impressions, who developed without that restraint so indispensable to men that is called education; rather, there grew strong in him that will of the spirit which in some men is tumultuous and disordered, and which—better directed—would have made of him a man of promise, perhaps of much utility to society," and added "it may be that time and age will correct this defect" (F. Cámara Zavala 1975, 23). Although it seems amazing that he was not hanged or shot for one or another of his mutinous involvements, he was declared *Benemérito* by the state congress following his death from natural causes in 1863 (Civeira Taboada 1975, 8, misquoting a portion of the passage just given).

43. Ancona (1889, 4:81–82).

44. Ancona (1889, 4:60–62, 81–83).

45. Secretary General of Yucatan to Superintendent of British Honduras, Dec. 31, 1847, ABH, R28.

46. Ancona (1889, 4:64; Aznar Pérez (1849–51, 3:182); LU (Jan. 29, 1848).

47. Ancona (1889, 4:67); Baqueiro (1878–79, 1:314–17).

48. Ancona (1889, 4:81–88).

49. Ancona (1889, 4:66).

50. Baqueiro (1878–87, 1:318). See also Ancona (1889, 4:66–67).

51. Baqueiro (1878–79, 1:319–20).

52. Ancona (1889, 4:69).

53. Baqueiro (1878–87, 1:301).

54. Baqueiro (1878–87, 1:318). That the region between Peto and Sacsucil was *barbachanista* country is implied by the fact that the intervening pueblo traditionally designated Dzitnup (see the Hübbe and Aznar map of 1878 [Berendt 1879]) was labeled *Barbachano* in the 1848 map of Regil and Peon (1853).

55. Ancona (1889, 4:69–70); Baqueiro (1878–87, 1:319–22). Duarte, a man with both real property and a lucrative mercantile business at Peto, was understandably distraught, but when Peto was retaken by the government the following year his property was among the small minority that had remained undisturbed, apparently respected by the rebels. When Duarte applied for its return, however, he was refused on the ground that it was war booty, and it was sold for the benefit of the government (Montilla Duarte 1955, 156, quoting other sources). His substantial fortune nearly eliminated, Duarte relocated in Tekax and entered business again, where over the next decade he recovered financially, and whence more will be heard of him.

56. Baqueiro (1878–87, 1:331).

6. Peace and War

1. There is no demographic information directly applicable to the rebels, of course. As I noted earlier, the population of Yucatan had been increasing extremely slowly through the 1840s, at a rate that apparently did not exceed 0.2 percent per year. In northern British Honduras, a region populated largely by Indian and other immigrants from eastern Yucatan, the life expectancy at birth in 1891 was somewhat less than twenty years (e.g., information from the 1891 census [CG, Mar. 16, 1895, 2–3] and in tables published as the *British Honduras Gazette*, 1894). A population with these characteristics—approximately stationary, with life expectancy at birth of around 20 years—can be expected to have roughly a third of its total population composed of males age fifteen or older (e.g., Coale and Demeny 1983, Model West, levels 1–3). Thus, under the fullest mobilization, one-third of the rebel population might conceivably have been active as soldiers, although a smaller proportion— perhaps one-fourth—seems more likely.

2. Villa Rojas (1945) in the 1930s; Bartolomé and Barabas (1977) in the 1970s. The description of the military organization and its prototypes is paraphrased from Dumond (1977).

3. Aznar Pérez (1849–51, 1:54–66); Mexico (1829, 134–38); Yucatan (1832, 108–23).

4. Various letters to Superintendent, British Honduras, or to Rev. John Kingdon and others, dated May 11, 1848, to Mar. 22, 1849 (ABH, R28).

5. These divisions were by no means fixed, however, for both Pec and Chi were closely involved in matters at Bacalar in 1849, to judge by their correspondence with the Superintendent and other residents of British Honduras (ABH, R28).

6. As it was rendered by Villa Rojas (1945).

7. For example, Villa Rojas (1945, plate 2b).

8. Villa Rojas (1945).

9. Baqueiro (1878–87, 1:260), paraphrasing Eulogio Rosado.

10. Anonymous (1866, 145–47). This account of the first nineteen years of the Caste War was attributed by the late Professor Antonio Canto López to General José Severo del Castillo, who commanded the military forces in Yucatan in the middle 1860s and authored the novel *Cecilio Chi* (first published in 1869); who was minister of war under Benito Júarez, then chief of staff of the emperor Maximilian, for which he was later imprisoned. Canto's opinion is seconded by Leopoldo Peniche Vallado (1980, 193–96). Careful examination of the anonymous manuscript, however, suggests that there were at least two authors and that one of them—but only one—was of substantial military acumen. It is this latter, whoever he may have been, who penned the words quoted here.

11. Baqueiro (1878–87, 1:338–39, 341, 349, 430).

12. Baqueiro (1978–87, 1:351).

13. Anonymous (1866, 149–51).

14. Fancourt to Alonso Manuel León, Feb. 1, 1848 (ABH, R22b).

15. Baqueiro (1878–87, 1:323, 327–29). Stephens (1963, 1:68–83) presents an engaging literary portrait of Padre Vela, the cura of Tekoh, who was his host in 1841.

16. Ancona (1889, 4:75–78); Baqueiro (1878–87, 1:333–39).

17. This is the brother of Justo Sierra O'Reilly, the author who was son-in-law of Santiago Méndez and at this time was in Washington DC representing Yucatan. See Sierra O'Reilly (1938, 1945).

18. "Bárbaros" (LU, Feb. 19, 1848, 4). There is confusion about dates. Both Ancona (1889, 4:88) and Baqueiro (1878–87, 1:358) correctly place the raid on Chancenote after the verbal presentation of peace conditions and the promise of armistice, which they date as February 13, and both take the raid to be an act of rebel perfidy. But Ancona (1889, 4:88, n. 7) gives the date of the raid as February 12 and Baqueiro (1878–87, 1:359) as February 10. The contemporary official periodical *La Union* specifically dates the attack on February 14, and it is followed here as the most nearly primary of the sources.

19. Baqueiro (1878–87, 1:357–59); "Bárbaros" (LU, Feb. 19 1848, 4).

20. For a translation evidently of Barbachano's letter, see Quintal Martín (1992, letter 4). According to Ancona (1889, 4:250), in 1847 the east (Valladolid area) was commanded by Florentino Chan, the center (Sotuta) by Cecilio Chi, and the south

(Tihosuco) by Jacinto Pat. In the exchanges, Chan and Pat sign a response from Tihosuco, while Chi did not sign any of the letters. Of the three named leaders, then, at least two of them were at Tihosuco, which was by now well away from the active front. The active forces before Valladolid and Sotuta appear to have been led by underlings or at least by others than the known principals. Two months later, Cecilio Chi would appear at Tinum.

21. Baqueiro (1878–87, 1:593–96, also 1:379–80).

22. Baqueiro (1878–87, 1:381–82, 596–97).

23. Baqueiro (1878–87, 1:382–83, 592–93); "Bárbaros" (LU, Feb. 29, 1848, 4).

24. Baqueiro (1978–87, 1:383, 385–86); "Bárbaros" (LU, March 7, 1848, 4); Quintal Martín (1992, letters 5, 6). One of the local whites at the Tzucacab meeting was Juan María Novelo, of whom more will be heard. The letter from Manuel Ignacio Tuz that led to the meeting is the subject of an exciting tale regarding Captain Mariano Ruiz, of Peto, who had volunteered to attempt the way from Tekax through rebel territory to contact Tuz. Captured en route at Tzucacab, Ruiz was released surreptitiously by an Indian friend of long standing and smuggled to Macmay, where Tuz expressed fears for Ruiz's safety because of the many eastern rebels who were about. But Tuz responded in a promising way, and Ruiz then returned to Tekax with Tuz's response to the peace commission, escaping aggressive rebels by passing himself off as engaged on a mission to obtain supplies for Tuz. See "Episodios de la Guerra Social," by B. Cuevas (RM, July 20–21, 1885).

25. Ancona (1889, 4:92–93); Baqueiro (1878–87, 1:366–68).

26. Ancona (1889, 4,78–80); Baqueiro (1878–87, 1:339–43), where there is a difference of opinion, the first giving the date of the siege from February 19–March 3, the second from March 7–10. The Virgin of Tabi had been important to an annual festival in Sotuta, although claimed and housed at Tabi. See Rugeley (1992, 290–93).

27. Baqueiro (1878–87, 1:331–32); "Bárbaros" (LU, Feb. 19, 1848, 4).

28. Ancona (1889, 4:93–94); Baqueiro (1878–87, 1:368–72).

29. Ancona (1889, 4:94–98); Baqueiro (1878–87, 1:372–76).

30. Ancona (1889, 4:97–98); Baqueiro (1878–87, 1:376–78); Sierra O'Reilly (1949, 127, 133, entries for Apr. 21, May 6), the latter referring to the U.S. vessel *Falcon* in particular.

31. Baqueiro (1878–87, 1:432–34). For the modern annual agricultural round at Chan Kom, see Redfield and Villa Rojas (1962, fig. 8). The fiestas at which Padre Sierra served included one for the patron of Tixcacalcupul, where he was invited by the rebel Crescencio Poot. This same part of the year is of ceremonial significance in eastern Yucatan because of the important fiesta for the Holy Cross that is held on May 3 (ibid., 84; Villa Rojas 1945, 125).

32. M. Barbachano to J. Pat, March 18, 1848 (Quintal Martín 1992, letter 7).

33. Baqueiro (1878–87, 1:388–91, 414).

34. Baqueiro (1878–87, 1:387, 391–95).

35. Baqueiro (1878–87, 1:415–16).

36. Baqueiro (1878–87, 1:409–15).

37. Baqueiro (1878–87, 1:416). There may be an error in dating, inasmuch as Baqueiro reports Barrera to have been in company with the commission on April 18 and April 20 but later indicates he was leading a column of rebels on April 19 at Iturbide, seventy-five kilometers to the southwest.

38. Baqueiro (1878–87, 1:416–18).

39. Baqueiro (1878–87, 1:418–19); "Tratado de paz . . ." (LU, Apr. 25, 1848, 4).

40. The full text is in Ancona (1889, 4:415–16).

41. For example, Anonymous (1866, 204–5); Baqueiro (1878–87, 1:420).

42. For example, "Tratado de paz . . ." (LU, Apr. 25, 1848, 4).

43. Ancona (1889, 4:111–12); Baqueiro (1878–87, 1:421); "Escriben de Tekax" (LU, Apr. 29, 1848, 3). According to Baqueiro (1878–87, 2:84–85), José María Barrera was a direct party to the murder of Tuz, although in view of Barrera's repeated contact with Vela, for whom he served as bodyguard, this does not seem credible.

44. Ancona (1889, 4:111); Baqueiro (1878–87, 1:422).

45. Ancona (1889, 4:111); Baqueiro (1878–87, 1:422–24). Baqueiro places this in Peto; Ancona puts it in Tzucacab, while saying the account is from Baqueiro, based on correspondence of rebels.

46. There was misunderstanding as fighting resumed. The Yucatecans saw the raid on Maní and Chi's continued attacks as a violation of the treaty and proof that Pat could not control the rebel forces. But leading officers of Pat's faction, as opposed to others, saw themselves as abiding by the treaty whereas it was the government's resumption of warfare that violated it (e.g., J. M. Barrera and others to J. C. Vela, Apr. 7, 1850 [Quintal Martín 1992, letter 42]).

47. Rugeley (1992, 147, n. 15).

48. "Tratado de paz . . ." (LU, Apr. 25, 1848, 4).

49. One can suggest that the agreement between Barbachano and Pat—calling for the evacuation of Tekax, the promise of 2,500 stand of arms to Pat's party, and the glorification of Pat himself—was intended to induce Pat's well-equipped army of pacified rebels to stand against the forces of Chi and the other leaders. If so, that position was clearly unacceptable to the bulk of Pat's followers.

50. Ancona (1889) vol. 4, 22.7 percent; Baqueiro (1878–87), vols. 1 and 2, 21 percent.

51. Rugeley (1992, 400) admits that "we have underestimated . . . the role of non-Indians in the rebellion" but provides no further resolution, whereas Patch (1993) provocatively demonstrates that later- and post-colonial Yucatecan society included

not only a landed elite and an Indian peasantry but a middle class of small farmers in which Indians and non-Indians were intermixed.

52. For example, see the discussion in Redfield (1938) as well as translations by Bricker (1981, app. A).

53. See compilations in *Diccionario maya Córdemex*, s.v. "masewal," "ts'ul." *Masewal* is a common modern spelling. In Yucatan, the Spanish-derived orthography renders it *mazehual* or *masehual* more often than *macehual* because of the local convention in which, as indicated earlier, *c* is given a hard pronunciation. I eschew the use of the term *ladino* to refer generally to hispanicized individuals for the word has never had that common meaning in Yucatan.

54. Bartolomé and Barabas (1977, 117) report that *mayero* is the term used by the rebel remnants for other Maya Indians of Yucatan—that is, for non-*masewalob*.

55. This view of the Caste War as a campesino rebellion is shared with other revisionists, although it will depart from most of them in still other respects. For a discussion see Joseph (1986, chap. 3, esp. 25–36).

7. Climax

1. Baqueiro (1878–87, 1:339–401). One of the sections was said to be commanded by José María Barrera, but either the report or the dating must be in error for as mentioned earlier he was in or near Tzucacab on both the day before and the day after the raid.

2. Baqueiro (1878–87, 1:402); "Hijo de la Patria" (LU, May 2, 1848, 3).

3. Baqueiro (1878–87, 1:403).

4. Baqueiro (1878–87, 1:404–7).

5. Supt. Fancourt to D. Martínez, and Fancourt to Peña de Loria, Feb. 24, 1848; Fancourt to Major Mends, various letters (ABH, R22b).

6. D. Martínez to Superintendent, Apr. 19, 1848; M. Esteves to superintendent, Apr. 20, 1848 (ABH, R28). W. Glubb to Supt. Fancourt, Apr. 27, 1848 (ABH, R29).

7. Supt. Fancourt to Major Mends, Apr. 23, 1848 (ABH, R22b).

8. Supt. Fancourt to Principal Civil Magistrate of Bacalar, May 9, 1848 (ABH, R22b). This permission for the rebels to trade would be repeatedly cited by Yucatan as evidence of active British aid to the rebellion.

9. C. S. J. Fancourt to Principal Magistrate of Bacalar, June 24, 1848 (ABH, R22b); T. Rhys to H. M. Superintendent, July 4, 1848 (ABH, R29).

10. J. P. Cocom and T. Villanueva to His Excellency, May 6, 1848 (ABH, R29); C. S. J. Fancourt to Principal Magistrate of Bacalar, May 13, 1848; C. S. J. Fancourt to the Chairman of the Public Meeting, July 18, 1848, C. S. J. Fancourt to P. Doyle, Oct. 13, 1848 (ABH, R22b).

11. Ancona (1889, 4:225).

12. H. H. Morant to Messrs. Cox and Lacroix, Dec. 30, 1848 (ABH, R22b); Ancona (1889, 4:225).

13. C. S. J. Fancourt to Principal Magistrate at Bacalar, July 12, 1848; H. H. Morant to Messrs. Cox and Lacroix, Dec. 30, 1848 (ABH, R22b).

14. Baqueiro (1878–87, 1:424–25).

15. Baqueiro (1878–87, 1:426–32). Before Ticul, some rebel Indians paraded wearing women's clothes, dancing to the strumming of guitars, while others who were dressed in European men's clothes—trousers, vest, jacket, and top hat—made broad sport of their enemies in town.

16. Ancona (1889, 4:120–24); Baqueiro (1878–87, 1:432–41).

17. Sierra O'Reilly (1953, 121, 137).

18. For example, a document appended by Reina (1980, 45), which indicates more than three hundred thousand.

19. Baqueiro (1881, 143–44).

20. Baqueiro (1878–87, 1:442).

21. Ancona (1889, 4:133).

22. For example, Bricker (1981, 102); G. D. Jones (1974, 666); Reed (1964, 99).

23. Thompson (1932, 70–71). I find no record that Acanceh was occupied by the rebels, although they must have been within twenty to thirty kilometers of it; nor was there time for feasting between the rebel success at Izamal and the Yucatecan reoccupation and ensuing counterattack. But who would quibble with folklore?

24. Bricker (1981, 102) entertains a similar possibility, attributing it to a suggestion from Philip C. Thompson.

25. F. Martínez de Arredondo to P. Regil y Estrada and J. García Rejón, July 4, 1848 (Baqueiro 1878–87, 2:512–17).

26. Ancona (1889, 4:129–32).

27. They would include, among others, Eligio Ancona (1889), Serapio Baqueiro (1878–87) and the author of the anonymous history used here (Anonymous 1866).

28. In early years, this would include Justo Sierra O'Reilly (1954), whose broad view also took account of many other factors as well. The view has also been expressed by authors such as Hector Pérez Martínez (1938), Antonio Canto López (1976) and Leopoldo Peniche Vallado (1980).

29. Among the more extreme in their blame of British Honduras would be, for instance, Sierra O'Reilly (1954). But see also Joaquín Hübbe (1940).

30. Sierra O'Reilly (1954) was early with such views. After Cline (e.g., 1950), Arnold Strickon (1965) gave an avowedly ecological twist to interpretation, to be followed with the heavily economic approaches of, among others, Moisés González Navarro (1970), Victor Suárez Molina (1977b), and Robert Patch (1985), who has

apparently modified his views somewhat more recently, as he provides a cogent if brief sketch of the history of the approach (Patch 1991). Terry L. Rugeley (1992) emphasizes the limited material opportunities open to Indian leaders and their consequent alienation.

31. Joseph (1986, esp. chap. 3), makes it clear that many of these later authors have taken as their datum for important rebel grievances the provisions of the Treaty of Tzucacab, which as shown here was by no means the first rebel attempt to express complaints and formulate conditions. Rebel statements made before the rebellion had spread as far west as Tzucacab include no reference to land. Rugeley (1992, 359–62) acknowledges this but attempts to explain it away.

32. In defense of the Yucatecan governments, a careful examination of the history of legislation and decrees does not show that clearly attested promises made to Indians or other troops failed to be kept, at least in large part. The official statement of Imán at Valladolid on the eve of his triumph included a promise to abolish the obventions in favor of a lesser tax, levied only on males, and this was done. But the eastern Indians—and perhaps others—obviously believed they had been promised more than this, just as they also believed that they received other, later promises in the same direction.

33. De Tocqueville (1856, 214). For much of this view I am indebted to a political scientist and colleague at the University of Oregon, James Davies (1962), who likened such a rise and threatened fall in expectations to an inverted J curve, arguing like de Tocqueville that people who revolt are not those who have been consistently oppressed but rather those who see their situation ameliorating, only to find the improvement cut suddenly short.

8. The Screw Tightens

1. Ancona (1889, 4:195–97); Baqueiro (1878–87, 2:14–16).

2. Taking Tekit from rebels, Cetina burned the town to prevent its further use as a base and filled the wells with rubble—into one of which he reportedly threw, alive, a little Indian boy (Baqueiro 1878–87, 2:22).

3. Ancona (1887, 4:137–41); Baqueiro (1878–87, 2:22).

4. Ancona (1887, 4:149) reports that the rebels were heard to yell that the English would soon take their revenge. In some of the complex action that occurred at this time a local Yucatecan government official of Sahcabá named Atanacio Espadas was said to have been impressed into the rebel army and compelled to lead it in continuing attacks (Baqueiro 1878–87, 2:28). His name will reappear.

5. Ancona (1887, 4:146–49). In Tekax, catching some rebels holed up in a second story overlooking the plaza, Cetina and his officers reportedly swung each by feet and arms and threw them onto the bayonets of soldiers in the plaza; this included a

little Indian boy—"*ángel de inocencia*"—who begged for mercy to no avail (Baqueiro 1878–87, 2:26).

6. Ancona (1887, 4:133–37); Baqueiro (1878–87, 2:16–21).

7. Baqueiro 1878–87, 2:20.

8. Ancona (1887, 4:159–65). A certain amount of assistance came from mercenary forces of U.S. citizens, some recruited from the U.S. army then evacuating Mexico after the settlement of the U.S.–Mexican War, some hired directly from the United States. Although an interesting sidelight of the conflict, their effect on the war was short lived and actually insignificant, and the clash of their attitudes with those of the Yucatecans clearly caused the latter to regret that the arrangement had ever been made, although they seemed to respect the foreigners' bravery (Baqueiro 1878–87, 2:36).

9. Baqueiro (1878–87, 2:75–76).

10. Ancona (1887, 4:181, 190–220).

11. Ancona (1887, 4:167); Aznar Pérez (1849–51, 3:221).

12. Ancona (1887, 4:166–68); Baqueiro (1878–87, 2:60).

13. Ancona (1887, 4:169).

14. Ancona (1887, 4:169–74); Baqueiro (1878–87, 2:62–72).

15. Ancona (1887, 4:175–77); Baqueiro (1878–87, 2:83–84). At about this same time, Padre Sierra made his escape from rebel hands. Going supposedly to visit his own parish, he traveled east through Chemax and Xcan, north to Chancenote, and finally to the north coast, where by canoe he slipped past the rebel garrison at Río Lagartos and made his way westward to Dzilam and the Yucatecan lines. He arrived on October 19 (Baqueiro 1878–87, 2:78–82).

16. "Guerra de barbaros" (EP, Nov. 15, 1848, 3). The full text of the decree is also given by Gonzalez Navarro (1970, 322) and Menéndez (1923, 22). Earlier in 1848 proposals had already been made to the government of labor-hungry Cuba to introduce Yucatecans as laborers. See Gonzalez Navarro (1970, 111–12).

17. Ancona (1887, 4:179–85); Baqueiro (1878–87, 2:84–94). There are various anecdotes deriving from this complicated sequence of maneuvers that throw light both on internal relationships in the *masewal* army and upon the character of some of their leaders. For one, when a force under *comandante* Juan Tomás Tzuc was outflanked, defeated, and dispersed after ambushing government troops at Tixcuitún, José María Barrera ordered Tzuc to Peto where he was given two hundred lashes for cowardice. In pique, as soon as Tzuc returned to the rear of his own sector he rounded up all the *masewal* soldiers who had left the front to attend funerals for their fellows and had them given fifty lashes apiece (Baqueiro 1878–87, 2:85). For another, Barrera engineered a clever ambush in which his forces were hidden at the end of thick plantings of sugarcane that crowded each side of the narrow road

and which he ordered set afire as the Yucatecans moved through the plantation. Barrera himself then strolled into the road directly in front of them, saying formally, "Pasen ustedes"—"come along." If they paused, the fire would ignite the powder they carried; if they retreated, they would be cut down by the ambush that was sure to be in place. But unexpectedly they attacked, catching Barrera off guard and almost capturing him, while they dispersed his men despite the fire and the ambush (Baqueiro 1878–87, 2:92–93).

18. Baqueiro (1878–87, 2:95–96). A number of regular Yucatecan clergymen were to be found within the rebel-controlled area (whether by design or abduction is not always clear), but the *masewal* troops also made use of more irregular priests to conduct ritual after the formal Christian fashion. We are told of one such case that illustrates this, as well as an ambivalence in the attitude of rebels toward their adversaries that mitigates the usual impression of unalloyed resentment and hatred. A Yucatecan captain named Acosta, evidently popular not only with his own men but with the rebels, was killed while defending the Yaxcabá plaza and hastily buried before the temporary Yucatecan withdrawal in September 1848. When the rebels took the pueblo, they lamented Acosta's death, located the body, and exhumed it in order to give him a proper burial after a grand funeral in which all their armed soldiers marched in solemn procession: "For this, the rebels relied on a counterfeit clergyman who served them as chaplain, and whom Apolinario Cel in Tiholop had consecrated priest by simply cautioning him that he should comport himself like one. . . . [He,] then, who practiced all the acts of his make-believe ministry with the appropriate vestments, presented himself with them at the hour of the ceremony, and . . . entoned the funeral cantations of the Church that he had had the opportunity to learn." (Baqueiro 1878–87, 2:68). This laxness with regard to institutional credentials, certainly not unknown among the Indian population in the early years after the Spanish conquest, would continue.

19. Ancona (1887, 4:185–87); Baqueiro (1878–87, 2:97–99).

20. In nine days, more than fifteen hundred people, both Indians and *vecinos*, presented themselves at Peto, while substantially all of the former population of Becanchén appeared at Tekax (Baqueiro 1878–87, 2:100–101). Among the former was Padre Manuel Meso Vales, who had recently officiated at the funeral of Marcelo Pat and who had earlier been one of the signatories of the Treaty of Tzucacab where he had served—presumably not voluntarily—as a peace commissioner for the rebels.

21. Baqueiro (1878–87, 2:101–2).

22. Ancona (1887, 4:189–90); Baqueiro (1878–87, 2:102).

23. Baqueiro (1878–87, 2:102).

24. The emphasis on the capture of corn from the enemy becomes increasingly evident in the historians' accounts of the Yucatecan eastward push of 1848, although

specific events are not recounted here. Some of the rebel complaints received during negotiations for the Treaty of Tzucacab had been to the same point, however.

25. Ancona (1889, 4:203–7). An *aguardiente* still at Pat's establishment was sampled immoderately, the entire government force becoming so drunk they could scarcely stand. Fortunately for them, before the counterattacking rebels finished them off a relief column from Tihosuco arrived and led the drunks home. Baqueiro (1878–87, 2:112–18) has a slightly different version of the story.

26. Ancona (1889, 4:208–12); Baqueiro (1878–87, 2:112–18).

27. Baqueiro (1878–87, 2:118–21, 204–6, 225–26).

28. Ancona (1889, 4:251–52); Baqueiro (1878–87, 2:103–4). Whether there was special significance to the color red in this situation is not clear, although on at least two occasions rebels were said by Baqueiro (1878–87, 1:435, 2:22) to be carrying red pennants into battle: some were captured by Yucatecans near Sitilpech, shortly before the successful rebel advance on Izamal, and others were mentioned at the rebel siege of Muna.

29. Ancona (1889, 4:251–52); Baqueiro (1878–87, 2:103–4, 200), the latter referring to some correspondence dated in May 1849. Bricker (1981, 102, 338, n. 32) reports a letter in ABH from "Cecilio Chi, Venancio Pec, et al., to Superintendent of Belize, June 15, 1849," which I have not seen. There is, however, one (in ABH, R29) from Chi, Pec, Juan Cez, Tomás Uc, Camilo Tus, and José Victor Reyes to "Excellent Sir Commander in Chief of the Liberating Law of Belize" that is dated June 15, 1848, which appears in both Spanish and English versions and is datelined Tihosuco—a place that had been recaptured by the Yucatecans before June 15, 1849. There are very few letters from Chi in ABH, and although it is certainly possible that Bricker's citation of the date is correct, one may also suspect the possibility of a misreading of a handwritten document in poor condition. In any event, letters to Belize from the rebels dated in October 1849 no longer carry Chi's name.

30. Pablo Encalada (in his deposition of Aug. 12, 1867, EP, Sept. 24, 1) alleged that one of Chi's successors, Venancio Pec, had been responsible for his death, as he later engineered Jacinto Pat's. I am unable to evaluate this suggestion.

31. Ancona (1889, 4:240); C. S. J. Fancourt to A. M. Peón, Feb. 1, 1848 (ABH, R22b).

32. Baqueiro (1878–87, 2:152); English translation of the interrogation of Pedro Garma, refugee from Bacalar at Motul, July 17, 1848, apparently originally an enclosure to a letter from M. Otero to P. W. Doyle, Aug. 31, 1848 (ABH, R29); "Refuerzos a los Bárbaros" (EF, Nov. 20, 1848, 4).

33. J. S. C. Fancourt to P. W. Doyle, Oct. 13, 1848 (ABH, R22b).

34. J. M. Tzuc to Estimado Señor, Dec. 29, 1848 (ABH, R28); the fighting is referred to in J. H. Faber to C. S. J. Fancourt, Jan. 22, Feb. 7, and Feb. 23, 1849 (ABH, R29) in which survivors are mentioned, and in J. Kingdon to Fancourt, Mar. 8, 1849 (ABH,

R28), where it is said that the attackers had burned to death at least one Indian rebel.

35. The first account referred to is the report of interrogation of Pedro Garma, Motul, July 17, 1848 (ABH, R29), the second is in Baqueiro (1878–87, 2:171–72) and is inconsistent with the report from a British Honduras magistrate (to be mentioned shortly) that Pacheco carried a commission in the Yucatecan army signed by Miguel Barbachano himself.

36. J. H. Faber to C. S. J. Fancourt, Jan. 22, 1849, with enclosed proclamation by Vito Pacheco, Jan. 18, 1849 (ABH, R29). At the bottom of the English translation of the proclamation someone, presumably J. H. Faber, the British magistrate at Punta Consejo, had written the following:

The writer of the original foregoing document is a murderer, robber, and pirate. In November 1834 Don Graciano Carras, European Spanish merchant, took passage in his bongo on the coast of Yucatan for Belize, with between $25 and $30,000. While still in sight of land he cut down the unfortunate Spaniard with an axe, threw his body overboard and then attacked the Carib servant to Señor Carras, who, though wounded, jumped overboard to effect his escape. . . . Persons . . . who are well informed in Yucateco affairs, have informed me that were he even to succeed in his contemplated enterprise, his sins toward his government are so great that if taken he will meet his reward.

37. J. H. Faber to C. J. S. Fancourt, Feb. 7, 1849 (ABH, R29). Faber's impression of Pacheco obviously had undergone a change, for he now described him as "about forty years of age, a little above the middle size, of a muscular frame and strongly sunburnt face, aquiline nose, quick small eyes, a black mustache, and long black curly hair. His features, gait, gestures announced a man of determined mind; . . . and his subsequent conversation about his battles proved him to be so."

38. "Guerra de bárbaros" (EF, Feb. 25, 1849, 3); "Belice" (EF, Mar. 10, 1849, 4), the latter also cited by Ancona (1889, 4:225).

39. Baqueiro (1878–87, 2:171–72).

40. Baqueiro (1878–87, 2:154, and elsewhere) and an eyewitness to later events near Bacalar whom he quotes (ibid. 2:329) indicate this to be Diego Ongay, who had been involved in the 1847 action at Tepich. The British magistrate later reports, possibly in error, that it was a Captain Fermín Ongay; see J. H. Faber to C. S. J. Fancourt, May 2, 1850 (ABH, R33).

41. G. D. Adolphus to C. S. J. Fancourt, May 2, 1849 (ABH, R29); Fancourt to J. D. Zetina, May 21, 1849 (ABH, R22b). One of the Belizeans was Henry Oswald, a Swiss by birth, who although prosecuted for attempting to assist the predominantly Indian rebels at this time, would later be acclaimed a hero for action against the pacified rebels of Icaiché.

42. Baqueiro (1878–87, 2:160).

43. George Fantesie was a Belizean known to Mayan-speaking rebels as Yach (i.e., George) or as Don Jorge; Silvestre Adolphus Lanabit was a native of France who for a time was Fantesie's partner in trade, illicit and otherwise, along the Río Hondo, and sometimes a partner of Henry Oswald in various enterprises. See depositions enclosed with J .H. Faber to C. S. J. Fancourt, May 20 and May 21, 1850 (ABH, R33).

44. Ancona (1889, 4:227–30); Baqueiro (1878–87, 2:153–59).

45. Ancona (1889, 4:230–37); Baqueiro (1878–87, 2:160–66). J. M. Barrera is mentioned as having returned northward from the Bacalar area in August in "Teatro de Guerra" (BO, Aug. 29, 1849, 2).

46. Baqueiro (1878–87, 2:170–71). In one case, Cetina reportedly formed his men and asked any who wanted to go to British Honduras to step forward. The unfortunates who did were immediately executed. When the executing officer hesitated to carry out the decree against a man and his young son, Cetina agreed to let the boy go and turned to the man and shot him himself.

47. Baqueiro (1878–87, 2:171–73), where Pacheco is reported to have repented and advised his children (who had never been mentioned before) to avoid the career of arms. One suspects elaboration by a sentimental hand.

48. For example, Alejandro Marcín dispatch of June 5, 1849, in "Teatro de la guerra" (BO, June 8, 1849, 1, also published in EF, same date).

49. M. Barbachano to the Superintendent, Sept. 12, 1849 (ABH, R33).

50. J. H. Faber to C. S. J. Fancourt, Oct. 13, 1849 (ABH, R33).

51. C. Trujillo dispatch, Oct. 29, 1849 (BO, Nov. 2, 1849).

52. For example, C. S. J. Fancourt to J. D. Zetina, Oct. 3, 1849, and Fancourt to M. Barbachano, Nov. 1, 1849 (ABH, R32b). See also Fancourt to C. Grey, dispatches numbered 48, 49, 50, all of Nov. 7, 1849 (ABH, R31).

53. P. W. Doyle to C. S. J. Fancourt, March 21, 1849 (ABH, R29).

54. J. D. Zetina dispatch of Sept. 25, 1849 (BO, Oct. 6, 1849, 1), in which *Four Sisters* is erroneously referred to as *Cuatro Hermanos*, "four brothers."

55. C. S. J. Fancourt to J. D. Zetina, Oct. 3, 1849 (ABH, R32b); P. W. Doyle to Fancourt, Nov. 15, 1849 (ABH, R33); Fancourt to G. W. Mehan, Oct. 3, 1849 (ABH, R32b); Fancourt to C. Grey, Misc. No. 42, Oct. 12, 1849 (ABH, R31). In complicated interplay, the magistrate J. H. Faber reported that the capture of *Four Sisters* was brought about through efforts of Juan Trujillo, a Yucatecan priest well known as an arms smuggler, and not long afterward Trujillo was refused a ticket of residence in British Honduras and apparently moved outside the boundary (J. H. Faber to C. S. J. Fancourt, Oct. 13, 1849, and summons of Faber to J. Trujillo, n.d., ABH, R33; Fancourt to G. W. Mehan, July 23, 1850, ABH, R32a). The Belizean captain of *Four Sisters*, William Longsworth, was imprisoned by the Yucatecans and sent to Mérida, while his cause

was a subject of correspondence (e.g., Fancourt to M. Barbachano, Feb. 18, 1850, ABH, R32b). Finally, although Austin Cox admitted trading with the rebels, there was not sufficient evidence of wrongdoing committed while in the colony for him to be charged (Fancourt to P. W. Doyle, Nov. 10, 1849, ABH, R32b).

56. Baqueiro (1878–87, 2:178–79).

57. Baqueiro (1878–87, 2:185–89). During these years, however, Barrera was likely to be credited with every rebel success, as Crescencio Poot would be later.

58. Baqueiro (1878–87, 2:190–97, quoted passage from 195). In the section (193) he also adds an accolade to the *hidalgos* who served in the advanced posts by clearing obstructions and carrying supplies, most of them unarmed an easy prey for rebel machetes: "Filthy, thin and pale as death, the *hidalgos* in the *cantones* were an object of compassion. . . . If there is justice in society, if there is reward, the government should exempt from every civil burden, extending the benefit to their unfortunate children, all those who served in this miserable campaign."

59. Baqueiro (1878–87, 2:199–200). The references to Chi are confusing, the use of the present tense, subjunctive mood, implying that he still was alive at this time. The vilification of Pat for allegedly committing the acts against which the war was being fought must reflect that wealthy and literate man's anomalous position among the rebels—a property owner with numerous commercial and personal contacts among Yucatecans of the Peto region, who had engaged in Yucatecan politics on a broader scale so that his support was actively sought by *barbachanistas*, a man regarded with such respect by contemporary Yucatecans that one historian could absolve him of guilt in the rebellion, declaring him "innocent, . . . unwilling to lend himself" to the cause except through coercive circumstances, "one of those beings whom destiny pushes to be the ruin . . . of their native land . . . in accordance with the inscrutable secrets of the Omnipotent" (Anonymous 1866, 110–11).

60. Baqueiro (1878–87, 2:198–201); J. H. Faber to C. S. J. Fancourt, Oct. 13, 1849 (ABH, R33); J. E. Rosado dispatch, Oct. 1, 1849 (BO, Oct. 5, 1–2); A. Marcín dispatch, Oct. 16, 1849 (BO, Oct. 19); "Guerra de bárbaros" (EF, Oct. 20, 1849, 4).

61. Deposition of Pablo Encalada, Aug. 12, 1867 (EP, Sept. 24, 1867, 1); J. E. Rosado dispatch, Oct. 15, 1949 (BO, Oct. 18, 1849, 1–2); "Guerra de bárbaros" (EF, Nov. 5, 1849, 4).

9. Olive Branches with Thorns

1. J. Kingdon, E. J. Rhys, E. Adolphus to C. S. J. Fancourt, Mar. 6, 1849 (ABH, R28), enclosing Kingdon and others to Chiefs of the Yucatecan Indians, Jan. 25, 1849, and Pat to Kingdon and others, Feb. 18, 1849.

2. J. Kingdon to C. S. J. Fancourt, March 8, 1849 (ABH, R28); Fancourt to Kingdon, March 9, 1849 (ABH, R22b).

3. C. Chi, V. Pec, and A. Espadas to C. S. J. Fancourt, March 22, 1849 (ABH, R28).

4. P .W. Doyle to C. S. J. Fancourt, Aug. 10 and Nov. 15, 1849 (ABH, R33); Baqueiro (1878–87, 2:226).

5. Baqueiro (1878–87, 2:232); Ancona (1889, 4:273) represents this as a move to beat the British to the attempt.

6. "Guerra de bárbaros" (EF, Oct. 25, 1849, 4).

7. F. Chan and V. Pec to Governor Barbachano, Oct. 9, 1849, in Baqueiro (1878–87, 2:553–55).

8. M. Barbachano to the Minister of External Relations, Oct. 20, 1849, in Baqueiro (1878–87, 2:548–50).

9. Baqueiro (1878–87, 2:312); J. Cadenas dispatch, Feb. 25, 1850 (BO, March 1, 1850, 2); Baqueiro (1878–87, 2:236–37), who also gives Cocom's letter in full (568–69).

10. Baqueiro (1878–87, 2:236–37).

11. J. C. Vela to A. M. Peón, Nov. 9, 1849, in Baqueiro (1878–87, 2:240–44).

12. Baqueiro (1878–87, 2:234, 244).

13. Baqueiro (1878–87, 2:247).

14. J. A. García to J. Sierra O'Reilly, in Baqueiro (1878–87, 2:279–80).

15. Baqueiro (1878–87, 2:275–76).

16. C. S. J. Fancourt to J. Pat, Sept. 17, 1849, Fancourt to V. Pec, Oct. 24, 1849, Fancourt to Chan and Pec, Oct. 30, 1849 (ABH, R32b).

17. Baqueiro (1878–87, 2:228).

18. C. S. J. Fancourt to M. Barbachano, Dec. 10, 1849 (ABH, R32b). Following the general practice of the time, Maya *masewalob* would be rendered in English as "Indians," although as I indicated in an earlier chapter the meanings are not completely parallel, for whereas *indio* had a strict legal meaning, *masewal* did not.

19. C. S. J. Fancourt to M. Barbachano, Dec. 10, 1849 (ABH, R32b). A complete version of the letter in Spanish, with emphases added, is given by Baqueiro (1878–87, 2:228–31), drawn from "Guerra de bárbaros" (EF, Jan. 25, 1850, 2).

20. P. W. Doyle to C. S. J. Fancourt, Jan. 16, 1850 (ABH, R33).

21. Baqueiro (1878–87, 2:227).

22. Baqueiro (1878–87, 2:239–40); G. Ruiz dispatch, Nov. 22, 1849 (BO, Dec. 1, 1849, 2); various articles in EF (Sept. 1, 5, 10, 15, 1849).

23. Baqueiro (1878–87, 2:228).

24. The letters referred to here are enclosures in Spanish to the letter from J. M. Lacunza to *Señor Ministro Plenipotenciario de S.M.B.*, May 3, 1850 (ABH, R33).

25. F. Castillo dispatch (BO, Dec. 1, 1849, 2).

26. Ancona (1889, 4:285); F. Castillo dispatch, Nov. 26, 1849 (BO, Dec. 1, 1849, 2); J. Cadenas dispatches, Jan. 18 and 19, 1850 (BO, Jan. 23, 1850, 2–4); J. E. Rosado dispatch, Jan. 13, 1850 (BO, Jan. 24, 1850, 3).

27. J. E. Rosado dispatch, Jan. 18, 1850 (BO, Jan. 22, 1850, 1–3). So ended the rebel career of Atanacio Espadas, former justice of the peace of Sahcabá, who (by his own account, at least) had been impressed by the rebels into their service and forced to lead them. That he did so enthusiastically cannot be doubted for he rose to be one of the major caudillos, claiming to have led the party that avenged the murder of Cecilio Chi, and probably appearing as a signatory with Chi and Venancio Pec in a letter of March 22, 1849, to Superintendent Fancourt (ABH, R28).

28. M. Barbachano to superintendent, Feb. 1, 1850 (ABH, R33).

29. Baqueiro (1878–87, 2:231).

30. C. S. J. Fancourt to Minister Bankhead, Sept. 17, 1850 (ABH, R32a).

31. The conditions were published as part of a letter from commissioner José Antonio García, Jan. 26, 1850 (BO, Feb. 6, 1850, 1–3), with versions reprinted in Baqueiro (1878–87, 2:571–77) and Ancona (1889, 4:429–33).

32. Baqueiro (1878–87, 2:338).

33. Baqueiro (1878–87, 2:292).

34. Baqueiro (1878–87, 2:325–26), who also describes encircled and panic-stricken rebels at Kekén (317–18).

35. See the contemporary characterization by Anthony Trollope (1858, 139–40) and the fictionalized but probably accurate account of the hazards of this contraband trade by Pío Baroja (1954).

36. González Navarro (1970, 120); Menéndez (1923, 100–34; 1925, 7–27). The former provides the most coherent account of the sale of prisoners through the entire period in which it occurred, cites evidence for the existence of contracts dated as late as July 1849, and presumes that it continued. Although there was talk of a shipment of captives to Veracruz as railroad workers, according to González Navarro the railroad people were outbid by the Cubans. The resources gained by Yucatan from the first two shipments, as well as the Spanish steamer that transported them, were used to raise the Seventh Division and deploy it to Chetumal Bay for Cetina's assault on Bacalar as mentioned in the preceding chapter (Baqueiro 1878–87, ii, 209; González Navarro 1970, 119).

37. S. López de Llergo to *Secretaría General de Gobierno*, Feb. 4, 1850 (BO, Feb. 6, 1850, 3–4).

38. According to Baqueiro (1878–87, 2:343–44), the roundup at an isolated settlement might begin with a public gang rape of young women. The people collected were then marshaled into ranks, loaded with whatever booty was taken, and force marched on their way, hungry, thirsty, and tired. The old and sick who faltered were killed in sight of their families; women approaching childbirth were abandoned, while the rest of their families were driven on; children cried and begged officers to take them on their horses because they could not keep up. Once at the *cantón* the

men were shut up in jail, from which they might be taken to work the commanders' farms or to be dispatched to acquaintances in Mérida or Campeche as de facto slaves. Their wives meanwhile ground corn and made tortillas for the garrison. Orphans were distributed among officers, siblings separated despite wailing, to be made an item of commerce. One officer was said to keep a stable of as many as twenty orphans to use as stakes in gambling or to sell to the sutlers who swarmed over the *cantones*.

39. Baqueiro (1878–87, 2:294–95).

40. Cob to Yam, Mar. 8, 1850, in Baqueiro (1878–87, 2:295); Quintal Martín 1992, letter 37).

41. Pec to C. Yam, Mar. 6, 1850, in Baqueiro (1878–87, 296).

42. Baqueiro (1878–87, 2:297–99).

43. Baqueiro (1878–87, 2:296–97).

44. Baqueiro (1878–87, 2:304–6). For related correspondence between Barrera and Vela see Quintal Martín (1992, letters 42, 43). As I indicated in chapters 6 and 7, Juan María Novelo was an adherent of Barbachano and of Felipe Rosado, the latter suspected of collusion with the faction of Jacinto Pat and later involved in the negotiations at Tzucacab. The greeting to Vázquez underscores the ambiguous nature of relationships during civil war.

45. Baqueiro (1878–87, 2:308–9). None of the letters is quoted in full, and although Baqueiro entertains the possibility that the letter from one *dzul* to another was a fiction of Chan's, he does not give the source of his information regarding Chan's correspondence. The term *masewalob* in the first quotation here is substituted for *indios*, the word used by Baqueiro. For a related letter from Chan to Barrera see Quintal Martín (1992, letter 45).

46. Baqueiro (1878–87, 2:309–10).

47. M. Micheltorena dispatch, Apr. 27, 1850 (BO, Apr. 30, 1850, 1). I am unaware of the identity of "Mister Gelas."

48. Baqueiro (1878–87, 2:232); J. E. Rosado dispatch, Jan. 13, 1850 (BO, Jan. 24, 1850, 3). Rosado reports that Pec took the north and Chan the south, whereas Baqueiro states the opposite. In the following months, however, Chan seemed to be associated with the rebel headquarters at Cruzchén in the northern district, Pec with the region around Chichanhá; it thus appears that Baqueiro was correct.

49. Baqueiro (1878–87, 2:300–1); M. Micheltorena dispatches, Apr. 13 and Apr. 27, 1850 (BO, Apr. 16, Apr. 30, 1850, 1). This may be an error for Felipe Ayala, who writes to rebels from the southern border regarding munitions, and on March 24 and May 4 signs himself as *comandante* (Quintal Martín 1992, letters 36, 38, 40).

50. Faber's account of the affair is in J. H. Faber to C. S. J. Fancourt, May 2, 1850, supplemented by Faber to Fancourt, May 3, May 11, May 20, May 21 (ABH, R33). The Yucatecan account is by "General Brito," evidently Celestino Brito, as given

to Baqueiro (1878–87, 2:328–32). There are certain inconsistencies within as well as between the two accounts. Brito apparently misremembered some place-names, and he also indicated that although the expedition was to have been commanded by Diego Ongay, an accident at the last moment left him, Brito, in charge. Faber, however, reported having talked to Ongay two or three different times and presumably already knew him by sight, although he reported his first name as Fermín. Ancona (1889, 4:288) gives Diego Ongay as the expedition leader. The claims of Fantesie and Lanabit are in depositions enclosed with Faber's letters of May 20 and May 21, respectively, the latter of which reported that Ongay was sent to Mérida for court-martial for having allowed Faber to pass him on the river, although shortly afterward he was in action in eastern Yucatan, where he died of illness (Baqueiro 1878–87, 2:377).

51. P. W. Doyle to J. M. Lacunza, July 22, 1850, and Lacunza to C. Bankhead, July 30, 1850 (ABH, R33). Because at Agua Blanca Faber improperly crossed the river to Yucatecan territory, he was relieved of his duties as magistrate and returned to his regular job of Assistant Crown Surveyor of the colony (Fancourt to C. Bankhead, Sept. 17, 1850, ABH, R32a).

52. C. S. J. Fancourt to Sir Charles Grey, Separate No. 34, July 11, 1850 (ABH, R31).

53. Baqueiro (1878–87, 2:345–47, 357–58, 360–62, 375).

54. Arista, Mexican Minister of War and Marine, to J. M. Lacunza, Mexican Minister of Exterior Relations, July 5, 1850 (ABH, R33).

55. Baqueiro (1878–87, 2:363–72), who felt the treatment of José María Vázquez to be unjust. A native of Tihosuco, educated in Mérida, friend of Jacinto Pat and supporter of Barbachano, Vázquez had fought against Trujeque but then fought with him when the rebels attacked Tihosuco. After his family was captured by the rebels, Vázquez made his way by sea to Belize and into rebel territory to seek them. Although judged a criminal and rebel by his military captors, Baqueiro reports that his name can be found in no rebel correspondence save for that with José María Barrera at the time that both were attempting to arrange a meeting with José Canuto Vela in Kampocolché to discuss peace (Baqueiro 1878–87, 2:372–74).

56. Baqueiro (1878–87, 2:358–59, 375–77).

57. E.g., J. E. Rosado dispatch of Oct. 3, 1850 (SD, Oct. 14, 1850, 1–2).

58. E. Rosado to M. Micheltorena, quoted in Baqueiro (1878–87, 2:378).

59. Baqueiro (1878–87, 2:377–79).

60. Baqueiro (1878–87, 2:380–81).

61. Baqueiro (1878–87, 2:384–86).

62. Baqueiro (1878–87, 2:444).

63. Reina (1980, 402–4), citing the Archivo Histórico de la Defensa Nacional. The list is suspect for other reasons as well: it omits mention of the most important leaders of the time (e.g., Venancio Pec, Florencio Chan, Bonifacio Novelo, José María Barrera,

Crescencio Poot, etc.), and it lists troop figures for some pueblos that are surely inflated (e.g., Tihosuco with 8,645, Oxkutzcab with 3,999). One must suppose that rather than a list of men still active in resistance in 1850, it must represent a composite of figures collected over the preceding two years or more, as local leaders were reported to have joined the rebels—possibly with their entire adherent population rather than simply fighting men.

64. Anonymous (1866, 416–17). For 1850, Nelson Reed (1964, 127) makes a similarly somewhat inflated "informed guess" of eighty thousand for the total surviving population.

65. Ancona (1889, 4:266–67); Baqueiro (1878–87, 2:223).

66. J. Cadenas dispatches of Feb. 16 (BO, Feb. 20, 1850, 2) and Feb. 25 (BO, Mar. 1, 1850, 2); J. H. Faber to C. S. J. Fancourt, Apr. 12, 1850 (ABH, R33).

67. J. H. Faber to C. S. J. Fancourt, Dec. 4, 1848 (ABH, R29).

10. A Parting of Ways

1. Baqueiro (1878–87, 2:385–86).

2. J. E. Rosado dispatch of Jan. 6 (SD, Jan. 10, 1951, 1). Rosado reported 28 rebel dead, but Baqueiro (1878–87, 2:389) claims a total of 108.

3. J. M. Novelo dispatch of Apr. 1, in M. Micheltorena to M. Barbachano, Apr. 2 (SD, Apr. 4, 1851, 2–3). He refers to the place of the crosses as a well [*pozo*], but later accounts indicate clearly that it was a natural well or cenote. Of the number of people, Novelo's words were "por falta de tropa que sirva de custodia, no recogí mas de dos mil personas," which I have interpreted (Dumond 1985, 294) to mean that he did take two thousand prisoners but could take no more for want to escort, whereas Baqueiro (1878–87, 2:390) apparently understood Novelo to mean that for want of escort he was unable to march back the more than two thousand people. The import with regard to the size of the pueblo is essentially the same in either case, of course.

4. F. Cámara Zavala (1928, quoted from Sept. 2, 3:5). The Mexican word *huipil* becomes *hipil* in Yucatan, where the *h* is aspirated; *fustán* is the skirt worn beneath the *hipil*.

5. Novelo dispatch of Apr. 1, in Micheltorena to Barbachano, Apr. 2 (SD, Apr. 4, 1851, 2–3).

6. Baqueiro (1878–87, 2:386–88). The name Nauat (or Náhuat in a more common Mexican spelling) is a dialectical variant of the word *náhuatl*, the common designation of the language spoken at the time of conquest by masses of Indians of central Mexico, including the Aztecs and a noun designating something of pleasant sound; the related verb *nahuati* designates certain modes of speaking (Molina 1944, s.v. "nahuatl," "nahuati"). The surprising appropriateness of this name borne by the

reputed ventriloquist has been remarked by Dumond (1970, 267, n. 2) and by Bricker (1981, 106), who asks "Is it only a coincidence . . . or was it an assumed name?" But despite its central Mexican derivation, Nauat is not uncommon as a Yucatecan surname (Roys 1940, 36), appearing for example in eight of twenty-two separate parish name lists available to me for the period 1803–52.

7. Anonymous (1866, 458).

8. J. M. Barrera and J. V. Reyes to Superintendent of Belize, Jan. 1851, ABH, R33. I found no counterpart in any language in British Colonial Office records of the period. In Maya original, *Indians* would have been rendered *masewalob* (although spelled differently). The English version has also been quoted in full by Bricker (1981, 107).

9. The entire document is published in Maya and in translation by Bricker (1981, app. A, text A-1), from whom this excerpt is taken (192), although rearranged here into prose format closer to that of the original document and with her *Kampokobche* changed to the more common Kampocolché. The original is in BCP and has been copied on microfilm roll No. 3 of UA (Bingham 1972); Quintal Martín (1992, letter 47) provides a Spanish translation of the first half. The content of the first four-fifths is exactly paralleled by the Spanish version of one of two Juan de la Cruz proclamations held by the Archivo Histórico de la Secretaría de Defensa Nacional, Mexico (Reina 1980, 408–10). *Balam Na*, translated by Bricker (1981, 218) as "Jaguar House," and by Villa Rojas (1945, 22, and n. 14) as "House of Officials and Priests," apparently referred to the central shrine or church in Chan Santa Cruz (Villa Rojas 1945, 22). Xocén is a village name; one so called lies a short distance south of Valladolid. Unlike many of the letters and exhortations, the signatures on this are not adorned with crosses.

10. Bricker (1981, 187–88).

11. Quintal Martín (1992, letter 35) dates a brief exhortation of Juan de la Cruz to Feb. 1, 1850. The document must be a fragment, for it begins in the middle of the cross's standard diatribe and thereafter parallels in a general but abbreviated way the second half of the proclamation translated by Bricker (1981, text A-1); it closes with a date rendered "día 1° febrero," (Feb. 1), which might be mistaken for February 10. One of the two cross proclamations held by Defensa Nacional (Reina 1980, 407) refers to commands issued by the cross to "the generals" on December 11, 1850. The proclamation translated by Bricker (1981, text A-1), its parallel published by Reina (1980, 408–10), and the fragment given by Quintal Martín (1992, letter 35), all refer to notifications to the generals "50 days ago." With the period from Dec. 11, 1850 to Feb. 1, 1851 closely approximating fifty days, I conclude that Feb. 1, 1851, rather than some day in 1850, is the most likely date for whatever was the original of the three documents last referred to. The repetitive proclamations or exhortations (of which there are a number of examples evidently of various dates) were addressed to the world in general, to *masewalob* and *dzulob* alike. Written to formula, the major

variations between them are in rearrangement of blocks of text devoted to standard assertions and commands, with certain of these eliminated entirely in the shorter documents. The early examples from Chan Santa Cruz are consistently signed Juan de la Cruz of Balamna and Juan de la Cruz of Xocén.

12. Baqueiro (1878–87, 2:391).

13. Bricker (1981, app. A, text A-2) translates the letter of Aug. 28, 1851, and compares it to all others of the series of five letters held in BCP. The letters are cataloged in Bingham (1972, 22) under "Juan de la Cruz, five letters in Maya," and are given in Spanish by Quintal Martín (1992, letters 50–52, 54, 58). Cenil is the name of more than one village in what is now Quintana Roo, one of which is said by Villa Rojas (1945, 163) to lie north and west of Chan Santa Cruz, and there are others of the name nearby in Yucatan.

14. Another case will appear in which the number of crosses reported by witnesses is expanded to three by Baqueiro or his informants. With regard to the dating of the letter, a brief reference to similar "ridiculous and extravagant communications to the government of the state" in a Campeche newspaper in July indicates they had begun to issue from the miraculous cross before, possibly well before, August 1851 ("Crónica peninsular," EF, July 25, 1851, 4). I refer to this again in a later chapter.

15. Chan and Novelo were headquartered at Cruzchén, Pec in a rancho of the far south called Chunkú; Pech had been centered at San Antonio until it was taken as a Yucatecan *cantón* during the summer of 1850. Baqueiro (1878–87, 2:392) presumes Novelo's aim was to support the foundation of Chan Santa Cruz. But Reina (1980, 385) cites a microfilmed letter from Colonel Rosado to Padre José Canuto Vela of Jan. 5, 1848, in which he reports that as early as that time Novelo was moving through rural pueblos with an image of the Virgin and the story that her apparition had announced the triumph of the rebel cause. One must wonder if this was a regular ploy of Bonifacio Novelo or if Baqueiro had his dates mixed.

16. Baqueiro (1878–87, 2:392–95; material quoted is from 393).

17. "La guerra" (EF, Feb. 10, 1851, 4).

18. M. Méndez to Governor of the State of Yucatan, Apr. 1, 1851 (SD, May 14, 1851, 1).

19. "Crónica peninsular" (EF, Aug. 10, 1851, 4); Baqueiro (1878–87, 2:427).

20. Baqueiro (1878–87, 2:429–32); "Crónica peninsular" (EF, Sept. 10, 1851, 4). An authorized copy of the agreement that was made on September 10, 1851, is located in the manuscript collection of BCP and appears on microfilm roll No. 3 of UA, although I have been unable to find it listed in the catalog of that collection (Bingham 1972). Hoil is a fairly common Yucatec Maya name. Angelino Itzá seems not to have been mentioned earlier as a leader at Chichanhá, while José María (or Felipe) Ayala, the former gunrunner who had been placed at Chichanhá by Venancio Pec to oversee the

logging operation, and who had issued letters in 1850 as *comandante* of Chichanhá (at least three of which are preserved in BCP), seems to have disappeared.

21. Baqueiro (1878–87, 2:431–32); J. M. Tzuc to M. Méndez, Aug. 25, 1851 (BCP; also microfilm roll No. 3, UA; see Bingham 1972).

22. "Crónica peninsular" (EF, Oct. 5, 1851, 4); Cocom and others to M. A. Sierra, Sept. 22, 1851 (Quintal Martín 1992, letter 57).

23. "Noticias de la campaña" (SD, Oct. 8, 1851, 4).

24. The situation is summarized by Baqueiro (1878–87, 2:345–50).

25. Baqueiro (1878–87, 2:415–19).

26. Baqueiro (1878–87, 2:422–28, 433–34).

27. Baqueiro (1878–87, 2:399). A letter received by a magistrate in British Honduras, however, stated that the rebels left twenty-four dead in the town as they retreated and took two Yucatecan officers and a drummer as their prisoners (W. Salmon to C. S. J. Fancourt, Apr. 1, 1851, ABH, R33).

28. The periodic reports of González were unanswered by the government (Baqueiro 1878–87, 2:395–401). Complaints about nonpayment for supplies by the Bacalar garrison were not new, however. On August 17, 1850, Domingo Martínez, a Yucatecan who had emigrated to Belize when Bacalar was taken by the rebels in 1848 and who (despite some legal difficulties mentioned earlier in the text) had maintained his residence there, petitioned the superintendent of British Honduras for assistance in collecting $12,217 owed him for more than a year for goods purchased in the name of the Yucatecan government for troops at Bacalar (D. Martínez to *Excelentísimo Señor Supremo*, Aug. 17, 1850, ABH, R29). I am not aware that he was given assistance.

29. For instance, in mid-December rebels had been able to enter the main street of Tihosuco before being repulsed (Baqueiro 1878–87, 2:433–35).

30. Baqueiro (1878–87, 2:436–38); T. Fajardo to M. Barbachano, Mar. 23 (SD, May 5, 1852, 2–3); F. Cámara Zavala (1928, Sept. 9, sec. 3, 6). The last does not mention the date on the tree, otherwise the three references are in agreement. As I reported earlier, Baqueiro had said there were three crosses carved on the tree marking the cenote. Despite the number of corpses mentioned, there is no reference to any raging disease.

31. F. Cámara Zavala (1928, Sept. 16, sec. 3, 4).

32. Baqueiro (1878–87, 2:433–40); F. Cámara Zavala (1928, Oct. 14, sec. 2, 2); T. Fajardo to M. Barbachano, Mar. 23 (SD, May 5, 1852, 2–3).

33. Baqueiro (1878–87, 2:440–41).

34. Rosado dispatch of May 6, 1851 (SD, May 14, 1851, 2).

35. Baqueiro (1878–87, 2:444–45).

36. Vega dispatch of Oct. 29, 1852 (SD, Nov. 4, 1852, 1–2).

37. Vega dispatch of Apr. 14, 1853 (ER, Apr. 18, 1853, 1).

38. Baqueiro (1878–87, 441); López de Llergo dispatch, Mar. 6, 1852 (sc, Mar. 8, 1852, 1–2); "Comunicado," June 15, 1852 (sd, June 21, 1852, 2–3); Vega dispatch, June 3, 1852 (sd, June 14, 1852, 1).

39. Vega dispatch of July 1, 1852 (sd, July 7, 1852, 2), and of Aug. 2, 1852 (sd, Aug. 9, 1852, 1).

40. For example, Vega dispatch of Oct. 30, 1852 (sd, Nov. 4, 1852, 2).

41. Baqueiro (1878–87, 2:442); Vega dispatch of June 28, 1852 (sd, July 8, 1852, 2). The inundations of the rainy season changed the character of warfare, wetting the priming pans of muskets and rendering them useless as anything but clubs or bayonet holders (e.g., Baqueiro 1878–87, 2:360). Although this would not have eliminated the customary shouting of the rebels, it would have reduced the total noise level considerably, for armies armed with the old flintlocks always burned a great deal of powder to little effect except the production of noise and smoke (e.g., Grant 1885, 1:95; for the rebels in particular, see Anonymous 1866, 149, 265). Juan Bautista Yam, here reported dead, turns up alive and well to sign the southern peace agreement of 1853.

42. Baqueiro (1878–87, 2:442); Vega dispatch of July 21, 1852 (sd, Aug. 6, 1852, 1–2).

43. Baqueiro (1878–87, 2:445, 482) gives the place as Yokdzadz, Baqueiro (1887) as Yokdzonot, where he also reports the full text of the eulogy.

44. Vega dispatch of June 9, 1853 (er, June 13, 1853, 1). As early as 1848 Reyes had appeared as secretary in correspondence from the rebels to the Superintendent of British Honduras (e.g., C. Chi, V. Pec, et al., to Excellent Sir, General of Belize, July 8, 1848, abh, r28; Chi, Pec et al., to Excellent Sir Commander in Chief of the Liberating Law of Belize, June 15, 1848, abh, r29) and presumably served the same function at the date of the letter from José María Barrera to the Superintendent of British Honduras that was cited earlier (Barrera and Reyes to Superintendent of Belize, Jan. 1851, abh, r33).

45. Baqueiro (1878–87, 2:445).

46. Hübbe (1940, 133).

47. Paraphrased from Vega to Excmo. Sr., May 5, 1852 (sd, extra edition, May 12, 1852). From the distribution of the military ranks, the rebels making peace were evidently a single company. One might expect that a *comandante* such as Zima would have two or more such companies under his command, but evidence to come later suggests that the usual pattern was for any isolated force to be led by a *comandante*, seconded by a captain.

48. Ancona (1889, 4:348–49); Hübbe (1940, 133); P. E. Wodehouse dispatch No. 20, June 11, 1853 (enclosed with C. Grey dispatch, Honduras No. 24, July 11, 1854, fo50/264). Actually, as Superintendent Wodehouse described it, "some Indians of

Yucatan headed by . . . José María Zuc [sic] came to Belize and stated that they had recently received from the Spanish commandant of Bacalar a proposal to enter into negotiations, . . . to which they had replied that they could only negotiate through the medium of the British authorities at Belize. They therefore requested that I would consent to take part in the negotiations."

49. Vega dispatch of June 21, 1853 (ER, June 24, 1853, 1).

50. Vega dispatch of July 15, 1853 (ER, July 20, 1853, 1).

51. Vega dispatch of July 15, 1853 (ER, July 20, 1853, 1).

52. M. F. Peraza dispatch of Sept. 6, 1853 (ER, Sept. 14, 1853, 2). This report is based on a single rebel prisoner's story. The parallel between it and the much better attested battle of December 26 in which José Isac Pat was driven toward the coast is enough to cause one to wonder if it was not perhaps the same incident.

53. The so-called treaty is given in full in Spanish by Hübbe (1940, 133–38) and by Anonymous (1866, 364–73), and in English as an enclosure to P. E. Wodehouse dispatch No. 53, Oct. 13, 1853 (FO50/264). The first also lists four secret instructions given by Díaz de la Vega to the commissioners, three of which related to the role the superintendent of British Honduras might take in negotiations, the fourth an insistence that talks take place on Yucatecan territory. The first three were nullified when Superintendent Wodehouse announced that he would be no more than a witness, the fourth was simply not followed, and apparently no excuse was submitted. It is remarkable that no copy of the peace agreement seems to have been preserved in the Archives of British Honduras or in records of the British Colonial Office now in the Public Record Office. The single English version I was able to find is in a volume of correspondence of domestic origin (FO50/264) that includes letters between the Colonial and Foreign offices in London. As will be seen from the text, there is possible ambiguity in the use of the term Indian, or *indio*, which at times appears to apply to all rebels, that is, all *masewalob*.

54. Letters from J. M. Novelo and E. López in Chichanhá to Díaz de la Vega in Mérida, Oct. 1853, (BCP; UA, microfilm roll 3, see Bingham 1972).

55. P. E. Wodehouse to P. Doyle, Sept. 24 and Oct. 13, 1853 (ABH, R40).

56. P. E. Wodehouse to Indian Chiefs, Oct. 12, 1853 (ABH, R40).

57. The agreement was acceptable to Yucatan in at least the short run, and appreciation for Superintendent Wodehouse's efforts was expressed graciously on behalf of the Mexican president (P. Doyle to P. E. Wodehouse, Mar. 4, 1854, enclosing the letter from M. Diez de Bonillo of Feb. 14, 1854, CO123/89).

58. Cadenas dispatch of Dec. 13, 1853 (ER, Dec. 19, 1853, 3–4).

59. Peraza dispatch of Nov. 28, 1853 (ER, Nov. 29, 1853, 3); Novelo dispatch of Jan. 9, 1854 (ER, Jan. 10, 1854, 4).

60. Anonymous (1866, 416–17).

11. Tribulations, Triumphs, Miraculous Crosses

1. Baqueiro (1978–87, 2:452–65, 470–73). Sebastián Molas was a stepson of Santiago Imán, behind whom Sebastián's mother, María Nicolasa Virgilio, was reputedly the power. Molas had his first military command when very young, became noted for his daring, and was thirty-four when executed (see Pérez Alcalá (1914, 14–30). His punishment, when compared with the lesser penalties visited on so many who were guilty of far more in the way of civil insurrection, was thought by many Yucatecans to be shockingly unjust. Baqueiro (1878–87, 2:484–86) refers to his death as martyrdom.

2. Rosado's troops joined Padre Vela in sorrowful vigil at the deathbed, Governor Vega wept, the church bells in Mérida pealed in sadness as all of government-controlled Yucatan mourned the man who ordered the execution of Manuel Antonio Ay, the officer most steadfast and effective in the fight against the rebels. His integrity was proclaimed by the poverty in which he left his family, who were finally aided by a public subscription (Baqueiro 1878–87, 2:465–66).

3. Baqueiro (1878–87, 2:468).

4. Baqueiro (1878–87, 2:445–58) is followed with regard to the civil revolt, with additional details regarding the massacre at Tizimín from Pérez Alcalá (1914, 38–41). Narciso Virgilio was, of course, a relative of Santiago Imán's wife and her son Sebastián Molas, all of them from Tizimín.

5. Anonymous (1866, 356).

6. Covian dispatch of Nov. 26, 1853 (ER, Dec. 9, 1853, 2–3).

7. Peraza dispatch of Dec. 27, 1853 (ER, Jan. 6, 1854, 4).

8. Novelo dispatch of Jan. 9, 1854 (ER, Jan. 10, 1854, 4). This would have been at the one time following the peace treaty of 1853 in which the *pacíficos* had moved to threaten the remaining rebels, as detailed in the preceding chapter.

9. Peraza dispatch of April 18, 1854 (ER, May 5, 1854, 2; see also Ancona 1889, 4:339). There is little doubt that this Moguel was the Baltazar Moguel who aided in enticing *comandante* Uch of Mabén to join Narciso Virgilio and then deserted rather than face the music.

10. No one knows if poison was involved. Baqueiro (1878–87, 4:488 ff.) was inclined to suppose it was simply cholera, although the popular tradition was otherwise. There is no reason that it need be other than cholera, however, which is a bacterial disease spread through fecal contamination of water and food, causing violent diarrhea and vomiting, killing chiefly by dehydration. With the state of the sanitation of Chan Santa Cruz that is attested by Yucatecan accounts, and with cholera raging in the region only a short time before, the presence of its organisms in the water there in May 1854 is more to be expected than surprised at. And the speed with which the government column approached and took the town on this occasion is hard to reconcile with a careful preparation of poisoned bait, although one can be sure that

the *masewalob* would have been happy to provide such fare for their unwelcome guests.

11. The most coherent account of this is in Ancona (1889, 4:339–41). Short descriptions are also in Pérez Alcalá (1914, 35–36, 58).

12. Ancona (1889, 4:341); Baqueiro (1878–87, 2:489–90).

13. Ancona (1889, 4:342–47); Baqueiro (1878–87, 2:490–99; passages quoted from 491–92). See also Pérez Alcalá (1914, 210–13). Yokdzonot—meaning, literally, "above the cenote"—is a common village name in Yucatan, where it often appears more or less interchangeably (for the same pueblo) with the name Dzonot ("cenote"). The pueblo chosen by González may have been the Dzonot shown ten to twenty kilometers southwest of Chan Santa Cruz in the map of Hübbe and Aznar, but another pueblo of Dzonot (marked Yokdzonot on some maps) is also located north of the rebel capital (Berendt 1879).

14. Ancona (1889, 4:343); Novelo dispatch of Jan. 2, 1855 (ER, Jan. 19, 1855).

15. Ancona (1889, 4:342–47); Baqueiro (1878–87, 2:491–97). This passage of Baqueiro places both Yokdzonot and Chunkulché south of Chan Santa Cruz, where I am unable to locate a Chunkulché. There was a pueblo so named northwest of Chan Santa Cruz, not a great distance from the northern Dzonot (Berendt 1879). If González was actually north of the rebel capital it would make it easier to understand his difficulty in communicating with Novelo at Pachmul.

16. Novelo dispatch (GS, Aug. 3, 1855, 1).

17. Ancona (1889, 4:350–55).

18. Baqueiro (1878–87, 3:10–17).

19. Ruiz dispatch of Dec. 30, 1855 (GS, Jan. 2, 1856, 2–3; see also GS, Dec. 26, 1855, 4).

20. Baqueiro (1878–87, 3:25–27).

21. Baqueiro (1878–87, 3:28–31); Peraza dispatches of Oct. 21 and Dec. 5, 1856 (GS, Oct. 24, 1856, 2–3 and Dec. 10, 1856, 1); Novelo dispatches of Oct. 28 and Nov. 24, 1856 (GS, Oct. 31, 1856, and Dec. 1, 1856, 3).

22. Novelo dispatch of Aug. 14, 1857 (GS, Aug. 10, 1857).

23. Baqueiro (1878–87, 3:41–43).

24. Peraza dispatch of March 18, 1856 (GS, March 24, 1856, 2–3). This "stone chapel" is presumably the stone apse section that still stands near the cenote at Felipe Carrillo Puerto.

25. Peraza dispatch of Oct. 17, 1856 (GS, Oct. 22, 1856).

26. F. Seymour dispatch, Confidential No. 1, May 15, 1857 (ABH, R52). One must presume that this was an overestimate by some thousands, but the number was anyway substantial.

27. Young, Toledo, and Co. to F. Seymour, June 15, 1857 (ABH, R58); F. Seymour dispatch, Confidential No. 2, June 17, 1857 (ABH, R52). Young, Toledo claimed that a

valid permit to work on the Yucatecan side of the river had been purchased from the Mexican government.

28. F. Seymour dispatch, unnumbered Confidential, August 17, 1857 (ABH, R52). In this levy of monetary charges, the Santa Cruz rebels and the *pacíficos* of the south were both following the same policy, as will be seen in a later chapter.

29. Ancona (1905, 17–18). There were three candidates for the governorship, Barrera, Pablo Castellanos, and Liborio Irigoyen. As the packages of votes from each locale were opened and certified, one from the *pacíficos del Sur* simply contained a statement purporting to bear the signatures of the major southern leaders and conveying the information that they and all their subordinates wished to cast their votes for Irigoyen, for a total of 4,674. At the same time, a legislator of an opposition party produced a letter purporting to bear the signatures of many of the same leaders, in which they assured him that they had not voted for Irigoyen. The *pacífico* votes were thrown out.

30. These events are summarized by Ancona (1905, 19–28), who is followed; and by Baqueiro (1878–87, 3:48–69), with some disagreement in minor details.

31. Baqueiro (1878–87, 3:72). Coherent accounts of these events appear in Ancona (1905, 28–32) and Baqueiro (1878–87, 3:70–77). Sections of the accounts that both drew upon, with other information, are in GS (Sept. 18, 1857), especially the letter from A. Duarte to P. Barrera of Sept. 16, 2, and that of J. M. Avila to the Governor, Sept. 17 (GS, Sept. 30, 3).

32. That the rebel "Indians" could be so easily mistaken for Campeche troops shows the fineness of the line that separated one side from the other in looks and comportment.

33. A somewhat flowery account of the heroism of Ramírez, as his family members were chopped up before his eyes, is given by R. Menéndez ("D. Eusebio Ramírez," RM, July 31, 1892, 3). According to the same author ("14 y 15 de setiembre de 1857 en Tekax," RM, Sept. 22, 1892, 2) no rapes were committed during the killings, for the cross had prohibited the behavior. I am not able to evaluate this.

34. It is ironic—if not worthy of outright suspicion—that the home of Anselmo Duarte should be one of only three that were untouched by the raiders, for it can be recalled that this same Duarte was a supporter of Felipe Rosado at Peto in 1848, was suspected strongly of traffic with the rebels, and was nearly shot by order of Eulogio Rosado (see chap. 7). A descendant reports that the reason the house was spared was that Duarte had given food and shown other kindnesses to rebel Indians jailed in Tekax, who presumably were those who then led the rebels to the lightly guarded town (Montilla Duarte 1955), although other sources say it was saved because the door was in the line of fire of the soldiers under Ramírez. In any event, after the massacre his public reputation was that of a great philanthropist.

See, for instance, R. Menéndez, "14 y 15 de setiembre de 1857 en Tekax" (RM, Sept. 22, 1892, 2).

35. For instance, Baqueiro (1878–87, 3:227) indicates that the leader was José Crescencio Poot, who "in 1857 when the Tekax catastrophe occurred made his name baneful" (see also Baqueiro 1887). Others (Ancona 1905, 28–32; Anonymous 1866, 407–15) are noncommittal. Evidently Zapata, Poot, and Claudio Novelo were all facile enough in Spanish to have performed as the bogus Campeche officers, and perhaps all of them did.

36. Peraza dispatches of Sept. 22 and Oct. 16, 1857 (GS, Sept. 28, 1857, 1, and 21 Oct., 1857, 3).

37. F. Seymour dispatches of Nov. 17 and Dec. 17, 1857 (ABH, R55); J. H. Faber to F. Seymour, Dec. 20, 1857 (ABH, R58).

38. Ancona (1905, 32–37). Andrés Cepeda was brother of Manuel Cepeda Peraza, who was leading the government forces against Campeche.

39. Peraza dispatches of Sept. 22 and Oct. 28, 1857 (GS, Sept. 28, 1857, 1, and Nov. 5, 1857, 1); J. M. Covian dispatch of Dec. 11, 1857 (GS, Dec. 18, 1857, 1–2).

40. Ancona (1905, 39–41). It was actually more complicated than this: Barrera resigned in favor of Peraza temporarily, to allow Peraza to attempt to make peace with Campeche; Peraza was unable to do so immediately and returned the government to Barrera on December 24, who four days later—now convinced that peace was impossible while he was governor—resigned permanently in Peraza's favor.

41. Ancona (1905, 32–52) summarizes these events. The agreement to separate is quoted in full on 52–56. Campeche was to consist of what were then the *partidos* of Carmen, Seibaplaya, Campeche, Hecelchakan, and Hopelchen, both names and boundaries changed from those of the beginning of the century (Rodríguez Losa 1989).

42. "Crónica peninsular" (EF, July 25, 1851, 4). Much of this section of the text parallels Dumond (1985). Although an event in the Chenes would seem too far from Chan Santa Cruz to be related to its cult leader, one of the letters of Juan de la Cruz to Barbachano, dated Aug. 11, 1851, datelined "Balamná"—that is, Chan Santa Cruz—was reportedly found near Becanchén (Quintal Martín 1992, letter 50).

43. Díaz de la Vega dispatches of April 14 (ER, Apr. 18, 1853, 1) and later (ER, July 8, 1853, 4). The location is shown in maps of both 1848 (Regil and Peón 1853) and 1878 (Hübbe and Aznar 1878 in Berendt 1879). Although it is surprising that the stronghold would be so close to Valladolid, the itineraries suggest that the Mabén in question should be somewhere in that vicinity: one force, for instance, went east-northeast of Xcan to a place called Chunkuché (not located), then south to Santa María (located on both maps cited), then began a return to Valladolid and Tizimín, which passed

through *Chan Santa Cruz del Oriente* from where one party went to Chemax, the other apparently to Tizimín (Peraza dispatch of Apr. 11, 1854, ER, May 3, 1854, 2–3).

44. López de Llergo dispatches of Feb. 14 and Feb. 24, 1854 (ER, Feb. 20, 1854, 1–2, and Mar. 6, 1854, 4). Although the given name of the Yucatecan deserter is not stated, circumstantial evidence suggests it was the same. According to Pérez Alcalá (1914, 39), the rebel Uch and his Mabén force were recruited by Yucatecan soldiers named Valencia, Gío, and Moguel, and he specifically reports that Valencia and Gío received for their pains sentences in San Juan de Ulúa. Moguel is not mentioned, I presume because he deserted in timely fashion and was able to explain himself in some manner satisfactory to the rebels of Mabén. I also presume it to be the same Moguel who in April 1854 was fighting on the side of the rebels of the original Chan Santa Cruz to the south, as I mentioned earlier. For in 1864 Baltazar Moguel was married to the daughter of Bonifacio Novelo and living in British Honduras, according to the report of P. Barrera and M. Sierra O'Reilly (LR, July 5, 1864, 2).

45. Peraza dispatch (ER, Apr. 4, 1855, 2–3).

46. J. Orihuela dispatch of Oct. 13, 1855, and its enclosure (GS, Oct. 17, 1855, 2–4). The presence of *Juan de la Cruz* three times in signatory position distinguishes this document from those apparently issued from Chan Santa Cruz.

47. Peraza dispatch of Dec. 28, 1855 (GS, Jan. 4, 1856, 3–4).

48. Peraza dispatches of March 18, 1856 (GS, Mar. 24, 1856, 2–3) and Oct. 17, 1856 (GS, Oct. 22, 1856). Pedro Acereto was son of Agustín Acereto, who was mentioned earlier and will be again.

49. Peraza dispatches of Feb. 27, Apr. 7, and May 26, 1857 (GS, Mar. 4, 1857, 1; Apr. 13, 1857, 3; and May 29, 1857, 1–2).

50. Peraza dispatch of May 26, 1857 (GS, May 29, 1857, 1–2).

51. Irigoyen decree of Dec. 18, 1858 (EC, Dec. 22, 1858, 1).

52. From Jan. 1, 1858, through Oct. 1, 1858, GS; from Oct. 4, 1858, EC.

53. Peraza dispatch of Dec. 23, 1856 (GS, Dec. 29, 1856, 1). It is interesting that the *hidalgo* from Tikuch, Onofre Xuluc—who proved the nemesis of local rebels—carried the same surname as Victor Xuluc, the rebel leader who had led the earlier raid on Tikuch.

54. As, for instance, Covian dispatch of Dec. 11, 1857 (GS, Dec. 18, 1857, 1–2); Cepeda P. dispatch, June 29, 1858 (GS, July 21, 1858, 1).

55. Martínez V. dispatch of July 27, 1858 (GS, July 30, 1858, 1); Peraza dispatch, Sept. 20, 1856 (GS, Sept. 24, 1856, 1–2).

56. J. M. Iturralde to the Governor, June 11, 1859 (EC, June 13, 1859, 3); letters from Dzib, Durán, and Moguel, and from Pérez, Sánchez, and Ayala, June 3, 1859 (EC, June 20, 1859, 1). "Montaña del Oriente," literally "forests of the east," apparently

referred to scattered hamlets in a relatively wide area; in any event, no pueblo of that name has been identified.

57. F. Osorio to the Governor, July 5, 1859 (EC, July 8, 1859, 2).

58. A map made in 1852 on orders of General Vega ("Carta de Yucatán formada con datos adquiridos sobre el terreno en la campaña que hizo el Sr. General de Brigada . . . Rómulo Díaz de la Vega, arreglado y delineado por Manuel Hernández," n.d.), the original now somewhat deteriorated and held by the Museo Yucateco de Antropología e Historia, includes in the northeastern part of the peninsula two points designated Kantunil—one in the far northeast immediately south of Cape Catoche, the other in the approximate location of modern Kantunil-kin. Anonymous (1866, 441–42) states that the earlier rebel Kantunil was located "between Chan Santa Cruz and Cape Catoche" and that the pacified rebels moved to a settlement of the same name "between Yalahau and . . . Tizimín." The latter appears to be the western Kantunil of Vega's map and the site Baqueiro (1878–87, 3:187) identified as Kantunil-kin, saying specifically that it was on lands belonging to the priest García (i.e., José Antonio García of Valladolid). The designation Kantunil-kin is used for the pacified town in an account of events of 1872 by Pérez Alcalá (1914, 226–27) and in some nineteenth-century references (e.g., Urcelay dispatch of Aug. 19, 1872, RP, Aug. 26, 1872, 1). The peace agreement itself and most nineteenth-century stories concerning the pacified town refer to it only as Kantunil. Fortunately, a few sources use both designators (e.g., attachments to the Urcelay dispatch cited above), indicating that at least after pacification Kantunil and Kantunil-kin were the same, presumably located at or near the present town of Kantunil-kin in northwest Quintana Roo. Hübbe and Aznar (Berendt 1879) place their Kantunil farther to the northeast, at a point written *Kantanihil* on the map of Anonymous 1848 and approximately at the eastern Kantunil of the Vega map.

59. P. Acereto and V. Marín to the governor, Oct. 3, 1859 (EC, Oct. 10, 1859, 3). It is not clear that this agreement covered the people from Chunchacalhaz, for those authorizing the signing of the treaty for the rebels apparently represented only people of Xpacchén and what was identified as Montaña del Oriente; but events to be described later make it evident that Chunchacalhaz was also pacified about this time.

60. Acereto dispatch of Mar. 9, 1860 (EC, Mar. 12, 1860); Iturralde to the governor (EC, June 28, 1861, 1).

61. J. Cadenas dispatches of Feb. 16 and Feb. 25, 1850 (BO, Feb. 20, 1850, 2, and Mar. 1, 1850, 2); J. H. Faber to C. J. S. Fancourt, Apr. 12, 1850 (ABH, R33).

62. Vega dispatch of June 21, 1853 (ER, June 24, 1853, 1).

63. Quintal Martín 1992, letters 29 and 30.

64. J. H. Faber (to F. Seymour, Dec. 20, 1857, ABH, R58), who says that Venancio Pec was murdered because of his interview with Superintendent Fancourt.

65. W. Anderson to the superintendent, Feb. 15, 1858 (ABH, R61).

12. Massacres and Machinations

1. F. Seymour dispatch No. 3, Jan. 12, 1858 (ABH, R55); M. A. Perdomo to Supt. of British Honduras, Feb. 5, 1858, and W. Anderson to Supt. of British Honduras, Feb. 15, 1858 (ABH, R61).

2. W. Anderson to Superintendent, Feb. 15, 1858 (ABH, R61). It would appear from the presence of a constructed "chapel" that this may have been a regular stopping place for *masewal* traders.

3. Baqueiro (1878–87, 3:138).

4. T. R. Esteves to Governor of Yucatan, Feb. 22, 1858 (GS, Mar. 31, 1858, 1); L. Canto to J. M. Novelo, Mar. 6, 1858 (GS, Apr. 7, 1858, 3); T. Rosado M. to J. M. Martínez, Feb. 23, 1856 (ABH, R61).

5. R. Menéndez, "Toma de Bacalar por los indios" (RM, Feb. 20, 1890, 2).

6. All direct quotations in this section are from F. Seymour dispatch 11, Mar. 13, 1858 (ABH, R55).

7. A part of the delay was because the presumably omniscient cross required that the letter, written in English, be translated first into Spanish and then into Maya before it would respond.

8. Interestingly, shortly before the British plea for mercy was rejected by the cross, Blake came to Captain Anderson "with some alarm to enquire if it were true that General Windham had been beaten in India, for the chiefs said so, and that the power of England was no longer to be feared" (F. Seymour dispatch No. 11, March 13, 1858, ABH, R55). The event referred to was in the early stage of the India mutiny, in which Sepoy and other Indian troops enjoyed remarkable success between May and September 1857, when the tide turned against them. Clearly, the *masewalob* were not entirely parochial in outlook.

9. The most coherent single source for the Bacalar executions is the Seymour dispatch just cited, which appears also as enclosure to Governor Darling's dispatch from Jamaica, Honduras No. 12, Mar. 24, 1858 (CO123/96). The dispatch is quoted almost verbatim, but without attribution, by Fowler (1879, 41–42), who in turn is quoted verbatim by Buhler (1975, 3–4). This account is supplemented by E. W. Burke to F. Seymour, Feb. 28 and Mar. 4, 1858 (ABH, R61), and by Rosado (1931). The Seymour dispatch is based on an interview with Anderson, represented by the almost illegible "notes taken under Cap^tn Anderson's dictation," dated Mar. 7, 1858 (ABH, R61). Anderson's observations are thus in Seymour's dispatch, Blake's in the letters of Edmund Burke. An account filled with much more in the way of atrocities—

certainly not written by an eyewitness and almost certainly unreliable—was drawn on by Ancona (1905, 57–59); with a Belize dateline of April 27, it appeared in the *New York Herald* of June 2, 1858, was translated into Spanish in Cuba and then published in Mérida (GS, June 23, 1858, 1). The manner of execution was apparently a standard one. Some years later, an eyewitness described a scene in which the executioner approached his male victim and "addressed him in Maya: . . . You must die. It is not our doing, it is the will of God. . . . The Indian's macheat then cleft the back of the unfortunate man's head, across. When he fell a second cut was then made diagonally to the first and the body was then run through with the macheat which was vigorously twisted round and round in the wound." See R. W. Pickwoad to Colonial Secretary, Apr. 18, 1892, encl. with A. Maloney dispatch No. 146, May 12, 1892 (CO123/198).

10. T. R. Esteves to Governor, Mar. 2 and Mar. 3, 1858, former with enclosed list (GS, Mar. 31, 1858, 1–2). There were a few survivors. One woman interviewed in the 1930s professed at the age of five or six years to have hidden for five days in a cave within Bacalar while the massacre went on, escaping one stormy night to the Río Hondo (G. Menéndez 1936, 173, 192).

11. Various letters and circulars in GS (Apr. 5, 1858, 1–2).

12. Baqueiro (1878–87, 3:139). Martínez V. dispatch of Apr. 5, 1858 (GS, Apr. 9, 1858, 1).

13. J. M. Novelo dispatches of Aug. 21, Aug. 24 (GS, Aug. 23, 1858, 4, Aug. 25, 1858, 2, Aug. 30, 2). The other four leaders listed were Pedro González, Pablo Castillo, Manuel Jesús Vitorín, and Juan Carlos Tzuc. Poot and González were reportedly wounded, Castillo killed.

14. Ancona (1905, 60–64).

15. "La situación" (EC, Dec. 27, 1858, 4); Salazar dispatch, Dec. 24, 1858 (EC, Dec. 29, 1858, 1).

16. The single *masewal* missive received in British Honduras between the Bacalar killings in March and the following October was, in the words of the governor, "a letter from a Junior Chief to Mr. [James Hume] Blake, a coloured gentleman. They . . . say that the English need not be afraid as the Indians only warred against 'los blancos,' an expression which Mr. Blake translated 'the Spaniards' " (F. Seymour dispatch No. 66, Oct. 17, 1858, ABH, R65). The majority of British Hondurans, of course, were people of color.

17. Quoted from Seymour dispatch No. 69, Nov. 17, 1858 (ABH, R65); see also Rosado (1931); L. Canto to Editors, Nov. 5, 1858 (EC, Nov. 8, 1858, 4). "Renouncing the religion of their conquerors" must be understood to mean renouncing the Catholic hierarchy of Yucatan, for the rebels clearly never ceased devoutly to regard themselves as Christians. Later estimates of the regular strength of the Bacalar detachment

are about half those cited from the Seymour dispatch. Both the church and the Santos house in Santo Cah are shown in a map in chapter 13 (see fig. 1).

18. Rosado (1931, material quoted from the issue of June 25, most spelling as in original), with editorial reference made to the republication by Buhler (1975), in which certain abridgements are apparent and some typographical errors in the former have been corrected, possibly by reference to manuscript material. Buhler (1975, 10) gives the name as Nazario, rather than Nazareo.

19. Rosado (1931). The given name of the "first General" is apparently misremembered for that of Dionisio (not Pantaleón) Zapata, who bore the title *Chikiwik*, as will be indicated later.

20. Rosado (1931).

21. Rosado (1931).

22. Rosado (1931). The Rosado account was written in 1915, nearly sixty years after the events (see Buhler 1975); an indication that his memory of some details may have suffered is given by Seymour's statement of November 17 (dispatch No. 69, Nov. 17, 1858, ABH, R65) that Rosado had already reached British Honduras by that date, and that he was accompanied in his release by the second boy, whom Rosado does not refer to at all. Seymour also remarks that upon the release "as an after-thought the loan of the boys was again applied for and forty lashes having been inflicted on each . . . they were restored to the English men." One must also suppose that Rosado's description of matters in the Chan Santa Cruz hierarchy was shaped by conversations and understandings acquired throughout his life in British Honduras, as well as by his experience as a prisoner for eight months at age eight.

23. Baqueiro (1878–87, 3:165–70).

24. C. Menéndez (1925, chaps. 3–11); P. E. Wodehouse to Vice Admiral Seymour, June 10, 1853, and Seymour to P. C. Doyle, Sept. 24, 1853 (ABH, R40); J. T. Crawford to the Earl of Clarendon, Feb. 23, 1854, and Marquis Peznela to the Mexican Consul in Havana, Jan. 5, 1854, both encl. with Foreign Office to Herman Merivale, Colonial Office, Apr. 4, 1854 (CO123/89). González Navarro (1970, 124–29) describes the same affair, adding that Martí held a commission in Cuban naval forces.

25. C. Menéndez (1923, 135; 1925, 81–87); González Navarro (1970, 132–39). The difference was that the new contracts did not allow beatings.

26. See, for instance, Suárez y Navarro (1979, 45).

27. Baqueiro (1878–87, 3:182, 199–200); González Navarro (1970, 138–43).

28. Suárez y Navarro (1979, 46).

29. Baqueiro (1878–87, 3:200–4). For the letter from Melchor Ocampo, see González Navarro (1970, 322–24).

30. Baqueiro (1878–87, 3:178–79); Aguayo dispatch of July 15, and Cetina dispatch of July 14, 1859 (EC, July 18, 1859, 1). Text of the Castellanos decree is in C. Menéndez (1923, 175).

31. Ancona (1905, 81–83).

32. Baqueiro (1878–87, 3:181–82); C. Menéndez (1925, 98–99).

33. Ancona (1905, 88–89); Baqueiro (1878–87, 3:183–85, 197). Actually, Acereto took over in his position as a member of the junta, not as governor. But by having son Pedro come to Mérida from Valladolid with his entire military force, Agustín was in a strong position from which he first offered Castellanos a chance to return to the governorship—an offer Castellanos, looking down the muzzles of Pedro's muskets, could easily refuse—and then accepted the dual positions of leadership that the pro-Irigoyen movement had offered him. Obviously, when he accepted he did not intend it to be only for the interim.

34. Anonymous (1866, 443), who also alleges that when the Aceretos did not acquire prisoners they shipped off peaceful Indians instead. This seems to have been more than rumor: Suárez y Navarro (1979, 48) reports the matter specifically; see also González Navarro (1970, 143).

35. P. Acereto dispatch of Jan. 23, 1860 (EC, Feb. 3, 1860, 1). The lack of finish to the church apparently referred simply to the absence of towers, which were never put in place.

36. The report was false, although consistently repeated by the historians, as will be clear later.

37. Pérez Alcalá (1914, 216–17).

38. A. Acereto dispatch of Feb. 16, 1860 (EC, Feb. 20, 1860, 1).

39. Baqueiro (1878–87, 3:188–97, the quotation is from 196); Ancona (1905, 92–101).

40. J. H. Faber to T. Price, July 6, 1860 (ABH, R71); the account is repeated in T. Price dispatch No. 50, July 9, 1860 (ABH, R68).

41. Baqueiro (1878–87, 3:204); Suárez y Navarro (1979, 48).

42. C. Menéndez (1925, 99–108).

43. Ancona (1905, 113–14) says that no formal plan was ever published but that the understanding was that Irigoyen was to be put into the office. There is an error in Ancona's text, in which the date of the pronouncement is given as May 1861, but revisions to it are dated in February of the same year.

44. This convoluted sequence of events is described fairly succinctly by Ancona (1905, 102–17).

45. The charges to the congress are given in full by González Navarro (1970, 146–48), who reports the British not willing to actually patrol, because the matter might involve less than outright slavery, but agreeing to provide intelligence.

46. Ancona (1889, 4:257, 310).

47. Bojórquez Urzáiz (1977).

48. Bojórquez Ur{á}iz (1977).

49. See, for example, the discussion of Rodríguez Losa (1978).

50. For example, Baqueiro (1881); Rodríguez Losa (1978); Suárez Molina (1977a, 1:49–50). Comparable figures, as well as others, are given by Cook and Borah (1974). The 1846–47 census figures are discussed in chapter 5.

51. González Navarro (1970, 148–50).

52. Suárez Molina (1977a, 1:169–70).

53. Joseph (1986, 41); Suárez Molina (1977a, 2:26).

54. See Bracamonte y Sosa (1993); G. Cámara Zavala (1977); Suárez Molina (1977, 1:250–81); Wells (1985).

13. Cross Triumphant, Cross Deposed

1. F. Seymour dispatch No. 7, Feb. 8, 1860 (ABH, R68).

2. These events are reported in T. Price dispatch No. 50, July 9, 1860 (ABH, R68) and in several documents of ABH (R71): J. H. Faber to the superintendent, July 6, 1860; E. Burke to T. Price, June 24, 1860; Deposition of Pierre Manrice, July 3, 1860; Deposition of Agapito Burgos, July 6, 1860, Deposition of A. Cámara, July 3, 1860; and Y. W. Cherrington to E. Burke, June 24, 1860.

3. Major Mends to Superintendent, July 9, 1860 (ABH, R71).

4. B. Puc to Sr. Gobernador del Majestad Britanico, n.d. (ABH, R71); Price dispatch No. 29, Mar. 12, 1861 (ABH, R68).

5. Price dispatches No. 29, Mar. 12, 1861, and No. 53, May 8, 1861 (ABH, R68). The name Bernardino Chi, apparently furnished to Price by a resident of Corozal, is almost certainly an error for Bernardino Cen, a name well known later. With regard to the rebel letter, both English and Spanish versions in the archives (B. Puc to Sr. Gobernador del Majestad Britanico, n.d., ABH, R71) bear as signature the name only of Puc and neither carries that of a scribe. The Spanish version is written in a very attractive hand, its spelling no worse than was common in nineteenth-century Yucatan. If the letter was the original rather than a translation from Maya (and there is nothing about it to indicate that it was such a translation), it would appear that Puc actually penned it and that no scribe was required to affix Puc's signature.

6. From ABH (R71): J. M. Castillo to Magistrate of Corozal, Feb. 27, 1861; depositions of J. Y. Tamay, Mar. 6, of F. Us, Mar. 2, F. Tun, Mar. 2, 1861.

7. T. Price to E. Burke, Mar. 12, 1861 (ABH, R72).

8. T. Price to V. Puc, Mar. 14, 1861 (ABH, R72).

9. This is apparently the same Trejo who had been instrumental in securing the release of the two boys from Santa Cruz somewhat more than two years earlier.

10. Firsthand accounts of the trip are in ABH (R71), dated 1861: Plumridge and Twigge to the Superintendent, Apr. 12; depositions of A. Orío, Apr. 9, and of J. M. Trejo of Apr. 9 and Apr. 12. The dates given by Plumridge and Twigge are uniformly one day later than those reported by their interpreters. A secondary account, but one that contains information apparently received directly from Plumridge or Twigge in 1861, and which is amplified beyond their own spare report, is in E. Rogers (1885). They also apparently provided a verbal estimate of the rebel soldiers as about five thousand in number (J. R. Longden dispatch No. 6, Nov. 28, 1867; ABH, R98). I have elsewhere erroneously identified the second of the two officer emissaries as J. Y. Twigge (Dumond 1977, 120), from misreading the handwritten documents. His name is corrected here from the army list (United Kingdom 1864).

11. E. Rogers (1885, 223).

12. Price dispatch No. 50, May 1, 1861 (ABH, R68).

13. E. Rogers (1885, 224–25). The description is clearly that of the massive church that is today in use in Felipe Carrillo Puerto.

14. Deposition of J. M. Trejo, Apr. 12, 1861 (ABH, R71).

15. E. Rogers (1885, 225).

16. Deposition of J. M. Trejo, Apr. 12, 1861 (ABH, R71).

17. T. Price dispatch No. 50, May 1, 1861 (ABH, R68).

18. Declaration of J. de los A. Loeza, Aug. 26, 1861 (ABH, R74).

19. Letters in "Parte oficial" (EC, June 14, 1861, 2–3): J. M. Martínez O. to Governor of Yucatan, Apr. 16; J. F. Sauri to Governor of Yucatan, Apr. 13, Apr. 30, with enclosures.

20. E. Burke to T. Price, Apr. 25, 1861, and J. Carmichael to T. Price, Apr. 27, 1861 (ABH, R71).

21. The map is drawn from a photographic copy generously given to me in 1974 by the late Alfredo Barrera Vásquez, then director of the Instituto Yucateco de Antropología e Historia. He had two such prints but was not able to find the identification of the archival source that had once been clipped to them. I have not been able to locate that source.

22. J. M. Castillo to Corozal Magistrate, Feb. 27, 1861 (ABH, R71).

23. Of these named individuals, Zapata, Santos, and Castillo were all dead by early 1864. Zacarías May is not known to have been active after the middle part of 1860 and can be presumed dead after that time, although his actual death is unreported; in any event, his name on the map should mean it was not drawn much if any after 1860. Jose María Canche is also not heard of again, although a Tomás Canche is mentioned as a *comandante* in 1861 and after and may be the individual intended.

24. Ancona (1905, 119).

25. Baqueiro (1878–87, 3:224–25).

26. Baqueiro (1878–87, 3:227–28); "Ultima correría de los bárbaros" (EC, Sept. 11, 1861, 3–4).

27. The raid is described by Ancona (1905, 121–23) and Baqueiro (1878–87, 3:227–28), and in "Ultima correría de los bárbaros" (EC, Sept. 11, 1861, 3–4). Preliminary reports of the event are in EC, Sept. 9, 1861, with additional details on Sept. 16.

28. F. Pren dispatch (EN, Feb. 19, 1862, 3).

29. L. Espinosa dispatch, Aug. 24, 1862 (EN, Aug. 27, 1862, 1–2). Women retained their own family names, so that Rodríguez was the original family name of Josefa (and her sister) as well as of her husband. The same escapees reported what they seemed to know of the leadership at this time: in addition to Puc these were identified as general Leandro Santos and *comandantes* Dionisio Zapata, Crescencio Poot, Claudio Novelo, Bonifacio Novelo, and Tomás Canche.

30. Ancona (1905, 124–37); Baqueiro (1878–87, 3:230–50).

31. Commercial deportation ended because of Irigoyen's policies (e.g., Ancona 1905, 138 ff) and also because of the distinctly paternalistic attitude of the Maximilian administration that followed.

32. Ancona (1905, 146–51);Baqueiro (1878–87, 3:257–62); R. Novelo dispatch (EN, Aug. 1, 1862, 1); Herrera dispatches (EN, Sept. 1, 1862, 1, and Sept. 4, 1862, 2); A. Maldonado dispatch of Sept. 4, 1862 (EN, Sept. 8, 1862, 2).

33. There is some suggestion that Acereto was here supported by the French; see Ancona (1905, 149).

34. Ancona (1905, 147–52); Baqueiro (1878–87, 3:260–66).

35. Baqueiro (1878–87, 3:266–76); reports in NE, Aug. 28, 1862 (2–4); Navarrete dispatches of Sept. 26, 1863 (NE, Sept. 26, 1863, 1), of Sept. 28, 1863 (NE, Oct. 2, 1863, 1–2), and of Oct. 1, 1863 (NE, Oct. 5, 1863, 1).

36. This complicated set of events is treated by Baqueiro (1878–87, 3:276–92), and perhaps more incisively by Ancona (1905, 165–85). The surrender concludes both historical works.

37. T. Briseño dispatch of Jan. 8, 1863 (EP, Feb. 3, 1863, 1); dispatches of C. M. Oca and R. López of Jan. 1–7 (EN, Jan. 9, 1863, 1–2); N. Novelo dispatches of Jan. 7 (EN, Jan. 12, 1863, 1) and Jan. 12 (EN, Jan. 23, 1863, 1).

38. S. Panting to P. Toledo, Apr. 26, 1863 (ABH, R83).

39. Deposition of J. I. Méndez, May 7, 1863 (ABH, R83). The *mecate* as a measure of area is equal to about four hundred square meters.

40. Puc, Santos, and Zapata to Magistrate at Corozal, June 11, 1863; E. Burke to F. Seymour, May 26, 1863, with enclosures; E. Burke to M. de los S. López, June 12, 1863 (all in ABH, R83). The matter is summarized in F. Seymour dispatches No. 70, June 14, 1863, and No. 72, July 13, 1863 (ABH, R81).

41. Baqueiro (1878–87, 3:279–80).

42. The translation to English, while amusing, is misleading. Written by Castillo, I presume the original was in Spanish, in which case the last phrase would go *que no era santo sino cristiano*, meaning literally "that he was no saint but a human being."

43. Santos, Zapata, and Castillo to His Excellency the Superintendent, Jan. 1, 1864 (ABH, R84).

44. E. Burke to G. Berkeley, Jan. 25, 1864 (ABH, R84). A common view in Yucatan would be that the peaceful bent of Zapata was owed to the influence of Yucatecan captives (e.g., Hübbe 1940, 150).

45. F. Navarrete to F. Seymour, Mar. 1864 (ABH, R84). The hope for peace even then was overly sanguine, for it was reported in early March that Zapata had been forced to allow a determined group of the rebels to leave in the customary way for an attack on Tekax (E. Burke to G. Berkeley, Mar. 5, 1864, ABH, R84).

46. Martínez de Arredondo letter of Mar. 18, "Remitado" (NE, Mar. 18, 1864, 3).

47. E. Burke to G. Berkeley, Apr. 4, 1864 (ABH, R84).

48. J. I. Montalvo dispatch of Feb. 12, 1864 (LR, Feb. 19, 1864, 2). But the fact that this event presumably occurred on December 31 and the letter to the British Honduras governor was written by Zapata, Santos, and Castillo on Jan. 1 casts doubt on the report. Santos does not appear again, however, and must have met death no later than did Zapata.

49. Report of the Commission of the Government of Yucatan, June 13, 1864 (LR, July 1, 1864, 3, and July 5, 1864, 2; the quotation is from the July 5 issue; the same report is published in NE, June 24, 1864, 1–3). The Campeche version (LR) lists one of the triumvirate as José Oa, the Mérida paper (NE) as José Na, the latter confirmed by J. I. Montalvo dispatch of Feb. 12, 1864 (LR, Feb. 19, 1864, 2). Balbino, Ake and Victoriano Villorín may be the rebels elsewhere called Albino Ake and Vitorio Vitorín.

50. Aldherre (1869).

51. Trebarra (1864).

52. Aldherre (1869, 75–76). This author speaks of both *tata Polin* and *tata Nohoch Dzul* as titles. As noted elsewhere, however (Dumond 1985), *tata* Polin almost certainly is based on the given name of Apolinar Sánchez, the incumbent of the position of Interpreter of the Cross in 1863–64. This is parallel to the nickname used by some for the *tatich* himself, *tata* Ve (or *tata* Be, in nineteenth-century Yucatan), "father Ve," for Venancio. It is also likely that *tata Nohoch Dzul* ("father Great Dzul") was similarly a personal rather than functional appellation of the particular person recognized as foremost spy: according to Barrera in his novel (Trebarra 1864), this name was applied to Bonifacio Novelo—a spy and also a general—as a jocular reference, I presume, to his Spanish name and mestizo origin.

53. E.g., Bricker (1981, 187); Villa Rojas (1945, 161).

54. I.e., "primer sacerdote de las cruces" (Baqueiro 1887).

55. Bricker (1981, 107) is inclined to identify *tata* Naz as Atanacio Puc, who is listed in late versions of the basic exhortation of the cross (as, for instance, that given by Villa Rojas 1945) as one of the early patrons, but there is no direct evidence to support this identification.

56. A partly parallel suggestion is made by Lapointe (1983, 88–89), who is determined to see the maintenance of British favor as the key factor in the rise of Novelo and Poot to top leadership at the expense of Zapata. I see no evidence whatever for this.

57. J. I. Montalvo dispatch of Feb. 12, 1864 (LR, Feb. 19, 1864, 2).

58. P. R. Lavalle dispatch of July 23, 1863 (NE, July 27, 1863, 2).

59. Trebarra (1864, 144).

60. A. Sandoval dispatch of July 2, 1864 (NE, July 8, 1864, 1, emphasis added).

14. Unsteady Peace in the South

1. G. Cantón and E. López to R. Díaz de la Vega, Sept. 17, 1853, quoted in full in Ancona (1889, 4:434–42); see also the summary of the course of the war in ER (Mar. 7, 1855, 2).

2. Díaz de la Vega to J. Cadenas, Nov. 22, 1854 (ER, Nov. 29, 1854, 3).

3. J. M. Novelo dispatch of Jan. 4, 1855 (ER, Jan. 21, 1855); summary of the course of the war, ER (Mar. 7, 1855, 2S).

4. W. Stevenson dispatch No. 72, Sept. 9, 1856 (ABH, R55) reports Luciano Tzuc as commander when he appeared on the Hondo to extort rents. On June 6, 1860, Asunción Ek, signing himself as general of Chichanhá (letter to E. Burke, ABH, R71), asked the British government's assistance in recovering rents from Zima for land he farmed on the Yucatecan side of the river. On June 3, 1864, a British magistrate (E. Burke to J. G. Austin, ABH, R84), reports that Tzuc's men committed depredations at San Román, on Albion Island, that included the burning of a boat of twenty tons belonging to Andrés Zima; On Aug. 17, 1868, a magistrate (E. Adolphus to J. R. Longden, ABH, R102) reports that Zima owned the settlement on the British side at Chunabá, where he operated a distillery, and also owned a house in Corozal.

5. See the discussion in Dobson (1973, 212–13).

6. British officials on the ground knew their settlers had overreached the territories allowed them by Spain. In 1854, the governor of Jamaica allowed that at the time "when Mexico threw off the Spanish yokes . . . Woodcutting Establishments had been formed by British Subjects far beyond the Northern frontier of the Honduras Settlement as . . . defined by the Convention" (H. Barkly to Sir George Grey, Oct. 4, 1854, CO123/89, enclosing related dispatch of W. Stevenson, Sept. 16, 1854). British Honduras Superintendent Stevenson in a secret letter to Secretary Leboucheve, of Dec. 16, 1856 (ABH, R52; also encl. with W. Bell dispatch, Honduras No. 27, Dec. 26,

1856, CO123/93) refers to the "boundary of our present occupations, authorized by (improper) 'grants' from former superintendents of this place: but I believe . . . those branches and portions of the Hondo and the works upon them from Blue Creek upwards are far beyond the limits defined by . . . treaty."

7. F. Seymour confidential dispatch No. 3, July 14, 1857 (ABH, R52).

8. Young, Toledo and Co. to F. Seymour, June 15, 1857 (ABH, R58); W. Stevenson dispatch No. 72, Sept. 9, 1856, and dispatch No. 76, Oct. 16, 1856 (ABH, R55); Young, Harrison, Bevan to Earl Granville, June 1873 (FO50/432).

9. F. Seymour dispatch No. 20, June 17, 1857 (ABH, R55); also W. Stevenson dispatch No. 76, Oct. 16, 1856 (ABH, R55).

10. Young, Toledo and Co. to F. Seymour, June 15, 1857 (ABH, R58); J. G. Austin dispatch No. 56, Aug. 14, 1866 (ABH, R92); Young, Harrison, Bevan to Earl Granville, June 1873 (FO50/432).

11. F. Seymour, confidential dispatch No. 3, July 14, 1857 (ABH, R52).

12. J. H. Faber to F. Seymour, Dec. 20, 1857 (ABH, R58); T. de Briceño to J. M. Novelo, July 22, 1858 (GS, Aug. 2, 1858, 2).

13. F. Seymour dispatch No. 127, Nov. 12, 1862, and dispatch No. 15, Feb. 13, 1863 (ABH, R81); M. Barbosa to Governor of Campeche, July 25, 1863 (EP, Aug. 11, 1863, 1). The best account of the succession from Uluac to Tzuc to Marcos Canul is statement of S. Cervera, May 12, 1866 (ABH, R93).

14. Baqueiro (1878–87, 2:323–24); P. Encalada statement of Aug. 12, 1867 (EP, Sept. 24, 1867, 1). Encalada's time count cannot be adjusted to the calendar: he claimed to have been captured by rebels as the war broke out (1847), to have then spent two years as Pat's servant, three years as his rural manager, and only then was present at Pat's death (1849). His claim to have been a noncombatant through the active stages of the war cannot be reconciled with repeated references in Yucatecan dispatches identifying him as a rebel leader in the thick of combat. Also, during most of 1852 Lochhá was held by Vega's army. From Encalada's account one cannot know whether his removal to Lochhá occurred before or after that interval of government occupation. Quintal Martín (1992, 127) cites oral history alleging Encalada to have been a native of Sabán.

15. J. H. Faber to Seymour, Dec. 20, 1857 (ABH, R58).

16. J. T. Briceño to J. M. Novelo, Oct. 30, 1857 (GS, Nov. 16, 1857, 2). Briceño writes—as he did frequently in this period—as the *pacífico* commander of Chansut, reporting to Colonel Juan María Novelo at Peto. It is not clear whether Briceño was acting here as a loyal subordinate or whether he was a self-seeking competitor of other *pacífico* commanders, particularly Encalada. In any event, his tone is clearly anti-Encalada; but although Briceño implies that Encalada was culpable (e.g., J. T. Briceño to J. M. Novelo, GS, Nov. 18, 1857, 3), there is no evidence that Encalada

ever responded as though he had received any such offer of high government position.

17. Encalada statement of Aug. 12, 1867 (EP, Sept. 24, 1867, 1).

18. J. T. Briceño to J. M. Novelo, May 8, May 10, 1858 (GS, May 17, May 24, 1858, 2).

19. "Indios bárbaros" (GS, June 23, 1858, 4).

20. Encalada statement of Aug. 12, 1867 (EP, Sept. 24, 1867, 1).

21. Letters of M. Be, June 7, P. García, June 12, and M. F. Peraza, June 19, 1858 (GS, Sept. 8, 1858, 1–2); see also Baqueiro (1878–87, 3:144–47).

22. Encalada statement of Aug. 12, 1867 (EP, Sept. 24, 1867, 1).

23. J. T. Briceño to Governor of Yucatan, Oct. 28, 1858 (EC, Nov. 5, 1858, 1). An unspecified number of sergeants were represented by seven named individuals, corporals and private soldiers by one each. The *mayor general* or "general major" stood next below the rank of lieutenant colonel in Yucatecan forces of the day.

24. "Los indios bárbaros" (EP, Dec. 25, 1860, 1; Aznar Barbachano and Carbó (1861, 181–88).

25. J. T. Briceño to Governor of Campeche, Jan. 8, 1863 (EP, Feb. 3, 1863, 1).

26. Aznar Barbachano and Carbó (1861, document No. 44).

27. Encalada statement of Aug. 12, 1867 (EP, Sept. 24, 1867, 1).

28. J. T. Briceño to Governor of Campeche, Jan. 8 (EP, Feb. 3, 1863, 1). Other details are in C. M. Oca dispatch of Jan. 4 and Jan. 7, 1863 (EN, Jan. 9, 1863, 1); N. Novelo dispatch of Jan. 7, 1863 (EN, Jan. 12, 1863, 1S).

29. M. Barbosa to Governor of Campeche, July 25, 1863 (EP, Aug. 11, 1863, 1); news item datelined Mérida, Oct. 31 (EP, Nov. 6, 1863, 4). Barbosa would be appointed to other positions by Governor García, the highest being that of *jefe político* of the partido of Chenes, in 1867 ("Conducto execrable de los disidentes," BY, Feb. 22, 1867, 2); at about the same time he was described as a merchant of Iturbide (Anonymous 1867).

30. "Rebellón de los cantones pacíficos del Sur" (EN, Oct. 30, 1863, 4).

31. This is discussed by Sánchez Novelo (1983, 45–49).

32. J. Escalante to F. Navarrete, Apr. 6, 1864 (LR, Apr. 12, 1864, 1, and NE, Apr. 4, 1864, 1–2).

33. P. Encalada to J. Escalante, Apr. 11, 1864 (LR, Apr. 26, 1864, 2, and NE, Apr. 22, 1864, 1); P. Encalada to J. Escalante, Apr. 27, with enclosure of Apr. 27, 1864 (LR, May 13, 1864, 3–4, and NE, May 6, 1864, 4). The enclosure, the formal announcement by the commanders, is signed by Encalada, Paulino Martínez (*sic*), Manuel Bak, Buenaventura Cruz, Lázaro Chan, Juan Camal, Mariano Tacu, José M. Pech, José A. Uc, Tomás Chabin, Pedro Góngora, Romualdo Us, Francisco Koh, Andrés Ku, and a Manuel Bojorquez, the latter possibly a misreading of handwritten Barbosa.

34. L. Tzuc to Sr. General, June 15, 1863, and an untranslated letter in Maya from Tzuc of June 20, 1863 (ABH, R83).

35. J. G. Austin dispatch No. 56, Aug. 14, 1866 (ABH, R92); see also notes of interview with R. G. Roberts, Sept. 1866 (ABH, R89).

36. L. Tzuc to E. Burke, May 15, 1864; E. Burke to J. G. Austin, May 23 and June 3, 1864; B. Grajales to E. Burke, May 23, 1864; L. Tzuc to Inhabitants of English Territory, May 31, 1864; statement of B. Grajales, June 6, 1864; L. Tzuc to Governor, June 6, 1864; and other correspondence (all in ABH, R84). Also J. G. Austin dispatches No. 70, June 7; No. 71, June 16; and No. 116, Nov. 12, 1864; and others (all in ABH, R81).

37. P. Toledo to V. M. MacDonald, May 31, 1864 (ABH, R84); J. G. Austin dispatches No. 83, July 13; and No. 89, Aug. 12, 1864 (ABH, R81).

38. A. Meda to E. Eyre, July 6, 1864 (ABH, R86).

39. D. Valencia to General in Chief, Aug. 2, and P. Encalada report of July 28, 1864 (NE, Aug. 8, 1864, 1).

40. J. G. Austin dispatch No. 123, Dec. 14, 1864 (ABH, R81).

41. Decree of Salazar Ilarregui of Sept. 19, 1864 (NE and LR, Sept. 23, 1864); J. G. Austin dispatch No. 120, Nov. 14, 1864 (ABH, R81). British protests against the statement made no headway.

42. M. Canul and R. Chan to British Honduras Co., Feb. 15, 1865 (ABH, R86).

43. J. Hodge to M. Canul and R. Chan, Mar. 21, 1865 (ABH, R86).

44. J. G. Austin dispatch No. 21, May 8, 1866 (ABH, R92); E. Adolphus to G. Berkeley, May 2, 1866 (ABH, R89); notes of interview with R. G. Roberts, Sept. 1866 (ABH, R89); E. Adolphus to G. Berkeley, May 19 and May 21, 1866 (ABH, R93), the latter with encl.

45. M. Canul to Mr. Panting, May 7, 1866, encl. with E. Adolphus to G. Berkeley, May 21, 1866 (ABH, R93); J. Hodge to J. G. Austin, May 8 and June 1, 1866 (ABH, R89).

46. G. Olafen to J. G. Austin, June 1 and June 15, 1866, and receipt signed by M. Canul and R. Chan, June 30, 1866 (ABH, R93).

47. P. Encalada to the Governor, Nov. 8, 1866, and P. Encalada to no addressee, same date (ABH, R93).

48. The powder proclamation, dated July 25, 1866, initially for three months but extended for periods totaling a year, prohibited "to be either exported from or carried coastwise in this Colony arms, ammunition, and gunpowder and military and naval stores, without a license first had and obtained under the hand of the Lieutenant Governor" (encl. with J. G. Austin dispatch No. 53, July 26, 1866, itself encl. with dispatch of the Governor of Jamaica, Honduras No. 6, Oct. 23, 1866, CO123/123). For periods involved see R. M. Mundy dispatch No. 102, July 29, 1874 (CO123/156). The troops were ordered to Orange Walk in September (J. G. Austin dispatch No. 81, Sept. 21, 1866, encl. with Governor of Jamaica dispatch No. 34, Oct. 23, 1866, CO123/123).

49. F. Seymour dispatch Confidential No. 1 and No. 2, May 15 and June 17 (ABH, R52). The San Pedro affair is also described by Jones (1977).

50. A. Ek to Magistrate of the Northern District, June 6, 1860 (ABH, R71). Although accounted a general, Ek does not seem to have ever been the actual commander at Chichanhá, to which his relationship is unclear.

51. F. Seymour dispatch No. 127, Nov. 12, 1862 (ABH, R81). Illustrated when a fugitive from British Honduras, wanted for purported extortionary raids on a logging company, was appointed a minor official in the Petén and began to act in ways thought repressive by villagers; he was seized by campesinos in what was thought Guatemala (the border not yet defined) and dragged across the frontier to Ek, who turned him over to the English.

52. E. Rhys to F. Seymour, Nov. 3, 1862 (ABH, R78), report in response to F. Seymour to E. Rhys, Oct. 4, 1862 (ABH, R72).

53. F. Seymour dispatch No. 72, July 13, 1863 (ABH, R81). The duties stated: "to catch all runaways accused of murder or escaped from the Belize jail gang, to respect the mahogany trees, to keep the peace, and to punish Indians who ill treated women or committed theft."

54. J. G. Austin dispatch No. 56, Aug. 14, 1866 (ABH, R92); T. Graham to Lt. Governor, Aug. 2, 1866 (ABH, R93).

55. Declaration of J. C. Hernández, Oct. 29, 1866 (ABH, R93); J. G. Austin dispatch No. 100, Nov. 1, 1866 (ABH, R92).

56. Report of Captain P. Delamere, Nov. 11, 1866 (ABH, R93), with nine attachments. The *masewalob* themselves said later there were only eighty men under arms at San Pedro; see unaddressed letter of E. Biffi, Jan. 23, 1867, and G. M. Arvaro to Lt. Governor, Jan. 25, 1867 (ABH, R89).

57. A. Ek to the Governor, Nov. 9 and Nov. 13, 1866 (ABH, R89); J. G. Austin to A. Ek, Nov. 20, 1866 (ABH, R89).

58. A. Ek to Alcaldes, Dec. 4, 1866 (ABH, R89).

59. For example, Declaration of L. Ortiz, Nov. 10, 1866 (ABH, R93).

60. M. Canul and R. Chan to J. Swasey and to G. Elliott, Dec. 3, 1866, and to General of Belize, Dec. 9, 1866 (ABH, R93).

61. G. M. Arvaro to Lt. Governor, Jan. 25, 1867 (ABH, R89). When this issue was raised it is evident that Lieutenant Governor Austin had a search made for a copy of the "treaty" of 1853, but none was apparently to be found anywhere in British Honduras. Neither was Canul able to produce one, although some of his men claimed to have accompanied José María Tzuc to Belize for the negotiations in 1853 and asserted the condition from memory. See, for instance, E. Adolphus to J. G. Austin, Feb. 17, 1867 (ABH, R89) and the Arvaro letter just cited.

62. Statement of J. Phillips, Dec. 14, 1866 (ABH, R93).

63. J. G. Austin to Major McKay [*sic*], Dec. 8, 1866 (ABH, R91); act of the Legislative

Assembly of Dec. 9, 1866, reported by Austin in dispatch No. 127, Dec. 12, 1866 (encl. with J. Grant dispatch Honduras No. 4, Jan. 8, 1867, CO123/126).

64. Gibbs (1883, 136).

65. J. G. Austin dispatch No. 133 (ABH, R92); R. Williamson to the Governor, Dec. 26, 1866, statements of J. Haylock and J. S. August, Dec. 27, 1866, M. Canul and R. Chan to Governor of Belize, Dec. 26, 1866 (ABH, R89). The debacle is summarized very briefly by Dobson (1973, 222) but is described far more entertainingly by Gibbs (1883, 134–38), who avers that Mackay had previously been on report for " 'tardiness' in meeting the enemy." The present spelling of Mackay's name, which is frequently rendered McKay in the documents, is from the army list (United Kingdom 1866).

66. J. Balam to Commandant General of Belize, Jan. 19, 1867 (ABH, R89).

67. Statement of the Commissioners of P. Encalada, Feb. 4, 1867 (ABH, R89).

68. J. G. Austin to Sir, Feb. 5, 1867 (ABH, R91); R. J. Downer to T. Graham, Feb. 7, 1867 (ABH, R89).

69. J. G. Austin dispatch No. 35, Feb. 25, 1867 (ABH, R92).

70. R. J. Downer to Acting Colonial Secretary, Feb. 26, 1867 (ABH, R89).

71. J. R. Longden dispatch No. 25, Dec. 27, 1867 (ABH, R98).

72. T. Edmunds to S. Cockburn, May 31, 1867; statement of D. Hernández, June 4, 1867; J. H. Faber to J. G. Austin, May 10, 1867 (ABH R96).

73. J. G. Austin dispatch No. 55, Apr. 9, 1867, and No. 69, Apr. 30, 1867 (ABH, R92); Austin refers to Canul's regained freedom in May (Austin to R. Harley, May 20, 1867, ABH, R91). Within a decade, Ek would again be an official at San Pedro, recognized by the British.

74. Although the original reorganization by Navarrete simply recombined Campeche and Yucatan as they had been under Santa Anna and earlier, a new law of March 3, 1865, separated them again as distinct departments of the empire; but less than two weeks later, March 16, 1865, the fifty departments of the country were allocated among eight administrative districts, with the district of Mérida to include both the departments of Campeche and Yucatan (see O'Gorman 1973, 164–65). As district commissary, Salazar governed both.

75. For example, Anonymous (1866, 490–91).

76. Proclamations of Salazar I., Oct. 13, 1864 (PM, Oct. 14, 1864, 1) and of Nov. 1864 (PM, Nov. 25, 1864, 1–2); Quintal Martín (1992, letter 64).

77. Valdés Acosta (1979, 235–38).

78. "Secretaría del excmo. tribunal superior de justicia de Yucatán" (PM, Oct. 7, 1864, 2), where the earlier proceedings are reported.

79. "Remitido" (NE, Mar. 18, 1864, 3). The December date of his visit is specified in "Mas sobre los indios del Sur de Yucatán" (LS, Jan. 26, 1865, 3).

80. "La redacción" (NE, Mar. 21, 1864, 4).

81. "Secretaría del excmo. tribunal superior de justicia de Yucatán" (PM, Oct. 7, 1864, 2).

82. L. Tzuc to J. M. Arredondo, Sept. 18, 1864 (BCP, 1865, "Documentos Guerra de Castas" folder). Whatever Arredondo's true role among the rebels of Santa Cruz, he showed his willingness to accept credit for their steps toward peace in his interview report from Mexico City, Jan. 1865 ("Mas sobre los indios del sur de Yucatán," LS, Jan. 26, 1865, 3), which said he "persuaded them to submit," but their "savage instincts rendered futile his work and difficult expedition."

83. Anonymous (1866, 511–20).

84. "Oficial" (PM, Jan. 13, 1865, 1). Manuscript original is in BCP (1865, "Documentos Guerra de Castas").

85. "Noticias, Yucatan" (DI, Jan. 30, 1865, 1); "Yucatan" (LS, Jan. 26, 1865, 2–3).

86. J. M. M. Arredondo to Comisario Imperial, various letters Mar. to June 1865 (BCP, 1865, "Documentos Guerra de Castas"). The appointment of Encalada as subprefect and of Briceño as tax collector took leaders of both Mérida and Campeche factions of the *pacíficos* into the new power structure.

87. Encalada's statement of Aug. 12, 1867 (EP, Sept. 24, 1867, 1); complaint of I. Chan, Sept. 16, 1865 (in Defensor de Indios to Comisario Imperial, Sept. 21, 1865, BCP, 1865, "Documentos Guerra de Castas"). See also Sánchez Novelo (1983, 89).

88. Arredondo to E. Salazar, Oct. 17, 1865 (BCP, 1865, "Documentos Guerra de Castas").

89. Hübbe (1940, 158) states Arredondo was killed at a public festival in which his body was dragged through the streets, Anonymous (1866, 511–40) that Pablo Encalada and four hundred men chopped him up with machetes in the Mesapich plaza. Encalada (statement of Aug. 12, EP, Sept. 24, 1867, 1) claimed the matter was brought on when Arredondo beat and injured the Mesapich *comandante* Feliciano Uch (or Uh), who then rebelled and occasioned the murder despite Encalada's efforts to thwart him. Yet a fourth account was that the actual murder was by three army deserters and an Indian of Xmabén, with the intimation that it was instigated by Manuel Barbosa, who earlier had been Governor Pablo García's personal appointee as *comandante general* of the pacified rebels (Anonymous 1867, probably a report made to Pablo Garcia's newly restored Campeche government shortly after the imperial defeat).

90. M. Negrón to Salazar I., Oct. 25, 1865 (BCP, 1865, "Documentos Guerra de Castas"); P. Encalada to Exmo. Sor., Oct. 27, 1865 (ibid); Encalada's statement of Aug. 12, 1867 (EP, Sept. 24, 1867, 1).

91. N. Carrillo statement, Oct. 24, 1865 (BCP, 1865, "Documentos Guerra de Castas"), much of it quoted by Sánchez Novelo (1983, 90).

92. Encalada et al., Oct. 24, 1865, without personal addressee, Spanish versions of copies sent both to Mérida and Iturbide exist in BCP (1865, "Documentos Guerra de Castas"); another sent to Tekax is in Anonymous (1866, 518–19). That these are renderings of missives originally in Maya seems clear from variations between them (i.e., in translation). At least two examples in Maya are in BCP (1865, "Documentos Guerra de Castas"); these carry the entire set of signatures, divided among thirteen evidently ranked as *comandantes* or higher, sixteen as captains, seven as lieutenants.

93. "Acta" of Nov. 10, 1865," and Encalada to J. Escalante, Nov. 18, 1865 (BCP, 1865, "Documentos Guerra de Castas," where there is also a copy of the act in Maya). Anonymous (1867) asserts that the document was actually contrived by Manuel Barbosa, who had been active in trade in the *pacífico* area and presumably wanted to eliminate the possibility of imperial taxes. In keeping with the noncommittal policy of the government with regard to the entire Arredondo fiasco, this declaration was apparently never made public.

94. For example, Governor to Vice Governor, Aug. 8, 1867 (EP, Aug. 9, 1867, 4).

95. Anonymous (1867).

96. P. Delamere to the Lieutenant Governor, Oct. 4, 1866 (ABH, R89). See also J. G. Austin dispatch No. 128, Nov. 20, 1866 (ABH, R92). As indicated above, Andrés Arana in 1860 was apparently a Campeche-appointed official in Mesapich, and in 1867 was reported to be a leader at Yakalcab.

97. "El Cristo de los bárbaros" (EP, July 19, 1867, 4). The only text known to me is in Spanish.

98. P. Encalada statement, Aug. 12, 1867 (EP, Sept. 27, 1867, 1).

99. Governor to Vice Governor, Aug. 8, 1867 (EP, Aug. 9, 1867, 4).

100. In his campaign against the empire, sometime before mid-1867 García had received aid from Encalada in the form of eighteen kegs of powder. See "Statement of the Commissioners of Pablo Encalada," July 4, 1867 (ABH, R89).

101. "Conducta execrable de los disidentes" (BY, Feb. 22, 1867, 2).

102. P. Encalada statement, Aug. 12, 1867 (EP, Sept. 27, 1867, 1); M. Barbosa to Governor, July 5, 1867 (EP, July 12, 1867, 2); various letters and "Los indios" in RP (July 23, 1867).

103. P. Encalada statement, Aug. 12, 1867 (EP, Sept. 27, 1867, 1).

104. M. Barbosa to Governor, July 18, 1867 (RP, July 23, 1867, 1); N. Novelo dispatch of July 22, 1867 (RP, July 30, 1867, 1); M. Barbosa to Governor, July 20, 1867 (EP, July 26, 1867, 1); J. A. Uc and P. Cuch to L. Preve, July 21, 1867 (EP, July 26, 1867, 4).

105. "Gobierno del estado" (EP, July 26, 1867, various letters); J. L. Santini dispatches of July 26, 27, 1867, L. Preve dispatch of unknown date (EP, July 30, 1867, 2).

106. J. L. Santini dispatch of Aug. 4, 1867 (EP, Aug. 9, 1867, 2); statement of F. Poot, enclosure to Santini dispatch of Aug. 19, 1867 (EP, Aug. 27, 1867, 2).

107. "Gobierno del estado" (EP, Aug. 9, 1867, various letters); J. D. Hernández dispatch, date unknown (EP, Aug. 27, 1867, 1).

108. F. Medina dispatch of Aug. 13, 1867 (RP, Aug. 19, 1867).

109. J. L. Santini dispatch of Sept. 13, (EP, Sept. 17, 1867, 1) and of Sept. 15, 1867 (EP, Sept. 27, 1867, 1). The Santa Rosa referred to is evidently a different settlement from that located on the direct road to Bacalar.

110. Statement of F. Poot, undated (EP, Aug. 27, 1867, 2); M. Canul, R. Chan, and others, to P. García, Aug. 24, 1867 (EP, Sept. 27, 1867, 2).

111. "Gacetilla" (EP, Dec. 6, 1867, 4).

15. Rebels and Friends

1. The tangled course of the Carmichael claims is detailed in documents in FO39/30–32. A statement of his major troubles is given by Carmichael to Lord John Russell, Jan. 3, 1853 (FO39/30). Notice of the bankruptcy is encl. with Fletcher and Hull to Russell, July 15, 1859 (FO39/31).

2. J. Carmichael to the Superintendent, Mar. 16, 1859 (ABH, R63).

3. Land dealings are summarized by Attorney General, Mar. 6, 1880 (encl. with F. P. Barlee dispatch No. 23, Mar. 8, 1880, CO123/165).

4. Various letters of April–June 1865 (ABH, R89). The status of the signatures is in J. H. Blake to J. G. Austin, June 9 and 29, 1865 (ABH, R89). The occurrence is reported in detail by Jones (1982b).

5. Burden (1931–35, 3:269), regarding the May 2, 1866 meeting of the Legislative Assembly, refers to "some 3,000 Chinese, distributed amongst seven estates," but the figures given in the Colonial Office list (Birch and Robinson 1867) for Honduras states that 474 were imported in 1865. Asian workers had been used in Cuba for some time.

6. J. G. Austin dispatch No. 14, May 5, 1866, encl. J. Carmichael to Governor, Feb. 11, 1866 (CO123/122); Austin dispatch No. 52, July 23, 1866, encl. Carmichael to A. W. Cox, July 16, 1866 (both encl. with Governor of Jamaica's dispatch Honduras No. 5, Oct. 23, 1866, CO123/123). Immigrants were said to be unsuited for the heaviest labor and not willing to work without some cash payment, whereas local practice—following the custom in logging works—was to pay in goods.

7. J. G. Austin dispatch No. 59, Aug. 22, 1866, with attachments (encl. with Governor of Jamaica dispatch No. 12, Oct. 23, 1866, CO123/123).

8. R. W. Harley dispatch No. 79, Apr. 25, 1872 (CO123/148).

9. E. Adolphus to T. Graham, Oct. 4, 1866 (ABH, R89). The general referred to is Bernardino (or Bernabé) Cen, the shortened form of whose given name was pronounced by Maya speakers (to whom the r phoneme is foreign) as Bel.

10. Later the same year Lieutenant Governor Austin reported that he was not happy with the Chinese experiment and would not renew it. In January 1870, 182 of the original importees were still alive and working in British Honduras, 49 of them at San Andrés. That year their indentures expired and the experiment was ended. See J. G. Austin to the Governor of Jamaica, Nov. 22, 1866 (CO123/124); J. H. Longden dispatch No. 19, Jan. 28, 1870 (CO123/339); W. W. Cairns dispatch No. 39, Mar. 27, 1871, with encl. draft of the Bluebook for 1870 (CO123/143). I have seen no indication of the numbers of those repatriated or of those who stayed in British Honduras.

11. "Indios" (LR, Dec. 9, 1864, 4, and Dec. 13, 1864, 3).

12. "Los indios bárbaros" (PM, Dec. 5, 1867, 2–3.)

13. J. Flowers (statement of Dec. 30, 1867, ABH, R96) reported such rebel arms. Apparently as late as the mid-1860s units of the Mexican army were still using the Brown Bess flintlock muskets purchased from England in the 1820s (e.g., Garavaglia and Worman 1984, 73).

14. Like the death of Arredondo, this military incident—embarrassing to the empire—did not appear in the controlled press. Accounts, however, appear in Molina Solís (1921–27, 2:382–86), Anonymous (1866, 499–506), and Pérez Alcalá (1914, 219–23), although in the last it is erroneously dated 1866 and is described as a preliminary to the siege of Tihosuco of that year. I have followed the first of these in most details.

15. Molina Solís (1921–27, 2:395–96). This was interpreted as an unqualified imperial success and widely announced (e.g., "Tihosuco," PY, Sept. 20, 1866, 3; Comandancia de la 7a División, dispatch of Sept. 22, PY, Sept. 24, 1866, 1; "Fuga de los bárbaros," PY, Sept. 27, 1866, 3), and Traconis was decorated. That it was the vigor of the imperial troops that brought the siege to an end is not so clear. October is an important month in the maize cycle, for then the drying stalks are doubled over to keep rainfall and birds from the ripening ears. Furthermore, it was in September 1866—precisely during the siege—that Andrés Arana appeared on the British Honduras frontier in his unsuccessful attempt to thwart the ban on powder and buy munitions for Santa Cruz. One suspects that agricultural and supply considerations weighed at least as heavily with the rebels as Yucatecan spirit.

16. For example, J. Carmichael to A. Ek, Nov. 5, and Ek to Carmichael, Nov. 5, 1866 (ABH, R93); John Carmichael Jr. summarized some of his own background in a letter to the Earl of Kimberley, Jan. 23, 1873 (CO123/155).

17. Resolutions of the Legislative Assembly of Feb. 11, 1867 (ABH, R89).

18. E. Adolphus to T. Graham, Feb. 16, 1867, with depositions of Moreno, Cervantes, and Majana, Feb. 15 and 16, 1867; Adolphus to Graham, Feb. 19, 1867 (all in ABH, R89). Despite Carmichael's interest in the shipment, the powder apparently

never passed through his hands; Moreno was an independent trader, and the transaction was presumably his.

19. J. M. Martínez to J. G. Austin, Feb. 27, 1867 (ABH, R89); "Un valiente menos" (RM, Sept. 9, 1888, 3).

20. E. Adolphus to the Acting Colonial Secretary, Feb. 26, 1867 (ABH, R89); W. Mundy dispatch No. 16, Feb. 11, 1875 (CO123/158; related material appears in ABH, R114, referring to the 1875 session of the Supreme Court, Corozal). The jury had recommended clemency, but with the concurrence of his council the lieutenant governor affirmed the sentence of death. There was feeling against the severity of the punishment, particularly by Yucatecan residents of the colony, given the circumstance and lapse of time before trial, and reportedly because Mena was earlier in custody and had been released without trial by a previous governor. See "México y Belice," pt. 8 (RM, Jan. 3, 2, and Jan. 10, 2, 1893). Miguel's brother Encarnación apparently died in 1888 in Espita, Yucatan, a minor hero for the powder adventure ("Un valiente menos," RM, Sept. 9, 1888, 3); he had been erroneously reported killed in action against rebels near Tekax in 1870 (M. Novelo dispatch, Jan. 16, RP, Jan. 21, 1870, 1).

21. Novelo, Cen, Poot to J. G. Austin, Feb. 16, 1867 (ABH, R89, a copy also in R96); J. Carmichael to J. G. Austin, Mar. 11, 1867 (two letters, ABH, R89). Unable to complete the transaction immediately, the rebels attacked a village on the eastern side of Chetumal Bay where they claimed the powder purloined by the Meneses party had been hidden until it could be shipped to Sisal (J. G. Austin dispatch No. 59, Apr. 9, 1867, ABH, R98).

22. J. Carmichael to J. G. Austin, May 11, 1867 (ABH, R96). The feast of the Holy Cross, or Santa Cruz, is May 3.

23. For example, Petition of A. J. Levy to J. G. Austin, n.d. (filed between two documents dated June 29, 1867, ABH, R96).

24. J. Carmichael to J. G. Austin, June 17 (two letters), and A. Mathé to J. G. Austin, June 21, 1867 (ABH, R96). This is the first time that a head of the colony government can be shown to have connived directly in any sale of munitions to the rebels, although as the century wore on the paternalistic attitude would become part of the customary stance of the colony's governors toward the Santa Cruz *masewalob*. The less than open manner of accomplishing this transaction may have been characteristic of Austin, who later that year was cashiered for showing illegal partiality to immigrants from the southern (post–Civil War) United States in the granting of crown lands. Dobson (1973, 246–47) takes a more charitable view of him, however.

25. Declaration of F. Poot (EP, Aug. 27, 1867, 2).

26. E. Esquivel dispatch (RP, Nov. 16, 1867, 1).

27. J. Carmichael to J. G. Austin, Aug. 8, 1867 (ABH, R96; spelling and capitalization as in the original).

28. T. Graham to J. G. Austin, Aug. 12, 1867 (ABH, R96).

29. Report of John Carmichael on his visit to the city of Santa Cruz, Nov. 15, 1867 (ABH, R93 and R96; appended to J. R. Longden dispatch No. 6, Nov. 28, 1867, CO123/130).

30. J. R. Longden dispatch No. 6, Nov. 28, 1867, and minute to J. Carmichael's report of Nov. 15, apparently by Sir F. Rogers (CO123/130). Cen's claim would place the total population of eastern rebels at more than twenty thousand, and that of the southern turncoat rebels more than twelve thousand, whereas the estimate of Plumridge and Twigge suggested a figure closer to fifteen thousand total. There are also two other estimates from this same period. In 1866, the author of a contemporary history (Anonymous 1866, 538) thought that Noh Cah Santa Cruz might count four thousand to five thousand people, with the entire rebel territory including fifteen thousand to twenty thousand. In 1867, the year of Carmichael's visit, Berendt (1872) reported educated estimates in British Honduras of ten thousand to fifteen thousand soldiers at Santa Cruz, which he took to indicate a total population of about forty thousand, with the *pacífico* population about equal. Both of Berendt's figures now seem excessive, but the Belizeans liked to impress themselves with the numbers of *masewalob* who surrounded them.

31. E. Adolphus to Acting Colonial Secretary, Feb. 18, 1867 (ABH, R89).

32. J. Carmichael Jr. to Lieutenant Governor Austin, Feb. 19, 1867 (ABH, R89). The date at which Yam appears in the rebel camp is several months before the real outbreak of warfare in the Lochhá region, still another indication that the loyalties of many of the *pacíficos* were eroding in the year following the murder of Arredondo.

33. J. O'Brian to T. Graham, May 24, 1867, and M. Pantí and J. B. Yam to the magistrate at Orange Walk, May 23, 1867 (ABH, R96).

34. Gacetilla (EP, Dec. 6, 1867, 4); see also J. R. Longden to the Duke of Buckingham, Nov. 2, 1868 (ABH, R98). This "proof" was a pair of letters written by Adolphus to Yam in the aftermath of the hijacking of the powder shipment, when all available hands were looking for Meneses and his men, and from which García concluded that Adolphus himself was selling powder. With regard to the Santa Cruz loss to Canul, the leadership at Noh Cah Santa Cruz said only that "at the rancho of Esteves the people met with a misfortune through the people of Icaiché" (Novelo, Cen, and Poot to the Governor, Jan. 9, 1868, ABH, R97).

35. E. Adolphus to P. Hankin, Dec. 26, 1867, enclosing statements of that date of A. González, J. M. Chan, M. Juan, A. Kituk, E. Chan, L. Aviles, P. Ek, and D. M. Taylor (ABH, R96).

36. J. R. Longden dispatches Nos. 5 and 12, Jan. 11 and 30, 1868 (ABH, R98). Carmichael's letters are particularly those of Dec. 31, 1867, and Jan. 6, 1868 (ABH, R96), and Feb. 15, 1868 (ABH, R97; other relevant correspondence is in R96, R97, and

R102). Adolphus took additional depositions indicating that the four men in rebel custody had been taken against their will and were prisoners (E. Adolphus to J. R. Longden, Jan. 10, 1868, ABH, R96, originally enclosing statements of P. Ek, A. Kituk, L. Aviles, and E. Chan, Jan. 6, 1868, now in ABH, R102).

37. Novelo, Cen, and Poot, Jan. 9, 1868 (ABH, R97); on the strength of their promise, Ake and his men were released. The letter with the powder request I read in poor text as also asking for twelve thousand guns and dated it Jan. 6, 1868 (ABH, R97). The correction of "guns" to "gun flints" and the January date to February 6, 1868, is according to personal communication from Paul Sullivan (1995).

38. E. Adolphus to J. R. Longden, Feb. 3, 1868, with "list of persons taken across the Río Hondo by the Santa Cruz Indians," n.d. (ABH, R97). Although Adolphus later made slight modifications to his figures, the magnitude remained comparable.

39. For example, J. Carmichael to Lieutenant Governor, Feb. 21, 1868, ABH, R97.

40. J. R. Longden dispatch No. 12, Jan. 30, 1868, ABH, R98. An interesting sidelight of the Ake affair involves the ammunition carried by the rebel party. One statement alleged that a percussion cap on one *masewal* firearm was a "rifle cap," said to have come, with cartridges, from "Don Juan Carmichael" (statement of J. Flowers, Dec. 30, 1867, ABH, R96). Adolphus also forwarded to the lieutenant governor "six of many similar cartridges found amongst the ammunition of the Indian prisoners, also two of those sent up for the Militia and Police in the early part of the year, of which a considerable quantity I understand, was under the charge of Captain John Carmichael of the British Honduras Militia" (E. Adolphus to P. I. Hankin, Jan. 2, 1868, ABH, R96). A month later Adolphus said that he could not find the source of an allegation that Ake or one of his men had admitted receiving the cartridges from Captain Carmichael, although he did locate witnesses to testify that rebels of the near region across the Hondo had stated they were being supplied with both cartridges and percussion caps by "Don Juan Carmichael" (Adolphus to Longden, Feb. 3, 1868, ABH, R97; statement of J. Magaña, Feb. 3, 1868, ABH, R97; statement of J. Flowers, Dec. 30, 1867, ABH, R96). Nothing seems to have come of these allegations, but they provide information about rebel armament. The "rifle cap" would have been a copper percussion cap specifically designed for the muzzle-loading Enfield rifle (but usable with other guns), which was adopted by the British in 1853 and by 1867 must have been fairly plentiful in the colonies. But because there is no mention at this time of Enfields in possession of the rebels—which would surely have been remarked—and because there are specific references to muskets, it can be concluded that the rebel arms were percussion-fired muskets which had superseded their earlier flintlocks. Brown Bess flintlocks began to be converted by the British army after the early 1840s, but the percussion conversions became surplus with adoption of the Enfield. The value of the percussion system to the rebels would have been in fewer misfires and

its lock that was far less likely to get wet when it rained. Its liability, however, was that it required an industrially produced cap of fulminate. The cartridges referred to would have been oiled paper packages, each containing one measured powder charge and a projectile. Although these could easily have been made by the rebels themselves, certain patterns were mass produced for the British soldiers, and it is apparently these that were the subject of the magistrate's complaint. For use these were ripped open, the powder dumped down the rifle or musket barrel, and the ball rammed home with the package used as wadding (e.g., Ellacott 1955).

41. J. Carmichael Jr. to Lieutenant Governor, Feb. 4, 1868 (ABH, R97).

42. For example, M. J. Castillo and eleven others, Dec. 27, 1867 (ABH, R96); J. R. Longden dispatch No. 62, May 4, 1868 (ABH, R98).

43. J. R. Longden dispatch No. 62, May 4, 1868, and No. 47, May 17, 1869 (ABH, R98); J. Plumridge to the Lieutenant Governor, Feb. 26 and Mar. 21, 1868 (ABH, R97). This was the same James Plumridge who as a lieutenant of the Third East India Regiment had visited Venancio Puc and Chan Santa Cruz in 1861. He had been forced to leave the military service because of serious deafness; see W. W. Cairns confidential dispatch of May 17, 1871 (CO123/144).

44. J. I. Blockley to J. R. Longden, July 10, 1868 (ABH, R102).

45. Longden dispatch No. 111, July 25, 1868; P. García to J. R. Longden, June 20, 1868 (ABH, R102).

46. J. R. Longden dispatch No. 62, May 4, 1868 (ABH, R98); M. Canul to Inspector, June 30, 1868, and Aug. 14, 1868, and Plumridge to Canul, Aug. 9, 1868 (ABH, R102).

47. J. R. Longden dispatch No. 127, Aug. 12, and No. 168, Oct. 2, 1868 (ABH, R98); J. Hodge to J. R. Longden, July 14, 1868; J. Plumridge to the Lieutenant Governor, July 31, 1868; M. Canul to His Excellency the Governor, July 29, J. J. Chan to Hodge and McDonald, Sept. 20, and various other letters of 1868 (ABH, R102).

48. For example, various entries in RP (Mar. 9, 16, Apr. 13, 17, 20, May 4, 6, June 28, July 1, 13, 15, 1868); EP (May 22, July 7, 1868).

49. "Censo General" (EP, Mar. 10, 1868, 2).

50. J. L. Santini to Governor, May 18, 1868, and various other letters (EP, May 22, 1868, 1–3).

51. E. Adolphus to J. R. Longden, Aug. 17 and 24, 1868 (ABH, R102).

52. Cen, Novelo, and Poot wrote on May 7, 1868 (ABH, R102) to warn that Yucatecans were at Isla Mujeres with seventeen ships of war and that they were bound for Belize with intent to burn that place. (Nothing of the sort happened.) The escapee's statement is in "Noticias de los indios" (EP, June 2, 1868, 4). The nature of this testimony—of a man who had been a prisoner for a year but the length of whose stay at Santa Cruz itself is not clear—warrants caution.

53. Bricker (1981, 112, 339, n. 58) states Novelo was active only until 1868, citing a letter from Lieutenant Governor Longden to Magistrate Adolphus of July 1868, which I have not seen.

54. Urzaiz (1946, 56–64).

55. Gacetilla (EP, July 27, 1869, 3–4).

56. E. Esquivel dispatch, July 3, 1869 (RP, July 5, 1869, 2–3); N. Novelo dispatch, July 7, 1869 (RP, July 12, 1869, 1); D. Traconis dispatch, Aug. 9, 1869 (RP, Aug. 11, 1869, 1); Gacetilla (EP, Aug. 17, 1869, 4).

57. Gacetilla (EP, Oct. 1, 1869, 4). Unfortunately, the general was not identified.

58. Humphreys (1961, 138).

59. J. Carmichael's report of his visit to Santa Cruz, Nov. 15, 1867 (ABH, R93 and R96, and encl. to J. R. Longden dispatch No. 6, Nov. 28, 1867, CO123/130).

60. J. Carmichael's report of his visit to Santa Cruz, Nov. 15, 1867 (ABH, R93 and R96, and encl. to J. R. Longden dispatch No. 6, Nov. 28, 1867, CO123/130); M. Cocom statement, in A. Espinosa dispatch, Feb. 28, 1871 (RP, Mar. 3, 1871, 1).

61. See Bricker (1981, 111) for such an argument.

62. J. I. Montalvo's dispatch, Feb. 12, 1864 (LR, Feb. 19, 1864, 2), reports the escapee as saying that Novelo had become priest even before Zapata was killed in the countercoup that brought Novelo, Cen, and Poot to complete power; for the governor's comment, see J. G. Austin dispatch No. 128, Dec. 20, 1866 (ABH, R92).

63. For example, E. Adolphus to T. Graham, Oct. 4, 1866 (ABH, R89).

64. Bricker (1981, 187).

65. Villa Rojas (1945, 161) in a version from X-Cacal that he published in 1945, renders it as *Heriana Uat*. Bricker (1981, 338, n. 37), her version also from X-Cacal, renders it as quoted, while showing it as "Ylaria Nauat" in her Maya text; she suggests that Villa's rendition involved a misreading of *Heria naUat*. In 1976, the late Alfredo Barrera Vásquez, then director of the Instituto Yucateco de Antropología e Historia, showed me the first few lines of a handwritten copy of the proclamation that he was transcribing—a document of uncertain provenience that he thought to date from about 1903—in which the same genealogy appeared but with the female's name written as *María Nauat*. With *Ylaria* a very possible misreading of *María*, it is equally possible that *Nauat* was a sometime misreading of handwritten *Uicab*.

66. Baqueiro (1887).

67. As noted earlier, Bricker (1981, 107) would like to identify Atanasio Puc with the "Tata Naz" who was one of the major functionaries of the cross cult in 1858, but I find no evidence for it.

68. Report of the Commission of the Government of Yucatan, June 13, 1864 (LR, July 5, 1864, 2); see chap. 13.

69. El Cristo de los bárbaros (EP, July 19, 1867, 4).

70. J. Carmichael to J. G. Austin, Mar. 11, 1867 (ABH, R89).

71. M. Cocom statement, in A. Espinosa dispatch, Feb. 28, 1871 (RP, Mar. 3, 1871, 3). Some such action as a pronouncement of the cross is likely in this case, inasmuch as Poot had been consistently referred to as the third in rank of the three leaders, and Baqueiro (1887) stresses his history of circumspection and lack of competitiveness toward his superiors, indicating that he simply had the qualities of a professional soldier.

16. *Bravo* Enterprises

1. Anonymous (1896, 117); "Repúblicas de indígenas" (RP, Nov. 30, 1868, 3–4; Jan. 29, 1869, 3).

2. See Urzaiz (1946, 49–83). Under the Díaz regime the government of Yucatan would be relatively placid.

3. In the absence of specific demographic information for the period, this statement assumes a stationary population with mortality equivalent to level 1 (males) of Coale and Demeny (1983).

4. Villa Rojas (1945) and Bartolomé and Barabas (1977). It was not only among the rebels, of course, that there was a breakdown in the colonial caste categories. Although invidious notions of the positions of *vecino* and *indio* have persisted into the twentieth century, the unsteady progress of *indio* to full citizenship had been evident before the colonial period ended—as detailed in earlier chapters—but was only brought to completion in 1869 with the final elimination of the *república de indígenas*. See, for instance, discussions in "Repúblicas de indígenas" (RP, Nov. 30, 1868, 3–4).

5. J. R. Longden dispatch No. 128, Nov. 13, 1869 (ABH, R98); Longden's speech to the Legislative Assembly, Jan. 1870 (encl. with his dispatch No. 25, Feb. 9, 1870, CO123/139); draft of the Bluebook for 1869, 56–61 (encl. with W. W. Cairns dispatch No. 127, Aug. 20, 1870, CO123/141).

6. Minute, encl. No. 22 to J. R. Longden dispatch No. 24, Jan. 29, 1870 (CO123/139).

7. W. W. Cairns dispatches No. 89, June 21, 1870 (CO123/140), and No. 110, June 25, 1872 (CO123/148).

8. R. W. Harley dispatch No. 68, Apr. 10, 1872 (CO123/148) discusses the desirability of Indian labor. J. R. Longden dispatch No. 28, Feb. 18, 1870, and the enclosed E. Adolphus to Longden, Jan. 15, 1870 (CO123/139), describe the preference.

9. R. W. Harley dispatch No. 68, Apr. 10, 1872, and enclosed draft of the Bluebook for 1871 (CO123/148).

10. R. W. Harley dispatch No. 153, Oct. 12, 1871 (CO123/145).

11. R. W. Harley dispatch No. 102, June 7, 1872 (CO123/148). Relative prosperity was not opulence, however. In these years, Carmichael acted as his own manager,

living while doing so "in a small cottage, primitive enough as regards its construction, but in which he dispenses a hospitality often wanting in more pretentious houses" (W. W. Cairns dispatch No. 89, June 21, 1870, CO123/140). In 1872, his residence of Pembroke Hall, nine miles from Corozal on the lower reaches of the New River, was in ruins (R. W. Harley dispatch No. 61, Apr. 6, 1872, CO123/148).

12. For example, D. Traconis dispatch of May 3, 1871 (RP, July 5, 1871, 2).

13. N. Aguilar dispatch of Aug. 23, 1870 (RP, Aug. 26, 1870, 1); "Lo de Chichimilá" (RP, Sept. 5, 1870, 3–4).

14. J. A. Cepeda Peraza dispatches of Dec. 19 and 23, 1870 (RP, Dec. 21, 1870, 2, and Dec. 26, 1870, 1).

15. The campaign is generally said to have lasted from Jan. 21 to Feb. 7, and on the former date the governor gave a rousing message to the departing troops (e.g., RP, Jan. 23, 1871, 1). But the Traconis diary of the march (RP, Feb. 22, 1871, 1–3) gives the departure as Jan. 22.

16. D. Traconis dispatch of Feb. 17, 1871 (RP, Feb. 22, 1871, 1–2; the passage was also translated by Villa Rojas 1945, 24, n. 22). The son, eleven years old, was named José M. Mukul y Uicab (Traconis dispatch of Feb. 7, RP, Feb. 13, 1871, 1). Throughout the nineteenth century, women of Yucatan retained their own names rather than take those of their husbands. But the use of *both* paternal and maternal family names was rare until the end of the century even in families of standing; the citation of both names here must have been to demonstrate that the boy was, indeed, the *reina*'s son. His father, presumably the *patrona*'s husband, was a Mukul. Information to be reported for 1872 will indicate that María Uicab lived not at Tulum but at the town of Muyil, although the account here suggests strongly that Tulum was her seat and the capture of her son there seems to say it was also her home in 1871.

17. "Sus habitantes se abastecen en Chan Santa Cruz, que dista 12 leguas, de donde les viene mensualmente un destacamento de 25 hombres para guarnecerlo" (Traconis dispatch of Feb. 17, 1871, RP, Feb. 22, 1871, 1–2). With regard to the iron rods, the wording is at first glance ambiguous: "palanquetas de hierro que allí se hacían del calibre de quince adarmes" would seem literally to mean "bar shot [or rods or crowbars] of iron that were being made there in caliber of one ounce." Bar shot—projectiles in which two balls are joined by an iron rod—commonly refers to projectiles used only in artillery considerably heavier than a shoulder musket, and such gunnery was not practiced seriously by the rebels; anyway, the weight of one ounce could not be meaningful in such a context. But an ounce was the approximate weight of the common lead musket ball, and it seems likely that the weight given here—fifteen *adarmes* or twenty-eight grams or about one ounce—actually refers to a musket bore diameter. The British Brown Bess musket, used to a great extent by both rebels and government troops in Yucatan, fired a ball of slightly more than

an ounce in weight, in a bore with a diameter of about three-quarter inches, or .75 caliber. The *palanquetas*, therefore, almost certainly were pieces of iron rod to be used as musket projectiles; Baqueiro (1878–87, 2:191, 202) uses the same term in describing such uses.

18. Sources are the dispatch of Traconis of Feb. 17, 1871 and the diary of the march (RP, Feb. 22, 1871, 1–3, republished in RM, Feb. 24, 26, and Mar. 1, 1871, and in DY, Apr. 28 and May 5, 1935), supplemented by the narrative of Pérez Alcalá (1914, 223–26), which adds some detail with regard to individual participants in the campaign. Much of the diary is quoted verbatim by Lapointe (1983, 134–36).

19. An early notice of the raid is the N. Urcelay dispatch of Aug. 18, 1872 (RP, Aug. 23, 1872, 1).

20. N. Urcelay, "Itinerario" dated Aug. 19, 1872 (RP, Aug. 26, 1872, 1–2).

21. N. Urcelay, "Itinerario," pt. 2, Aug. 19, 1872 (RP, Aug. 28, 1872, 1). The "dustcovers" [*guardapolvos*] must have referred to the sorts of embroidered cloth adornments that were referred to as *hipiles* in the earliest raids on Chan Santa Cruz in 1851.

22. Sources include the Nicolás Urcelay dispatch and itinerary of Aug. 19, 1872 (RP, Aug. 26, 1872, 1–2, and Aug. 28, 1). Additional details are in Pérez Alcalá (1914, 226–29). Information regarding the extent of damage to Kantunil-kin is in Juan de la C. Valle to the Governor, Nov. 12, 1872 (RP, Nov. 22, 1872). Later information indicated that one of the actual leaders of the raid was Encarnación Cahum, whose propensity for warfare would finally bring him no good. Some of the implications of prisoners' testimony appears at odds with that gained by Traconis the year before, for the men of San Antonio said specifically that the military force from Chunpom was under the orders of María Uicab, thus suggesting no direct subservience of Chunpom to Santa Cruz. The name given for the leader at San Antonio—Juan de la Cruz Pomol—seems to suggest that he was also the chief priest, a supposition strengthened by the evident presence of a sacred cross on the raiding trip to Kantunil-kin.

23. F. Cantón dispatch of Jan. 18, 1875 (RP, Jan. 24, 1873, 1); M. Navarrete dispatch of Jan. 25, 1873 (RP, Jan. 29, 1873, 1).

24. F. Rosado Lavalle dispatch, Feb. 12, 1873 (RP, Feb. 14, 1873, 1); R. Erosa dispatch, Mar. 25, 1873 (RP, Mar. 28, 1873, 2); F. Díaz dispatch, July 29, 1874 (RP, Aug. 5, 1874, 1). Poot's properties were said to be named Chunlla (Chunya) and San Isidro. Another source refers to a Rancho San Felipe as his (RP, Mar. 11, 1876).

25. E. Esquivel dispatch of Apr. 5, 1873 (RP, Apr. 7, 1873, 1); N. Aguilar dispatch, May 24, 1873 (RP, May 27, 1873). Vitorin's property was not referred to by name, Moguel's as San Miguel. This is the same Moguel who had been involved in Virgilio Narciso's massacre of *bravos* at Tizimín, who deserted, and who is last heard of living in British Honduras after having married the daughter of Bonifacio Novelo. There

were other private ranchos mentioned at about this time. Bel Cen, for instance, had one at Rancho Derrepente (RP, Mar. 8, 1875).

26. S. Piña dispatch, July 28, 1874 (RP, July 31, 1874, 1); declaration of M. May, J. Carbó dispatch of Aug. 1, 1874 (RP, Aug. 5, 1874, 1–2).

27. J. B. Cueto and R. A. Hernández to the governor of Campeche, July 3, 1873 (LD, July 8, 1873, 1).

28. Statement of I. R. Alatorre, May 16, 1873 (LD, May 20, 1873, 4).

29. For example, F. Cantón dispatch, July 9, 1873 (RP, July 14, 1873, 1); P. Osorio dispatch, July 29, 1873 (RP, Aug. 1, 1873, 1). The background is described by Urzaiz (1946, 73–76).

30. For example, dispatches of M. J. Cámara, Jan. 27, Jan. 29, 1874 (RP, Jan. 30, 1, and Feb. 2, 1874, 2); D. S. Osorio dispatch, Feb. 24, 1874 (RP, Feb. 27, 1874, 3).

31. F. Díaz dispatch of July 29, 1874 (RP, Aug. 5, 1874, 1).

32. Confidential enclosure to C. B. H. Mitchell secret dispatch of Apr. 15, 1874 (CO123/156).

33. Confidential enclosure to C. B. H. Mitchell secret dispatch of Apr. 15, 1874 (CO123/156).

34. M. Navarrete dispatch, Mar. 6, 1875 (RP, Mar. 8, 1875, 1).

35. J. Carmichael Jr. report on his visit to Santa Cruz, Nov. 15, 1867 (ABH, R93, 96, also CO123/130).

36. N. Urcelay dispatch of Aug. 19, 1872 (RP, Aug. 28, 1872, 1).

37. J. B. Cueto and R. A. Hernández to Governor of Campeche, July 3, 1873 (LD, July 8, 1873, 1).

38. C. B. H. Mitchell secret dispatch of Apr. 15, 1874 (CO123/156).

39. J. M. Vásquez statement, Apr. 16, 1877 (encl. with F. Appleford to the Earl of Carnarvon, June 15, 1877, CO123/161).

40. "Visito oficial del estado," (EP, Mar. 29, 1870, 1).

41. "El corresponsal" to D. Moreno Cantón, Mar. 24, 1888 (RM, Mar. 27, 1888), says that there were three sons, of whom Leandro Poot, friend and informant of Edward Thompson (1932) was one. Baqueiro (1887) provides no name for Poot's second spouse but indicates that it was a pretty Yucatecan prisoner who had two children by him. As a young captive, Pastora was evidently the model for the heroine of Pantaleón Barrera's novel of Santa Cruz (Trebarra 1864), whom he named Pastora Naré (by a simple rearrangement of letters in the surname) and paired romantically with the young musician Gerardo Castillo, who in real life was killed in 1864 at the time of the overthrow of Dionisio Zapata (e.g., A. Sandoval dispatch, June 12, 1864, LR, June 21, 1864, 1).

42. For example, L. Espinosa dispatch of Aug. 24, 1862 (EN, Aug. 27, 1862, 1–2). More fully, the third woman mentioned was Josefa Rodríguez y Romero de

Rodríguez Solís, her own paternal family name (Rodríguez) being—as noted in connection with events of an earlier chapter—the same as that of her husband.

43. F. Díaz dispatch of July 29, 1874 (RP, Aug. 5, 1874, 1); José Patricio Nicoli, "Yucatan y los ingleses" (LD, Nov. 30, 1875, 3–4). The second may be less credible, simply because neither children nor deserted husband are referred to elsewhere. It is just possible that this account confused Josefa Rodríguez with Pastora Rean.

44. The implication is that the *masewalob* had heard of the death of Manuel Rodrígues Solís earlier that year and expected his wife to inherit.

45. First letter of E. Adolphus to Acting Colonial Secretary, Dec. 26, 1874, ABH, R114.

46. Second letter from Adolphus to the Acting Colonial Secretary, Dec. 26, 1874 (ABH, R114).

47. E. Adolphus to J. C. Poot, B. Cen, and other commanders, Dec. 27, 1874 (ABH, R114).

48. J. C. Poot to Magistrate, Northern District, Feb. 7, 1875, and E. Adolphus to Acting Colonial Secretary, Feb. 15, 1875 (ABH, R114).

49. A very brief notice of her arrival is given by a Progreso correspondent (RM, Mar. 4, 1875, 3). Only J. P. Nicoli, "Yucatan y los ingleses" (LD, Nov. 30, 1875) provides a few more lurid details: "Thirteen years of captivity . . . had nearly destroyed the prisoner's mind. She had forgotten the language of her forebears, and when she was interrogated about . . . the barbarians . . . she resisted all revelation, keeping complete silence." This is the same source who said she had been married and had children at Santa Cruz. There was no indication in the Adolphus letters of the language in which he and Doña Josefa communicated, but had she been unable to speak Spanish he would probably have mentioned it.

50. B. M. Montilla dispatch of Oct. 15, 1875 (RP, Oct. 20, 1875, 1); D. Evia to the Governor, May 29, 1875 (RP, June 2, 1875, 2). This is the second "Juan de la Cruz" identified as leader at San Antonio Muyil, again probably because he was chief priest of the cross.

51. For example, letters from the U.S. Consul in Mérida and from the Governor of Yucatan, in RP (Nov. 1, 1875, 1–2). The affair was complicated by earlier complaints Stephens had made against Montilla for allegedly violating his property and by the fact that Montilla had a criminal record. See "Sección Judicial" (RP, Feb. 2, 1876, 2). According to Alice Le Plongeon, who misnamed the murdered man Alexander Stephens, he had been the engineer in charge of building harbor facilities at Progreso ("Notas sobre Yucatan," RM, Jan. 1, 1891, 2).

52. R. A. Pérez dispatches of Oct. 12, Oct. 16, 1875 (RP, Oct. 15 and Oct. 20, 1875, 1).

53. S. Escamilla statement in S. Piña dispatch, Mar. 11, 1876 (RP, Mar. 17, 1876, 1). The same captive reported the garrison at Santa Cruz to consist of four hundred men

relieved every two weeks, that of Bacalar of two hundred relieved each two months. The traders no doubt were Jose María Trejo and Domingo Andrade.

54. R. M. Mundy dispatch No. 7, Jan. 7, 1876 (CO123/129). The .577 caliber Enfield rifle was the last British army muzzle loader, and in 1855 the first rifle of general issue, finally replacing the Brown Bess musket everywhere in the British service (Ellacott 1955). After 1866, certain military units were issued the single-shot Snider breech-loading rifle, some of which saw service in British Honduras beginning in 1872, when furnished to the corps of frontier scouts that replaced the frontier police (see W. W. Cairns dispatch No. 226, Dec. 16, 1872, CO123/150).

55. Although much more accurate than any musket, the Enfield must have been limiting for the rebels, for it fired not a simple ball but a manufactured, compound bullet with a boxwood plug in its base that upon firing was driven forward into the projectile, expanding it to engage the rifling and so impart twist to the flight. Although in a pinch the gun could be fired with a ball smaller than .577-inch diameter in the manner of a musket, such a small projectile would be only about 40 percent of the weight of the old military musket ball of approximately .75 caliber. In the absence of its own special ammunition the Enfield would be inferior to the Brown Bess.

56. Statement of Benito Te and Bernardina Can in J. I. Vázquez dispatch, Dec. 12, 1876 (RP, Dec. 15, 1876, 1). Despite the apparent familiarity of this witness with Noh Cah Santa Cruz and rebel affairs in general, neither the relative sizes of the garrisons nor the lengths of their tours accords with statements of other witnesses, all of whom insist that Santa Cruz had the largest guard and that the soldiers at Bacalar were relieved much less frequently than those at Santa Cruz or Tulum.

57. F. P. Barlee dispatch of Nov. 13, 1877 (CO123/161); the points for discussion and treaty are listed in enclosures 5 and 6 to that dispatch. That a distinction between Tulum and Noh Cah Santa Cruz was recognized seems indicated by the wording of the statement regarding payment to the soldiers (from enclosure 6).

58. F. P. Barlee dispatch of Nov. 13, 1877 (CO123/161). This is at least the second order of four hundred firearms made by the rebels within two years. The newer .45-caliber single-shot rifle with Martini breech-loading action and Henry rifling system—which Barlee proposed to give to the rebel leaders—was adopted by the British Army for general use in 1871 (Ellacott 1955), but the fact that the lieutenant governor had to secure the four from Jamaica shows they were not yet current in British Honduras.

59. News items, NE (Feb. 28, 1879, 2; Mar. 4, 1879, 3). See also F. P. Barlee to M. E. Hicks Beach, Confidential, Apr. 15, 1879 (CO123/163).

60. Baqueiro (1887). His place of residence is identified in "Ecos de la excursión a Santa Cruz de Bravo" (RM, June 26, 1901, 2).

61. For example, Bricker (1981, 111).

62. D. G. Gamble, "Report on Military Arrangements, British Honduras," Feb. 14, 1880 (CO123/165). He specified one hundred to two hundred soldiers for Icaiché although he allowed that these might also draw reinforcements from the more numerous *pacíficos* to the west.

63. Based on a Belize newspaper article of 1882 professing to report "the third such visit, by Dn. Juan Chuc the second, and Dn. Alonzo Chablé the third, in command—the principal Chief Dn. Crescencio Poot, being too aged to travel" ("The Chiefs of the Santa Cruz Indians," CG, Jan. 21, 1882, 2).

64. For example, Bartolomé and Barabas (1977, 118–19); Villa Rojas (1962, 227) laments an event of 1958 (which he dates to 1957) when representatives of the rebel-derived village of Señor traveled to Belize to pay their respects to the visiting Princess Margaret as the great granddaughter of Queen Victoria, "the person they . . . honour next to God" ("Maya Indians Come from Quintana Roo, . . ." *Belize Billboard*, May 3, 1958, 8).

65. F. P. Barlee to the Earl of Kimberley, Confidential, June 15, 1881 (CO123/166).

66. F. P. Barlee dispatch No. 33, Mar. 30, 1882 (CO123/167). By this date all British Honduras dispatches were sent direct to London.

67. F. P. Barlee dispatch No. 70, July 6, 1882 (CO123/167). Avila was also said to have acted as interpreter for General Santiago Pech of Icaiché in a visit to Mexico City that will be mentioned later. The Belize press reported that Avila's wife had lived among the rebels since their second taking of Bacalar; it is possible he was himself from that region ("Intertribal War amongst Maya Indians," CG, Nov. 22, 1884, 2).

68. R. W. Harley dispatch No. 13, June 19, 1883 (CO123/169).

69. H. Fowler dispatch No. 2, Jan. 15, 1884, with letter dated Nov. 19, 1883, as encl. 2 (CO123/172).

70. H. Fowler dispatch No. 2, Jan. 15, 1884 (CO123/172). Lapointe (1983, 143–44), drawing on archival material, alleges that the Canto-Avila operation was directed by Porfirio Díaz, who was already planning the erection of a federal territory in eastern Yucatan.

71. H. Fowler dispatch No. 2, Jan. 15, 1884, encl. 5 (CO123/172). The treaty is also included, with a description of the proceedings signed by R. J. Norris, Secretary to the Administrator, in ABH (R118). The British Foreign Office took exception to the proceedings, saying the administrator "was not to allow himself to be made the medium of negotiations between the Government of Mexico and the Santa Cruz Indians, without special instructions from Her Majesty's Government." See FO to Undersecretary of State, Colonial Office, Apr. 7, 1884 (CO123/174).

72. J. C. Poot to H. Fowler, Jan. 30, 1884 (encl. with Fowler dispatch No. 15, Feb. 14, 1884, CO123/172, and in ABH, R118). But it might well not have been accepted. Although the tolerance apparently shown to General Canto's blandishments on this

occasion seem to mark a real change in rebel attitudes, acceptance of the treaty would mean abandonment by the *masewalob* of their steadfast insistence on sovereignty in their own territory.

73. "Chan-Santa-Cruz" (RM, Dec. 7, 1884, 3); "Intertribal War amongst Maya Indians" (CG, Nov. 22, 1884, 2). According to the Belize paper, Avila's death was the first stroke in the rebellion against Poot ("Tribal Revolution in Chan Santa Cruz, CG, Sept. 5, 1885, 2).

74. Events surrounding the break are recapitulated on a Colonial Office scratch sheet that accompanies H. Fowler to H. T. Holland, Confidential, Mar. 7, 1887 (CO123/183), and touched on in "Memorandum: The Santa Cruz Indians, Mexico, and British Honduras" of Mar. 1887 (FO15/241, fol. 180).

75. R. T. Goldsworthy dispatch No. 127, Sept. 8, 1885 (CO123/176); see also "Crescencio Poot" (RM, July 14, 1885, 3); items in CG (Sept. 5, Sept. 12, and Sept. 19, 1885).

76. The course of hostilities is described briefly in enclosures to Goldsworthy's dispatch No. 127, of Sept. 8, 1885 (CO123/176). Dzul announced his triumph in a letter to the Governor of Belize, Sept. 8, 1885 (enclosed with H. Fowler dispatch No. 134, Sept. 21, 1885, CO123/176). A list of those killed is given in "Chan Santa Cruz" (EEC, Feb. 13, 1886, 3). Although another source indicates Poot's family was murdered, this could not have included all of his sons, for one of them lived to be an informant to Edward H. Thompson (1932). A version of the basic exhortation of the speaking cross that is translated by Bricker (1981, 187, n. to line 6) seems to indicate that Chuc was killed on August 23, 1885; the date is in keeping with such evidence as is available. Baqueiro (1887) in his brief biography of Poot adds no very specific details of the time or place of his death but does provide him with a curtain line as he is shot: "Death has always been close to me, and you well know it is not unknown to me. Finish me off, that's what you're looking for; but you too will have to die the same way." But the prediction was inaccurate with regard to Dzul, who seems to be among that few who met their end in bed.

17. *Pacífico* Affairs

1. R. J. Downer to the Colonial Secretary, Apr. 15, 1870 (encl. with J. R. Longden dispatch No. 47, May 7, 1870, CO123/140).

2. J. Plumridge to J. R. Longden, n.d. (encl. with J. R. Longden dispatch No. 47, May 7, 1870, CO123/150).

3. No such looting is mentioned in contemporary accounts, but more than two decades later a priest would report the presence at Icaiché of "the famous cross taken by Canul from Xaibe" (TA, May 1895, 87).

4. The event is described in J. R. Longden dispatch No. 47, May 7, 1870 (with numerous enclosures, CO123/140).

5. W. W. Cairns dispatches No. 125, Aug. 2, 1870, and No. 159, Sept. 17, 1870 (CO123/141). The Yucatecan prisoners were all released on bail within three months (W. W. Cairns dispatch No. 104, July 2, and No. 116, July 28, 1870, CO123/140); apparently none was ever tried.

6. W. W. Cairns dispatch No. 77, June 6, 1870 (CO123/140); R. W. Harley dispatch No. 119, Aug. 30, 1871 (CO123/145). I am unable to reconcile conflicting sums given in these two documents; that quoted was the amount mentioned by Harley in his dispatch just cited.

7. M. Canul and R. Chan to the Governor, May 4, 1870 (encl. with W. W. Cairns dispatch No. 80, June 6, 1870, CO123/140).

8. W. W. Cairns dispatch No. 87, June 20, 1870 (CO123/140).

9. P. García and F. Carvajal to the National Government, Mar. 19, 1870 (EP, Mar. 22, 1870, 1–2); P. García to Secretary of State, Mexico, Apr. 1, 1870 (EP, Apr. 5, 1870, 1).

10. See articles in EP (June 3, 6, 14, 21, and July 15, 1870); Anonymous (1896, 111–15).

11. J. A. Cepeda Peraza dispatch, Dec. 19, 1870 (RP, Dec. 21, 1870, 2); see also news items in LD (Jan. 31, 1871, 4).

12. "Revista de los Chenes, by R. J. Piña, LD (Apr. 11, 1871, 2).

13. "Memoria anual del partido de los Chenes," by C. Penelo y Ruiz, Feb. 3, 1872 (LD, Feb. 16, 1872, 1–4).

14. "Los cantones pacíficos del Sur" (LD, Jan. 3, 1871, 3) and news items in LD (Jan. 31, 1871, 4). While this delegation was in Campeche, Arana himself made a trip to Icaiché, returning to Xkanhá with Laureano Flores, late of Corozal, who was now being referred to as a secretary of Marcos Canul; see "El General Arana" (LD, Feb. 14, 1871, 4).

15. Decree of J. Baranda, Mar. 8, 1871 (LD, Mar. 10, 1871, 1).

16. C. Pinelo y Ruiz dispatch, Sept. 23, 1871 (LD, Sept. 29, 1871, 1), and news item, LD (Sept. 29, 1871, 4).

17. Budget (LD, Dec. 1, 1871, 2–3); C. Pinelo y Ruiz dispatch of Oct. 10, 1871 (LD, Oct. 24, 1871).

18. M. Cervera y Molina dispatch, Dec. 9, 1872 (LD, Dec. 17, 1872, 2).

19. Editorial (LD, Nov. 29, 1872, 1).

20. W. W. Cairns dispatches No. 65, Apr. 25, 1871 (CO123/143) and No. 87, June 9, 1871 (CO123/144).

21. R. J. Downer to the Colonial Secretary, June 20, 1871 (encl. with R. W. Harley dispatch No. 106, June 23, 1871, CO123/144).

22. R. J. Downer to Colonial Secretary, Aug. 12, 1872 (encl. with W. W. Cairns dispatch No. 169, Sept. 15, 1872, CO123/149).

23. Report of Officer Commanding the Troops, Sept. 21, 1872 (encl. with W. W. Cairns dispatch No. 169, CO123/149). According to a later statement, Canul was irritated because he had understood that wrongdoers would be returned to their own territory for justice; see J. L. Moo to Lieutenant Governor, Jan. 20, 1874 (encl. with W. W. Cairns dispatch of Feb. 28, 1874, FO50/433). Much later, Lieutenant Governor Barlee (dispatch No. 72, July 20, 1882, CO123/168) expressed belief that Canul had overnighted at San Antonio and that Manuel Castillo could have warned Orange Walk. But this opinion was expressed after Castillo was tried for treason on another, possibly trumped-up, charge.

24. Memorial of R. J. Downer to the Earl of Kimberley, n.d. (encl. with W. W. Cairns dispatch No. 230, Dec. 16, 1872, CO123/150, copied in FO50/432).

25. A coherent description of the preliminary trial and of the fight, with a map, are in W. W. Cairns dispatch No. 169, Sept. 15, 1872, with its numerous enclosures (CO123/149). See also Memorial of R. J. Downer to the Earl of Kimberley, n.d. (encl. with W. W. Cairns dispatch No. 230, Dec. 16, 1872, CO123/150). Other details are in FO50/432. For his bravery Oswald was made Companion of the Order of St. Michael and St. George—a remarkable climax to an eventful career in which he had been one of the early traders to the *masewal* rebels as the partner of Lanabit, had been accused of abetting those rebels against the Yucatecans, and had finally settled as a sugar planter; a sketch of his life is in CG (Mar. 17 through Apr. 14, 1883).

26. R. Chan and L. Moo to the Governor of the Colony of Belize, Sept. 26, 1872 (ABH, R111, and in FO59/432).

27. General D. J. Gamble, "Report on Military Arrangements, British Honduras," Feb. 14, 1880 (CO123/165).

28. For example, news item, LD (Mar. 4, 1873, 4).

29. J. M. Lafragua to the Minister of Foreign Affairs of Great Britain, Feb. 12, 1873 (FO50/432). Whereas the governments of Yucatan and Campeche had fully recognized that the Icaiché commandant could claim to act under their authority, the central government consistently refused to acknowledge the relationship. As noted earlier, in 1864 following a British complaint the Yucatecan government had sent a messenger to the south to inquire into the activities of Luciano Tzuc, and in 1868 Governor García of Campeche had not only explained his relationship to Canul but had taken measures to curb activities of Canul that might lead to trouble with the British colony. Yet in both 1866 and 1873 the central government—first of Maximilian, then of Juárez—had insisted there was no relationship.

30. Earl of Derby to J. M. Lafragua, July 28, 1874 (FO50/433).

31. For example, P. Campbell Scarlett's "Memorandum on the Boundary Question of British Honduras," Oct. 31, 1872 (FO50/432).

32. J. Carmichael Jr. to the Earl of Kimberley, Jan. 23, 1873 (CO123/155), with minutes by various people. See W. W. Cairns dispatch No. 40, Mar. 13, and Confidential, Mar. 13, 1873 (CO123/152), in which Lieutenant Governor Cairns discusses the suggestions and implicit issues.

33. HG (Sept. 14, 1878, 117) carried a notice that his will was approved; creditors were advised to file claims.

34. R. Chan and L. Moo to the Governor of the Colony of Belize, Sept. 26, 1872 (ABH, R111, and FO50/432).

35. R. Chan and J. L. Moo to the Governor of Campeche, Dec. 23, 1872 (LD, Jan. 28, 1872, 2).

36. W. W. Cairns to R. Chan, Oct. 10, 1872 (LD, Jan. 28, 1873, 2, and FO50/432).

37. R. Chan to W. W. Cairns, Mar. 8, 1873, and E. Arana to W. W. Cairns, Mar. 8, 1873 (FO50/432).

38. There was a brief interlude when Chan's position was usurped by his second in command. On January 20, 1874, José Luis Moo wrote to the lieutenant governor of British Honduras to say that Chan was unable to act as commander because of habitual drunkenness and to the magistrate at Orange Walk to ask if he could "enter into an amicable treaty to enable my troops to enter the colony to seek employment, and to send their products as formerly." Governor Cairns responded that there had never been a bar to any people's entering the colony for trade or work and that he was not empowered to make treaties. He pointed out that no apology or reparation had been made for the raid on Orange Walk (Moo to the Lt. Governor, Jan. 20, 1874; Moo to Magistrate, Orange Walk, n.d.; and W. W. Cairns to Moo, Feb. 1874, all encl. with W. W. Cairns dispatch No. 28, Feb. 13, 1874, FO50/433). Evidently, Moo's position was neither secure nor obtained according to Icaiché custom, for on February 12, 1874, Arana wrote that Rafael Chan had complained that Moo had expelled him from his position, "wounding him and sacking his home, and murdering the citizen Dolores Sarmiento" and that Moo had been apprehended and sent to Campeche for trial. The following month Arana wrote again, this time to say it was Chan who had captured Moo and ten others accused of raising insurrection at Icaiché and that Chan had taken them to Xkanhá (E. Arana to no addressee, Feb. 12, 1874, ABH, R119; Arana to Lieutenant Governor, Mar. 16, 1874, ibid., and encl. with C. B. H. Mitchell dispatch No. 68, Apr. 15, CO123/156). Arana also said that Moo had been sentenced to ten years' imprisonment, which turns out not to have been the case; Moo was tried in Campeche on Dec. 28, 1874, and found innocent ("Jurados," LD, Jan. 1, 1875, 1). The murdered Sarmiento was that former secretary of Canul who had been sentenced for horse stealing after the 1870 "invasion"' of Corozal.

39. For example, E. Arana to the Governor of Belize, Feb. 12, 1874, and W. W. Cairns to Arana, Mar. 14, 1874 (encl. with Cairns dispatch no. 46, Mar. 13, 1874, co123/156); Arana to the Lieutenant Governor, June 2, 1874, and R. M. Mundy to Arana, July 25, 1874 (encl. with R. M. Mundy dispatch No. 100, July 25, 1874, fo50/433).

40. See various documents in fo50/433, especially G. von Ohlafen to the Acting Colonial Secretary, Nov. 6, 1874; R. M. Mundy to E. Arana, Nov. 11, 1874; and Mundy dispatch No. 140, Dec. 14, 1874.

41. G. von Ohlafen to the Acting Colonial Secretary, Nov. 6, 1874 (fo50/433).

42. I. L. Vallarta to the Earl of Derby, March 23, 1878 (fo50/434), in which the Mexican minister took the opportunity to remind the British that the convention of 1786 had included their promise to avoid trade with hostile Indians on the borders of Spanish possessions. He went again through the question of trade in munitions, taking issue with the trial of Mena, who he stated had not been involved in an act of piracy, as the British claimed, but in trying to forestall the crime of selling powder to the Indians and further that the killing by Mena took place not in British but in Mexican waters, there being no British waters anywhere in the region. This exchange of letters is also published in Anonymous (1878).

43. See Humphreys (1961, chaps. 6, 7). This convention did not end the dispute between Guatemala and Britain, for one provision—the mutual construction of a road from Guatemala City to the Atlantic coast—was never carried out, and the problems it raised virtually sank Anglo-Guatemalan relations. This is outside the focus of the present work, however.

44. F. P. Barlee dispatches No. 77, Aug. 1, and No. 90, Aug. 27, 1879, with enclosures (co123/163).

45. See fo50/433 (esp. Phillips and Co. to Acting Colonial Secretary, Mar. 22, 1875, with encl.).

46. G. von Ohlafen to Acting Colonial Secretary, Apr. 29, 1875, with encl. (fo50/433).

47. R. H. Mundy dispatch No. 57, June 14, 1875, with encl., and C. B. H. Mitchell dispatch No. 82, Sept. 14, 1876, with encl. (fo50/433).

48. C. B. H. Mitchell dispatches No. 106, with encl. (fo50/433), and No. 7, Jan. 5, 1877, with encl. (co123/160); F. P. Barlee dispatch No. 68, June 16, 1877 (fo50/434).

49. F. P. Barlee dispatch No. 101, Sept. 3, 1877 (co123/161); S. S. Plues to R. H. Pickwoad, Aug. 31, 1877 (fo50/434).

50. F. P. Barlee dispatch No. 118, Nov. 13, 1877, with two enclosed letters from Arana, both dated Sept. 27, 1877 (co123/161); and letters from Arana to Governor of Belize, Nov. 30, 1877 (encl. with F. P. Barlee dispatch No. 1, Jan. 4, 1878, co123/162).

The letters of September were uncharacteristically unfriendly, leading the lieutenant governor to suspect they were written by Arana's secretary without his knowledge; those of November were in Arana's usual conciliatory style.

51. F. P. Barlee dispatch No. 9, Jan. 16, 1878 (CO123/162). Chan's removal had been rumored somewhat earlier (Barlee dispatch No. 118, Nov. 13, 1877, CO123/161). He had been little inclined to take decisive military action of any kind and was particularly well disposed to the British; he had even contemplated moving his family to the colony. See, for instance, the statement attributed to him and encl. with F. P. Barlee confidential dispatch, May 16, 1878, (FO50/434, apparently originally included with a letter from A. L. Kindred to the Secretary of the Belize Estate and Produce Co., May 15, 1877, the latter in Misc. Offices of CO123/161).

52. J. C. Hernández statement of Oct. 29, 1866 (ABH, R93).

53. F. P. Barlee dispatch No. 15, Feb. 20, 1878, with undated Arana letter encl. (CO123/162).

54. F. P. Barlee dispatch No. 77, Aug. 1, 1879 (CO123/163); reports of G. Marriner, Inspector of Police, and of Lieutenant D. M. Allen, Aug. 22 and Aug. 14, 1879, respectively, (encl. with F. P. Barlee dispatch No. 90, Aug. 27, 1879, CO123/163).

55. F. P. Barlee dispatch No. 119, Nov. 5, 1879, with encl. (CO123/164).

56. F. P. Barlee dispatch No. 123, Nov. 22, 1879, with encl. (CO123/164). People bitten by snakes were believed to be so susceptible to the evil eye that anyone looking at them might prove lethal to them (because anyone could unwittingly have evil power), and so others would considerately stay away. Thus, it was hoped to keep the affair secret.

57. F. P. Barlee dispatch No. 127, Dec. 10, 1879, with encl. (CO123/164). The official account of the incident was not accepted by a large number of British Honduras residents, for a memorial to the secretary of state for the colonies that bore two full pages of signatures (and that primarily focused on spendthrift aspects of Barlee's administration) defended Pech, saying that although he had been accused by Governor Barlee of masterminding " 'a determined raid into this Territory,' . . . it will be found that 'General Santiago Pech,' . . . had rather the best of the Argument with Lieutenant Governor Barlee, and shewed clearly that a murder having been committed near the Boundary of a disputed territory: the British Authorities having taken no notice of it, the Indians took steps to punish the Culprits, . . . outstripping our 'tardy British Justice.' " See memorial of Sept. 8, 1880 (Misc., CO123/165). A similar view of the affair was held by Henry Fowler, then colonial secretary in Belize, who in a lengthy letter to the Under Secretary of State, Colonial Office, of May 7, 1883 (Misc. Offices, CO123/171) laid out his argument that Pech had acted with intelligence

and circumspection, while Barlee had been unreasonable. Fowler was no admirer of Barlee, however.

58. F. P. Barlee dispatch No. 24, Mar. 8, 1880 (CO123/165), also the source of the quotation. For the spelling of Socotz (which appears as Soccoths on recent maps of Belize) I follow articles in Jones (1977).

59. S. Pech to F. P. Barlee, Mar. 21, 1882 (encl. with Barlee dispatch No. 33, Mar. 30, 1882, CO123/167; also see other encl.). The treaties extracted were those that first agreed to the presence of the British settlement on Spanish territory and then specified a boundary that in its last (1786) statement included the Hondo on the north and the Sibun on the south. The treaty of December 26, 1826, recognized sovereignty neither of Mexico nor of Britain in the formerly Spanish territory occupied by the British but did provide that British subjects should not be molested "within the limits described and laid down in a Convention . . . [with] the King of Spain, on the 14th of July, 1786" (Humphreys 1961, 27, also chap. 1). The Mexicans—and Pech—took the statement of 1826 as confirming the boundaries of the settlement set out in 1786, while the position of Britain was now that all territory under British control at the time Spain recognized Mexico and Guatemala (i.e., 1836 and 1863) had been ceded to the British crown. It was on this trip of Pech to Mexico that Francisco Avila served as his interpreter (F. P. Barlee dispatch No. 70, July 7, 1882, CO123/167).

60. S. Pech to the Lieutenant Governor of British Honduras, May 16, 1882, (encl. in English translation with F. P. Barlee dispatch No. 52, June 3, 1882, CO123/167).

61. F. P. Barlee to S. Pech, May 29, 1882 (encl. with Barlee dispatch No. 52, June 3, 1882, CO123/167).

62. C. Peña to Magistrate at Orange Walk, June 2, 1882, and F. Escalante statement of June 8, 1882 (encl. with F. P. Barlee dispatch No. 58, June 22, 1882, CO123/167).

63. F. P. Barlee dispatch No. 58, June 22, 1882 (CO123/167).

64. F. P. Barlee dispatch No. 72, July 20, 1882 (CO123/167) with enclosed report of proceedings of W. H. Dillet, July 17, 1882; also, "Special Sitting of the Supreme Court" (CG, July 15, 1882, 2–3). According to the latter source, the jury deliberated only ten minutes to bring its unanimous verdict of guilty, and "after the evidence . . . had been heard, . . . almost every one present expressed his approval of the finding, and some of them rather boisterously." At least one man on the street expressed his satisfaction in a letter to the newspaper (letter from "A Bayman," CG, Nov. 25, 1882, 3). But there was a counter opinion that the sentence was unjust, that the matter had not been serious enough to warrant the colony's legal attention. This view is articulated in a letter from the colonial secretary, Henry Fowler (by now at odds in almost all ways with Lieutenant Governor Barlee) to the Undersecretary of State, Colonial Office, May 7, 1883 (Misc. Offices, CO123/171). This summarizes the entire affair, from Pech's imprisonment to the trial—the most coherent single description

but slanted heavily against Barlee. A similar opinion is in a letter from R. Niven of the Belizean firm of William Gill Co. to Professor James Bryce, a member of parliament, June 22, 1883 (Misc. Offices, CO123/171). But Colonel Sir Robert Harley, who followed Barlee as governor, disagreed, having concluded on the basis of the court proceedings and an interview with Castillo (then in jail) that there had indeed been a conspiracy but that the elderly (and illiterate) Castillo had probably been "the dupe of his more astute advisors, such as López, Sevilla, and others" (Harley to the Undersecretary of State, Colonial Office, June 28, 1883, Misc. Offices, CO123/171).

65. F. P. Barlee dispatch No. 70, July 6, 1882 (CO123/167).

66. H. Fowler to the Lieutenant Governor, July 11, 1882 (encl. with F. P. Barlee dispatch No. 72, July 20, 1882, CO123/167).

67. Colonial Secretary to Colonel Harley, Aug. 7, 1882, and Acting Magistrate, Western District, to Colonial Secretary, Aug. 18, 1882 (encl. with R. W. Harley dispatch No. 94, Sept. 14, 1882, CO123/167). The show of force at Yaloch took Fowler into Guatemala and extracted allegiance from the wrong people, although at the time he thought the village was in British Honduras. There was apparently another side to this affair, however. Four years earlier Fowler had been a member of an exploring party into the inaccessible western region (Fowler 1879), and he had become the holder of logging interests there. As the somewhat muckraking Belize newspaper put it ("The Way the Money Goes," CG, June 16, 1883, 2): "The person in charge of Mr. Fowler's land . . . was the informant of the intended disturbances. . . . It gradually leaked out that the whole affair arose from a dispute between his agent and his tenants. . . . The whole affair amounted . . . to an expedition to protect Major Fowler's agent and his mahogany cutters, which . . . cost the Government nearly $2,000."

68. S. Pech to the Lieutenant Governor, July 18, 1882 (encl. with R. W. Harley dispatch No. 79, Aug. 17, 1882, CO123/167); see also J. S. López to Magistrate of Orange Walk District, Mar. 11, 1882 (ibid.).

69. Memorandum between Colonel R. W. Harley and General S. Pech, Oct. 13, 1882 (encl. with Harley dispatch No. 111, Oct. 20, 1882, CO123/168; also in ABH, R93). A much less bland description of Peña's death—in which he was tied around a spiny palmetto branch, left in the sun for three days, kicked, beaten, and finally shot—is given in "Pech's Inhumanity" (CG, Dec. 9, 1882, 2).

70. B. Travers undated report to the Lieutenant Governor (encl. with R. W. Harley dispatch No. 16, Jan. 30, 1883, CO123/169). The alcalde at San Pedro was no longer Asunción Ek, but was José Domingo Vela, appointed in August 1882 (List of Alcaldes, ibid).

71. R. S. Turton dispatch No. 75, May 30, 1883 (CO123/169); Turton dispatch No. 93, July 3, 1883, and H. Fowler dispatch No. 133, Aug. 31, 1883 (CO123/170); also

Fowler dispatches No. 127, Aug. 23, 1883, with enclosures, and No. 142, Sept. 24, 1883 (ibid.).

72. G. Tamay to the Lieutenant Governor, June 7, 1883 (encl. with R. S. Turton dispatch No. 88, June 21, 1883, co123/169); H. Fowler dispatch No. 144, Sept. 24, 1883, with encl. (co123/170).

73. On the face of it, this act is surprisingly naive of *pacífico* officials who so legalistically reaped financial gain behind international treaties. It is possible that Icaiché had suffered some rebuff from Campeche in requests for arms; and the adroit Arana may have known that he had no very strong support there. For as the *jefe político* of the *partido* of the Chenes had said officially only a few years before, Arana's territory was not only the home of Indians who had vacillated between war and peace with the government but also provided a den for criminals, fugitives, and absconded servants. And, "these *cantones*, obedient, seemingly, to the government, . . . make surreptitious war that does not cease to cause us great evil. Their inhabitants live without laws to regulate their actions, with a theocratic-military form of government still more despotic than that established in Poland by the Czar of Russia, ruled only by the all-encompassing will of the so-called General Eugenio Arana, . . . man of terrible antecedents, habitually drunk and capable . . . of any disorder." (Solís 1878, 43). The second witness, Eustaquio Avila, did not report Arana to have been in Mérida, and it is possible that Arana did not accompany Tamay that far.

74. Statement of Andrés Ongay, Nov. 19, 1883 (encl. with H. Fowler dispatch No. 23, Apr. 3, 1884, co123/172).

75. Statement of Eustaquio Avila, quoted in F. E. Gabb to the Acting Colonial Secretary, Nov. 30, 1883 (encl. with H. Fowler, dispatch No. 23, Apr. 3, 1884, co123/172). A similar account is in "Further Particulars about López and the Icaichés" (cg, Dec. 8,1883, 2).

76. R. T. Goldsworthy dispatch No. 101, Oct. 2, 1884 (co123/173). On October 31 of that year Goldsworthy was elevated from Lieutenant Governor to Governor and Commander in Chief, as British Honduras was raised from Colony to Crown Colony.

77. H. Fowler dispatch No. 42, June 2, 1884 (co123/173). The Belize Estate and Produce Co. had been in doubt about making such payments after Lieutenant Governor Barlee proclaimed his ban on all communication with Icaiché, but upon referring the matter to the Colonial Office in London it received word from Lord Kimberley to make the payment and inform the acting governor, who would not prosecute. See exchange of memoranda dated Aug. 13–15, 1882 (Misc., co123/168).

78. D. M. Allen to the district magistrate, Orange Walk, May 7, 1884 (encl. with Fowler dispatch No. 42, June 1, 1884, co123/173).

79. Humphreys (1961, 143).

80. Humphreys (1961, chap. 10).

81. These adventures in demarcating the boundary are included in H. Fowler confidential dispatches of Oct. 9, 19, 30, Nov. 19, and R. T. Goldsworthy confidential dispatch of Dec. 28, 1885, all with enclosures (CO123/177); the phrases quoted are from G. Tamay to Surveyor in Charge, Oct. 19, 1885 (encl. with the Fowler dispatch of Oct. 30).

18. The World Moves Closer

1. See, for instance, figures summarized by Rodríguez Losa (1989, pt. 2).

2. Cámara Zavala (1977); Suárez Molina (1977a, 1:146–47); Wells (1985).

3. Suárez Molina (1977a, 2:34–40).

4. Wells (1985, 164–66; 1991); Turner (1911, chap. 1).

5. See, for instance, "La cuestión de Belice, Yucatán y Campeche" (RM, July 18, 1889, 2).

6. Careaga Viliesid (1990a, 126–27); Suárez Molina (1977a, 1:212–15); see also Konrad (1991).

7. R. W. Pickwoad to Colonial Secretary, Dec. 19, 1885 (encl. with R. T. Goldsworthy confidential dispatch of Dec. 18, 1885, CO123/177).

8. "Icaiché" (RM, Sept. 29, 1895, 3); see also an account of defections in A. Milson to Colonial Secretary, May 4, 1886 (encl. with R. T. Goldsworthy dispatch No. 102, May 27, 1886, CO123/179).

9. S. St. John to Earl of Rosebery, Apr. 3, 1886 (Foreign Office sect., CO123/181); "Grave noticia" (RM, Feb. 7, 1886, 3), and news item, RM (Feb. 10, 1886). Leaders are also identified in "Dos chinos de Santa Cruz" (RM, May 5, 1886, 3). A comment in "Mas de indios bárbaros" (RM, Feb. 12, 1886, 1) attributes repeating rifles to the rebels, but this is unlikely. The repeating Spencer rifle was patented in 1860, leading to the tube-magazine Winchesters of 1866 and 1873, the former of which saw limited military use in eastern Europe. But the British adopted a magazine rifle for military uses only in 1888, Mexico not until 1895 (Ellacott 1955; Fuentes 1983). For their part, the rebels were said always to prefer muzzle-loaders, for these did not force them to depend on factory-made metallic cartridges. See, for instance, "Belize and the Indians of Yucatan" (CG, Dec. 15, 1888, 2).

10. "Cantón en Tihosuco" (RM, Feb. 11, 1886, 3).

11. E. A. H. Schofield to A. H. Hall, May 25, 1886 (encl. with R. T. Goldsworthy dispatch No. 104, June 8, 1886, CO123/179).

12. "The Chiefs of the Santa Cruz Indians" (CG, Jan. 21, 1882, 2) records the third such visit, during which they were treated to a tour of a British ship, where they "were greatly delighted, amazed, and slightly scared at the terrific effects produced by their turning the handles of the Gattling-guns."

13. Memorandum "The Santa Cruz Indians, Mexico, and British Honduras," Mar. 28, 1887 (FO15/241); A. Dzul, J. M. Puc, and J. Aguilar to the Governor, Oct. 1, 1885 (encl. with H. Fowler dispatch No. 146, Oct. 19, 1885, CO123/176).

14. "De Tulum" (RM, Mar. 16, 1886, 1); "Los de Tulum" (RM, Mar. 17, 1886, 1). Neither is it indicated how they arranged their journey. Apparently they were allowed to return home without hindrance.

15. R. T. Goldsworthy dispatch No. 89, May 6, 1886, with enclosures (CO123/179); E. Thomson to H. B. M. Minister, Washington, May 18, 1886, and S. St. John to Earl of Iddesleigh, Oct. 30, 1886 (Foreign Office sec., CO123/181). A firsthand account of the captivity is provided anonymously in "Narrative of a Mexican Captive" (CG, Jan. 8, 15, 22, 1887).

16. "Memorandum: The Santa Cruz Indians, Mexico, and British Honduras," March 1887 (CO15/241, 180 ff).

17. H. Fowler dispatch No. 24, Feb. 28, 1887 (CO123/182), where the name of the Tulum leader is *Xiab*; I have corrected the spelling to that given by Roys (1940), and as will be detailed later I presume him to be the high priest rather than governor at Tulum. The Chinese mentioned, of course, were remnants of those who had fled from British Honduras in the 1860s. These occupants of *masewal* territory had evidently graduated from the status of laborers to that of wandering peddlers who provided most of the commercial needs of the *masewalob* and had largely cornered the export pig market. Resentment of them was strong; by one account most of them lived in a small village about fifteen kilometers from Noh Cah Santa Cruz, but unlike ordinary *masewalob* they were required to pay an annual tax of two kegs of powder per person. See "El corresponsal a D. Moreno Cantón" (RM, Mar. 27, 1888); "El indio de Santa Cruz capturado" (RM, Aug. 7, 1894, 2).

18. H. Fowler dispatch No. 80, June 18, 1887 (CO123/184).

19. A. Dzul to the Governor, Jan. 30, 1887 (encl. with H. Fowler dispatch No. 21, Feb. 10, 1887, CO123/182).

20. H. Fowler dispatch No. 68, May 9, 1887 (CO123/184). The merchant vessel of his return passage was afraid to stop at Tulum for fear of attack, and it dumped him at Belize.

21. H. de Villamil to R. T. Goldsworthy, n.d. (encl. with Goldsworthy to Secretary of State for Colonies, Jan. 17, 1887, Misc. sec., CO123/188).

22. E. A. H. Schofield to A. H. Hall, May 25, 1886, and other enclosures to R. T. Goldsworthy dispatch No. 104, June 6, 1886 (CO123/179); H. de Villamil to R. T. Goldsworthy, n.d. (encl. with Goldsworthy to Secretary of State for Colonies, Jan. 17, 1887, Misc. sec., CO123/188).

23. "El corte de maderos" (RM, Feb. 15, 1887, 3); "Noticias estadísticas y geográficas de Yucatán" (RM, Feb. 21 through Mar. 13, 1888). The concession to Ibarra Ortoll in

1887 must be related to the reported grant in 1889 of 673,850 hectares along the coast to a firm operating as Faustino Martínez y Compañía (Careaga Viliesid 1990a, 127; Suárez Molina 1977a, 1:215–16), possibly Ibarra's successor. See also Lapointe (1983, 148–49). Rights of Faustino Martínez y Cia. passed to the British-financed East Coast of Yucatan Colonization Co. in 1896 (Suárez Molina 1977a, 1:215).

24. Younger brother of José Peón y Contreras, the poet and playwright whose name now adorns the major theater in Mérida, Juan Peón in his later days took the maternal name of his mother (Pilar Contreras Elizalde de Peón) to append to his own. As museum director he had been influential in restricting the use of dynamite in the excavation of Maya ruins and in preventing the export of Maya sculpture by Auguste Le Plongeon. Personal details are summarized by Peón Ancona (1985); details of his mission as Forerunner II, as well as some other personal notes, are in a disjointed work by Peón Contreras himself (1888), much of which is a sixty-seven-stanza poem of uneven quality.

25. "La expedición de D. Juan Peón Contreras," by M. E. Monteagudo (RM, May 19, 1887, 2–3). Although his plan—whatever it was—was convincing enough to secure backing from one of the Belizean commercial houses, it seemed wild enough to the local creoles that he was referred to as *Pañaful*, "Spaniard fool." According to Bricker (1981, 339, n. 60), Peón announced his project in a bilingual (Maya-Spanish) newspaper, possibly of only a single issue, published in Mérida in March 1887. Although the paper presented what was said to be a statement of the archbishop of Mexico authorizing him to undertake a peace mission to the rebels of Santa Cruz, his own announcement, couched in the "same idiom as the proclamation of Juan de la Cruz," also implied his intention to log the forests of the east coast. I have not seen this source.

26. Tancah lies fifteen kilometers north of both the ruins and the pueblo of Tulum; the ruins are on the coast, the pueblo three or four kilometers inland. There is also a building in the ruins of Tancah that is known as the *castillo*, or castle.

27. "La expedición" (RM, May 24, 1887, 2–3).

28. Peón's early successes are described in "D. Juan Peón y los indios" (RM, Apr. 17, 1887, 3); "La expedición de D. Juan Peón Contreras," by M. E. Monteagudo (RM, May 19, May 24, 1887, 2–3). An account by one of the survivors, as well as the story of Arjonilla's perfidy, is in "The Tragedy at Tulum" (CG, July 23, 1887, 2). Basic reports of the debacle are "Noticias de los bárbaros" (RM, June 14 and June 21, 1887, 2), and "Del campo enemigo" (EC, June 14, 1887, 2), in the latter of which the *gobernador* is named as Luciano Canul, and Peón's bride is said to be widow of a "Colonel Pech." It was to Luciano Pech as "Chief of Tulum" that administrator Henry Fowler of British Honduras wrote sometime around May 10, 1887 (H. Fowler to L. Pech, two letters without date, ABH, R117, with a single similar but not duplicate letter to

an unnamed Tulum official dated May 10, 1887, encl. with Fowler dispatch No. 68, May 9, 1887, CO123/184), and it seems likely that it was Pech who was killed by Dzul. But Cruz Ciau—who there is reason to suspect was high priest—seems to have been still alive in 1892, as I will indicate later. An entirely different account of the whole affair was given by an Indian former prisoner and fugitive from Santa Cruz, who stated that Dzul had been friendly throughout with Peón and that it was people of Chunpom who had killed Peón's collaborators, resulting in enmity between Dzul and the Chunpom commander; see J. M. Ay statement, in El corresponsal to D. M. Cantón, Mar. 24, 1888 (RM, Mar. 27, 1888), where the personal name of Peón's bride is also given.

29. R. T. Goldsworthy confidential dispatch of July 24, 1890 (CO123/194). Konrad (1991, 149) and Lapointe (1983, 148) date the Mexican Exploration Company concession to 1892, but Goldsworthy indicates that activity began before that date on lands originally conceded to Ibarra Ortoll. Ibarra's concession was canceled in 1890, and by 1895 the area from Blue Creek to a point north of Ascension Bay was held on concession by another Belizean, who intended to let logging rights in the same way (M. O. Melville dispatch No. 22, Feb. 19, 1891, with encl., CO123/196; A. Maloney dispatch No. 431, Dec. 27, 1895, with encl., CO123/215).

30. "Bacalar, terrenos baldíos mexicanos invadidos por extranjeros" (RM, Apr. 5, 1888, 2). Bacalar was said to be occupied day by day more completely by Carlos Melhado, operator of a major works cutting dyewood, cedar, and mahogany for shipment to Belize. Melhado was also alleged to act as agent of the rebels and to pay his own rent to them in arms and ammunition. Bacalar and Noh Cah Santa Cruz, the papers said, both flew the British flag. The reports about Melhado were almost certainly accurate, although much of the description of Bacalar was from an earlier era, lifted without attribution from Acevedo (1846). The exchange with British Honduras continued throughout much of the series "Noticias estadísticas y geográficas de Yucatán" (RM, Feb. 21 through Mar. 13, 1888).

31. CG also asserted that the only reason the British flag did not fly permanently was that Britain refused to accede to rebel requests for incorporation into the colony—and, indeed, had refused to accept sovereignty over the entire peninsula when it was offered by the Yucatecan government at the outbreak of the Caste War. See "Yucatan Indians" (CG, June 2, 1888, 2); the exchange continued in an editorial series "Belize and the Indians of Yucatan" (CG, Sept. and Dec., 1888).

32. H. Fowler confidential dispatch of Mar. 7, 1887 (CO123/183). Given the extent of British logging around Bacalar Lagoon, it is hard to believe that there were not British subjects living relatively permanently around Bacalar, although there were apparently no actual trading houses. In the account of a journey from Bacalar to Santa Cruz in January 1888, however, there is no mention of anyone other than *masewalob*

at Bacalar or on the lagoon (Miller 1889). But by 1892 Cramer and Co. had a resident agent there, as indicated in A. Maloney dispatch No. 20, Jan. 20, 1892 (co123/198).

33. A. Dzul, R. Pec, and A. Chi to the Governor, Jan. 8, 1888, encl. with R. T. Goldsworthy confidential dispatch of Jan. 26, 1888 (co123/189); paragraphs of the English manuscript translation are consolidated here. It seems evident from the tone of the letter that to these leaders, forty years after the initial rebellion, the prewar social state of Indians was hearsay.

34. R. T. Goldsworthy dispatch No. 92, July 12, 1888 (co123/189).

35. R. T. Goldsworthy dispatch No. 92, July 12, 1888 (co123/189). Goldsworthy himself was not in town when the meetings occurred. The Mexican ploy was to offer the protection of the Mexican president against harm by the Yucatecans.

36. R. T. Goldsworthy, confidential letter to Lord Knutsford, Oct. 24, 1888, with enclosures (Individuals sec., co123/191).

37. S. St. John to Foreign Office, telegraph of Apr. 26, 1887 (FO to CO, May 2, 1887, co123/187).

38. S. Montalvo and J. Quijano to G. Tamay, Dec. 1, 1886, encl. with H. Fowler dispatch No. 12, Jan. 25, 1887 (co123/182).

39. H. Fowler dispatch No. 30, Feb. 28, 1887, with encl. B. Travers to the Acting Colonial Secretary, Feb. 7, 1887 (co123/182); W. Miller to Colonial Secretary, Mar. 16, 1887 (encl. with H. Fowler dispatch No. 43, Mar. 28, 1887, co123/183). Miller was actually unable to locate any physical evidence of the line Abbs had previously cleared.

40. The Mexicans were even willing to accept what was mapped as Snosha Creek, a very northern tributary of Blue Creek, as the boundary, thereby giving extra territory to Britain, who for her own part considered seriously accepting the Río Bravo as the Hondo headwater and so yielding more land to Mexico. See, for instance, FO to CO communications of July 9, 1887 (co123/187); FO to CO communication, May 28, 1889, with enclosures (co123/193).

41. R. T. Goldsworthy confidential dispatches of Mar. 8, 1889 (two of that date); of Mar. 22, 1889; of June 13, 1989; all with enclosures (co123/192).

42. W. Miller to Acting Colonial Secretary, Nov. 18, 1889 (encl. with W. McKinney confidential dispatch, Nov. 18, 1889, co123/193).

43. Among the British gestures, accepted by Mexico as a token of friendship, was the granting of a pardon to José Santos López, then a fugitive serving as Tamay's secretary. See S. St. John to Marquis of Salisbury, Sept. 8, 1887 (in FO to CO, Sept. 28, 1887, co123/2187); communications and scratch sheets in FO to CO, Oct. 31, 1887 (ibid).

44. S. St. John to Marquis of Salisbury, Nov. 23, 1887 (FO to CO, Dec. 16, 1887, co123/187). The Mexican excuse for the delay in military action was the fighting

then in progress with the Yaqui Indians of northwestern Mexico, which Mariscal indicated must be settled before any force could be fielded against Santa Cruz. The Yaqui troubles were in fact not ended when Noh Cah Santa Cruz was finally taken in 1901, although decisive battles against the Yaqui were won by Mexican government forces in the early 1890s (Hu-DeHart 1984).

45. S. St. John to Marquis of Salisbury, confidential of Nov. 4, 1887 (FO to CO, Jan. 13, 1888) and communication in FO to CO, Feb. 6, 1887 (CO123/191); see Humphreys (1961, 146–48).

46. S. St. John to Earl of Rosebery, n.d. (FO to CO, Sept. 4, 1886, CO123/181); P. W. Currie to CO, June 15, 1888 (FO to CO, June 15, 1888, CO123/191); S. St. John to FO, July 28, 1888 (FO to CO, Aug. 27, 1888, ibid). A second bit of pressure was applied when Mexico asked if, to better fill its commitment in protecting British Honduras from the Santa Cruz, it would be allowed to land some of its troops south of the Hondo, to which St. John's response was that such a possibility could be entertained only after a convention had been signed. (St. John to FO, Sept. 27, 1888, FO to CO, Oct. 19, 1888, CO123/191).

47. R. T. Goldsworthy, confidential dispatch of May 10, 1888 (CO123/189).

48. Fabela (1944, 387–90), appended document 7.

49. E. B. Sweet Escott dispatch No. 301, Sept. 20, 1893 (CO123/204); Sweet Escott to D. Crescencio Puc, Oct. 4, 1893 (encl. in Sweet Escott confidential dispatch of Oct. 6, 1893, ibid).

50. E. B. Sweet Escott confidential dispatch of Oct. 6, 1893, and of Oct. 13, 1893 (CO123/204); T. Schofield to Secretary of State for Colonies, Oct. 18, 1893 (CO123/205).

51. The decision was developed through correspondence FO to CO, Feb. 24, Mar. 1, Mar. 20, Apr. 5, Aug. 17, 1893 (CO123/205); ratification was announced in P. Le Poer Trench to Earl of Rosebery, Oct. 20, 1893 (FO to CO, CO123/205).

52. FO to CO, Jan. 19, Mar. 2, Mar. 20, May 11, Nov. 16, Nov. 30 (CO123/209).

53. Santa Cruz toleration for their jittery British neighbors is conveyed in H. P. C. Strange to Colonial Secretary, Oct. 24, 1893 (encl. in private letter of A. Maloney to Wingfield, Oct. 27, 1893, CO123/204), and in A. Maloney confidential dispatch of Nov. 16, 1893 (CO123/205). Belizean attitudes are included in A. Maloney confidential dispatch of Mar. 14, 1895 (CO123/211); E. B. Sweet Escott dispatch No. 241, July 16, 1895, with enclosures, and dispatches No. 243, July 18, 1895, No. 257, July 26, 1895 (CO123/213), and dispatch No. 300, Aug. 28, 1895 (CO123/214).

54. "Icaiché" (TA, July supplement; Sept., 277–79; Oct., 298–301, all 1889); published in translation as "Icaiché" (RM, May 5, 1892, 2) and included without source attribution in "Breve reseña de Yucatán," vol. 2, a collection of Yucatecan memorabilia compiled for the Paris Exposition of 1900 by José Antonio Alayón, to which I was kindly given access by the late Alfredo Barrera Vásquez. Although no byline is

included in any of these, this first priestly visit is said elsewhere (TA, July, 277) to have been by the priest Pastor Molina. "Icaiché" (TA, May, 1895, 87–88) covers the second visit; again no byline, but "Colony Notes" (TA, Apr. 1895, 62) indicates it was by Molina and the priest Silvin Gillet; internal evidence marks Gillet as the author.

55. Sapper (1904).

56. "Mas sobre Icaiché" (RM, May 10, 1892, 2); see also "Icaiché," by Aristarco (RM, Sept. 29, 1895, 3).

57. Although Sapper (1904, 626) speaks of "houses of sun-dried brick or stone which existed before the rebellion" which were "either destroyed or . . . fallen into ruins," I have seen no other suggestion that the site was occupied in historic times before the removal from Chichanhá. He also places the population at only five hundred, whereas Molina ("Icaiché," TA, 1889, cited previously) conveys an estimate of seventeen hundred and Aristarco ("Icaiché," RM, 1895, cited above) of thirty-five hundred.

58. TA (May 1895, 87).

59. The second in command might also be referred to, in British Honduras at least, as *chiquito general*. See A. Maloney dispatch No. 21, Jan. 11, 1895 (CO123/210).

60. J. H. Hugh Harrison, "Report on the Small Pox Epidemic, 1891, 1892," (encl. with A. Maloney dispatch No. 211, July 8, 1892, CO123/199); news item in RM (June 18, 1891, 3).

61. A. Maloney to G. Tamay, Nov. 23, 1891, and Tamay's response of Dec. 21, 1891 (encl. with A. Maloney dispatch No. 211, Dec. 31, 1891, CO123/197).

62. "Icaiché" (TA, May 1895, 87); Sapper (1904, 627).

63. R. W. Pickwoad to the Colonial Secretary, Apr. 5, 1892 (encl. with A. Maloney dispatch No. 125, Apr. 15, 1892, CO123/198). This secretary was then Sico Figuero, or Figueroa, who had been banished from the colony earlier, as I noted in the previous chapter.

64. The most coherent account of this is R. W. Pickwoad to Colonial Secretary, n.d. [apparently Apr. 18, 1892] (encl. with A. Maloney dispatch No. 146, May 12, 1892, CO123/198). One rather suspicious element in the story is that the shortage of officers at Icaiché led Tamay to place command of the party of retribution with Avila's logging captain rather than an Icaiché soldier. A rather different version of the affair is given by Flores's partner, Gregorio Suárez González, who escaped with a simple whipping, and who claimed that the affair had been entirely trumped up by Avila while Flores was blameless ("Mas sobre Icaiché," RM, May 10, 1892, 2, and in EC, May 21, 2). This Suárez story does not account for the deposing of Tamay, however, which the other information suggests really occurred. Tamay's announcement of his resumption of control is in his letter to Magistrate of Orange Walk District, Apr. 10, 1892 (encl. with A. Maloney dispatch No. 125, Apr. 17, 1892, CO123/198). The district

magistrate had been recently retitled district commissioner. Eustaquio Avila was one of those who had described the visit of Tamay and Santos López to Mérida in 1883.

65. A. Maloney dispatch No. 40, Feb. 22, 1893, with encl. (CO123/202); passage quoted is from A. B. R. Kaye to Colonial Secretary, Feb. 22, 1893, one of the enclosures.

66. Sapper (1904).

67. Mexico (1897–99); the refusal to be enumerated is reported by González Navarro (1957, 8), apparently on the basis of contemporary Mexico City press reports.

68. "La comisión del Gral. Canto" (RM, Nov. 14, 1895, 3). Sapper (1904) mentions that although funds for a schoolmaster in Xkanhá were regularly budgeted by the Campeche government, there were never applicants for the position.

69. "El censo de los cantones de Campeche" (RM, Oct. 17, 1895, 2).

70. F. Lara to D. Contreras, n.d. (encl. in A. Maloney dispatch No. 419, Dec. 5, 1895, CO123/215). "Icaiché Indians," minute by Maloney dated Dec. 13, 1895 (encl. with Maloney dispatch No. 426, Dec. 14, 1895, CO123/215).

19. Determination and Dissolution

1. "Noticias de los bárbaros" (RM, Mar. 25, 1888, 2–3); "El corresponsal to D. Moreno Canton, Mar. 24, 1888 (RM, Mar. 27, 1888); "Noticias de Chan Santa Cruz" (RM, Aug. 8, 1886, 3).

2. "El indio de Sta. Cruz capturado" (RM, Aug. 7, 1894, 2); "En el territorio de Belice" (RM, Aug. 30, 1894, 2).

3. "Noticias de los redeldes [sic]" (RM, June 23, 1895, 2).

4. Representatives of Noh Cah Santa Cruz and of Tulum had been received by the acting governor of British Honduras as equals in early 1887 (e.g., H. Fowler dispatch No. 24, Feb. 28, 1887, CO123/182), and when the surveyor Miller (1889) visited Noh Cah Santa Cruz in 1888 he mapped Santa Cruz territory as separate from Tulum. See the map enclosed in A. Maloney dispatch No. 20, Jan. 20, 1892 (CO123/198).

5. "Cosas de Belice" (RM, Feb. 11, 1892) and "Los indios rebeldes" (RM, Feb. 14, 1892, 2).

6. "Muerte del jefe de Tulum" (RM, May 5, 1892, 2). The 1887 visit to British Honduras is described in H. Fowler dispatch No. 24, Feb. 28, 1887 (CO123/182). Identification of the two references as applying to the same Tulum official involves an interpretation of variant transcriptions of his surname (Xiab in Fowler's dispatch, Quial in the RM account of his death) as indicating Ciau (Roys 1940) and a rejection of the report that this Tulum high priest had been killed by Dzul following the visit to Tancah of Peón Contreras.

7. Bartolomé and Barabas (1977, 49) document activities at Tulum in years before the 1930s, when the cross and its priest moved to Xcacal (or X-Cacal) to avoid

exposure to travelers at Tulum. One wonders if the loss of the major cult in 1892 may be parallel to Tulum's loss of a cult object in the 1940s, when a commercial baby doll found under "miraculous" circumstances and venerated by the Tulum folk was forcibly taken from them by men from another Maya town; see Heydn (1951; 1967). That there was no important cross center at Tulum in 1897, whereas there was one located at Chunpom, can be inferred by the account of the capture of Juan Bautista Vega, to be related shortly.

8. E. A. H. Schofield to A. H. Hall, May 25, 1886 (encl. with R. T. Goldsworthy dispatch No. 104, June 8, 1886, CO123/119); annex D to Memorial, Dec. 1, 1886 (encl. with H. Fowler dispatch No. 12, Jan. 25, 1887, CO123/182); Dzul's lower figure is cited in H. Fowler dispatch No. 24, Feb. 28, 1887 (CO123/182).

9. Sapper (1904, 628);"Un jefe de los rebeldes capturado" (RM, Aug. 5, 1894, 2); E. B. Sweet Escott dispatch No. 306, Aug. 30, 1895 (CO123/214).

10. The extremes were considerably wider than indicated: one Yucatecan logger working near Ascension Bay in the mid-1890s placed the maximum number under arms at eight hundred ("Noticias de los redeldes [sic]," RM, June 23, 1895, 2), while a bellicose Santa Cruz general asserted he could raise ten thousand (A. J. Beattie to Officer Administering the Government, Sept. 10, 1895, encl. with E. B. Sweet Escott confidential dispatch of Sept. 11, 1895, CO123/214).

11. A. Maloney dispatch No. 20, Jan. 20, 1892 (CO123/198); "Importantes noticias de Bacalar y Belice" (RM, June 4, 1895, 2). See also Konrad (1991).

12. E. B. Sweet Escott dispatch No. 249, July 22, 1895 (CO123/213); A. Maloney dispatch No. 431, Dec. 27, 1895 (CO123/215).

13. "Muerte de Aniceto Dzul" (RM, Aug. 12, 1888, 2); "Editorial and Local Notes" (CG, Aug. 11, 1888, 2); S. St. John dispatch of July 11, 1888, (FO to CO, Oct. 1, 1888, CO123/191).

14. A. Dzul to the Governor, Dec. 20 and Dec. 26, 1889, and R. T. Goldsworthy to A. Dzul (encl. in R. T. Goldsworthy confidential dispatch of Jan. 18, 1889, CO123/192).

15. A. Dzul et al. to the Governor (encl. in R. T. Goldsworthy confidential dispatch of Feb. 20, 1889, with a slightly differing translation also enclosed in his confidential dispatch of Feb. 25, 1889, both in CO123/192).

16. Miller (1889); Dzul blamed his problem on witchcraft and had just killed two people he suspected of causing it.

17. "Muerte de Aniceto Dzul" (RM, Feb. 20, 1890, 2–3); also "Noticias de los bárbaros" (RM, Aug. 12, 1890, 2). So much for Crescencio Poot's prediction.

18. R. Pec et al. to Governor, Sept. 23, 1894 (encl. with A. Maloney dispatch No. 246, Oct. 17, 1894, CO123/208); "Del campo de los rebeldes" (RM, Nov. 22, 1894, 1).

19. A. B. R. Kaye to Acting Colonial Secretary, Aug. 24, 1895 (encl. with E. B. Sweet Escott dispatch No. 306, Aug. 30, 1895, CO123/214); "Del campo de los rebeldes" (RM, Oct. 15, 1895, 2).

20. "Noticias de los bárbaros" (RM, Aug. 12, 1890, 2); "El indio de Santa Cruz capturado" (RM, Aug. 7, 1894, 2). Villa Rojas (1945, 72) reports that Pedro Pascual Barrera was Nohoch Tata or chief priest at the time of his work with the Xcacal Maya in 1931–36 and that Pedro Barrera had received the office from his father, Agustín Barrera, who in turn had it from his father José María Barrera. Although the sources cited here confirm the order and relationship of Agustín and Pedro, there is no historical evidence that José María Barrera was ever chief priest of the cult, and such evidence as there is seems to say that the ranking priest at Noh Cah Santa Cruz included several individuals between the time of the death of José María Barrera in the early 1850s and the assumption of the priestly office by Pedro Barrera.

21. Miller (1889). Apparently the jaunt was unofficial, for I find no mention of it in the governor's dispatches from Belize in 1889. The map of Miller's route, published with his account of the trip, was reproduced for an official dispatch in 1892 (A. Maloney dispatch No. 20, Jan. 20, CO123/198); added to it was an indication of the limits of the territory then controlled directly from Noh Cah Santa Cruz, which was said specifically to be separate from the territory of Tulum. This was immediately before the wholesale dispersal of the Tulum population.

22. H. P. C. Strange to Colonial Secretary, Oct. 24, 1893 (encl. with A. Maloney to Mr. Wingfield, Oct. 27, 1893, CO123/204); A. J. Beattie to Officer Administering the Government, Sept. 10, 1895 (encl. with E. B. Sweet Escott confidential dispatch, Sept. 11, 1895, CO123/214).

23. Chan Santa Cruz was the more common local name for this hamlet, a designation contrasting with Noh Cah Santa Cruz or Nohoch Santa Cruz for the rebel capital. But because Chan Santa Cruz is so often used for the major center in the period long after it lost that name, I use Santa Cruz Chico here for clarity of reference.

24. A. J. Beattie to Officer Administering the Government, Sept. 10, 1895 (encl. with E. B. Sweet Escott confidential dispatch, Sept. 11, 1895, CO123/214).

25. Miller (1889, 27).

26. This presumably was the feast of the Holy Cross, held in early May (see Villa Rojas 1945, 24). With Beattie's letter written in September, there appears to have been the lapse of some months between his visit and his communication with the government. Chan Cah Vera Cruz is the designation of today's holy village south of Felipe Carrillo Puerto (Noh Cah Santa Cruz), which is the seat of active cross worship (Bartolomé and Barabas 1977, 112). That locale, however, was apparently not occupied by a cross center before 1915 (ibid, 46), at which time it was moved

there from the earlier site known as Dzonot-Guardia, located north of old Noh Cah Santa Cruz (see Villa Rojas 1945, 34, also fig. 3; Bartolomé and Barabas 1977, 46). One must suppose that this Dzonot-Guardia was the same settlement as the Dzonot or Yokdzonot that was the home of Felipe Yama at the end of the nineteenth century (to be mentioned shortly), a hamlet fifteen or sixteen kilometers from Santa Cruz, slightly east of due north. The Chan Cah Vera Cruz of Beattie may have been near or even at this same Dzonot (see also Dumond 1985, 302), although Beattie described it as "slightly to the northwest of Santa Cruz."

27. Miller (1889, 26).

28. For instance, when young José María Rosado (1931) was a prisoner in 1858, his rebel mentor, Leandro Santos, spent time at his rancho and then removed to Noh Cah Santa Cruz (chap. 12).

29. As I have noted elsewhere (Dumond 1985, 302), the location described for Chan Cah Vera Cruz seems to accord with that of Dzonot-Guardia, a major center of cross worship in the early decades of the present century and possibly a seat of worship at the time of the Mexican conquest in 1901.

30. For example, R. M. Mundy dispatch No. 7, Jan. 7, 1876 (CO123/159). In 1886, Aniceto Dzul was reported to take delivery of arms, presumably military arms, that had been bought in the colony. A report of the following year said the same thing, for in March 1888 a fugitive stated that the rebels had received about five hundred guns six months before. The same year the surveyor Miller described the guard at Santa Cruz as armed with Enfield rifles (E. A. H. Schofield to A. H. Hall, May 25, 1886, encl. with R. T. Goldsworthy dispatch No. 104, June 8, 1886, CO123/179; El corresponsal to D. Moreno Cantón, Mar. 24, 1888, RM, Mar. 27, 1888; Miller 1889). These rifles repeatedly caused minor problems in British Honduras because they were considered to be the property of the Santa Cruz polity rather than of individual soldiers, and when defectors carried them into the colony the rebel officers insisted loudly on the return of their firearms (e.g., R. H. Pickwoad to Colonial Secretary, Jan. 20, 1888, encl. with R. T. Goldsworthy confidential dispatch of Jan. 26, 1888, CO123/189; P. W. Currie to Under Secretary of State for Colonies, Mar. 14, 1888, in FO to CO, CO123/191).

31. J. W. McKinney to Colonial Secretary, Feb. 27, 1894 (encl. with A. Maloney dispatch No. 97, Apr. 19, 1894, CO123/206). He reported that the previous December some two hundred of these cheap hunting arms had been brought into the colony for sale to their Indian neighbors.

32. J. E. Plummer to the Governor, Dec. 26, 1895 (encl. with A. Maloney dispatch No. 431, Dec. 27, 1895, CO123/215); "Santa Cruz Indians," minute of A. Maloney, dated Dec. 13, 1895 (encl. with Maloney dispatch No. 426, Dec. 14, 1895, CO123/215).

33. H. N. Dering to FO, Dec. 31, 1895 (FO sec., CO123/226).

34. The major such colony was evidently that established at Punta Corcho, later Puerto Morelos, in 1896 by the East Coast of Yucatan Colonization Co., using English and some Mexican capital. See Careaga Viliesid (1990a, 127–28); Konrad (1991); Lapointe (1983, 148–49, 152–53, map 5); Súarez Molina (1977a, 1:215–18).

35. E. B. Sweet Escott confidential dispatch of July 19, 1895, with enclosures (CO123/213); A. Maloney confidential dispatch of Oct. 5, 1896, with enclosure (CO123/219).

36. E. B. Sweet Escott confidential dispatch of July 19, 1895 (CO123/213).

37. R. W. Pickwoad, report on the Northern District, 1895 (encl. in A. Maloney dispatch No. 139, May 18, 1896, CO123/218). Terms of the Mexican royalty arrangements are outlined by J. E. Plummer, Jan. 15, 1896 (encl. with A. Maloney dispatch No. 17, Jan. 16, 1896, CO123/217).

38. Negotiations are described in Humphreys (1961). Actions in Belize are described in D. Wilson dispatch No. 296, Nov. 26, 1897, with enclosures (CO123/226). There were minor provisions allowing weapons to be held by colony residents while working outside the British boundaries.

39. R. W. Pickwoad to Colonial Secretary, Mar. 11, 1896 (encl. with A. Maloney dispatch No. 86, Mar. 12, 1896, CO123/217); "Indios sublevados de Chan Santa Cruz en Mérida" (RM, Aug. 12, 1897, 2); F. Angel Ortiz Monasterio to Acting Colonial Secretary, n.d. (encl. with F. Newton dispatch No. 149, Sept. 23, 1898, CO123/230). One of the Mexican measures was the decree of a two-year period in which Belizean loggers in Yucatan might import foodstuffs to their camps free of duty—again, simply to encourage commerce with the rebels.

40. A. Maloney dispatch No. 273, Oct. 29, 1896 (CO123/219), No. 290, Nov. 11, 1896, (CO123/220), both with enclosures. Although there seems to have been some altercation regarding payment for the vessel in New Orleans, Lieutenant Blanco was able to remove it from its dock—possibly by stealth—and move it to Mexico (RM, May 25, and Dec. 19, 1897).

41. D. Wilson dispatch No. 316, Dec. 30, 1897 (CO123/226); see also RM (Dec. 23, 1897).

42. D. Wilson dispatch No. 13, Jan. 28, and confidential dispatch of Jan. 19, 1898 (CO123/228).

43. A. Maloney dispatch No. 22, Jan. 17, 1896 (CO123/217).

44. R. W. Pickwoad to Colonial Secretary, Apr. 23, 1897 (encl. with D. Wilson dispatch No. 110, Apr. 30, 1897, CO123/223).

45. R. Pec et al. to Governor, Feb. 8, 1896 (encl. with A. Maloney dispatch No. 57, Feb. 19, 1896, CO123/217).

46. A. Maloney dispatch No. 86, Mar. 12, 1896, with encl. (CO123/217); R. Pec

to Governor, June 30, 1896 (encl. with A. Maloney dispatch No. 203, July 31, 1896, CO123/219).

47. A. Maloney dispatch No. 245, Sept. 10, 1896, with encl. (CO123/219).

48. A. Maloney dispatch No. 254, Sept. 21, 1896, with encl. (CO123/219). A news item in RM (Feb. 23, 1897, 2), reported that Pec and Felipe Ake had fallen on Tulum to punish the inhabitants for contemplating surrender, killing one hundred people, at which Ake was so disgusted that he turned his machete on Pec, then fled to Corozal—where, indeed, other reports showed Felipe Ake to be living. But fugitive rebel officers confirmed Pec's death by sickness; see "Indios sublevados de Chan Santa Cruz en Mérida" (RM, Aug. 12, 1897, 2).

49. A. Maloney dispatch No. 281, Oct. 20, 1896, with encl. (CO123/219). Presumably the selections were made, as was the case in the twentieth century when deciding delicate matters, by either a council of all officers or a still more general council of all adult males; see Villa Rojas (1945, 93).

50. F. Yama et al. to Governor, Oct. 15, 1896 (encl. with A. Maloney dispatch No. 289, Nov. 11, 1896, CO123/220). The brown paper was for the manufacture of cartridges.

51. Basic accounts are in D. Wilson dispatches No. 106 and 110, Apr. 27 and 30, 1897, with encl. (CO123/223); details regarding alleged shortages in funds are in "Indios sublevados de Chan Santa Cruz en Mérida" (RM, Aug. 12, 1897, 2). George Pennington was a young black man from British Guiana who as a boy "came to Belize as servant to one of the W. I. R. [West India Regiment] officers, and ran away to the Santa Cruz Indians" (A. Maloney dispatch No. 20, Jan. 20, 1892, CO123/198).

52. D. Wilson dispatches No. 125, May 14, 1897 (CO123/223) and No. 207, Aug. 5, 1897 (CO125/224), both with encl.; "Indios sublevados de Chan Santa Cruz en Mérida" (RM, Aug. 12, 1897, 2).

53. News items (RM, Feb. 23, June 10, 1897, 2).

54. D. Wilson dispatch No. 8, Jan. 19, 1898, with encl. (CO123/228).

55. F. Yama, L. Pat, D. Noh to Our Lady Queen Victoria, Jan. 24, 1898, (encl., with other related correspondence, with D. Wilson dispatch No. 26, Feb. 16, 1898, CO123/228).

56. Letters from F. Yama and L. Pat dated Mar. 8, 1898 (encl. with D. Wilson dispatch No. 64, Apr. 15, 1898, CO123/228); see also the attitude indicated in news items (RM, Sept. 16, 1898).

57. R. W. Pickwoad to Colonial Secretary, Nov. 30, 1898 (encl. with D. Wilson dispatch No. 180, Dec. 6, 1898, CO123/230).

58. News item datelined Valladolid, May 30, 1898 (RM, June 30, 1898, 2). This estimate of the total number of rebels who could be called to arms was probably too high, as will be seen. The fact that Muyil had been depopulated suggests that its

people were allied to those of Tulum, a union also implied by the remark by Colonel Traconis that the priestess María Uicab of Tulum actually lived at Muyil (chap. 16).

59. G. Tamay to Magistrate of Orange Walk, Dec. 14, 1895 (encl. with A. Maloney dispatch No. 10, Jan. 9, 1896, co123/217), and Tamay to Magistrate of The Cayo (source of passage quoted), May 14, 1896, (encl., with other relevant documents, with A. Maloney confidential dispatch of June 4, 1896, co123/218).

60. D. Wilson dispatch No. 93, May 20, 1898 (co123/229).

61. F. Newton dispatches No. 150 and 158, Sept. 23 and Oct. 18, 1898, with encl. (co123/230); D. Wilson dispatch No. 29, Feb. 15, 1899 (co123/232). It was evidently in 1898 that Blanco was transported up the Río Hondo on the steamer Stanford, property of a U.S. company legitimately exploiting dyewood on Mexican territory, and at the company station at Agua Blanca he was outfitted for a visit to Icaiché. Once there, he and his guide were treated as prisoners in Tamay's absence, interrogated with suspicion on Tamay's return—when fear was expressed that he might have come with a military escort—and finally fed and sent back to Agua Blanca under a guard of honor, with an invitation to return. See "Audaz visita del comandante Blanco a Icaiché" (G. A. Menéndez 1936, 144, 150–53). Clearly, despite Tamay's claim to official Mexican government status, Mexican soldiers were counted as the enemy.

62. D. Wilson dispatches No. 231 and 263, Sept. 3 and Oct. 15, 1897, with encl. (co123/225).

63. D. Wilson dispatches No. 272, Oct. 21, 1898 (co123/225) and 301, Dec. 7, 1898 (co123/226), both with encl.

64. "Desde Tizimín" (RM, Mar. 5, 1891, 2).

65. "Indios de Kantunil in Mérida" (RM, Dec. 16, 1897); see also news item (RM, June 1, 1897, 2).

66. Ferrer de Mendiolea (1977, 552–53). The line was not completed until 1900, just in time for the final military thrust against Noh Cah Santa Cruz.

67. "El gral. Arana en Oxkutzcab" (RM, Aug. 1, 1897, 2); "El gobernador Arana en Mérida" (RM, Aug. 3, 1897, 3); "La llegada del gobernador de Xkanhá" (RM, Aug. 5, 1892, 2); news item (RM, Aug. 10, 1897, 3). Although there was little public notice of it, this did not end communications between Mérida and Xkanhá (despite the fact that Xkanhá was subject to Campeche). In January of the following year, a *pacífico* officer, not identified, was in Mérida on official business with the governor, presumably related to the military campaign (RM, Jan. 29, 1898, 2). One wonders how many of the traveling peddlers may have been the same Chinese entrepreneurs who had cornered commerce in the *bravo* area.

68. News item (RM, Apr. 24, 1898, 3).

69. The Xkanhá trip is briefly described in "La misión en los cantones pacíficos del Sur" (RM, Jan. 28, 1898, 1), and news item in RM (Feb. 10, 1898, 2). That to Icaiché

is touched on in various articles of RM (Apr. 19, May 12, June 26, 1898). "Icaiché" (RM, June 29, 1898, 1) presents a brief description of the town evidently proceeding from the bishop's visit, but adding nothing to the accounts cited in earlier chapters. The visit is also treated in "The Colony" (TA, May 1898, 84) and "La visita pastoral del Sr. Obispo de Campeche" (TA, June 1898, 104a).

70. Encl. to A. Maloney dispatch No. 57, Feb. 19, 1896 (CO123/216).

71. News items, RM (Feb. 12, Nov. 30, Dec. 18, Dec. 20, 1898).

72. "Las tragas de la campaña" (RM, July 1, 1899, 1); "De Valladolid a Tihosuco" (RM, Aug. 1 and Aug. 8, 1899, 2). As I noted earlier, roads from the Valladolid area toward the east coast were projected as early as 1897, when fear was expressed that they would be so effective in speeding transport that they would encourage rebel attacks (RM, June 1, 1897, 2).

73. "Colonos contratados por la campaña" (RM, July 12, 1896, 3); see also Careaga Viliesid (1990a, 127–28). Two of the settlements, stations of what began as the British firm and later became the Mexican Compañia Colonizadora y Explotadora de la Costa Oriental de Yucatán, S.A. (Suárez Molina 1977a, 1:216), were visited in 1907 and described very briefly by Arnold and Frost (1909, 153–56).

74. Juan Bautista Vega spent his life at Chunpom, becoming secretary of one of the most important of the centers of the vanquished rebels and ending as one of the two ranking *masewal* leaders. After his death in 1969 at age eighty-three a plaque in his honor was set into a fountain at the former Noh Cah Santa Cruz. On the plaque in the nonoperative fountain in present-day Felipe Carrillo Puerto, Vega's age at his death in 1969 is given as eighty, but overall the evidence is that he was born in 1886 and was aged eleven at his capture. A garbled contemporary account of what must be the killing of Vega's companions is in RM (Oct. 12, 1897, 2), corrected the following year (RM, May 12, 1898, 2). The next January (RM, Jan. 22, 1899, 2), it was reported that Juan had written his mother to say he was alive. More extensive accounts of his capture, based on interviews with him but differing in details, are in Adrian (1924), Mendizabal (1929), and Pacheco Cruz (1934, 89–92; 1959, 128–31, the latter was first published in DY, Apr. 1934). The clearest account, however, with the most specific identification of places, is that of Wright (1962), an account also used by Careaga Viliesid (1981) to whom I am indebted for the reference. Further confirmation of the reading of the bottled notes is in the account of Fernando Tamayo, director of the school at Chunpom in 1950, quoted in Pacheco Cruz (1962, 70–71). The mysterious Dr. Fábregas, whoever he may have been, had appeared earlier in the region, for in late summer 1892 he arrived in Corozal from Yucatan and left toward Noh Cah Santa Cruz, where he was said to think he could effect the rebel submission by arranging for them to govern their own territory independently. There is no indication that this attempt bore fruit either among rebels or Yucatecans. See news item, RM (Sept. 22,

1892, 2). According to Wright (1962) Vega served Cituk until 1917, Perfecto Dzul until 1935, Tiburcio Cen to 1955, Segundo Coh thereafter.

75. "Los indios rebeldes amenazan" (RM, Apr. 23, 1899, 2).

20. The End of Independence

1. The provisions of the basic document issued by the *Ministro de Fomento* on Oct. 15, 1895, are set out in "El territorio ocupado por los rebeldes" (RM, May 23, 1901, 1).

2. For example, FO sec. (CO123/234).

3. For example, D. Wilson confidential dispatch, July 13, 1899 (CO123/232).

4. Preliminary arrangements are described in several dispatches of Governor Sir David Wilson (CO123/233). Results of Pickwoad's visit are described in Wilson's confidential dispatch, Oct. 13, 1899, with encl. (CO123/233). The first passage quoted is from a private letter from Pickwoad that is quoted by Wilson in the confidential dispatch cited, the second from Pickwoad's "Report of District Commissioner of Corosal," Oct. 6, 1899, encl. with the same dispatch.

5. "La campaña contra los rebeldes" (RM, July 22, 1899, 2); news items (RM, Oct. 22, 1899, 2).

6. D. Wilson dispatch No. 188 and confidential dispatch, Oct. 13, 1899 (CO123/233). The Mexican force moving into Chetumal Bay was permitted passage through British waters on condition that no parts of British territory be used as a base (D. Wilson dispatch No. 189, Oct. 18, 1899, CO123/233).

7. D. Wilson dispatch No. 10, Jan. 11, 1900, CO123/235.

8. D. Wilson confidential dispatches of Jan. 12, Feb. 1, and Feb. 15, 1900 (CO123/235).

9. "Del campo de operaciones . . ." (RM, Jan. 10, 1900, 1). More than twenty rebel deaths are indicated in "Del campo de operaciones" (RM, Feb. 14, 1900, 2).

10. D. Wilson confidential dispatch of Mar. 1, 1900 (CO123/235). The Mexican communications are enclosed with H. N. Dering to Marquis of Salisbury, Feb. 7, 1900 (in FO to CO, Feb. 26, 1900, CO123/237).

11. "Otro encuentro con los rebeldes" (RM, Feb. 23, 1900, 2); "El combate del 24" (RM, Mar. 1, 1900, 3) and news items (ibid., 4–5).

12. "Del campo de operaciones" (RM, Apr. 6, 1900, 2).

13. R. W. Pickwoad report of Oct. 6, 1899, encl. with D. Wilson confidential dispatch of Oct. 13, 1899 (CO123/233); D. Wilson confidential dispatch of Mar. 2, 1900 (CO123/235).

14. "Del campo de los rebeldes" (RM, May 2, 1900, 2).

15. D. Wilson confidential dispatch of Apr. 6, 1900 (CO123/235) with encl.; the quotation is from encl. letter of Pat, Cob, Yama, and May, Mar. 23, 1900.

16. Mexico adopted the Remington single-shot, breech-loading military rifle in the 1880s and issued it into the 1890s (Fuentes 1983, 210–11; Janvier 1893). The Spanish pattern Mauser bolt-action repeater was adopted about 1895; twenty-six thousand were imported in 1897 and issued to the regular troops (Fuentes 1983, 211), who used it against the Yaquis (Turner 1911, 441). The regular Mexican army units in Yucatan were armed with Mausers (as well as with precursors of the modern machine gun), although Yucatecan militia units (about 10 percent of the total force) probably carried the Remingtons, as did most Mexican reserve troops (Fuentes 1983, 211). Both guns were significantly more effective than the best rebel muzzle-loaders.

17. MM (1, 195, 409).

18. Where not otherwise indicated, the account of the military campaign and description of equipment and tactics is from MM, vols. 1 and 2, July 1900–June 1902. The condition as well as the supplying of Zaragoza is described by D. Wilson dispatch No. 47, Mar. 12, and his confidential dispatch of Mar. 22, 1900 (CO123/235).

19. Accounts of the affair begin with "Los indios de Yok-Dzonot en armas . . ." (RM, Nov. 21, 1900, 2) and continue in later RM (Nov. 25, Dec. 1, Dec. 4, Dec. 19, 1900). A comic sidelight on emotions of the time is that immediately before the renewed uprising, a party of men from Kantunil-kin had walked to the east coast in search of work, not war, where they were arrested, protesting innocence, by nervous colonists; finally receiving the call to come back and protect their homes, they were allowed their jobless freedom ("Declaración de los 33 detenidos," RM, Dec. 5, 1–2); "Los 33 de Kantunil," RM, Dec. 9, 2; and "Cuatro indígenas aprehendidos en Solferino," RM, Dec. 16, 2).

20. News items, RM (Jan. 3, Jan. 20, 1901); MM (1, 439).

21. MM (2, 17). This is probably one of the more accurate estimates of rebel military strength, although given Bravo's propensities and the publicity paid the campaign it was if anything an overestimate.

22. Notice was promptly published in the British Honduras gazette. See D. Wilson confidential dispatch of Feb. 21, 1901 (CO123/238).

23. MM (1, 484). Governor Wilson (dispatch No. 77, Apr. 13, 1901, CO123/238) reports that about fifteen-hundred Mexican troops were in Bacalar shortly after its recapture.

24. MM (1, 484).

25. News item, RM (Apr. 13, 1901, 1); " 'El General' Felipe Yamá asesinado . . ." (RM, Apr. 19, 1901, 2).

26. For example, "No hay indios en Chan Santa Cruz" (RM, Apr. 27, 1901, 2).

27. "La toma de Chan Santa Cruz" (RM, May 5, 2).

28. See, for example, RM (May 8, 2).

29. The decree is reproduced in RM (June 18, 1901, 2).

30. "Peregrina expedición a Tulum" (MM 2, 132).

31. "La campaña de pacificación en el Oriente . . ." (RM, Aug. 22, 1901, 1); "Los sublevados de Yok-Dzonot" (Nov. 19, 1901, 2); "La campaña de pacificación . . ." (RM, Mar. 25, 1902, 2).

32. "Nuevo encuentro con los rebeldes" (RM, July 11, 1901, 2).

33. For example, "Depredaciones de los indios rebeldes" (RM, Aug. 13, 1901, 1).

34. This was evidently not San Antonio Muyil that was taken by the officer who would become president of Mexico after the apparent murder of his predecessor, but the village of San Antonio nearer to, and almost due north of, Noh Cah Santa Cruz.

35. "La erección del Territorio Federal en Yucatan" (RM, Nov. 8 and 9, 1901, 2); "El Territorio Federal" (RM, Apr. 24, 1892, 6). The name chosen, of course, was that of the famous son of Yucatan, Andrés Quintana Roo (see chap. 4).

36. For example, "La campaña de Yucatan" (RM, Jan. 29, 1902, 2).

37. "Un combate con los mayas . . ." (RM, Mar. 1, 1902, 2); "Un ataque de los rebeldes mayas" (RM, Apr. 2, 2).

38. "Reorganización de los mayas rebeldes" (RM, Dec. 9, 1902, 2).

39. "La campaña contra los mayas" (RM, Dec. 31, 1902, 1; similar reports in RM (Jan. 1, Jan. 9, Jan. 13, 1903).

40. For example, "Noticias de la campaña" (RM, Jan. 21, 6); "La campaña contra los mayas" (RM, Feb. 18, 1903, 1).

41. "Muerte de Gral. León Pat" (RM, Mar. 17, 1903, 2); "El jefe maya Victorín [*sic*] herido" (RM, Mar. 21, 1903, 5).

42. With, for example, the clear statement of the progression of leadership at Chunpom in Wright (1962).

43. The history of the region after "pacification" is detailed most clearly by Careaga Viliesid (1981).

44. "Como está Chan Santa Cruz actualmente" (RM, May 11, 1901, 2).

45. The description suggests this to be the masonry structure, still standing, that was apparently the altar end of the first substantial church at Chan Santa Cruz, built at the edge of the cenote at which appeared the miraculous crosses. The significance of the skulls is not at all clear, although early visitors more than once had reported the presence of unburied bodies scattered carelessly around the town.

46. "Ecos de la excursión a Santa Cruz de Bravo" (RM, June 22, 1901, 2).

47. "Ecos de la excursión a Santa Cruz de Bravo" (RM, June 22, 1901, 2).

48. He should not be confused with José María Ake, whom Yama had ordered killed in 1897. In that same year, Felipe Ake was reported living in Corozal (F. Yama et al. to Sir, June 12, 1897; encl. with D. Wilson dispatch No. 207, Aug. 5, 1897, CO123/224).

49. F. Yama et al. to Sir, June 12, 1897; encl. with D. Wilson dispatch No. 207, Aug. 5, 1897, CO123/224); "Como está Chan Santa Cruz actualmente" (RM, May 11, 1901, 2). The fact that prisoners could specify locations of houses of rebel leaders dead for forty years and more bespeaks a consistently low level of actual use of Santa Cruz. One must suppose that Santa Cah ("Holy Settlement") and Chan Cah Vera Cruz ("True Cross Village") were one and the same. Yet in figure 2 the road to Santo Cah is shown departing from the southeast, whereas the statement quoted in the preceding chapter indicated the ceremonial village to be north of the capital.

50. Mexico (1904). There are discrepancies between the numbers listed settlement by settlement and those given in the synthesis of the published census of 1900, but either way Xkanhá numbered about six thousand, Icaiché between two thousand and twenty-five hundred. Interestingly, there was a significant difference between the two *pacífico* centers in native speakers of Spanish, recorded as thirty-six males and twelve females in Icaiché but only seven males and no females in much larger Xkanhá. One would suppose this was related to the tendency for Icaiché to acquire various fugitives from the border areas of British Honduras, largely populated by one-time Yucatecan residents of Bacalar.

51. "El general Gabriel Tamay . . ." (RM, June 15, 1901, 2).

52. D. Wilson dispatch No. 97, May 31, 1902, and D. Wilson confidential dispatch of Dec. 10, 1902 (FO50/547), the former with encl. Correspondence regarding the claims dragged on for two years, with the Mexican position—strangely enough—being that Lewis was in the wrong because he had not obtained his concession legitimately from the Mexican government for work in Guatemala (see various letters in FO50/547).

53. See, for example, Thompson (1963, 179).

54. For example, budget projections for 1901 in PC (Nov. 1, 1900, 8). But in 1908 the governor's annual message (PC, Aug. 9, 1908, 2–3) referred to the difficulty of maintaining a teacher there. And in some years the money for the Xkanhá school seems to have been omitted (e.g., projections for 1903, PC, Dec. 10, 1902).

55. "Arana en Iturbide" (RM, Dec. 28, 1902, 2).

56. See the Campeche governor's annual address of Aug. 7, 1907 (PC, Aug. 13, 1907, 1).

57. "Ley orgánica de la administración interior del Estado de Campeche" (PC, Sept. 26, 1903, 1–8); in Article 2 Xkanhá is named a *municipio* of the *partido* of Bolonchenticul. Elections are announced in PC (Oct. 2, 1903, 1).

58. Announcement of election results, PC (Dec. 13, 1905, 1) and PC (Dec. 11, 1906). Some other isolated *municipios* were also omitted from these results.

59. PC (Dec. 12, 1908, 4, and Dec. 18, 1909, 4).

60. See changes to the Law of Interior Administration, dated Oct. 18, 1910 (PC, Oct. 20, 1–3).

61. As I indicated in these pages, Campeche had claimed jurisdiction over the *pacíficos* since the formation of the state. Although Campeche's southeastern boundary with Yucatan was not defined in the legislation that created the state (Núñez y Escalante 1980, 14–15), the map (Fremont 1861) that formed part of the comprehensive Campeche argument for autonomy (Aznar Barbachano and Carbó 1857) placed that boundary at a meridian that in modern measurement falls at about 89°25' west longitude. When the Territory of Quintana Roo was proclaimed, its southwestern boundary was simply declared to abut Campeche. But when the positions of major settlements of the former *pacíficos* were finally fixed by astronomical measurement, nearly all were found to be east of the commonly accepted border (Alvarez Coral 1971, 152–53). This led first to a loud complaint from Campeche, which argued that the intent at the time of the state's separation from Yucatan had been to include the *pacíficos* (Gobernador de Campeche 1939) and then to a meeting between the governors of Campeche and Yucatan (without representation of Quintana Roo) in which they agreed that the southeastern boundary of Campeche should be moved eastward nearly ten degrees to the meridian of Garbutt's Falls—that is, to form a northward extension of the boundary between Belize and Guatemala. The effect of this shift was not only to place virtually all of the still important and former *pacífico* settlements in Campeche, but to adjust southeastward the southeast boundary of Yucatan so as to place the pueblos of Tihosuco and Tepich within that state rather than Quintana Roo. In 1940, this accord was pronounced binding by President Lazaro Cárdenas (Alvarez Coral 1971, 154–55; Núñez y Escalante 1980, 18–21). Nevertheless, the border of Quintana Roo effective on the ground today remains that of 1902, which embraces almost all of the former *pacífico* settlements. Either one or both of the two boundaries may appear on recent maps, however, to the traveler's confusion.

62. Arnold and Frost (1909, 158–59).

63. The insurrection is described by Urzaiz (1946, 182–83), the anecdote is from González Avilés (1970, 9–16).

Retrospect

1. Konrad (1991, 156) cites figures for 1903 from the Mexican Archivo General de la Nación that place the total population of Quintana Roo, including all surviving rebels, at only 12,500.

2. These are discussed by Rodríguez Losa (1978).

3. Baqueiro (1881, 144) concludes a decline of 180,000 between rebels, emigrants, and dead; García Cubas (1870) notes the decrease of about 205,000 between 1846 and 1856 but concludes the real decline was only 65,000, for he allows some 140,000 for the rebels as late as the 1860s—a figure patently impossible, exceeding by 65 percent

even the unbelievably high figure for the rebels drawn by Reina (1980, 402–4) from the military archives in Mexico City.

4. For example, Dobson (1973, 251).

5. The Bacalar population of 1846 was reported by Regil and Peón (1853, tables C, D) to be about seventy-six hundred, of whom no more than two thousand were legally *vecinos*. The original estimate of the 1857 immigrants is in F. Seymour dispatch, confidential No. 1, May 15, 1857 (ABH, R52).

6. Regil and Peón (1853, 267), where the role of mosquitoes, of course, is not recognized; the disease is attributed to the exhalation of miasmas by the swamps.

7. Steggerda (1941, 229, and table 63).

8. Quotation from MM (2, 527). The hospital is mentioned in MM 2, 360, and in "La Campaña de Yucatan" (RM, Jan. 29, 1902, 2).

9. Colonial Surgeon to Colonial Secretary, Jan. 22, 1895 (encl. with A. Maloney dispatch No. 105, Mar. 26, 1895, CO123/211).

10. Current thinking would impute nearly all of the truly major killers—smallpox, cholera, measles, as well as insect-borne malaria and yellow fever—to importations from the Old World at the time of the conquest or after (e.g., Burnet and White 1972; Crosby 1972). Patch (1993, 23) adds that the concurrent depopulation of the coast by native Maya was in significant part because of the rapid transmission of the new diseases along these major traditional pathways of commerce.

11. See, for instance, Steggerda (1941, esp. table 61).

12. "Life and Death in the Colony," by C. H. Eyles, Colonial Surgeon (CG, Mar. 16, 1895, 2–3); Colonial Surgeon to Colonial Secretary, Jan. 22, 1895 (encl. with A. Maloney dispatch No. 105, Mar. 26, 1895, CO123/211). Neither of the sets of figures in these sources matches those published in HG for 1894, where the crude birth and death rates are given, respectively, as Corozal 58.2 and 40.9 and Orange Walk 30.2 and 23.6, with both populations apparently growing. The HG figures do not accord with the life table published with them, part of which was also published in the CG article just cited for some of the differing birth and death rates. If the life table is at all accurate and if the population is anywhere near stability, a condition of growth could be expected only with *both* birth and death rates above fifty per thousand, with the former exceeding the latter; with birth rates below fifty, the population surely was in decline. See, for instance, Coale and Demeny (1983, stable population tables Model West Female and Model West Male, level 1).

13. For example, Steggerda (1941); Ryder (1977). In the former, crude birthrates for three towns are between fifty and seventy-five per thousand, which is credible for a long-term trend. But they are coupled with death rates from twenty-three to thirty-four per thousand, and it is the resulting combinations that are not believable as a long-term condition, for the following reason: Except for very old age categories,

age-specific death rates are always highest for infants, and any increase in birthrate is therefore inevitably accompanied by an increase in death rate, even when the population is growing. Because of this universal condition, crude death rates that are only half the value of crude birthrates are simply not to be found in relatively stable circumstances unless the expectancy of life at birth is some forty years or more (e.g., Dumond 1990), a condition almost certainly not to be found in early rural Yucatan. Ryder's figures are less extreme, but questionable for the same reason.

14. Sapper (1904, 629).

15. Aznar Barbachano and Carbó (1861, document 44).

16. With regard to these arguments see Coale and Demeny (1983, appropriate tables of stable populations, Model West, mortality level 1).

17. For these considerations, I made use of ages below fifteen, rather than some lower age, because fifteen seemed an age an observer could be expected to recognize with moderate accuracy, when all ages of the individuals counted are almost certainly estimated rather than derived from records.

18. See, for instance, the list of rebel soldiers and leaders by locale, in Reina (1980, appended document 7).

19. See also Villa Rojas (1945, 93), who explains the system as it operated in the 1930s.

20. Villa Rojas (1945, table 13).

21. For example, Bricker (1981, 114); Dumond (1970).

22. Villa Rojas (1945, 91–92).

23. It is tempting to wonder if this was the brainchild of Bonifacio Novelo. It appeared in or near his region of real interest, and his earlier perambulations with the image of a saint he claimed had appeared miraculously showed his interest in establishing control through means that transcended the mundane.

24. This policy of capital punishment continued; in 1890, for example, a *masewal* who insisted to a friend that the crosses could not speak was denounced and sentenced to die—but he ran away ("Noticias de los bárbaros, RM, Aug. 12, 1890, 2).

25. Dumond (1970, 1977). Revitalization movements are discussed specifically by Wallace (1956).

26. See, for instance, Reed (1964, chap. 11).

27. Lapointe (1983, 181) argues that Britain was more interested in expanding her commercial empire in Central America, and she points out that she raised British Honduras from settlement to colony while the United States was involved in civil war and its enthusiasm for the Monroe Doctrine was perforce on the back burner.

28. There can be no doubt that the British attitude was a direct violation of the spirit of the Convention of London, the 1786 treaty with Spain, Article 14 of which states that "Great Britain had undertaken to prevent the settlers from furnishing arms

and supplies to the Indians" (Humphreys 1961, 65). However, with the independence of the former Spanish colonies the validity of that treaty could be questioned.

29. J. L. Solís, "Memoria del Partido de los Chenes" (LD, May 26, 1874, 2).

30. See, for instance, the discussion by Joseph (1986, 40–44), with numerous references.

31. According to the story of the leaders of the brief 1910 insurrection in Valladolid who fled to Chunpom, mentioned in the preceding chapter, the Valladolid fugitives were key figures in the attack on the railway (González Avilés 1970).

32. I write this *Xcacal* to conform with the style used elsewhere here. In the anthropological literature it is usually written X-Cacal, after Villa Rojas. The local highway signs and the maps of Quintana Roo identify it now as Tixcacal Guardia.

33. Aspects of the twentieth-century history of the region are drawn from Alvarez Coral (1971); Avila Zapata (1974); Bartolomé and Barabas (1977); Careaga Viliesid (1981); and Villa Rojas (1945, 1962, and 1978, app. E). There are inconsistencies in stories about Francisco May, in some of which he seems to be given single-handed credit for leading the fight against Bravo and spurring the rebel resistance after Bravo triumphed; probably the high point in his glorification can be found in the label of a photograph taken at the time the Governor of Yucatan visited Bravo in conquered Santa Cruz in 1901, which is displayed in the small museum by the sacred cenote of Santa Cruz (now the town of Felipe Carrillo Puerto): for one of the prominent, elderly, and bearded Mexican generals—possibly Ignacio Bravo himself—is identified as "General Francisco May." May lived until 1969.

34. The first instance is described by Villa Rojas (1962, 227), the second by Wright (1962). See also Bartolomé and Barabas (1977, 118–19).

Works Cited

Abbreviations

ABH   Archives of British Honduras. For years before 1885 this set of records was organized by J. A. Burdon into various series, the most numerous of which is the serially numbered *Records* (hereafter R). ABH are now a part of the Archives of Belize, in Belmopan.

BCP   Biblioteca General Manuel Cepeda Peraza, Sección Yucateca, in Mérida.

BO   *Boletin Oficial del Gobierno de Yucatan.* Official gazette of Yucatan, published in Mérida.

BY   *Boletin Oficial del Departmento de Yucatan.* Official gazette of the Department of Yucatan in February and March 1867, published in Mérida.

CG   *Colonial Guardian.* Commercial newspaper published in Belize.

CO   British Colonial Office documents in the Public Record Office, London and Kew (followed by numerical designation of document class and volume number).

DI   *Diario del Imperio.* Official newspaper and gazette of the imperial government, published in Mexico DF. Examined for parts of January 1865 only.

DY   *Diario de Yucatán.* Commercial newspaper published in Mérida.

EC   *El Constitutional.* Official newspaper of Yucatan, published in Mérida.

EEC   *El Eco del Comercio.* Commercial newspaper published in Mérida.

EF   *El Fénix.* Newspaper published in Campeche by Justo Sierra O'Reilly.

EN   *El Espíritu Nacional.* Official newspaper of Yucatan, published in Mérida.

EP   *El Espíritu Público.* Official newspaper of Campeche, published in Campeche.

ER   *El Regenerador.* Official newspaper of Yucatan, published in Mérida.

FO   British Foreign Office documents in the Public Record Office, London and Kew (followed by numerical designation of document class and volume number).

GS   *Las Garantías Sociales.* Official newspaper of Yucatan, published in Mérida.

HG   *Honduras Gazette.* Official gazette of British Honduras, published in Belize.

LD   *La Discusión.* Official newspaper of Campeche, published in Campeche.

LN   *La Nueva Era.* Official newspaper of Campeche, published in Campeche.

LR   *La Restauración.* Official newspaper of Campeche, published in Campeche.

LU   *La Unión.* Official newspaper of Yucatan, published in Mérida.

LS   *La Sociedad.* Political and literary newspaper published in Mexico DF. Examined for January 1865.

MM   *México Militar.* Monthly journal of local military affairs, published in Mexico DF. Examined vols. 1 and 2, July 1900–June 1902.

NE   *La Nueva Epoca.* Official newspaper of Yucatan, published in Mérida.

PC   *Periódico Oficial del Estado Libre y Soberano de Campeche*. Gazette of Campeche, published in Campeche.

PM   *Periódico Oficial del Departamento de Mérida*. Official newspaper of Yucatan, published in Mérida.

PY   *Periódico Oficial del Departamento de Yucatán*. Official newspaper of Yucatan, published in Mérida.

RM   *Revista de Mérida*. Commercial newspaper published in Mérida.

RP   *La Razón del Pueblo*. Official newspaper of Yucatan, published in Mérida.

SD   *El Siglo XIX*. Official newspaper of Yucatan, published in Mérida.

TA   *The Angelus*. Monthly Catholic newspaper published in Belize.

UA   University of Alabama Yucatan Collection, cataloged in Bingham (1972).

Map Sources

References relied on especially heavily or that provide crucial information for specific maps are cited in map captions. Major sources include Anonymous (1787, 1848), Berendt (1879), Faber and Rhys (1867), Hernández (1854–55), López (1801), Heller (1847), México, Instituto Geológico (1895), Sapper (1895), and Usher (1888). Locations were also checked against the more recent maps listed next, none of which is cited specifically in the text or captions. Not listed are sketch maps of minor utility found among ABH and CO records.

American Geographical Society of New York. 1927–35. North America. Scale 1:1,000,000. Sheets N.E-15 (1930), N.E-16 (1935), N.F-16 (1927).

Guatemala, Dirección General de Cartografía. 1959. Mapa preliminar de la República de Guatemala. Scale 1:750,000.

Libreria Patria. [1981]. Mapas de los estados. Scale 1:600,000–1:800,000. Sheets of Campeche, Quintana Roo, Yucatan.

Mexico, Comisión Coordinadora del Levantamiento de la Carta Geográfica. 1958. República Mexicana. Scale 1:500,000. Sheets 15Q-IV, 15Q-VI, 16Q-III to 16Q-VII.

Mexico, Dirección General de Geografía. 1985. Carta topográfica. Scale 1:1,000,000. 2d. ed. Mérida sheet.

Mexico, Instituto Nacional de Estadística, Geografía e Informática 1985. Carta Topográfica. Scale 1:50,000. Sheets for Campeche, Quintana Roo, Yucatan.

Mexico, Secretaría de Agricultura y Ganadería. 1963 n.d. Dirección de Geografía y Meteorología. Scale 1:1,000,000. Sheets Campeche (1963), Quintana Roo (1969), Yucatan (n.d.).

Mexico, Secretaría de Obras Públicas. 1971. Estado de Yucatán, red de caminos. Junta Local de Caminos.

———. [1972]. Estado de Campeche. Dirección General de Carreteras en Cooperación. Scale 1:500,000.

————. [1972]. Quintana Roo, red de carreteras. Junta Local de Caminos.

————. 1975. Estado de Yucatán.

United Kingdom, Directorate of Overseas Surveys. 1963. British Honduras. Scale 1:250,000. 2d ed.

————. 1965. British Honduras. Scale 1:800,000. 2d ed.

Works Cited

Acereto, Albino. 1977. Historia política desde el descubrimiento europeo hasta 1920. *Enciclopedia yucatanense.* 2d ed., 3:5–388. Mexico DF: Gobierno de Yucatán.

Acevedo, M. 1846. Bacalar. *El registro yucateco* 4:311–15.

Adrian, H. 1924. Einiges über die Maya-Indianer von Quintana Roo. *Zeitschrift der Gesellschaft für Erdkunde zu Berlin,* nos.5–7: 235–47.

Aldherre, Fed. 1869. Los indios de Yucatán. *Boletín de la Sociedad Mexicana de Geografía y Estadística* (época 2) 1:73–76.

Allen, G. 1886. Map of Yucatan. Compiled from Faber and Rhys (1867) and other sources, showing territories of active and pacified rebels according to H. Fowler. Encl. 3, H. Fowler confidential dispatch, Nov. 29, 1886, CO123/180.

Alvarez Coral, Juan. 1971. *Historia de Quintana Roo.* 3d ed. Mexico DF: B. Costa-Amic.

Ancona, Eligio. 1889. *Historia de Yucatán.* 4 vols. Barcelona: Jaime Jepús Roviralta.

————. 1905. *Historia de Yucatán.* Vol. 5. Mérida: El Peninsular.

Anonymous. 1787. A map of a part of Yucatan of that part of the eastern shore within the Bay of Honduras alloted to Great Britain . . . by a Bay-Man. London.

————. 1848. Plano de Yucatan [map]. In Estadística de Yucatán, by J. M. Regil and A. M. Peón. *Boletín de la Sociedad Mexicana de Geografía y Estadística* (época 1) 3(5): 237–340.

————. 1866. Guerra de Castas en Yucatán: Su origen, sus consecuencias, y su estado actual. Manuscript in BCP.

————. [1867]. Untitled, unsigned, fragmentary document on official government stationary, dated on the basis of internal evidence. Property of the late Alfredo Barrera Vásquez.

————. 1878. *Correspondencia diplomática cambiada entre el gobierno de la República y el de su Majestad Britanica con relación al territorio llamado Belize, 1872–1878.* Campeche: Imprenta de la Sociedad Tipográfica. First published in signature form for binding, LN, July 30 to Oct. 18, 1878.

————. 1884. Map of part of the Republic of Yucatan shewing the occupation of the Chan Santa Cruz Indians from information given in 1881 by the Indian Chiefs to Henry Fowler. Encl. with H. Fowler dispatch No. 2, Jan. 15, 1884, CO123/173.

————. 1896. *In memoriam: Corona funebre y apuntes biográficos del licenciado D. Pablo García.* Mérida: Tipografia de G. Canto.

———. 1901. *Album fotográfico: Recuerdo de la excursion del sr. gobernador a Sta. Cruz de Bravo*. Mérida.

Arnold, Channing, and Frederick J. Tabor Frost. 1909. *The American Egypt: A Record of Travel in Yucatan*. New York: Doubleday, Page.

Asociación Cívica Yucatán. 1956. *De la "Guerra de Castas" causa de Manuel Antonio Ay el primer indio maya rebelde fusilado en Valladolid el 30 de julio de 1847*. Mexico DF: Ediciones Asociación Cívica Yucatán.

Avendaño y Loyola, Fray Andés de. 1987. *Relation of Two Trips to Peten: Made for the Conversion of the Heathen Ytzaes and Cehaches*. Translated by C. P. Bowdich and G. Rivera, edited by F. Comparato. Culver City, CA: Labyrinthos.

Avila Zapata, Felipe Nery. 1974. *El general May, último jefe de las tribus mayas*. Mérida: Ediciones del Gobierno de Yucatán.

Aznar Barbachano, Tomás, and Juan Carbó. 1861. *Memoria sobre la conveniencia, utilidad y necesidad de la erección constitucional del Estado de Campeche*. Compilation presented to the Mexican congress in 1861. Mexico DF: Imprenta de Ignacio Cumplido.

Aznar Pérez, Alonso. 1849–1851. *Colección de leyes, decretos y órdenes o acuerdos de tendencia general del poder legislativo del Estado libre y soverano de Yucatán*. 3 vols. Mérida: Rafael Pedrera.

Baqueiro, Serapio, 1878–87. *Ensayo histórico sobre las revoluciones de Yucatán desde el año de 1840 hasta 1864*. 3 vols. Mérida: Imprenta de Manuel Heredia Argüelles.

———. 1881. *Reseña geográfica, histórica y estadística del Estado de Yucatán*. Mexico DF: Francisco Díaz de León.

———. 1887. Estudios históricos y biográficos: Crescencio Poot. *El Eco del Comercio*, June 18–28.

Baqueiro Anduze, Oswaldo. 1943. *La ciudad heroica: Historia de Valladolid*. Mérida: García Franchi.

Baroja, Pío. 1954. *Los pilotos de Altura*. Buenos Aires: Espasa-Calpi Argentina.

Bartolomé, Miguel Alberto. 1978. La insurrección de Canek. *Cuadernos de los Centros Regionales*. Mexico DF: Centro Regional de Antropología e Historia del Sureste.

Bartolomé, Miguel Alberto, and Alicia Mabel Barabas. 1977. La resistencia maya. *Colección científica, etnología* 53. Mexico DF: Centro Regional de Antropología e Historia del Sureste.

Berendt, Carl Herman. 1872. Report of explorations in Central America. *Annual Report of the Board of Regents of the Smithsonian Institution . . . for the Year 1867*, 420–26. Washington DC: Government Printing Office.

———. 1879. Karte der Halbinsel Yucatán, Hauptsächlich nach der von Joachim Hübbe und Andrés Aznar Pérez . . . 1878 [map]. *Petermann's Geographische Mittheilungen*, Tafel 11.

Bingham, Marie Ballew. 1972. *A Catalog of the Yucatán Collection on Microfilm in the University of Alabama Libraries.* University, Alabama: University of Alabama Press.

Birch, Arthur N., and William Robinson. 1867. *The Colonial Office List for 1867.* London: Harrison.

Bojórquez Urzáiz, Carlos E. 1977. El Yucatán de 1847 hasta 1851: Breves apuntes sobre el trabajo y la subsistencia. *Boletín de la Escuala de Ciencias Antropológicas de la Universidad de Yucatán* 27:18–25.

Bracamonte y Sosa, Pedro. 1993. *Amos y sirvientes: Las haciendas de Yucatán 1789–1860.* Mérida: Universidad Autónoma de Yucatán.

Bray, Warwick. 1977. Maya metalwork and its external connections. In *Social Process in Maya Prehistory,* edited by N. Hammond, 365–404. New York: Academic.

Bricker, Victoria Reifler. 1981. *The Indian Christ, the Indian King.* Austin: University of Texas Press.

Buhler, Richard. [1975]. A refugee of the War of the Castes makes Belize his home: The memoirs of J. M. Rosado. BISRA *Occasional Publications,* no. 2. Belize: Belize Institute for Social Research and Action.

Burdon, Sir John Alder. 1931–35. *Archives of British Honduras.* 3 vols. London: Sifton Praed.

Burnet, Sir MacFarlane, and David O. White. 1972. *Natural History of Infectious Disease.* 4th ed. Cambridge: Cambridge University Press.

Calzadilla, José M., Policarpo Antonio de Echánove, Pedro Bolío y Torresillas, and José M. Zuaznavar. [1814] 1977. *Apuntaciones para la estadística de la Provincia de Yucatán.* 3d ed. Mérida: Ediciones del Gobierno del Estado.

Cámara Zavala, Felipe de la. 1928. Las memorias inéditas de D. Felipe de la Cámara Zavala. Relación circunstanciada de la expedición practicada por el gral. don Rómulo Díaz de la Vega . . . que comienzan desde el 15 de diciembre de 1851. *Diario de Yucatán,* Sundays, Aug. 12–Oct. 21.

———. 1975. *Memorias de don Felipe de la Cámara y Zavala, 1836–1841.* Mexico DF: Editorial Yucalpetén.

Cámara Zavala, Gonzalo. 1977. Historia de la industria henequenera hasta 1919. In *Enciclopedia yucatenense.* 2d ed., 3:657–725. Mexico DF: Gobierno de Yucatán.

Canto López, Antonio. 1976. *La Guerra de Castas en Yucatán.* Mérida: Ediciones de la Universidad de Yucatán.

Cantón Rosado, Francisco. 1943. *Historia de la instrucción pública en Yucatán.* Mexico DF: Ediciones de la Secretaría de Educación Pública.

Caravaglia, Louis A., and Charles G. Worman. 1984. *Firearms of the American West, 1803–1865.* Albuquerque: University of New Mexico Press.

Careaga Viliesid, Lorena. 1981. *Chan Santa Cruz: Historia de una comunidad cimarrona de Quintana Roo*. Thesis in social anthropology. Mexico DF: Universidad Ibero-americana.

———. 1990a. *Quintana Roo: Una historia compartida*. Mexico DF: Instituto de Investigaciones Dr. José Luis Mora.

———. 1990b. *Quintana Roo: Textos de su historia*. 2 vols. Mexico DF: Instituto de Investigaciones Dr. José Luis Mora.

Carrillo y Ancona, Crescencio. 1895. *El obispado de Yucatán: Historia de su fundación y de sus obispos*. 2 vols. Mérida: Ricardo B. Caballero.

Chamberlain, Robert S. 1948. *The Conquest and Colonization of Yucatan, 1517–1550*. Washington DC: Carnegie Institution.

Civeira Taboada, Miguel. 1975. Introducción. In *Memorias de don Felipe de la Cámara Zavala*, 7–17. Mexico DF: Editorial Yucalpetén.

Cline, Howard F. 1950. Regionalism and society in Yucatan, 1825–1847: A study of "progressivism" and the origins of the Caste War. *Related Studies in Early Nineteenth Century Yucatecan Social History*, pt. 5. University of Chicago Library, Microfilm Collection of Manuscripts on Middle American Cultural Anthropology, no. 32.

Coale, Ansley J., and Paul Demeny. 1983. *Regional Model Life Tables and Stable Populations*. 2d ed. New York: Academic.

Cook, Sherburne F., and Woodrow Borah. 1960. The Indian population of central Mexico, 1531–1610. *Ibero-Americana* 44.

———. 1974. The population of Yucatan, 1517–1960. In *Essays in Population History, Mexico and the Caribbean*, by S. F. Cook and W. Borah, 2:1–179. Berkeley and Los Angeles: University of California Press.

Cortés, Hernán [Hernando]. 1928. *Five Letters, 1519–1526*. Translated by J. Bayard Morris. Reprint, New York: W. W. Norton, n.d.

Crosby, Alfred W., Jr. 1972. *The Columbian Exchange*. Westport, CT: Greenwood.

Davies, James C. 1962. Toward a theory of revolution. *American Sociological Review* 27(1): 5–19.

Díaz del Castillo, Bernal. [1632] 1956. *The True Story of the Conquest of Mexico, 1512–1521*, Translated by A. P. Maudsley, edited by I. A. Leonard. New York: Farrar, Straus, and Cudahy.

Diccionario maya Córdemex. 1980. Mérida: Ediciones Córdemex.

Dobson, Narda. 1973. *A History of Belize*. Trinidad and Jamaica: Longman Caribbean.

Dumond, Don E. 1970. Competition, cooperation, and the folk society. *Southwestern Journal of Anthropology* 26:261–86.

———. 1976. An outline of the demographic history of Tlaxcala. In *The Tlaxcaltecans: Prehistory, Demography, Morphology and Genetics*, edited by M. G. Crawford, 13–28. University of Kansas Publications in Anthropology 7.

————. 1977. Independent Maya of the late nineteenth century: Chiefdoms and power politics. In *Anthropology and History in Yucatan*, edited by G. D. Jones, 105–37. Austin: University of Texas Press.

————. 1985. The talking crosses of Yucatan: A new look at their history. *Ethnohistory* 32(4): 291–308.

————. 1990. Fertility, mortality, and the mean age at death: A model of a population under stress. *American Anthropologist* 92:179–87.

Dumond, Carol Steichen, and Don E. Dumond, eds. 1982. Demography and parish affairs in Yucatan. *University of Oregon Anthropological Papers* 27.

Eggan, Fred. 1934. The Maya kinship system and cross-cousin marriage. *American Anthropologist* 36:188–202.

Ellacott, S. E. 1955. *Guns.* New York: Roy.

Fabela, Isidro. 1944. *Belice.* Mexico DF: Editorial Mundo Libre.

Faber, J. G., and E. L. Rhys. 1867. A map of British Honduras. London.

Farriss, Nancy M. 1978. Nucleation versus dispersal: The dynamics of population movement in colonial Yucatan. *Hispanic American Historical Review* 58(2): 187–216.

————. 1984. *Maya Society under Colonial Rule.* Princeton: Princeton University Press.

Ferrer de Mendiolea, Gabriel. 1977. Historia de la comunicaciones. *Enciclopedia yucatenense.* 2d ed., 3:507–626. Mexico DF: Gobierno de Yucatán.

Flannery, Kent V., ed. 1982. *Maya Subsistence: Studies in Memory of Dennis E. Puleston.* New York: Academic.

Fowler, Henry. 1879. *A Narrative of a Journey across the Unexplored Portion of British Honduras, with a Short Sketch of the History and Resources of the Colony.* Belize: Government Press.

Fremont, H. 1861. Plano del Estado de Campeche. In *Memoria sobre la conveniencia, utilidad y necesidad de la erección constitucional del Estado de Campeche,* by Tomás Aznar Barbachano and Juan Carbó. Mexico DF: Imprenta Ignacio Complido.

Fuentes, Gloria. 1983. *El ejército mexicano.* Mexico DF: Grijalbo.

Garavaglia, Louis A., and Charles G. Worman. 1984. *Firearms of the American West, 1803–1865.* Albuquerque: University of New Mexico Press.

García Bernal, Manuela Cristina. 1972. *La sociedad de Yucatán, 1700–1750.* Seville: Escuela de Estudios Hispano-Americanos.

————. 1978. Indios y encomenderos en el Yucatán español. In *Memorias de la primera semana de la historia de Yucatán* 1:165–87. Mérida: Universidad de Yucatán.

García Cubas, Antonio. 1870. *Apuntes relativos á la población de la república Mexicana.* Mexico DF: Imprenta del Gobierno.

Gerhard, Peter. 1972. *A Guide to the Historical Geography of New Spain.* Cambridge: Cambridge University Press.

————. 1979. *The Southeast Frontier of New Spain*. Princeton: Princeton University Press.

Gibbs, Archibald R. 1883. *British Honduras: An Historical and Descriptive Account of the Colony from Its Settlement, 1670*. London: Sampson Low, Marston, Searle & Rivington.

Gibson, Charles. 1964. *The Aztecs under Spanish Rule*. Stanford: Stanford University Press.

Gobernador de Campeche. 1939. *Documentos relacionados con los limites entre el Estado de Campeche y el Territorio de Quintana Roo*. Mérida: Imp. Oriente.

González Avilés, José. 1970. *Stephens y el pirata Molas y otras narraciones y estudios*. Mérida.

González Navarro, Moisés. 1957. *El Porfiriato: La vida social*. Vol. 4 *Historia Moderna de México*, Edited by D. Cosío Villegas. of Mexico DF: Editorial Hermes.

————. 1970. *Raza y tierra: La Guerra de Castas y el henequén*. Mexico DF: El Colegio de México.

Grant, U. S. 1885. *Personal Memoirs of U. S. Grant*. 2 vols. New York: Charles L. Webster.

Harrison, Peter D., and B. L. Turner II, eds. 1978. *Pre-Hispanic Maya Agriculture*. Albuquerque: University of New Mexico Press.

Heller, Carl. [1847] 1953. Karte von Yucatan. Nach der handschriftlichen Karte von Juan José de León [map]. In *Reisen in Mexiko en den Jahren 1845–48*, by C. Heller. Reprint, Leipzig: Wilhelm Engelmann.

Hernández, Manuel. 1854–55. Carta de Yucatán. Formado con datos adquiridos sobre el terreno en la campaña que hizo el Sr. General de Brigada . . . Dn Rómulo Díaz de la Vega [map]. Hand-drawn copy in the Museo Regional de Antropología del Estado de Yucatán.

Heydn, Doris. 1951. Tulum: The walled city. *Pemex Travel Club Bulletin*, (Mar. 1): 12–14.

————. 1967. Birth of a deity. *Tlalocan* 5:235–42.

Hu-DeHart, Evelyn. 1984. *Yaqui Resistance and Survival*. Madison: University of Wisconsin Press.

Hübbe, Joaquín. 1940. *Belice*. Edited by C. R. Menéndez. Mérida: Tipográfica Yucateca.

Huerta, María Teresa, and Patricia Palacios, eds. 1976. *Rebeliones indígenas de la época colonial*. Mexico DF: Instituto Nacional de Antropología e Historia, Departamento de Investigaciones Históricas.

Humphreys, R. A. 1961. *The Diplomatic History of British Honduras, 1638–1901*. London: Oxford University Press.

Janvier, Thomas A. 1893. The Mexican army. In *Armies of Today*, 361–96. New York: Harper & Brothers.

Jones, Grant D. 1974. Revolution and continuity in Santa Cruz Maya society. *American Ethnologist* 1(4): 659–83.

———. 1977. Levels of settlement alliance among the San Pedro Maya of western Belize and eastern Petén, 1857–1936. In *Anthropology and History in Yucatán*, edited by G. D. Jones, 103–38. Austin: University of Texas Press.

———. 1982a. Agriculture and trade in the colonial period southern Maya lowlands. In *Maya Subsistence*, edited by K. V. Flannery, 275–94. New York: Academic.

———. 1982b. Mayas, Yucatecans and Englishmen in the nineteenth century fiesta system of northern Belize. *Belizean Studies* 10(3–4): 25–42.

———. 1989. *Maya Resistance to Spanish Rule: Time and History on a Colonial Frontier.* Albuquerque: University of New Mexico Press.

Joseph, Gilbert M. 1986. *Rediscovering the Past at Mexico's Periphery.* University: University of Alabama Press.

Konrad, Herman W. 1991. Capitalism on the tropical-forest frontier: Quintana Roo, 1880s to 1930. In *Land, Labor, and Capital in Modern Yucatan*, edited by J. T. Brannon and G. M. Joseph, 143–78. Tuscaloosa: University of Alabama Press.

Lapointe, Marie. 1983. *Los mayas rebeldes de Yucatán.* Zamora, Michoacán: El Colegio de Michoacán.

Liss, Peggy K. 1983. *Atlantic Empires: The Network of Trade and Revolution, 1713–1826.* Baltimore: John Hopkins University Press.

López, Tomás. 1801. Mapa geografico de la Península y Provincia de Yucatan segun las mejores notícias . . . [map]. Madrid.

López de Cogolludo, Diego. [1688] 1954. *Historia de Yucatán.* 3 vols. Campeche: Comisión de Historia.

López de Gómara, Francisco. [1552] 1964. *Cortés, the Life of the Conqueror by His Secretary.* Translated and edited by Lesley Byrd Simpson. Berkeley and Los Angeles: University of California Press.

Lyon, Capt. G. F. [1828] 1971. *Journal of a Residence and Tour in the Republic of Mexico in the Year 1826.* 2 vols. Port Washington, NY: Kennikat.

Martínez Parédez, Domingo. 1967. *El idioma maya hablado y el escrito.* Mexico DF: Editorial Orion.

Means, Philip A. 1917. History of the Spanish conquest of Yucatan and of the Itzas. *Papers of the Peabody Museum of American Archaeology and Ethnology, Harvard University* 7.

Mendizabal, Miguel de. 1929. Juan Bautista Vega, el secretario de Dios. *El Universal*, Nov. 21, sec. 1, 3, 5.

Menéndez, Carlos R. 1923. *Historia del infame y vergonzoso comercio de indios vendidos a los esclavistas de Cuba por los políticos yucatecos desde 1848 hasta 1861.* Mérida: Talleres Gráficos de "La Revista de Yucatán."

———. 1925. *Las "memorias" de Don Buenaventura Vivó y la venta de indios yucatecos en Cuba*. Mérida: Compañía Tipográfica Yucateca.

Menéndez, Gabriel Antonio, ed. 1936. *Quintana Roo, album monográfico*. Mexico DF.

México, Gobierno de. 1829. *Colección de órdenes y decretos de la Soberana Junta Provisional Gubernativa, y Soberanos Congresos Generales de la Nación Mexicana*. Vol. 3. Mexico DF: Galvan.

———. 1897–99. *Censo general de la República Mexicana verificado el 30 de Octubre de 1895*. Dirección General de Estadística. Mexico DF: Secretaría de Fomento.

———. 1904. *Censo y división territorial del Estado de Campeche, verificados en 1900*. Dirección General de Estadística. Mexico DF: Secretaría de Fomento.

México, Instituto Geológico. 1895. Bosquejo de una carta geológica de la península de Yucatán [map]. In La geografía física y la geología de la péninsula de Yucatán, by Karl Sapper. *Instituto Geológico de México, Boletín* (1896) 3:1–57.

Miller, William. 1888. Map of the road from Bacalar to Santa Cruz. Encl. with A. Maloney dispatch No. 20, Jan. 20, 1892, CO123/198.

———. 1889. A journey from British Honduras to Santa Cruz, Yucatan. *Proceedings of the Royal Geographical Society of London*, n.s. 11:23–28.

Molina, Alonso de [1571] 1944. Vocabulario en lengua castellana y mexicana. *Colección de incunables americanos, siglo XVI*. Vol. 4. Madrid: Ediciones Cultura Hispánica.

Molina Solís, Juan Francisco. 1904–13. *Historia de Yucatán durante la dominación Española*. 3 vols. Mérida: Imprenta de la Lotería del Estado.

———. 1921–27. *Historia de Yucatán desde la independencia de España hasta la época actual*. 2 vols. Mérida: La Revista de Yucatán.

Montilla Duarte, Felipe. 1955. Don Anselmo Duarte de la Ruela en la Guerra de Castas. In *Cuentos mayas y fantasías*, by F. Montilla Duarte, 145–73. Mexico DF: Editora Ibero-Mexicana.

Morley, Sylvanus G. 1947. *The Ancient Maya*. Stanford: Stanford University Press.

Núñez y Escalante, Roberto. 1980. *La cuestión de limites del Estado de Campeche*. Mexico DF: Ediciones de la Muralla.

O'Gorman, Edmundo. 1973. *Historia de las divisiones territoriales de México*. 5th ed. Mexico DF: Editorial Porrua.

Pacheco Cruz, Santiago. 1934. *Estudio etnográfico de los maya del ex Territorio Quintana Roo*. Mérida.

———. 1959. *Diccionario de etimologías toponímicas mayas*. 2d ed. Mérida.

———. 1962. *Antropología cultural maya*. Vol. 1. Mérida.

Patch, Robert W. 1985. Agrarian change in eighteenth-century Yucatán. *Hispanic American Historial Review* 65(1): 21–49.

———. 1991. Decolonization, the agrarian problem, and the origins of the Caste War,

1812–1847. In *Land, Labor, and Capital in Modern Yucatan*, edited by J. T. Brannon and G. M. Joseph, 51–82. Tuscaloosa: University of Alabama Press.

———. 1993. *Maya and Spaniard in Yucatan*. Stanford: Stanford University Press.

Peniche Vallado, Leopoldo. 1980. *Promotores e historiadores de la rebelión maya de 1847 en Yucatán*. Mérida: Fondo Editorial de Yucatán.

Peón Ancona, Juan Francisco. 1985. Cucherías de la historia, XXXI. *Diario de Yucatán*, Sunday, May 26, tabloid feature section, 1–2.

Peón Contreras de Elizalde, Juan. 1888. *La sacra y real misión de Jesus, el Incognito, el Buhonero, el Gran Consolador, por Juan su precursor, el peregrino el real confirmador ¡a Yucatán y al universo entero!* Havana: Imprenta El Aerolito.

Pérez Alcalá, Felipe. 1914. *Ensayos biográficos, cuadros históricos, hojas dispersas*. Mérida: La Revista de Yucatán.

Pérez Martínez, Hector, ed. 1938. Preface to *Diario de nuestro viaje a los Estados Unidos*, by Justo Sierra O'Reilly, ix–l. Mexico DF: Antigua Librería Robredo.

Quintal Martin, Fidelio. 1992. *Correspondencia de la Guerra de Castas: Epistolario documental, 1843–1866*. Mérida: Universidad Autónoma de Yucatán.

Raisz, Edwin. 1964. *Landforms of Mexico*. 2d ed. Prepared for Geography Branch, Office of Naval Research, Cambridge, Massachusetts.

Real Academia Española. 1956. *Diccionario de la lengua española*. 18th ed. Madrid: Espasa Calpe.

Redfield, Robert. 1938. Race and class in Yucatan. In *Cooperation in Research*, by staff members and research associates of the Carnegie Institution of Washington, 511–32. Pub. No. 501. Washington DC: Carnegie Institution.

Redfield, Robert, and Alfonso Villa Rojas. 1962. *Chan Kom: A Maya village*. Chicago: University of Chicago Press.

Reed, Nelson. 1964. *The Caste War of Yucatan*. Stanford: Stanford University Press.

Regil, José M., and Alonso M. Peón. 1853. Estadística de Yucatán. *Boletín de la Sociedad Mexicana de Geografía y Estadística* (época 1) 3(5): 237–340.

Reina, Leticia. 1980. *Las rebeliones campesinas en México, 1819–1906*. Mexico DF: Siglo Veintiuno Editores.

Ríos, Eduardo Enrique. 1940. La rebelión de Canek, Yucatan, 1761. *Boletín de la Sociedad Mexicana de Geografía y Estadística* 54(7–8): 483–95.

Rodríguez Losa, Salvador. 1978. Población y "Guerra de Castas." In *Memorias de la Primera Semana de la Historia de Yucatán* 2:149–64. Mérida: Universidad Autónoma de Yucatán.

———. 1985. Censo inédito de 1821. *Geografía política de Yucatán*. Vol. 1. Mérida: Universidad Autónoma de Yucatán.

———. 1989. División territorial, gobierno de los pueblos y población 1821–1900. *Geografía política de Yucatán*. Vol. 2. Mérida: Universidad Autónoma de Yucatán.

Rogers, E. 1885. British Honduras: Its resources and development. *Journal of the Manchester Geographical Society* 1:197–227.

Rogers, H. C. B. 1960. *Weapons of the British Soldier.* London: Seeley Service.

Rosado, José María. 1931. Memoirs. *The Clarion*, June 18 (656–73); June 25 (681–84); July 2 (5–9). Belize. Reprinted in Buhler (1975).

Roys, Ralph L. 1933. *The Book of Chilam Balam of Chumayel.* Carnegie Institution of Washington. Pub. No. 438. Washington DC: Carnegie Institution.

———. 1940. Personal names of the Maya of Yucatan. In *Contributions to American Anthropology and History* 31:35–48. Washington DC: Carnegie Institution.

———. 1957. *Political Geography of the Yucatan Maya.* Washington DC: Carnegie Institution.

———. [1943] 1972. *The Indian Background of Colonial Yucatan.* Norman: University of Oklahoma Press.

Rubio Mañé, J. Ignacio. 1977. Andrés Quintana Roo. *Enciclopedia yucatanense.* 2d ed., 7:9–50. Mexico DF: Gobierno de Yucatán.

Rugeley, Terry L. 1992. Origins of the Caste War: A social history of rural Yucatan, 1800–1847. Ph.D. diss., University of Houston.

Ryder, James W. 1977. Internal migration in Yucatán: Interpretation of historical demography and current patterns. In *Anthropology and History in Yucatán*, edited by G. D. Jones, 191–231. Austin: University of Texas Press.

Sánchez Novelo, Paulo. 1983. *Yucatán durante la intervención francesa.* Mérida: Maldonado Editores.

Sanders, William T. 1970. The population of the Teotihuacan Valley, the Basin of Mexico, and the Central Mexican Symbiotic Region in the 16th century. In *The Teotihuacan Valley Project, Final Report*, 1:385–457. University Park: Pennsylvania State University.

Santamaría, Francisco J. 1959. *Diccionario de mejicanismos.* Mexico DF: Editorial Porrúa.

Sapper, Karl. 1895. Die unabhängigen Indianerstaaten von Yucatan [map]. Scale 1:3,100,000. In Die unabhängigen Indianerstaaten von Yucatan, by K. Sapper. *Globus* 67(13): 197–201.

———. [1895] 1904. The independent states of Yucatan [map]. In Mexican and Central American antiquities, calendar systems, and history," edited by C. P. Bowditch. *Bureau of American Ethnology, Bulletin* 28: 623–34. Translated from original German in *Globus* 67, no. 13 (1895):197–201.

Scholes, France V., and Eleanor B. Adams. 1936. Documents relating to the Mirones expedition to the interior of Yucatan. *Maya Research* 3:153–76, 251–76.

———. 1938. Don Diego Quijada, Alcalde Mayor de Yucatán. *Biblioteca Histórica Mexicana de Obras Inéditas.* Vols. 14 and 15. Mexico DF: Antiqua Libería Robredo.

Scholes, France V., and Ralph L. Roys. 1938. Fray Diego de Landa and the problem of idolatry in Yucatan. In *Cooperation in Research*, by staff members and research associates of the Carnegie Institution of Washington, 585–620. Pub. No. 501. Washington DC: Carnegie Institution.

———. 1948. *The Maya Chontal Indians of Acalan-Tixchel*. Pub. No. 560. Washington DC: Carnegie Institution.

Scholes, France V., and Sir Eric Thompson. 1977. The Francisco Perez *probanza* of 1654–1656 and the *matrícula* of Tipu (Belize). In *Anthropology and History in Yucatan*, edited by G. D. Jones, 43–68. Austin: University of Texas Press.

Sierra O'Reilly, Justo. 1938. *Diario de nuestro vieja a los Estados Unidos*. Mexico DF: Antigua Librería Robredo, de José Porrúa e Hijos.

———. 1949. *Segundo libro del diario de mi viaje a los Estados Unidos*. Mexico DF: Librería de Manuel Porrúa.

———. 1950. *La hija del judío*. 2 vols. Mérida: Editorial Yucatanense "Club del Libro."

———. [1848–51] 1954. *Los índios de Yucatán*. Edited by C. R. Menendez. 2 vols. Mérida: Tipográfica Yucateca.

Simpson, Lesley B. 1966. *Many Mexicos*. 4th ed. Berkeley and Los Angeles: University of California Press.

Smith, Colin, Manuel Bermejo Marcos, and Eugenio Chang-Rodriguez. 1971. *Collins Spanish-English English-Spanish Dictionary*. London: Collins.

Solís, José Leandro. 1878. *Memoria del Partido de los Chenes*. Campeche: Imprenta de la Sociedad Tipográfica. First published in LN, Oct. 22–Dec. 6, 1878.

Steggerda, Morris. 1941. *The Maya Indians of Yucatan*. Washington DC: Carnegie Institution.

Stephens, John L. [1843] 1963. *Incidents of Travel in Yucatan*. 2 vols. New York: Dover.

Strickon, Arnold. 1965. Hacienda and plantation in Yucatan. *América Indígena* 25(1): 35–63.

Suárez Molina, Victor M. 1977a. *La evolución económica de Yucatán*. 2 vols. Mexico DF: Ediciones de la Universidad de Yucatán.

———. 1977b. La Guerra de Castas y el problema de la tierra. *Revista de la Universidad de Yucatán* 19:49–55.

Suárez y Navarro, Juan. 1979. *Yucatán ante la creación del Estado de Campeche*. Mexico DF: Ediciones de la Muralla. Originally published as *Informe sobre las causas y caracter de los frecuentes cambios políticos en el Estado de Yucatan*, (1861).

Thompson, Donald E. 1954. Maya paganism and Christianity. Middle American Research Institute Publication 19:1–36.

Thompson, Edward H. 1932. *People of the Serpent: Life and Adventure among the Mayas*. Boston: Houghton-Mifflin.

Thompson, J. Eric S. [Sir Eric]. 1963. *Maya archaeologist*. Norman: University of Oklahoma Press.

———. 1970. *Maya History and Religion*. Norman: University of Oklahoma Press.

———. 1977. A proposal for constituting a Maya subgroup, cultural and linguistic, in the Petén and adjacent regions. In *Anthropology and History in Yucatan*, edited by G. J. Jones, 3–42. Austin: University of Texas Press.

Tocqueville, Alexis de. 1856. *The Old Regime and the French Revolution*. Translated by J. Bonner. New York: Harper & Brothers.

Tozzer, Alfred M. 1941. Landa's relación de las cosas de Yucatán. *Papers of the Peabody Museum of American Archaeology and Ethnology, Harvard University* 18.

Trebarra, Napoleón. 1864. *Los misterios de Chan Santa Cruz*. Mérida: M. Aldama Rivas.

Trollope, Anthony. 1858. *The West Indies and the Spanish Main*. New York: Harper & Brothers.

Turner, John Kenneth. 1911. *Barbarous Mexico*. Chicago: Charles H. Kerr.

United Kingdom. 1864. *A list of the Officers of the Army 1863–1864*. London: Her Majesty's Stationary Office.

———. 1866. *The Army List*. London: Her Majesty's Stationary Office.

Urzaiz, Eduardo. 1946. *Del Imperio a la Revolución, 1865–1910*. Mérida: Talleres Gráficos del Sudeste.

Usher, Alfred. 1888. Map of British Honduras. Rev. ed. London.

Valdes Acosta, J. M. [1931] 1979. *A través de las centurias*. 2d ed. Mexico DF: Bravo.

Villa R[ojas], Alfonso. 1945. *The Maya of East Central Quintana Roo*. Carnegie Institution of Washington, Pub. No 559. Washington DC: Carnegie Institution.

———. 1962. Notas sobre la distribución y estado actual de la población indígena de la Península de Yucatán, Mexico. *América Indígena* 22(3): 209–40.

———. 1978. *Los elegidos de Dios*. Mexico DF: Instituto Nacional Indigenista.

Villagutierre Soto-Mayor, Juan de. [1701] 1983. *History of the Conquest of the Province of the Itzá*. Translated by R. D. Wood. Culver City, CA: Labyrinthos.

Wagner, Philip L. 1964. Natural vegetation of Middle America. In *Natural Environment and Early Cultures*, edited by R. C. West, 216–63. Vol. 1 of *Handbook of Middle American Indians*. Austin: University of Texas Press.

Wallace, Anthony F. C. 1956. Revitalization movements. *American Anthropologist* 58:264–81.

Wells, Allen. 1985. *Yucatan's Guilded Age*. Albuquerque: University of New Mexico Press.

———. 1991. From hacienda to plantation: The transformation of Santo Domingo Xcuyum. In *Land, Labor, and Capital in Modern Yucatán*, edited by J. T. Brannon and G. M. Joseph, 112–42. Tuscaloosa: University of Alabama Press.

West, Robert C., ed. 1964. Natural Environment and Early Cultures. *Handbook of Middle American Indians.* Vol. 1. Austin: University of Texas Press.

Wright, Norman Pelham [N.P.W.]. 1962. The remarkable saga of Juan Bautista Vega. *Intercambio,* no. 223 (June 30): 55–65. Mexico DF: British Chamber of Commerce.

Yucatán, Estado de. 1832. *Colección de leyes, decretos y órdenes del Augusto Congreso del Estado de Yucatán.* Vol 2. Mérida: Lorenzo Segui.

Index

Acanbalam, 91, 96

Acanceh, 132, 450 n.23

Acereto, Agustín: death of, 250; as government officer, 232, 233, 235, 247–48, 447 n.33; insurrections of, 68, 77, 187–88, 249; and rebels, 232–34

Acereto, Pedro: death of, 251; insurrections of, 226, 232, 235, 250–51; military positions of, 215, 240, 247; and rebels, 215, 240

Act of Valladolid, 71, 72. *See also* Imán, Santiago

adelantado, Montejo as, 25, 30

Adolphus, Edwin: and J. Carmichael, 289–90, 299; and Icaiché, 333–34; and rebels, 299, 302, 322–24

Agua Blanca, 172–73, 190, 460 n.50

aguardiente, 46, 66, 88; in Treaty of Tzucacab, 119, 121

Aguilar, Gerónimo de, 10

Aguilar, José María, 380–81

Aguilar, Juan, 304

Ake, [B]albino, 256, 302

Ake, Diego, 295

Ake, Felipe, 400–401, 530 n.48

Ake, Isidro, 299–300

Ake, José María, 373, 380–81

Albion Island, 173–74, 252, 334, 366–67

alcalde, 30

alguacil, 30

Ambergris Cay, 354, 369, 377

amnesty, decrees of: 1848, 146; 1849, 160; 1858, 215; response to, 216

Ampudia, Pedro de, 76, 207

Anderson, James, 373, 375, 380, 392

Anderson, W., 221–23, 223–25

Andrade, [José] Domingo, 291, 306, 324, 326, 329, 331

Anduce, Juan Bautista, 230–31

Arana, Andrés, 269; of Yakalcab, 283, 302, 489 n.96

Arana, Eugenio, 283, 367, 384–85, 403; and *bravos*, 302, 403; and British Honduras, 339–40, 342–43, 366–67; and Icaiché, 339, 340, 342–43, 347–48, 505 n.14, 512 n.73; at Xkanhá, 332, 336–68, 512 n.73

Arjonilla, Gumesindo, 356–58

armistice, 163, 167, 171

Arredondo, José María Martínez de, 280–83, 488 n.82

Ascension Bay: in Mexican campaign, 395–97; and munitions trade, 155, 175; as rebel port, 155, 175, 192, 230

audiencia, 29, 30, 51

Austin, John Gardiner, 294–95, 492 n.24

Avila, Eustaquio, 366, 382, 519 n.64

Avila, Francisco, 328, 330, 503 n.67, 510 n.59

Avila, José María, 210–11

Ay, Manuel Antonio, 91–93, 442 n.22. *See also* conspiracy, alleged (1847)

Ayala, José María 172, 464 n.20

ayuntamiento, 18, 52

Azueta, Manuel, 396

B. Cramer and Company, 360, 371, 373, 516 n.32

Bacalar, [Salamanca de]: British Hondurans residents at, 159; and British Honduras, 127, 229, 241, 334,